Bind Up the Testimony

Explorations in the Genesis
of the **Book of Isaiah**

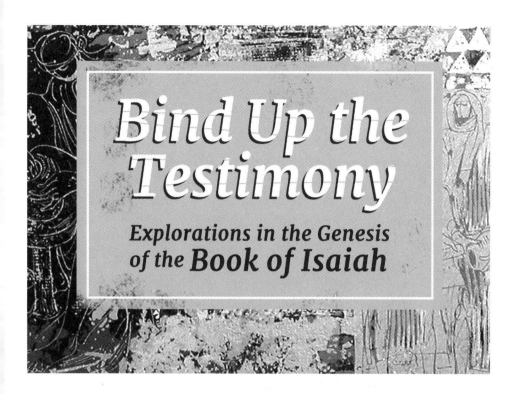

Bind Up the Testimony

Explorations in the Genesis of the Book of Isaiah

Edited by

DANIEL I. BLOCK and **RICHARD L. SCHULTZ**

HENDRICKSON
PUBLISHERS

Bind Up the Testimony: Explorations in the Genesis of the Book of Isaiah

© 2015 by Hendrickson Publishers Marketing, LLC
P. O. Box 3473
Peabody, Massachusetts 01961-3473

ISBN 978-1-61970-599-9

Printed in the United States of America

First Printing—December 2015

Cover Art: Shraga Weil, "Writing of Dead Sea Scrolls" (detail). Used with permission of the Safrai Fine Art Gallery, Jerusalem.

Library of Congress Cataloging-in-Publication Data

Bind up the testimony : explorations in the genesis of the Book of Isaiah / edited by Daniel I. Block and Richard L. Schultz.
    pages cm
  Includes bibliographical references and index.
  ISBN 978-1-61970-599-9 (alk. paper)
    1. Bible. Isaiah—Criticism, interpretation, etc. I. Block, Daniel Isaac, 1943- editor.
  BS1515.52.B43 2015
  224'.1066—dc23

2015026996

Contents

Editors' Preface and Acknowledgments

After Moses, no prophet of ancient Israel stands taller than Isaiah. From the waning years of Israel's history as a Davidic monarchy to the present, the person of Isaiah and the book that goes by his name have captured the imagination of lay readers, clergy, and scholars. For Christians especially, Isaiah is extremely significant for its anticipation of the Messiah, both as a royal ruler and as the suffering Servant. In their portrayal of Christ and his mission, New Testament writers—both the Gospel writers and the authors of the epistles—referred to and made use of Isaiah more than any other book of the Hebrew Bible.

The present volume reflects the ongoing interest of biblical scholars in Isaiah, and in particular the tension that exists among evangelical scholars on the genesis of the book. With a few exceptions, the essays included here were first presented at a colloquium on "The Genesis of the Book of Isaiah" held at Wheaton College, September 26–28, 2013. Our expressions of gratitude must begin with those who made this colloquium possible. We are grateful to the administrators of Wheaton College for creating a climate in which conversations like this may be held freely and openly, and for providing the facilities for the colloquium. Harbor House and its Board Room in particular provided a delightful venue for formal and informal conversation among the participants. To the scholars who participated in the program we express our appreciation for their hard work and the cordiality with which they engaged in discussion. We owe special thanks to Michelle Knight, Ellen Block, and Carol Schultz for their assistance in the administration of the social aspects of the event. This colloquium could not have been held without the generous support of interested persons. The major portion of the funding for the event was provided by the Daniel and Ellen Block Fund for Old Testament Studies, established by their son and daughter-in-law, Jason and Carolyn Block. This was supplemented by monies from the Blanchard and Gunther H. Knoedler Chairs of Old Testament and the Carl Armerding and Hudson T. Armerding Chair of Biblical Studies.

Converting presented papers into forms suitable for publication involved another set of persons, without whose assistance this published product would never have seen the light of day. We are deeply grateful to Hendrickson Publishers for making these essays available to the public in printed form. From the beginning, their enthusiasm and support has sustained all who have had a hand. We are especially grateful to Allan Emery III, for his initial support for the project, and to Jonathan Kline, the Hendrickson editor charged with making what scholars do look acceptable to the public. Not only has he worked tirelessly on the editing of the manuscripts, but he has also consistently dealt with the idiosyncrasies and infelicities of the contributors' submissions with grace and respect. This volume is a monument to his disciplinary expertise, close attention to detail, energy, industry, and sensitivity. We also would like to express our appreciation to all of the other staff at Hendrickson who have contributed to the production and marketing of this book, for their obvious commitment to both excellence and Christian ministry in their publications.

It has been a privilege to work with the scholars whose essays are included here. We are grateful for the seriousness and grace with which they presented their material at the colloquium and responded to our edits. We express special thanks to Greg Beale for allowing us to republish his work on New Testament perspectives on the book of Isaiah. This essay fills in what otherwise would have been a gap in the list of subjects treated. I (Dan) am also very grateful to my colleague Richard Schultz, who agreed to contribute a second essay on the reception of Isaiah in the Hebrew Bible, thereby filling a second significant gap.

This volume could not have been produced without the assistance of our graduate students. While they have not signed their names, the work of Holly Brackin, Eva Dittmann, Michelle Knight, Daniel Lanz, Cooper Smith, and Franklin Wang underlies many aspects of the work: proofreading essays, creating bibliographies and lists of abbreviations, checking footnotes for stylistic consistency, and indexing. We are deeply grateful to them. We are also grateful to our wives, Carol Schultz and Ellen Block, for standing by us and giving us space to work on projects like this.

With great respect, we dedicate this volume to the memory of Thomas E. McComiskey (Trinity Evangelical Divinity School) and Brevard S. Childs (Yale University), who introduced us and so many others to the poetic beauty, theological richness, and compositional complexity of the book of Isaiah.

While many associates have contributed to this project, ultimate praise must go to the "The Holy One of Israel," who inspired the ministry of Isaiah and whose presence among us in human flesh was announced by John the Baptist in adopting the immortal words of Isaiah the prophet, "I am the voice of one calling in the wilderness, 'Make straight the way for the Lord'" (John 1:23; cf. Isa 40:3). May this volume bring glory to God our Savior and contribute to making straight his way.

Permissions

Chapter 4 of this book is a slightly revised version of Chapter 5 ("A Specific Problem Confronting the Authority of the Bible: Should the New Testament's Claim That the Prophet Isaiah Wrote the Whole Book of Isaiah Be Taken at Face Value?") of *The Erosion of Inerrancy in Evangelicalism: Responding to New Challenges to Biblical Authority*, by G. K. Beale © 2008. This material is used by permission of Crossway, a publishing ministry of Good News Publishers, Wheaton, IL 60187, www.crossway.org.

Portions of chapter 9, "Characteristics of the Hebrew of the Recognized Literary Divisions of Isaiah," reproduce or otherwise draw on material from Mark F. Rooker, *Biblical Hebrew in Transition: The Language of the Book of Ezekiel*, JSOTSup 90 (Sheffield: Sheffield Academic Press, 1990). This material is reproduced by permission of Bloomsbury/T&T Clark.

Scripture quotations marked (ESV) are from The Holy Bible, English Standard Version® (ESV®), copyright © 2001 by Crossway, a publishing ministry of Good News Publishers. Used by permission. All rights reserved.

Scripture quotations marked HCSB® are taken from the Holman Christian Standard Bible®, copyright © 1999, 2000, 2002, 2003 by Holman Bible Publishers. Used by permission. Holman Christian Standard Bible®, Holman CSB®, and HCSB® are federally registered trademarks of Holman Bible Publishers.

Scripture quotations marked (NASB) are taken from the NEW AMERICAN STANDARD BIBLE®, copyright © 1960, 1962, 1963, 1968, 1971, 1972, 1973, 1975, 1977, 1995 by The Lockman Foundation. Used by permission. (www.Lockman.org)

Scripture quoted by permission. Quotations designated (NET) are from the NET Bible® copyright © 1996–2006 by Biblical Studies Press, L.L.C. http://bible.org. All rights reserved.

Scripture quotations marked (NIV) are taken from the Holy Bible, New International Version®, NIV®. Copyright © 1973, 1978, 1984, 2011 by Biblica, Inc.™ Used by permission of Zondervan. All rights reserved worldwide. www.zondervan.com.

Contributors

G. K. Beale
Westminster Theological Seminary (Philadelphia, Pennsylvania)

Daniel I. Block
Wheaton College (Wheaton, Illinois)

Mark J. Boda
McMaster Divinity College, McMaster University (Hamilton, Ontario, Canada)

Seulgi L. Byun
Oak Hill College (London, United Kingdom)

Peter J. Gentry
The Southern Baptist Theological Seminary (Louisville, Kentucky)

Michael W. Graves
Wheaton College (Wheaton, Illinois)

Knut M. Heim
Trinity College (Bristol, United Kingdom)

John W. Hilber
Grand Rapids Theological Seminary (Grand Rapids, Michigan)

John N. Oswalt
Asbury Theological Seminary (Wilmore, Kentucky)

Mark F. Rooker
Southeastern Baptist Theological Seminary (Wake Forest, North Carolina)

Richard L. Schultz
Wheaton College (Wheaton, Illinois)

Gary V. Smith
Union University (Jackson, Tennessee)

Abbreviations

General Abbreviations

1 Esd	1 Esdras
11QTemple	Temple Scroll
1QH	*Hodayot* or *Thanksgiving Hymns*
1QIsaᵃ	Isaiahᵃ, the "Great Isaiah Scroll"
1QIsaᵇ	Isaiahᵇ, the "Hebrew University Isaiah Scroll"
1QM	*Milḥamah* or *War Scroll*
1QS	*Community Rule* or *Manual of Discipline*
4QFlor	*Florilegium*, also *Midrash on Eschatology*ᵃ
Ag. Ap.	*Against Apion*
Ant.	*Jewish Antiquities*
ARM	Archives royales de Mari
AT	Altes Testament
b.	Babylonian version of the Talmud
B. Bat.	*Baba Batra*
B. Qam.	*Baba Qamma*
BCE	before the Common Era
Ber.	*Berakot*
ca.	circa
CD	Cairo Genizah copy of the Damascus Document
CE	Common Era
cf.	*confer*, compare
ch(s).	chapter(s)
com.	common
Comm. Isa.	Ibn Ezra's *Commentary on Isaiah*
diss.	dissertation
Dreams	*On Dreams*
EBH	Early Biblical Hebrew
ed(s).	editor(s), edited by; edition
e.g.	*exempli gratia*, for example
ʿErub.	ʿErubin
esp.	especially
ESV	English Standard Version
ET	English translation
et al.	*et alii*, and others
f(f).	and the following one(s)

fem.	feminine
Ḥag.	*Ḥagigah*
HCSB	Holman Christian Standard Bible
Heb.	Hebrew
Ḥul.	*Ḥullin*
i.e.	*id est*, that is
ibid.	*ibidem*, in the same place
idem.	the same
J.W.	*Jewish War*
Kil.	*Kilʾayim*
LBH	Late Biblical Hebrew
LXX	Septuagint (the Greek Old Testament)
m.	Tractate of the Mishnah
Maʿaś. Š.	*Maʿaśer Šeni*
Mak.	*Makkot*
Mart. Isa.	*The Martyrdom and Ascension of Isaiah*
masc.	masculine
Meg.	*Megillah*
Mid.	*Middot*
Midr.	*Midrash*
MT	Masoretic Text
n	note
n.s.	new series
Names	*On the Change of Names*
NASB	New American Standard Bible
Naz.	*Nazir*
Ned.	*Nedarim*
Neg.	*Negaʿim*
NIV	New International Version
NJPS	*Tanakh: The Holy Scriptures: The New JPS Translation according to the Traditional Hebrew Text*
NRSV	New Revised Standard Version
NT	New Testament
OG	Old Greek version of the Old Testament
OT	Old Testament
p(p).	page(s)
Pesaḥ.	*Pesaḥim*
pl.	plural
prol.	prologue
R.	Rabbi
Rab.	*Rabbah* (+ biblical book)
repr.	reprint
rev.	revised (by)
Rewards	*On Rewards and Punishments*
Roš. Haš.	*Roš Haššanah*

RSV	Revised Standard Version
SAA	State Archives of Assyria
Šabb.	*Šabbat*
Sanh.	*Sanhedrin*
sg.	singular
sec.	section
sic	*thus,* used to indicate a typographical or other error in the original
Siloam	Siloam Inscription
Sir	Sirach/Ecclesiasticus
Tg. Onq.	*Targum Onqelos*
trans.	translator, translated by
v(v).	verse(s)
viz.	*videlicet,* namely
vol(s).	volume(s)
y.	Jerusalem Talmud
YHWH	the consonants of the divine name in the Hebrew Bible, conventionally rendered LORD in English translations
Zebaḥ.	*Zebaḥim*

Series, Periodicals, and Reference Works

AB	Anchor Bible
ABD	*Anchor Bible Dictionary.* Edited by D. N. Freedman, 6 vols. New York, 1992.
ABRL	Anchor Bible Reference Library
ADPV	Abhandlung des Deutschen Palästina-Vereins
ANET	Ancient Texts Relating to the Old Testament. Edited by J. B. Pritchard. 3rd. ed. Princeton: Princeton University Press, 1969
AOAT	Alter Orient und Altes Testament
ATD	Das Alte Testament Deutsch
ATDan	Acta theological Danica
AYBRL	Anchor Yale Bible Reference Library
BAR	*Biblical Archaeology Review*
BBET	Beiträge zur biblischen Exegese und Theologie
BBR	*Bulletin for Biblical Research*
BDAG	Danker, F. W., W. Bauer, W. F. Arndt, and F. W. Gingrich. *Greek-English Lexicon of the New Testament and Other Early Christian Literature*, 3rd ed. Chicago, 1999.
BDB	Brown, F., S. R. Driver, and C. A. Briggs. *A Hebrew and English Lexicon of the Old Testament.* Oxford, 1907.
BHT	Beiträge zur historischen Theologie
Bib	*Biblica*
BibInt	*Biblical Interpretation*
BibInt	Biblical Interpretation Series

BibSem	The Biblical Seminar
BibS(N)	Biblische Studien (Neukirchen, 1951–)
BJRL	*Bulletin of the John Rylands University Library of Manchester*
BJS	Brown Judaic Studies
BKAT	Biblischer Kommentar, Altes Testament. Edited by M. Noth and H. W. Wolff
BNP	*Brill's New Pauly: Encyclopedia of the Ancient World.* Edited by Hubert Canick. 22 vols. Leiden: Brill, 2002–2011
BSac	*Bibliotheca sacra*
BWA(N)T	Beiträge zur Wissenschaft vom Alten (und Neuen) Testament
BZ	*Biblische Zeitschrift*
BZAW	Beihefte zur Zeitschrift für die alttestamentliche Wissenschaft
BZNW	Beihefte zur Zeitschrift für die neutestamentliche Wissenschaft
CahRB	Cahiers de la Revue biblique
CANE	*Civilizations of the Ancient Near East.* Edited by J. Sasson. 4 vols. New York, 1995
CBQ	*Catholic Biblical Quarterly*
Chm	*Churchman*
ConBOT	Coniectanea biblica: Old Testament Series
COS	*The Context of Scripture.* Edited by W. W. Hallo. 3 vols. Leiden, 1997–
DBSup	*Dictionnaire de la Bible: Supplément.* Edited by L. Pirot and A. Robert. Paris, 1926–
DJD	Discoveries in the Judean Desert
DSD	*Dead Sea Discoveries*
ECC	Eerdmans Critical Commentary
EdF	Erträge der Forschung
EDSS	*Encyclopedia of the Dead Sea Scrolls.* Edited by Lawrence H. Schiffman and James C. VanderKam. 2 vols. New York: Oxford University Press, 2000.
EncJud	*Encylopedia Judaica*
ET	English Translation
EvQ	*Evangelical Quarterly*
FAT	Forschungen zum Alten Testament
FRLANT	Forschungen zur Religion und Literatur des Alten und Neuen Testaments
HALOT	*The Hebrew and Aramaic Lexicon of the Old Testament.* Ludwig Koehler, Walter Baumgartner, and Johann J. Stamm. Translated and edited under the supervision of Mervyn E. J. Richardson. 4 vols. Leiden: Brill, 1994–1999
HAR	*Hebrew Annual Review*
HCOT	Historical Commentary on the Old Testament
Heb.	Hebrew
HKAT	Handkommentar zum Alten Testament
HS	*Hebrew Studies*

HSM	Harvard Semitic Monographs
HSS	Harvard Semitic Studies
HThKAT	Herders Theologischer Kommentar zum Alten Testament
HUCA	*Hebrew Union College Annual*
IB	*Interpreter's Bible.* Edited by G. A. Buttrick et al. 12 vols. New York, 1951–1957
IBC	Interpretation: A Bible Commentary for Teaching and Preaching
ICC	International Critical Commentary
IEJ	*Israel Exploration Journal*
Int	*Interpretation*
ISBE	*International Standard Bible Encyclopedia.* Edited by G. W. Bromiley. 4 vols. Grand Rapids, 1979–1988.
JANESCU	*Journal of the Ancient Near Eastern Society of Columbia University*
JAOS	*Journal of the American Oriental Society*
JBL	*Journal of Biblical Literature*
JCS	*Journal of Cuneiform Studies*
JE	*The Jewish Encyclopedia.* Edited by I. Singer. 12 vols. New York, 1925.
JEOL	*Jaarbericht van het Voorasiatisch-Egyptisch Gezelschap (Genootschap) Exoriente lux*
JETS	*Journal of the Evangelical Theological Society*
JNES	*Journal of Near Eastern Studies*
JNSL	*Journal of Northwest Semitic Languages*
JQR	*Jewish Quarterly Review*
JSNTSup	Journal for the Study of the Old Testament: Supplement Series
JSOT	*Journal for the Study of the Old Testament*
JSOTSup	Journal for the Study of the Old Testament: Supplement Series
JSP	*Journal for the Study of the Pseudepigrapha*
JSPSup	Journal for the Study of the Pseudepigrapha: Supplement Series
JSQ	*Jewish Studies Quarterly*
JSS	*Journal of Semitic Studies*
KHC	Kurzer Hand-Commentar zum Alten Testament
LHBOTS	The Library of Hebrew Bible/Old Testament Studies
LS	*Louvain Studies*
LSAWS	*Linguistic Studies in Ancient West Semitic*
LTQ	*Lexington Theological Quarterly*
MdB	*Le Monde de la Bible*
NAC	New American Commentary
NBD[3]	*New Bible Dictionary.* Edited by D. R.. Wood, Howard Marshall, J. D. Douglas, and N. Hillyer. 3rd ed. Downers Grove, IL: InterVarsity Press, 1996
NCB	New Century Bible
NIBCOT	New International Biblical Commentary on the Old Testament
NICOT	New International Commentary on the Old Testament
NovT	*Novum Testamentum*

NSBT	New Studies in Biblical Theology
NTApoc	*New Testament Apocrypha*. 2 vols. Revised ed. Edited by Wilhelm Schneemelcher. English trans. Ed. Robert McL. Wilson. Cambridge: Clarke; Louisville: Westminster John Knox, 2003
NTSI	New Testament and the Scriptures of Israel
OAC	Orientis Antiqui Collectio
OBO	Orbis biblicus et orientalis
OBT	Overtures to Biblical Theology
OG	Old Greek
OIS	Oriental Institute Seminars
OLA	Orientalia Lovaniensia Analecta
OTL	Old Testament Library
OTP	*Old Testament Pseudepigrapha*. Edited by J. H. Charlesworth. 2 vols. New York, 1983, 1985
OtSt	Oudtestamentische Studiën
PAAJR	*Proceedings of the American Academy of Jewish Research*
RevQ	*Revue de Qumran*
SAA	State Archives of Assyria
SAAS	State Archives of Assyria Studies
SBL	Society of Biblical Literature
SBLAIL	Society of Biblical Literature Ancient Israel and Its Literature
SBLDS	Society of Biblical Literature Dissertation Series
SBLMS	Society of Biblical Literature Monograph Series
SBLSP	Society of Biblical Literature Seminar Papers
SBLSup	Society of Biblical Literature Supplement Series
SBLSymS	Society of Biblical Literature Symposium Series
SBLWAW	Society of Biblical Literature Writings from the Ancient World
SBS	Stuttgarter Bibelstudien
SEÅ	*Svensk Exegetisk Årsbok*
SemeiaSt	Semeia Studies
SJOT	*Scandinavian Journal of the Old Testament*
SNTSMS	Society for New Testament Studies Monograph Series
SSLL	Studies in Semitic Languages and Linguistics
STDJ	Studies on the Texts of the Desert of Judah
TJ	*Trinity Journal*
TynBul	*Tyndale Bulletin*
VT	*Vetus Testamentum*
VTSup	Supplements to Vetus Testamentum
WAW	Writings from the Ancient World
WBC	Word Biblical Commentary
WMANT	Wissenschaftliche Monographien zum Alten und Neuen Testament
WTJ	*Westminster Theological Journal*
WUNT	Wissenschaftliche Untersuchungen zum Neuen Testament
ZAW	*Zeitschrift für die alttestamentliche Wissenschaft*

Introduction

RICHARD L. SCHULTZ

In the course of Sirach's praise of "famous men, our ancestors in their generations" (Sir 44:1), the author highlights the visionary powers of the prophet Isaiah: "By his dauntless spirit he saw the future, and comforted the mourners in Zion [τοὺς πενθοῦντας ἐν Σιων, *tous penthountas en Siōn*; cf. Isa 61:3 LXX: τοῖς πενθοῦσιν Σιων, *tois penthousin Siōn*]. He revealed what was to occur to the end of time, and the hidden things [τὰ ἀπόκρυφα, *ta apokrypha*; cf. Isa 45:3 LXX: ἀποκρύφους, *apokryphous*] before they happened" (Sir 48:24–25 NRSV). Here Sirach affirms that the same eighth-century BCE prophet Isaiah who supported Hezekiah in a time of national distress (Sir 48:20–23; cf. Isa 36–39) also addressed the "mourners in Zion" in Isa 61. It is precisely this assertion that has been the focus of considerable scholarly discussion and debate for more than three centuries.

On the one hand, modernist interpreters claim that their goal is simply to interpret the various prophetic messages contained in the canonical book of Isaiah in light of their original historical-cultural settings. According to these interpreters, there is an abundance of compelling evidence that many of these compositional units stem from a much later period in Israelite history than the reigns of King Hezekiah and his immediate predecessors. On the other hand, traditionalist interpreters claim that, since the book of Isaiah itself acknowledges only one prophetic source, it should be read as an original compositional unity from the period of the divided monarchy. These interpreters argue that none of the book's content exceeds that which the inspiring Spirit could reveal to and through the special messenger of Israel's God. An even-handed assessment, however, would acknowledge that numerous texts within this prophetic work lack sufficient indication of their exact period of origin.

Too often, proponents of opposing interpretive positions talk past, ignore, or even denigrate the publications of the others. Some are skeptical that an open conversation between those holding long-standing contrasting positions would prove to be constructive. All but two of the essays in the following volume were prepared for the first biennial Wheaton College Old Testament Colloquium.[1] The purpose of the colloquium was to provide a venue in which evangelical scholars who have

---

1. G. K. Beale's essay, "'Isaiah the Prophet Said': The Authorship of Isaiah Re-examined in the Light of Early Jewish and Christian Writings," is a revision of ch. 5 of his book *The Erosion of Inerrancy in Evangelicalism: Responding to New Challenges to Biblical Authority* (Wheaton, IL: Crossway, 2008). Richard Schultz's essay "Isaianic Intertextuality and

expertise in a particular Old Testament sub-discipline and who represent a range of interpretive viewpoints regarding disputed issues related to it can meet together for several days to discuss openly and irenically the pertinent textual and extratextual evidence and its theological and hermeneutical implications. Ten academic papers addressing various aspects of the contents, compositional history, and history of interpretation of the book of Isaiah were read in advance by the participants, summarized and discussed at length during the colloquium, and subsequently revised in light of our academic conversations.

All the contributors to this volume are evangelical biblical scholars, but they hold to divergent positions regarding the compositional process by which the book of Isaiah was created and the resultant degree of unity the book possesses. Two of them expressly defend a multi-author viewpoint in their essays, others defend a one-author position, and still others simply synthesize textual or historical data without drawing firm conclusions regarding questions of authorship and dating. The diversity of the participants' interpretive frameworks and disciplinary specializations enlivened and enriched our dialogue during the colloquium and, hopefully, make this publication a more balanced and substantial presentation of issues that have often divided scholars. This diversity of perspectives also means, not surprisingly, that the co-editors do not agree with all the positions presented in the following essays.

The initial five essays explore the history of the interpretation of the book of Isaiah. Richard Schultz's opening essay briefly summarizes major developments in Isaianic studies during recent decades, including progressive evangelical proposals. The majority of the essay traces the rise of the multi-author view of the composition of Isaiah, from Campegius Vitringa through Bernhard Duhm, noting the primary factors that led to the development of this view. The essay concludes with discussions of (1) the difficulty of dating, delimiting, and determining the meaning of individual texts in the book of Isaiah, and (2) the warrant for positing Spirit-directed editorial work in the formation of the text, as well as (3) a proposal that Isaiah might be considered the primary source of the prophecies in the book rather than their sole author/editor. These topics are provided as points of departure for the following essays in this collection.

Richard Schultz's second essay explores the relationship between Isaiah and other Hebrew Bible texts—both those dated earlier and those dated later than their Isaianic intertexts—as well as intratextual parallels within the book of Isaiah itself. Though such explicit verbal parallels and allusions offer ample evidence of the influence of the Isaianic tradition on other biblical writers, as well as the receptivity of those responsible for the Isaianic tradition toward other Israelite traditions, scholars' common employment of them in reconstructing the compositional growth of the book of Isaiah is assessed as being methodologically problematic. This is due primarily to difficulties involved both in tracing the direction of literary borrowing

---

Intratextuality as Composition-Historical Indicators: Methodological Challenges in Determining Literary Influence" was written later for inclusion in this volume.

within the prophetic corpus and in assessing the significance of such borrowing, as is illustrated by several representative intratextual and intertextual studies.

Gregory Beale continues the intertextual emphasis with a detailed study of early quotations of and references to the book and/or prophet Isaiah outside of the Hebrew Bible. He argues that the attributions of quotations to the prophet Isaiah in early Judaism, the New Testament, and early Christian texts offer such compelling evidence in support of the active, personal role of Isaiah the prophet in writing and prophesying in all parts of the book that arguing instead for multiple authors requires one to conclude that Jesus and the New Testament writers were fundamentally wrong in their assessment of the book's authorship.

Michael Graves seeks to identify and explain the most important ancient and medieval Jewish sources that potentially address the authorship of Isaiah, giving special attention to the Talmudic tractate *Baba Batra* and the writings of Ibn Ezra. He also traces how Jewish thinking on this topic has developed in recent years in light of modern biblical criticism, noting that many questions raised by contemporary scholars regarding the composition of Isaiah were already raised by early rabbis and medieval scholars, though the latter usually offered different answers than many modern Jewish thinkers.

In the final essay in this section, Seulgi Byun surveys the Qumran manuscripts of Isaiah and their relation to the Masoretic Text, and examines whether scribal features in 1QIsa^a indicate "editions," "volumes," or other structural features. Similarly to Beale, he analyzes the attributions of quotations of Isaiah in the nonbiblical texts at Qumran in order to determine how the community approached the questions of the authorship and coherence of the book.

The next section consists of four essays that focus on the historical context of the book of Isaiah. Taking a multi-author perspective, Knut Heim proposes that the book called Isaiah has been shaped to form a larger whole that transcends the various perspectives of its constituent parts and thus, in its final canonical form, contains editorial clues that overtly encourage readers to note the diachronic dimensions of various parts of the book. He develops his thesis by examining several shorter texts and one longer text (Isa 13–23), concluding that the book wants to be read both as a unified composition, inspired by the historical figure of the prophet Isaiah of Jerusalem, and as a "prophetic chronicle," in which "the original compositions from Isaiah's own lifetime" are interspersed with "divinely inspired theological and equally prophetic reflections in the form of shorter comments *and* carefully crafted, longer literary units" (p. 150).

John Hilber explores the contribution of ancient Near Eastern prophecy to questions about the prophet Isaiah and the book that bears his name. He establishes that Mesopotamian texts refer to individual prophets who produced written prophecy, sometimes with the assistance of a scribe. However, extrabiblical prophetic texts from the ancient Near East offer no evidence that scribes "recontextualized" prophetic oracles by rewriting them or expanded prophetic oracles in any substantial way. Nor were these Mesopotamian and Egyptian texts regarded as "prophetic" in the same sense as the biblical books, due to the very different mechanism for mediating divine revelation involved in the former (i.e., omen divination and magic).

Hilber concludes that, since prophetic literature in the Bible has no analogy in the ancient Near East, the comparative method contributes little to our understanding of the composition of Isaiah as a whole.

Gary Smith considers historical issues that bear on the interpretation of Isa 40–55. After highlighting the historical arguments for an exilic provenance of these chapters, he argues, unconventionally, that the historical allusions and war imagery contained in these chapters fit best in the world of preexilic Judah, and specifically that they refer to Sennacherib's attack on Jerusalem (chs. 36–37), during which Hezekiah was considering entering an alliance with Babylon (ch. 39). The oracles referring to Cyrus in 44:28 and 45:1, in turn, assert that, if God raised up a strong king like Sennacherib (41:2–3, 25) and redeemed his people from the power of this king in the past (37:36; 41:10–13), God's people should be able to trust him to use the unknown king Cyrus to restore the people of Jerusalem from exile in the future (44:24–45:7).

Mark Rooker undertakes a detailed linguistic analysis of Isa 1–39 and 40–66 to determine whether the language of the latter chapters derives from a later period than the language of the former. Responding in particular to Shalom Paul's recent work, he seeks to demonstrate that, while the precise date of Isaiah cannot be established on linguistic grounds alone, Isa 40–66 does not employ the same features found in documents from the exilic and postexilic periods, as represented by Esther, Ezra-Nehemiah, and 1–2 Chronicles. Rather, the language of Isa 40–66 appears to reflect the same period of linguistic development as the language found in chapters 1–39.

The final section consists of three essays that consider evidence for the literary and theological coherence or incoherence of the book of Isaiah. Peter Gentry gives special attention to the role of text linguistics, the features of Hebrew discourse and literature, the character of the author, and the nature of Hebrew prophecy in the presentation of his case that the book of Isaiah exhibits literary and theological coherence issuing from a single mind. Emphasizing the recursive and resumptive character of the oracles incorporated into the book of Isaiah, Gentry seeks to demonstrate that the themes of social justice, judgment and restoration, and the role of the Davidic king combine to unite the sections of the book in the form of one grand essay.

In contrast, Mark Boda focuses on the voices of the various speakers in Isaiah in proposing that the autobiographical voices of Isa 40–66—especially in chapter 40—are distinct from the autobiographical voice of chapters 1–39, which is clearly that of the eighth-century prophet Isaiah of Jerusalem. Appealing to New Testament texts that highlight the role of the Holy Spirit in guiding the authors of Scripture into truth, Boda suggests that, although the autobiographical voices of chapters 40–66 are distinct from the voice of the earlier prophet, they nevertheless articulate the Isaianic message anew for those who return from the exile.

John Oswalt counters that the person(s) responsible for the final form of the book wanted the prophecies in it to be read as the work of a single prophet, the eighth-century prophet Isaiah son of Amoz. He observes that chapters 40–66 neither hint at the identity of any other author nor offer geographical or historical information that would ascribe the material in these chapters to any other person. The exceptional reference to Cyrus appears in an explicitly predictive context, which demonstrates that, unlike other gods, YHWH is able not only to predict the future but also to determine the course of future events.

Daniel Block's epilogue briefly reviews the perspectives represented by the papers in this volume, identifying both the common threads and the divergent viewpoints. Evangelical scholars recognize that, while the processes by which prophetic books were produced may have varied from book to book, a high view of Scripture requires that we acknowledge the role of the Holy Spirit in each phase of a book's growth, with the result that the final product remains authoritative Scripture for the church.

For more than a century, the standard academic account of the composition of the book of Isaiah has posited two or three major authors or tradition circles and two and a half centuries of editorial growth. During recent decades, evangelical scholars have increasingly adopted this viewpoint, thereby raising some basic questions about the theological compatibility of these conclusions with traditional understandings of divine inspiration, predictive prophecy, and the apparent association in Isa 1:1 of the (entire) book with the eighth-century prophet. The scholars invited to our Isaiah Colloquium voiced a variety of perspectives regarding these disputed issues. They also encouraged each other to give serious attention to the possible contributions of divinely inspired editors, as well as to the internal evidence for a complex and lengthy process of composition and later editorial supplementation.

The colloquium did not result in any definite consensus regarding these matters, but the open and honest exploration of interpretive options was both illuminating and refreshing. It is the hope of the co-organizers of the colloquium in our role as co-editors of this book that the essays contained herein will serve not only to offer new and refined arguments in support of the one-author view of the book of Isaiah, but also to promote ongoing, irenic evangelical conversations regarding its contents and composition. All the contributors are agreed that the prophet Isaiah as divine spokesperson "was great and trustworthy in his visions" (Sir 48:22 NRSV). As such, any effort made to understand the book of Isaiah more fully is, at the same time, an effort to discern more accurately the voice of the God of Israel. And so we continue to ponder the words of the ancient prophet, despite all of our still unanswered—and perhaps unanswerable—questions.

The Origins and Basic Arguments of the Multi-Author View of the Composition of Isaiah: Where Are We Now and How Did We Get Here?

1

RICHARD L. SCHULTZ

Introduction: Evangelicals and the Critical Analysis of the Book of Isaiah

The purpose of this essay is to provide an historical context for the essays to follow in this volume by addressing three foundational introductory questions: (1) How is the composition of the book of Isaiah generally understood in the academy today? (2) What are the key textual phenomena that led, or even compelled, scholars gradually to reject the traditional view of unified authorship? and (3) How did that process unfold?

At the outset, it should be acknowledged that the majority viewpoint of the Christian church extending backwards in time to its first-century origins and encompassing local congregations around the world is that the entire book of Isaiah essentially had its origins in the prophetic ministry of one eighth-century Israelite prophet. The apparent claim of Isa 1:1 that the book of Isaiah records the "vision concerning Judah and Jerusalem that Isaiah son of Amoz saw during the reigns of Uzziah, Jotham, Ahaz and Hezekiah, kings of Judah"—a public ministry that presumably lasted for at least a half century—suffices for them to support this view, buttressed by repeated quotations from the *book* of Isaiah attributed by New Testament authors to the *prophet* Isaiah.[1] Nevertheless, most critical biblical scholars, including a growing percentage of evangelical scholars, no longer affirm this traditional position, positing instead a multi-author origin for the book.[2] Thus Hugh Williamson concludes that the view "that the book was all written by a single

---

1. See Bill T. Arnold and Bryan E. Beyer, *Encountering the Old Testament* (Grand Rapids: Baker Books, 1999), 371: "Over the centuries most Jews and Christians have believed the prophet Isaiah wrote the entire book that bears his name." G. K. Beale, *The Erosion of Inerrancy in Evangelicalism: Responding to New Challenges to Biblical Authority* (Wheaton, IL: Crossway, 2008), 123–59, a version of which appears below, offers a defense of traditional authorship along these lines.

2. Arnold and Beyer, *Encountering the Old Testament*, 370.

individual . . . is still defended [only] from time to time,"[3] but he himself considers this position to be neither "plausible" nor "necessary."[4]

Recent Trends in the Study of Isaiah

The Gradual Collapse of the Duhm Consensus

How did we arrive at the current multi-author (and multi-editor) analysis of the book of Isaiah? Most discussions of Isaiah begin with Bernhard Duhm, since he is to the modern historical-critical study of the book of Isaiah what Julius Wellhausen is to contemporary Pentateuchal studies. Already building on more than a century of critical studies of Isaiah, in his 1892 commentary Duhm offered a persuasive synthesis of the compositional origins of the book, which set the agenda for Isaiah studies for the next century. Most influential was Duhm's distinction between three primary and completely independent authors—one preexilic, associated with Isa 1–39; one late exilic, associated with Isa 40–55; and one postexilic, associated with Isa 56–66—authors who later became known, respectively, as "First," "Second," and "Third" Isaiah. However, according to Duhm, the three subsections of the book he attributed to these authors were hardly monolithic in nature, since, in his view, Isa 13–23 was added in the second half of the second century BCE, Isa 24–27 was composed around 128 BCE, Isa 34–35 originated in the Maccabean period, Isa 36–39 was derived from 1–2 Kings, and four "Servant Songs" were inserted into Isa 40–55. Duhm did not view these later additions as necessary supplements to the already-existing oracle collections that had been included as part of some larger, theologically driven editorial plan.[5]

On the one hand, those accustomed to reading about only two or three "Isaiahs" in the standard textbooks might be surprised to learn that, already by the end of the nineteenth century, Duhm and others had posited the contributions of additional authorial and editorial hands stretching far beyond the early postexilic era. This is a detail that Evangelicals affirming the existence of a "Second Isaiah" or "Third Isaiah" seldom acknowledge. On the other hand, except for Duhm's assertion of multiple authors and editors having been involved in the composition of the book of Isaiah, the consensus that resulted from his work on Isaiah has crumbled in almost all respects, some of which will be discussed below.[6]

---

3. H. G. M. Williamson, "Recent Issues in the Study of Isaiah," in *Interpreting Isaiah: Issues and Approaches*, ed. David G. Firth and H. G. M. Williamson (Downers Grove, IL: InterVarsity Press, 2009), 21.

4. H. G. M. Williamson, "Isaiah, Book of," in *Dictionary of the Old Testament: Prophets*, ed. Mark J. Boda and J. Gordon McConville (Downers Grove, IL: InterVarsity Press, 2012), 370.

5. Bernhard Duhm, *Das Buch Jesaia*, 4th ed., Göttinger HKAT (Göttingen: Vandenhoeck & Ruprecht, 1922), 7–15.

6. For a more detailed discussion of how recent scholars have disputed Duhm's key claims, see Richard L. Schultz, "How Many Isaiahs Were There and What Does It Matter?

Redefining the Identity and Roles of Second and Third Isaiah

In this regard, one growing trend within Isaianic studies is the questioning of the identity or even the existence of Third Isaiah. There are several variations on this view, but all basically involve a return to the pre-Duhm position of ascribing most of chapters 40–66 to one author/editor/group. One version, endorsed by Christopher Seitz, claims a Palestinian provenance for the entire book,[7] rejecting the claim that Second Isaiah originated in the Jewish exilic community in Babylon sometime between 586 and 536 BCE. Lena-Sofia Tiemeyer describes this long-held claim as "a house built on sand without a firm textual foundation," arguing instead that Isa 40–55, along with 56–66, is part of a continuous Judahite prophetic tradition produced by those who remained in the land, not by members of the "*golah* group."[8] This opens up the possibility that the person or group behind Second Isaiah might have been the same as the one behind Third Isaiah, which has led Richard Coggins to ask, "Do we still need Deutero-Isaiah?"[9] Whether Third Isaiah consequently vanishes or is simply equated with Second Isaiah, the effect is essentially the same: the "three Isaiahs" viewpoint no longer commands a consensus. An alternative view, argued by Williamson and Jacob Stromberg, understands Second Isaiah as both a primary author of chapters 40–55 and editor of chapters 1–55, while Third Isaiah similarly served as a primary author of chapters 56–66 and editor of chapters 1–66.[10]

The Increasing Literary-Critical Atomization of Texts

For more than a century since Duhm, literary and redaction critics have continued to identify later explanatory glosses, expansions, and additions in Isaianic texts. This approach has not abated as a result of the development of newer synchronic/literary/holistic/final-form approaches. To the contrary, it seems that no text is safe from the textual surgeon's scalpel. For example, Ronald Clements distinguishes within a single textual unit, Isa 2:6–22, *nine* authorial or editorial

---

Prophetic Inspiration in Recent Evangelical Scholarship," in *Scripture in the Evangelical Tradition: Tradition, Authority, and Hermeneutics*, ed. Vincent Bacote, Laura C. Miguélez, and Dennis L. Okholm (Downers Grove, IL: InterVarsity Press, 2004), 153–54.

7. Christopher R. Seitz, "Isaiah, Book of (First Isaiah), (Third Isaiah)," *ABD* 3:472–88, 501–7; *Zion's Final Destiny: The Development of the Book of Isaiah; A Reassessment of Isaiah 36–39* (Minneapolis: Fortress, 1991). Seitz is not alone in claiming a Palestinian provenance for the entire book.

8. Lena-Sofia Tiemeyer, *For the Comfort of Zion: The Geographical and Theological Location of Isaiah 40–55*, VTSup 139 (Leiden: Brill, 2011), 363–65.

9. Richard J. Coggins, "Do We Still Need Deutero-Isaiah?," *JSOT* 81 (1998): 77–92.

10. See Williamson's summary of this view in "Recent Issues in the Study of Isaiah," 28–29, as well as the fuller treatments in H. G. M. Williamson, *The Book Called Isaiah: Deutero-Isaiah's Role in Composition and Redaction* (Oxford: Clarendon, 1994), and Jacob Stromberg, *Isaiah After Exile: The Author of Third Isaiah as Reader and Redactor of the Book*, Oxford Theological Monographs (Oxford: Oxford University Press, 2011).

hands spanning at least three centuries,[11] while Williamson and Stromberg point to numerous editorial insertions by "Second" and "Third" Isaiah within sections of the book not usually attributed to them.[12]

The Shrinking Profile of the Eighth-Century Prophet and a Half Millennium of Other "Isaiahs"

As a result of the ongoing effort to identify later additions in the book of Isaiah, the number of verses attributed to the eighth-century prophet Isaiah continues to shrink, although there is clearly no consensus regarding how many (or which) verses are "genuine." Historical-critical "maximalists" who follow the broad parameters of the critical consensus regarding the origins of Isa 36–39, 40–55, and 56–66 reduce by nearly one half the portion of the book stemming from the eighth-century prophet, while some scholars limit Isaiah of Jerusalem's contribution to only chapters 7–8 and 28–31. For example, Matthijs de Jong attributes only ninety-five verses in the book "to prophetic activity in the eighth century"—and these, according to de Jong, do not necessarily even derive from the prophet Isaiah himself.[13]

Ironically, at the same time some scholars continue to emphasize the remarkable *personal* influence exercised on the formation of the book by Isaiah of Jerusalem, whose eighth-century ministry spawned a "circle" or "school" of disciples that continued to treasure, transmit, reinterpret and expand his prophetic legacy for two or more centuries. In fact, many Isaiah scholars today trace an ongoing compositional process for centuries after "Third Isaiah" supposedly authored chapters 55–66. For example, building on the tradition-historical and redactional work of Odil Hannes Steck, Judith Gärtner locates the final editor of the book as late as the third century BCE.[14] It appears that the only operative *termini ad quem* are the reference to Isaiah (mostly likely to 61:3) in Sir 48:24–25 and the discovery of copies of Isaiah at Qumran!

---

11. Ronald E. Clements, *Isaiah 1–39*, NCB (Grand Rapids: Eerdmans, 1980), 42–46.

12. See Williamson, *Book Called Isaiah*, chs. 6–8; and Stromberg, *Isaiah After Exile*, chs. 5–6. See also H. G. M. Williamson, *Isaiah 1–5*, ICC (London: T&T Clark, 2006).

13. Matthijs J. de Jong, *Isaiah among the Ancient Near Eastern Prophets: A Comparative Study of the Earliest Stages of the Isaiah Tradition and the Neo-Assyrian Prophecies*, VTSup 117 (Leiden: Brill, 2007), 465. According to an earlier calculation by George L. Robinson, "Isaiah," *ISBE*, 1st (1915) ed., 3:1505, the "moderate" scholars of the early twentieth century concluded that forty-four out of sixty-six chapters were not written by Isaiah (i.e., approximately 800 out of 1,292 verses, or 62 percent, are not genuine). "Radicals," such as Cheyne, Duhm, Marti, and Gray, rejected approximately 1,030 verses, accepting only about 262 out of 1,292 verses, or 20 percent, as genuine.

14. Judith Gärtner, *Jesaja 66 und Sacharja 14 als Summe der Prophetie: Eine traditions- und redaktionsgeschichtliche Untersuchung zum Abschluss des Jesaja- und des Zwölfprophet- enbuches*, WMANT 114 (Neukirchen-Vluyn: Neukirchener, 2006). These late editors were not conceived as merely rearranging previously existing materials. Steck, for example, argues that chs. 56–59 were added to the growing complex of Isaianic tradition sometime before 302/301 BCE (Odil H. Steck, "Beobachtungen zu Jesaja 56–59," *BZ*, n.s., 31 [1987]: 236n40).

In sum, one of the longest Old Testament books is sometimes understood as having been generated by the proclamation of an eighth-century prophet, the extent of whose personal literary record is approximately the same length as the book of Micah. So small has the contribution of the traditional prophet become in the wake of critical analysis that Stromberg considers it a positive statement to concede that "some of the prophecies in the book are actually authentic."[15] At the same time, there has been a shift in how some scholars view what they consider to be substantial additions to the original prophetic core. To again cite Stromberg, "later developments are now being appreciated as much as original sources" (or, one might argue, even more), so that " 'authentic' is not better than 'secondary.' "[16]

The Ascendance of the "One Canonical Book of Isaiah" View

One of the most remarkable developments in the post-Duhm world is the "one book of Isaiah" perspective, which focuses on unifying features of the book rather than on its critical dissection.[17] This approach has been gaining an increasing number of adherents for nearly four decades. Although there certainly were earlier contributions pointing in this direction, one major impetus for this new emphasis was the publication, in 1976, of Roy Melugin's dissertation on Isa 40–55 and this scholar's subsequent role in helping to establish and lead the "Formation of the Book of Isaiah Group" within the Society of Biblical Literature.[18] The approach advocated by this group should be understood neither as a return to the pre-critical "one Isaiah" viewpoint nor as a radical departure from the critical consensus.[19] Rather, the new contributions involved the identification of "large structural features" within the book of Isaiah and the claim that redactional activity

---

15. Jacob Stromberg, *An Introduction to the Study of Isaiah*, T&T Clark Approaches to Biblical Studies (London: T&T Clark, 2011), 2. In a similar vein, Williamson speaks of the "search" for "the pre-exilic Isaiah," in which one seeks to hear the voice of the original prophet amidst the tangle of textual accretions incorporated within the canonical book (H. G. M. Williamson, "In Search of the Pre-Exilic Isaiah," in *In Search of Pre-Exilic Israel*, ed. John Day [London: T&T Clark, 2004], 181–206).

16. Stromberg, *Introduction to the Study of Isaiah*, 2.

17. A helpful summary of the "one-book" approach to Isaiah and its proponents is offered by Marvin E. Tate, "The Book of Isaiah in Recent Study," in *Forming Prophetic Literature: Essays on Isaiah and the Twelve in Honor of John D. W. Watts*, ed. James W. Watts and Paul R. House, JSOTS 235 (Sheffield: Sheffield Academic, 1996), 22–56. Tate contrasts what he calls the "One-Book Interpretation" with the "One-Prophet" and the "Three-Book" interpretations.

18. Roy F. Melugin, *The Formation of Isaiah 40–55*, BZAW 141 (Berlin: de Gruyter, 1976). For a discussion of the most influential precursors of this movement and a summary of the work of this SBL seminar since its establishment in 1990, see Patricia Tull, "One Book, Many Voices: Conceiving of Isaiah's Polyphonic Message," in *"As Those Who Are Taught": The Interpretation of Isaiah from the LXX to the SBL*, ed. Claire Mathews McGinnis and Patricia K. Tull, SBLSymS 27 (Atlanta: Society of Biblical Literature, 2006), 279–314.

19. See Tull's affirmation of the continuity of the seminar's work with precursors such as Duhm ("One Book, Many Voices," 290).

often involved "[r]einterpretation and recontextualization of the prophet's words for generations beyond his horizon," activity that applied these words to later circumstances in which they offered comfort or rebuke.[20] Not all recent advocates of the "one book of Isaiah" approach have employed this methodology; nevertheless, in their work tradition-historical, redactional, canonical, sociological, literary, rhetorical, and thematic approaches complement one another in a unique, even remarkable, way to create "new visions" of the unity of the book of Isaiah.[21]

To summarize the current state of Isaiah studies, although there is a great diversity in critical approaches, the following perspectives predominate:

(1) Duhm's view that the major contributors to the book were three single independent authors and that the book constitutes a loosely organized anthology has been largely rejected. This position has been replaced by the view that later contributors, loosely designated "Second" and "Third" Isaiah, consciously supplemented the oracles of First Isaiah, perhaps viewing themselves as his "disciples," and the book was carefully edited over the course of three to five centuries to produce a theologically coherent whole.

(2) Each of the major sections of the book is much more heterogeneous than previously thought, with editorial insertions and interpretive glosses clarifying and updating statements in nearly every textual unit.

(3) The distinction between Second and Third Isaiah is becoming increasingly blurred and, as a result, it is treated as less crucial for the overall interpretation of the book.

(4) The significant influence of the eighth-century prophet on the entire complex and protracted compositional process is emphasized, even as his actual literary deposit continues to shrink as a result of literary-critical analysis.

(5) The most striking "discovery" during the past quarter century has been the undeniable "unity" of the book, though this is diversely described.[22]

---

20. Tull, "One Book, Many Voices," 291.

21. See Roy F. Melugin and Marvin A. Sweeney, eds., *New Visions of Isaiah* (Sheffield: Sheffield Academic, 1996). In contrast to the SBL group, when the evangelical Tyndale Fellowship Old Testament Study Group met in Cambridge in July 2008 to discuss the book of Isaiah, no paper was devoted primarily to its compositional unity or to internal indications of how the canonical book wishes to be read. See the resultant conference volume edited by David G. Firth and H. G. M. Williamson, *Interpreting Isaiah: Issues and Approaches* (Downers Grove, IL: InterVarsity Press, 2009).

22. Shalom Paul's recently published commentary (*Isaiah 40–66*, ECC [Grand Rapids: Eerdmans, 2012], 1–12) illustrates some of these trends. According to Paul, (1) the prophecies of First and Second Isaiah were not combined arbitrarily but, rather, due to their "linguistic affinity," a reflection of the former's influence on the latter. (2) There are clear linguistic and thematic links between Isa 55 and 56 that negate the standard redaction-critical claim that

The Evangelical Response to the
Historical-Critical Assessment of Isaiah

The Current Denigration of and Disregard for
"One Prophet" Proponents

Most scholars feel so confident in the critical consensus regarding the complex and lengthy compositional history of the book of Isaiah that a detailed rehearsal of the key arguments in support of this consensus is often deemed unnecessary. Furthermore, proponents of this view have sometimes engaged in snide denigration of or have disregarded the remaining proponents of the "one prophet" interpretation. For example, Brevard Childs accuses conservatives of turning Isaiah into "a clairvoyant of the future,"[23] while Marvin Tate criticizes Alec Motyer's "shopworn appeals to verbal inspiration."[24] In Tate's assessment, "[t]he substance of the work of scholars along this line has not improved over the past century" and thus "faces a marginalized future."[25] Proponents of the multiple authorship of Isaiah widely dismiss defenders of the "one prophet" approach as merely relying on "slogans or theological dicta."[26]

Progressive Evangelical Perspectives Today

As noted above, a growing number of evangelical scholars (i.e., those who identify themselves as such and/or who teach at evangelical institutions) no longer affirm the "one prophet Isaiah" position. These "progressive"[27] evangelical biblical scholars typically share at least four claims:

(1) They affirm without qualification the historical-critical view that the book of Isaiah has at least two or three major authors and, in some cases, acknowledge the presence of additional authorial and editorial hands contributing to

---

a major subdivision of the book begins in the latter. (3) Isa 40–66 constitutes one coherent work composed by a single prophet who spent time in both Babylon and Jerusalem. Accordingly, there was no Third Isaiah (a rather conservative position today).

23. Brevard S. Childs, *Isaiah: A Commentary*, OTL (Louisville: Westminster John Knox, 2001), 3–4.

24. Tate, "Book of Isaiah," 27. See J. A. Motyer, *The Prophecy of Isaiah* (Downers Grove, IL: Inter Varsity Press, 1993), 25–33; idem, "Three in One or One in Three: A Dipstick into the Isaianic Literature," *Chm* 108 (1994): 22–36.

25. Tate, "Book of Isaiah," 52.

26. Here Tate ("Book of Isaiah," 52) cites Raymond B. Dillard and Tremper Longman III, *An Introduction to the Old Testament* (Grand Rapids: Zondervan, 1994), 75.

27. This term is preferred by Kenton Sparks to designate those Evangelicals who *accept* rather than *oppose* the "assured results" of modern critical scholarship, even if that requires them to revise their doctrine of Scripture (Kenton L. Sparks, *God's Word in Human Words: An Evangelical Appropriation of Critical Biblical Scholarship* [Grand Rapids: Baker Academic, 2008], 169).

the composition of the book. They find the evidence cited by many scholars in support of multiple authors convincing.

(2) Despite stemming from various authors, the prophetic writings included within the book of Isaiah are basically in continuity with each other rather than contradictory. This agreement may be attributed to the work of the one inspiring Spirit as well as to careful editing. This coherence is to be seen in the overall structure and flow of the book rather than in specific affirmations. As John Goldingay describes it, in the book one can hear a quartet (or quintet) of harmonious voices, which he labels, in sequence, the ambassador, disciple, poet, preacher (and visionary).[28]

(3) Above all, this harmony stems from the fact that these later authors viewed themselves as disciples of Isaiah who operated "under the influence" of and constantly imitated their prophetic master.[29] Accordingly, the superscription in Isa 1:1 is "less a matter of authorship or proprietary claims made on behalf of Isaiah than it is a statement of belief, made on the part of those who shaped the Isaiah traditions, that what followed was a faithful rendering of the essence of Isaiah's preaching as vouchsafed to him by God."[30]

(4) The nature, extent, and (non-)fulfillment of "predictive" prophecy constitutes the primary objection adherents of the progressive evangelical view raise against the traditional one-author view. This includes the claim that Cyrus' role in releasing the exiles and rebuilding Jerusalem would not (or could not) be predicted by Isaiah long in advance. An astonished John Goldingay asks, "What would God be doing giving Isaiah in the eighth century words to write down that were addressed to people two centuries later?"[31]

But the problems extend beyond the mention of the Persian ruler in Isa 44–45. Numerous prophecies are also judged to be inaccurate, i.e., not fulfilled by later historical events. These lead Amber Warhurst, Seth B. Tarrer, and Christopher M. Hays, the co-authors of a chapter on prophecy in a recent work, to claim that such texts (e.g., Ezek 36:1–21; Isa 13:17–19; Jer 51:11–12; Jer 34:1–5 [cf. 52:3–11 and 2 Kgs 25:7]; Jer 22:18–19 and 36:30–31 [cf. 2 Kgs 24:6 and 2 Chr 36:8]) should be understood not as specific predictions but as prophecies that dynamically set forth God's general plans in history so that a "broad range of

---

28. John Goldingay, *Isaiah*, NIBCOT (Peabody, MA: Hendrickson, 2001), 2–5. Goldingay adds to the four, as a secondary voice, the apocalyptic voice heard in Isa 24–27.

29. I discuss three evangelical publications that illustrate this emphasis in my "How Many Isaiahs Were There and What Does It Matter?," 154–58.

30. Christopher R. Seitz, *Isaiah 1–39*, IBC (Philadelphia: Westminster John Knox, 1993), 24.

31. John Goldingay, "What Are the Characteristics of Evangelical Study of the Old Testament?," *EvQ* 73 (2001): 105.

fitting events can fill up a prophetic word."[32] Not only can these prophecies be expressed by means of obscure and imprecise figurative language, but they are also always conditioned by God's freedom to act differently than anticipated in response to the behavior of the prophecy's initial audience. In other words, such prophecy should be viewed as "unpredictable."[33] These co-authors also affirm the validity of *vaticinium ex eventu*[34] as a non-deceptive (i.e., not intended to be predictive) convention of apocalyptic texts that served to affirm God's sovereignty over history.[35]

To summarize, despite the risk of being reductionistic, progressive Evangelicals affirm a multi-author approach to the composition of the book of Isaiah, whether limiting this to two or three "Isaiahs" or identifying more extensive editorial additions throughout the book. They usually conceive of the major contributors to the book as consciously building on and, as necessary, clarifying (or even correcting), and thereby continuing, the prophetic legacy of the eighth-century prophet Isaiah into the following centuries of Israelite history, and of doing so under the inspiration and guidance of the same divine Spirit.

Open Questions for Traditionalist Evangelical Scholarship

Some of these "progressive" discussions of the composition of Isaiah not only wrestle honestly with perceived conceptual differences and tensions within the book but also uphold a high view of the scriptural authority of OT prophecy as a *divine* word and not merely a *human* word. Therefore they challenge conservative scholars to take seriously the charge that the traditional evangelical understanding of biblical prophecy in general, and in the book of Isaiah in particular, is simply driven by dogmatic—rather than textual—claims. Such discussions also prompt reconsideration of the counter-accusation that historical-critical conceptions of prophecy are fundamentally driven by God-denying rationalism.

As noted above, if Williamson is correct in claiming that the one-author view of Isaiah is neither "plausible" nor "necessary," one must ask why it continues to be defended. Or, to express the matter differently: What do proponents of a one-author model consider to be at stake here? Here are a few concerns that help to explain the reluctance of some critically informed scholars to abandon a traditionalist position:[36]

---

32. Amber Warhurst, Seth B. Tarrer, and Christopher M. Hays, "Problems with Prophecy," in *Evangelical Faith and the Challenge of Historical Criticism*, ed. Christopher M. Hays and Christopher B. Ansberry (London: SPCK, 2013), 101.

33. Ibid.

34. That is, prophecy composed *after* the prophet already knew the outcome of the events that he appeared to be predicting.

35. Warhurst, Tarrer, and Hays, "Problems with Prophecy," 111–13.

36. The following should not be understood as the strongest arguments that I would offer in support of the one-author position, but rather as issues that, in my view, ought to

(1) Such scholars wonder whether the superscription in Isa 1:1 places any constraints on one's model of compositional growth, especially given the absence of any comparable superscription in Isa 40–66.

(2) They find unconvincing the positing of the existence of a succession of "disciples"—usually argued for largely on the basis of Isa 8:16—who sustained a prophetic movement inspired by Isaiah for several centuries and who were responsible for producing half or more of the present book.

(3) On the basis of specific OT and NT texts, they consider "prediction" to be a feature of biblical prophecy and therefore resist efforts to explain texts that appear to be predictive in nature as non-specific poetic visions of a better (or worse) future or as *vaticinium ex eventu*, troubled as they are by the potentially deceptive nature of the latter. Rather, such scholars understand the ability to predict and bring about the foretold future as one of the abilities that distinguishes Israel's God from the deities of its neighbors (see Isa 44:26).

(4) They are generally satisfied with explanations of stylistic and theological diversity within the book of Isaiah that do not involve attributing divergent texts to different authors.[37]

Given these convictions and concerns, although proponents of the one-author approach to Isaiah are open to engaging historical-critical findings (for example, those regarding "unfulfilled" prophecies), they wonder whether a new, more "progressive" consensus position can be found that adequately addresses—or dispels— these concerns for those who affirm the work of the divine Spirit through the human prophet.

The Origins of the Historical-Critical Consensus: A Brief Historical Sketch

How did we arrive at the current scholarly situation, in which most have moved from a position where the dominant—or even exclusive—contribution of the eighth-century prophet Isaiah to the canonical book that bears his name was largely assumed, leaving only a stubborn few to still hold to this position and requiring one to offer detailed arguments in order to claim any words for the "original" prophet? One could justify tracing this development back to the first

---

restrain those with a high view of scriptural authority from hastily abandoning this position in favor of a multi-author approach.

37. See Schultz, "How Many Isaiahs Were There and What Does It Matter?," and idem, "Isaiah, Isaiahs, and Current Scholarship," in *Do Historical Matters Matter to Faith? A Critical Appraisal of Modern and Postmodern Approaches to Scripture*, ed. James K. Hoffmeier and Dennis R. Magary (Wheaton, IL: Crossway, 2012), 243–61.

millennium CE.[38] For the purposes of this essay, it will suffice to go back only a century and a half to examine the initial stages in critical scholars' dismantling of the unity of the prophetic book of Isaiah that led to Bernhard Duhm's influential synthesis, and to note both the basis for and the implications of their analyses.[39]

The Intellectual Background of Early Eighteenth-Century Biblical Scholarship

Substantial developments in biblical studies do not occur within a vacuum, but instead are significantly influenced by and thus reflect broader cultural and philosophical developments. Accordingly, despite the risk of oversimplifying the prevailing intellectual climate, it is useful to sketch briefly some of the major movements that preceded, accompanied, and facilitated the rise of the multi-author approach to the book of Isaiah in eighteenth- and nineteenth-century Europe. It is appropriate to begin earlier, with the rise of Renaissance humanism, which was marked by a new historical consciousness that would come to challenge the prevailing biblical understanding of history as the sphere within which the sovereign purposes of God were carried out. Scholars began to focus instead on the immanent human forces that shaped events and to investigate the biblical sources rather than simply accepting traditional accounts of the past. According to Hans-Joachim Kraus, "the opposition between the Reformation and humanism has been felt throughout the course of Protestant biblical research."[40] Scholars in Britain and France, prompted largely by Deism's insistence on applying reason to approve of revealed truths and its rejection of biblical rituals and miracles, led the way in biblical criticism prior to 1750, after which point Germans took the lead.[41]

In the second half of the eighteenth century, early German neologists such as Johann Salomo Semler and Johann David Michaelis abandoned their Pietist roots and engaged in exegesis unconstrained by traditional Christian doctrines, including that of the verbal inspiration of the Bible.[42] Rationalism, which grew in prominence in the following century and focused on human reason, further undermined claims of divine inspiration and supernatural intervention in human affairs

---

38. See the essay in this volume by Michael Graves.

39. One of the most helpful historical studies in this regard is Marvin A. Sweeney, "On the Road to Duhm: Isaiah in Nineteenth-Century Critical Scholarship," in *"As Those Who Are Taught": The Interpretation of Isaiah from the LXX to the SBL*, ed. Claire Mathews McGinnis and Patricia K. Tull, SBLSymS 27 (Atlanta: Society of Biblical Literature, 2006), 243–62. See also the lengthy introduction in Joseph A. Alexander, *The Prophecies of Isaiah* (1865; repr., Grand Rapids: Zondervan, 1977).

40. Hans-Joachim Kraus, *Geschichte der historisch-kritischen Erforschung des Alten Testaments*, 3rd ed. (Neukirchen-Vluyn: Neukirchener, 1982), 27. Unless otherwise noted, all translations of German sources in this article are my own.

41. This is the claim of John W. Rogerson, *Old Testament Criticism in the Nineteenth Century: England and Germany* (London: SPCK, 1984), 16.

42. Rogerson, *Old Testament Criticism*, 16–17.

and shifted the focus to the human authors. Scholars emphasized the inferiority
of Old Testament religion and accounted for the diversity and discrepancies they
discovered within biblical thought by positing a lengthy compositional history for
the biblical documents.[43] This shift, in turn, combined with nineteenth-century
Romanticism, led to greater attention to the emotions and creative imagination
of the human author and their literary expression in the biblical texts, especially
poetic ones. The developments summarized here led scholars to shift their focus
from studying what they considered to be messianic prophecies in the book of Isaiah that predicted the ministry of Jesus Christ to studying the historical setting(s)
that gave rise to the book's oracles. This freed scholars to question fundamentally
the one-author view of the book that was generally assumed.

Developments in Pentateuchal Studies as a Model and Warrant for Historical Criticism of the Prophetic Corpus

Before tracing the impact of these broader developments on the critical analysis of the book of Isaiah, we must note the significance of critical developments
within Pentateuchal studies for how the prophetic books were approached in the
nineteenth century. The source-critical analysis of the Pentateuch basically entailed
the denial of the revealed nature, Mosaic authorship, and premonarchic origin
of (at least the majority of) its narratives and law collections. Instead, scholars
assigned these portions of the text to various periods throughout the monarchic
and postexilic eras. As a result, the Pentateuch was no longer viewed as the basic
source for understanding Israelite religion, with the prophets as Moses' successors.
Instead, "one could glimpse the prophets as the real progenitors of Israelite religion," and accounting for "the inspired character of the prophets would become the
central fascination."[44] At the same time, the detailed attention nineteenth-century
scholars gave to determining the historical setting and audience of specific texts led
them to distinguish the individual prophets from the books traditionally associated
with them, the latter coming to be viewed instead (like the Pentateuch) as complex
anthologies of diverse materials that originated and were brought together over
the course of several centuries. Emphasis on the historical origin and meaning of
prophecy led to the denial of its apologetic value for demonstrating the validity
of the Christian religion. However, the abiding religious authority that Scripture
had for most Christian scholars compelled them to seek to identify the "authentic
words" of the traditional prophets as sources of religious and moral insight. The
following section will investigate how these developments influenced the critical
analysis of the book of Isaiah during the eighteenth and nineteenth centuries.

---

43. John H. Hayes and Frederick C. Prussner, *Old Testament Theology: Its History and
Development* (London: SCM, 1985), 70–71.

44. Christopher R. Seitz, "Prophecy in the Nineteenth Century Reception," in *Hebrew
Bible / Old Testament: The History of Its Interpretation*, vol. 3/1, *The Nineteenth Century*, ed.
Magne Sæbø (Göttingen: Vandenhoeck & Ruprecht, 2013), 7.

Important Isaianic Stations on the Road to Duhm

Campegius Vitringa (1659–1722)[45]

Although my historical journey could commence with influential figures like Richard Simon, Benedict Spinoza, or Wilhelm M. L. de Wette, the road leading to Duhm begins most directly with Campegius Vitringa, a Dutch Protestant Hebraist and disciple of Johannes Coccceius who published a two-volume commentary on Isaiah (1714 and 1720) that is usually considered to be the first complete exposition of the book. John Sandys-Wunsch describes Vitringa as "a good scholar caught between two worlds"—the world of orthodoxy and of emerging criticism—who insisted on attending to both the biblical text and extrabiblical data bearing on the interpretation of the text, even when the latter threatened the former.[46] According to Kraus,[47] Vitringa's major contribution was his *sensus historicus*–oriented exegesis, which determined the text's meaning on the basis of its historical background and linguistic features rather than on theological convictions about its inspiration and its primarily messianic message. By giving priority to the historical meaning of the text without denying its theological contents, Vitringa sought to steer a middle course between Coccceius' salvation-historical approach, which "found Christ everywhere in Scripture," and that of Hugo Grotius, who "found him practically nowhere."[48] Although Vitringa accepted the possibility of some prophecy speaking about the distant future, he doubted that its recipients would have had much interest in what would not occur in their own day. This helped to lay the foundation for the dominant critical view today that prophets only addressed the immediate circumstances and concerns of their contemporaries.

Johann Christoph Döderlein (1745–1792)

According to Shalom Paul, the road to Duhm began when the distinction between the two parts of the book of Isaiah already noted by Abraham Ibn Ezra[49] was "rediscovered" by Johann Christoph Döderlein in 1776, as manifested in his Latin commentary on Isaiah.[50] Döderlein is commonly, though probably incorrectly, declared to be the first to assert that Isa 40–66 is the work of an exilic poet who was either anonymous or, like the eighth-century prophet, also named Isaiah. In

---

45. Vitringa is sometimes confused with his youngest child, who also was named Campegius (1698–1723).

46. John Sandys-Wunsch, "Early Old Testament Critics on the Continent," in *Hebrew Bible / Old Testament: The History of Its Interpretation*, vol. 2, *From the Renaissance to the Enlightenment*, ed. Magne Sæbø (Göttingen: Vandenhoeck & Ruprecht, 2008), 976.

47. Kraus, *Geschichte der historisch-kritischen Erforschung*, 91–92.

48. This is a paraphrase of a claim made by Richard Simon and cited by Ernestine van der Wall, "Between Grotius and Coccceius: The 'Theologica Prophetica' of Campegius Vitringa (1659–1722)," in *Hugo Grotius, Theologian: Essays in Honour of G. H. M. Posthumus Meyjes*, ed. Henk J. M. Nellen and Edwin Rabbie, Studies in the History of Christian Traditions 55 (Leiden: Brill, 1994), 199.

49. See the discussion of Ibn Ezra in the essay in this volume by Michael Graves.

50. Paul, *Isaiah 40–66*, 3. Other sources give the publication date as 1775.

a lengthy annotation to Isa 40 in the second (1780) edition of his work, Döderlein spoke more cautiously of the poet encouraging the people regarding their future liberation, "whether before they would be led into captivity or when they were held captive."[51] However, his clearest statement regarding the independent origin of Isa 40–66 is found in the preface to the third edition of the commentary. Since this edition is dated 1789, Döderlein's claim that the author of Isa 40–66 is not the same as the author of Isa 1–39 is later than similar claims made by some of the other German contributors to the authorship discussion—he refers to Michaelis, Lowth, and Koppe in his preface—and is likely influenced by them.[52]

Ernst Friedrich Karl Rosenmüller (1768–1835)

Ernst Friedrich Karl Rosenmüller, who from 1813 to 1835 was professor of Oriental languages at Leipzig, is credited with being the first to list specific reasons for dating the second half of the book of Isaiah to the exilic period, which he does in a lengthy preface to the third volume of his commentary on Isaiah.[53] His discussion includes the following points:

(1) The latter part of the book, beginning with chapter 40, contains a very different argument and character than the previous part.

(2) The author of Isa 40–66 writes as one residing in the midst of ruined cities in a land laid waste and not as one simply viewing these things with the mind's eye. References to the destruction of the temple, the desolation of Jerusalem, and many other details in this part of the book clearly betray a writer who flourished near the end of the Babylonian exile.

(3) The descriptions in Isa 40–66 of the destruction of Babylon and the liberation of the exiles would have been of no benefit to Jews who were still residing peacefully and quietly in their homeland. A poet always counsels, comforts, or admonishes the people of his own age.

---

51. Johann Christoph Döderlein, *Esaias ex recensione textus hebraei ad fidem codd. quorundam mss. et versionum antiquarum latine vertit notasque varii argumenti subiecit*, 2nd ed. (Altorf: Officina Schupfeliana, 1780), 166: "After he [Isaiah] set forth in his first book [i.e., chapters 1–39] the subject of the impending Babylonian captivity, now he has added a consoling address, which runs in its entirety from Chapter 40 down to the end of the book. This address is crammed full of all kinds of various subjects, by means of which he consoles the people—whether before they would be led into captivity or when they were held captive—already confidently proclaiming how they are to be miraculously set free." All translations from the Latin in this essay are by my former Wheaton College colleague Mark Thorne.

52. Döderlein, *Esaias ex recensione*, 3rd ed. (Altorf: Georg. Petr. Monath, 1789), xv: "For which reason, it appears reasonable to assign the speech or rather the latter book from Chapter 40 to a later time period than Isaiah, and to acknowledge that it was composed toward the end of the exile by some anonymous person or by an ancient prophet with the same name." In the same edition (p. 183), Döderlein modifies the lengthy annotation to Isa 40 translated in the preceding footnote to "the prophet—whoever he is—comforts a people in exile."

53. Ernst Friedrich Karl Rosenmüller, *Scholia in Vetus Testamentum partis tertiae Jesajae vaticinia complectensus volumen tertium*, 2nd ed. (Leipzig: Joh. Ambros. Barthii, 1820), 1–8.

(4) In Isa 40–66, the prophet's vague descriptions of the future do not correspond to the detailed accounts of Ezra, Nehemiah, Haggai, and Malachi. Hence, it is very probable that Isa 40–66 was written earlier than these books, when the Jews were first given the opportunity to return to the land by Cyrus.

Rosenmüller concludes:

> But each prophet looks to the interests of his own time period, whether through [the avenue of] comfort or admonition or encouragement. Since these things are so, it will be reasonable to assign this latter part of the collection of prophets, which takes its name from Isaiah, to a period of time later than that prophet, and to place its composition toward the end of the Babylonian exile by some anonymous prophet.[54]

Robert Lowth (1710–1787) and Johann Benjamin Koppe (1750–1791)

Bishop and Oxford professor Robert Lowth's influential English translation of Isaiah, first published in 1778,[55] helped to establish that the prophetic writings were poetry, not prose. Lowth's emphasis on poetic genius rather than on divine inspiration furthered the shift toward focusing on the human authors, rather than the divine author, of Scripture. As Seitz expresses it, "What in Lowth's hands were essentially aesthetic and appreciative observations about the genius of the prophetic consciousness quickly became a warrant for seeing the prophets as men of like nature with ourselves in virtually all respects."[56] Lowth acknowledged that, beginning with Isa 40, the prophet makes clear reference to the return from Babylonian exile, but nevertheless conceives of the prophecies as "probably delivered in the latter part of the reign of Hezekiah."[57] In Lowth's view, the prophet Isaiah "sometimes is so fully possessed with the glories of the future more remote kingdom, that he seems to leave the more immediate subject of his commission almost out of the question."[58] Although Lowth was still able to conceive of an inspired prophet who could both speak to his own day and foresee much later events, including those with a "double-sense" fulfillment in the coming of the Messiah,[59] his German translator could not. In 1780, Johann Benjamin Koppe, a professor in Göttingen, added annotations to his German translation of Lowth's Isaiah in which he questioned the genuineness of many of Isaiah's prophecies, suggesting, for example, that Isa 50 was written by

---

54. Rosenmüller, *Scholia in Vetus Testamentum*, 3–4 (translated by Mark Thorne).

55. Robert Lowth, *Isaiah: A New Translation; With A Preliminary Dissertation, and Notes, Critical, Philological, and Explanatory* (London: J. Dodsley & T. Cadelle, 1778). In his comments, Lowth interacted frequently with Vitringa's earlier commentary. Lowth's poetic translation of Isaiah was preceded by his *De sacra poesi Hebraeorum: Praelectiones academicae* (Oxford: Clarendon, 1753), published in English in 1787 as *On the Sacred Poetry of the Hebrews* and published in German by Rosenmüller in 1815. For a more detailed discussion of Lowth's contributions to the interpretation of Isaiah, see Gary Stansell, "The Poet's Prophet: Bishop Robert Lowth's Eighteenth-Century Commentary on Isaiah," in *"As Those Who Are Taught": The Interpretation of Isaiah from the LXX to the SBL*, ed. Claire Mathews McGinnis and Patricia K. Tull, SBLSymS 27 (Atlanta: Society of Biblical Literature, 2006), 223–42.

56. Seitz, "Isaiah, Book of (First Isaiah)," 472.

57. Lowth, *Isaiah*, 14th ed. (London: William Tegg, 1848), 307.

58. Ibid., 308.

59. Ibid., 310–11.

Ezekiel or another prophet residing in Babylon. These conclusions provoked the criticism of Wilhelm Gesenius, who strongly opposed Koppe's "critical system of dismembering" the book, according to which "the entire collection appears to be a loose (nearly as in a card game) pile of prophetic fragments by various authors from various times."[60]

Johann Gottfried Eichhorn (1752–1827)

Johann Gottfried Eichhorn, a student of Johann David Michaelis, is often viewed as the founder of modern Old Testament criticism. Eichhorn incorporated the new multi-author approach to the book of Isaiah into his introduction to the Old Testament, devoting fifty pages to his discussion of the book.[61] His analysis of the Old Testament prophetic corpus and of Isaiah in particular anticipated many of Duhm's conclusions by more than a century. In Eichhorn's view, the current book of Isaiah came into being because sufficient space remained on the scroll after chapters 1–39 had been incorporated, leading the collector to add the historical account in which Isaiah the prophet was involved (chs. 36–39), as well as the anonymous oracles (chs. 40–66). This resulted in the scroll of Isaiah achieving approximately the same length as the scrolls of Jeremiah and Ezekiel. In the canonical ordering reflected in the Babylonian Talmud tractate *Baba Batra*, Isaiah was listed after Jeremiah and Ezekiel but before the Book of Twelve, since Isaiah, according to Eichhorn's analysis, contained oracles originating later than any of the material in Jeremiah or Ezekiel, while the Book of Twelve contained some material that was later still.[62]

Since it was clear to Eichhorn that the present book of Isaiah contains "many oracles that do not belong to this prophet," he accused his contemporaries who affirmed the canonical ascription of all of the oracles contained therein to Isaiah as doing so out of "blind faith." Rather, to him "it appears that oracles from the most diverse times and from completely diverse prophets have been collected under the same name and strung like so many individual anonymous pearls on a long cord."[63] Eichhorn cited various stylistic considerations in support of his analysis. For example, he considered the Moab oracle (Isa 15–16) a later editorial insertion since it displays a harsh style and contains an abundance of geographical names. Similarly, in his view the unnamed prophet of Isa 24–27 manipulated sounds "in an unmanly manner" in striving to achieve aesthetically pleasing wordplay, alliteration, and assonance (e.g., in Isa 24:3, 4, 16–19, 21, and 27:7).[64] Eichhorn believed that both

---

60. Wilhelm Gesenius, *Philologisch-kritischer und historischer Commentar über den Jesaia*, vol. 1, bk. 1, *Die Einleitung und Auslegung von Kapitel 1–12* (Leipzig: Vogel, 1821), xiii. See the summary of Gesenius' own views below.

61. Johann Gottfried Eichhorn, *Einleitung ins Alte Testament: Dritter Theil*, 2nd ed. (Leipzig: Weidmanns Erben und Reich, 1787).

62. Ibid., 41–42.

63. Ibid., 57–58. This kind of claim would lead Eichhorn's contemporary Wilhelm de Wette to conclude that "Isaiah" functions not to designate an actual author but rather as a symbolic "collective name" to embrace the most diverse traditions arising in the community (Kraus, *Geschichte der historisch-kritischen Erforschung*, 179).

64. Eichhorn, *Einleitung*, 60–61.

early (i.e., genuine) and late oracles are mixed together in Isaiah and considered the latter to be distinguishable from the former because their contents and language are incompatible with the period of the divided monarchy (e.g., according to Eichhorn, Isa 15–16, 21:1–10, and 40–52 could not have been composed prior to the Babylonian exile). Eichhorn was willing to concede the possibility that a prophet like Isaiah could, through "a flight of fantasy," transport himself into the period of the exile, but affirmed that no author can completely remove from his writings the trace of the historical setting in which he actually lives. Accordingly, he concluded that what one finds in Isa 40–52 exhibits the kind of specificity of detail that only a person actually living in exile could give. This includes descriptions of Babylon's downfall, Cyrus' rise, and the exiled Jews' preparation to return to their homeland. By contrast, prophecies about the distant future found elsewhere in the book speak exclusively in general, even vague, terms.[65] Nevertheless, Eichhorn admitted that, in the absence of more objective evidence, he ultimately had to rely on his "trained" feelings and on his impression that a given text is late rather than early.[66]

Wilhelm Gesenius (1786–1842)

In Eichhorn's analysis, no distinct late-exilic prophetic figure (i.e., a Second Isaiah) emerges to rival Isaiah of Jerusalem. This, however, would be a major focus of Wilhelm Gesenius' analysis of Isaiah. Having studied under Eichhorn in Göttingen during the peak of the latter's popularity, Gesenius echoed the opinion of his teacher:

> The oracles gathered under the name of Isaiah have experienced a fate unlike that of any of the other prophetic works: at least in the respect that a very significant number of oracles are included that, on the basis of content, language, and historical circumstances, must be denied as originating with the contemporaries of Ahaz and Hezekiah.[67]

Instead, according to Gesenius, these oracles stem from the late exilic period. Such texts include all of chapters 40–66, as well as chapters 13–14, 21, 24–27, 34–35, and other briefer passages, all of which reflect "such a similarity of language, manner, and perspective that one is inclined to ascribe them to the same author"[68] (except perhaps, in his view, chs. 24–27, which exhibit stylistic artificiality). Consequently at least *two* authors are represented in the collection (Gesenius called the later one "Pseudojesaia"), but certainly not *many* more. In fact, Gesenius suggested that the entirety of Isa 40–66 may be viewed as an original written composition, an open letter sent to the exilic community, even though not all of its sections were written at the same time.[69]

---

65. Ibid., 62–66.

66. Ibid., 71–72.

67. Gesenius, *Der Prophet Jesaia*, 1/1:15–16. Gesenius sets forth in some detail the distinctive styles and expressions of Isaiah and the later prophet (ibid., 1/1:35–36).

68. Ibid., 1/1:16

69. Wilhelm Gesenius, *Der Prophet Jesaia*, vol. 3, *Commentar über Kapitel 40–66, nebst einigen Beylagen und den Registern* (Leipzig: Vogel, 1821), 2–3, see also 15–16.

Gesenius cited the following arguments as the basis for his distinguishing the prophecies of Pseudo-Isaiah from those of Isaiah:[70]

(1) All detailed descriptions of the conditions of the Jewish people in the portions of the book that originated with Pseudo-Isaiah point irrefutably to the late exilic period, not to the time of Isaiah.

(2) The same applies to Pseudo-Isaiah's descriptions of other peoples.

(3) Pseudo-Isaiah refers to previous prophecies regarding the return of the people from exile that have been fulfilled and to which he now adds new ones.

(4) Whenever Isaiah describes the current circumstances of his people or political relationships, he stands on firm historical ground and everything corresponds to the historical reality. Whatever he says regarding future circumstances, on the other hand, constitutes ideals and joyful, enthusiastic hopes, which fell far short of being achieved. If Isaiah had truly been enabled supernaturally to predict the achievements of Cyrus, then he also would have predicted accurately the postexilic conditions that actually obtained rather than never-realized ideal circumstances.

(5) The chapters attributed to Pseudo-Isaiah exhibit a distinctive style, which can also be found in other late texts.

(6) These chapters also use late Hebrew idioms or "Chaldeanisms" (Aramaisms), which one would expect to find in texts written in the exilic period.

(7) Had these texts been written and in circulation earlier under the name of Isaiah, then a prophet like Jeremiah would surely have referred to them when condemned as treasonous for announcing the coming destruction of Jerusalem and the exile.

How do we account for the fact that more non-genuine oracles are contained in the current book of Isaiah than genuine ones? According to Gesenius, this may be due to the ancient practice of ascribing anonymous texts to a well-known author or authority figure. However, he felt that a more important role was played by chance, accompanied by the uncritical faculties and other limitations of those who collected the oracles after the exile.[71] Gesenius' massive three-volume commentary on Isaiah laid the foundational defense of the "two Isaiahs" hypothesis, which his successors would merely simplify and refine. This is not only the viewpoint that many popular treatments of the book of Isaiah present exclusively, but also, as

---

70. Ibid., 19–35.
71. Gesenius, *Der Prophet Jesaia*, 2/1:16–18.

noted above, it is the perspective to which a growing number of scholars have now returned, having jettisoned the "three Isaiahs" hypothesis.

Georg Heinrich August Ewald (1803–1875)

Like Gesenius, Heinrich Ewald studied with Eichhorn in Göttingen. Unlike Gesenius, however, in his three-volume study of the Hebrew prophets, Ewald offered no detailed defense of the contribution of Pseudo-Isaiah to the book of Isaiah.[72] Instead, he declared with remarkable certitude that one can recognize late prophecies in the book "on the basis of a hundred indicators, and the closer one compares them with older texts, the more proofs one finds that they could not have been composed earlier than during this extraordinary time [i.e., at the end of the exile]."[73] Ewald dismissed all efforts to demonstrate that allegedly later texts actually originated with Isaiah as not only unsuccessful but also as incapable of ever succeeding; he therefore considered them "completely reprehensible" rather than "scientific" efforts.[74] By this time, a number of conservative German scholars had taken up the defense of the traditional view of Isaianic authorship, led by Berlin professor Ernst Wilhelm Hengstenberg (1802–1869).[75] For example, in a discussion of Isa 53, Hengstenberg offered an extensive refutation of Gesenius' and de Wette's arguments for a non-messianic interpretation of this text, concluding, "One can characterize the arguments against the messianic interpretation as insignificant. None of them is capable of intimidating the one who is capable of examining it critically."[76]

As Bernhard Duhm's teacher, and since his influence can be seen throughout his student's commentary, Ewald merits special attention. Rather than treating the book of Isaiah as a whole, Ewald devoted separate chapters in his commentary on the prophets to the authentic Isaianic oracles and to the anonymous later prophecies. According to his account of the book's composition, in the excitement that accompanied the conclusion of the exile and the reestablishment of the Jewish community in their homeland, many prophetic pamphlets were quickly composed (though some of these were apparently mere writing exercises imitating texts other than Isaiah). Since they reflected the mood of the age, these pamphlets became popular, but they remained anonymous because their authors were not public figures. Accordingly, Ewald considered attributing such texts to a "Pseudo-Isaiah"

---

72. Heinrich Ewald, *Die Propheten des Alten Bundes*, 2 vols. (Stuttgart: Adolph Krabbe, 1840). The second edition, published in 1867–68 in Göttingen by Vandenhoeck & Ruprecht, devoted a third volume to the postexilic prophets: *Die jüngsten Propheten des alten Bundes mit den Büchern Barukh und Daniel.*

73. Ewald, *Die Propheten des Alten Bundes*, 3:4–5.

74. Ibid., 6n1.

75. For a more detailed discussion of their opposition to the historical-critical conclusions, see Rogerson, "Confessional Opposition to the Critical Method," ch. 5 (pp. 79–90) in *Old Testament Criticism in the Nineteenth Century*; also Kraus, *Geschichte der historisch-kritischen Erforschung*, 222–26.

76. Ernst W. Hengstenberg, *Christologie des Alten Testaments und Commentar über die messianischen Weissagungen* (Berlin: Ludwig Dehmigke, 1854–57; 1st ed., 1829–35), 2:360, cited in Kraus, *Geschichte der historisch-kritischen Erforschung*, 224.

figure, as Gesenius did, to be completely inappropriate; instead, he preferred to call the author of Isa 40–66 "the Great Unnamed One." Furthermore, in Ewald's view texts like Isa 13–14 and 21 are not to be attributed to the author of Isa 40–66.[77] Contrary to Gesenius, Ewald concluded that the prophetic author of chapters 40–66 inserted several lengthy *earlier* texts into this section, including 40:1–31, 52:13–54:12, and 56:9–57:11, all of which, he believed, originated in the time of Manasseh. On the other hand, Ewald believed that insertions in Isa 58 and 59 resemble Ezekiel. Anticipating later redactional studies, Ewald also identified coherent subdivisions within Isa 40–66 (40–48, 49–60, 61:1–63:6, and 63:7–66:24), each of which he considered to reflect further developments in the life of the author and in the community.[78]

Bernhard Lauardus Duhm (1847–1928)

The preceding survey suggests that a major contribution of Bernhard Duhm's 1892 Isaiah commentary was its persuasive synthesis of critical positions already current in his day.[79] One result was that these positions set the agenda for the scholarly discussion of the book of Isaiah during the following century. But Duhm's views also went significantly beyond those of his teacher Ewald and his most influential contemporaries. According to Seitz, although no scholars who preceded Duhm had seen a significant break between Isa 40–55 and 56–66,[80] Duhm "discovered" "Trito-Isaiah" (or Third Isaiah) as the last major contributor to a series of unrelated additions to what ultimately constituted the canonical book of Isaiah in the Hasmonean period, ca. 70 BCE. Whereas, according to Duhm, Second Isaiah wrote in Phoenicia (not Babylon, as others argued) in the sixth century BCE, Third Isaiah wrote in postexilic Judah during the mid-fifth century BCE, shortly before the time of Nehemiah. In Duhm's analysis, the section of the book authored by Third Isaiah constitutes a more corrupt text than Isa 40–55, is full of glosses and additions, and is less poetically refined and degenerates into a more prosaic style.

Unlike his teacher Ewald, who posited a compositional history for the book that extended for only about two centuries, for Duhm the book of Isaiah experienced editorial expansion for more than six centuries. Each of the three "Isaiahs" reflects the respective prophet's own historical setting and does not consciously build on the work of his predecessors. In fact, Duhm stated that "the majority of the authors and even several collectors could not have dreamed that they were engaged in producing a single book of Isaiah."[81] Another of Duhm's lasting contributions was his labeling of Isa 42:1–4, 49:1–6, 50:4–9, and 52:13–53:12 as four "servant songs," which he considered to be both independent of and later than either Second or Third Isaiah.[82]

---

77. Ewald, *Die Propheten des Alten Bundes*, 3:5–7.

78. Ibid., 27–30.

79. Duhm, *Das Buch Jesaia*.

80. Seitz, "Isaiah, Book of (Third Isaiah)," 502.

81. Duhm, *Das Buch Jesaia*, 7–8.

82. Rogerson (*Old Testament Criticism in the Nineteenth Century*, 23), however, notes that Rosenmüller had already isolated these four texts nearly a century earlier, in 1793.

Like his predecessors, Duhm argued that genuine and non-genuine texts (some of the latter of which he considered very late) were frequently placed side by side in small collections, sometimes accidentally. He rigorously applied historical-critical, literary-critical, and redaction-critical criteria in his analysis, as is illustrated by the following examples of his conclusions regarding texts from Isa 1–39:

(1) Isa 2:2–4 is a late addition within chapters 2–4, since in these chapters an initial threat is typically followed by a promise. Therefore, the unit should not *begin* with this glorious promise.

(2) In 9:7[ET 8]–11:16 the reference to the desire for the subordination of the Philistines and the Moabites indicates that the collector of this collection could not have lived prior to the Maccabean period.

(3) Since the brief collection of oracles in Isa 5 lacks any promise, the expected promise was probably lost due to material damage to the papyrus scroll and ended up being inserted in another collection.

(4) In Isa 34–35, the threat against Edom points to the subjugation of the Edomites by John Hyrcanus in 110 BCE. Furthermore, these chapters presuppose late eschatology, and 34:16 ("Look in the scroll of the LORD and read . . .") betrays a scribal style. The editor of Isa 40–66 also incorporated numerous foreign additions, such as 42:5–7, 44:9–20, 46:6–8, some material in chapter 48, 49:22–50:3, 50:10–11, 52:3–6, 58:13–14, 59:5–8, and 66:22–23.[83]

This kind of detailed approach to the text of Isaiah, which Duhm refined and which focuses almost exclusively on the genesis of the text rather than on the meaning of the text as it stands, continues to flourish today.

The Continuing Search for the Historical Isaiah

The foregoing historical survey has been intentionally selective and has highlighted the major contributors and claims that have produced the current multi-author view of the book of Isaiah. I have given minimal attention to the early opponents of these historical-critical developments and refrained from critiquing them myself. My goal, instead, has been to help the reader feel the weight of three centuries of careful analysis of the book of Isaiah (beginning with Vitringa's 1714 commentary) that initially questioned and then rejected the traditional one-author view. My final task in this essay is to summarize the major reasons that have led and continue to lead to this rejection and to indicate some of the issues and questions that the critical consensus raises for the evangelical interpreter of Isaiah.

---

83. Duhm, *Das Buch Jesaia*, 10–14.

Primary Reasons for Opposing the One-Author View in General and for Denying the Isaianic Origin of Chapters 40–66 in Particular

Interpreters of Isaiah have cited various reasons—historical, stylistic, and theological—for claiming that the eighth-century prophet Isaiah was not the source of all of the prophetic texts included in the present book of Isaiah.[84] Even conservative interpreters of Isaiah acknowledge that such differences exist between Isa 1–39 and 40–66, though they account for them differently than by attributing the divergences to different authors.

Historical

If one assumes that a prophet lives and addresses the people and circumstances in the period that his prophecy describes, there is no suitable occasion during the lifetime of the eighth-century prophet Isaiah that chapters 40–66 (and even much of 1–39) could plausibly address, especially his announcement of the imminent deliverance of the people from exile and restoration of the temple through Cyrus.

Stylistic

Chapters 40–66 are markedly different from chapters 1–39 with respect to literary style, employing words, phrases, rhetorical devices, and images that are unique to the book and cannot be accounted for simply by different subject matter. Furthermore, characteristic expressions of chapters 1–39 that occasionally appear in chapters 40–66 are often used in a distinctive manner in the latter. And even Isa 1–39 contains shorter passages whose style diverges from the prevailing style within these chapters.

Theological

The major theological themes of Isa 40–66—God as Creator, Lord of history, and Redeemer, Israel as servant, the inclusion of the nations within his salvation—are distinctive to this section of the book. Conversely, major theological ideas present in chapters 1–39, such as the future Davidic ruler, the remnant, and the call to faith in the midst of concrete military threats, are missing from chapters 40–66.[85] Furthermore, Isa 1–39 deals with some theological themes, such as the resurrection of the dead (Isa 26:19), that many deem too advanced for an eighth-century prophet to have uttered.

---

84. Since all of these have been mentioned and documented previously in this essay, I will not repeat the documentation here, but see esp. the claims of Keil and Bredenkamp, two nineteenth-century opponents of this developing critical approach, in Carl F. Keil, *Introduction to the Old Testament* (Edinburgh: T&T Clark, 1869) 2, 265–81, and C. J. Bredenkamp, *Der Prophet Jesaia* (Erlangen: Andreas Deichert, 1887), 7–10.

85. This reason was not emphasized by the early proponents of the multi-author approach.

Philosophical/Rationalist

One additional factor underlying the critical consensus should be noted here. With the rise of modern biblical criticism, prophetic literature was increasingly viewed as a solely human product, devoid of any revelatory content or source, especially the divinely enabled foretelling of near or distant events that God would bring about in the future. As a result, everything within the book of Isaiah needed to be accounted for on the basis of purely human processes. This approach was supported, in part, by the identification of "unfulfilled" prophecies, as well as of "fulfilled" prophecies that were so detailed and specific that they were best explained as composed "after the fact." More foundational, however, was the rise of a naturalistic worldview that perceived the world as a sphere in which supernatural intervention in human affairs was extremely rare or nonexistent. As a result, biblical prophecy was basically reduced to political projections, idealistic portrayals of a better future, and propagandistic efforts to support a particular party or cause.

Points of Departure for Ongoing Evangelical Discussion

Although evangelical scholars lack consensus regarding how to account for supposed "unfulfilled" or *ex eventu* prophecy, they reject the philosophical/rationalist presuppositions described above. Nevertheless, the arguments for distinguishing Isa 1–39 and 40–66 that are based on historical, stylistic, and theological differences between these chapters present a greater challenge, since they are based substantially on careful textual analysis. Lay interpreters of Isaiah may readily agree with Thomas K. Cheyne's claim that "the principal thing for the student of a prophecy is, not to know who wrote it, but to understand its essential ideas; this is important for all—the rest can be fully utilized only by the historical critic. . . . There is no absolute necessity for an honest exegete to give any detailed treatment to the higher criticism."[86] However, the disputed issues regarding the genesis of the book of Isaiah must concern evangelical biblical scholars because they have a direct impact on both the exegesis of the book and its use in the church. The questions raised by the proposed complex compositional histories are not easily answered, but they need to be discussed openly and honestly in efforts to explore whether new answers *must be* offered out of scholarly integrity and *can be* discovered through new research and fruitful collaboration among scholars.

I will conclude this essay with three foundational theses that arise from my ongoing engagement with Isaiah and that could provide a point of departure for future evangelical responses to critical claims regarding the book's compositional history:

(1) We should admit how difficult it is (a) to assign specific dates to many Isaianic texts, (b) to determine specific developments to which figurative poetic

---

86. T. K. Cheyne, *The Prophecies of Isaiah: A New Translation with Commentary and Appendices*, 4th ed. (New York: Thomas Whittaker, 1890), 2:224.

expressions point, and (c) to discern the exact delimitation of specific textual units and the underlying logic that accounts for the juxtaposition and sequencing of various sub-units. Despite the superficial impression of a critical consensus, in Isaianic studies today there is significant disagreement not merely over which methodologies are appropriate for analyzing the book but also over how to distinguish between and date primary and secondary texts. Interpreters differ significantly with regard to the number of redactional layers that they identify within a given section of the book and which texts they assign to each of them, and also with regard to how they use intratextual relationships in constructing their arguments.

(2) We should affirm that an evangelical doctrine of Scripture does not in principle rule out Spirit-directed editorial work, including additions and updates, but claims of (much) later material within the book of Isaiah need to be thoroughly defended and not simply asserted. Moving from the "microscopic" to the "macroscopic" level, in recent decades the identification of complex patterns of compositional organization and design within the book of Isaiah seems to offer evidence of overarching editorial design (rather than merely a display of interpretive creativity). Although such observations do not necessarily help one determine the date of the book's final editing, they do raise the possibility of a later inspired editor ordering and shaping the collections of earlier oracles in order to produce an authoritative final composition whose whole is able to address in a coherent manner future generations of faithful readers better than the sum of its parts.

(3) We should distinguish between Isaiah as the primary or sole prophetic voice heard in the oracles contained in the book of Isaiah and Isaiah as the sole *author or editor* of this book. In a recently published book, John Walton argues on the basis of his comparative studies of compositional practices and processes in the ancient Near East and the Old Testament that "when later reference is made to what has become the book of Isaiah, Isaiah is being identified as the authority figure behind the material, not as an 'author' of a 'book.'" Therefore, New Testament references to Isaiah should be understood as referring to the *book* called "Isaiah," not to Isaiah as *author* of that book.[87] This claim deserves serious consideration when we seek to describe Isaiah's role as a "writing prophet." At the same time, we need to ponder carefully to what extent the ancient Near Eastern comparative material should play a *decisive*— rather than merely a *possible*—explanatory role regarding the compositional processes underlying biblical books.

Since the purpose of this essay has been primarily the historical one of tracing the rise of the dominant critical position on the composition of Isaiah, as synthe-

---

87. John H. Walton and D. Brent Sandy, *The Lost World of Scripture: Ancient Literary Culture and Biblical Authority* (Downers Grove, IL: InterVarsity Press, 2013), 64–65.

sized by Duhm and summarizing recent developments within Isaiah studies, I will refrain here from offering my own responses to the scholarly claims I have surveyed.[88] The essays that follow in this volume will address various aspects of the issues noted in this one. The theological richness of the book of Isaiah, which, in my view, reflects its divinely inspired origin, continues to beckon diverse interpreters, while its compositional complexity resists all efforts to offer a definitive explanation for its current shape and particular contents. And so we persevere in studying both it and the publications of others, in an ongoing effort to understand and appreciate more fully this profound and influential prophetic work.

---

88. I have done this in previous publications. See notes 6 and 37 above and "How Many Isaiahs Were There?," *Areopagus Journal: The Journal of the Apologetics Resource Center* (Spring 2012): 16–23.

Isaianic Intertextuality and Intratextuality as Composition-Historical Indicators: Methodological Challenges in Determining Literary Influence

RICHARD L. SCHULTZ

Introduction

The influence of the book of Isaiah on the New Testament and early Christian authors is so pervasive that John Sawyer refers to it as "the fifth gospel."[1] Its influence on Second Temple Judaism is similarly extensive.[2] It is therefore not unexpected that modern interpreters would find numerous echoes of Isaianic prophecies in later prophetic books within the Old Testament, as well. In fact, Joseph Blenkinsopp claims that "*the first stage in the interpretation of a prophetic book is to be found in the book itself*," citing as illustrations the way in which Isa 51:4–6 and 61:1–3 draw on the preceding "Servant Songs."[3] Whether found within or outside of the Old Testament, these intertextual links[4] with Isaianic texts are rich in hermeneutical and theological implications and rightly have been the focus of much recent study.

---

1. John F. A. Sawyer, *The Fifth Gospel: Isaiah in the History of the Church* (Cambridge: Cambridge University Press, 1996).

2. For example, according to Darrell D. Hannah, the two Old Testament books (Psalms and Isaiah) most often cited or alluded to in the New Testament are also among the three best-attested books (along with Deuteronomy) at Qumran ("Isaiah within Judaism of the Second Temple Period," in *Isaiah in the New Testament*, ed. Steven Moyise and Maarten J. J. Menken, NTSI [New York: T&T Clark, 2005], 7).

3. Joseph Blenkinsopp, *Opening the Sealed Book: Interpretations of the Book of Isaiah in Late Antiquity* (Grand Rapids: Eerdmans, 2006), 252–53. Blenkinsopp italicizes the statement. See also H. G. M. Williamson, *Variations on a Theme: King, Messiah and Servant in the Book of Isaiah*, The Didsbury Lecture Series (Carlisle: Paternoster, 1998), 174–88.

4. It is necessary to acknowledge at the outset that, within contemporary literary theory and biblical studies, the term "intertextuality" frequently is used in a broader, Kristevan manner to describe the synchronic tracing of all possible relationships existing between texts or even between a text and the larger cultural reservoir from which it has drawn. However, it is also used as a now-favored cover term for designating inner-biblical quotation, allusion, and echo, which are identified and evaluated as a primarily diachronic process. I am using it in this essay in the latter sense. See Richard L. Schultz, "The Ties that Bind: Intertextuality, The Identification of Verbal Parallels, and Reading Strategies," in *Thematic Threads in the Book of the Twelve*, ed. Paul L. Redditt and Aaron Schart, BZAW 325 (Berlin: de Gruyter, 2003), 28–29; also idem, *The Search for Quotation: Verbal Parallels in the Prophets*, JSOTSup 180 (Sheffield: JSOT Press, 1999), 98–99.

But their implications for various theories regarding the compositional history of the book of Isaiah are less clear. For example, most contemporary interpreters would attribute Isa 61:1–3 to "Third Isaiah," though they would argue that it was influenced by the earlier Servant Songs, whereas some early twentieth-century interpreters (e.g., W. W. Cannon, O. Procksch, and C. C. Torrey) labeled it a fifth "Servant Song" from the same source as the other four.[5] Similarly, recent studies of the intertextual relationship between the book of Jeremiah and Isa 40–55—with the exception of those authored by conservative scholars who view the eighth-century BCE prophet Isaiah of Jerusalem as the primary source of the prophetic messages contained in the entire book of Isaiah—almost uniformly "conclude" (or perhaps assume) that "Second Isaiah" appropriated the text of Jeremiah, rather than vice versa.

Those studying the citations of and allusions to Isaiah in the New Testament have to contend with complex methodological issues such as text form, hermeneutical precursors, and contextual awareness. However, those studying the reuse and reinterpretation of Isaiah elsewhere in the Old Testament, as well as the reuse and reinterpretation of other biblical texts or traditions within the book of Isaiah, have to contend with the more intractable problem of the relative dating of the "borrowing" and the "borrowed" texts. In light of the wide range of redaction-critical reconstructions of the lengthy compositional histories of various canonical books, any attempt to use Isaianic intertextuality as an argument in dating any given text or texts is likely to succeed in convincing only those whose compositional theories already fit such claims.

As a result, my goals in this essay are modest. I will begin by briefly setting forth and illustrating the difficulties involved both in tracing the direction and in assessing the significance of literary borrowing within the prophetic corpus. I will then summarize and critique several representative intertextual studies (i.e., concerning verbal parallels between Isaiah and other Old Testament books) that analyze literary influences *on* or *of* the book of Isaiah, as well as some intratextual studies (i.e., concerning verbal parallels within the book of Isaiah) that argue for the interpretive reuse of earlier Isaianic material by the authors and editors who, it is claimed, later reworked and supplemented his prophetic "tradition." In the process, I will examine a number of verbal parallels and consider their potential composition-historical implications.

Methodological Problems in Using Intertextuality in Dating Prophetic Literature

Relative but Not Absolute Dating

There are at least three major methodological problems related to using inter- or intratextuality to date prophetic literature. I begin with an example from the

---

5. Herbert Haag, *Der Gottesknecht bei Deuterojesaja*, EdF 233 (Darmstadt: Wissenschaftliche Buchgesellschaft, 1985), 6. Haag notes that Hans Kosmala also considers Isa 51:4–8 to be a "Servant Song."

book of Daniel that highlights the difficulty of using intertextual links to draw conclusions regarding the date of composition. Long before interpreters such as Blenkinsopp argued that Isa 61:1–3, because it is found within the book of Isaiah itself, offers the earliest interpretation of the Servant Songs, H. L. Ginsberg claimed that the oldest interpretation of the fourth Servant Song is found in Dan 11.[6] The verbal links cited as support include the description in Dan 12:3 of sufferers as "those who are wise"[7] (הַמַּשְׂכִּלִים, *hammaśkîlîm*; cf. 11:35), based on Isa 52:13, "my servant will act wisely" (יַשְׂכִּיל עַבְדִּי, *yaśkîl ʿabdî*), and as "those who lead many to righteousness" (וּמַצְדִּיקֵי הָרַבִּים, *ûmaṣdîqê hārabbîm*), derived from Isa 53:11, "my righteous servant will justify many" (יַצְדִּיק צַדִּיק עַבְדִּי לָרַבִּים, *yaṣdîq ṣaddîq ʿabdî lārabbîm*). Furthermore, as Darrell Hannah notes, both Daniel's *wise* and Isaiah's *servant* "suffer . . . are condemned as lawbreakers . . . are executed . . . and are subsequently vindicated."[8]

If one considers this striking repetition of Hebrew verbs in Dan 12:3, one from Isa 52:13 and one from 53:11 (both in the Hiphil stem), along with other cited parallels, as a sufficient basis for labeling this an "interpretive" reuse of Isaiah, this would, at best, indicate that the fourth Servant Song was composed prior to the Maccabean period (i.e., the second century BCE), since that is the date most commonly ascribed to Daniel by modern scholars. Similarly, on a weaker textual basis than in the preceding example, Choon-Leong Seow claims that Eccl 12:2 ("before the sun and the light and the moon and the stars grow dark, and the clouds return after the rain") is dependent on eschatological prophetic texts such as Isa 5:30 and, especially, 13:10 ("The stars of heaven and their constellations will not show their light. The rising sun will be darkened and the moon will not give its light").[9] If Seow's analysis of intertextual dependence here is accepted, this is only minimally useful for assigning relative dates to the two texts, since Ecclesiastes is typically assigned today to the third century BCE, while a redaction critic like Ronald Clements dates the eschatological expectation found in Isa 13:9–16 to "no earlier than the fourth century BC."[10] Such analyses show that dating texts based on intertextual observations requires both a presumed direction of borrowing and a presumed date of composition for the borrowing text while only providing a *terminus ad quem* for what is claimed to be the "earlier" (i.e., borrowed) text.

---

6. H. L. Ginsberg, "The Oldest Interpretation of the Suffering Servant," *VT* 3 (1953): 400–404; Hannah, "Isaiah within Judaism," 30, rearticulates Ginsberg's interpretation.

7. Unless otherwise noted, all biblical citations in this article are from the NIV 2011.

8. Hannah, "Isaiah within Judaism," 30.

9. Choon-Leong Seow, "Qoheleth's Eschatological Poem," *JBL* 118 (1999): 209–34. For a critique of the claims that the book of Ecclesiastes is dependent on Isaiah, see Richard L. Schultz, "Qoheleth and Isaiah in Dialogue," in *Reading Ecclesiastes Intertextually*, ed. Katharine Dell and Will Kynes, LHBOTS 574 (London: Bloomsbury, 2014), 60–61.

10. Ronald E. Clements, *Isaiah 1–39*, NCB (Grand Rapids: Eerdmans, 1980), 135. A conservative interpreter might argue to the contrary that the eighth-century prophet Isaiah has appropriated the language used by Solomon but more likely would suggest that the cited poetic imagery is too commonplace to posit any dependence.

Multiple Explanatory Options

Even well-known verbal parallels are of minimal use in establishing the direction of dependence and dates of composition, since a variety of explanations for the similarities can be offered. The most extensive verbal parallel between Isaiah and another text within the prophetic corpus involves the "swords into plowshares" texts in Isa 2:2–4(5) and Mic 4:1–4(5), as well as the converse of this "peacetime" image in Joel 4:10 [ET 3:10]. In light of this and many other verbal, conceptual, and formal similarities between the books of Isaiah and Micah,[11] it would be logical to conclude that one of these eighth-century prophets took over this dramatic vision of Zion's future exaltation from his contemporary, leaving us merely with the task of determining who borrowed from whom. Although the use of vocabulary statistics and tradition-critical analysis has failed to link this oracle definitively to the ministry and message of either prophet, a significant number of interpreters prefer to name either the prophet Micah (e.g., Calvin, Caspari, Nägelsbach) or, more often, Isaiah (e.g., Duhm, Gunneweg, Motyer, von Rad, Rudolph, Wildberger, van der Woude) as the originator. In grounding their decision, they use criteria such as the fullness of expression or smoothness of the text, its contextual fit, and its consistency with the prophet's style, vocabulary, imagery, and theology elsewhere. Among the more unusual reasons are psychological explanations, such as that Isaiah would never have stooped to quote a younger, less prominent prophet, or labeling the superscription in Isa 2:1 an early redactor's effort to claim the oracle for Isaiah.

But this is certainly not viewed as the only option. Another favored conclusion is that the oracle has been incorporated into *both* books from a no-longer-extant third source. This could have been a preexilic addition, perhaps by the prophets Micah and Isaiah (an explanation mostly held prior to the twentieth century), or a postexilic addition to both books reflecting an "advanced" eschatology, perhaps by the same editor who added Isa 2:5 and Mic 4:5 (as is more commonly suggested today). A primary problem is presented by the specific content of the oracle, which lacks any clear parallel within the prophetic corpus. Elsewhere, when the nations head for Zion, they do so either in order to attack or to join the Israelites in worshipping YHWH in the temple; here they do neither. To sum up the discussion related to this problem, even in the case of such an extensive and well-known parallel text, there is no consensus today regarding the relative dating and direction of dependence of the "swords into plowshares" text in Isa 2 and Mic 4—and little likelihood that one will be achieved in the foreseeable future.[12]

---

11. See, for example, the study by Gary Stansell, *Micah and Isaiah: A Form and Tradition Historical Comparison*, SBLDS 85 (Atlanta: Scholars Press, 1988).

12. For more detailed discussion and documentation of these options, see Schultz, *Search for Quotation*, 290–307, esp. 295–302. For an example of how one can engage these texts canonically, see Irmtraud Fischer, "World Peace and 'Holy War'—Two Sides of the Same Theological Concept: 'YHWH as Sole Divine Power' (A Canonical-Intertextual Reading of Isaiah 2:1–5, Joel 4:9–21, and Micah 4:1–5)," in *Isaiah's Vision of Peace in Biblical and*

Inadequate Criteria

Intertextual connections have been employed frequently in modern biblical scholarship in determining the relative chronology of biblical books, subsections, texts, or even phrases thereof, although contemporary interpreters are more likely to give more weight to tradition-historical considerations.[13] Despite the attention given to such intertextual connections, consensus over criteria for determining the direction of borrowing remains elusive. For example, with regard to Isa 2 and Mic 4, discussed above, John Thompson argues that, since Joel twice gives "the reverse of ideas" (i.e., "plowshares into swords" and "pruning hooks into spears") in Joel 4:10 [ET 3:10], each of which, in turn, is found twice elsewhere (i.e., in both Isa 2:4 and Mic 4:3), the latter probably represents the original.[14] The presence of this parallel text in Isaiah and Micah is hardly a telling argument for priority. One could as easily argue that Isaiah alone reversed Joel in formulating his oracle regarding Zion's future exaltation and that his contemporary Micah (or a later editor) incorporated the same oracle into the book of Micah without any knowledge of Joel's prior influence. In sum, Thompson's criteria are inadequate to justify his assertion.

Richard Hays, whose approach to identifying intertextual echoes is widely employed in intertextual studies today, suggests seven criteria (or tests) for determining their *presence*: availability, volume, recurrence or clustering, thematic coherence, historical plausibility, history of interpretation, and satisfaction.[15] However, here it must be noted that in his study of Paul's use of Isaiah, Hays obviously assumes, in each case, that Paul is echoing Isaiah and not vice versa! What he is seeking to determine by using these criteria is merely *whether* an Isaianic echo is indeed present in a given Pauline text. Of the seven criteria, the most important is what Hays labels "volume," that is, "*the degree of verbatim repetition of words and syntactical patterns*" as well as "*the distinctiveness, prominence, or popular familiarity of the precursor text*."[16] Most of these criteria can be utilized in identifying intertextual relationships within the Hebrew Bible as well, although they may

---

Modern International Relations: Swords into Plowshares, ed. Raymond Cohen and Raymond Westbrook, Culture and Religion in International Relations (New York: Palgrave Macmillan, 2008), 151–65.

13. For example, in Elie Assis' recent discussion of the date of Joel in the initial chapter of his *The Book of Joel: A Prophet between Calamity and Hope*, LHBOTS 581 (New York: Bloomsbury, 2013), he makes no mentions of verbal parallels between Joel and other Hebrew Bible texts.

14. John A. Thompson, *The Book of Joel*, IBC 6 (Nashville: Abingdon, 1956), 732. Thompson also cites two other examples of probable borrowing. He suggests that the phrase "that I, the LORD, am your God and there is none else" (Joel 2:27; RSV) comes from Deutero-Isaiah and that "So you shall know that I am the LORD your God" (Joel 4:17[ET 3:17]; RSV) is drawn from Ezekiel, where "variations of [it] . . . occur over fifty times."

15. Richard B. Hays, "'Who Has Believed Our Message?' Paul's Reading of Isaiah," in *The Conversion of the Imagination: Paul as Interpreter of Israel's Scripture* (Grand Rapids: Eerdmans, 2005), 34–45.

16. Ibid., 35–36. The emphases here are original.

involve considerable uncertainty (as in the case, e.g., of "availability"). Few (if any) of them, however, offer much help in determining *priority*, that is, which text is being intertextually enriched and which text is the "source."

There is a substantial body of secondary literature, much of it from recent decades, that discusses examples of biblical intertextuality, including those involving the Latter Prophets.[17] Most of these publications offer methodological reflections in order to provide a warrant for their interpretive work. In my earlier study of this topic, I noted four problematic assumptions plaguing such studies[18] relating to the accessibility of previous oracles, the stability of the text (or underlying tradition), the incipient authority of these sayings supposedly being quoted or alluded to, and the identifiability of "quotations" of allusions, given the almost complete absence of "introductory formulae" within the Hebrew Bible. Numerous criteria have been commended for determining the directionality of literary borrowing: prominence of the original author, interpretive reuse, fullness of expression, awkward contextual fit, typical vocabulary, and style. Furthermore, it is commonly held that such textual reuse is a secondary, even a "late," compositional feature. Many assume that ancient authors would not "recycle" an especially striking formulation from an "earlier" text, incorporating it into a later literary context, even if the striking formulation were in one of their own texts. It is even claimed that such intertextual reuse stems from an era lacking in prophetic inspiration.[19]

Unfortunately, some (perhaps even most) of the suggested criteria have been employed to support opposite conclusions, i.e., that a later editor either expanded or abbreviated a borrowed text, either producing a literary-critical "bump" by incorporating a "foreign" text into a later literary context or modifying it in the process to produce a "smooth," almost undetectable fit.[20] In sum, various features can

---

17. From a methodological standpoint, some of the more useful contributions are Mark J. Boda and Michael H. Floyd, eds., *Bringing out the Treasure: Inner Biblical Allusion in Zechariah 9–14*, JSOTSup 370 (New York: Sheffield Academic, 2003); D. A. Carson and H. G. M. Williamson, eds., *It is Written: Scripture Citing Scripture; Essays in Honour of Barnabas Lindars* (Cambridge: Cambridge University Press, 1988); Lyle M. Eslinger, "Inner-Biblical Exegesis and Inner-Biblical Allusion: The Question of Category," *VT* 42 (1992): 47–58; Michael A. Fishbane, *Biblical Interpretation in Ancient Israel* (Oxford: Clarendon, 1985); Karl W. Weyde, "Inner-Biblical Interpretation: Methodological Reflections on the Relationship between Texts in the Hebrew Bible," *SEÅ* 70 (2005): 287–300; Ina Willi-Plein, *Vorformen der Schriftexegese innerhalb des Alten Testamentes*, BZAW 123 (Berlin: de Gruyter, 1971); and Walther Zimmerli, "Prophetic Proclamation and Reinterpretation," in *Tradition and Theology in the Old Testament*, ed. Douglas A. Knight (Philadelphia: Fortress, 1977), 69–100.

18. Schultz, *Search for Quotation*, 109–12.

19. See, for example, Wolfgang Lau, *Schriftgelehrte Prophetie in Jes 56–66*, BZAW 225 (Berlin: de Gruyter, 1994), 318.

20. For example, Will Kynes disputes the claim of Risto Nurmela that "the awkwardness in the later text" results from the incorporated allusion, stating that if "later authors can smooth out vocabulary, then they could also adapt allusions to new contexts" ("Job and Isaiah 40–55: Intertextualities in Dialogue," in *Reading Job Intertextually*, ed. Katharine Dell and Will Kynes, LHBOTS 574 [London: Bloomsbury: 2013], 97). Here Kynes is interacting with the discussion in Risto Nurmela, *The Mouth of the Lord Has Spoken: Inner-Biblical*

legitimately be noted in constructing an intertextual argument, but they supply us with little objective evidence for use in determining the relative dating of specific texts or redactional layers. It is not surprising, therefore, that some scholars have opted for more non-committal labels such as "interdependence"[21] or employ a reader-oriented focus on the *effect* of recognizing such intertextual connections.[22] Nevertheless, most biblical scholars have not abandoned the "historical" enterprise, and this is methodologically foundational for the intertextual studies that I will discuss in the following major sections of this essay.

Intertextuality and the Composition of the Book of Isaiah

What can we learn with any degree of certainty about the compositional history of Isaiah from the numerous intertextual studies that have been published in recent decades? We actually can learn very little, as a brief examination of several such studies will illustrate. I will begin with a shorter study by William Tooman, in which he examines the reuse of Scripture in Ezekiel's "Gog Oracles."[23] In one example, he notes that Ezek 38:7–13 has "adapted" Isa 10:3–6 and Jer 49:30–33, which have "dictated" its shape. According to his analysis, "the day of visitation . . . when the devastation will come" (תָבוֹא . . . לְיוֹם פְּקֻדָּה וּלְשׁוֹאָה, *lĕyôm pĕquddâ ûlĕšôʾâ . . . tābôʾ*) from Isa 10:3 is reflected in Ezek 38:8–9 ("after many days you will be visited . . . like a devastation you will come"; מִיָּמִים רַבִּים תִּפָּקֵד . . . כַּשֹּׁאָה תָבוֹא, *miyyāmîm rabbîm tippāqēd . . . kaššôʾâ tābôʾ*), while the phrase "to take spoil and to seize plunder" is found in identical form in Isa 10:6 and Ezek 38:12 (cf. also 38:13 and 39:10: לִשְׁלֹל שָׁלָל וְלָבֹז בַּז, *lišlōl šālāl wĕlābōz baz*).[24] According to Tooman, the author of the Gog Oracles uses Isa 10 and Jer 49 "typologically," "not as *prophecies* about Israel's future *per se*, but paradigmatically, as if future events will be patterned on events from the past."[25] Tooman argues further that Ezek 39:1–8 draws on Isa 14:4b–21 for

Allusions in Second and Third Isaiah, Studies in Judaism (Lanham, MD: University Press of America, 2006), 32–37.

21. See Andrew E. Hill, "Appendix C: Intertextuality in the Book of Malachi," in *Malachi*, AB 25D (New York: Doubleday, 1998), 401–12.

22. Peter D. Miscall, *Isaiah*, 2nd ed., Readings (Sheffield: Sheffield Phoenix, 2006).

23. William A. Tooman, "Transformation of Israel's Hope: The Reuse of Scripture in the Gog Oracles," in *Transforming Visions: Transformations of Text, Tradition, and Theology in Ezekiel*, ed. William A. Tooman and Michael A. Lyons, Princeton Theological Monograph Series 127 (Eugene, OR: Pickwick, 2010), 50–110. By "Scripture," Tooman implies that the reused texts are already authoritative but not yet canonical (p. 51). Tooman considers the Gog Oracles to be a later addition to—but deeply influenced by and frequently borrowing from—the earlier parts of the book of Ezekiel. In an appendix (pp. 94–105), he lists about twenty examples of the "scriptural reuse" of Isaiah texts in Ezek 38–39. Tooman has authored a fuller study of this section of Ezekiel, *Gog of Magog*, FAT II/52 (Tübingen: Mohr Siebeck, 2011).

24. Tooman, "Transformation of Israel's Hope," 66–67. The translations cited here are from Tooman.

25. Ibid., 68. The emphases here are original.

its images of a ruler from the north who is slain and remains unburied, that Isa
34:6–7 is the "direct inspiration for" the "motif of animals devouring the slain" in
Ezek 39:17–20, and that the motifs of "glory, witness of the nations, and vindication
of Israel" in Ezek 39:21–29 are all "distinctive expressions of Isaiah 40–66" (i.e.,
42:8b; 52:10; 62:2; and 66:19).[26]

If Tooman is correct, what implications does his analysis have for the issues of
compositional history and dating? Unlike many scholars, in this regard Tooman is
strikingly honest and reserved:

> The surest method of dating is from evidence of literary dependence. That is, if the
> author's sources could be dated with some certainty, they would establish a *terminus ad
> quo* [*sic*] for GO [= the Gog Oracles]. . . . But scholars can seldom agree on the date of
> any scriptural text, which renders any judgment in this regard indeterminate.[27]

That is, minimally, Tooman has demonstrated only that Isa 10, whenever he
dates it, is earlier than the Gog Oracles, whenever he dates them. And since his
examples are drawn from various critically-distinguished sections of the book of
Isaiah (i.e., Isa 10, 14, 34, 42, 52, 62, and 66) without him noting any significant
differences in how the Gog Oracles draw on these various Isaiah texts, his study
has no implications whatsoever for his understanding of the composition of the
book of Isaiah. Since he dates Joel and Third Isaiah (e.g., Isa 62 and 66) to the fifth
century BCE, following the critical consensus, he dates the Gog Oracles later, but
a considerably earlier date for either of the first two texts probably would have no
impact on his study.

Turning to another example, Will Kynes argues that Job is dependent on Isa
40–55, but *not* on the basis of the scholarly consensus regarding the relative dates of
these compositions (i.e., between the fifth and third centuries and the sixth century
BCE, respectively). Rather, according to his analysis, in each claimed parallel, it appears that Job is offering a "parody and dialogical interpretation" of the Isaiah text.[28]
One wonders how strong a case one can build with just four examples. The first
of these is based primarily on the occurrence of the phrase "cannot be fathomed"
(אֵין חֵקֶר, *'ên ḥēqer*) in Isa 40:28 and in the nearly identical verses Job 5:9 (spoken
by Eliphaz) and 9:10 (spoken by Job). In Isa 40, the phrase refers to God's "understanding" (תְּבוּנָה, *tĕbûnâ*), while in Job it refers to the "great things" (גְדֹלוֹת, *gĕdōlôt*)
God does. An arguably closer parallel for the Joban verses can be found in Ps 145:3,
in which the phrase refers to God's "greatness" (וְלִגְדֻלָּתוֹ אֵין חֵקֶר, *wĕligdullātô 'ên
ḥēqer*) using the same Hebrew root (ג-ד-ל, *g-d-l*) as the Joban verses, and presumably refers to God's "works" (מַעֲשֶׂיךָ, *ma'ăśêkā*) mentioned in the following verse
(v. 4). Thus, it is not certain that in 9:5 Job is alluding to Isa 40; nor is it apparent

---

26. Ibid., 71–79.

27. Ibid., 91.

28. Kynes, "Job and Isaiah 40–55," 94–105. Kynes (pp. 100–104) examines only four such
intertextual allusions: (1) Job 9:10; 5:9; and Isa 40:28; (2) Job 9:12; 25:2–4; and Isa 45:9; (3) Job
9:12; 11:10; and Isa 43:13; and (4) Job 5:12–13; 12:17; and Isa 44:25.

that Job has "taken [Isaiah's] praise and turned it into an accusation,"[29] since in Isa 40 it actually occurs in the context of an admonitory theological argument (see Isa 40:27).

Kynes does not explain the focus in his study on "allusions to Isaiah 40–55 in Job," as expressed in the title of his essay, especially since the four examples cited are confined to Isa 40–45. It may be because he is building on prior studies of these texts that proceed from the assumption that Isa 40–55 represents an independent composition within the larger canonical book. However, if his intertextual argument for the priority of Isa 40–55 over Job is accepted, he has minimally demonstrated only that the book of Job cannot predate the eighth-century ministry of Isaiah of Jerusalem (the traditional source of the oracles in the canonical book) and that the author of Job was especially attracted to the portrayal of God's actions in Isa 40–55.⊠Lest this essay be viewed as merely critiquing the work of others, it is important to consider a couple of textual examples in which I will argue for the presence of intertextual allusion, although these are all disputed by other scholars.[30] Not surprisingly, in light of the scope and rhetorical richness of its vision of Israel's future, Deut 32 appears to have made a significant impact on the prophetic books of the Hebrew Bible. The verbal, theological, and thematic parallels between Deut 32 and "First" (Ronald Bergey) and "Second" Isaiah (Thomas Keiser and Hyun Chul Paul Kim) have been thoroughly examined. Bergey and Keiser strongly affirm the prophetic dependence on Deut 32, while Kim is more reserved in asserting the direction of dependence.[31]

The parallels between Deut 32 and Isa 1:2–4 are particularly striking. First of all, both texts begin by calling on the heavens and the earth to serve as witnesses, as clarified in Deut 31:28 (cf. 4:26; 30:19):[32]

---

29. Kynes, "Job and Isaiah 40–55," 101.

30. In Schultz, *Search for Quotation*, 307–29, I make a lengthy case for the dependence of the Moab oracle in Jer 48 on the Moab oracle in Isa 15–16. Even if this claim is accepted, it only indicates that Isa 15–16 is prior to Jer 48, rather than, for example, undercutting the frequent claim of Deutero-Isaiah's dependence on Jeremiah, since (1) Deutero-Isaiah is commonly dated around 150 years later than Proto-Isaiah and (2) the "oracles concerning the nations" section in both books is often dated later than the period when the traditional prophets Isaiah and Jeremiah addressed the people of God.

31. Ronald Bergey, "The Song of Moses (Deuteronomy 32.1–43) and Isaianic Prophecies: A Case of Early Intertextuality?," *JSOT* 28 (2003): 33–54; Thomas A. Keiser, "The Song of Moses as a Basis for Isaiah's Prophecy," *VT* 55 (2005): 486–500; Hyun Chul Paul Kim, "The Song of Moses (Deuteronomy 32:1–43) in Isaiah 40–55," in *God's Word for Our World*, ed. J. Harold Ellens et al., JSOTSup 388 (London: T&T Clark, 2004), 1:141–71. See also Paul Sanders, *The Provenance of Deuteronomy 34*, OtSt 37 (Leiden: Brill, 1996), 354–56, 360–62. My discussion in this section is indebted to the analysis of Brittany D. Kim, "'Enlarge the Place of Your Tent': The Metaphorical World of Israel's Household in the Book of Isaiah" (PhD diss., Wheaton College, 2014), 33–35.

32. In the parallel texts displayed in the remainder of the essay, full underlining indicates that both texts use the same Hebrew root though not necessarily the same grammatical forms or even the same word order. Broken underlining indicates that both texts use corresponding or similar concepts but not the same Hebrew roots. The use of a specific

Deut 32:1

הַאֲזִינוּ הַשָּׁמַיִם . . . וְתִשְׁמַע הָאָרֶץ

ha'ăzînû haššāmayim . . . wĕtišmaʿ hā'āreṣ

Listen, you heavens, . . . **hear, you earth!**

Isa 1:2a

שִׁמְעוּ שָׁמַיִם וְהַאֲזִינִי אֶרֶץ

šimʿû šāmayim wĕha'ăzînî 'ereṣ

Hear me, you heavens! Listen, earth!

Deut 32:5a

שִׁחֵת לוֹ לֹא בָּנָיו

šiḥēt lô lō' bānāyw

They [Israel] are **corrupt** and not his **children.**

32:19

וַיַּרְא יְהוָה וַיִּנְאָץ מִכַּעַס בָּנָיו וּבְנֹתָיו

wayyar' yhwh wayyin'āṣ mikkaʿas bānāyw ûbĕnōtāyw

The Lᴏʀᴅ saw this and **rejected** them because he was angered by his **sons** and daughters.

Isa 1:4b

בָּנִים מַשְׁחִיתִים . . . נִאֲצוּ אֶת־קְדוֹשׁ יִשְׂרָאֵל

bānîm mašḥîtîm . . . ni'ăṣû 'et-qĕdôš yiśrā'ēl

children given to corruption! . . . they have **forsaken** the Holy One of Israel

The verbs א-ז-ן (*'-z-n*) and שׁ-מ-ע (*š-m-ʿ*) and the nouns שָׁמַיִם (*šāmayim*) and אֶרֶץ (*'ereṣ*) occur together in the Hebrew Bible only in Deut 32:1 and Isa 1:2. In Isaiah the two verbs take the opposite objects, which lack definite articles (unlike in Deut 32:1), resulting in a pleasing alliteration that is lacking in Deut 32. This could point to Isaiah as the borrower in this verbal pair. As displayed above, both Deut 32 (in vv. 5a and 19) and Isa 1 (in v. 4b) also employ the metaphor of Israel as YHWH's "children," who are described as "corrupt," using the verb שׁ-ח-ת (*š-ḥ-t*). The second verb, נ-א-ץ (*n-'-ṣ*), occurs twenty-four times in the Hebrew Bible, predominantly to describe Israel or others rejecting God or things associated with God. Only in Deut 32:19; Jer 14:21; 33:24; and Lam 2:6 (see also Prov 1:30) is God the subject rather than

---

published translation—rather than a more literal rendering—sometimes obscures these verbal correspondences.

the object of this verb. God's actions toward his "children" in Deut 32:19 correspond to their similar actions toward God in 31:20 (וַיְנַאֲצוּנִי, *wĕni'ăṣûnî*), which involved blatant apostasy (31:20; see also 32:17).

These close verbal parallels between Deut 32 and Isa 1:2–4 suffice to indicate a relationship of dependence (rather than coincidental verbal overlap) between these two texts.[33] Though not often involving as close verbal parallels as here, the additional parallels with Deuteronomy throughout the book of Isaiah that are noted by Bergey, Keiser, and Kim may offer additional support for the claim that Isaiah is the borrower. If accepted as such, this would not necessarily constitute support for the compositional unity of the book of Isaiah; one would also have to demonstrate, for example, that Deut 32 is used similarly in both Isa 1–39 and Isa 40–66.[34] At the very least, however, it would require that Deut 32 (but not necessarily the entire canonical book of Deuteronomy) predate "Proto-Isaiah."

On the other end of the canonical spectrum, Risto Nurmela has devoted detailed attention to biblical allusions in Zechariah. In an essay summarizing the implications of his analyses for an understanding of this book's relationship to the book of Isaiah,[35] he cites five parallel texts. By focusing not on the basis of the (claimed) relative dating of the two books but rather on "the integration of the verbal elements shared by Zechariah and other Old Testament writings [i.e., Isaiah] in their respective contexts," he argues that in most of these examples "a dependence on the book of Isaiah can be demonstrated."[36] In order to assess the cogency

---

33. The verb ה-נ-ק (*q-n-h*, "create, acquire") also occurs in both Deut 32:6 and Isa 1:3.

34. See H. G. M. Williamson, "Deuteronomy and Isaiah," in *For Our Good Always: Studies on the Message and Influence of Deuteronomy in Honor of Daniel I. Block*, ed. Jason S. DeRouchie, Jason Gile, and Kenneth J. Turner (Winona Lake, IN: Eisenbrauns, 2014), 251–68. Williamson generally attributes parallels between Deuteronomy [including Deut 32] and the first part of Isaiah to late editors who may have been "influenced by their knowledge of Deuteronomy . . . but not in any exclusive or scholastic sense" (p. 257), while concluding that one finds "within Isaiah 40–55 a use of themes and terminology that have their closest parallels in Deuteronomy [including Deut 32] and that seem to have been influenced by that book" (p. 268).

35. Risto Nurmela, *Prophets in Dialogue: Inner-Biblical Allusions in Zechariah 1–8 and 9–14* (Åbo: Åbo Akademi University Press, 1996); ibid., "The Growth of the Book of Isaiah Illustrated by Allusions in Zechariah," in *Bringing Out the Treasure: Inner Biblical Allusion in Zechariah 9–14*, ed. Mark J. Boda and Michael H. Floyd, JSOTSup 370 (New York: Sheffield Academic, 2003), 245–59; see also Nurmela, *Mouth of the Lord Has Spoken*.

36. Nurmela, "Growth of the Book of Isaiah," 247–48. In *Prophets in Dialogue*, Nurmela analyzes the following additional allusions involving these two Old Testament books, but considers them to be weaker examples: Zech 1:15–16 // Isa 47:6; 60:10; Zech 4:7 // Isa 40:4; 42:16; Zech 9:13 // Isa 49:2; Zech 9:16 // Isa 62:3, 10; Zech 10:11 // Isa 11:15–16; Zech 11:1–2 // Isa 2:13; Zech 11:7, 10, 14, 16–17; 13:7–9 // Isa 1:25 and Ezek 5:1–12; 34:2–5; 37:15–28. In monograph-length studies of allusion in "Second" Isaiah, Patricia Tull Willey (*Remember the Former Things: The Recollection of Previous Texts in Second Isaiah*, SBLDS 161 [Atlanta: Scholars Press, 1997]) and Benjamin D. Sommer (*A Prophet Reads Scripture: Allusion in Isaiah 40–66*, Contraversions [Palo Alto, CA: Stanford University Press, 1998]), both argue consistently that Second Isaiah is dependent on Jeremiah rather than vice versa, raising the question whether this conclusion is based on their relative dating of the two texts rather

of Nurmela's claims, we must first examine the texts in Zechariah that he considers to be allusive:[37]

1

Isa 12:6

צַהֲלִי וָרֹנִּי יוֹשֶׁבֶת צִיּוֹן כִּי־גָדוֹל בְּקִרְבֵּךְ קְדוֹשׁ יִשְׂרָאֵל:

ṣahălî wārōnnî yôšebet ṣiyyôn kî-gādôl běqirbēk qědôš yiśrāʾēl

"Cry aloud and **shout for joy**, O inhabitant of **Zion**, **for** great *in your midst* is the Holy One of Israel."

Zech 2:14[ET 10]

רָנִּי וְשִׂמְחִי בַּת־צִיּוֹן כִּי הִנְנִי־בָא וְשָׁכַנְתִּי בְתוֹכֵךְ נְאֻם־יְהוָה:

ronnî wěśimḥî bat-ṣiyyôn kî hiněnî-bāʾ wěšākantî bětôkēk ně'um-yhwh

"**Sing for joy** and *be glad*, *O daughter* of Zion; *for* behold I am coming and I will dwell *in your midst*," declares the LORD.

2

Isa 14:1

וּבָחַר עוֹד בְּיִשְׂרָאֵל . . . וְנִלְוָה הַגֵּר עֲלֵיהֶם וְנִסְפְּחוּ עַל־בֵּית יַעֲקֹב:

ûbāḥar ʿôd běyiśrāʾēl . . . wěnilwâ haggēr ʿălêhem wěnispěḥû ʿal-bêt yaʿăqōb

"**and again** [the LORD will] **choose** Israel. . . . *then strangers* **will join** them and attach themselves to the house of Jacob."

Zech 2:15–16[ET 11–12]

וְנִלְווּ גוֹיִם רַבִּים אֶל־יְהוָה בַּיּוֹם הַהוּא וְהָיוּ לִי לְעָם . . . וּבָחַר עוֹד בִּירוּשָׁלָםִ:

wěnilwû gôyim rabbîm ʾel-yhwh bayyôm hahûʾ wěhāyû lî lěʿām . . . ûbāḥar ʿôd bîrûšālāim

"[**And**] *many nations* **will join** themselves *to* the LORD in that day and will become My people. . . . **and** [the LORD] **will again choose** *Jerusalem*."

* See also the use of the verb ל-ח-נ (*n-ḥ-l*), "to inherit," in Isa 14:2 and Zech 2:16.

---

than on their analyses of the respective literary contexts. See also Shalom M. Paul, *Isaiah 40–55*, ECC (Grand Rapids: Eerdmans, 2012), 53–55, who lists about two dozen examples of the "influence" of Jeremiah on Deutero-Isaiah, a considerably looser term than Nurmela's and Sommer's preferred term, "allusion."

37. The NASB translation is used in the following texts in order to indicate the verbal correspondence more fully, but the NASB's practice of capitalizing the first word of each clause has not been followed.

3

Isa 6:10–11

וְאָזְנָיו הַכְבֵּד . . . וּבְאָזְנָיו יִשְׁמָע . . . וְהָאֲדָמָה תִּשָּׁאֶה שְׁמָמָה:

wĕ'oznāyw hakbēd . . . *ûbĕ'oznāyw yišmā'* . . . *wĕhā'ădāmâ tiššā'ê*
šĕmāmâ

"**Render** . . . **their ears dull.** . . . [Otherwise, they might] **hear** with
their ears. . . . [until] the *land* is utterly **desolate**."

Zech 7:11, 14

וְאָזְנֵיהֶם הִכְבִּידוּ מִשְּׁמוֹעַ: . . . וַיָּשִׂימוּ אֶרֶץ־חֶמְדָּה לְשַׁמָּה

wĕ'oznêhem hikbîdû *miššĕmôa'* . . . *wayyāśîmû 'ereṣ-ḥemdâ lĕšammâ*

"[They] **stopped their ears** from **hearing.** . . . for they made the pleasant *land* **desolate**."

* The hardening of the heart (לֵב, *lēb*) is mentioned in both Isa 6:10
and Zech 7:12.

4

Isa 1:26

יִקָּרֵא לָךְ עִיר הַצֶּדֶק קִרְיָה נֶאֱמָנָה:

yiqqārē' lāk 'îr haṣṣedeq qiryâ ne'ĕmānâ

"**You will be called** the city of righteousness, a **faithful** city."

Zech 8:3

וְנִקְרְאָה יְרוּשָׁלַ͏ִם עִיר־הָאֱמֶת

wĕniqrĕ'â yĕrûšālaim 'îr-hā'ĕmet

"Then Jerusalem **will be called** the **City of Truth**."

5

Isa 2:2–4

וְנָהֲרוּ אֵלָיו כָּל־הַגּוֹיִם: וְהָלְכוּ עַמִּים רַבִּים וְאָמְרוּ לְכוּ וְנַעֲלֶה אֶל־הַר־יְהוָה
אֶל־בֵּית אֱלֹהֵי יַעֲקֹב

wĕnāhărû 'ēlāyw kol-haggôyim wĕhālĕkû 'ammîm rabbîm wĕ'āmĕrû
lĕkû wĕna'ălê 'el-har-yhwh 'el-bêt 'ĕlōhê ya'ăqōb

"And all the **nations** *will stream* to it. **And many peoples will come**
and **say**, '**Come**, let us go up *to the mountain of the* Lord*, to the house*
of the God of Jacob.'"

Zech 8:20–23

לֵאמֹר נֵלְכָה הָלוֹךְ . . . וּבָאוּ עַמִּים רַבִּים וְגוֹיִם עֲצוּמִים לְבַקֵּשׁ אֶת־יְהוָה
צְבָאוֹת בִּירוּשָׁלָם

*lēʾmōr nēlĕkâ hālôk . . . ûbāʾû ʿammîm rabbîm wĕgôyim ʿăṣûmîm
lĕbaqqēš ʾet-yhwh ṣĕbāʾôt bîrûšālāim*

"saying, 'Let us go at once'. . . . So many peoples and mighty nations
will come to seek the LORD of hosts in Jerusalem."

6

Isa 52:8

בְּשׁוּב יְהוָה צִיּוֹן (בְרחמים = 1QIsaᵃ)

bĕšûb yhwh ṣiyyôn (1QIsaᵃ = brḥmym)

"when the LORD **restores** [NIV: returns to] *Zion* . . ."

Isa 52:9

כִּי־נִחַם יְהוָה עַמּוֹ גָּאַל יְרוּשָׁלָם:

kî-niḥam yhwh ʿammô gāʾal yĕrûšālāim

"for the LORD **has comforted** His people, He has redeemed
Jerusalem."

Zech 1:16–17

שַׁבְתִּי לִירוּשָׁלַם בְּרַחֲמִים . . . וְנִחַם יְהוָה עוֹד אֶת־צִיּוֹן וּבָחַר עוֹד
בִּירוּשָׁלָם:

*šabtî lîrûšālāim bĕraḥămîm . . . wĕniḥam yhwh ʿôd ʾet-ṣiyyôn ûbāḥar
ʿôd bîrûšālāim*

"[thus says the LORD,] 'I will **return** to *Jerusalem* with **compassion** . . .
and the LORD will again **comfort** Zion and again choose **Jerusalem**.' "

7

Isa 29:3

וְחָנִיתִי כַדּוּר עָלָיִךְ וְצַרְתִּי עָלַיִךְ מֻצָּב

wĕḥānîtî kaddûr ʿālāyik wĕṣartî ʿālayik muṣṣāb

"**I will camp** against you encircling (you), and I will raise up **battle
towers** against you."

Zech 9:8

וְחָנִיתִי לְבֵיתִי מִצָּבָה

wĕḥānîtî lĕbêtî miṣṣābâ

"But **I will camp** around My house **because of an army.**" [NRSV: "**as a guard**"]

8

Isa 31:5

כְּצִפֳּרִים עָפוֹת כֵּן יָגֵן יְהוָה צְבָאוֹת עַל־יְרוּשָׁלָם

kĕṣippŏrîm ʿāpôt kēn yāgēn yhwh ṣĕbāʾôt ʿal-yĕrûšālāim

"Like flying birds, **the LORD of hosts will protect Jerusalem.**"

Zech 9:15

יְהוָה צְבָאוֹת יָגֵן עֲלֵיהֶם

yhwh ṣĕbāʾôt yāgēn ʿălêhem

"**The LORD of hosts will defend** *them.*"

Zech 12:8

בַּיּוֹם הַהוּא יָגֵן יְהוָה בְּעַד יוֹשֵׁב יְרוּשָׁלַם

bayyôm hahûʾ yāgēn yhwh bĕʿad yôšēb yĕrûšālaim

"In that day **the LORD will defend** the inhabitants of **Jerusalem.**"

9

Isa 5:26; 7:18

וְשָׁרַק לוֹ

wĕšāraq lô

"and **will whistle for** it . . ."

יִשְׁרֹק יְהוָה לְ

yišrōq yhwh la

"The LORD **will whistle for** [the fly] . . ." (also: Egypt and Assyria)

Zech 10:8, 10

אֶשְׁרְקָה לָהֶם

ʾešrĕqâ lāhem

"**I will whistle for** them" (Egypt and Assyria)

10

Isa 51:13

יְהוָה עֹשֶׂךָ נוֹטֶה שָׁמַיִם וְיֹסֵד אָרֶץ

yhwh ʿōśekā nôṭê šāmayim wĕyōsēd ʾāreṣ

"the LORD your Maker, **who stretched out the heavens and laid the foundations of the earth**"

Zech 12:1

נְאֻם־יְהוָה נֹטֶה שָׁמַיִם וְיֹסֵד אָרֶץ

nĕʾum-yhwh nōṭê šāmayim wĕyōsēd ʾāreṣ

"the LORD who stretches out the heavens, lays the foundation of the earth, . . ."

11

Isa 1:25

וְאָשִׁיבָה יָדִי עָלַיִךְ וְאֶצְרֹף כַּבֹּר סִיגָיִךְ וְאָסִירָה כָּל־בְּדִילָיִךְ׃

wĕʾāšîbâ yādî ʿālayik wĕʾeṣrōp kabbōr sîgāyik wĕʾāsîrâ kol-bĕdîlāyik

"**I will also turn My hand against** you, **and will smelt away** your dross as with lye and will remove all your alloy."

Zech 13:7, 9

וַהֲשִׁבֹתִי יָדִי עַל־הַצֹּעֲרִים׃ . . . וּצְרַפְתִּים כִּצְרֹף אֶת־הַכֶּסֶף וּבְחַנְתִּים כִּבְחֹן אֶת־הַזָּהָב

wahăšibōtî yādî ʿal-haṣṣōʿărîm . . . ûṣĕraptîm kiṣrōp ʾet-hakkesep ûbĕḥantîm kibḥōn ʾet-hazzāhāb

"**and I will turn My hand against** the little ones. . . . [and] **refine** them as silver **is refined**, and test them as fine gold is tested."

12

Isa 41:17

אֲנִי יְהוָה אֶעֱנֵם אֱלֹהֵי יִשְׂרָאֵל לֹא אֶעֶזְבֵם:

'ănî yhwh 'e'ĕnēm 'ĕlōhê yiśrā'ēl lō' 'e'ezbēm

"**I, the Lord, will answer them** Myself, (as) the God of Israel I will **not** *forsake them*."

Zech 10:6

וְהָיוּ כַּאֲשֶׁר לֹא־זְנַחְתִּים כִּי אֲנִי יְהוָה אֱלֹהֵיהֶם וְאֶעֱנֵם:

wĕhāyû ka'ăšer lō'-zĕnaḥtîm kî 'ănî yhwh 'ĕlōhêhem wĕ'e'ĕnēm

"And they will be as though I had **not** *rejected them*, for **I am the Lord** their God and **I will answer them**."

13

Isa 66:23

וְהָיָה מִדֵּי־חֹדֶשׁ בְּחָדְשׁוֹ וּמִדֵּי שַׁבָּת בְּשַׁבַּתּוֹ יָבוֹא כָל־בָּשָׂר לְהִשְׁתַּחֲוֹת לְפָנַי אָמַר יְהוָה:

wĕhāyâ middê-ḥōdeš bĕḥodšô ûmiddê šabbāt bĕšabbattô yābô' kol-bāśār lĕhištaḥăwôt lĕpānay 'āmar yhwh

" '**And it shall be from** *new moon to new moon* **and from** *sabbath to sabbath*, all mankind *will come* **to bow down** before Me,' says the **Lord**."

Zech 14:16

וְהָיָה כָּל־הַנּוֹתָר מִכָּל־הַגּוֹיִם הַבָּאִים עַל־יְרוּשָׁלָָם וְעָלוּ מִדֵּי שָׁנָה בְשָׁנָה לְהִשְׁתַּחֲוֹת לְמֶלֶךְ יְהוָה

wĕhāyâ kol-hannôtār mikkol-haggôyim habbā'îm 'al-yĕrûšālāim wĕ'ālû middê šānâ bĕšānâ lĕhištaḥăwōt lĕmelek yhwh

"**Then it will come about** that any who are left of all the nations that went against Jerusalem *will go up year after year* **to worship** the King, the **Lord** . . ."

* Both Isa 66:24 and Zech 14:12 describe loathsome physical punishment.

We cannot take the space here to examine each of these parallels and consider the case Nurmela makes in each for the direction of the dependence, but it is useful to summarize his conclusions: First of all, examples ##1–5 involve the dependence of passages in Zech 1–8 on passages in Isa 1–39 (i.e., Proto-Isaiah), while in example #6, Isa 52:8–9 is dependent on Zechariah. Second, examples ##7–9 and 11 involve the dependence of texts in Zech 9–12 on texts in Proto-Isaiah, while #10 involves dependence on Deutero-Isaiah. Third, examples ##12 and 13 involve the dependence of passages in Deutero- and Trito-Isaiah, respectively, on passages in Zech 9–14. For Nurmela, these findings "might indicate that both parts of the book of Zechariah can be dated to a period when the book of Isaiah did not yet include Deutero-Isaiah." He notes furthermore that all the allusions in Zechariah are from the original "core" (i.e., chs. 2–11 and 28–31 or the slightly later ch. 1) of Proto-Isaiah, except for examples ##1–2, from Isa 12 and 14 respectively, which probably involve redactional additions to Zechariah taken from "sections very close to that core." Thus Nurmela concludes that the dependence of Zechariah on Deutero- and Trito-Isaiah "seems to be negligible."[38]

Nurmela's careful study of allusion in Zechariah indicates the kind of implications for understanding the compositional history of the book of Isaiah that the study of intertextuality could have. However, one can rightly ask how justified one is in drawing these conclusions on the basis of just thirteen allusions (in addition to the seven "weaker" examples examined in his longer study), especially when conflicting evidence (i.e., examples ##1, 2, and 10) is discounted as stemming from "later additions" to Zechariah. Furthermore, Nurmela's use of a criterion similar to the text-critical principle of *lectio difficilior* to determine the direction of dependence still does not guarantee objectivity. An example of the remaining subjectivity is found in Nurmela's example #6, in which he claims that Isa 52:8–9 is dependent on Zech 1:16–17. He concludes this because (a) Isaiah's description of God's return is, in his view, "very vivid" and thus reflects an "intensification" of Zechariah and (b) the "addition" in 1QIsa^a from Zech 1:16 results in a "clearly overloaded" line. The latter involves a questionable *metri causa* argument, especially when one could claim the same about the corresponding line in Zech 1:16:

שַׁבְתִּי לִירוּשָׁלַ͏ִם בְּרַחֲמִים // בֵּיתִי יִבָּנֶה בָּהּ

šabtî lîrûšālaim bĕraḥămîm // bêtî yibbānê bāh

I will return to Jerusalem with mercy, // and there my house will be rebuilt.

In concluding this section, I would simply (and somewhat disappointingly) state that there are numerous close verbal parallels that already have been identified—and may yet be identified—between the book of Isaiah and other passages now included in the Hebrew Bible. This suggests that the author(s)/editor(s) responsible for the present canonical book frequently drew on earlier texts and traditions and, in turn, the text they wrote was drawn on frequently by later authors and editors. Some of these verbal parallels can yield fascinating hermeneutical and

---

38. Nurmela, "The Growth of the Book of Isaiah," 258–59.

theological insights into how earlier texts were alluded to, not merely for the purpose of stylistic enhancement but rather to reaffirm or reverse "prophetic" promises or threats and indicate that these were now in the process of being fulfilled by
divine action. However, we have noted the following:

(1) the current redaction-critical disagreement regarding the duration and
complexity of the compositional process for each biblical book and, thus,

(2) the lack of consensus regarding the coherence and relative dating of many,
if not most, prophetic texts,

(3) the diversity in criteria employed by "intertextualists" in identifying
allusions,

(4) the subjectivity of nearly all arguments for the direction of dependence.

And to these points we might add:

(5) the possibility that many claimed "allusions" may, in fact, result either from
commonplace expressions in the ancient Hebrew language, despite their infrequent occurrence in the Hebrew Bible, or from unpreserved oral or written
sources.

As a result, there probably is insufficient warrant for using these allusions to draw
any firm conclusions regarding the compositional history of the book of Isaiah.

Intratextuality and the Composition of the Book of Isaiah

This brings me to the second major, albeit shorter, section of my essay—the implications of *intra*textual relationships (i.e., relationships *within* the book of Isaiah),
rather than *inter*textual relationships (i.e., relationships *between* Isaiah and other
books in the Hebrew Bible), for the book's compositional history. At the outset, it
must be acknowledged that not all scholars consider the distinction between these
two categories of allusions to be significant or even legitimate. Benjamin Sommer, for example, offers a study involving "inner-biblical allusion in Isa 40–66"
(which he refers to as "Deutero-Isaiah") in which he argues for the dependence of
these chapters on texts in "the first part of Isaiah" (which Sommer simply refers
to as "Isaiah") as well as in Jeremiah.[39] In that essay, Sommer uses the existence

---

39. Benjamin Sommer, "Allusions and Illusions: The Unity of the Book of Isaiah in
Light of Deutero-Isaiah's Use of Prophetic Tradition," in *New Visions of Isaiah*, ed. Roy F.
Melugin and Marvin A. Sweeney (Sheffield: Sheffield Academic, 1996), 156–86. Sommer sets
forth his methodology for identifying allusions in greater detail in *A Prophet Reads Scripture:
Allusion in Isaiah 40–66*, published in 1998.

of allusions in Deutero-Isaiah to passages in both (Proto-)Isaiah and Jeremiah in seeking to deconstruct the recent claim of "canon critics" that chapters 40–66 were composed to complement or complete chapters 1–39. His argument can be summarized as follows: since Deutero-Isaiah uses texts from both Isa 1–39 and Jeremiah in an indistinguishable manner (i.e., in confirming the fulfillment of prophecies, reversing "tropes of condemnation to ones of comfort," reissuing unfulfilled prophecies, linking individuals or nations with others), there is no intertextual support for the claim that Deutero-Isaiah was written to "complete" Proto-Isaiah. Instead, one could just as convincingly argue that Deutero-Isaiah was once (intended to be) joined to Jeremiah![40] Thus Sommer feels warranted in concluding that Isaiah 40–66 was originally an independent prophetic work and not a "Deutero," becoming the latter only through a later editorial decision. Hence, in Sommer's opinion, the study of verbal parallels between Deutero-Isaiah and (Proto-)Isaiah is just as "intertextual" an analysis as is the study of its parallels with Jeremiah.

In theory, Sommer's analysis of the compositional history of the book of Isaiah could be correct, but such a claim must be based on a *comprehensive* rather than merely an *illustrative* comparison of *intratextual* verbal parallels within Isaiah with *intertextual* links with other prophetic books. More problematic, however, is Sommer's methodology with regard to the identification and analysis of "allusions." First of all, it appears that Sommer simply assumes that Deutero-Isaiah is later than Jeremiah on the basis of a priori considerations, since he does not seek to establish any relative dating for these "books" in his essay.[41] Second, as a result, he assumes that all the allusions he identifies involving Isaiah and Deutero-Isaiah are flowing from the former to the latter rather than vice versa. However, this must be demonstrated rather than simply assumed, since Williamson has argued, for example, that Isa 1:27–31 originated with Third Isaiah.[42] Third, Sommers employs four questionable stylistic features in identifying allusions. These are (1) the "split-up pattern," in which a borrowed phrase is broken up into two or more parts that are separated from each other by several words or even several verses; (2) sound play, involving similar-sounding but not identical words; (3) word play (i.e., homonyms); and (4) parallel word pairs, in which a synonym or related word in the alluding text replaces one of the paired words in the source text.[43] Focusing on these stylistic features rather than on exact or close verbal and grammatical correspondence allows Sommer considerable (and

---

40. Idem, "Allusions and Illusions," 172–78. A related claim by Sommer is that Isa 65–66 should not be viewed as forming an inclusio with Isa 1 that resulted from an author intentionally alluding to the opening chapter of the book (pp. 178–83).

41. For example, Sommer, *Prophet Reads Scripture*, 36, omits Jer 50–51 from his study "because it is altogether likely that Jeremiah 50–51 or large sections thereof were written at the same time as (or even later than) Deutero-Isaiah."

42. H. G. M. Williamson, *A Critical and Exegetical Commentary on Isaiah 1–27*, vol. 1, *Commentary on Isaiah 1–5*, ICC (London: T&T Clark, 2006), 151–55. To be more precise, Williamson attributes these verses to "post-exilic . . . circles very close to those attested in Isaiah 56–66" (p. 154). Sommer sees here instead an allusion of Isa 65:12, 13; 66:17, 24 to Isa 1:28–29, 30 (*Prophet Reads Scripture*, 180–81).

43. Sommer, "Allusions and Illusions," 158–60. See Schultz, *Search for Quotation*, 39–41.

possibly too much) freedom in identifying "evidence" in support of the presence of allusions within the verses included in the passages being analyzed.

To cite an example, Sommer identifies in Isa 28:1–5 and 40:1–10 the following six parallels. According to Sommer, "not only the repetition of vocabulary and themes" but also the stylistic features found here (i.e., the split-up pattern and sound play)—"which are typical of Deutero-Isaianic allusion—mark the relationship between these passage as a borrowing."[44]

	28:1–5	40:1–10
1	הִנֵּה חָזָק וְאַמִּץ לַאדֹנָי (hinnê ḥāzāq wěʾammiṣ laʾdōnāy; v. 2)	הִנֵּה אֲדֹנָי יְהוִה בְּחָזָק יָבוֹא (hinnê ʾădōnāy yhwh běḥāzāq yābôʾ; v. 10)
2	צְבִי (ṣěbî; v. 1) צְבִי (ṣěbî; v. 4) צְבָאוֹת (ṣěbāʾôt; v. 5) צְבִי (ṣěbî; v. 5)	צְבָאָה (ṣěbāʾāh; v. 2)
3	וְצִיץ נֹבֵל (wěṣîṣ nōbēl; v. 1) צִיצַת נֹבֵל (ṣîṣat nōbēl; v. 4)	כְּצִיץ הַשָּׂדֶה (kěṣîṣ haśśādê; v. 6) נָבֵל צִיץ (nābēl ṣ.îṣ.; vv. 7–8)[45]
4	גֵּיא־שְׁמָנִים (gêʾ-šěmānîm; v. 1) גֵּיא (gêʾ; v. 4)	כָּל־גֵּיא (kol-gêʾ; v. 4)
5	בְּיָד (běyād; v. 2)	מִיַּד (miyyad; v. 2)
6	עַמּוֹ (ʿammô; v. 5)	עַמִּי (ʿammî; v. 1)

According to Sommer, this allusion involves a "reversal," in which "figures that served to rebuke and to predict doom in 28.1–5 reappear in 40.1–10 as harbingers of hope" as Deutero-Isaiah "shifts the referent of Isaiah's vocabulary to . . . the return of Judean exiles from Babylonia," an example of "historical recontextualization."[46]

This sounds quite convincing until one considers Sommer's evidence in support of seeing an allusion here. Since verbal parallel 1 consists of three Hebrew words that occur together in Isaiah only in these two texts, it offers the strongest evidence, in Sommer's view, that "the similarity between these passages may result from Deutero-Isaiah's deliberate reference to the older text."[47] However, even in

---

44. Sommer, "Allusions and Illusions," 160.

45. Incorrectly listed twice by Sommer in reverse word order.

46. Sommer, "Allusions and Illusions," 158–60. The emphasis is original.

47. Ibid, 159.

this cited sequence of words we do not have the same phrase but only some of the same commonly used words in different order (i.e., Sommer's "split-up pattern"): "See, the Lord has one who is powerful and strong" (28:2—הִנֵּה חָזָק וְאַמִּץ לַאדֹנָי, *hinnê ḥāzāq wě'ammiṣ la'dōnāy*) // "See, the Sovereign LORD comes with power" (40:10—הִנֵּה אֲדֹנָי יְהוִה בְּחָזָק יָבוֹא, *hinnê 'ădōnāy yhwh bĕḥāzāq yābô'*). The word "See" (הִנֵּה, *hinnê*) occurs seventy-eight times in Isaiah, "Lord" (אֲדֹנָי, *'ădōnāy*) fifty-seven times, and the root ח-ז-ק (*ḥ-z-q*; "strong") twenty-four times (although the adjectival form occurs only in Isa 27:1, 28:2, and 40:10).[48] In Sommer's interpretation, the threat of the Assyrian army in Isaiah (28:2) as the "strong" agent of YHWH's judgment is "reversed" in Deutero-Isaiah in the new context of the Babylonian exile by the promise of YHWH's "strong" deliverance.

If Sommer's identification of an allusion here is accepted (and Isa 40:10 is referring specifically to deliverance from the Babylonian exile), then his interpretation is hermeneutically and theologically significant. But should it be accepted? Sommer's practice of not requiring a sequence of identical words exhibiting a similar syntactic structure increases the subjectivity of his method; indeed, the non-identical nature of the claimed alluding and alluded-to texts (i.e., what Hays might call "low volume") constitutes the very evidence on which he relies. This raises the question again of probability. How likely is it that a reader (or hearer) of Deutero-Isaiah would recall the recurrence of three Hebrew words from Isa 28:2 in Isa 40:10, especially in a section of the book not considered to be particularly "scribal"? A more likely source for the phrase under discussion in Isa 40:10 is found in Exod 13:3, 14, and 16, which describe YHWH as the deliverer of Israel from Egyptian oppression: Isa 40:10—"See, the Sovereign LORD comes with power" (הִנֵּה אֲדֹנָי יְהוִה בְּחָזָק יָבוֹא, *hinnê 'ădōnāy yhwh bĕḥāzāq yābô'*; Exod 13:3—"the LORD brought you out with a mighty hand" (בְּחֹזֶק יָד הוֹצִיא יְהוָה אֶתְכֶם, *bĕḥōzeq yād hôṣî' yhwh 'etkem*).[49]

Sommer acknowledges that the words and themes in the additional parallels either "occur quite often" or may "stem from a stock vocabulary cluster" and may have been used by the authors of both Isa 28 and 40 "coincidentally."[50] These parallels nevertheless contribute to Sommer's overall assessment that "figures" and "vocabulary" from Isa 28:1–5 have been subjected to "reversal" and "historical recontextualization" by the author of Isa 40:1–10, and thus warrant brief discussion, as well:

> Parallel 2: It is questionable that what Sommer terms "sound play" involving the roots צ-ב-י (*ṣ-b-y*; "beauty") and צ-ב-א (*ṣ-b-'*; "hard service") constitutes clear evidence of allusion—or that any early reader (or hearer) of these two texts would recognize it as such.

> Parallel 3: The noun צִיץ (*ṣîṣ*) occurs with the verb נ-ב-ל (*n-b-l*; "fade") in the Hebrew Bible only in Isa 28:1 and Isa 40:7–8. However, since the actual phrases are not identical in the two passages, this suggests that we merely have a paral-

---

48. These statistics were obtained using Accordance Bible software.
49. Note also note the mention of YHWH's "hand" in Isa 40:2, Sommer's parallel 5, and the contrasting verbs: "to bring out" in Exod 13 versus "to enter in" in Isa 40:10.
50. Ibid, 159, 160.

lel botanical metaphor here, which may even have been a common literal or figurative expression in ancient Israel and in ancient Hebrew (i.e., "a stock vocabulary cluster," according to Sommer). Since the metaphor in both texts designates the brevity of urban (regarding Samaria in Isa 28) or human "loveliness" (in Isa 40 [NASB]; or "faithfulness" [NIV]: חֶסֶד, ḥesed), this parallel involves no "reversal," nor any common or contrasting referent.

Parallel 4: "Valley" (גַּיְא, gayʾ) occurs elsewhere in Isaiah only in 22:1, 5, but a total of thirty-six times in the Hebrew Bible. It is a topographically specific referent in Isa 28 but a general term contrasted with "mountain and hill" (הַר וְגִבְעָה, har wĕgibʿâ) in Isa 40.

The words "hand" and "people" in parallels 5 and 6, respectively, are frequently used in Isaiah and throughout the Hebrew Bible. The fact that these two nouns occur in the two passages, respectively, with different prepositions and pronominal suffixes, minimizes their allusive value. In Isa 28, "hand" occurs in a simile comparing the military conquest of Samaria with picking a ripe fig, while in Isa 40 "hand" occurs in an anthropomorphic expression; furthermore, both occurrences refer to divine judgment.

Although many "intertextualists" cite the presence of additional parallels (e.g., parallels ##2–6 above) within the immediate context of the primary parallel (e.g., parallel #1 above) as increasing the probability of the existence of an allusion (what Hays labels "clustering"), it is important to point out here that multiplying weak parallels may actually reduce the probability. Furthermore, in my view, offering several similar examples of claimed allusions to "Isaiah" in "Deutero-Isaiah" does not necessarily lend much support to Sommer's assertion that the author of the latter used the former in the same manner as he used Jeremiah, which, according to Sommer, justifies treating both Isa 1–39 and Jeremiah as originally independent sources.

Regardless of what one concludes with respect to Sommer's claim concerning the original independence of "Second" Isaiah, an argument can be made that, from the synchronic perspective of the readers of Isaiah, *intratextual* allusion produces a different reading dynamic than *intertextual* allusion, one that transcends composition-historical considerations. Whether or not one views internal verbal parallels as "self-quotation," which in principle could be the case, one encounters them sequentially in the reading process, resulting in a layering of semantic content that enriches the later recurrence of a specific verse, clause, or distinctive phrase from the textually "earlier" verbal parallel, even if it is composition-historically "later." Conversely, an awareness of the verbal parallel can lead one to enrich the "earlier" text semantically in a "retroactive" reading.[51] Even from a diachronic perspective, verbal parallels that ultimately were included within the canonical boundaries of one book deserve to be considered differently from those that bridge two

---

51. Schultz, "Intertextuality, Canon, and 'Undecidability': Understanding Isaiah's 'New Heavens and New Earth' (Isa 65:17–25)," *BBR* 20 (2010): 29, 36–37. The term "retroactive" is suggested by the French literature scholar Michael Riffaterre.

different books in the Hebrew Bible, regardless of origin, since, in the case of Isaiah, the former unavoidably raise the question of whether they originated through the effort of an author or editor consciously invoking, imitating, or linking their content to the growing prophetic collection that is now known as the "book" of Isaiah.

What are the data that form the basis of intratextual studies in Isaiah? In the course of my dissertation research, I sought to compile a list of the most striking verbal parallels within the book.[52] Then I went through my list and eliminated nearly half of them as consisting merely of (1) repeated near synonyms or "word pairs," such as "lofty" (ר-ו-ם/נ-שׂ-א, r-w-m/n-ś-ʾ; 2:13; 6:1; 52:13; 57:14) or "briars" (שָׁמִיר/שַׁיִת, šāmîr/šayit; 5:6; 7:23–25; 10:17; 27:4), or of (2) similar imagery that often involves some verbal correspondence, such as the highway (11:16; 19:23; 35:8; 40:3; 42:16; 43:19; 49:11; 57:14; 58:11; 62:10) or the revivification of the desert (35:6–7; 41:18; 43:19–20; 48:21; 49:10), even though some of these also may involve inner-Isaianic allusions. In addition, perhaps exhibiting excessive caution, I eliminated verbal parallels involving (3) physical gestures, such as hiding one's face (54:8; 59:2); (4) similar grammatical structures that lack verbal correspondence, such as 2:3 ("The law will go out from Zion, the word of the LORD from Jerusalem') // 37:32 ("For out of Jerusalem will come a remnant, and out of Mt. Zion a band of survivors"; both verses using תֵּצֵא . . . כִּי מִן, kî min . . . tēṣēʾ); (5) construct chains consisting of only two members, such as "the glory of Lebanon (35:2; 60:13); and (6) rare expressions in the Hebrew Bible but not necessarily in the Hebrew language, such as "not missing" (לֹא נֶעְדָּר/נֶעְדָּרָה, lōʾ neʿdār/neʿdārâ; 34:16; 40:26). In the end, only the fifty verbal parallels shown on the following page remained.

In my view, but without making any claim regarding comprehensiveness, these verses contain the verbal parallels within the book of Isaiah that are least likely to be coincidental and that are most likely to be recognized by the alert reader. Interestingly, of these fifty passages, fifteen occur within Isa 1–39 and thirty within 40–66, while only five "link" these two major sections of the book (##7–8, 10, 14, and 47). Furthermore, five "link" adjoining chapters, while nearly half of the thirty within chapters 40–66 (#14) link "Second" and "Third" Isaiah. On the basis of these passages, one can suggest that, although close verbal repetition is more typical of Isa 40–66 than of 1–39, it is typical of the style of the book throughout. The best known of the five verbal parallels linking Isa 1–39 with 40–66 is clearly the "wolf with the lamb" passages, in which the more expansive description of the "peaceful kingdom" (the "lion lying down with the lamb" description is a later artist's creation) from Isa 11:6–9 is apparently summarized in 65:25. Also noteworthy is the nearly identical description of the "ransomed of YHWH" returning to Zion in 35:10 and 51:11. We may understand both of these verbal parallels to have a significant structural function. Isaiah 11, the penultimate chapter of the opening section of the book, with its portrayal of the harmonious messianic kingdom, is thereby linked to the penultimate chapter of the entire book, with its portrayal of the "new Jerusalem" within the context of the new heavens and earth. Similarly, the repeated

---

52. The following material is abbreviated from Schultz, *The Search for Quotation*, "Appendix: Verbal Parallels in the Book of Isaiah," 339–41.

descriptions in 35:10 and 51:11 strongly link the transitional chapters 34–35 with the extensive description of the restoration from exile in 40–55.[53]

1.	2:9, 11, 17	// 5:15		26.	49:2	// 51:16
2.	2:20	// 31:7		27.	49:18, 22–23	// 60:4
3.	4:6	// 25:4		28.	49:26	// 60:16
4.	5:30	// 8:22		29.	50:2	// 59:1
5.	8:15	// 28:13		30.	51:5	// 60:9
6.	10:23	// 28:22		31.	51:9	// 52:1
7.	11:6–9	// 65:25		32.	51:16	// 59:21
8.	11:12	// 56:8		33.	52:12	// 58:8
9.	13:21–22	// 34:13–14		34.	53:6	// 56:11
10.	14:27	// 43:13		35.	55:3	// 61:8
11.	24:4	// 33:9		36.	55:5	// 60:9
12.	25:12	// 26:5		37.	55:13	// 56:5
13.	29:17	// 32:15		38.	57:14	// 62:10 (40:3)
14.	35:10	// 51:11		39.	58:12	// 61:4
15.	40:10	// 62:11		40.	59:16	// 63:5
16.	40:21	// 48:8		41.	60:21	// 61:3
17.	40:25	// 46:5		42.	61:9	// 65:23
18.	41:8–10	// 44:1–2		43.	65:12	// 66:4
19.	41:19	// 60:13		44.	5:25; 9:11, 16, 20[ET 12, 17, 21]; 10:4	
20.	42:6–7	// 49:8–9		45.	18:2	// 18:7
21.	43:18–19	// 65:17		46.	45:5, 6, 14, 18, 21–22; 46:9	
22.	44:23	// 49:13 // 52:9		47.	1:20; 40:5; 58:14	
23.	45:23	// 55:11		48.	8:11; 18:4; 21:16; 31:4	
24.	46:13	// 51:5		49.	9:6[ET 7]	// 37:32
25.	48:22	// 57:21		50.	21:20	// 28:22

---

53. From a reader's perspective, even if Isa 35:10 may be later than and literarily dependent on Isa 51:11, as some scholars, such as Odil H. Steck, claim (*Bereitete Heimkehr: Jesaja 35 als redaktionelle Brücke zwischen dem Ersten und dem Zweiten Jesaja*, SBS 121 [Stuttgart: Katholisches Bibelwerk, 1985]), from a readerly perspective the former anticipates or adumbrates the latter within the book of Isaiah.

Within biblical scholarship as a whole, the extensive intratextuality within the book of Isaiah is viewed rather differently. To be sure, it serves as one of the data points supporting what Marvin Tate labels "the one-book interpretation" of Isaiah, in contrast to the traditional "one-prophet" and the Duhm-inspired "three-book" interpretations.[54] Nevertheless, the original "inspired" prophet is usually conceived of as having had no need for self-quotation. Instead, nearly all instances of intratextuality within Isaiah are viewed as the work of subsequent authors and editors who are engaged in either uncreative but respectful imitation and redactional insertions or in learned reflection, reinterpretation, and reapplication. To illustrate this claim, I will now briefly summarize the work of Williamson, Hibbard, and Lau.

Contrary to the view of Tull Willey and Sommer (who deny an original relationship between Second and First Isaiah),[55] Williamson sought to demonstrate, in a book published shortly before theirs, that the literary deposit of Isaiah was the primary influence on Deutero-Isaiah. The latter understood his role as heralding the arrival of post-judgment salvation, as previously announced by his prophetic predecessor in a subsequently sealed book. He therefore placed his prophecies following those of Isaiah and carefully edited the expanded collection so as to emphasize the ongoing involvement of God in Israel's national history. Williamson cites verbal parallels identified within Isa 1–55 as offering evidence in support of his thesis, some of them being explained as Deutero-Isaiah's imitations, especially within Isa 40–55, of Proto-Isaiah, while others are labeled as later redactional insertions within Isa 1–39, often by Second Isaiah, that were made with the effect (or goal) of binding the two sections of the book more closely together. Williamson claims that one can distinguish between imitation and insertions on the basis of whether or not a given expression or thematic emphasis is more typical of the style of First or of Second Isaiah. Such verbal parallels, then, are typically viewed not as the result of "self-quotation" but rather as the result of a later author or editor repeating the words of another, even if both texts constituting a given verbal parallel occur within Isaiah 1–39.[56]

Accordingly, the verbal parallel "and he will raise a banner for the nations" (וְנָשָׂא־נֵס לַגּוֹיִם, *wĕnāśāʾ-nēs laggôyim*), which occurs identically in Isa 5:26 and

---

54. Marvin E. Tate, "The Book of Isaiah in Recent Study," in *Forming Prophetic Literature: Essays on Isaiah and the Twelve in Honor of John D. W. Watts*, ed. James W. Watts and Paul R. House, JSOTSup 235 (Sheffield: Sheffield Academic, 1996), 22–56.

55. Willey, *Remember the Former Things*, 270; Sommer, *Prophet Reads Scripture*, 74, 97, 104–7.

56. Williamson, *The Book Called Isaiah: Deutero-Isaiah's Role in Composition and Redaction* (Oxford: Clarendon, 1994). Jacob Stromberg, a former doctoral student of Williamson, has recently extended Williamson's thesis, claiming that Trito-Isaiah played a similar role in joining his prophecies to and further editing Deutero-Isaiah's edited work: see Stromberg, *Isaiah after Exile: The Author of Third Isaiah as Reader and Redactor of the Book*, Oxford Theological Monographs (Oxford: Oxford University Press, 2010). Although Williamson frequently focuses on close verbal parallels, which he subjects to both a *quantitative* and a *qualitative* test, his preference for the term "influence" allows him to discuss a wider range of parallels as well. See also Paul's discussion of "Influence of First Isaiah on Deutero-Isaiah" on pp. 50–52 of his *Isaiah 40–55*.

11:2, is *not* First Isaiah's creation. Rather, Isa 5:26 has influenced Second Isaiah, who turned the negative image in 5:26 into a positive one in the similarly worded verse Isa 49:22: "See, I will beckon to the nations, I will lift up my banner to the peoples" (הִנֵּה אֶשָּׂא אֶל־גּוֹיִם יָדִי וְאֶל־עַמִּים אָרִים נִסִּי, *hinnê ʾeśśāʾ ʾel-gôyim yādî wĕʾel-ʿammîm ʾārîm **nissî***). Each of these three texts also contains a reference to God's "hand" in the immediate context. According to Williamson, Second Isaiah, as editor, subsequently relocated 5:25–29(30) to conclude a "condemnatory section" of the book (Isa 1–5) and also pluralized the word "nation" to better express his view of the future role of the nations in both judging and restoring Israel. As a final step, he created 11:11–16, incorporating both the specific banner formulation of 5:26 and the positive use of the image in 49:22 in concluding the next, more promissory, section (Isa 6–11).[57] However, one wonders whether divergent uses of a particular image (here, a banner summoning the nations both to judge and to restore Israel) offer clear indications that a later editorial hand is at work, rather than simply being a reference to two moments within God's plan for Israel and the nations that one prophet, in principle, could have announced. It is also unclear how often the relative frequency (Williamson's qualitative test) of infrequent words or concepts (Williamson's quantitative test) actually warrants the claim that these are "more at home" in Second Isaiah than in First Isaiah, and thus editorial additions to Isa 1–39 by Second Isaiah. The more one points out how much Second Isaiah was influenced by and inserted himself into First Isaiah, the more their messages coincide and the more difficult it becomes at various points for us to distinguish them.

In his revised Notre Dame dissertation, Todd Hibbard builds on the scholarly near-consensus that Isa 24–27 constitutes one of the latest sections to have been composed and added to the book of Isaiah, as reflected in its designation as the "Isaiah Apocalypse" (which, by definition, means that it is late).[58] Hibbard's particular goal is to demonstrate the close intertextual relationship of these chapters to "earlier material" in the rest of the book, as well as to other prophetic traditions utilized in shaping its depiction of "worldwide judgment followed by the establishment of YHWH's kingship on Zion."[59] What Hibbard discovers is that these chapters are marked by an effort to universalize earlier prophetic announcements of both judgment and salvation and to respond to "unfulfilled" prophecies, in addition to contributing to "a larger thematic discourse that runs through Isaiah."[60] To a greater extent than some of the scholars previously mentioned, Hibbard views the author of Isa 24–27 as using earlier texts because they can serve as "exemplars of a message . . . [he] wishes to deploy" rather than in order to "reinterpret" them. Although leaving such a larger diachronic synthesis to a later study, he concludes

---

57. Williamson, *Book Called Isaiah*, 63–67, 125–43. Ronald Clements assigns the entire section 11:10–16 to the fourth century BCE (*Isaiah 1–39*, 125).

58. J. Todd Hibbard, *Intertextuality in Isaiah 24–27*, FAT II/16 (Tübingen: Mohr Siebeck, 2006).

59. Ibid., 210.

60. Ibid., 216. An earlier, similar analysis by Donald C. Polaski, *Authorizing the End: The Isaiah Apocalypse and Intertextuality*, BibInt 50 (Leiden: Brill, 2001), gives greater attention to the social context of proto-apocalyptic.

that the intertextuality in these chapters (along with the latest stages of Third Isaiah) can give us "a glimpse into a fairly late stage of the book's formation."[61]

To cite one example, Hibbard notes the similarities (in his words, "the overwhelming verbal connections") between Isa 12:1–6 and 26:1–6, with both texts containing the words or phrases "salvation" (יְשׁוּעָה, yĕšûʿâ), "trust" (ב-ט-ח, b-ṭ-ḥ), "strength" (עֹז, ʿaz), "exalted" (נִשְׂגָּב, niśgab), "in that day" (בַּיּוֹם הַהוּא; bayyôm hahûʾ), and "Yah YHWH" (יָהּ יְהוָה, yah yhwh; found only in these two texts in the Hebrew Bible), in addition to the fact that both texts can be labeled "songs."[62] Hibbard acknowledges the diachronic complication that Isa 12 is often considered to be a late redactional addition and thus not clearly "earlier" than Isa 26, which, combined with his assessment that "Isa 26:1–6 is not reusing Isaiah 12 in any meaningful way," leads him to dismiss seeing here any "intertextual" relation in the narrower sense.[63] He does, however, see an intertextual connection between Isa 26:1 ("God makes salvation its walls and ramparts"; יְשׁוּעָה יָשִׁית חוֹמוֹת וָחֵל, yĕšûʿâ yāšît ḥômôt wāḥēl) and 60:18 ("but you will call your walls Salvation"; וְקָרָאת יְשׁוּעָה חוֹמֹתָיִךְ, wĕqārāʾt yĕšûʿâ ḥômōtayik), with "righteous" in Isa 60:21 (צַדִּיקִים, ṣaddîqîm) serving as the basis for the description of the people in 26:2 as "the righteous nation" (גּוֹי־צַדִּיק, gôy-ṣaddîq) in its "more inclusive vision."[64] Furthermore, he thinks that the author of Isa 26 may have "redeployed language and imagery" from the depiction of the "overthrow of human pride" from Isa 2:6–21 in his portrait of "the overthrown exalted city," though he rejects Marvin Sweeney's judgment that Isa 26:1–6 involves an "exegetical/interpretive reappropriation" of the earlier text.[65]

Studies like Hibbard's emphasize how much verbal and thematic repetition is found throughout the book of Isaiah, and these phenomena should be taken into consideration by the careful interpreter. At the same time, Hibbard's study also illustrates the ongoing terminological and methodological debate regarding how one identifies, labels (for example, as "exegetical/ interpretive"), and assesses the composition-historical and hermeneutical/theological implications of "intertextuality" within the book. It also reveals the extent to which scholars can offer *ad hoc* explanations for individual texts that support their foundational composition-critical theories. More importantly, in my view, it reflects their reticence to give sufficient attention to the synchronic "effect" on the reader of the present canonical book of Isaiah of identifying such verbal parallels, since most scholars focus almost exclusively on the diachronic origins of these parallels.[66]

A contrasting approach to Hibbard's is found in Wolfgang Lau's study of "scribal prophecy" in Isa 56–66.[67] Lau distinguishes multiple "hands" within these

---

61. Hibbard, *Intertextuality in Isaiah 24–27*, 217.

62. Ibid, 129–30.

63. Ibid, 131.

64. Ibid, 125–28.

65. Ibid., 133–34; cf. Marvin A. Sweeney, "Textual Citations in Isaiah 24–27: Toward an Understanding of the Redactional Function of Chapters 24–27 in the Book of Isaiah," *JBL* 107 (1988): 47–48.

66. Miscall's "deconstructive" commentary, *Isaiah*, may go too far in the opposite direction.

67. Lau, *Schriftgelehrte Prophetie*.

chapters on the basis of their divergent interpretive approaches to earlier prophetic material: Trito-Isaiah (the source of chs. 60–62), three separate "tradition circles," and individual traditions. The scribal *Fortschreibung* ("continuation") of Deutero-Isaiah's oracles commenced with their literary fixation, as the exilic "prophet's" messages were actualized, (re)interpreted, and reapplied to the constantly changing circumstances of the people of God. Lau views these interpreters as *authors* (or "desk prophets") rather than *editors*, thereby distinguishing his approach from that of Odil Hannes Steck. In Lau's opinion, scribal prophets normally signaled their intended references to other texts through the use of word-for-word quotation, requiring a learned readership, rather than through countless cross-references, as Steck suggests. These desk prophets could juxtapose or recombine various "authoritative" texts without this necessarily resulting in "contradiction," though this often involved the texts taking on different meanings in their new contexts.[68]

This interpretive procedure is illustrated by Lau's identification of a trajectory in the development of the phrase "prepare the way" (פַּנּוּ דֶרֶךְ, *pannû derek*), which refers to the "highway of the return" image in Isa 40:3, 57:14, and 62:10, as well as of the expression "Build up, build up" (סֹלּוּ־סֹלּוּ, *sōllû-sōllû*), which occurs only in 57:14 and 62:10. In Lau's interpretation, because the author of 57:14 no longer expected a real exodus to take place, this author must be distinguished from (and later than) both "Second" (40:3) and "Third" Isaiah (62:10), whose texts (40:3 and 62:10) are quoted in 57:14.[69] This example displays two questionable premises that appear to undergird much of Lau's analysis (as well as that of many other Isaiah scholars). First, if an expression occurs only twice (or three times, as with פַּנּוּ דֶרֶךְ [*pannû derek*]) within the Hebrew Bible, one (or more) of the texts likely stems from a later, dependent author/editor. Second, an image or concept cannot be used in significantly different ways by the same author. Such a rigid view of verbal parallels—which virtually rules out self-quotation, downplays the effect of literary context on meaning, and understands authors as consciously and constantly drawing on a limited range of texts when addressing any subject—is bound to lead to an inflated assessment of the amount of "scribal prophecy" to be found in "Third" Isaiah.

In my view, it is more useful—and less speculative—to see in Isa 40:3, 57:14, and 62:10 a thematic progression rather than a reconstructed redaction-compositional sequence, expressed verbally through a gradual "building up" of imperative verbs from "In the wilderness **prepare** the way for the Lord; **make straight** in the desert a highway for our God" (פַּנּוּ דֶרֶךְ יְהוָה יַשְּׁרוּ בָּעֲרָבָה מְסִלָּה לֵאלֹהֵינוּ, *pannû derek yhwh yaššěrû bā'ărābâ měsillâ lē'lōhênû*) in 40:3 to "**Build up, build up**, **prepare** the road! **Remove** the obstacles out of the way of my people" (סֹלּוּ־סֹלּוּ פַּנּוּ־דָרֶךְ הָרִימוּ

---

68. Ibid.; Steck, *The Prophetic Books and their Theological Witness* (St. Louis: Chalice, 2000). The discussion of Lau in this section is adapted from Schultz, *Search for Quotation*, 95–96. In Lau's view, Zion, the servant of God, the Holy One of Israel, and the exodus are the foundational themes that prompted the majority of the scribal utilizations of earlier Isaianic texts.

69. Lau, *Schriftgelehrte Prophetie*, 8–9, 14–18.

מְכְשׁוֹל מִדֶּרֶךְ עַמִּי, *sōllû-sōllû pannû-dārek hārîmû mikšôl midderek ʿammî*) in 57:14 to "**Build up, build up** the highway! **Remove** the stones" (פַּנּוּ דֶרֶךְ הָעָם סֹלּוּ סֹלּוּ הַמְסִלָּה סַקְּלוּ מֵאָבֶן, *pannû derek hāʿām sōllû sōllû haměsillâ saqqělû mēʾeben*) in 62:10. Whereas in 40:3 the highway is constructed in the wilderness and 57:14 specifies no location, in 62:10 the construction apparently extends to the very gates of the city. Furthermore, while 40:3 focuses on YHWH's coming, and 57:14 focuses on the sinful condition of the people and the continuing divine judgment that hinder restoration, 62:10 completes the portrayal with the return of the exiled, assisted by the nations, reconstituting God's people. Although it could be coincidental, interestingly, each passage contains a Hiphil form of the verb ר-ו-ם (*r-w-m*; "raise"), each time occurring with a different object: "the voice" in 40:3, "obstacles" in 57:14, and "a banner for the nations." Even if 57:14 emphasizes spiritual obstacles rather than physical obstacles to restoration, this does not mean that the highway image also has been "spiritualized" here, since the book of Isaiah frequently blurs the line (and alternates) between the literal and the metaphorical.[70]

Conclusion

This examination of representative scholars who have studied Isaianic intertextuality and intratextuality must come to an end not with a call to curtail future efforts to identify and assess such verbal parallels but rather with a call to continue such efforts—with more methodological rigor and less interpretive certitude. There is every reason to expect prophetic figures within Israel to have repeated the words of their predecessors (see Isa 16:13–14; Zech 1:4), whether their intention was thereby to emphasize continuity, announce imminent fulfillment, "borrow" authority, or enhance style, and all of these certainly appear to be the case with the book of Isaiah. Given the subjective nature of identifying verbal parallels, it is beneficial to give priority to texts that manifest a higher degree of verbal and grammatical correspondence in analyzing allusions and citations, although "influence" can be expressed in ways that involve less quantitatively "measurable" agreement. Furthermore, due to the wide divergence in current redaction- and composition-critical theories regarding Isaiah and the other prophetic books, few broad theories are likely to garner widespread support. Accordingly, interpreters should acknowledge more readily that a given verbal parallel can prompt several plausible explanations and that no set of criteria can definitively determine the direction of dependence in most texts. The intertextual studies examined in this essay would give the impression that some parts of the book of Isaiah involve denser intertextual connections than others and that some types of interpretive reuses are more characteristic of some sections of the book than others. This may be correct, but this may also re-

---

70. An example of such alternation would be the multiple descriptions of physical impairment and healing in the book of Isaiah: Isa 6:9; 29:9–10, 18; 30:10–11; 32:3–4; 33:23; 35:5–6; 42:7, 18–20; 43:8; 44:18; 59:10. I offer a contrasting interpretation of the three "highway texts" in Schultz, *Search for Quotation*, 270–90.

sult from a given scholar's selection of textual examples and the theory-supporting analyses he or she offers. At the very least, however, we must affirm Stromberg's claim that a significant part of "Isaiah's rhetoric is achieved by making overt references to other texts that would have been familiar to its readers/hearers,"[71] and, accordingly, this cannot be ignored by any serious interpreter.

---

71. Jacob Stromberg, *An Introduction to the Study of Isaiah*, T&T Clark Approaches to Biblical Studies (London: T&T Clark, 2011), 65.

3

The Biblical Texts of Isaiah at Qumran

Seulgi L. Byun

Introduction

The discovery of the "Dead Sea Scrolls" is, arguably, the most significant find in biblical archaeology to date. Fragments from nearly one thousand texts dating to the third and second centuries BCE were discovered, approximately two hundred of which are copies of biblical books. These scrolls are indispensable for text-critical purposes, but they also shed light on other areas, such as the development of the Hebrew language, formation of the Hebrew canon, and the theology of the Qumran covenanters.

Isaiah is one of the most prominent and most copied biblical books among the texts found in the Judean desert.[1] Between 1947 and 1952, twenty-one copies of the book were discovered in the caves near the Dead Sea, and another copy was found at Wadi Murabbaʿat. In addition to the biblical texts, six pesher manuscripts on Isaiah were found at Qumran.[2] Isaiah is also one of the most frequently cited books in the Qumran corpus.[3] For these reasons, George Brooke rightly

---

1. Only Psalms (thirty-six copies) and Deuteronomy (twenty-six copies) are attested in more copies. The popularity of the book of Isaiah in the Qumran community is especially apparent when one compares the manuscript evidence with that of the other Major Prophets: only six copies of Jeremiah and five copies of Ezekiel have been found. As Joseph Blenkinsopp reminds us, Isaiah is the book of the Hebrew Bible that is quoted, cited, and alluded to most frequently in the NT (*Opening the Sealed Book: Interpretations of the Book of Isaiah in Late Antiquity* [Grand Rapids: Eerdmans, 2006], 89).

2. The pesharim constitute a genre of Qumran sectarian literature that essentially involves commentary on prophetic texts whose exegesis is based chiefly on eschatology.

3. G. J. Brooke has identified at least twenty-three explicit citations of Isaiah in the sectarian texts ("Isaiah in the Pesharim and Other Qumran Texts," in *Writing and Reading the Scroll of Isaiah: Studies of an Interpretive Tradition*, ed. Craig C. Broyles and Craig A. Evans, VTSup 70 [Leiden: Brill, 1997], 609–32). By comparison, the two other Major Prophets, Jeremiah and Ezekiel, are cited only four times each. Allusions are admittedly more difficult to identify (and define), but for 1QH alone S. Holm-Nielsen lists 154 possible allusions to Isaiah (*Hodayot: Psalms from Qumran*, ATDan 2 [Aarhus: Universitetsforlaget, 1960], 354–56); by way of comparison, Jeremiah is alluded to forty-three times and Ezekiel is alluded to twenty-six times in 1QH. See also Chaim Rabin, *The Zadokite Documents*, 2nd, rev. ed. (Oxford: Clarendon, 1958), 81–85, for a list of allusions and quotations in CD.

concludes: "Of the prophetic books Isaiah was by far and away the most popular at Qumran."[4]

The aim of this study is to survey the texts at Qumran relating to the book of Isaiah in order to determine how the scribes who wrote these documents and the members of the Qumran community perceived it. There is not enough space here to discuss all these texts; I will simply focus on three aspects of them. In the first section I will survey the biblical manuscripts of Isaiah and consider their relation to the MT; in the second section I will examine, in brief, scribal features in 1QIsa[a], focusing primarily on division markers and any implications they may have on the literary structure of the book; and in the final section I will look at the attributions that accompany quotations of Isaiah in the non-biblical texts at Qumran.

The Biblical Manuscripts of Isaiah

There are twenty-one copies of Isaiah at Qumran:[5] two from Cave 1, eighteen from Cave 4, and one from Cave 5.[6] A cursory glance at these disproportionate figures might lead one to think that Cave 4 is the most significant of the three, but, unfortunately, most of the manuscripts in Cave 4 are very fragmentary and preserve only a handful of words or letters.[7] In fact, as Emanuel Tov points out, the two

---

4. Brooke, "Isaiah in the Pesharim," 631.

5. The consensus today is that there are twenty-one copies of Isaiah from Qumran, but since most of the copies of Isaiah at Qumran are fragmentary in nature and contain only small portions of the book, it is difficult to determine the precise number of actual copies of the book. New identifications and fresh analysis of the orthographic and paleographic evidence may alter the number. One must keep in mind that, at one stage, Patrick W. Skehan thought there were sixteen copies ("The Qumran Manuscripts and Textual Criticism," in *Volume du Congrès Strasbourg*, VTSup [Leiden: Brill, 1957], 150), though he later revised his estimate to eighteen ("Qumran, Littérature de Qumran, A. Texts bibliques," *DBSup* [Paris: Letouzey et Ané, 1979], 9:805–22).

6. Qumran scholars have published many helpful studies on the text, character, and paleography of the individual manuscripts. For a brief overview of Isaiah at Qumran, see F. García Martínez, "Le livre d'Isaïe à Qumrân: Les textes. L'influence," *MdB* 49 (1987): 43–45, and Eugene Ulrich, "Isaiah," in *EDSS*, ed. L. H. Schiffman and J. C. VanderKam (New York: Oxford University Press, 2000). For a comprehensive list and description of the manuscripts, see Peter W. Flint, "The Isaiah Scrolls From the Judean Desert," in *Writing and Reading the Scroll of Isaiah: Studies of an Interpretive Tradition*, ed. Craig C. Broyles and Craig A. Evans, VTSup 70 (Leiden: Brill, 1997), 2:481–89. For a helpful summary of the paleographic dating, see Dwight Swanson, "The Text of Isaiah at Qumran," in *Interpreting Isaiah: Issues and Approaches*, ed. David G. Firth and H. G. M. Williamson (Downers Grove, IL: InterVarsity Press, 2009), esp. pp. 194–95. For facsimiles of the texts, see Emanuel Tov, ed., *The Dead Sea Scrolls on Microfiche: A Comprehensive Facsimile Edition of the Texts from the Judean Desert*, vol. 2, *Companion Volume* (Leiden: Brill, 1993).

7. For example, 4QIsa[h] (4Q62) contains limited portions of Isa 42:2–11; 4QIsa[i] (4Q62a) preserves several words from Isa 56:7–8 and 57:5–8; 4QIsa[j] (4Q63) is a single fragment preserving just seven complete words from Isa 1:1–6; 4QIsa[l] (4Q65) preserves several words from Isa 7:14–15 and 8:11–14; 4QIsa[n] (4Q67) is a single fragment preserving ten words from

copies of Isaiah from Cave 1 cover more of the text of Isaiah than all eighteen copies from Cave 4.[8]

1QIsa[a] and 1QIsa[b], both from Cave 1, were among the first Qumran texts to be discovered and published, and are considered to be of more value than any other Isaianic texts as far as contributions to the textual history of Isaiah are concerned. This section will focus primarily on 1QIsa[a] and its many apparent variants and scribal features, but first I will make a few observations on the text of 1QIsa[b].

1QIsa[b]

1QIsa[b], also known as the Hebrew University Isaiah Scroll, is dated to the late Hasmonean period, around 50 BCE. It is a significant scroll insofar as it covers a large amount of the text of Isaiah (from 7:20 to 66:8),[9] but much of it is fragmentary. Initial studies on this scroll suggested that the differences between it and the MT were minor and that only a few variants changed the meaning of the text.[10] Eliezer Sukenik, the first editor of the scroll, noted only a few textual variants and described it as "quite close to the Masoretic Text of the Book of Isaiah in both its readings and in its spellings."[11] Bleddyn Roberts went so far as to say that "the almost complete absence of textual variants is the clearest indication of the close affinity between the two text-forms [1QIsa[b] and MT], for in one instance only can a case be made for a significant variant reading. It is in 53.11."[12] Emanuel Tov and Dominique Barthélemy have also concluded that the variants in 1QIsa[b] are minor and concern only minutiae.[13] However, more recently Peter Flint has stirred the pot by suggesting that there may be up to six variant readings that are textually superior to those of Codex Leningradensis, a few of which I think are plausible.[14] Be that as it may,

---

Isa 58:13–14; 4QIsa[p] (4Q69) preserves several words from Isa 5:28–30; 4QIsa[q] (4Q69a) is a single fragment preserving just a few letters from Isa 54:10–13; and 4QIsa[r] (4Q69b) consists of just two complete words from Isa 54:10–13.

8. Emanuel Tov, "The Text of Isaiah at Qumran," in *Writing and Reading the Scroll of Isaiah: Studies of an Interpretive Tradition*, ed. Craig C. Broyles and Craig A. Evans, VTSup 70 (Leiden: Brill, 1997), 2:493.

9. See Eva Jain, "Die materielle Rekonstruktion von 1QJes[b] (1Q8) und einige bisher nicht edierte Fragmente dieser Handschrift," *RevQ* 20/79 (2002): 389–409, for an excellent reconstruction of the entire scroll of 1QIsa[b].

10. See Eliezer L. Sukenik, *The Dead Sea Scrolls of the Hebrew University* (Jerusalem: Magnes, 1955), published posthumously by Nahman Avigad.

11. Ibid., 30.

12. Bleddyn J. Roberts, "The Second Isaiah Scroll from Qumrân (1QIsb)," *BJRL* 42 (1959): 134. In Isa 53:11, the MT reads יִרְאֶה נַפְשׁוֹ מֵעֲמַל ([mēʿămal napšô] yirʾê). However, 1QIsa[a], 1QIsa[b], 4QIsa[d], and LXX Isaiah (δεῖξαι αὐτῷ φῶς) add אור (ʾwr).

13. Emanuel Tov, *Textual Criticism of the Hebrew Bible*, 2nd ed. (Minneapolis: Fortress, 1992), 30–31, and Dominique Barthélemy, *Critique textuelle de l'Ancien Testament*, OBO 50/3 (Göttingen: Vandenhoeck & Ruprecht, 1992), cii–cxvi.

14. Peter W. Flint, "Non-Masoretic Variant Readings in the Hebrew University Scroll (1QIsa[b]) and the Text to be Translated," in *The Dead Sea Scrolls and Contemporary Culture:*

the text of 1QIsa[b], on the whole, follows the consonantal text of the MT, and there is insufficient evidence as yet to suggest that this scroll should not be characterized as a Proto-Masoretic text.

1QIsa[a]

1QIsa[a], commonly known as the Great Isaiah Scroll,[15] is without doubt the most famous of the Dead Sea Scrolls texts. It was kept safely in a jar, and, with the exception of a few lacunae owing to leather damage, it contains all sixty-six chapters of Isaiah. The paleographical evidence and radiocarbon dating suggest that the scroll was written sometime around 150–125 BCE. Since 1QIsa[a] is a complete scroll that predates Codex Leningradensis by more than one thousand years, it is not surprising that this scroll has been studied more than any of the other biblical texts at Qumran.

Of great interest to scholars are the many apparent variant readings of 1QIsa[a] vis-à-vis the MT.[16] Since these variants have been scrupulously analyzed by others,[17] it will suffice to summarize the main characteristic differences:[18]

(1) **Extensive use of *matres lectionis*:** In 1QIsa[a] *wāw* is consistently employed for "o" and "u" vowels and, to a lesser extent, *yôd*, *hê*, and *ʾālep* as *matres*; combinations of אי, יא, אי, and או (ʾy, yʾ, wʾ, and ʾw) occur as medial *matres* for "e" and "o" vowels; and וה (*wh*) is employed as a final *mater* for "o." Frank Moore Cross was not surprised by the heavy use of *matres* in 1QIsa[a] since he

---

Proceedings of the International Conference Held at the Israel Museum, Jerusalem (July 6–8, 2008), ed. Adolfo D. Roitman, Lawrence H. Schiffman, and Shani Tzoref, STDJ 93 (Leiden: Brill, 2011), 117.

15. Also called "St. Mark's Isaiah," after the monastery that initially owned the scroll.

16. Opinions vary on the correct use of the designation MT. The majority position is that it refers to the Hebrew text as fixed by the Masoretes, Jewish scribes in Tiberias during the eighth and ninth centuries CE who devised a system of vocalization, cantillation, and marginal annotations. By MT, most scholars are referring to the text of Codex Leningradensis B19a, the most familiar of the ben Asher family manuscripts. There is, however, another Masoretic text, the Aleppo Codex, which predates Codex Leningradensis by almost a hundred years and is considered by many Jewish scholars to be the most accurate and authoritative Masoretic text. The Aleppo Codex has recently been digitized, and printed editions should become more accessible. For an excellent critical version of the text of Isaiah based on the Aleppo Codex, see Moshe H. Goshen-Gottstein, ed., *The Book of Isaiah* (Jerusalem: Magnes, 1995).

17. For detailed discussions on the differences between 1QIsa[a] and the MT, see M. Burrows, "Orthography, Morphology, and Syntax in the St. Mark's Isaiah Manuscript," *JBL* 68 (1949): 195–211; Malachi Martin, *The Scribal Character of the Dead Sea Scrolls*, 2 vols. (Leuven: Publications Universitaires, 1958); and, esp., E. Y. Kutscher, *The Language and Linguistic Background of the Isaiah Scroll (1QIsa[a])*, STDJ 6 (Leiden: Brill, 1974). The literature on this topic is very extensive, but these are a few of the most significant studies.

18. See Jesper Høgenhaven, "The First Isaiah Scroll from Qumran (1QIs[a]) and the Massoretic Text: Some Reflections with Special Regard to Isaiah 1–12," *JSOT* 28 (1984): 17–35, for an excellent summary of the linguistic and orthographic differences between 1QIsa[a] and the MT text of Isaiah.

regarded *plene* orthography as the conventional style in Palestine during the Hasmonean period.[19]

(2) **Weakening of gutturals**: The number of cases in which gutturals in the MT are omitted, exchanged, or added in 1QIsaᵃ is surprisingly large. The fact that such alterations were rarely corrected suggests that they were not errors, but rather reflect the linguistic background of the scribes who wrote 1QIsaᵃ (see below).

(3) **Pronouns and pronominal suffixes**: The second- and third-person plural personal pronouns and pronominal suffixes often end with a final ה (*h*); the second-person feminine singular possessive pronoun ‏ךְ‎- (-*k*) sometimes appears as ‏כִי‎- (-*ky*).

(4) **Substitution of familiar words for rare or archaic ones**: Edward Kutscher lists 235 cases where the scribe appears to replace an older MT word with one that was known to him and his audience, that is, a word derived from a more common root in Late Biblical Hebrew, Rabbinic Hebrew, or Aramaic.[20]

(5) **Verbal forms**: There are differences between the way the Qal imperfect and imperative are written in 1QIsaᵃ and in the MT; for example, 1QIsaᵃ often has *wāw* after the second radical in these forms. Also, in 1QIsaᵃ the preposition ‏ל‎ (*l*) is added to infinitives where the MT has no preposition, which accords with the way infinitives are written in Mishnaic Hebrew.

The vast majority of the variants in 1QIsaᵃ are orthographical or morphological in nature and do not offer more original readings than those of the MT. There are, however, a handful of textual variants of consequence, which have been noted by various scholars, but these are relatively few and far between.[21] Thus, as Peter Flint concludes, the scroll "is mostly in agreement with the received Masoretic Text," and the broad consensus is that 1QIsaᵃ is of limited value for text-critical purposes.[22] If 1QIsaᵃ is mostly in agreement with the MT, how then do we explain the numerous variant readings? Are they the result of incompetent scribes? Or are they simply stylistic differences?

In his seminal monograph *The Language and Linguistic Background of the Isaiah Scroll (1QIsaᵃ)*, Edward Kutscher argued that most of the variants in 1QIsaᵃ

---

19. F. M. Cross, "The Contribution of the Qumrân Discoveries to the Study of the Biblical Text," *IEJ* 16 (1966): 81–95.

20. Kutscher, *Language and Linguistic Background*, 216–315.

21. Brownlee suggests a number of readings from 1QIsaᵃ that he considers superior to those of the MT. See also Gary V. Smith, *Isaiah 1–39*, NAC 15a (Nashville: Broadman & Holman, 2007), 44, which provides a list of variants where the Dead Sea Scrolls may offer a more original reading.

22. Flint, "Isaiah Scrolls," 483. So also Smith, who says of the Isaianic texts at Qumran: "Once the plene readings, Aramaic influences, scribal errors, and modernizations are eliminated, there are only a few cases where the Qumran texts preserve a more authentic Hebrew text than the MT" (*Isaiah 1–39*, 49).

have to do with the linguistic situation of the late Second Temple period.[23] Hebrew was a highly fluid language during the Qumran period for the following reasons: Classical Hebrew had declined as a spoken language; colloquial Aramaic had expanded in the Levant; and there had emerged a Postbiblical, or "proto-Mishnaic," Hebrew dialect.

Kutscher proposed that the scribe of 1QIsa[a] updated the Classical Hebrew text to reflect the contemporary Hebrew dialect. Practically speaking, *plene* orthography was used to aid pronunciation, especially for Aramaic speakers. For example, the negative particle is spelled לוא (*lw'*) to emphasize Hebrew לֹא (*lō'*) against Aramaic לָא (*lā'*);[24] and the third-person *yiqtol* verb יֹאמַר (*yō'mar*), "he said," is written יואמר (*yw'mr*) in 1QIsa[a] to distinguish it from Aramaic יֵאמַר (*yē'mar*).

In addition, the scribe updates the text by replacing rare words and archaic forms with more familiar ones (see point 4 above). For instance, in Isa 33:7 and 42:4 the root צ-ע-ק (*ṣ-ʿ-q*) is replaced by ז-ע-ק (*z-ʿ-q*), which is attested frequently in Chronicles, Nehemiah, and Esther and is the common word meaning "cry out" in the Second Temple period. Even the spellings of proper nouns are updated. Damascus, which is normally spelled דַּמֶּשֶׂק (*dammeśeq*) in Biblical Hebrew, occurs as דרמשק (*drmśq*) in 1QIsa[a], the form that is attested in Postbiblical Hebrew, and in rabbinic texts.

These features suggest that 1QIsa[a] was a "popular" or "vulgar" text designed to help those who may have struggled with Classical Hebrew, but one that largely resembles the MT. As Kutscher summarizes, "the stylistic and orthographical changes really brought the [scroll of Isaiah] closer to the semi-literate masses."[25] The MT, on the other hand, appears to reflect the standard text that was kept in the temple and used in synagogues and centers of education.

In sum, despite the many variants in 1QIsa[a]—which might be characterized as "stylistic" in nature—and Flint's recent reassessment of 1QIsa[b], both Isaiah manuscripts from Cave 1, as well as those from Caves 4 and 5,[26] not only support the MT but also indicate that the Hebrew text of Isaiah was relatively stable by the second century BCE at the very latest. Tov's summary of the evidence at Qumran is instructive: "The bottom line of any comparative analysis of the texts of Isaiah is

---

23. For a different view, see Paulson Pulikottil, *Transmission of Biblical Texts in Qumran: The Case of the Large Isaiah Scroll 1QIsa[a]*, JSPSup 34 (Sheffield: Sheffield Academic, 2001), who not only challenges Kutscher's linguistic approach but also attributes many of the variants to the "traditio of the scroll," that is, interpretive or theological exegesis. However, many of Pulikottil's arguments are not convincing because they lack evidence and are based on some questionable assumptions.

24. Kutscher, *Language and Linguistic Background*, 215.

25. Ibid., 73. Kutscher maintained that 1QIsa[a] was used as a personal copy, used for study in the home or, possibly, the synagogue (pp. 77–89).

26. Almost all the texts of Isaiah from Cave 4 agree with the MT (Codex Leningradensis); 4QIsa[c] may be the lone exception (see Tov, "Text of Isaiah," 506–7). G. J. Brooke comments: "Study of the Cave 4 Isaiah manuscripts reveals a largely stable text tradition" ("On Isaiah at Qumran," in *"As Those Who Are Taught": The Interpretation of Isaiah from the LXX to the SBL*, ed. Claire Mathews McGinnis and Patricia K. Tull, SBLSymS 27 [Atlanta: Society of Biblical Literature, 2006], 82).

that the amount of variation is relatively limited. The present textual data for Isaiah thus point to a picture of textual unity."[27]

Scribal Features in 1QIsa[a]

Johann Gottfried Eichhorn (1783) and Johann Christoph Döderlein (1789) advanced the theory that Isaiah is a composite of two individual works and that chapters 40–66 are a product of postexilic Yehud.[28] Since then, scholars have divided the text of Isaiah between chapters 39 and 40, and even between 55 and 56. A representative example is Robert Pfeiffer, who, in his celebrated *Introduction to the Old Testament*, posited that sometime around 200 BCE a scribe copied the text of Isaiah 40–66 onto a scroll that already had Isaiah 1–39 (which itself was a collection of disparate oracles). According to Pfeiffer, the simple reason for adding Isaiah 40–66 onto a preexisting scroll was that "sufficient space remained on the scroll,"[29] as if the scribe only had pragmatic considerations in mind. But is there any evidence, textual or otherwise, to support such a claim?

In what follows, I will focus on two scribal issues relating to 1QIsa[a] that may shed light on how the scribe(s) who composed it understood the structure of the book of Isaiah: (1) spacing and division markers in the scroll; and (2) a gap of about three lines between chapters 33 and 34 found at the bottom of column 27 (out of fifty-four columns, i.e., the midpoint of the scroll).

Spacing and Division Markers

In recent years, there has been a revival of sorts on research into the scribal features and physical attributes of 1QIsa[a], with particular emphasis on spacing and division markers. Several studies have been published on this subject and are worth mentioning.

In 1993, John Olley proposed a structure to the book of Isaiah on the basis of division markers. He isolated all sentences that immediately followed a *petuḥah* or *setumah* in 1QIsa[a] and found that they almost always began with words or phrases that fell into five distinct categories: (1) the speech of YHWH; (2) summons to hear; (3) designation of time; (4) exclamations; or (5) oracles against the nations.[30]

In a comprehensive, two-volume study on the text of 1QIsa[a], Odil Hannes Steck nuanced Olley's work by taking a more hierarchical approach, giving more

27. Tov, "Text of Isaiah," 505.

28. Abraham Ibn Ezra was, by all accounts, the first to question the authorship of Isaiah in certain sections, but the salient discussions in his commentary are terse and not explicit (*The Commentary of Ibn Ezra on Isaiah*, ed. and trans. M. Friedländer [New York: Philipp Feldheim, 1964], 169–71, 223–24).

29. Robert H. Pfeiffer, *Introduction to the Old Testament* (New York: Harper & Brothers, 1941), 447–48.

30. John W. Olley, "Hear the Word of YHWH," *VT* 43 (1993): 19–49.

weight to certain delimiting markers. Steck concluded that the spaces and blank lines can be attributed to one system, which subdivided the book into "subsections" (*Unterabschnitte*). A second system, marked by *paragraphoi* (that is, paragraph markers designated by a horizontal line or a "Mexican hat"), breaks the text into "large divisions" (*Großabteile*).[31] When Isaiah is read according to the divisions of this second system, the structure of the book focuses the reader's attention on YHWH's actions with regard to his people. The breakdown of the structure of 1QIsa[a] according to Steck's criteria is plausible at points, but more analysis is needed, especially at the "subsection" level.

One of the most significant works on scribal features is Tov's *Scribal Practices and Approaches Reflected in the Texts Found in the Judean Desert*, which examines many of the technical aspects of the production of scrolls found at Qumran, including 1QIsa[a]. Specifically, Tov examines details such as scribal marks, columns, margins, ruling, division between words and units, and the length and contents of scrolls. Tov explains that the habits and features of individual scribes often leave clues to the interpretation of a given text: "These details are important in their own right for improving our understanding of these scribes and the compositions they copied."[32] However, Tov maintains that the scribes made their decisions on an ad hoc basis and that some scribal marks may even have been added by later scribes.[33]

I should also mention Delimitation Criticism, a relatively new critical method that examines the delimitation of "sense units" based on internal graphic systems.[34] One of its chief aims is to determine the extent to which section dividers such as indentations, paragraphs, *petuḥah*, and *setumah* represent a scribe's understanding of how a particular text or book was to be understood. Marjo Korpel's statement in the introduction to the definitive book *Delimitation Criticism* is representative of this approach: "I believe that unit delimitation determines to a large extent the interpretation of a given passage."[35] Joseph Oesch goes further, suggesting that an

---

31. Odil Hannes Steck, *Die erste Jesajarolle von Qumran (1QIs^a)*, SBS 173, 2 vols. (Stuttgart: Katholisches Bibelwerk, 1998).

32. Emanuel Tov, *Scribal Practices and Approaches Reflected in the Texts Found in the Judean Desert*, STDJ 54 (Leiden: Brill, 2004), xix.

33. Ibid., 144–47. Even if Tov is right that some marks were added by later scribes, this does not undermine the general observation that scribes involved with 1QIsa[a] divided the book into smaller sections and units.

34. For an introduction to Delimitation Criticism, see Marjo Korpel and Josef Oesch, eds., *Delimitation Criticism: A New Tool in Biblical Scholarship*, Pericope: Scripture as Written and Read in Antiquity 1 (Assen: Van Gorcum, 2000); and idem, eds., *Studies in Scriptural Unit Division*, Pericope: Scripture as Written and Read in Antiquity 3 (Assen: Van Gorcum, 2002). See Emanuel Tov, "Sense Divisions in the Qumran Texts, the Masoretic Text, and Ancient Translations of the Bible," in *The Interpretation of the Bible: The International Symposium in Slovenia*, ed. J. Krasovec (Sheffield: Sheffield Academic, 1998); and idem, "The Background of the Sense Divisions in the Biblical Texts," in *Delimitation Criticism*, ed. Korpel and Oesch, 312–50, for an application of Delimitation Criticism to the biblical texts at Qumran and in the MT tradition.

35. Marjo Korpel, "Introduction to the Series Pericope," in *Delimitation Criticism: A New Tool in Biblical Scholarship*, ed. Marjo Korpel and Josef Oesch, Pericope: Scripture as Written and Read in Antiquity 1 (Assen: Van Gorcum, 2000), 1.

author or scribe might use division markers to preserve what he believed to be the correct interpretation of a text: "It is . . . likely that the author or latest redactor of a work sought to safeguard the correct understanding of the text by dividing it into text-units."[36] Thus, in contrast to Tov, delimitation critics argue that scribal marks reflect intentional and careful exegesis by the scribes. Further discussion of these recent developments in research is beyond the scope of this study, but suffice it to say that there is a growing consensus that scribal marks and division markers in 1QIsa[a] may represent the scribe's (or scribes') understanding of the structure and meaning of the book.

The "Gap" between Isaiah 33 and 34

One of the most important scribal features in 1QIsa[a] is a gap of about three or four lines between chapters 33 and 34 found in column 27 (out of fifty-four columns, i.e., the midpoint of the scroll; see Figure 1). There is no evidence in 1QIsa[a], or any of the biblical texts of Isaiah at Qumran, of a division between chapters 39 and 40, or between chapters 55 and 56. There are no significant breaks in 1QIsa[b], and in this scroll the salient sections of chapters 39, 40, 55, and 56 are missing.

This raises the question: What is the significance of this gap in 1QIsa[a], and does it inform us in any way about the scribe's understanding of the book of Isaiah and its structure?

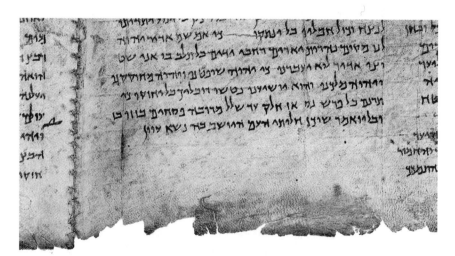

**Figure 1. Image of the bottom of column 27 of the Great
Isaiah Scroll (1QIsa[a]). From the Digital Dead Sea Scrolls.
Used by permission of the Israel Museum, Jerusalem.**

---

36. Joseph Oesch, *Petucha und Setuma: Untersuchungen zu einer überlieferten Gliederung im hebräischen Text des Alten Testaments*, OBO 27 (Göttingen: Vandenhoeck & Ruprecht, 1979), 339.

Various explanations for this gap have been proposed. Paul Kahle was the first to bifurcate the scroll at chapters 33 and 34.[37] He further contended that this lends support to the theory that Second Isaiah begins with chapter 34 and not chapter 39, as first advocated by Charles Torrey and later by Marvin Pope.[38] Tov took a text-critical approach by examining the orthography and morphological features in the two segments. He concluded that chapters 1–33 and 34–66 were copied by two different scribes and that the gap at the bottom of column 27 simply marks the end of the first scribe's section.[39] On balance, however, the differences in orthography, morphology, and style between the two sections are relatively minor.

Perhaps the most detailed and important study on this subject is an article published by William Brownlee, who was one of the first to have seen and photographed the scroll.[40] Brownlee noted that the gap between chapters 33 and 34 occurs precisely at the midpoint of the scroll. He then divided the scroll into two sections, chapters 1–33 and chapters 34–66, and looked at the text of each section to see if there were any patterns of literary organization. He noticed that these two segments are strikingly similar "in their overall structure and outline,"[41] forming two "volumes" that consist of "seven parallel sections":[42]

Volume I (Chapters 1–33)	**Volume II (Chapters 34–66)**
The Ruin and Restoration of Judah (1–5)	Paradise Lost and Regained (34–35)
Biography (6–8)	Biography (36–40)
Agents of Divine Blessing and Judgment (9–12)	Agents of Deliverance and Judgment (41–45)
Anti-foreign Oracles (13–23)	Anti-Babylonian Oracles (46–48)
Universal Judgment and the Deliverance of God's People (24–27)	Universal Redemption through the Lord's Servant, also the glorification of Israel (49–55)

---

37. Paul Kahle, *Die hebräischen Handschriften aus der Höhle* (Stuttgart: Kohlhammer, 1951), 72–77.

38. C. C. Torrey, *The Second Isaiah* (New York: Scribner's, 1928). See Marvin H. Pope, "Isaiah 34 in Relation to Isaiah 35, 40–66," *JBL* 71 (1952): 235–43, for an excellent study on the similarities in vocabulary, style, and usage between Isa 34–35 and 40–66.

39. Tov, "Text of Isaiah," 501. See Tov, *Scribal Practices and Approaches*, 19–23, for a discussion on the production of scrolls and the use of multiple scribes at Qumran. Unfortunately, Tov does not elaborate on the reason(s) for two different scribes; he concedes that "the background of these changes [of hand, i.e., scribes] is often not evident" (p. 20).

40. William H. Brownlee, "The Literary Significance of the Bisection of Isaiah in the Ancient Scroll of Isaiah from Qumran," in *Trudy Dvardtsat Pyatogo Mezhdunarodnogo Kongressa Vostokokovedov*, vol. 1 (Moscow: Tzolatel'stvo Vostochnoi Literatary, 1962), 435–36.

41. Brownlee, "Literary Significance," 431.

42. Brooke, "On Isaiah," 78. The following chart, based on Brownlee's fuller outline (and following his capitalization and punctuation), is a slightly modified version of the chart found in Brooke, "On Isaiah," 78–79, and is reproduced with permission from SBL Press. For Brownlee's more comprehensive outline, see Brownlee, "Literary Significance," 435–36.

Ethical sermons, indicting Israel and Judah (28–31)	Ethical Sermons, the Ethical Conditions for Israel's Redemption (56–59)
The Restoration of Judah and the Davidic Kingdom (32–33)	Paradise Regained: The Glories of the New Jerusalem and the New Heavens and the New Earth (60–66)

Brownlee highlighted three aspects of this outline in particular: (1) the presence of a biography after an introduction in each section; (2) the second exodus motif in both sections (11:11–16 and 43:14–44:5), as well as the balancing of oracles against the foreign nations with oracles against Babylon in particular; and (3) the function of the narrative section in Isa 34–39 within "Volume II," Isa 34–66.[43] In the end, Brownlee concluded that 1QIsaᵃ is a work of two "volumes" but that they existed as one larger work:

> I was uncertain whether the former manuscript [chapters 1–33] preserved the tradition of a First Isaiah Scroll or should be regarded as Vol. I of Isaiah, which had become separated from Vol. II. I now feel certain that it is to be regarded as Vol. I, that indeed this body of material never existed in this form, except as the first tome of the larger work.[44]

In addition to the internal evidence, a few external factors support Brownlee's bisection of the scroll. First, as Brooke has noted, there is a "remarkable" pattern in the biblical copies of Isaiah found in Cave 4.[45] As he observes, some "copies of Isaiah contain only portions from Isa 1–33 (4QIsaᵃ, 4QIsaᵉ, 4QIsaᶠ, 4QIsaʲ, 4QIsaᵏ, 4QIsaˡ, 4QIsaᵒ, 4QpapIsaᵖ, 4QIsaʳ), while several others contain only portions from Isa 34–66 (4QIsaᵈ, 4QIsaᵍ, 4QIsaʰ, 4QIsaⁱ, 4QIsaᵐ, 4QIsaⁿ, 4QIsaᑫ, 5QIsᵃ [sic])."[46] One must keep in mind, however, that, with the exceptions of 4QIsaᵇ and 4QIsaᶜ, the manuscripts from Cave 4 are very fragmentary, and any evidence derived from this cave should be received with caution. Nevertheless, Brooke's observation must be taken into consideration

Second, a distinct marginal mark (the so-called "Mexican hat") is found several times at key junctures in 1QIsaᵃ.[47] Brooke speculates that these signs "mark a theologically important text division."[48] What is most remarkable about the placement of these marks is that several of them correspond to significant breaks in Brownlee's literary structure.[49]

---

43. Brownlee, "Literary Significance," 433. As Brownlee stated, "Linguistically, Chapter 34 is most intimately related to Chapters 55–66; and Chapter 35 finds its closest verbal parallels in Chapters 40–55. Together they make a superb introduction to Chapters 40–66" (ibid.).

44. Ibid., 432.

45. Brooke, "On Isaiah," 79.

46. Ibid.

47. E.g., between 35:10 and 36:1; 39:8 and 40:1; 41:13 and 41:14; 44:28 and 45:1; 52:6 and 52:7; and 59:21 and 60:1.

48. Brooke, "On Isaiah," 80.

49. For a more detailed breakdown of Brownlee's outline, see the chart on the previous page.

Third, Josephus[50] curiously stated that Isaiah "wrote down all his prophecies, and left them behind him in books [Βίβλοις]."[51] It is difficult to know exactly what Josephus meant by "books," but he seems to refer to multiple scrolls that make up the prophecies of Isaiah. A similar reference is made earlier in *Antiquities* with regard to Ezekiel: "Ezekiel . . . left behind him in writing two books concerning these events [the impending Babylonian invasion]."[52] The phenomenon of bisecting longer works for practical purposes, such as handling of texts, copying, and storage, has been noted by Henry Thackeray and others.[53]

In sum, the scribal features of 1QIsaᵃ and other external factors suggest that the gap between chapters 33 and 34 reflects an ancient understanding of the book of Isaiah that divides the book into a two-part tome. It is difficult to know whether the purpose of the division was purely pragmatic—to divide the tome into two smaller, manageable volumes—or whether the book of Isaiah was compiled with a bipartite literary structure in mind. Recent studies on gaps and scribal features suggest the latter, namely, that these marks are an indication of the scribe's interpretation of the literary structure of the book. If so, Brownlee's proposal that the scribe of 1QIsaᵃ understood Isaiah as a bipartite book with parallel themes must be taken seriously.[54] At the very least, the scribe(s) of 1QIsaᵃ considered Isaiah to be one book with a complex and coherent structure.

Quotations of Isaianic Texts at Qumran

Thus far the focus of this study has been on the biblical texts of Isaiah at Qumran, but these texts by themselves cannot tell us what those who wrote them, or the Qumran community, considered to be authoritative scriptures. In order to determine how these groups viewed questions of authority and authorship, the biblical

---

50. For more on Josephus' view on Isaiah, see pp. 87–88 of G. K. Beale's essay in the present volume. By all indications, Josephus attributed all the prophecies in the book of Isaiah to the eighth-century prophet.

51. *Ant.* 10.35.

52. *Ant.* 10.5. The "two books" here probably refer to two scrolls that contained Ezek 1–24 and 25–48, respectively. Cf. Brownlee, "Literary Significance," 431.

53. For a discussion of the bisection of Old Testament books, see H. St. J. Thackeray, *The Septuagint and Jewish Worship: A Study in Origins*, Schweich Lectures 1920 (London: Oxford University Press, 1921), 130–36. Brownlee went too far when he suggested that in some cases long books "were so composed as to yield a natural literary division at about the mid-point of the work" ("The Literary Significance," 431).

54. Some scholars today espouse a "bifid" structure for the book of Isaiah, the gap in column 27 of 1QIsaᵃ being one of the chief reasons for doing so. For more on "bifid" outlines, see John D. W. Watts, *Isaiah 1–33*, WBC 24 (Waco: Thomas Nelson, 1985); E. W. Conrad, *Reading Isaiah*, OBT (Minneapolis: Fortress, 1991); R. K. Harrison, *Introduction to the Old Testament* (Grand Rapids: Eerdmans, 1969); and Craig A. Evans, "On the Unity and Parallel Structure of Isaiah," *VT* 38 (1988): 129–47.

texts must be examined alongside citations of them and the use that was made of them in the sectarian texts.

The book of Isaiah is the most frequently quoted prophetic book in the sectarian texts, and the latter contain numerous Isaianic allusions as well. Additionally, there are no rewritten forms or apocryphal versions of Isaiah extant anywhere, which, according to some, is further evidence of the authority of the text.[55] Isaiah is also one of the few prophetic books that receive treatment as pesher.[56] In light of what has just been mentioned, the consensus view is that Isaiah was viewed by the Qumran community as authoritative scripture,[57] carrying with it a higher status than most of the other biblical books.[58] It should not be surprising, then, that the book of Isaiah's claims regarding its authorship are generally taken at face value by the scribes, as is reflected by their attribution of quotations from the book to the eighth-century prophet. In the remainder of this article, I will briefly look at some of the citations of Isaiah in the sectarian texts at Qumran, keeping in mind questions surrounding authority and authorship.

In the sectarian documents, quotations from all sections of Isaiah are almost always attributed to a person (e.g., "the prophet Isaiah") or a book (e.g., "the book of the prophet Isaiah"), and in a few instances the designation is simply "Isaiah."[59] For example:

CD VI, 8

אמר ישעיה מוציא כלי למעשיה

ʾmr yšʿyh mwṣyʾ kly lmʿśyh

Isaiah said, "He produces a tool for his labor." (Isa 54:16)

---

55. Cf. Jeremiah Apocryphon and Pseudo-Ezekiel. Fragments of both of these works were found in Cave 4.

56. As many as six distinct pesharim are attested at Qumran. On the authority of the cited biblical texts in the pesharim, Timothy H. Lim states: "There is little doubt that the pesher functioned authoritatively in the sectarian community . . . the pesher presents itself as a comment. The lemma, almost invariably in the form of a verbatim biblical citation, is authoritative, because it requires comment" (*The Formation of the Jewish Canon*, AYBRL [New Haven: Yale University Press, 2013], 139).

57. By authoritative, I refer to a text or collection of writings that were accepted and used by a group of people and considered to be divinely inspired.

58. The Pentateuch and some other prophetic books are in the same category and were considered authoritative scripture (Brooke, "Isaiah in the Pesharim," 609–10). Lim describes the sliding scale of influence among the biblical books as follows: "The sectarian scrolls imply a broadly bipartite collection of authoritative scriptures consisting of the 'Torah of Moses,' referring to the Pentateuch, and an undefined collection of writings that are considered prophetic" (*Formation of the Jewish Canon*, 120).

59. See G. K. Beale's essay in the present volume, esp. pp. 88–89, for a list of eight such examples.

4Q176 1–2 I, 4

ומן ספר ישעיה תנחומים[—נחמו נחמו עמי] יומר אלוהיכם

wmn spr yšʿyh tnḥwmym[—nḥmw nḥmw ʿmy] ywmr ʾlwhykm

And from the book of Isaiah, words of comfort

[... "'Comfort, comfort, my people,'] says your God." (Isa 40:1)

Attributions like these are quite generic and could easily refer to a tradition or a literary composition known as "Isaiah." As John Walton and Brent Sandy have recently argued, modern conceptions of authorship and books are anachronistic, and ancient scribes were not necessarily concerned with who wrote a book. Rather, they were interested in the figure that lies behind the text, the true locus of biblical authority.[60] It is certainly possible that the Qumran community had similar understandings of authorship and authority, but a few quotations from the book of Isaiah in documents from Qumran that are more specific and refer to the words of "Isaiah the prophet" or "Isaiah ben Amoz" seem to indicate otherwise:

4Q265 1, 3[61]

כתוב בס[פר] ישעיה הנביא [—]

ktwb bs[pr] yšʿyh hnbyʾ [—]

It is written in the bo[ok of] Isaiah the prophet [...] (Isa 54:1–2)

11Q13 II, 15–16

הזואת הואה יום ה[שלום א]שר אמר[—ביד ישע]יה הנביא אשר אמר]
מה [נאוו על הרים רגל]י[מבש]ר מ[שמיע שלום מב]שר טוב משמיע
ישוע]ה [א]ומר לציון [מלך]אלוהיך

*hzwʾt hwʾh ywm h[šlwm ʾ]šr ʾmr[—byd yšʿ]yh hnbyʾ ʾšr ʾmr[mh]nʾww
ʿl hrym rgl[y] mbś[r m]šmyʿ šlwm mb[śr ṭwb mšmyʿ yšwʿ]h [ʾ]wmr
lṣywn [mlk]ʾlwhyk*

This is the day of [peace about wh]ich he said[... through Isa]iah the prophet, who said: "How pleasant on the mountains are the feet of one proclaiming good news, announcing peace, proclaiming good tidings, announcing salvation, saying to Zion, 'Your God reigns!'" (Isa 52:7)

---

60. John H. Walton and D. Brent Sandy, *The Lost World of Scripture: Ancient Literary Culture and Biblical Authority* (Downers Grove, IL: InterVarsity Press, 2013), 60–74, 226–27.
61. For more examples of attributions to "the book of Isaiah the prophet," see 4Q174 1 I, 21, 2, 15; 4Q177 5 VI, 2; 4Q285 7 1; and 11Q14 2 9–11.

CD IV, 13–14[62]

בליעל משולח בישראל כאשר דבר אל ביד ישעיה הנביא בן אמוץ לאמר
פחד ופחת ופח עליך יושב הארץ

bly'l mšwlḥ byśr'l k'šr dbr 'l byd yš'yh hnby' bn 'mwṣ l'mr pḥd wpḥt
wpḥ 'lyk ywšb h'rṣ

Belial will be set loose against Israel, as God has said by the prophet Isaiah, son of Amoz, saying: "Panic, pit, and net are against you, earth-dweller." (Isa 24:17)

The example from 11Q13 (*Melchizedek*) quoted above is significant insofar as it cites a prophetic text from Second Isaiah and attributes it to ישעיה הנביא (*yš'yh hnby'*).[63] Again, it is possible that the phrase "the prophet Isaiah" is a stylistic convention referring to a book, the tradition of the prophet himself, or a postexilic prophet called Isaiah. However, a straightforward reading suggests that the scribe of 11Q13, and by extension the Qumran community, understood Isa 52:7 as the words of God spoken through Isaiah ben Amoz.

The citation of Isa 24:17 in the Damascus Document (CD IV, 13–14) as divine words spoken through ישעיה הנביא בן אמוץ (*yš'yh hnby' bn 'mwṣ*) is particularly striking, as many scholars date Isa 24–27, the so-called "Little Apocalypse of Isaiah," to the late sixth century BCE,[64] with some dating it as late as the mid-second century BCE.[65] Not only did the Qumran covenanters attribute this verse to Isaiah son of Amoz, but they also understood his role in his prophetic ministry to be that of God's spokesperson.[66]

Conclusion

A few conclusions may be drawn from the preceding study. First, evidence from the biblical copies of Isaiah at Qumran generally supports the MT tradition and

---

62. See also CD VII, 10, "that is when the oracle of the prophet Isaiah son of Amoz came true" (in reference to Isa 7:17). A parallel text, 4Q266 3i 7, cites "the prophet Isaiah, son of Amoz."

63. See also 11Q13 II, 4, a slightly damaged text, which appears to read "just as [Isaiah said . . .]," followed by the text of Isa 61:1.

64. So Paul D. Hanson, *The Dawn of Apocalyptic: The Historical and Sociological Roots of Jewish Apocalyptic Eschatology* (Philadelphia: Fortress, 1975), 313.

65. For example, Otto Kaiser characterizes Isa 24–27 as "advanced apocalyptic speculation" and assigns it a *terminus ad quem* of 164 BCE (*Isaiah 13–39: A Commentary*, trans. R. A. Wilson, OTL [London: SCM, 1974], 178–79). Bernhard Duhm dates Isa 24–27 to around 128 BCE (*Das Buch Jesaia*, Göttinger HKAT 3.1, 4th ed. [Göttingen: Vandenhoeck & Ruprecht, 1922], 13).

66. This is confirmed in other citations of Isaiah elsewhere in the Damascus Document. Cf. CD VI, 8, "Isaiah said, 'he produces a tool for his labor'" (Isa 54:16), and VI, 10, "that is when the oracle of the prophet Isaiah came true."

points to a stable text by the second century BCE at the latest. There are some text-critical matters to consider, such as the orthographic and morphological variants in 1QIsaᵃ and a few notable variants in 1QIsaᵇ, but most of these can be explained by the linguistic situation of the Second Temple period or as scribal errors.

Second, recent research has shown that scribal marks and divisions, such as indentations and paragraph markers, are an indication that the scribe(s) of 1QIsaᵃ sought to identify structural and literary breaks within the book. More research is needed to determine the structure of Isaiah as the scribe(s) envisaged it, but suffice it to say that these scribal marks reflect early exegesis of the book of Isaiah. One of the most debated "marks" is the gap in column 27 of 1QIsaᵃ, which effectively bisects Isaiah into two volumes with, as Brownlee argued, parallel outlines and corresponding themes. It is possible that the gap simply marks the point at which a second scribe took over, but even this would not undermine the fact that the scribe(s) responsible for 1QIsaᵃ considered Isaiah a coherent and unified book.

Third, the attributions of Isaianic quotations in the sectarian texts cannot be viewed as decisive, as they occur several hundred years after the historical events of Isaiah. Most of them are fairly generic and could refer to the eighth-century BCE prophet, a book called Isaiah, or even a prophetic tradition that traces its origin to Isaiah the prophet. However, a straightforward analysis of the citations, especially those that are accompanied by explicit and detailed attributions, such as CD IV, 13–14, suggests that the Qumran covenanters considered Isaiah ben Amoz to be the author of the book.

4

"Isaiah the Prophet Said": The Authorship of Isaiah Reexamined in the Light of Early Jewish and Christian Writings

G. K. BEALE

Introduction

The debate about the authorship of Isaiah represents just one of a variety of issues related to the inspiration of the Scriptures that are being debated by Evangelicals today.[1] Some contemporary evangelical scholars do not take at face value the repeated affirmations by Jesus and the New Testament writers that the prophet Isaiah wrote the entire Old Testament book known as Isaiah. The debate on this issue has significant bearing on the debate about the Bible's authority, since if Isaiah did not write the book attributed to him, the New Testament's assertion that he wrote the book is wrong. Perhaps of even greater significance, if the prophet Isaiah was not responsible for the contents of the whole book, we are left with a christological problem, since Jesus understood that the prophet Isaiah wrote the entire book attributed to him.

Some Evangelicals who contend that Isaiah was not the author of the book by that name do not think this position is inconsistent with the inspiration of Scripture. Some believe that the New Testament refers only to a collection of writings known as "Isaiah," so that such allusions need not be understood as referring to a personal prophet whose handprint is over the whole work.[2] Others believe that Jesus' intention was not to convey that the historical prophet Isaiah was the author, but that his focus was on communicating only the meaning of the prophecy.

I will contend that these views are problematic, and that it is difficult to see how the Bible could be authoritative while espousing the view of multi-authorship of Isaiah.

---

1. The present essay is a lightly revised version of "A Specific Problem Confronting the Authority of the Bible: Should the New Testament's Claim That the Prophet Isaiah Wrote the Whole Book of Isaiah Be Taken at Face Value?," ch. 5 in G. K. Beale, *The Erosion of Inerrancy in Evangelicalism: Responding to New Challenges to Biblical Authority* (Wheaton, IL: Crossway, 2008), 123–59.

2. For example, see H. G. M. Williamson, "Isaiah: Book of," in *Dictionary of the Old Testament: Prophets*, ed. Mark J. Boda and J. Gordon McConville (Downers Grove, IL: InterVarsity Press, 2012), 366–71, who says the New Testament references to Isaiah do not disallow multiple authorship of Isaiah, "since the use of those contexts of 'Isaiah' may be perfectly well understood as a reference to the book, not the author."

Current Evangelical Dispositions toward New Testament Views of Old Testament Books

Until the late 1970s, evangelical scholars generally accepted the Bible's claims about the human authorship of some of its books, whether regarding the Isaianic authorship of the book of Isaiah,[3] the Mosaic authorship of the Pentateuch, or the attribution of the *lĕdāwīd* psalms to David. This was the position taken by the Chicago Statement on Biblical Inerrancy. However, in less than thirty years American Evangelicals have become increasingly willing to accept higher-critical views of the Bible's claims about authorship of particular biblical books like Isaiah,[4] though some contemporary Old Testament evangelical scholars still hold to the traditional view about Isaiah.[5]

The main conservative arguments for the single authorship of Isaiah were helpfully summarized in the mid-twentieth century by Oswald Allis:

(1) Since all fifteen of the Latter Prophets of the Old Testament begin with a heading that includes the prophet's name, but Isa 40–66 does not, the author of Isa 1–39 was probably the same as that of chapters 40–66.

(2) For twenty-five centuries no one questioned the authorship of Isaiah, except for one insignificant Jewish medieval interpreter.

(3) The New Testament writers quoted from all parts of the book of Isaiah and considered all quotations to be the words of the prophet Isaiah.

(4) The Qumran scroll of Isaiah 1QIsa[a] shows no literary break between chapters 39 and 40, where critics locate the major break in the authorship of the book.[6]

---

3. For example, see E. J. Young, *The Book of Isaiah*, 3 vols. (Grand Rapids: Eerdmans, 1972), 3:538–49; Roland K. Harrison, *Introduction to the Old Testament* (Grand Rapids: Eerdmans, 1969), 765–95.

4. See, e.g., Raymond B. Dillard and Tremper Longman III, *An Introduction to the Old Testament* (Grand Rapids: Zondervan, 1994), 268–74, which is used at many evangelical institutions and is published by a traditionally conservative evangelical publisher.

5. John N. Oswalt, *The Book of Isaiah: Chapters 1–39*, NICOT (Grand Rapids: Eerdmans, 1986), 23–28; J. A. Motyer, *The Prophecy of Isaiah* (Downers Grove, IL: InterVarsity Press, 1993), 25–30. See also N. H. Ridderbos, "Isaiah: Book of," *NBD*[3] 513–16, who holds a mediating position, that it is acceptable to affirm that Isa 40–66 contains an Isaianic core that Isaiah's disciples expanded according to the spirit of Isaiah, but that it is not possible to determine what belongs to the core and what to the later editors. See also Bruce K. Waltke, *An Old Testament Theology* (Grand Rapids: Zondervan, 2007), 67, who holds to single authorship of Isaiah by the prophet Isaiah, though he allows for the possibility that a disciple of Isaiah could have authored Isa 40–66.

6. Oswald T. Allis, *The Unity of Isaiah: A Study in Prophecy* (Phillipsburg, NJ: Presbyterian & Reformed, 1950), 39–43.

Reconsideration of Jesus' and the
New Testament's References to Isaiah

Old Testament scholars have presented cogent arguments for multiple authorship of Isaiah, which is the ruling model today for understanding the book's authorship.[7] But others continue to offer viable arguments for the unity of Isaiah's authorship. Interestingly, scholars have devoted less study to evidence for diversity of authorship in the last ten to fifteen years, while still affirming multiple authorship, and many recognize an overall unity of subject matter, though they propose that this is the result of a final editor's work. Since the cumulative effect of these arguments has been to highlight the book's literary unity,[8] the longer these arguments are made, the thinner the line becomes between a final redactor, who imposed unity on the diverse strands of the book, and Isaiah as the original author, who was responsible for its unity from the beginning.[9]

Though the book of Isaiah itself has much to contribute to the discussion about its authorship, the present article will consider the authorship of Isaiah primarily on the basis of the claims made in references to "Isaiah" found in the New Testament and other early Jewish and Christian sources. Most Christian Old Testament scholars who hold to multiple authorship consider their arguments so convincing that New Testament evidence must fit their conclusion. They argue that, like other early Jews, Jesus and his followers were wrong, that Jesus knowingly accommodated himself to false Jewish tradition, or that the New Testament merely refers to a literary collection known as "Isaiah."

In this article, I will argue that the New Testament evidence that the whole book of Isaiah was authored by the prophet Isaiah is so strong that arguing for multiple authors must inevitably lead to one conclusion: that Jesus and the New Testament writers were wrong in their assessment of the book's authorship. However, I believe that the New Testament evidence vindicates the traditional arguments that Isaiah wrote the whole book and best explains the book's literary and theological unity that scholars have recently been recognizing, but which they attribute to later redactors. In presenting my argument, I will develop in more detail the traditional arguments for Isaianic authorship based on New Testament evidence, which I view to be significant and which cannot lightly be dismissed.

---

7. For the typical critical arguments, see the summary and responses in Harrison, *Introduction to the Old Testament*, 765–95.

8. E.g., see Williamson, "Isaiah: Book of," 368–71.

9. See Richard L. Schultz, "How Many Isaiahs Were There and What Does It Matter? Prophetic Inspiration in Recent Evangelical Scholarship," in *Evangelicals and Scripture: Tradition, Authority and Hermeneutics*, ed. Vincent Bacote, Laura C. Miguélez and Dennis L. Okholm (Downers Grove, IL: InterVarsity Press, 2004), 150–70, for a convenient survey of this issue, as well as the current status of evangelical views on the authorship of Isaiah with respect to the Old Testament data.

Attributions of Quotations to Isaiah the Prophet in Early Judaism, the New Testament and Early Christianity

A study on how the ancients viewed the authorship of the book of Isaiah should begin by surveying the actual evidence about Isaiah in early Judaism and Christianity. Without exception, this literature understands that the prophet Isaiah was the author of the entire book. In the following study, I consider all the references to Isaiah in the Dead Sea Scrolls, Josephus, Philo, the Old Testament Apocrypha and Pseudepigrapha, the New Testament, the New Testament Apocrypha, and the Apostolic Fathers. This evidence shows that early authors of Jewish and Christian literature quoted from all parts of the book of Isaiah (so-called First, Second, and Third Isaiah) and that they attributed all of their quotations to the person of Isaiah. In the citations below, I have highlighted with italics and underlining the expressions that reflect the personal agency of "Isaiah."

The New Testament

Matthew 3:3
> For this is the one referred *to by Isaiah the prophet when he said,*
> "THE VOICE OF ONE CRYING IN THE WILDERNESS,
> 'MAKE READY THE WAY OF THE LORD,
> MAKE HIS PATHS STRAIGHT!' "[10]

Matthew 4:14
> This was to fulfill what *was spoken through Isaiah the prophet*:

Matthew 8:17
> This was to fulfill what *was spoken through Isaiah the prophet*:
> "HE HIMSELF TOOK OUR INFIRMITIES
> AND CARRIED AWAY OUR DISEASES."

Matthew 12:17
> This was to fulfill what *was spoken through Isaiah the prophet*:

Matthew 13:14
> In their case the *prophecy of Isaiah* is being fulfilled, which says,
> "YOU WILL KEEP ON HEARING, BUT WILL NOT UNDERSTAND;
> YOU WILL KEEP ON SEEING, BUT WILL NOT PERCEIVE."

Matthew 15:7
> You hypocrites, *rightly did Isaiah prophesy of you.*

---

10. Unless otherwise noted, all Scripture references are taken from the NASB (1977). Italics have been added for emphasis. Text in small capital letters indicates quotations from the book of Isaiah.

Mark 1:2

As it is written *in Isaiah the prophet*:
"BEHOLD, I SEND MY MESSENGER AHEAD OF YOU,
WHO WILL PREPARE YOUR WAY."

Mark 7:6

And He said to them, *"Rightly did Isaiah prophesy of you* hypocrites, as it is written:
'THIS PEOPLE HONORS ME WITH THEIR LIPS, BUT THEIR HEART IS FAR AWAY FROM ME.'"

Luke 3:4

As it is written *in the book of the words of Isaiah the prophet,*
"THE VOICE OF ONE CRYING IN THE WILDERNESS,
'MAKE READY THE WAY OF THE LORD,
MAKE HIS PATHS STRAIGHT.'"

Luke 4:17

And the book *of the prophet Isaiah* was handed to Him. And He opened the book and found the place where it was written.

John 1:23

He said, "I am A VOICE OF ONE CRYING IN THE WILDERNESS,
'MAKE STRAIGHT THE WAY OF THE LORD,' *as Isaiah the prophet said."*

John 12:38–39

This was to fulfill *the word of Isaiah the prophet which he spoke*:
"LORD, WHO HAS BELIEVED OUR REPORT?
AND TO WHOM HAS THE ARM OF THE LORD BEEN REVEALED?"
For this reason they could not believe, for *Isaiah said again....*

Acts 8:28, 30–35

And he was returning and sitting in his chariot, and *was reading the prophet Isaiah.*
... Philip ran up and *heard him reading Isaiah the prophet,* and said, "Do you understand what you are reading?" And he said, "Well, how could I, unless someone guides me?" And he invited Philip to come up and sit with him. Now the passage of Scripture that he was reading was this:
"HE WAS LED AS A SHEEP TO SLAUGHTER;
AND AS A LAMB BEFORE ITS SHEARER IS SILENT,
SO HE DOES NOT OPEN HIS MOUTH.
IN HUMILIATION HIS JUDGMENT WAS TAKEN AWAY;
WHO WILL RELATE HIS GENERATION?
FOR HIS LIFE IS REMOVED FROM THE EARTH."
The eunuch answered Philip and said, "Please tell me, *of whom does the prophet say this? Of himself or of someone else?"* Then Philip opened his mouth, and beginning from this Scripture he preached Jesus to him.

Acts 28:25

And when they did not agree with one another, they began leaving after Paul had spoken one parting word, *"The Holy Spirit rightly spoke through Isaiah the prophet to your fathers...."*

Romans 9:27, 29

Isaiah cries out concerning Israel, "THOUGH THE NUMBER OF THE SONS OF ISRAEL BE LIKE THE SAND OF THE SEA, IT IS THE REMNANT THAT WILL BE SAVED." . . . And *just as Isaiah foretold,* "UNLESS THE LORD OF SABAOTH HAD LEFT TO US A POSTERITY, WE WOULD HAVE BECOME LIKE SODOM, AND WOULD HAVE RESEMBLED GOMORRAH."

Romans 10:16

However, they did not all heed the good news; for *Isaiah says,* "LORD, WHO HAS BELIEVED OUR REPORT?"

Romans 10:20

And *Isaiah is very bold and says,* "I WAS FOUND BY THOSE WHO DID NOT SEEK ME, I BECAME MANIFEST TO THOSE WHO DID NOT ASK FOR ME."

Romans 15:12

Again Isaiah says, "THERE SHALL COME THE ROOT OF JESSE, AND HE WHO ARISES TO RULE OVER THE GENTILES, IN HIM SHALL THE GENTILES HOPE."

Philo

Names 169

But it is not allowed to every wicked man to rejoice, *as it is said in the predictions of the prophet,* "There is no rejoicing for the wicked, says God" [Isa 47:22].[11]

Dreams 2.172

They then very fairly compare this vine of which we were only able to take a part, to happiness. *And one of the ancient prophets bears his testimony in favour of my view of the matter, who speaking under divine inspiration has said,* "The vineyard of the Lord Almighty is the house of Israel" [Isa 5:7].

Rewards 158

Then, like an affectionate mother, it shall pity the sons and the daughters whom it has lost, who now that they are dead are, and still more were, when alive, a grief and sorrow to their parents; and becoming young a second time, it will again be fertile as before, and will produce an irreproachable offspring, an improvement on its former progeny; for she that was desolate, *as the prophet says,* [Isa 54:1] is now become happy in her children and the mother of a large family. Which prophetic saying has also an allegorical meaning, having reference to the soul.

---

11. Citations of Philo are from *The Works of Philo*, trans. C. D. Yonge (Peabody, MA: Hendrickson, 1993).

Josephus

Ant. 9.276

But king Hezekiah was not concerned at his threatenings, but depended on his piety towards God, and upon *Isaiah the prophet, by whom he inquired, and accurately knew all future events:*—and thus much shall suffice for the present concerning this king Hezekiah.[12]

Ant. 10.35

Now *as to this prophet* [clearly Isaiah in context], he was by the confession of all, *a divine and wonderful man in speaking truth; and out of the assurance that he had never written what was false, he wrote down all his prophecies, and left them behind him in books, that their accomplishment might be judged of from the events by posterity. Nor did this prophet do so alone; but the others, which were twelve in number, did the same.* And whatsoever is done among us, whether it be good, or whether it be bad, comes to pass according to their prophecies; but of every one of these we shall speak hereafter.

Ant. 11.5

This was known to Cyrus by his reading the book which Isaiah left behind him of his prophecies; for this prophet said that God had spoken thus to him in a secret vision:— "My will is, that Cyrus, whom I have appointed to be king over many and great nations, send back my people to their own land, and build my temple."

Ant. 13.64

The chief reason why he was desirous so to do, was, that he relied upon the prophet Isaiah, who lived about six hundred years before, and foretold that there certainly was to be a temple built to Almighty God in Egypt by a man that was a Jew. Onias was elevated with this prediction, and wrote the following epistle to Ptolemy and Cleopatra:—

Ant. 13.68

For the prophet Isaiah foretold, that "there should be an altar in Egypt to the Lord God:" and many other such things did he prophesy relating to that place.

Ant. 13.71

But since *thou sayest that Isaiah the prophet foretold this long ago*, we give thee leave to do it, if it may be done according to your law, and so that we may not appear to have at all offended God herein.

J.W. 7.431–432

Accordingly, he [Onias] thought that by building this temple he should draw away a great number from them to himself. *There had been also a certain ancient prediction made by a [prophet] whose name was Isaiah, about six hundred years before, that this temple should be built by a man that was a Jew in Egypt.* And this is the history of the building of that temple.

---

12. Citations of Josephus are from *The Works of Flavius Josephus*, trans. William Whiston (Peabody, MA: Hendrickson, 1987).

The above references to a temple in Egypt are likely to Isa 19:18–25, which pertains to the final eschatological restoration of Egyptians and Assyrians, portrayed as occurring at the same time as Israel's end-time restoration.

Qumran

CD IV, 13–14

Belial is unrestrained in Israel, *just as God said by Isaiah the prophet, the son of Amoz,* saying, "Fear and pit and snare are upon thee, dweller in the land" (Isa. 24:17).[13] The true meaning of this verse . . .[14]

CD VII, 10

. . . to them that is *when the oracle of the prophet Isaiah son of Amoz came true* [in context the reference is to Isa 7:17].

4Q174 III, 15–16

. . . as it is written *in the book of Isaiah the prophet* in reference to the Last Days, "And it came to pass, while His hand was strong upon me, [that He warned me not to walk in the way of] this people" (Isa. 8:11). These are they about whom it is written in the book of Ezekiel the prophet . . ."

4Q177 5–6 I, 2

. . . [as it is written *in the book of Isaiah the*] *prophet,* "This year eat what grows [by itself, and next year the aftergrowth" (Isa. 37:30). The meaning of] "what grows by itself" is [. . .]

4Q177 5–6 I, 5

[. . . that is written] about them *in the book of [Isaiah the prophet . . .* for] the Law of the [. . .]

4Q177 I, 6

[. . .] it calls them, as [it is written about them *in the book of Isaiah the prophet,* "He] thinks up plots to [destroy the humble with lying words" (Isa. 32:7) . . .]

4Q265 1 3–5

[. . .] it is written *in the b[ook] of Isaiah the prophet,* ["Sing, O barren one who did not bear; burst into song and] shout, you who have not been in labor! For the children of the desolate will be more [than the children of her that is married, says the LORD.] Enlarge the site of [your] ten[t] [and stretch out the curtains of your dwelling; do not hold back" (Isa. 54:1–2).

---

13. Many scholars consider this text non-Isaianic.

14. Unless otherwise noted, all quotations from Qumran are from M. O. Wise, M. G. Abegg, and E. M. Cook, eds., *The Dead Sea Scrolls: A New English Translation* (New York: Harper Collins, 1996). Most of the brackets indicate lacunae filled in by the editors, though occasionally they indicate my additions.

4Q266 3i 7–3ii 2

> . . . in Israel, just *as God said by Isaiah the prophet, the son of Amoz,* (CD 4:14) *sayin]g,*
> . . . [against] them. Al[l of them are kindlers and lighters of brands (Isa. 50:11); the
> webs of (CD 5:14) a spider are their webs]. . . . [and the eggs of vip]ers are t[heir] eggs
> (Isa. 59:5). [Whoever touches them (CD 5:15) shall not be clean. The more he does so,
> the more he is guilty].[15]

Old Testament Apocrypha

2 Esdras 2:18

> I will send you help, my servants Isaiah and Jeremiah. According to their counsel I
> have consecrated and prepared for you twelve trees loaded with various fruits. [This
> is in a clear context of this chapter involving God's promise to bring Israel out of
> captivity into all the blessings of the restoration promises.][16]

Sirach 48:20–25

> But they called upon the Lord who is merciful, spreading forth their hands toward
> him; and the Holy One quickly heard them from heaven, and delivered them by
> the hand of Isaiah. . . . For Hezekiah did what was pleasing to the Lord, and he held
> strongly to the ways of David his father, which *Isaiah the prophet commanded, who
> was great and faithful in his vision.* In his [Isaiah's] days the sun went backward, and
> he lengthened the life of the king. *By the spirit of might he [Isaiah] saw the last things,
> and comforted those who mourned in Zion. He revealed what was to occur to the end of
> time, and the hidden things before they came to pass.*

4 Maccabees 18:14

> He reminded you of the Scripture of Isaiah, which says, "Even though you go
> through the fire, the flame shall not consume you" [Isa 43:2].

Old Testament Pseudepigrapha

Martyrdom and Ascension of Isaiah 3:6:

> *Isaiah and the prophets who (are) with him prophesy* against Jerusalem and against the
> cities of Judah that they will be laid waste, and also (against) Benjamin that it will go
> into captivity, and also against you, lord king, that you will go (bound) with hooks
> and chains of iron.[17]

---

15. This text is not found in the 1996 edition of Wise, Abegg, and Cook, *Dead Sea Scrolls*, but is instead cited from M. O. Wise, M. G. Abegg, and E. M. Cook, eds., *The Dead Sea Scrolls: A New English Translation*, rev. ed. (San Francisco: HarperOne, 2005).

16. Citations of the Apocrypha are from the RSV.

17. Translations of the Martyrdom and Ascension of Isaiah are from M. A. Knibb, "Martyrdom and Ascension of Isaiah," in *The Old Testament Pseudepigrapha*, ed. James H. Charlesworth (Garden City, NY: Doubleday, 1985), 2.143–76.

Martyrdom and Ascension of Isaiah 4:8:[18]

> And the rest of the words of the vision [by Isaiah] are written in the vision of Babylon [Isa 13]. And the rest of the vision about the LORD, behold it is written in parables in the words of mine [Isaiah] that are written in the book which I prophesied openly. And the descent of the Beloved into Sheol, behold it is written in the section where the LORD says, "Behold, my son shall understand" [Isa 52:13, LXX].

New Testament Apocrypha

Acts of Pilate 18:1 (2.1)

> O Lord Jesus Christ, the resurrection and the life of the world, give us grace that we may tell of thy resurrection and of thy miracles which thou didst perform in Hades . . . And at the hour of midnight there rose upon the darkness there [in Hades] something like the light of the sun and shone, and light fell upon us all . . . the prophet Isaiah, who was present there, said: This shining comes from the Father and the Son and the Holy Spirit. *This I prophesied when I was still living*: The land of Zabulon and the land of Nephthalim, the people that sit in darkness saw a great light (9:1, 2[ET 2, 3]).[19]

Acts of Pilate 21:2 (5.2)

> [Referring to Christ's death and resurrection victory over the powers of evil in Hades,] Isaiah said: "I foresaw this by the Holy Spirit and wrote: *The dead shall arise, and those who are in the tombs shall be raised up, and those who are under the earth shall rejoice* (26:19). O death, where is thy sting? O Hades, where is thy victory?"[20]

The Apostolic Fathers

2 Clement 3:5

> And in Isaiah he also says, "This people honors me with their lips, but their heart is far from me" [Isa 28:13][21].

Barnabas 12:4

> And *again in another prophet [Isaiah] he says:* "All day long I have stretched out my hands to a disobedient people who oppose my righteous way" [Isa 65:2].

---

18. In the Charlesworth edition of the pseudepigrapha, this reference is *Mart. Isa.* 4:20–21. The Martyrdom and Ascension of Isaiah is dated variously either to the first or second century CE.

19. Citations of the Acts of Pilate are from F. Scheidweiler, "The Gospel of Nicodemus / Acts of Pilate and Christ's Descent into Hell," in *NTApoc*, ed. Wilhelm Schneemelcher, trans. A. J. B. Higgins, George Ogg, Richard E. Taylor, and R. M. Wilson, 2 vols. (Philadelphia: Westminster, 1963), 1:444–84.

20. This last clause is actually a quotation from Hos 13:14, but the author has taken the verse as an interpretation of the resurrection prophecy of Isa 25:8 (LXX), probably under the influence of 1 Cor 15:54–55, where the same Hosea text directly follows the same Isa 25:8 citation as an interpretation of it. This resembles the same phenomenon we observe in the use of the Old Testament in Mark 1:2–3.

21. All translations from the Apostolic Fathers are from Michael W. Holmes, ed. and trans., *The Apostolic Fathers: Greek Texts and English Translations*, 3rd ed. (Grand Rapids: Baker Academic, 2007).

Barnabas 12:11

> And *again, Isaiah says as follows*: "The Lord said to the Messiah my Lord, whose right hand I held, that the nations would obey him [Isa 52:15? 60:11–12], and I will shatter the strength of kings" [Isa 45:1]. Observe how David calls him "Lord," and does not call him "son."

Observations on the Isaiah Quotations Above

The ancient sources quoted above attribute references to all parts of the book of Isaiah to the personal prophet Isaiah (in distinction to an impersonal literary collection). Admittedly, some of the general references to "Isaiah" could refer figuratively to a literary collection known as "Isaiah." However, the majority of the citations from early Judaism, the New Testament, and early Christianity cannot refer only to a literary collection. It is apparent from the specific personal language often used that they refer to sayings spoken by the personal prophet Isaiah. For example, in context the following expressions allude not merely to the "prophecy" or "prophecies" of "Isaiah" (which possibly could refer to a literary collection or to a personal prophet), but to "Isaiah" as a personal "prophet": "Isaiah the son of Amoz," "what was spoken through Isaiah the prophet," "referred to by Isaiah the prophet," "the prophecy of Isaiah," "rightly did Isaiah prophesy" (a literary collection cannot prophesy), "as it is written in the book of the words of Isaiah the prophet," "the book of the prophet Isaiah," "the word of Isaiah the prophet that he spoke," "of whom does the prophet [Isaiah] say this," "the Holy Spirit rightly spoke through Isaiah the prophet to your fathers," "Isaiah cries out," "Isaiah foretold," "Isaiah says," "the predictions of the prophet," "one of the ancient prophets bears his testimony," "as the prophet says," "Isaiah the prophet . . . and [he] accurately knew all future events," "reading the book that Isaiah left behind him of his prophecies," "he relied upon the prophet Isaiah, who lived about six hundred years before, and foretold," "the prophet Isaiah foretold," "there had been also a certain ancient prediction made by a [prophet] whose name was Isaiah, about six hundred years before," "as God said by Isaiah the prophet," and "the oracle of the prophet Isaiah."

Hugh Williamson contends that statements in the New Testament referring to Isaiah as "speaker" or "author" can easily be understood as references only to the literary book called "Isaiah" and not to the personal prophet "Isaiah."[22] However, if these references are read straightforwardly in a historical-grammatical exegetical manner, the majority of them refer to *the active personal role of Isaiah the prophet in writing and prophesying in all parts of the book*. These references to prophecies by Isaiah offer no substantial evidence that they derive merely from a literary work known as "the book of Isaiah." A literary collection does not "speak" or "cry out." Expressions that allude to the personal activity, role, or involvement of a person named Isaiah are best taken as personal references to the prophet named "Isaiah," rather than references to an anonymous prophet responsible for a literary

---

22. Williamson, "Isaiah: Book of," 370.

collection, or personifications of a literary collection speaking. The reference in
Acts 8:34 is telling; with respect to the citation of the suffering servant from Isa 53,
the Ethiopian eunuch asks, "Please tell me, of whom does the prophet [earlier said
to be Isaiah] say this? Of himself or of someone else?" The use of Isa 6:9–10 and
Isa 52:1 in John 12:38–40 in relation to 12:41 supports this argument (on which see
below). The citations from the Acts of Pilate declare expressly that Isaiah's prophecies were issued by the personal prophet Isaiah when he was "alive on earth." It
would never occur to readers to interpret these statements as figuratively referring
only to a literary collection unless they had concluded in advance that the personal
prophet Isaiah was not the author of these texts quoted in these statements, something that has happened only in recent critical scholarship.

Significantly, the quotations come from all parts of the book of Isaiah (so-called
First, Second, and Third Isaiah), and all are attributed to the personal prophet Isaiah. The first-century Christian and Jewish view was that the single prophet Isaiah
wrote the entire book attributed to him. The stylistic convention of attributing the
name of an Old Testament prophet, like Isaiah, to a quotation not written by that
prophet finds no support in the evidence surveyed above. Therefore, when Jesus,
the book of Acts, and Paul quote Isaiah, they have in mind the personal prophet
himself—a conclusion supported by references in early Judaism and other early
Christian literature. Jesus, the book of Acts, and Paul were either wrong or correct
in referring to Isaiah this way. Early evidence regarding Isaianic authorship seems
to exclude the view that these references reflect a stylistic convention that referred
only to a literary work known as "Isaiah." Josephus' summary of the early Jewish
view of Isaiah bears repeating:

> Now as to this prophet [clearly Isaiah in context], he was by the confession of all, a di-
> vine and wonderful man in speaking truth; and out of the assurance that he had never
> written what was false, he wrote down all his prophecies, and left them behind him
> in books, that their accomplishment might be judged of from the events by posterity.
> Nor did this prophet do so alone; but the others, which were twelve in number, did
> the same. And whatsoever is done among us, whether it be good, or whether it be bad,
> comes to pass according to their prophecies; but of every one of these we shall speak
> hereafter. (*Ant.* 10.35)

Some have argued that when Jesus and the New Testament writers referred to
"Isaiah," they did not intend to speak specifically about human authorship but were
concerned only about the divine meaning of the text they quoted. Even if a real
person known as Isaiah did not actually write the entire book, if the New Testament writers did not intend to communicate the identity of the human author, they
cannot be charged with inaccuracy. When someone says, "I went to work when the
sun rose this morning," the intent is not to make a scientific statement about the
movement of the sun, but merely to communicate at what time the person went to
work. Accordingly, references to "Isaiah" are like window dressing through which
the divine message is conveyed.

However, this view is problematic. The preceding list of references to Isaiah
in early Jewish writings and especially in the New Testament includes repeated

references to the active role of Isaiah in writing and prophesying in all parts of the book. Such references are not merely the pipes through which the water of the real message flows, but are part of the actual message. These references assume the authority of the personal prophet who was appointed by God, so that his message was to be seen as having divine authority. Note again the following examples of such expressions: "*rightly* did Isaiah prophesy of you [hypocrites]" (Matt 15:7; Mark 7:6); "*to fulfill* what was spoken through Isaiah the prophet," and similar phrases (six times); "the Holy Spirit *rightly* spoke through Isaiah the prophet to your fathers" (Acts 28:25). The word translated "rightly" is καλῶς (*kalōs*), which can also be rendered "correctly" or "accurately" (as elsewhere in the NT).[23] That the authority of the personal prophet Isaiah is integral to the message communicated is apparent also in Jesus' comparable appeal to the persons of Moses (Luke 20:37; 24:27, 44; John 1:17, 45) and David. These texts underscore the authority of the message, which means that the authority of these personages is inextricably bound up with the message. For example, note Jesus' appeal to David in Mark 12:35–37, quoting Ps 110:1:

> And Jesus began to say, as He taught in the temple, "How is it that the scribes say that the Christ is the son of David? David himself said in the Holy Spirit, 'THE LORD SAID TO MY LORD, "SIT AT MY RIGHT HAND, UNTIL I PUT YOUR ENEMIES BENEATH YOUR FEET."' David himself calls Him 'Lord'; so in what sense is He his son?" And the large crowd enjoyed listening to Him.

Significantly, Jesus modeled parts of his ministry after the prophetic vocation of the actual prophet Isaiah. For example, Jesus viewed his use of parables in his ministry as a recapitulation of the ministry of Isaiah, as explained in Isa 6:9–10:

> "Therefore I speak to them in parables; because while seeing they do not see, and while hearing they do not hear, nor do they understand. In their case the prophecy of Isaiah is being fulfilled, which says,
> 'YOU WILL KEEP ON HEARING, BUT WILL NOT UNDERSTAND;
> YOU WILL KEEP ON SEEING, BUT WILL NOT PERCEIVE;
> FOR THE HEART OF THIS PEOPLE HAS BECOME DULL,
> WITH THEIR EARS THEY SCARCELY HEAR,
> AND THEY HAVE CLOSED THEIR EYES,
> OTHERWISE THEY WOULD SEE WITH THEIR EYES,
> HEAR WITH THEIR EARS,
> AND UNDERSTAND WITH THEIR HEART AND RETURN,
> AND I WOULD HEAL THEM.'" (Matt 13:13–15)

In Jesus' mind, what applied to the ministry of the historical Isaiah also applied to his own ministry. Indeed, Isa 6:9–10 involves a commission for the prophet to fulfill, and Jesus understood that it "is fulfilled again" (ἀναπληρόω, *anaplēroō*) in him

---

23. See BDAG 505–6, which surveys ranges of meaning and correctly places the occurrences in Matt 15:7, Mark 7:6, and Acts 28:25 in the category of meaning "being in accord with a standard, rightly, correctly."

(Matt 13:14). The historical Isaiah's ministry foreshadowed the even greater ministry of Jesus. Thus, in part the authority of this statement derived from its origin with the prophet Isaiah. Jesus believed that Isaiah was a historical figure and that Isaiah's historical ministry was a model for his own. Though most scholars accept the Isaianic authorship of Isa 6, it is remarkable that Jesus' quotation of Isa 6:9–10 in John 12:39 is said to be written by the same "Isaiah" whom Jesus had credited in verse 38 with prophesying the words of Isa 53:1, which is commonly attributed by critical scholars to an anonymous author living after the time of Isaiah:

John 12:38–40
> This was to fulfill *the word of Isaiah the prophet, which he spoke*: "LORD, WHO HAS BE-
> LIEVED OUR REPORT? AND TO WHOM HAS THE ARM OF THE LORD BEEN REVEALED?"
> [quoting Isa 53:1]. For this reason they could not believe, for *Isaiah said again*, "HE
> HAS BLINDED THEIR EYES AND HE HARDENED THEIR HEART,
> SO THAT THEY WOULD NOT SEE WITH THEIR EYES
> AND PERCEIVE WITH THEIR HEART,
> AND BE CONVERTED AND I HEAL THEM."

In addition, that Jesus interlaced the quotation with allusions to other passages later in Isaiah typically attributed to an author other than Isaiah is striking. The phrases "he has blinded their eyes" and "he hardened their heart" are interpretive paraphrases, respectively, of "make dim their eyes" and "make the hearts of this people fat," both of which derive from Isa 6:10. Jesus formulates these two paraphrases on the basis of allusions from parts of the book of Isaiah usually thought to have been written by writers other than Isaiah the prophet:

John 12:40	Isaiah	
He has blinded their eyes	29:9–10	blind yourselves and be blind . . . he [YHWH] has shut your eyes
	29:18	the eyes of the blind
	42:18–19	look you blind . . . Who is so blind . . . as the servant of the Lord (cf. Isa 56:10; 59:10).
He hardened their heart	63:17	Why . . . do you harden our heart . . .?[24]

In fact, Isa 29:9–10,[25] 42:18–19, and 63:17 all reflect some of the intertextual developments of Isa 6:9–10 later in Isaiah.[26] Williamson considers the use of Isa 6 in John

---

24. Most of these interlaced allusions in John 12:40 have been observed by Craig A. Evans, "The Function of Isaiah 6:9–10 in Mark and John," *NovT* 24 (1982): 134–37.

25. Though Isa 29:9–10 is less often attributed to an author other than Isaiah.

26. For developments of Isa 6:9–10, see also John L. McLaughlin, "Their Hearts *Were* Hardened: The Use of Isaiah 6,9–10 in the Book of Isaiah," *Bib* 75 (1994): 1–25, who sees parts of Isa 29 and 44 to be direct developments from Isa 6:9–10. See similarly Ronald E. Clements, "Patterns in the Prophetic Canon: Healing the Blind and the Lame," in *Canon, Theology, and Old Testament Interpretation: Essays in Honor of Brevard S. Childs*, ed. Gene M. Tucker, David L. Petersen, and Robert R. Wilson (Philadelphia: Fortress, 1988), 192–94, 198, who considers such passages as Isa 29:18, 20–21; 32:3; 33:23; 35:5–6; 42:18–21; and 44:18 to have

12:40 to be an exception to the many other references to Isaiah that refer only to a literary collection. In the context of John 12:40, Isaiah is not referred to merely as a speaker or author but as involved in an *action* of seeing God's glory.[27] For Williamson, this is not a problem, since Isa 6 is generally regarded to be from the personal prophet Isaiah anyway. Williamson's conclusion is problematic because the citation from Isa 53:1 (from so-called Second Isaiah) in John 12:38 is inextricably linked to the Isa 6 citation. It is included in "these things" that introduces verse 41, which concerns what Isaiah "saw."[28] Furthermore, as we have just seen, other passages from Isa 56 and 63 are also woven into the Isa 6 reference.

In conclusion, in Jesus' mind this development of Isa 6:9–10 in later parts of the book, such as Isa 42 and 53, was not to be credited to later anonymous writers, but to Isaiah the prophet. None of the references to Isaiah cited above support the view that these attributions are insignificant husk that surrounds the intended message. Rather, they are part of the message.

Ancient Stylistic Conventions Regarding Literary Works and Their Purported Authors

Those who reject Isaianic authorship of the whole book of Isaiah argue that the treatments of Isaiah by Jesus, the book of Acts, and Paul follow a common stylistic convention in the ancient world according to which people would refer to passages from literary works by names of persons who had not actually authored those works. However, there is no evidence for such a conventional way of referring *to particular passages from ancient works*. Although more work needs to be done in this area, we are well served by Christopher D. Stanley's book on Paul's use of the Old Testament.[29] After surveying early Greco-Roman and Jewish writers contemporary with the New Testament, Stanley observes that when later authors would quote earlier authors, they often made changes, small and larger. While sometimes the changes did not affect the meaning of the text, at other times the changes represent interpretations

---

demonstrable links with and to be developments of the themes of blindness and deafness in Isa 6:9–10; see also idem, "Beyond Tradition-History: Deutero-Isaianic Development of First Isaiah's Themes," in *The Prophets*, ed. Philip R. Davies, BibSem 42 (Sheffield: Sheffield Academic, 1996), 95–113, which mentions most of the preceding texts in Isa 29–55 but also adds Isa 43:8; likewise idem, "The Unity of the Book of Isaiah," *Int* 36 (1982): 125–26, which discusses the passages from Isa 42 and 43, as well as Isa 32 and 35. For Clements, these are some of the best examples of allusions to early chapters of Isaiah later in the book.

27. Williamson, "Isaiah: Book of," 370.

28. On this point, see Daniel J. Brendsel, *"Isaiah Saw His Glory": The Use of Isaiah 52–53 in John 12*, BZNW 208 (Berlin: de Gruyter, 2014), 123–34, who also cites significant commentators in agreement.

29. Christopher D. Stanley, *Paul and the Language of Scripture: Citation Technique in the Pauline Epistles and Contemporary Literature*, SNTSM 69 (Cambridge: Cambridge University Press, 1992).

by the quoter.[30] Stanley argues that Paul's technique of quotation followed the same general procedure used by nonbiblical writers of his time.

Stanley's work helpfully demonstrates how, on the one hand, authors often depended on earlier textual traditions and how, on the other hand, changed wording may reflect the author's independent interpretation. Although he provides many examples of such quotations (especially in Paul), he rarely discusses the interpretive significance of these changes. This applies both to examples that reflect later authors' own alterations and to those that represent a secondary textual tradition that appears already to have reinterpreted the earlier text (such as the LXX in relation to the MT). Stanley also demonstrates that this style of quoting was not unique to the ancient world but continues in modern times.[31]

With regard to the specific issue at hand, Stanley presents no evidence for a stylistic convention current in New Testament times where someone attributes to a known author a quotation that was not actually written by that author. (Nor does he adduce any textual support that Jesus might have attributed to Isaiah the prophetic quotations in so-called Second and Third Isaiah that Jesus did not believe were actually written by Isaiah the prophet.) And even if there were evidence of such a convention in Greco-Roman writings, one would have to show it operating in early Judaism.[32] Stanley demonstrates that later writers may "correct" an earlier

---

30. Ibid., 242–43.

31. See ibid., 355–56; though on pp. 345 and 350 Stanley contradicts this assessment.

32. Jewish pseudepigrapha could offer parallels to taking Isa 40–66 as written by a different author than Isaiah but in the name of Isaiah, which would have been assumed from chapters 1–39. However, our concern here is Jesus and the apostles quoting particular verses from "Isaiah" and attributing them to the prophet Isaiah. I do not consider the pseudepigraphic writings here because their authors do not quote from or expand on specific passages composed by ancient biblical figures in the precise way as argued by some scholars for the anonymous authorship of Isa 40–66, though allusions to Old Testament passages are common. Rather, pseudepigraphic works attribute completely new and later compositions to earlier biblical characters. Their authors attached pseudepigraphic names to "new" works, rather than to citations of existing Old Testament writings. Furthermore, some of the names identify persons who wrote nothing of which we know (e.g., Enoch, Abraham, Jacob, etc.). Isaiah presents a different case. Those who argue for multiple authorship contend that chs. 40–66 were composed by a school of disciples or editors who expanded on chs. 1–39, which were written by the historical Isaiah. Indeed, it seems the large collection of pseudepigraphic works were not included in the Old Testament canon because people likely knew at least by the time of the close of the Old Testament canon that they were not written by the biblical person whose name was attached to them, and thus concluded that these compositions lacked the authority of those composed by the Old Testament writers. Most scholars who recognize two or three Isaiahs believe that chs. 40–66 were written in the sixth century BCE, long before the literary genre of Jewish pseudepigrapha arose and flourished (the beginning of the second century BCE). Furthermore, if Isa 40–66 were a pseudepigraph, the author should have inserted the name of Isaiah at various points in these chapters, as happened typically in the pseudepigraphical books. The survey of early Jewish and Christian views of Isaianic authorship found above in this article demonstrates that early writers did not view the book to be a pseudepigraph. Moreover, neither Jesus nor the apostles ever explicitly

ancient text to "bring it into line with later sensibilities."³³ However, New Testament writers never quote Old Testament texts and then "correct" them. While Stanley concludes that "modern notions of the inviolability of an author's original text simply cannot be transferred to the ancient world,"³⁴ he also inconsistently asserts that such practices of changing earlier texts occur in modern quotations.³⁵ Stanley observes that Heraclitus "can quote two or more verses back-to-back with no indication of their diverse origins [i.e., from different parts of Homer]. In every case the materials thus combined deal with similar topics, producing a single 'quotation' that better supports or exemplifies the author's [Heraclitus'] point."³⁶ He offers a specific example:

> One peculiarity worth noting is a single instance in which an introductory formula that anticipates a quotation concerning Athena . . . is actually followed by a "quotation" that combines one passage on Athena with another that originally referred to Artemis. Though a memory lapse is always possible, it may be that here again one sees a certain willingness on the part of the author to adapt the Homeric text to his own purposes.³⁷

If this is not a memory lapse, then it is an interpretive attempt to describe Athena with the attributes of Artemis.³⁸ However, both quotations appear to be from Homer, rather than Homer and a different author.

None of Stanley's evidence parallels attributing a specific quotation to an author (like "Isaiah") that was not really from that author. Indeed, while his survey of Greco-Roman authors focuses on their quotations of Homer, nowhere does any author attribute to Homer statements that come from another author.³⁹ But Stanley cites the following statements from 1 Esdras that may have a bearing on this discussion:

> And they were servants to him and to his sons until the Persians began to reign, in fulfilment of the word of the Lord by the mouth of Jeremiah: "Until the land has enjoyed its sabbaths, it shall keep sabbath all the time of its desolation until the completion of seventy years." (1 Esd 1:57–58 [= 1:54–55, Rahlfs LXX ed.])

---

quoted from a pseudepigraphic book, presumably because they believed that these books lacked divine, canonical authority.

33. Stanley, *Paul and the Language of Scripture*, 274. For example, later writers may correct an ancient author's wrong geographical reference or a statement apparently contrary to the morality of a later age. Sometimes such "corrections" consist of additional statements set alongside the original without comment.

34. Ibid., 274.

35. Ibid., 356.

36. Ibid., 283–84.

37. Ibid., 284.

38. For a similar move by John in Revelation, note the phrase "the one who was and is and is coming," which originated as an epithet for Zeus but was applied to the God of the Bible. For additional examples like this in Acts and Revelation, see G. K. Beale, "Other Religions in New Testament Theology," in *Biblical Faith and Other Religions: An Evangelical Assessment*, ed. D. W. Baker (Grand Rapids: Kregel, 2004), 79–105.

39. See Stanley's conclusion in *Paul and the Language of Scripture*, 339.

In the first year of Cyrus as king of the Persians, that the word of the Lord by the mouth of Jeremiah might be accomplished,

The Lord stirred up the spirit of Cyrus king of the Persians, and he made a proclamation throughout all his kingdom and also put it in writing. (1 Esd 2:1–2)

According to Stanley, in 1 Esd 1:58, "a verse framed as an indirect statement in 2 Chr 36.21 (a midrashic conflation of Jer. 25.12 and Lev. 26.34), appears as a direct quotation and is attributed in its entirety to the prophet Jeremiah."[40] On the surface, one might say that 1 Esdras attributes to Jeremiah words from Moses (Leviticus) and the Chronicler. But the line between what Stanley calls "an indirect statement in 2 Chr 36.21" and "a direct quotation" in 1 Esdras is very thin, since both are introduced by virtually the same formula, "to fulfill the word" [or "for fulfillment of the saying"] of YHWH through the mouth of Jeremiah."[41] The relationship between these texts is evident in the following synopsis (Rahlfs LXX ed.):[42]

Leviticus 26:34	Jeremiah 25:12
τότε εὐδοκήσει ἡ γῆ **τὰ σάββατα αὐτῆς** καὶ **πάσας τὰς ἡμέρας τῆς ἐρημώσεως αὐτῆς** καὶ ὑμεῖς ἔσεσθε ἐν τῇ γῇ τῶν ἐχθρῶν ὑμῶν τότε σαββατιεῖ ἡ γῆ καὶ εὐδοκήσει **τὰ σάββατα αὐτῆς**	καὶ ἐν τῷ **πληρωθῆναι τὰ ἑβδομήκοντα ἔτη** ἐκδικήσω τὸ ἔθνος ἐκεῖνο φησὶν κύριος καὶ θήσομαι αὐτοὺς εἰς ἀφανισμὸν αἰώνιον
*tote eudokēsei hē gē **ta sabbata autēs** kai **pasas tas hēmeras tēs erēmōseōs autēs** kai hymeis esesthe en tē gē tōn echthrōn hymōn tote sabbatiei hē gē kai eudokēsei **ta sabbata autēs***	*kai en tō **plērōthēnai ta hebdomēkonta etē** ekdikēsō to ethnos ekeino phēsin kyrios kai thēsomai autous eis aphanismon aiōnion*
Then the land shall enjoy its sabbaths all the days of its desolation, and you shall be in the land of your enemies; then the land shall also keep its sabbaths."	And when the seventy years are fulfilled, I will take vengeance on that nation, and will make them a perpetual desolation.

2 Chronicles 36:21–22	1 Esdras 1:54–55
τοῦ **πληρωθῆναι** *λόγον κυρίου* *διὰ στόματος Ιερεμιου* *ἕως τοῦ* προσδέξασθαι **τὴν γῆν τὰ σάββατα αὐτῆς** σαββατίσαι **πάσας** τὰς ἡμέρας **τῆς ἐρημώσεως αὐτῆς** ἐσαββάτισεν *εἰς συμπλήρωσιν ἐτῶν* **ἑβδομήκοντα** μετὰ τὸ **πληρωθῆναι** ῥῆμα κυρίου διὰ στόματος Ιερεμιου	*εἰς ἀναπλήρωσιν τοῦ ῥήματος τοῦ κυρίου* *ἐν στόματι Ιερεμιου* *ἕως τοῦ* εὐδοκῆσαι **τὴν γῆν τὰ σάββατα αὐτῆς** **πάντα** τὸν χρόνον **τῆς ἐρημώσεως αὐτῆς** σαββατιεῖ *εἰς συμπλήρωσιν ἐτῶν* **ἑβδομήκοντα**

---

40. Ibid., 309.
41. These renderings of the Greek are my own.
42. The bold font highlights common features.

tou plērōthēnai logon kyriou	*eis anaplērōsin tou rhēmatos tou kyriou*
dia stomatos Ieremiou	*en stomati Ieremiou*
heōs tou prosdexasthai *tēn gēn ta sabbata autēs*	*heōs tou* eudokēsai *tēn gēn ta sabbata autēs*
sabbatisai **pasas** *tas hēmeras*	**panta** *ton chronon*
tēs erēmōseōs autēs esabbatisen	*tēs erēmōseōs autēs sabbatiei*
eis symplērōsin etōn hebdomēkonta	*eis symplērōsin etōn hebdomēkonta*
meta to plērōthēnai rhēma kyriou	
dia stomatos Ieremiou	

. . . that the word of the LORD	. . . in fulfillment of the word of the Lord
by the mouth of Jeremiah might be fulfilled	by the mouth of Jeremiah;
until the land should enjoy its sabbaths	until the land has enjoyed its sabbaths,
in resting [and] sabbath-keeping	it shall keep sabbath
all the days of its desolation	all the time of its desolation
until the fulfillment of seventy years . . .	until the completion of the seventy years.
after the fulfillment of the word of the LORD	
by the mouth of Jeremiah.	

The chart above demonstrates that 1 Esd 1:54b–55 is essentially a quotation of 2 Chr 36:21.[43] Therefore, like 2 Chr 36:21, 1 Esd 1:54b–55 attributes this statement to Jeremiah. Stanley correctly notes that 2 Chronicles itself combines Lev 26:34 and Jer 25:12. However, the problem is not how 1 Esdras could attribute to Jeremiah a saying that includes what Moses said, but how the Chronicler could do so.[44] The following answer seems plausible: Jeremiah could be developing Leviticus (though it does so more conceptually than verbally), or the Chronicler could understand Jeremiah to be developing Leviticus, and so he combines the two. It seems the Chronicler attributes the entire saying to Jeremiah because that is the part of the prophecy that he mainly had in mind; Leviticus was subsumed interpretively in Jeremiah. This is classic midrash, in which one key biblical text is combined with another in order to be interpreted by it. The Chronicler does not cite a segment of chapters and attribute them to an author who really did not write them. Rather, the Chronicler interprets one verse in Jeremiah by another verse in Leviticus. His primary concern is the author he mentions (Jeremiah), whom he interprets by borrowing from the secondary author (Moses in Leviticus).[45]

Therefore, this is not an issue of authorship but of midrashic interpretation. The same phenomenon occurs with the attribution of Malachi to Isaiah in Mark 1:2–3. Rikki Watts has demonstrated that this happened because Isaiah dominates Mark throughout the book[46] and that other Old Testament references throughout

---

43. Indeed, 1 Esd 1:1–2:5 essentially copies 2 Chr 35:1–36:23 verbatim.

44. However, 1 Esdras also appears to supplement two additional words from Leviticus, under the influence of the precedent-setting 2 Chronicles, which had already combined other parts of Leviticus with Jeremiah: εὐδοκήσει (*eudokēsei*) and σαββατιεῖ (*sabbatiei*)— though the latter involves only a minor change in verbal form.

45. Stanley concludes his discussion by noting the lack of clarity in the 1 Esdras quotation: "The origins of this conflation and adaptation remain obscure [in 1 Esd 1:55]" (*Paul and the Language of Scripture*, 309). Therefore, one should be cautious about basing too much on this example.

46. Note especially Mark's describing Jesus as inaugurating the end-time second exodus predicted by Isaiah.

Mark supplement interpretively the Isaianic picture.[47] Reading Isa 40:3 in the light of Malachi suggests that Malachi has been subsumed interpretively into Isaiah.[48] This does not point to a forgetful memory, a stylistic convention, or an author mistakenly understood to have written a passage that he did not actually write.[49]

It is possible that in some cases only the primary text to be interpreted is mentioned. Since in 1 Esd 1:54–55 several secondary texts have been used to interpret the focus text, it would have been too cumbersome to mention all three texts or their authors.[50]

If Isa 40–66 represents one large midrashic interpretation of the preceding part of Isaiah, then Jesus could attribute parts of this latter section to the prophet Isaiah, even though not they were not written by him; the anonymous author of Isa 40–66 has interpretively expanded the focus text of the first part of the book called and penned by "Isaiah." However, this phenomenon belongs to the Jewish pseudepigraphical genre, which, as we have shown, suggests an unlikely context for the production of Isa 40–66. Citing specific quotations or combining parts of verses for interpretive purposes—which is the topic of concern here—is a different matter.

Jesus' References to "Isaiah" and Accommodation to Incorrect Jewish Traditions

Some who reject the view that New Testament references to Isaiah followed an understandable stylistic convention, as just discussed above, might contend that early Judaism's and Christianity's belief in the authorship of Isaiah was historically incorrect and that this conviction was part of their socially constructed tradition. Therefore, Jesus naturally expressed this belief, since he not only had a divine nature but he was also human, speaking Aramaic and accepting customs of his Jewish culture, presumably including unbiblical traditions that were historically inaccurate. As part of the "kenosis" theory of Christ's incarnation, Jesus "emptied himself" or "gave up the use" of his divine attributes. Accordingly, he was in part a typical person of his time and culture, naturally and unconsciously accepting some false traditions of that culture, which may be referred to as Jesus' "unconscious accommodation" to his culture.

---

47. On which see Rikki E. Watts, *Isaiah's New Exodus in Mark*, WUNT 88 (Tübingen: Mohr Siebeck, 1997), 53–90.

48. Malachi 3:1 alludes to the leading angel of Exod 23:20 guiding Israel in the first exodus, which fits well with the reference to the messenger preparing for the second exodus in Isa 40:3.

49. For a similar phenomenon in Matt 27:9–10 (Jeremiah and Zechariah are combined, but the entire passage is attributed to Jeremiah), see D. A. Carson, *Matthew, Chapters 13 through 28*, Expositor's Bible Commentary (Grand Rapids: Zondervan, 1995), 562–66.

50. This could be the case in Mark 1:2–3, where both Mal 3:1 and Exod 23:20 contribute as secondary texts enhancing the focus text of Isaiah. Watts discusses the influence of Exod 23:20 in Mal 3:1, but concludes that only Malachi is present in Mark 1 (*Isaiah's New Exodus in Mark*, 53–90).

To support this view, some suggest that, though the main thrust of Christ's message was reliable, he admitted his ignorance of certain facts and, therefore, fallibility in his knowledge. In Matt 24:36, he declared that the "day and hour" of the end of history "no one knows, not even the angels of heaven, nor the Son, but the Father alone." However, ignorance of the future is not the same as the making of erroneous statements: if Christ predicted something that did not take place, that would be an error. Ironically, in the verse immediately before Matt 24:36, Jesus had declared, "Heaven and earth will pass away, but my words shall not pass away," which means that the truth of any assertion by him about past, present, or future reality cannot be blunted.[51]

Some postmodern Evangelicals argue that this tradition was not "wrong" for first-century Jews, even though modern historical standards would deem it erroneous. We should not impose our standards of historical correctness on ancient literature. God communicated fully inspired truths to the original readers in their own linguistic and cultural language. However, Jesus declared in Matt 24:35 that no matter how many cultures come and go, his word remains the same. While cultures and even heaven and earth may come and go until Christ returns, Christ's words "will not pass away." The truth of Christ's words is not culturally bound but transcends all cultures and remains unaltered by cultural beliefs. Declared another way in Isa 40:7–8, and quoted in part in Jas 1:10–11 and more fully in 1 Pet 1:24–25, "the grass withers, the flower fades, but the word of our God stands forever" (see also Isa 55:11; Matt 5:17–18). Ancient peoples' categories for observing and assessing the observable world and distinguishing truth from falsehood were commensurate with modern categories in significant respects.[52] Accordingly, Jesus' propositional statements about matters like sin, his deity, his saving death, his resurrection, the final resurrection of humanity, and the end of world history declare truths that transcend all time.

Other postmodern Evangelicals contend that, as the God-man, Jesus may well have known that Isaiah did not author the work that went by his name, but he consciously "accommodated" himself to a false Jewish view to facilitate his own communication of the message from the book. Accordingly, to have exposed the error of the false Jewish tradition about Isaiah would have shifted attention from the main point of his message from Isaiah to a technical point about historical authorship.

---

51. I am grateful to J. I. Packer for this point about the link between Matt 24:35 and 24:36 (*"Fundamentalism" and the Word of God* [Grand Rapids: Eerdmans, 1957], 60–61). In this connection, note also B. B. Warfield's comment on Christology: "[I]n the case of our Lord's person, the human nature remains truly human while yet it can never fall into sin or error because it can never act out of relation with the Divine nature into conjunction with which it has been brought" (*The Inspiration and Authority of the Bible* [Nutley, NJ: Presbyterian & Reformed, 1970], 162–63 [cited by Packer, ibid., 83]). However, I have been unable to find this precise quotation in Warfield's book, though he says as much on pp. 158–76.

52. On which see G. K. Beale, "The Issue of Socially Constructed Cultures, Presuppositions, and Biblical Interpretation," in ch. 1 of *Erosion of Inerrancy in Evangelicalism*, 44–48.

These perspectives reflect a common problem in some Evangelicals' understanding of Christ's "accommodation": obviously, part of Jesus' mission was to con-
front and expose false traditions of Judaism that had developed by the first century
CE.[53] As far back as the late 1950s, J. I. Packer identified this problem when he
concluded that Jesus "did not hesitate to challenge and condemn, on His authority,
many accepted Jewish ideas which seemed to him false;"[54] and that

> Scripture, indeed, contains emphatic warnings against uncritical deference to tradi-
> tions and speculations in theology. Christ deals with the question of the authority of
> tradition in Mk. vii.6–13. The Pharisees claimed their oral law was derived from Moses
> and should therefore be treated as an authoritative supplement to and exposition of
> the written law. Christ rejects this idea, contrasting the written word with the oral law
> as "the commandment *of God*" and "the commandments *of men*" respectively. . . . The
> fact that they are bowing to man-made tradition rather than God-given Scripture, He
> says, shows that their hearts are far from God. To Christ, ecclesiastical tradition was no
> part of the word of God; it must be tested by Scripture and, if found wanting, dropped.[55]

Significantly, the Jews believed that since a well-known Old Testament figure,
Moses, was the author of their oral law,[56] the authority of their oral laws equaled
the authority of written Scripture that had come from Moses. Jesus rejected this
view. In fact, in Mark 7:1–13, he contrasts Isaiah's prophesying (v. 6, citing Isa 29:13)
and Moses' written word (v. 10), both of which had divine authority, with "the
tradition of the elders," which lacked divine authority. While Jesus opposed the
pseudo-authority of untrue Jewish traditions, he consistently affirmed the authority of the Old Testament (e.g., John 10:35, "the Scripture cannot be broken") and
"never qualified the Jewish belief in its absolute authority in the slightest degree."[57]

This raises the question of whether Jesus could have gone along with a false
Jewish view of the authorship of Isaiah. This seems unlikely, especially since the
Old Testament was foundational for Jesus' teaching about his own vocation and
identity; he appealed repeatedly to the Old Testament as the primary warrant for
what he did and said. Could he, then, have knowingly or unknowingly been wrong
about the identity of the author of what some refer to as the "gospel of Isaiah"? The
significance of this question intensifies when we realize that the book of Isaiah
(especially chs. 40–66) was formative for the Gospel of Mark[58] and the book of

---

53. On which see further N. B. Stonehouse, *The Witness of Matthew and Mark to Christ*
(Philadelphia: Presbyterian Guardian, 1944; repr. Grand Rapids: Eerdmans, 1958), 195–211;
R. V. G. Tasker, *The Old Testament in the New Testament* (Grand Rapids: Eerdmans, 1954),
32. I am thankful to Packer, *"Fundamentalism" and the Word of God*, 56n2, for alerting me
to these two sources.

54. *"Fundamentalism" and the Word of God*, 55.

55. Ibid., 70–71.

56. On which see Jacob Neusner, "Rabbinic Literature: Mishnah and Tosefta," in *Dictionary of New Testament Background: A Compendium of Contemporary Biblical Scholarship*,
ed. C. A. Evans and S. E. Porter (Downers Grove, IL: InterVarsity Press, 2000), 895.

57. Packer, *"Fundamentalism" and the Word of God*, 55.

58. On which see Watts, *Isaiah's New Exodus in Mark*.

Acts,[59] and that it underlay the other Gospels.[60] Had Jesus been wrong in his view of Isaiah's authorship, we would have no reason to trust him in his appeals to the Old Testament elsewhere.[61] As R. V. G. Tasker has concluded, "If He [Christ] could be mistaken on matters which He regarded as of the strictest relevance to His own person and ministry, it is difficult to see exactly how or why He can or should be trusted anywhere else."[62]

Reconsideration of the Material in the Book of Isaiah Itself

Superscriptions referring to "Isaiah" occur repeatedly in the book of Isaiah itself:

Isaiah 1:1

> The *vision of Isaiah* the son of Amoz concerning Judah and Jerusalem, which he saw during the reigns of Uzziah, Jotham, Ahaz and Hezekiah, kings of Judah.

Isaiah 2:1

> *The word which Isaiah the son of Amoz saw* concerning Judah and Jerusalem.

Isaiah 13:1

> *The oracle concerning Babylon which Isaiah the son of Amoz saw.*

Isaiah 20:2

> At that time *the Lord spoke through Isaiah the son of Amoz, saying,* "Go and loosen . . ."

Note also the witness of 2 Chr 26:22: "Now the rest of the acts of Uzziah, first to last, *the prophet Isaiah, the son of Amoz, has written.*" Based on this evidence, I agree with Richard Schultz's conclusion about the superscriptions and prefer the traditional view of Isaianic authorship for the whole book.[63] According to Schultz,

---

59. David Pao, *Acts and the Isaianic New Exodus,* WUNT 2/130 (Tübingen: Mohr Siebeck, 2002).

60. See Brendsel, *"Isaiah Saw His Glory,"* 214–20, who argues that the new exodus of Isa 40–55 was formative for John's gospel. For significant influence of Isaiah in Luke, see M. L. Strauss, *The Davidic Messiah in Luke-Acts: The Promise and Its Fulfillment in Lukan Christology,* JSNTSup 110 (Sheffield: JSOT Press, 1995).

61. Packer, *"Fundamentalism" and the Word of God,* 60, though Packer speaks generally about Christ's view of the authority of the Old Testament, rather than focusing merely on Jesus' appeals to Isaiah.

62. Tasker, *Old Testament in the New Testament,* 37.

63. Schultz has recently presented a brief but viable conservative view of the unity of the book: "How Many Isaiahs Were There?," *Areopagus Journal: The Journal of the Apologetics Resource Center* (Spring 2012): 16–23. See also his monograph *The Search for Quotation: Verbal Parallels in the Prophets,* JSOTSup 180 (Sheffield: Sheffield Academic, 1999), which focuses not on authorship issues but on intertextuality in the Old Testament, with a particular focus on Isaiah.

Given 1) the clear assertion in Isaiah 1:1 that what follows is "the vision of Isaiah son of Amoz, which he saw concerning Judah and Jerusalem in the days of Uzziah, Jotham, Ahaz, and Hezekiah, kings of Judah" and 2) the absence of any additional ascriptions of authorship within the book, the "one Isaiah" position may be the only one that takes the book's own claims seriously.[64]

Scholars have reconsidered the authorship of Isa 40–66 because this section reflects specific awareness of circumstances in Babylon, and it addresses those who were in exile there instead of Isaiah's earlier audience in the land of Israel.[65] These facts fit the presupposition of the majority of Old Testament scholars, who insist that prophecy had to be relevant primarily for the prophet's contemporary audience and could not predict events that had no relevance for the present. Therefore, they view most predictions as *vaticinium ex eventu* utterances ("prophecy after the event"). Events that had happened recently were written down as if they had been prophesied many years, or even centuries, earlier. Accordingly, those who argue that chapters 40–66 were written by a different hand than chapters 1–39 believe that that person lived after (or perhaps during) the time the prophecies were fulfilled, but that he wrote history to make it look like prophecy. However, a minority of scholars holding to non-Isaianic authorship of Isa 40–66 still affirm that the anonymous author of these chapters lived in exile in Babylon and genuinely prophesied concerning events soon to happen (in thirty to forty years or so).

But Isa 13 is as specific as and even more extreme than chapters 40–66 in its portrayal of the decisive judgment of Babylon at the hand of the Persians. This chapter begins: "The oracle concerning Babylon which Isaiah the son of Amoz saw." A superscription like this suggests that Isa 40–66 could have been written by "Isaiah the prophet" only if he had a vision of the future. The "oracle" that follows Isa 13:1 includes 14:1–23, which declares repeatedly that Israel was in bondage to Babylon, that Babylon would be judged, and that Israel would be restored from Babylon. Similarly, Isa 21:1–2 refers to Isaiah's "oracle"/"vision" that concerns the judgment of Babylon ("Fallen, fallen is Babylon," 21:9). Many commentators date Isa 13–14 and parts of 21:1–10 late as well,[66] and many date Isa 24–27 late, in part because of its eschatology (e.g., resurrection, Israel's restoration, etc.).[67] I find these arguments unpersuasive, not just because they are driven by questionable presuppositions, but, more fundamentally, because I think they misread the evidence. First, continuing the pattern in Isa 6–21 (fifteen times), the first-person pronoun "I" in 24:16 and in 25:1 must also refer to Isaiah the prophet. Furthermore, Isa 24:16 ("But I say, 'Woe to me! Woe to me! Alas for me!'") uniquely resembles Isa 6:5 within the book of Isaiah ("Then I said, 'Woe is me, for I am ruined!'"). The

---

64. Schultz, "How Many Isaiahs Were There and What Does It Matter?," 153.

65. Williamson summarizes many different compositional views not only of Isa 40–55 and 56–66, but also of Isa 1–39 ("Isaiah: Book of," 366–71).

66. With respect to Isa 13–14, see, e.g., Seth Erlandsson, *The Burden of Babylon: A Study of Isaiah 13:2–14:23*, ConBOT 4 (Lund: Gleerup, 1970), as well as Williamson, "Isaiah: Book of," 367.

67. See Williamson, "Isaiah: Book of," 367, who summarizes others.

"I" in Isa 24:16 is likely best identified with the "I" of 6:5, since both employ "woe" together with "I" without linking it with the name "Isaiah," and most scholars agree that the use in Isa 6:5 is, indeed, Isaiah the prophet speaking. (Of course, other scholars might view Isa 24:16 as a later author imitating the earlier Isaiah.)

Second, the word "oracle" (מַשָּׂא, maśśā'; Isa 21:1) occurs twelve times in Isa 13–30, and expressions for "vision" (ח-ז-ה, ḥ-z-h; e.g., Isa 21:2) occur six times in the same segment. Third, the name Isaiah occurs sixteen times in Isa 1–39. The tenfold use of the name in Isa 37–39 seems especially significant, particularly in the reports that Isaiah prophesied the exile to Babylon:

Isaiah 39:3

> Then Isaiah the prophet came to King Hezekiah and said to him, "What did these men say, and from where have they come to you?" And Hezekiah said, "They have come to me from a far country, from Babylon."

Isaiah 39:6

> "Behold, the days are coming when all that is in your house and all that your fathers have laid up in store to this day will be carried to Babylon; nothing will be left," says the LORD.

Isaiah 39:7

> And some of your sons who will issue from you, whom you will beget, will be taken away and they will become officials in the palace of the king of Babylon.

Associated with the prophecies of Israel's bondage to Babylon in chapters 13–14 and of her restoration in chapters 24–27, these predictions of the same events foreseen in Isa 40–66 are not unique. Except for the specific reference to the idols of Babylon (Isa 46:1; cf. 21:9),[68] the main difference between Isa 1–39 and Isa 40–66 involves the extended nature of this latter section. However, even the theme of idolatry in chapters 40–66 is clearly rooted in Isa 1–39.[69] Note, in this respect, for example, Isa 21:1–10:

> The oracle concerning the wilderness of the sea.
> As windstorms in the Negev sweep on,
> It comes from the wilderness, from a terrifying land.
> A harsh vision has been shown to me;
> The treacherous one still deals treacherously, and the destroyer still destroys.
> Go up, Elam, lay siege, Media;
> I have made an end of all the groaning she has caused.
> For this reason my loins are full of anguish;
> Pains have seized me like the pains of a woman in labor.
> I am so bewildered I cannot hear, so terrified I cannot see.

---

68. References to idolatry in general appear in Isa 40:19–20; 42:8, 17; 44:9–20; 45:16–20; 48:5; 57:13; 66:3. Intriguingly, "Babylon" appears nine times in Isa 13–39 and only four times in chs. 40–66.

69. On which see G. K. Beale, "Isaiah 6:9–13: A Retributive Taunt against Idolatry," *VT* 41 (1991): 257–78. See also the expanded comments in G. K. Beale, *We Become What We Worship: A Biblical Theology of Idolatry* (Downers Grove, IL: InterVarsity Press, 2008), 36–70.

My mind reels, horror overwhelms me;
    The twilight I longed for has been turned for me into trembling.
They set the table, they spread out the cloth, they eat, they drink;
    "Rise up, captains, oil the shields,"
For thus the Lord says to me,
    "Go, station the lookout, let him report what he sees.
When he sees riders, horsemen in pairs,
    A train of donkeys, a train of camels,
    Let him pay close attention, very close attention."
Then the lookout called,
    "O Lord, I stand continually by day on the watchtower,
    And I am stationed every night at my guard post.
    Now behold, here comes a troop of riders, horsemen in pairs."
And one said, "Fallen, fallen is Babylon;
    And all the images of her gods are shattered on the ground."
O my threshed people, and my afflicted of the threshing floor!
    What I have heard from the LORD of hosts,
    The God of Israel, I make known to you.

Here Isaiah sees a vision of the fall of Babylon and hears the message from God about this event that will occur several generations after his own, including the judgment of Babylon's idols, a theme expanded on in Isa 40–48. Isaiah 21:2 not only prophesies concerning the fall of Babylon but also explicitly names the nation ("Media") that will defeat Babylon (cf. Isa 13:17). While not as specific, this resembles Isa 44:28 and 45:1–3, 12–13. Is the Isa 21 narrative not virtually equivalent to Isaiah being transported to the future, or seeing a vision of the future, or hearing about it in an oracular manner and then prophesying about it?[70]

The same applies to Isa 2:1–4, which is introduced as "the vision that Isaiah the son of Amoz saw" and prophesies concerning the eschatological temple and the Gentiles streaming to Jerusalem. This is also a specific restoration prophecy of distant eschatological events. If all of Isa 1–39 is from Isaiah's hand, it would seem that the nature of chapters 13–14, 21, 24–27, and 39 especially would assuage one's unease at the same (though more extended) material in Isa 40–66.[71]

During the time of Isaiah the prophet, the Assyrians took the people of the northern kingdom into exile, and "Sennacherib claimed to have conquered forty-six walled cities in Judah and deported more than two hundred thousand of its

---

70. For support of the ideas offered in this paragraph, see Young, *Book of Isaiah*, 2:59–75.

71. Of course, again, if these earlier eight chapters are not from Isaiah, that would change the nature of this conclusion. The most specific prophecy in Isa 40–66 involves the prediction of Cyrus (Isa 44–45). However, this text is a smaller problem for an exilic prophet than for a preexilic prophet, inasmuch as Cyrus could have been reigning at the time of the purported exilic prophet's writing. Although Harrison considers the mention of the name Cyrus a later scribal gloss that does not *necessarily* compromise a "unity of Isaiah" view (*Introduction to the Old Testament*, 794), if genuine prophecy is allowed, then such a prophecy is possible, especially since (1) the coming Messiah is specifically predicted, (2) the "Medes" are already anticipated in chs. 13 and 21, and (3) in all parts of Isaiah predictive prophecy provides evidence of God's sovereignty over history.

citizens."[72] Combined with the fact that Babylon was already emerging (see Isa 39), it makes sense that Isaiah would have foreseen captives belonging eventually to Babylon (which he actually predicted in ch. 39) and that Israel must be restored from Babylon in the future.

The appeal by early Jewish writers and the authors of the New Testament to "Isaiah" as the author of Isa 40–66 underscores in part God's ability to predict the end from the beginning, even in cases involving long-range prophecies. These early authors seem to have read Isa 40–66 at face value, believing that this portion of the book, like chapters 1–39, was written by Isaiah long before the exile and restoration. To claim that the predictions in Isa 40–66 were not predictions of the future but history written to appear as prophecy obscures and nullifies the fundamental polemic of Isa 40–66, namely, idols' inability to predict the future. Although technically affirming real predictions, to say that an anonymous prophet living during the exile issued actual short-term prophecies suggests that such predictions resembled prognostications regarding weather or politics. Presumably, living close to the events that he prophesied, the author was able from the human perspective to predict what would happen. Nevertheless, even according to the short-range view, that these events actually happened as predicted demonstrates the divine inspiration of the prophecies. It requires special pleading to say that, although the prophecies came from an anonymous exilic prophet living on the verge of the events prophesied, such events were in the prophetic mind of God centuries earlier. Even short-range prophecy dilutes the argument that idols cannot make long-range predictions. While it may be admitted that short-range prophecy is found in both the Old and New Testaments, the Isaianic statements involve a long-range perspective, as the following texts support. These long-range predictions of Israel's restoration from Babylonian exile continue a theme begun before the Assyrian exile, most likely by Isaiah the prophet:

Isaiah 40:21
> Do you not know? Have you not heard?
> Has it not been declared to you from the beginning?
> Have you not understood from the foundations of the earth?

Isaiah 41:4
> Who has performed and accomplished it,
> Calling forth the generations from the beginning?
> "I, the LORD, am the first, and with the last. I am He."

Isaiah 41:26
> Who has declared this from the beginning, that we might know?
> Or from former times, that we may say, "He is right!"?
> Surely there was no one who declared,
> Surely there was no one who proclaimed,
> Surely there was no one who heard your words.

---

72. Schultz, "How Many Isaiahs Were There and What Does It Matter?," 164.

Isaiah 44:6–8
> Thus says the LORD, the King of Israel and his Redeemer, the LORD of hosts:
> "I am the first and I am the last,
> And there is no God besides Me.
> Who is like Me? Let him proclaim and declare it;
> Yes, let him recount it to Me in order,
> From the time that I established the ancient nation.
> And let them declare to them the things that are coming
> And the events that are going to take place.
> Do not tremble and do not be afraid;
> Have I not long since announced it to you and declared it?
> And you are My witnesses.
> Is there any God besides Me,
> Or is there any other Rock?
> I know of none."

Isaiah 46:10–11
> . . . declaring the end from the beginning,
> And from ancient times things which have not been done,
> Saying, "My purpose will be established,
> And I will accomplish all My good pleasure";
> Calling a bird of prey from the east,
> The man of My purpose from a far country.
> Truly I have spoken; truly I will bring it to pass.
> I have planned it, surely I will do it.

Isaiah 48:3, 5–6
> I declared the former things long ago
> And they went forth from My mouth, and I proclaimed them.
> Suddenly I acted, and they came to pass.
> . . .
> Therefore I declared them to you long ago,
> Before they took place I proclaimed them to you,
> So that you would not say, "My idol has done them,
> And my graven image and my molten image have commanded them."
> You have heard; look at all this.
> And you, will you not declare it?
> I proclaim to you new things from this time,
> Even hidden things which you have not known.[73]

---

73. Cf. also Isa 43:9–19. Though compare the following text, which uses the same language as the above Isaiah texts in affirming that the king of Assyria's recent past victories over other nations were planned long ago by God:
> Have you not heard?
> Long ago I did it,
> From ancient times I planned it.
> Now I have brought it to pass,
> That you should turn fortified cities into ruinous heaps. (Isa 37:26)

The New Testament concurs that Old Testament prophets made long-range predictions. For example, 1 Pet 1:10–12 affirms,

> As to this salvation, the prophets who prophesied of the grace that would come to you made careful searches and inquiries, seeking to know what person or time the Spirit of Christ within them was indicating as He predicted the sufferings of Christ and the glories to follow. It was revealed to them that they were not serving themselves, but you, in these things which now have been announced to you through those who preached the gospel to you by the Holy Spirit sent from heaven—things into which angels long to look.

This statement underscores that Israel's prophets consciously predicted events that would occur in the distant future.[74] This contradicts the presupposition of many in the contemporary Old Testament guild that what appears to be predictive prophecy was really "prophecy after (or during) the fact"[75] and that true prophecy was restricted only to messages relevant for audiences contemporary with the prophets.[76]

The text from 1 Peter is significant particularly because Peter's purview involved Old Testament prophecies like Isa 40:6–8 and Isa 53 (which predicted the restoration of Israel).[77] Because of the guild's presuppositions regarding the importance of prophecy for the prophet's contemporary audience, the texts cited above are typically attributed to "Second Isaiah," rather than to the prophet Isaiah himself. However, 1 Pet 1:10–12 connects these very texts to the programmatic statement about long-range prophecy. Indeed, New Testament writers understand that Isa 53 was fulfilled in Christ, which means that some prophet predicted the Messiah's coming long before the event (i.e., seven centuries, if it be granted that the prophet is Isaiah son of Amoz; cf. Matt 8:17; Mark 15:28; Acts 8:28–35). This being the case, it is not difficult to believe that, two centuries before the event, Isaiah could have predicted Israel's return from Babylonian captivity or the rise of Cyrus, who would be instrumental in that restoration (Isa 45:1–13).[78]

---

74. For additional New Testament passages making the same point, see Matt 13:16–17; John 8:56; and Heb 11:13.

75. According to Williamson, if the long-range prophecies are *vaticinium ex eventu*, "there is still predictive prophecy included in all parts of the book even on the most radical of critical positions" ("Isaiah: Book of," 367). Since Williamson tends to view the prophecies in Isa 13–14, 24–27, and 40–66 as "prophecies after (or during) the fact," it would have been helpful for him to identify those prophecies.

76. See Williamson, "Isaiah: Book of," 367, who views long-range prophecy (which he deems unintelligible to the original recipients) as flying "in the face of Christian understandings of the word of God, seen ultimately in incarnation." Christian understanding of prophecy certainly includes both "forthtelling" for the present and "foretelling" for the distant future, even if such prophecy exhibited an element of imminence.

77. With Isa 40:6–8 compare 1 Pet 1:24–25, and with Isa 53 compare 1 Pet 2:22–25, which alludes repeatedly to Isa 53. On these texts, see, most recently, D. A. Carson, "1 Peter," in *Commentary on the New Testament Use of the Old Testament*, ed. G. K. Beale and D. A. Carson (Grand Rapids: Baker, 2007), 1019–22, 1033–35.

78. Following Schultz, "How Many Isaiahs Were There and What Does It Matter?," 162–63.

Critics of the view proposed here tend to argue that the New Testament writers did not share the perspective of their Old Testament counterparts, and that the authorship of Isaiah may be settled only by studying the book itself. This response is fueled by two notions. The first—which is related to the fact that the study of the Old Testament is a separate discipline from the study of the New Testament—is that the New Testament's interpretation of the Old Testament is secondary and often misrepresents truth or original meanings as presented in the Old Testament. According to this view, the New Testament reflects primarily the evolved beliefs and traditions of first-century Judaism. The second notion is that the Bible is not fully inspired, which means there is no ultimate divine author of the whole and that the New Testament's commentary on the Old (e.g., the authorship of Isaiah) is unreliable. There are Old Testament scholars, indeed, who believe in the inspiration of the entire Bible yet hold to multiple Isaiahs, though I have tried to point out the inconsistencies of such a view. In this essay, I have argued that reasonable and cogent arguments for the unity of Isaiah are found within the book. Furthermore, I contend that the New Testament provides vital evidence for discussions of the authorship issue that reinforce arguments for the unity of authorship based on the book of Isaiah itself.

Based on the degree of "intratextuality" (some would say "intertextuality") between Isa 1–39 and 40–66, many Isaiah scholars who hold to multiple authorship for the book recognize a "final literary unity."[79] However, the line between "unity of authorship" and "final literary unity" is becoming increasingly fine, and Schultz points us in the right direction:

> Rather, the issue is whether we legitimately can posit a series of inspired authors or editors when the involvement of multiple "prophets" is *not* acknowledged in the text and when one of the reasons for positing such a complex compositional process is the claim that the Spirit of God *could not* (or at least probably *did* not) reveal the diversity of contents identified in the book of Isaiah to just one individual.[80]

The critical position raises many additional questions. If Isa 40–66 was written by an unknown prophet, why was it attached to Isaiah's book (Isa 1–39)? Why was it not preserved as a separate book and placed after Isaiah, without any attribution of authorship? Such an extended composition (twenty-seven chapters) attributed to a pseudonymous author finds no precedent or analogue in the Old Testament.

The Possibility of Minor Editing of Isaiah

One final question remains: Does minor updating or editing of Isaiah nullify or undermine the New Testament's witness to the fact that the entire book of Isaiah was written by one author? Recently, J. H. Wood has criticized Oswald Allis for

---

79. See ibid., 169.
80. Ibid., 161.

admitting that the account of Moses' death at the end of the Pentateuch was written not by Moses but by a subsequent editor, which is to say that not every word in the Pentateuch comes from Moses' pen, but for not also granting the same for the book of Isaiah. Wood has asked, "if the NT authors assert that the Pentateuch is from Moses even though he did not write every word, then is it possible that NT ascriptions of Isaianic origin do not necessarily imply that the eighth-century prophet wrote every word?"[81] This critique assumes that allowance for some statements as not being originally from Moses or Isaiah dilutes New Testament ascriptions of Mosaic and Isaianic authorship to the Pentateuch and the book of Isaiah and raises questions about the traditional view of authorship of these two corpora. However, as Wood recognizes, this view of authorship is unnecessarily legalistic and narrow. The notion of single authorship does not demand that every word was written verbatim by that author. Two examples will suffice. Clearly, much of what Moses said in the Pentateuch was written down by scribes, and this scribal record has become the written pentateuchal record.[82] Although these scribes may have exercised some liberty in their recording, it is unlikely that Moses and subsequent religious officials would have allowed such scribal records to circulate if they did not genuinely reflect Moses' speech.

Similarly, while it is unlikely that Paul did not write any part of the epistle to the Romans, Rom 16:22 explicitly identifies Tertius as his secretary who wrote down what he dictated. Nevertheless, the epistle has always been called Paul's Epistle to the Romans because he, not Tertius, was responsible for the book. In the first century CE, dictation happened either by reading a whole segment of a work and having the secretary transcribe it at the end, or by having the scribe copy a text syllable by syllable.[83] The former mode probably allowed for some creative composition by the secretary. Even if Tertius transcribed Paul's words in this way, the letter would have been read back to the apostle to ensure that the text said what Paul intended. But this means that, even if at various points we may not have Paul's exact words, we certainly hear his clear conceptual "voice." For example, Paul begins his letter to the Romans by declaring that it is from him to them (Rom 1:1–7), rather than from Tertius to the Romans.[84] Similarly, Oswald Allis could rightfully see Moses as the ultimate author of the Pentateuch, even if he did not write every word. The record of Moses' death (Deut 34) was probably intended as a transition to the book of Joshua. Moses may have commissioned its author—perhaps one of his scribes or even Joshua[85]—to record this event after the fact. Even so, the New

---

81. John H. Wood, "Oswald T. Allis and the Question of Isaianic Authorship," *JETS* 48 (2005): 256–57.

82. On which see, for example, Daniel I. Block, "Recovering the Voice of Moses: The Genesis of Deuteronomy," *JETS* 44 (2001): 385–408.

83. See Cicero, *Att.* 13.25.3.

84. The same applies to 1 Pet 5:12, where Peter identifies Sylvanus as his secretary for the letter.

85. In light of the repeated references to his commissioning by Moses, Joshua is an excellent candidate (cf. Num 27:18–23; Deut 3:27–28; 31:7–23; 34:9; Josh 1:1).

Testament writers could attribute the entire Pentateuch to Moses because it was ultimately from him—his handprint is over the whole.[86]

Isaiah may well have had scribes and disciples who wrote down his discourses, which might account for variations of literary style within the book. Furthermore, later inspired editors could have engaged in minor editing of Isaiah's prophecies. But the conceptual essence of each prophecy must stem from the historical Isaiah, and each prophecy bears his handprint. This is not unlike the situation with the Gospels. Gospel writers may have paraphrased Jesus' sayings, thereby preserving distinctive nuances that may not have been explicit when Jesus spoke them. Nevertheless, the later evangelists brought out Jesus' true intention without altering the conceptual essence of his utterances. This also resembles the kind of creative secretarial activity spoken of above with respect to Paul.

Even if Isaiah did not write down every word found in the book that bears his name, like the compositions attributed to Moses, the apostles and New Testament writers could rightly attribute prophetic sayings throughout Isaiah to the prophet Isaiah; Isaiah's historical, conceptual handprint pervades the whole. Some acknowledge that Isa 40–66 may have an Isaianic core upon which later editors built and expanded, but they argue that no one is able to identify precisely what words or sections derive from Isaiah and which come from his editors.[87] This position is too loose. It seems that each prophecy derives entirely from the historical Isaiah in a conceptual sense, though some words and phrases may have been altered later for interpretive purposes. The position laid out here requires further refinement and elaboration, but limitations of space preclude this.[88]

Conclusion

Of the views on the authorship of Isaiah presented above, the only perspective that is compatible with the use of Isaiah in the New Testament is the one that understands that the actual prophet Isaiah wrote the entire book that goes by that name. Other views conflict with the traditional evangelical notion of the inspiration of Scripture, treating the repeated New Testament references to Isaiah ultimately as an irrelevant husk that contains the "true" message of the particular Isaiah texts being quoted. For such views, this irrelevant husk plays no significant role in determining what Scripture *intends* to say. This is what I have argued against throughout this essay. I think that this amounts to the "insignificant part" of Scripture not being inspired, and thus this leads to a limited view of the inspiration of the Bible and of

---

86. Significantly, the record of Moses' death (Deut 34:5–8) is never specifically attributed to Moses.

87. See the earlier reference to Ridderbos, "Isaiah: Book of," 513–16. Similarly Schultz, "How Many Isaiahs Were There and What Does It Matter?," 158–59.

88. For example, further work needs to be done on how the genres of the Pentateuch, the Gospels, and epistolary literature bear upon the issue of secretarial/scribal/editorial work.

Jesus Christ himself, who accordingly could make errors even in his affirmations about holy Scripture itself. Though those with whom I disagree, especially Evangelicals holding to multiple Isaiahs, might cry "foul" and say that I am mischaracterizing their view at this point, it is difficult for me to see that this is not what their view inevitably entails.

Packer's conclusion about proposals concerning pseudonymity of New Testament books applies equally to Old Testament books:

> [The] position, that their canonicity cannot be affirmed if their authenticity is denied, thus seems to be the only one possible; and we may lay it down as a general principle that, when biblical books specify their own authorship, the affirmation of their canonicity involves a denial of their pseudonymity. Pseudonymity and canonicity are mutually exclusive.[89]

The goal of this essay has been to demonstrate that the New Testament's repeated affirmation of Isaiah as the personal author of the entire book with that name is so sufficiently clear and reasonable that to maintain multiple authorship leads unavoidably down one path: that the New Testament writers and Jesus were mistaken in their conviction about the authorship of the book of Isaiah. For some scholars, this conclusion may not be problematic, but for those with a high view of Scripture, this position is difficult to hold.

The clear New Testament stance on this subject reinforces the evidence provided by the book of Isaiah itself that the prophet Isaiah authored the complete book. The New Testament view of a single author for Isaiah also provides the best explanation for the book's literary and theological unity that many Old Testament scholars over the past two decades have recognized, even while crediting that unity to final redactors. The authorship of Isaiah should not be a litmus test for a biblical view of the inspiration of Scripture, any more than any other aspect of Scripture that is not being affirmed as true. However, in recent times it has become apparent that one's position on this issue reflects one's overall view of the authority of Scripture.

---

89. Packer, *"Fundamentalism" and the Word of God*, 184.

The Composition of the Book of Isaiah in Jewish Tradition

MICHAEL W. GRAVES

Introduction

The common assumption in ancient Jewish sources is that the book of Isaiah consists of divine pronouncements spoken by the prophet Isaiah. Yet, one cannot describe a single Jewish view on the composition of the book of Isaiah. The first and perhaps most significant complication is that the topic of the actual writing of the book received little attention in Jewish sources of the Greco-Roman and early Byzantine periods. A second complication is that Jewish texts that appear to address the human authorship of Isaiah do not all present the same picture. Differences can already be found in classical Jewish sources, and the range of ideas expressed by Jewish scholars on the origins of the book of Isaiah have only increased in modern times. The goal of this essay is to present and explain the most important indications in ancient and medieval Jewish sources that touch on the human authorship of Isaiah, and also to provide some sense of how Jewish thinking on this topic has developed in recent years in light of modern biblical criticism.

Early Jewish Views on the Writing of Isaiah

The earliest references that offer any sort of window into early Jewish opinions about the authorship of the book of Isaiah come from the late Second Temple period. A few of these references are general in nature and indicate only the association of Isaiah with the entirety of the book. Thus, Sir 48:24–25 states that Isaiah, who is mentioned by name, "saw the last things and comforted those mourning in Zion," and "made known what will take place until the end of time, and hidden things before they happen."[1] The statement alludes to the second half of the book of Isaiah (see Isa 40:1), and in particular to the passages that speak to YHWH's capacity to make known the future (Isa 41:26; 42:9; 45:21; 46:10; 48:3–8). Numerous New Testament texts also mention Isaiah, often as the speaker of a prophecy, in connection with quotations from the second half of the book of Isaiah, including

---

1. J. Ziegler, *Sapientia Iesu Filii Sirach*, Septuaginta: Vetus Testamentum Graecum Auctoritate Societatis Litterarum Gottingensis editum XII.2 (Göttingen: Vandenhoeck & Ruprecht, 1965), 354. All English translations in this essay are my own.

Isa 40:3 (Matt 3:3; Mark 1:2; John 1:23), 40:3–5 (Luke 3:4), 42:1–3 (Matt 12:17), 53:1 (John 12:38; Rom 10:16), 53:4 (Matt 8:17), 53:7–8 (Acts 8:28, 30), 61:1–2 (Luke 4:17), and 65:1 (Rom 10:20). On at least three occasions Philo quotes or alludes to the book of Isaiah, introducing these traditions simply as the saying of a prophet (Isa 54:1; *Rewards* 158–59), as the oration of a prophet (Isa 48:22; *Names* 169), and as a saying of one of the ancient prophets who spoke under divine inspiration (Isa 5:7; *Dreams* 2.172–73), without specifically identifying Isaiah by name.

The historian Josephus portrays Isaiah as an author who accurately predicted future events. Josephus' summary comment on Isaiah is as follows:

> This prophet was recognized as godly and extraordinary in truthfulness, confident that he had never spoken anything that was false. He wrote everything that he prophesied in books, and he left these books so that people in the future would commend them as true based on the events coming to pass. (*Ant.* 10.35)[2]

A first significant point is that Josephus portrays Isaiah as writing his own prophecies in books. Josephus similarly depicts Jeremiah and Ezekiel as authors, underscoring their prestige and reliability.[3] Josephus criticizes pagan Greek historians for their contradictory reports and lack of reliable records (*Ag. Ap.* 1.3–5, 8), and it no doubt suited his purpose to show what precise and careful records had been handed down among the Jews.

A second key point is that Isaiah's essential role in Josephus' narrative is to prophesy future events.[4] When threatened by the Assyrians, Hezekiah's confidence was strengthened by Isaiah's assurance of safety specifically because Isaiah could accurately predict the future (*Ant.* 9.276; 10.12–13, 16–17). Josephus states that Isaiah secretly predicted two hundred and ten years ahead of time that Cyrus would send the Jews back to their land and rebuild the Jerusalem temple. In fact, according to Josephus, Cyrus was stirred to act on these matters by reading what Isaiah had written about him so many years in advance, one hundred and forty years before the temple was destroyed (*Ant.* 11.5–7). Josephus claims that the Jewish temple built by Onias IV ca. 160 CE at Leontopolis in Egypt was the fulfillment of Isa 19:19, "an ancient prediction made some six hundred years before" (*J. W.* 7.432), and that Onias himself referred to the Isaiah text in justifying this temple (*Ant.* 13.68).[5]

---

2. B. Niese, ed., *Flavii Iosephi Opera*, 2nd ed. (Berlin: Weidmann, 1955), 2:338.

3. On Jeremiah as the author of a lament for Josiah (see 2 Chr 35:25) and Ezekiel as the author of "two books," on the destruction of Jerusalem and the fall of Babylon, see *Ant.* 10.79–80. On the classical prophets as authors in Josephus, see Christopher T. Begg, "The 'Classical Prophets' in Josephus' *Antiquities*," *LS* 13 (1988): 350, 352, 355, 357.

4. Josephus frequently refers to Isaiah as a "prophet" even in places where the underlying biblical source does not do so; see Louis H. Feldman, *Studies in Josephus' Rewritten Bible* (Leiden: Brill, 1998), 389. Also, Josephus does not mention Isaiah's unfulfilled prophecy regarding Hezekiah's illness in Isa 38:1; see Christopher T. Begg, *Josephus' Story of the Later Monarchy (AJ 9,1–10,185)* (Leuven: Peeters, 2000), 439.

5. On Isa 19:18–25 and the Jewish temple at Leontopolis, see Emil Schürer, Geza Vermes, Fergus Millar, and Martin Goodman, eds., *The History of the Jewish People in the Age of Jesus Christ*, rev. ed., vol. 3/1 (London: T&T Clark, 1993), 48.

Whereas some early sources offer no more than the general notion that quotations from the book of Isaiah come from the prophet Isaiah, Josephus clearly imagines Isaiah as the writer of his book and particularly emphasizes the predictive nature of Isaiah's prophecies.

One slightly later text worth mentioning is the composite work *The Martyrdom and Ascension of Isaiah*. The core narrative of the *Martyrdom of Isaiah*, which is found within the first five chapters of the composite work, appears to be a Jewish composition perhaps from the second or first century BCE. What is transmitted to us from this Jewish composition does not directly address the question of the authorship of Isaiah.[6] Yet, a theme found in the Christian interpolations and expansions to this work anticipates later Jewish traditions and may reflect some stream of Jewish thought, perhaps as refracted through late first- or second-century CE Jewish-Christian writers.[7] The theme in question is the role of Hezekiah as transmitter of Isaiah's prophecies. In the brief Christian interpolation in chapter 1 (vv. 2b–6a), Hezekiah is said to pass on to Manasseh words that Isaiah gave to him (v. 5), and reference is made to Isaiah handing on prophetic words to Josab, his son (v. 6). Moreover, the Christian expansion describing Isaiah's ascension (chs. 6–11, the *Ascension of Isaiah*) often depicts Isaiah recounting visions to Hezekiah and Josab (6:16; 8:24; 11:16). The work ends with Isaiah communicating his visions to Hezekiah, who eventually passes them on to Manasseh (11:36–43). The role of Hezekiah as transmitter of Isaiah's prophecies was likely encouraged by the reference to the "writing" (מִכְתָּב, *miktāb*) or "prayer" (LXX: προσευχή, *proseuchē*) produced by Hezekiah after his recovery from illness (Isa 38:9; cf. *Mart. Isa.* 1:4). Although this theme is found only in the Christian sections of the *Martyrdom and Ascension of Isaiah*, the authors of these sections either drew upon Jewish traditions that emerged only in later sources, or else independently followed similar lines of reasoning that associate Hezekiah with writing Isaiah's prophecies.

The Writing of Isaiah in Classical Rabbinic Sources

The most important rabbinic text touching on the composition of the book of Isaiah is the well-known passage in *Baba Batra* 14b–15a, which discusses the order of biblical books and indicates who wrote them. As straightforward as this passage may seem, several difficulties arise in its interpretation and in determining what significance it holds for understanding how ancient Jews thought about the writing of Scripture.

---

6. Likewise, the treatment of Isaiah in the non-canonical work called the *Lives of the Prophets* (perhaps first century CE) says nothing about the authorship of the book of Isaiah.

7. The Christian interpolations can be identified by the presence of New Testament allusions and by the frequent references to "the Beloved." On this text, see M. A. Knibb, "Martyrdom and Ascension of Isaiah," in *The Old Testament Pseudepigrapha*, ed. J. H. Charlesworth (Garden City, NY: Doubleday, 1985), 2:143–76.

The order of the Mishnah dealing with legal issues surrounding property, *Ne-ziqin*, begins with three tractates, *Baba Qamma* ("first gate"), *Baba Meṣiʿa* ("middle gate"), and *Baba Batra* ("last gate"). Each deals with specific issues related to property, such as damages (e.g., the goring ox), theft, purchases, found objects, renting, wages, and inheritance. *Baba Batra* begins with a discussion of the division of property jointly owned by two or more people. The passage dealing with biblical books comes in the Gemara's treatment of Mishnah *Baba Batra* 1:6, which presents rules for dividing various possessions, such as a courtyard, a garden, or a cloak, when the possession in question is jointly owned. This is the general principle: "Anything that can be divided and still keep its name, they may divide it; but if not, they may not divide it" (*m. B. Bat.* 1:6; *b. B. Bat.* 11a).[8] For example, if two people jointly own a field, but dividing the field would make it too small to use for growing crops, then one owner cannot sell his portion and force the other owner to divide the field, because the resulting half portion would be too small to call a "field." Yet, if both parties are willing, then the property can be divided, even if the resulting half portions lose their identity. Nevertheless, the Mishnah concludes, "They may not divide Sacred Books, even if both of them are willing" (*m. B. Bat.* 1:6). The tradition regarding the order and writers of biblical books comes from the Talmud's discussion of this final statement.

The Gemara on this statement begins by addressing the question of whether one might make a division of biblical scrolls in the case where two scrolls are jointly owned. The topic of possibly dividing a biblical scroll leads to a discussion on fastening scrolls to cylinders and on the size of scrolls. This opens a conversation about the size of the ark, how the tablets were placed in the ark, whether a scroll of the Torah was inside the ark or merely next to it, and whether or not the fragments of the first tablets were kept in the ark. At this juncture comes the *baraita* concerning biblical books (*b. B. Bat.* 14b–15a). The *baraita* itself is in Hebrew and likely dates to sometime before 225 CE.[9] Inserted into the *baraita* is analysis offered mostly by the anonymous voice of the Talmud, written primarily in Aramaic. The

---

8. On the text of the Talmud, see note 10 below.

9. It is typical to date this *baraita* to roughly 200 CE, as in Philip S. Alexander, "The Formation of the Biblical Canon in Rabbinic Judaism," in *The Canon of Scripture in Jewish and Christian Tradition*, ed. Philip S. Alexander and Jean-Daniel Kaestli (Lausanne: Éditions du Zèbre, 2007), 76–77. In the end, however, we cannot know with certainty that this *baraita* is earlier than the Amoraic period or that it has been preserved verbatim, since evidence exists to suggest that at least some *baraitot* were partially invented, or at least creatively updated, by the compilers of the Talmud; see Louis Jacobs, "Are There Fictitious Baraitot in the Babylonian Talmud?," *HUCA* 42 (1971): 185–96. J. N. Lightstone suggests that this *baraita* "is probably not earlier than the second half of the third century C.E., and may well be substantially later" ("The Rabbi's Bible: The Canon of the Hebrew Bible and the Early Rabbinic Guild," in *The Canon Debate*, ed. Lee M. McDonald and James A. Sanders [Peabody, MA: Hendrickson, 2002], 178). Against this view, however, it is reasonable to assume that this *baraita* comes from the Tannaitic period, because evidence is lacking to suggest a later date. Nevertheless, it should be kept in mind that the wording of the *baraita* as it appears in the Talmud might reflect later reworking.

Rabbi Johanan mentioned here is the well-known third-century CE Palestinian amora. The text is presented below with the *baraita* in bold and the amoraic material in italics.[10]

Our rabbis taught:

The order of the Prophets is Joshua and Judges, Samuel and Kings, Jeremiah and Ezekiel, Isaiah and the Twelve.

Of course Hosea came first, as it is written, "At first the LORD spoke to Hosea" (Hos 1:2). But did He speak first to Hosea? Were there not many prophets from Moses to Hosea? R. Johanan said: He was the first of the four prophets who prophesied during that period: Hosea and Isaiah, Amos and Micah. So then Hosea should come first at the beginning? (No.) Since his prophecy is written close to Haggai, Zechariah, and Malachi, and Haggai, Zechariah, and Malachi are at the end of the prophets, he is reckoned as one of them. So then it should be written by itself and placed first? (No.) Because it is small, it would be lost. Of course Isaiah came first before Jeremiah and Ezekiel.[11] So then Isaiah should come first? (No.) Since the ending of Kings is about destruction and all of Jeremiah is about destruction, and Ezekiel begins with destruction and ends with consolation, and all of Isaiah is about consolation, we put destruction next to destruction and consolation next to consolation.

The order of the Writings is Ruth and Psalms and Job and Proverbs, Ecclesiastes and Song of Songs and Lamentations, Daniel, the scroll of Esther, Ezra, and Chronicles.

As for one who says that Job lived in the days of Moses, and so Job should come first at the beginning: We do not begin with misfortune. (But) Ruth likewise is about misfortune. (Yet,) it is about misfortune that has something (better) afterwards. As R. Johanan said: Why was her name called Ruth? Because there came forth from her David, who saturated[12] the Holy Blessed One with songs and praises.

And who wrote them? Moses wrote his book and the book of Job and the portion of Balaam.[13] And Joshua wrote his book and eight verses from the Torah. Samuel wrote his book and the book of Judges and Ruth. David wrote the book of Psalms through ten elders, through the first Man, and through

---

10. The text of *Baba Batra* used for this essay is that of Hamburg 165, a late twelfth-century Spanish manuscript, as available through the Sol and Evelyn Henkind Talmud Text Databank, at the Saul Lieberman Institute of Talmud Research of the Jewish Theological Seminary of America (accessed August 22, 2013, at http://www.lieberman-institute.com). Significant differences from the standard printed edition of the Talmud are indicated in the footnotes.

11. The words "and Ezekiel" are absent from Hamburg 165. This is probably an accidental omission. The words are supplied in the Lieberman Institute databank as found in the standard printed edition and other witnesses; see also Shraga Abramson, ed., *Masekhet Baba Batra*, in *Talmud Babli ʿim targum ʿIvri u-ferush ḥadash*, edited by J. N. Epstein (Jerusalem: Debir and Massadah, 1958), 24.

12. The word for "saturate" (רוה, *rwh*) is graphically similar to "Ruth" (רות, *rwt*).

13. The standard printed edition has "Moses wrote his book and the portion of Balaam and Job."

> Melchizedek,[14] and through Abraham, and through Moses, and through
> Heman, and through Yeduthun, and through Asaph, and through the three
> sons of Korah. Jeremiah wrote his book and the book of Kings and Lamenta-
> tions. Hezekiah and his company wrote[15] Isaiah, Proverbs and Song of Songs,
> (and) Ecclesiastes. The Men of the Great Synagogue wrote *qndg*:[16] Ezekiel
> and the Twelve, Daniel and the scroll of Esther. Ezra wrote his book and the
> genealogy in Chronicles up to his own.

What follows this passage is a discussion of whether Moses or Joshua wrote
the end of Deuteronomy. This discussion is not clearly resolved. After this, the
anonymous voice of the Talmud suggests that the book of Joshua was actually completed by Eleazar, and that the book of Samuel was completed by Gad the seer and
Nathan the prophet. After some brief comments related to the Psalms, the Gemara
devotes considerable attention to issues pertaining in various ways to Job (*b. B. Bat.*
15a–16b). The *sugya* ends with a series of traditions on Abraham, Isaac, and Jacob.
These traditions are reached by means of an association between God's blessing of
Job (Job 42:12) and God's blessing of Abraham in "all things" (Gen 24:1), which is
then explained. The *sugya* in this case does not return to its original topic. Regarding the *baraita* at 14b–15a, several important points require comment.

First, the only Talmudic statement on the order and composition of biblical books is an incidental reference in *Baba Batra* within a context dealing with
property division. No section within the Mishnah or Talmud is devoted to these
topics, and no specific treatment is found in the Midrash or in the post-Talmudic
tractate *Soperim*. Clearly the composition and order of biblical books was not of
great concern to the Jewish sages of antiquity. The *baraita* at *Baba Batra* 14b–15a
was obviously regarded as an important tradition worthy of being preserved and
discussed. Yet, it was not afforded a prominent place in the structure of the Talmud.

Second, since the *baraita* begins with a statement on the order of biblical books,
we may wonder why this topic needed to be addressed at all. Nahum Sarna suggested that the early rabbinic interest in the order of books evidenced in *Baba Batra*
14b–15a reflects influence from the Hellenistic world, in particular the practice of
cataloguing works as known from the library in Alexandria, and ultimately from
ancient Mesopotamian scribal practices.[17] H. M. I. Gevaryahu likewise traced the
roots of this *baraita* to the ancient Near Eastern world. According to Gevaryahu,
a seventh-century BCE catalogue from the Library of Assurbanipal that ascribes
specific texts to "authors" suggests a model by which Israel might also have had

---

14. Hamburg 165 reads מלכי צדקה (*mlky ṣdqh*), whereas the standard printed edition
has מלכי צדק (*mlky ṣdq*).

15. The standard printed edition adds ימשק (*ymšq*), i.e., the acronym for Isaiah (ישעיה,
yšʿyh), Proverbs (משלי, *mšly*), Song of Songs (שיר השירים, *šyr hšyrym*), Qohelet (קהלת, *qhlt*).

16. *Qndg* is an acronym made from ק (*q*) in Ezekiel (יחזקאל, *yḥzqʾl*), נ (*n*) in the
Twelve (שנים עשר, *šnym ʿśr*), ד (*d*) in Daniel (דניאל, *dnyʾl*), and ג (*g*) in the Scroll of Esther
(מגלת אסתר, *mglt ʾstr*).

17. Nahum M. Sarna, "The Order of the Books," in *Studies in Jewish Bibliography, History, and Literature in Honor of I. Edward Kiev*, ed. C. Berlin (New York: Ktav, 1971), 407–13.

catalogues of books and authors as early as the Babylonian exile.[18] These suggestions may be valid as a broad cultural explanation for early Jewish interest in the order and perhaps authorship of books. Yet, it is also worth noting regarding the *baraita* in *Baba Batra* that earlier in the *sugya* the Talmud contains a discussion of whether or not biblical books can be bound together. Furthermore, while the "sages" (חכמים, *ḥkmym*) say that each book should be written separately, multiple opinions are offered permitting all of the Tanak, or at least canonical units, to be written on the same scroll (*b. B. Bat.* 13b).[19] Sarna was correct that in the era of this *baraita* Jews were not using the codex format for biblical texts.[20] However, the immediate context of the passage suggests that the whole question of order may have become significant because of the practice of writing more than one biblical book on a scroll.[21] When this was done, in what order should the books be written?

As to the rationale behind the particular order given, the two most likely factors are chronology and size. As for the first factor, Louis Jacobs argues that the "order" refers simply to chronological order.[22] For the Writings, Ruth (Judges period) comes first, then Psalms (David), Job (whose author and period are unknown), Proverbs, Ecclesiastes, Song of Songs (Solomon), Lamentations (Jeremiah), Daniel, Esther, Ezra, and Chronicles (postexilic). The problematic book is Job, whose chronology the Rabbis discuss at length after the *baraita*.[23] For the Prophets, the order is: Joshua, Judges, Samuel, Kings (following the chronology),

---

18. H. M. I. Gevaryahu, "Biblical Colophons: A Source for the 'Biography' of Authors, Texts and Books," in *Congress Volume, Edinburgh 1974*, VTSup 28 (Leiden: Brill, 1975), 46–51. See W. G. Lambert, "A Catalogue of Texts and Authors," *JCS* 16 (1962): 59–77. According to Lambert, authorship in this catalogue is usually expressed by the phrase *ša pî* ("of the mouth"), and texts are ascribed in this way to men, legendary figures, and gods (p. 72). It is uncertain whether this catalogue really serves as a parallel to ancient Israel's interest in authorship, but its potential relevance to the question of the order of books is evident.

19. R. Meir and "Rabbi" (i.e., R. Judah the Patriarch) permit binding together the whole Tanak (in theory, at least); R. Judah allows the whole Torah or all of the Prophets or all of the Writings to be bound together; and R. Eleazar b. Azariah is said to have suggested binding together the eight prophetic books (cf. *y. Meg.* 3:1, 73b). As illustrated by the case of a man who threw a knife with the intention of sticking it into the wall and it inadvertently ritually slaughtered an animal on the way (*Ḥul.* 31a), the Talmud is perfectly capable of working out its principles and values (e.g., the role of intentionality in ritual sacrifice) by extending arguments into purely hypothetical cases. The practice of writing more than one book on a single scroll would be enough to raise the question of order for the whole Tanak, even if the whole Tanak was not yet being written in a single volume.

20. Sarna, "Order of the Books," 408.

21. See Timothy H. Lim, *The Formation of the Jewish Canon* (New Haven: Yale University Press, 2013), 35–36, 218–19; Menahem Haran, "Archives, Libraries, and the Order of the Biblical Books," *JANESCU* 22 (1993): 61. Haran does not think that Jews in antiquity had libraries or catalogues similar to those found in the ancient Near East.

22. Louis Jacobs, *Structure and Form in the Babylonian Talmud* (Cambridge: Cambridge University Press, 1991), 33–35. See also Alexander, "Formation of the Biblical Canon," 76.

23. *B. Bab.* 15a–16b. The Talmud explains that the Writings do not begin with Job so as not to begin with suffering. Jacobs suggests that the sages did not want to give too much prominence to a pagan hero (*Structure and Form*, 35).

and then Jeremiah, Ezekiel, Isaiah, and the Twelve. In this unit the book of Isaiah seems out of place. According to Jacobs, the rationale given in the Talmud for the placement of Isaiah is artificial: Kings and Jeremiah are put together because of their linked theme of destruction and Ezekiel and Isaiah are put together because of their linked theme of consolation.[24] Jacobs thinks that Isaiah is placed after Ezekiel because the former foresaw events that would take place after Ezekiel.[25] Nachmann Krochmal, however, proposed that Isaiah was placed after Ezekiel because the early sages recognized that the book of Isaiah contains material that was written after the time of Ezekiel.[26] This is an intriguing idea, but it seems unlikely. A better explanation is that a second factor, the size of books, also played a role in ordering some biblical books. Following Hermann L. Strack, Ludwig Blau argued that the prophetic books (Jeremiah, Isaiah, Ezekiel, and the Twelve) were placed in order of decreasing size, following the pattern seen in the organization of tractates in the Mishnah. Blau showed that the issue of book length also explains certain features in the ordering of the Writings.[27] In sum, although chronology (as understood by the early sages) was a factor in ordering the books, the relative size of the books was also considered in ordering specific units, such as the Latter Prophets. Consequently, the order of the books does not bear on the question of the chronology or composition of Isaiah.[28]

Third, the *baraita* in *Baba Batra* 14b–15a evidently uses the word כ-ת-ב (*k-t-b*, "wrote") in different senses. When it says that Moses "wrote" his book, or that Joshua "wrote" his book and the final eight verses of the Torah, it apparently means that these men were the human authors of these texts in the most direct sense. Yet, when it states that the Men of the Great Synagogue "wrote" the books of Ezekiel and the Twelve Prophets, the word כ-ת-ב (*k-t-b*) cannot mean that the Men of the Great Synagogue were the sole "authors" of these books, in the sense of being the creators of the content. As Max Margolis observed, "it must at once be conceded that the term 'wrote' cannot possibly have been used with the same

---

24. Jacobs, *Structure and Form*, 35. David Weiss Halivni proposes that "forced explanations" in the Talmud often resulted from the compilers of the Talmud not having access to the original argumentation underlying their sources and therefore needing to reconstruct this argumentation (*The Formation of the Babylonian Talmud*, trans. J. L. Rubenstein [Oxford: Oxford University Press, 2013], 41, 143–45).

25. Jacobs, *Structure and Form*, 35.

26. Nachmann Krochmal, *More Nebuche ha-seman* (Leopoli: Joseph Schnayder, 1851), ch. 11, sec. 2, pp. 114–15. Joseph Blenkinsopp also sees a connection between Isaiah's placement in the list of books in *Baba Batra* and modern critical theories on the composition of Isaiah ("The Formation of the Hebrew Bible Canon: Isaiah as a Test Case," in *The Canon Debate*, ed. Lee M. McDonald and James A. Sanders [Peabody, MA: Hendrickson, 2002], 61).

27. Ludwig Blau, "Bible Canon," *JE* 3:143–44. See also Roger Beckwith, *The Old Testament Canon of the New Testament Church* (Grand Rapids: Eerdmans, 1985), 160–62.

28. It is notable that the order stated in the *baraita* was not consistently followed in later biblical manuscripts, particularly regarding the order of the Latter Prophets and the Writings. See Christian D. Ginsburg, *Introduction to the Massoretico-Critical Edition of the Hebrew Bible* (London: Trinitarian Bible Society, 1897), 1–8, and Beckwith, *Old Testament Canon*, 208–11, 450–68.

meaning throughout."[29] According to Wilhelm Bacher, כ-ת-ב (*k-t-b*) is used in the *baraita* with reference to the Men of the Great Synagogue and Hezekiah and his company to indicate that these assemblies included the books in question in the canon.[30] Bacher argued that Ezekiel, Daniel, and Esther required canonical certification from the Men of the Great Synagogue because they were written outside the land of Israel. Louis Ginzberg suggested the meanings "edited" or "declared canonical" for כ-ת-ב (*k-t-b*) as used with Hezekiah and his company and the Men of the Great Synagogue.[31] Maurice Simon proposed the meanings "edited" or "published."[32] Margolis, for his part, agreed that the Men of the Great Synagogue "edited" or "completed" the Twelve, but he maintained that, from the perspective of the *baraita*, Isaiah wrote his own book, on the grounds that Isaiah was considered to be a member of Hezekiah's company.[33] This interpretation, however, seems very unlikely. Ezra was one of the Men of the Great Synagogue, and yet he is also singled out for the individual works that he wrote. Why would this not have been the case for Isaiah? Moses, Joshua, Samuel, Jeremiah, and Ezra are all said to have written their own book. Why not Isaiah? The obvious meaning of the *baraita* is that someone other than Isaiah, namely, "Hezekiah and his company," copied down, edited, published, or canonized the book of Isaiah.[34]

A later rabbinic tradition lends some support to the idea that the men of Hezekiah "canonized" or "ratified" biblical books. Proverbs 25:1 introduces a collection of sayings with the words, "These are the Proverbs of Solomon that the Men of Hezekiah copied" (הֶעְתִּיקוּ, *heʿtîqû*). In expounding *m. ʾAbot* 1:1, "Be deliberate" (מתונין, *mtwnyn*) in judgment," *ʾAbot de Rabbi Nathan* 1:4 first says that the meaning of הֶעְתִּיקוּ (*heʿtîqû*) in Prov 25:1 is that the Men of Hezekiah "deliberated" (המתינו, *hmtynw*) on these sayings. Then, a second opinion is given according to which the Men of Hezekiah "explained" (פירשו, *pyršw*) them, indicating that the books of Proverbs, Ecclesiastes, and Song of Songs were formerly "stored away" (גנוזים, *gnwzym*) because they contained problematic content, and they were only rendered acceptable later when they had been rightly explained.[35] Thus, according

---

29. Max L. Margolis, *The Hebrew Scriptures in the Making* (Philadelphia: JPS, 1922), 20. On this point, Margolis is followed by Sid Z. Leiman, *The Canonization of Hebrew Scripture: The Talmudic and Midrashic Evidence* (New Haven: Transactions of the Connecticut Academy of Arts and Sciences, 1991), 163.

30. Wilhelm Bacher, "Synagogue, The Great," in *JE* 11:642.

31. Louis Ginzberg, *The Legends of the Jews* (Philadelphia: JPS, 1938; repr., Baltimore: Johns Hopkins University Press, 1998), 6:448.

32. Maurice Simon, trans., *Baba Bathra*, in *The Babylonian Talmud*, ed. I. Epstein (London: Soncino, 1938), 71n7.

33. Margolis, *Hebrew Scriptures in the Making*, 21.

34. An alternative tradition is preserved in certain medieval manuscripts that "Isaiah wrote his own book, and Proverbs, and Song of Songs, and Ecclesiastes"; see Leiman, *Canonization of Hebrew Scripture*, 165.

35. At the end of this passage, the transmitted text of *Abot de-Rabbi Nathan* 1:4 has "the Men of the Great Synagogue" as the ones who explained these texts, but, based on the content of the whole passage, this is widely regarded as a copying error for "the Men of

to one opinion expressed in *'Abot de Rabbi Nathan*, the Men of Hezekiah enabled
Proverbs, Ecclesiastes, and Song of Songs to achieve canonical status. However,
this tradition is not really about the activities of the Men of Hezekiah as much as
it is about the interpretation of the Solomonic books. Moreover, the activities of
the Men of Hezekiah are described using the word פ-ר-ש (p-r-$š$, Piel), not כ-ת-ב
(k-t-b). If the *baraita* in Baba Batra 14b–15a had wished to refer to Hezekiah and his
company "rendering canonical" the book of Isaiah, it is hard to see why they would
have used the word כ-ת-ב (k-t-b) for this. Such an idea stretches the meaning of
the word כ-ת-ב (k-t-b) too far. It is much more likely that the *baraita* means to say
that Hezekiah and his company copied out or compiled the book of Isaiah, that is,
they engaged in literary activity.[36]

Rashi (1040–1105 CE) and the Tosafot (twelfth to thirteenth centuries CE)
provide medieval Jewish perspectives on why Hezekiah and his company were
involved in composing the book of Isaiah. Rashi identifies the "company" (סיעה,
sy'h) of Hezekiah as the people of his generation who outlived him. According to
Rashi, the prophets typically did not write their books until just before they died.
Thus, because Isaiah was killed unexpectedly by Manasseh, he did not actually get
to write his own book, with the result that the task was left to his surviving sup-
porters. The Tosafot add that Hezekiah himself could not have written the book of
Isaiah, since he died before Isaiah did. Yet, the "company" responsible is called by
Hezekiah's name because he was the one who caused them to engage in the study of
Torah.[37] Rashi and the Tosafot see Hezekiah and his company as the composers of
the book of Isaiah, but they imagine this as having taken place shortly after Isaiah's
death. This is a reasonable interpretation of the *baraita* in Baba Batra 14b–15a.[38]

Hezekiah." Examples of problematic passages listed by *Abot de-Rabbi Nathan* include Prov
7:7, 10–20; Song 7:11–13[ET 10–12]; and Qoh 11:9. See also *Midr. Prov.* 25.

36. Jed Wyrick argues that the *baraita* in *b. B. Bat.* 14b–15a is not concerned with authorship or human composition but with "textual transmission" and "the process whereby
prophecies and histories achieved a written form" (*The Ascension of Authorship* [Cambridge:
Harvard University Press, 2004], 22). I agree that the Talmud is not concerned with creative
human agency in composition (cf. ibid., 78–79), since the rabbis see God as the ultimate
author of Scripture and often depict the writing process as having occurred by means of
dictation. But this does not mean that the verb כ-ת-ב (k-t-b) in the *baraita* means "to copy
down" in the sense of "transmission," rather than "composition" or "editing" (cf. ibid., 73–75).
In *b. B. Bat.* 14b–15a, כ-ת-ב (k-t-b) probably means, in some sense, "to put into writing" the
divinely created scriptural content so as to produce the biblical books as we now have them.
For some books, this can be equivalent to "to edit."

37. On the great success of Hezekiah in seeing that his generation learned Torah, see
b. Sanh. 94b.

38. Most early rabbinic texts treat the book of Isaiah as testimony to the prophecies of
Isaiah, without special comment. Statements that are relevant to the composition of Isaiah
are rare. Two interesting texts are as follows: (1) In *Lev. Rab.* 6:6 and 15:2, it is asserted that
Beeri, father of Hosea (Hos 1:1), spoke Isa 8:19 and its "companion" (חברו, *ḥbrw*) verse,
which refers either to Isa 8:20 or Isa 29:4. Yet, because these prophecies were too brief to
constitute a book on their own, they were "attached" (נטפלו, *ntplw*) to the book of Isaiah (see
also Rashi on Isa 8:19). (2) *Eliyahu Rabbah* 16:83 claims that Isaiah prophesied all of God's

There is no way to determine the source of the information preserved in the *baraita*. It is possible that the tannaitic sages responsible for this tradition possessed independent information related to the authorship of biblical books. Several considerations, however, work against this hypothesis. First, the simplicity of the traditions reported in the *baraita*, which are problematized even in the subsequent discussion in the Gemara, suggests an idealized scheme rather than a historical record. Second, part of the haggadic impulse was to fill in missing details, to identify anonymous figures in the text, and to assign anonymous verses to known biblical characters.[39] It might be expected that the Rabbis would supply the names of famous biblical characters this way. Third, the sages of the *baraita* lived within the context of the Greco-Roman world and might have been expected to pay particular attention to questions of authorship appropriate to that cultural setting.[40] Therefore, the most likely explanation of this *baraita* is that it represents early Jewish haggadah that was generated entirely out of the biblical texts themselves.

Ibn Ezra on the Composition of Isaiah

The earliest figure in preserved Jewish tradition to suggest that the second half of the book of Isaiah was written by someone other than the prophet Isaiah is the Spanish scholar Abraham Ibn Ezra (1089–1164). Ibn Ezra was one of the most important biblical commentators of the Middle Ages. He was also a grammarian, poet, philosopher, and scientist, who wrote in both Hebrew and Arabic. In his *Commentary on Isaiah*, Ibn Ezra presented an innovative view on the authorship of the book of Isaiah through his application of philological principles to the biblical text. While Ibn Ezra's perspective on Isaianic authorship anticipated modern scholarship in some of its critical presuppositions, he nevertheless retained traditional beliefs about God and the supernatural.

Near the beginning of his commentary, Ibn Ezra indicates his understanding that the book of Isaiah falls into two halves: "The majority of his prophecies concern the cities of Judah that the king of Assyria captured, and Jerusalem which escaped from his hand. In the second half of the book (וכן מחצי הספר, *wkn mḥṣy hspr*) it concerns the exile of Judah, since it does not mention the rest of the tribes" (*Comm. Isa.* 1:1).[41] This initial comment relates to subject matter rather than authorship, but looking ahead in the commentary one sees that, while Ibn Ezra freely

---

mercy and consolations to Israel in the twenty-ninth year of Hezekiah's life (see 2 Kgs 18:2), thus affirming the belief that Isaiah himself spoke the prophecies contained in the second half of the book of Isaiah.

39. Isaac Heinemann, *Darkhei ha-Aggadah* (Jerusalem: Magnes, 1954), 21–22, 60–61.

40. See Johannes Renger, "Authors: I. Ancient Orient and Egypt," and Ulrich E. Schmitzer, "Authors II. Classical Antiquity," in *BNP (Antiquity)*, ed. H. Cancik and H. Schneider (Leiden: Brill, 2003), 2:399–403.

41. I am following the edition of Ibn Ezra's commentary presented in Menachem Cohen, ed., *Mikra'ot Gedolot 'Haketer': Isaiah* (Ramat-Gan, Israel: Bar-Ilan University, 1996). I have also consulted the Hebrew text and commentary offered by M. Friedländer, *Commentary of*

uses Isaiah's name with reference to the first half of the book (e.g., *Comm. Isa.* 2:2; 6:1; 7:14), in his discussion of the text after chapter 40 he avoids mentioning Isaiah and refers almost exclusively to "the prophet."[42] In keeping with a characteristic of his writings, Ibn Ezra was reserved in expressing novel conclusions. He only allows his perspective to emerge subtly as the commentary unfolds.

Ibn Ezra explains his general approach to the second half of the book of Isaiah in his remarks on the beginning of chapter 40, where he contrasts his own view with that of R. Moses Hakkohen Ibn Chiquitilla, an eleventh-century Jewish scholar whose commentary on Isaiah is no longer extant. Ibn Ezra divides Isa 40–66 into two parts, chapters 40–51 and chapters 52–66. He sums up these two divisions as follows:

> These earlier comforts at the start of this half of the book [i.e., chs. 40–51] concern the Second Temple according to the opinion of R. Moses Hakkohen, may his rest be Paradise; but according to my opinion, all of it concerns our exile,[43] except that within [this part of] the book there are words dealing with the Babylonian exile, as an allusion [זכר, *zkr*], in that Cyrus sent back the exiles;[44] nevertheless, in the latter part of the book [i.e., chs. 52–66], the words deal with the future, as I will explain. (*Comm. Isa.* 40:1)

We learn from this statement and many others by Ibn Ezra that Ibn Chiquitilla interpreted most of Isa 40–66 as relating to the return from Babylon, both by imagining historical events that could serve as near fulfillments for certain details and by taking some of the language metaphorically.[45] In contrast to this, we might expect Ibn Ezra to focus primarily on the redemption of the Jews from their present exile (chs. 40–51) and the future (chs. 42–66), with only occasional allusions to Babylon. In fact, however, Ibn Ezra interprets the majority of passages in Isa 40–51 as prophetic promises announcing the rescue from Babylon brought about through Cyrus the Great.[46] In this way, Ibn Ezra is able to explain Isa 40–51 in accordance

---

Ibn Ezra on Isaiah, Edited from MSS. and Translated, with Notes, Introductions, and Indexes (New York: Philipp Feldheim, 1873).

42. On "the prophet" in Isa 40–66, see, e.g., *Comm. Isa.* 42:1, 19; 43:10; 44:26; 49:1, 7, 9; 50:10; 57:1; 59:1, 12; 61:1; 63:14–15. Isaiah is mentioned by name at *Comm. Isa.* 50:1, where Ibn Ezra compares Isaiah's prophecy with quotations from Jeremiah and Amos, and therefore he needs to invoke Isaiah's name to distinguish him (or his book) from these other prophets.

43. According to Ibn Ezra, the Jews of his day still lived in exile among the nations and awaited a future redemption (e.g., see *Comm. Isa.* 59:1; 62:8–11; 65:8–9).

44. The difficulty of the text at this point (כי כורש ששלח הגולה, *ky kwrš ššlḥ hgwlh*) has been noted by Friedländer, *Commentary of Ibn Ezra on Isaiah*, 170, and Uriel Simon, "Ibn Ezra between Medievalism and Modernism: The Case of Isaiah XL–LXVI," in *Congress Volume, Salamanca 1983*, ed. J. A. Emerton, VTSup 36 (Leiden: Brill, 1985), 263. The ש (*š*, "who") appears unnecessary. Perhaps the sense is, "in that it is Cyrus who sent back the exiles," or perhaps the ש (*š*) should be deleted.

45. See Simon, "Ibn Ezra between Medievalism and Modernism," 260.

46. Ibn Ezra explicitly mentions the Babylonian exile or redemption from exile in his comments on the following verses: Isa 41:2, 9, 11, 14–17, 22, 25; 42:7, 10, 13; 43:2, 5, 14, 16–17, 19, 21–23; 44:8, 27; 45:14, 20; 46:1–4; 47:1; 48:14, 22; 49:2, 7, 12; 51:7. Verses that Ibn Ezra explicitly applies to Cyrus include Isa 41:2, 5–6; 44:28; 45:3, 5, 8, 13–14; 46:11; 48:14–15.

with what he thinks the language of the text indicates (i.e., the Babylonian exile and the promise of return), but he is also able to see the past deliverance of the Jews from Babylon as a "hint" or "allusion" to God's coming deliverance of the Jews from their present exile.[47]

As for chapters 52–66, Ibn Ezra argues that these prophecies relate directly to a yet-to-come future restoration.[48] As Ibn Ezra explains, the language of these texts cannot possibly refer to the return from Babylon under Cyrus, as demonstrated by passages such as "never again shall the uncircumcised and the unclean come to you" (*Comm. Isa.* 52:1) and "nations that do not know you will run to you" (*Comm. Isa.* 55:5).[49] Furthermore, Ibn Ezra points out that Babylon is not mentioned in the last chapters of the book of Isaiah (*Comm. Isa.* 52:11). As seen by Isaiah and explained by Ibn Ezra, in the future God will bless Israel so that they no longer suffer at the hands of the nations, but Israel will treat the nations with compassion and pray for them (*Comm. Isa.* 53:11). Only rarely when commenting on chapters 52–66 does Ibn Ezra raise the possibility that the return from Babylonian exile could be in view (this may be the case in *Comm. Isa.* 54:4; 55:6; 56:8; 57:18). In general, Ibn Ezra sees Isa 40–51 as predicting the future blessing of the Jews as hinted at through a detailed prophetic description of the restoration from Babylon under Cyrus, and Isa 52–66 as promising future blessing for the Jews in more direct and grand language.

As noted previously, Ibn Ezra avoids talking about "Isaiah" in chapters 40–66, preferring to refer simply to "the prophet." Yet, he touches directly on the question of authorship in only a few brief remarks, and these select comments are delicately expressed.

The first and most detailed statement on the authorship of the second half of the book appears among Ibn Ezra's comments on Isa 40:1:

> Understand that the transmitters of the commandments, of blessed memory, said that Samuel wrote the book of Samuel, and this is correct up to the statement, "And Samuel died" (1 Sam 25:1). And the book of Chronicles demonstrates (this principle), for it

---

47. For an example of Ibn Ezra seeing a double reference in a single text, applying the text both to Babylon and also to a future redemption, see *Comm. Isa.* 55:12. Notable is the parallel with "typological" interpretation by Antiochene Christian commentators, who see historical events as "types" of greater events in the future; see Diodore of Tarsus, *Comm. Ps. 118*, in *Biblical Interpretation in the Early Church*, ed. and trans. Karlfried Froehlich (Philadelphia: Fortress, 1984), prol.; Theodore of Mopsuestia, *Commentary on the Twelve Prophets*, trans. Robert C. Hill, Fathers of the Church (Washington: Catholic University of America Press, 2004), *Comm. Joel 2:28–32 (LXX)*; Theodoret of Cyrus, *Commentaries on the Prophets*, vol. 1, *Commentary on Jeremiah*, trans. Robert C. Hill (Brookline: Holy Cross Orthodox, 2006), *Comm. Jer. 23:4*.

48. Texts identified as having a future fulfillment and discussed in an illuminating way by Ibn Ezra include Isa 52:11; 53:7, 9–12; 54:1, 8, 14, 17; 55:1, 3–5; 56:1; 59:19–20; 65:17, 20, 22, 25; 66:23–24. In *Comm. Isa.* 53:12, Ibn Ezra notes that the "servant" referenced at Isa 53:12 is the same one spoken of at 42:1; 49:3; and 50:6.

49. Based on Isa 62:8, Ibn Ezra argues that God has made these great promises in the last chapters of Isaiah to Israel through an unbreakable decree, and so there must be a fulfillment fitting the language that still lies in the future (see *Comm. Isa.* 62:8).

(contains) the names for several generations after Zerubbabel (1 Chr 3:19–24). And (in this book) there is this testimony: "Kings will see and arise; princes, and they will bow down" (Isa 49:7). Some may reply: "(This will happen) when they hear the name of the prophet." And if (this is so), (then) (my view) is not (correct). The one who is wise will understand.[50]

Ibn Ezra argues that Samuel only wrote the book of Samuel down to the point where the prophet died. Someone else must have added to the book the material beyond that. This is supported by the fact that Chronicles, which was supposedly written during the time of Zerubbabel, contains genealogies for generations after Zerubbabel that must have been added later by someone else. According to Ibn Ezra, Isa 49:7 says that kings will arise and bow down to God when they see the prophet (see Ibn Ezra's comments on Isa 49:7). This implies that the prophet was alive at the time of Cyrus. Therefore, this prophet cannot be Isaiah but must be someone who lived after his time. This prophet must have added to Isaiah's book, just as someone did with the books of Samuel and Chronicles. This is Ibn Ezra's view, but he offers an alternative explanation, namely, that Cyrus and other kings will bow down at the mention of Isaiah's name. In the end, Ibn Ezra leaves the matter up to the judgment of the reader.

Ibn Ezra alludes to his view that the second half of the book of Isaiah comes from a prophet living in the time of Cyrus in at least three other brief comments. First, in addition to Ibn Ezra's belief that Isa 49:7–12 implies a prophet contemporaneous with Cyrus, which has already been discussed, in his commentary on 49:9 ("saying to the captives"), he says, "He [the prophet] hints concerning Israel, indicating that the prophet prophesied (just) before the redemption."[51] Second, at Isa 55:6 ("seek the Lord!"), Ibn Ezra states, "In my opinion, this section is an admonition *for the men of his generation*; the sense is: (seek the Lord,) since you know that you will be redeemed from Babylon, and from all the nations thereafter."[52] Because the prophet is understood to be admonishing and assuring his contemporaries who will be redeemed from Babylon, the prophet is presumed to live shortly before that redemption. Third, Ibn Ezra comments on Isa 57:18 ("I have seen his ways") as follows: "This is an indication of the correctness of my interpretation of the book,"[53] because "his ways" refers either to the repentance or to the disposition

---

50. ‏ודע כי מעתיקי המצות ז״ל אמרו כי ספר שמואל כתבו שמואל והוא אמת עד וימת שמואל‎ והנה דברי הימים יוכיח ששם דור אחר דור לבני זרובבל והעד מלכים יראו וקמו שרים ויש להשיב כאשר ישמעו שם הנביא ואם איננו והמשכיל יבין‎ (wdʿ ky mʿtyqy hmṣwt z″l ʾmrw ky spr šmwʾl ktbw šmwʾl, whwʾ ʾmt ʿd wymt šmwʾl, whnh dbry hymym ywkyḥ, šśm dwr ʾḥr dwr lbny zrwbbl. whʿd: mlkym yrʾw wqmw śrym wyśtḥww. wyš lhśyb: kʾśr yśmʿw šm hnbyʾ. wʾm ʾynnw. whmśkyl ybyn).

51. ‏רמז על ישראל שהתנבא הנביא קודם הגאולה‎ (rmz ʿl yśrʾl šhtnbʾ hnbyʾ qwdm hgʾwlh).

52. ‏לפי דעתי כי זאת הפרשה תוכחה על אנשי דורו הטעם שתדעו כי תגאלו מבבל וגם מכל‎ ‏הגוים פעם שנית‎ (lpy dʿty, ky zʾt hpršh twkḥḥ ʿl ʾnšy dwrw. hṭʿm: ʾḥr štdʿw ky tgʾlw mbbl, wgm mkl hgwym pʿm šnyt).

53. ‏הנה זאת לאות על יושר פירוש הספר‎ (hnh zʾt lʾwt ʿl ywšr pyrwš hspr). This follows the reading proposed by Friedländer, *Commentary of Ibn Ezra on Isaiah*, 100. Cohen (*Mikraʾot Gedolot ʿHaketerʾ: Isaiah*, 361), follows manuscripts that read ‏הסתר‎ (hstr), referring to 57:17.

of those who are already in exile and are about to be rescued. This is taken to imply that the prophet personally saw the ways of the exilic community. In his comments on these passages Ibn Ezra recalls the suggestion he made in his remarks on the beginning of chapter 40, that a prophet living in the time of Cyrus wrote Isa 40–66. The whole tenor of Ibn Ezra's commentary on Isa 40–66 fits with a late exilic date (especially in chs. 40–51), but he does not belabor the point. He is content to pursue his exegetical task and to leave the critical question in the background.

Ibn Ezra's approach to the second half of Isaiah may be regarded as historical-critical, but he also intended to remain faithful to Jewish traditions and beliefs. One may speak generally of Ibn Ezra's "search for logic and rationality, his critical, philological attitude."[54] At the same time, Ibn Ezra regularly softened the tone of his conclusions if he perceived that they were in tension with traditional views, and he often left open an alternative explanation for those who might reject his position.[55] Ibn Ezra showed this caution and respect in his *Commentary on Isaiah*. Moreover, it is important to point out that Ibn Ezra had no aversion to miracles. Commenting on Isa 45:24, Ibn Ezra emphasizes that the prophet does not know what he knows by his own knowledge, but by the Lord's informing him. In his comments on Isa 47:10, Ibn Ezra condemns "heretical knowledge that denies God." The notion that God might reveal to the eighth-century prophet Isaiah events that would take place two centuries later did not trouble Ibn Ezra, as shown by his commentary on Isa 13:1, 4, 11, and 14:1, where he identifies Cyrus and the end of the Babylonian captivity as the fulfillment of prophecies spoken by Isaiah. Ibn Ezra's problem with Isa 40–66 was that the language of the speaker seemed to fit the situation of a later time, rather than predict it. Ibn Ezra's philological training and historical convictions led him to believe that language, even scriptural language, corresponds to the specific historical context of the writer. A natural convergence should exist between the wording of the text and the context that the text is addressing. Because the language of Isa 40–66 appeared to Ibn Ezra to arise out of the period just before the redemption from Babylon, he suggested that these chapters were written at that time.

The nature of Ibn Ezra's pious philology may be illustrated by a passage from his *Commentary on Exodus*. Regarding the word וַיּוֹרֵהוּ (*wayyôrēhû*; "And [the Lord] showed him [a tree]") in Exod 15:25, the suggestion had been made that God "taught" (י-ר-ה, *y-r-h*; cf. תּוֹרָה, *tôrâ*) Moses about a type of tree that possessed the natural quality of making water sweet.[56] This reading grows out of a midrash on the

---

Friedländer's reading makes good sense in context, and it is easy to see how הספר (*hspr*) could become הסתר (*hstr*) in the mind of a copyist who is not thinking of Ibn Ezra's interpretation of the book as a whole but has in mind the previous verse.

54. Angel Sáenz-Badillos, "Abraham Ibn Ezra: Between Tradition and Philology," *Zutot* 2 (2002): 85. For illustrations of Ibn Ezra's rational bent in the *Commentary on Isaiah*, see his comments on Isa 40:21–22 ("by the weighing of ideas, which is the essence of knowledge"), 40:28 ("there is no need for a verse, for the matter is known by decisive evidence"), and 51:6 ("Men of wisdom [philosophers] learn from this verse that the soul of humanity is eternal; yet, although their idea is true, that is not the sense of this verse").

55. Sáenz-Badillos, "Abraham Ibn Ezra," 88.

56. See Ramban and Rashbam, probably reflecting an older interpretation.

word וַיּוֹרֵהוּ (*wayyôrēhû*).[57] Ibn Ezra regards this sort of interpretation as untenable, and offers this explanation: "We do not know what kind of tree this was, only that the matter was a miracle."[58] In this case, the midrashic reading could actually lead to a non-supernatural explanation. Committed to the natural sense of the language in context, Ibn Ezra rejects this explanation and insists that the use of the tree to make the water sweet described in this verse was simply a miracle. This serves as a helpful parallel for understanding Ibn Ezra on Isa 40–66. The interpretive difficulty does not reside in the ability of God to do the miraculous, but in properly interpreting the sense of the language in its context.

It would have benefited future readers of Isaiah if the issues raised by Ibn Ezra had been discussed further by subsequent commentators. Unfortunately, virtually nothing is preserved of any such discussion for centuries afterwards. Don Isaac Abrabanel (1437–1508), the great Jewish intellectual of Portugal and then Italy, suggested that certain biblical books such as Samuel and Kings were the work of a later editor (מתכן, *mtkn*) and assembler (מקבץ, *mqbṣ*). Abrabanel justified his willingness to deviate from the *baraita* in *Baba Batra* 14b–15a by pointing out that the rest of the discussion in the Talmud reports disagreements on matters of authorship, such as whether Moses wrote Job or whether Joshua wrote the end of the Torah. If the sages of the Talmud expressed uncertainties on these points, Abrabanel reasoned, it is acceptable for later thinkers to attempt their own explanations.[59] Yet, despite the insights of Ibn Ezra and Abrabanel, Jewish thinkers did not seriously address the question of who wrote the second half of Isaiah until the rise of historical criticism of the Bible in the wake of the Enlightenment.[60]

The Authorship of Isaiah in Modern Jewish Thought

Prominent Jewish thinkers who adopted the critical view on Isaianic authorship include Nachmann Krochmal (1785–1840) and Solomon Judah Rapoport

---

57. Cf. Midrash *Tanḥuma*, Beshallah 24.

58. Menachem Cohen, ed., *Mikraʾot Gedolot ʾHaketerʾ: Exodus, part 1* (Ramat-Gan, Israel: Bar-Ilan University, 2012), 128.

59. Eric Lawee, "Don Isaac Abarbanel: Who Wrote the Books of the Bible?" *Tradition* 30 (1996): 70. On Isa 53, Abrabanel says that the prophecies in this chapter are not all connected or related to each other, but some of them refer to king Josiah and some of them speak of the future redemption of the Jews; see S. R. Driver and A. Neubauer, *The Fifty-Third Chapter of Isaiah According to the Jewish Interpreters* (Oxford: James Parker and Co., 1877), 188.

60. It is debatable whether Spinoza's views belong in this discussion. Let it suffice to say that, in spite of his critical inquiries into the Pentateuch, Spinoza did not contribute anything to the study of the authorship of Isaiah. Spinoza seems to have taken at face value the statement that Isaiah wrote a record of king Uzziah's acts (see 2 Chr 26:22). Spinoza regarded as a myth the story that Isaiah was put to death by Manasseh, but he took this myth simply as evidence that the rabbis did not believe that all of Isaiah's prophecies are extant; see Benedict de Spinoza, *A Theological-Political Treatise and a Political Treatise*, trans. R. H. M. Elwes (London: G. Bell & Son, 1883), ch. 10, p. 147.

(1790–1867). A notable defense for the essential unity of Isaiah was made by the Italian Jewish scholar Samuel David Luzzatto (1800–1865).[61] Interestingly, Luzzatto had accepted the ideas that Solomon was not the author of Ecclesiastes and that Zechariah did not write Zech 9–10 or 13–14.[62] Furthermore, Luzzatto believed that Isa 56:9–57:13 was not written by Isaiah but was composed as a lament for Isaiah by an anonymous prophet who wrote during the reign of Manasseh.[63] Nevertheless, Luzzatto rejected the standard critical view that denied the second half of the book of Isaiah to the prophet Isaiah on the grounds that the critical view makes the book out to be a forgery and denies the possibility of predictive prophecy.[64] According to Luzzatto, Isa 34:16 illustrates how Isaiah's futuristic prophecies were not announced publicly but were written in a book for posterity, which explains why they do not seem to relate to Isaiah's contemporaries.[65] Luzzatto supposed that in Isa 65–66 the prophet Isaiah rebuked future Israel for sins they had not yet committed because he saw these future people through the lens of his sinful contemporaries.[66] Luzzatto firmly dismissed the idea that God could not have revealed to Isaiah detailed knowledge such as the name of Cyrus.[67] Luzzatto's views on the composition of Isaiah and other biblical books reflect his desire to maintain the core of traditional viewpoints while still presenting his arguments as critical and objective.[68]

Many traditionally oriented Jews today continue to affirm that the prophet Isaiah composed the whole book of Isaiah.[69] At the same time, since the late nineteenth century many Jewish scholars have adopted the view that significant parts of the book of Isaiah were written at a later time. Heinrich Graetz argued for the postexilic date of Isa 34, 35, and 40–66 in an article published in 1891 in the *Jewish Quarterly Review*.[70] Julian Morgenstern published a volume on Deutero-Isaiah that reflects the fruits of his seminars on Isaiah at the Hebrew Union College from 1939 to 1957. According to Morgenstern, the majority of the members of the seminar agreed that Isa 34–35 and 49–66 arose out of the late sixth or early fifth century BCE.[71] The standard view of many contemporary Jewish intellectuals on the composition of Isaiah can be summed up by this statement of J. H. Hertz (1872–1946),

---

61. See Shmuel Vargon, "S. D. Luzzatto's Approach Regarding the Unity of the Book of Isaiah," *Review of Rabbinic Judaism* 4 (2001): 272–96.

62. Max Seligsohn, "Samuel David (ShaDaL) Luzzatto," *JE* 8:225; Shmuel Vargon, "Isaiah 56:9–57:13: Time of the Prophecy and Identity of the Author According to Samuel David Luzzatto," *JSQ* 6 (1999): 232; and Vargon, "S. D. Luzzatto's Approach," 290–91.

63. Vargon, "Isaiah 56:9–57:13," 220–21, 226–30.

64. Vargon, "S. D. Luzzatto's Approach," 286–95.

65. Ibid., 279.

66. Ibid., 282.

67. Ibid., 276–77, 287.

68. Ibid., 275–77; cf. Vargon, "Isaiah 56:9–57:13," 232.

69. E.g., A. J. Rosenberg, *Mikraoth Gedoloth: The Book of Isaiah*, vol. 1, *Translation of Text, Rashi and Other Commentaries*, Judaica Books of the Prophets (Brooklyn: Judaica Press, 1982; repr., 2007), ix, xi.

70. H. Graetz, "Isaiah XXXIV and XXXV," *JQR* 4 (1891): 1–8.

71. Julian Morgenstern, *The Message of Deutero-Isaiah in its Sequential Unfolding* (Cincinnati: Hebrew Union College Press, 1961), 1–3.

for many years the chief rabbi of the United Hebrew Congregations of Great Britain, as quoted in the *Encyclopaedia Judaica*: "This question can be considered dispassionately. It touches no dogma, or any religious principle in Judaism; and, moreover, does not materially affect the understanding of the prophecies, or of the human conditions of the Jewish people that they have in view."[72] In his recent *Theological and Critical Introduction to the Jewish Bible*, Marvin Sweeney mentions the reference to Hezekiah and his colleagues in the Talmud and the views of Ibn Ezra, David Kimchi, and Samuel David Luzzatto in his own presentation of the standard critical view of the composition of Isaiah.[73]

Conclusion

Much can be learned about Judaism and the history of biblical interpretation from even a brief account of Jewish reflection on the composition of Isaiah. It is not surprising that the perspectives of Jewish scholars from different times and places were shaped by the contexts in which they worked. Josephus' depiction of Isaiah as prophet, advisor, and author probably reflects the desire of Jews in the Greco-Roman world to present positive portrayals of their great men of the past. The sages of the Talmud and Midrash did not treat prophetic books as coherent documents and apparently gave little thought to how they were composed.[74] The Talmudic *baraita* discussed at length above likely reflects the Greco-Roman interest in authorship, and it functions within its context in *Baba Batra* as part of a practical discussion, namely, the need to determine the order in which books should be written when more than one book is copied on a scroll. Ibn Ezra cautiously suggested

---

72. Theodore Friedman, "Isaiah: Introduction," *EncJud*, 2nd ed., ed. F. Skolnik (Detroit: Thomson Gale, 2007), 10:58.

73. Marvin A. Sweeney, *TANAK: A Theological and Critical Introduction to the Jewish Bible* (Minneapolis: Fortress Press, 2012), 270. Sweeney points to Luzzatto's suggestion that Isaiah wrote Isa 40–66 for the sake of future readers to show that Luzzatto recognized that the prophecies contained in these chapters address a later time period. Sweeney also mentions David Kimchi's questions regarding the date and character of Isa 6. In contrast to Rashi and Ibn Ezra, Kimchi did not think that the scene described in Isa 6 constituted the beginning of Isaiah's prophetic ministry, pointing out 2 Chr 26:22, which states that Isaiah wrote about the deeds of King Uzziah, "first and last." In other words, Isaiah was already active in the early days of Uzziah's reign and did not begin prophesying in the year of Uzziah's death (Isa 6:1); see Kimchi's preface to the book of Isaiah and his discussion at Isa 6:1. These comments are not necessarily relevant to the issue of the composition of Isaiah. In his comments on Isa 40:1, Kimchi says that these comforts will come about in the days of the Messiah.

74. See the conclusions of Jacob Neusner, *The Rabbis and the Prophets*, Studies in Judaism (Lanham, MD: University Press of America, 2011), 194–95, regarding the books of Hosea and Amos. Neusner argues that the rabbis do not treat the prophets systematically, but "dismantle" the prophetic texts and quote "random samples of opinions" in order to "prove propositions that emerge from the Rabbinic program," not from the coherent program of the prophetic book. These observations based on the study of Hosea and Amos hold true for Isaiah as well.

a later date for Isa 40–66 in keeping with the best principles of philological analysis as practiced among scholars of the Iberian Peninsula in the twelfth century. Samuel David Luzzatto's agreement with certain critical views but his rejection of any postexilic "Isaiah" shows his desire to adopt the scholarly methods of the nineteenth century without yielding to the radical skepticism common among certain intellectuals of his day. Recent Jewish scholarship of most varieties has tended to accept some version of the multiple-authorship theory for Isaiah. This reflects contemporary Jewish engagement with modern biblical criticism and also shows that the authorship of Isaiah is not of critical significance for modern Judaism.

Jewish traditions on the composition of the book of Isaiah also raise at least two important questions for contemporary thinking about the origins of this prophetic work. First, are the earliest Jewish traditions about Isaiah and his book derived in any way from independent historical memories dating back to the preexilic era? The earliest traditions affirm that Isaiah wrote his own book (Josephus), or else they connect him with the entirety of the book (e.g., Sirach) and ascribe a significant role to Hezekiah (e.g., the *baraita* in *Baba Batra*). These opinions could potentially be explained as merely products of the Greco-Roman mindset (e.g., in the case of Josephus) and as derived from inferences within Scripture (e.g., the statements about Hezekiah in Isa 38:9 and Prov 25:1). However, it is possible that genuine traditions were handed down from earlier centuries and simply took on new significance within the Greco-Roman context. The fact that a tradition fits well within a later time period does not necessarily demonstrate that it was invented to address the needs of that later period. It is important to recognize that the earliest Jewish traditions connect Isaiah with the whole book of Isaiah. At the same time, these traditions are somewhat late. Even the reference to Isaiah in Sir 48:24–25 is at least two hundred years later than the setting of the purported Third Isaiah, which would be sufficient time for misunderstandings about the nature of the book to arise. In the end, if the earliest Jewish evidence points in any direction, it points to the essentially Isaianic origins of the whole book, but the evidence is ultimately inconclusive.

Second, does Ibn Ezra's perception that material in the second half of Isaiah speaks to the late exilic community as if speaking to contemporaries constitute a strong argument that these parts of the book were written during that time? One potential benefit of the history of interpretation is that sometimes readings from different times and places that run along the same lines uncover features of the text that are genuinely there. Ibn Ezra provides an example of a reader outside of the context of the Enlightenment who saw a prophet other than Isaiah as the speaker in the second half of the book of Isaiah. Ibn Ezra's testimony is all the more interesting because his arguments do not arise out of skepticism about the existence of God or the reality of the supernatural. A key issue that must be addressed in evaluating Ibn Ezra's position is whether he sufficiently understood the conventions of discourse that would have been used in writing a prophetic book in the era of biblical Judah. Did Ibn Ezra correctly identify the relationship in the text between the presumed speaker and hearers of the message of Second Isaiah, and does this mode of speaking suggest that Isaiah is not the author? As with many aspects of the prophetic books, such as the precise significance of the superscriptions, it is difficult to answer these questions with certainty based on the evidence we possess. And yet these remain important questions to ask. At the very least, Ibn Ezra serves as a valuable example of one who attempted to engage Scripture both critically and theologically.

6

The Diachronic Perspective of the Book of Isaiah's Final Form

KNUT M. HEIM

Introduction

This study concentrates on literary features of the book of Isaiah through a particular lens—the dimension of time—to determine how the book itself wants to be read.[1] There is a lively debate about diachronicity and synchronicity in the book called Isaiah. Should the various parts of the book be read from the perspective of the entire book's final form, and thus synchronically, or should its various parts be read against their reconstructed historical backgrounds, and thus diachronically?[2] This study proposes an approach that attempts to draw on the strengths of both sides of the debate. On the one hand, I will propose that modern readers need to take seriously that the book called Isaiah has been shaped into a larger whole that transcends the various perspectives of its constituent parts. Here I follow Brevard Childs' canonical approach.[3] On the other hand, I propose that the book, even in its final, canonical form, contains editorial clues that deliberately encourage readers

---

1. I am grateful to Prof. Hugh Williamson, Prof. Alan Millard, and Prof. Daniel Falk for reading and helpfully commenting on an earlier version of this study. Any remaining weaknesses remain my responsibility. Elements of this essay were presented as an academic paper in another context, a paper currently accessible at https://oimts.files.wordpress .com/2013/01/2007-1-heim.pdf and at https://www.yumpu.com/en/document/view/6471138/ israel-and-other-nations-in-isaiah-duke-divinity-school/15.

2. Cf., e.g., H. G. M. Williamson, *The Book Called Isaiah: Deutero-Isaiah's Role in Composition and Redaction* (Oxford: Clarendon, 1994). A recent, book-length survey of scholarship on Isaiah dedicates no fewer than fifty-one of its 146 pages to scholarship treating the book of Isaiah as an artfully constructed unity: Peter Höffken, *Jesaja: Der Stand der theologischen Diskussion* (Darmstadt: Wissenschaftliche Buchgesellschaft, 2004), 40–90. Odil Hannes Steck represents a radically diachronic methodology. See esp. his *Bereitete Heimkehr: Jesaja 35 als redaktionelle Brücke zwischen dem Ersten und dem Zweiten Jesaja*, SBS 121 (Stuttgart: Katholisches Bibelwerk, 1985); *Studien zu Tritojesaja*, BZAW 203 (Berlin: de Gruyter, 1991); *Gottesknecht und Zion: Gesammelte Aufsätze zu Deuterojesaja*, FAT 4 (Tübingen: Mohr Siebeck, 1992).

3. E.g., Brevard S. Childs, *Introduction to the Old Testament as Scripture* (London: SCM, 1979); idem, *Biblical Theology of the Old and New Testaments: Theological Reflection on the Christian Bible* (London: SCM, 1992); idem, *Isaiah: A Commentary*, OTL (Louisville: Westminster John Knox, 2001).

to take note of several diachronic dimensions in the different parts of the book.[4] In support of my proposal, I will present case studies of several short, representative passages that display diachronic and synchronic features side by side.

The aim of this study is not to argue for multiple authorship for the book of Isaiah. This I will assume, although the third section of my essay will build on a key argument for multiple authorship. Rather, my aim is to seek to account for two prominent features of the book that have puzzled readers on either side of the debate on Isaianic authorship, traits that, in my opinion, neither side has explained satisfactorily. The first characteristic, the frequent juxtaposition of apparently conflicting statements in the book, is the main feature in the book that those who hold to single authorship struggle to explain. The second, the regular juxtaposition of carefully edited and highly integrated sections in Isaiah with apparently unedited materials, is the main feature in the book that those who hold to multiple authorship struggle to explain.

The aim of my study is to develop a model of the textual genesis of the book called Isaiah that better accounts for both of these features. This model has three components: (1) a multi-dimensional understanding of explicit and implicit temporal aspects of synchronicity, diachronicity, and eschatology in Isaiah; (2) a nuanced model of textual production and transmission that draws on recent progress in our understanding of scribal practices in biblical times; and (3) a consideration of how both the topos of "former things" and the related topos of "sealed" prophetic utterances are used in Isaiah to demonstrate divine sovereignty. I will begin with some reflections on explicit and implicit temporal aspects of the book in order to set the following parts of my study into an appropriate temporal framework.

Synchronicity, Diachronicity, and Eschatology in Isaiah

In the book's final form, synchronicity and diachronicity depend on each other because the book called Isaiah was edited over several centuries before it reached its final, canonical form. As we will see, carefully edited materials that have been almost seamlessly integrated with each other stand side by side with portions of text in which apparently conflicting materials are juxtaposed with little or no mediation. This suggests that the book is composed in such a way that diachronicity is written into the synchronic level of its final form. Those responsible for the book as we now have it did not "iron out" some of the book's features that reflect previous stages of its formation.

---

4. On the debate in general, see the various essays in Johannes C. de Moor, ed., *Synchronic or Diachronic? A Debate on Method in Old Testament Exegesis*, OtSt 34 (Leiden: Brill, 1995), esp. H. G. M. Williamson, "Synchronic and Diachronic in Isaian Perspective," 211–26. Other important contributions to this debate include Rolf Rendtorff, "The Book of Isaiah: A Complex Unity: Synchronic and Diachronic Reading," in *Society of Biblical Literature Seminar Papers*, ed. E. H. Lovering Jr. (Atlanta: Scholars Press, 1991), 8–20, and David M. Carr, "Reaching for Unity in Isaiah," *JSOT* 57 (1993): 61–80.

However, we need to highlight that the book of Isaiah is "diachronic" in two distinct respects. First, the book is "diachronic" in the usual sense in which "diachronic" is employed in the academic study of biblical texts, that is, in the sense that statements that originated in different historical periods are interwoven throughout it. Second, the book is "diachronic" in the sense that all parts of the book contain statements that reflect an acute awareness of a divine plan that can be traced through events from the past, that is being fine-tuned in the authors' or editors' present, and that will be worked out *in various ways* through *several* periods in the future. There is, then, an acute sense of past, present, and various alternative futures in the book.[5]

Furthermore, there are different kinds of references to the future in Isaiah. Some are more "eschatological" than others, referring to different time spans in the future. The word "eschatology" commonly concerns the *eschaton*, i.e., the time of the end. In the book of Isaiah, however, the *eschaton* itself is layered, and it is therefore better to speak of "end times" in the plural. Many statements about *different* future periods, often in the form of small, self-contained but similar sub-units, stand side by side in the editorial arrangement of the final form of the book. (Two examples, Isa 7:21–22 and 17:1–14, are discussed below.)

"Eschatology" in Isaiah, then, is multilayered in two respects. First, there are different levels of awareness about the "eschatological" import of relatively brief editorial comments about events of the future, reflecting a sliding scale of "eschatological consciousness" on the part of the various editors who introduced them. Second, and partly dependent on the first point, various statements refer to different kinds of future scenarios that are not necessarily envisaged as happening at the same time or even as being connected through direct causality—other than that God is envisaged as the originator of these events.

Although a full investigation of all future references in the book of Isaiah with a view to this layered eschatology lies outside the scope of this study, later in the essay I will present some case studies to support the hypotheses presented in the preceding paragraphs. The following examples show that the pervasive polyvalence of eschatology in Isaiah owes much to the practicalities of editorial work during the formative period of the book, which extended over several centuries.

Canonical Shaping, Editorial Inconsistencies, and the Nature of Editorial Processes in Isaiah

Following the publication of Bernhard Duhm's groundbreaking commentary on Isaiah in 1892,[6] there was a tendency during most of the twentieth century to see numerous editorial strands reflecting conflicting theologies in the book of Isaiah. More recently, Childs and others have developed a "canonical approach" to the

---

5. On eschatology in the Old Testament, see Knut M. Heim, "The (God-)Forsaken King of Psalm 89: A Historical and Intertextual Enquiry," in *King and Messiah in Israel and the Ancient Near East*, ed. John Day, JSOTSup 270 (Sheffield: Sheffield Academic, 1998), 303–4.

6. Bernhard Duhm, *Das Buch Jesaia* (Göttingen: Vandenhoeck & Ruprecht, 1892).

interpretation of Isaiah in which the final form of the book overrides all previous editorial levels. While previous editorial levels, visible through what Childs called "editorial seams" or "traces," are important for the canonical approach, they mainly serve to cast the "canonical intention(s)" of the final redactor(s) into sharper focus and so help to highlight the theological profile of the final form of the text.[7]

However, the final form of the book of Isaiah contains so many rough edges that this view is less than convincing. The book's final form is not an editorially polished monolith. Rather, it contains finely honed sections side by side with materials in their raw state. As an example that illustrates this point, let us look at Isa 7:21–22:[8]

> On that day one will keep alive a young cow and two sheep, and will eat curds because of the abundance of milk that they give; for everyone that is left in the land shall eat curds and honey.

These two verses belong to a series of oracles (7:18–19, 20, 21–22, 23–24).[9] Since each of these oracles is introduced by the phrase "on that day," a phrase that usually functions as an eschatological formula, they are often considered "eschatological." Following in this vein in his comments on 7:15–25, Childs suggests that "[s]ome of the complexity of the final form of the passage lies in the exegetical activity of those editorial tradents of the Isaianic tradition who struggled in response to the coercion of the text for further understanding of God's purpose with Israel."[10] Regarding 7:21–22 in particular he writes:

> In v. 21 the devastation is such that a man struggles for a subsistence level of life with a young cow and two sheep. Yet at this point, the meaning of the imagery shifts. These few pitiful animals produce such an abundance of milk that all those survivors who are left now feast on curds and honey.[11]

This interpretation may be challenged on several grounds. First, not all "eschatological" formulae refer to an unspecified "end time" of peace, liberty, and justice for Israel. Here, for example, the phrase refers to a specific time of judgment for Judah through an Assyrian invasion in the *foreseeable* future. This suggests that such formulae are either not eschatological at all,[12] or it supports my point made earlier that "eschatology" in Isaiah (and perhaps elsewhere in the Hebrew Bible)

---

7. For a comprehensive study of Childs' canonical approach, see Paul R. Noble, *The Canonical Approach: A Critical Reconstruction of the Hermeneutics of Brevard S. Childs*, BibInt 16 (Leiden: Brill, 1995).

8. Biblical citations in this article will be taken from the NRSV, unless otherwise indicated.

9. On the section as a whole, see also H. G. M. Williamson, "Poetic Vision in Isaiah 7:18–25," in *The Desert Will Bloom: Poetic Visions in Isaiah*, ed. A. Joseph Everson and Hyun Chul Paul Kim, SBLAIL 4 (Atlanta: Society of Biblical Literature, 2009), 77–89.

10. Childs, *Isaiah*, 68.

11. Ibid. Willem A. M. Beuken, by contrast, argues that the oracle describes a situation of bare survival (*notdürftiges Leben*); see Willem A. M. Beuken, *Jesaja 1–12*, HThKAT (Freiburg: Herder, 2003), 208–9. This interpretation ignores the expression מֵרֹב עֲשׂוֹת חָלָב (*mērôb ʿăśôt ḥālāb*), which indicates an *abundance* of milk.

12. So, e.g., John D. W. Watts, *Isaiah 1–33*, WBC 24 (Waco, TX: Word, 1985), 106.

is multilayered. The oracles in Isa 7:15–25 refer to *different* eschatological periods. Second, Childs' language betrays how difficult he finds it to integrate this passage with his overall approach. Terms like "complexity" and phrases like "struggled in response to the coercion of the text for further understanding" point not so much to the labors of the canonical editors as to his own. Third, the oracle found in verses 21–22 is not what it is made out to be by Childs and others; it is not another oracle of judgment that, by means of strenuous editorial activity, has been made into an eschatological promise of future bliss. Verse 21, supposedly the "judgment" part of the oracle, is simply too short to act as such. Rather, the whole of verses 21–22 is a promise of divine help. The oracle has been added *in its raw form* to introduce a glimmer of hope in the midst of the surrounding oracles of doom. It introduces a vision of supernatural provision *in the midst of* divine judgment.[13] Isaiah 7:21–22 is indeed an editorial addition that enhances the final form of the book of Isaiah in its canonical shape. However, within the series of the surrounding oracles, this "counter-oracle" stands out like a sore thumb.

The book of Isaiah contains numerous other passages like Isa 7:21–22. For example, the "Oracle concerning Damascus" in 17:1–14, probably related to the period of the Syro-Ephraimite crisis, contains three subsections (17:4–6, 7–8, 9–11) each of which is introduced by the eschatological formula "on that day." In this context, 17:7–8 is an editorial addition that constitutes an eschatological word of hope that is in stark contrast with the surrounding sections in vv. 4–6 and 9–11. As with 7:21–22, no effort has been made to integrate 17:7–8 with the surrounding material. Childs' comments are instructive. He writes: "the *pattern of shifting without mediation* from judgment to eschatological salvation *is used so frequently* as an *editorial technique* . . . that it tends to support a redactional shaping of the larger passage."[14] The highlighted sections of the text just quoted indicate underlying problems in Childs' analysis. It is true, as Childs points out, that the unmediated juxtaposition of materials is so regular in Isaiah as to form a "pattern," and this supports my earlier claim that editorial inconsistencies are frequent in the book. However, Childs makes a virtue out of necessity when he calls the stark juxtaposition of judgment oracles and "eschatological" oracles a "pattern of shifting without mediation." More likely, repeated unmediated juxtapositions are not evidence of an "editorial technique," as Childs calls it, but rather point to a *lack* of editorial intervention.

---

13. Cf. Williamson, "Poetic Vision," 85–86: "[A]lthough these verses certainly envisage a small population surviving the disaster of the previous verses, there is no implication that they should expect to be entering some new age of blessing and plenty; rather, it seems they will survive with a minimum of livestock and with a diet that results from the milk of the animals together with naturally produced honey." I agree with Williamson that what is in view here is less than a blessed age of bliss. However, the combination of milk/butter and honey in other texts (e.g., Gen 18:8; Deut 32:14; Judg 5:25; 2 Sam 17:29) consistently suggests considerably more than simple survival. See Etan Levine, "The Land of Milk and Honey," *JSOT* 87 (2000): 43–57. Contra Levine's claim that Isa 7:22 is a sarcastic inversion of this theme (ibid., 54), the passage should be read in the light of the normal meaning suggested by the mention of milk and honey.

14. Childs, *Isaiah*, 137; emphases added.

This is not to say that there is no editorial shaping in the book of Isaiah or even in the kind of sections under discussion—quite the opposite. Indeed, I believe that Childs is correct in his overall assessment of canonical shaping in the book of Isaiah and elsewhere in the Hebrew Bible. However, I would like to suggest that examples like the ones just cited show that the persons responsible for canonical shaping, at least in the book called Isaiah, did not aim for absolute editorial consistency.[15] The main problem for the canonical approach of Childs and his followers is the uneven nature of the results of the proposed editorial process(es) that are evident in the biblical text of Isaiah itself. On the one hand, very sophisticated editorial activity has shaped various parts of the book of Isaiah into a larger whole. On the other hand, one finds the kinds of editorial inconsistencies just described, as well as rough transitions between major parts of the book—for example, the way chapters 36–39 are positioned between chapters 1–35 and chapters 40–66, or the abrupt way in which chapter 40, with its focus on the return from exile in the sixth century, follows biographical court materials of the eighth-century King Hezekiah.[16]

Similarly, why is there no narrative account in Isaiah of the exile of the northern kingdom to Assyria similar to chapters 36–39? Perhaps the brief editorial gloss in Isa 7:8b constituted an attempt to remedy this perceived gap in the historical record. The phrase "within sixty-five years Ephraim will be shattered, no longer a people" in Isa 7:8—marked as an editorial comment in the NRSV by means of parentheses—is one of a number of references to specific time periods (see also "seventy years" in 23:15) that introduce a mid-term diachronic perspective (i.e., longer than a few years but not an "end times" reference).[17] Isaiah 7:8b seems quite obviously to interrupt the flow of vv. 8a–9, and should therefore not be understood as a deliberate attempt to "deceive" readers but rather as *a way of introducing a gloss into the text that was meant to be recognized as such*. This seems to be an example of a short editorial gloss whose brevity was due to lack of space on the scroll. Apparently the phrase was simply copied subsequently in its unaltered form as part of the main text when a new copy of the book was produced.

The book of Isaiah, then, contains numerous instances of editorial additions that have been integrated into their contexts with varying degrees of sophistication. In a recent study of Isaiah, Blenkinsopp states:

> The history of the interpretation of Isaiah begins in the book itself. . . . We can detect throughout the book an ongoing process of commentary and supplementation,

---

15. Cf. Carr, "Reaching for Unity," 62, 70–71, 77–78. Contra Carr, however, it is not the *content* of the non-integrated materials that made them "not amenable to final closure" (ibid., 62). Rather, as I will demonstrate below, seamless editing was complicated by the nature of the writing materials available and the writing conventions of the time.

16. Cf. the fundamental critique of sophisticated editing in the Pentateuch and the historical books of the Hebrew Bible mustered by John Van Seters in his *The Edited Bible: The Curious History of the "Editor" in Biblical Criticism* (Winona Lake, IN: Eisenbrauns, 2006). Carr ("Reaching for Unity," 68–70) proposes an interesting explanation for the role of chs. 36–39 in easing the transition, but even this fails to explain why there is no mention of defeat and exile at the hand of Babylon; so also Beuken, *Jesaja 1–12*, 29.

17. For the temporal references, see Beuken, *Jesaja 1–12*, 199.

of cumulative and incremental interpretive activity, until the point is reached where such activity had to be carried on outside the book, in the form of commentary on it.[18]

A similar scenario is envisaged by Hugh Williamson. Building on a discussion by David Carr,[19] he notes that

> these later editors worked at the margins, introducing their material at the opening and close of sections in order to invite a particular reading of the whole while nevertheless respecting the integrity of the material which they inherited. In many cases this material includes passages which run counter to the later editors' dominating perceptions. For modern scholars to attempt to force the whole book into a synthesis on the basis of these redactional passages can never, therefore, be more than partially successful. Their limited impact on the growth of the book as a whole needs be respected.[20]

I largely agree with Williamson's and Carr's reconstructions. The diachronic dimensions of the final form of Isaiah need to feed into synchronic interpretations of the book. Nonetheless, many of the book's diachronic features may not reflect the degree of incompatibility between earlier material and the views of later editors that Carr and Williamson suggest. In the following section, I will propose a scenario of extended editing over time that may better account for the juxtaposition of highly integrated with less integrated editorial materials.

How, practically, did such editing happen, and who were the people who did the editing? Works like Isaiah would, in their various editorial stages, have been heard in public by many, but would have been read by few. Even fewer individuals had the means to own such materials. The most likely owners would have been the temple in Jerusalem, the royal court, and the more important synagogues in Judah and the Diaspora, with important priests and scribes situated at the temple and/or the court having the motivation, the means, and the opportunity to carry out editorial work on the text.[21]

Like the book of Isaiah in its various incarnations, substantial pieces of writing were committed to "scrolls" in the form of sheets of papyrus or animal skin (parchment) that were sewn together to produce long panels about twenty to thirty centimeters wide and up to several meters long, which were then rolled up for easy storage.[22] The Great Isaiah Scroll (1QIsa[a]) is 734 centimeters long and contains all sixty-six chapters of the book of Isaiah, written in fifty-four columns.[23]

---

18. Joseph Blenkinsopp, *Opening the Sealed Book: Interpretations of the Book of Isaiah in Late Antiquity* (Grand Rapids: Eerdmans, 2006), 7.

19. Carr, "Reaching for Unity," 61–80.

20. Williamson, "Synchronic and Diachronic," 219.

21. See David M. Carr, *Writing on the Tablet of the Heart: Origins of Scripture and Literature* (Oxford: Oxford University Press, 2005).

22. See Emanuel Tov, "The Writing of Early Scrolls and the Literary Analysis of Hebrew Scripture," *DSD* 13 (2006): 339–47. For fuller discussions of the technical aspects of writing on early scrolls, see idem, *Scribal Practices and Approaches Reflected in the Texts Found in the Judean Desert*, STDJ 54 (Atlanta: Society of Biblical Literature, 2009).

23. Eugene Ulrich and Peter W. Flint, *Qumran Cave 1: II. The Isaiah Scrolls*, part 1, *Plates and Transcriptions*, DJD 32 (Oxford: Clarendon, 2010); see also idem, *Qumran Cave*

Significantly, the width of the columns varies considerably from sheet to sheet and even on the same sheet. Furthermore, the length of the various sheets varies significantly, as does the number of lines per column. The following table shows the number of columns on the seventeen sheets of parchment that were sewn together to make up the Great Isaiah Scroll:

Sheet	Columns	Sheet	Columns	Sheet	Columns
1	3	7	3	13	3
2	4	8	2	14	3
3	4	9	3	15	3
4	4	10	3	16	3
5	4	11	3	17	2
6	3	12	4		

**Figure 1. The Number of Columns on Each Sheet
of the Great Isaiah Scroll (1QIsaᵃ)**

The average number of columns per sheet is three, but there are five sheets with four columns and two sheets with two columns. Some sheets are significantly wider than others (e.g., Sheet 12 compared with Sheet 8).

In the light of the editorial inconsistencies observed above, I would like to propose a sketch of how various kinds of editorial activities may have contributed to the final form of the book. Since we lack any primary evidence (i.e., scrolls from the time period under consideration), I should acknowledge that I am basing my comments on what we know about scribal practices from Qumran and elsewhere and drawing reasonable inferences to imagine the situation.

There is a fundamental difference between modern and even medieval literature, on the one hand, and ancient literature, on the other: "ancient texts were primarily written to be heard, not seen."[24] Ancient reading practice involved reading texts out loud, whether they were read by individuals or to a larger audience. Furthermore, ancient writing materials, especially papyrus and parchment, were expensive and therefore writers and copyists, for financial reasons, generally put as much

---

1: II. *The Isaiah Scrolls*, part 2, *Introductions, Commentary, and Textual Variants*, DJD 32 (Oxford: Clarendon, 2010). See also the online publication of 1QIsaᵃ in *The Digital Dead Sea Scrolls* project (http://dss.collections.imj.org.il/isaiah, accessed February 2, 2014), and Donald W. Parry and Elisha Qimron, *The Great Isaiah Scroll (1QIsaᵃ): A New Edition*, STDJ 32 (Leiden: Brill, 1999).

24. David A. Dorsey, *The Literary Structure of the Old Testament: A Commentary on Genesis–Malachi* (Grand Rapids: Baker Academic, 1999), 15–16.

text on a given writing surface as possible.[25] This had two consequences: First, unlike most modern printed materials, biblical texts were written by authors, editors, and copyists continuously, with few breaks or spaces between sentences or paragraphs or even larger sections that might have visually presented a text's structure. Second, ancient writers, authors, editors, glossators, copyists, and readers were forced to use *audible* means to explain the relationships between the various parts of the text on the page. "Signals were geared for the ear, not the eye, since visual markers would be of little value to a listening audience."[26] There were no italics or underlining to highlight words, no brackets to mark interpolations, no footnotes or text boxes for additional explanatory materials.[27] However, this does not mean that ancient texts contained no means for marking such materials. For example, sophisticated combinations of repetition and variation could act as structural markers. The reversal of word order and repetition acted to highlight specific words or parts of a sentence.

We may therefore draw an analogy from audible *structural* markers to audible *interpretive* markers and reconstruct possible scenarios for the various editorial activities.

(1) To save space, editorial additions were often limited to brief glosses and bare editorial additions, without including elegant literary padding that would have integrated the new materials smoothly into their immediate contexts on the page.

(2) Interpretive comments and contextual links may have been provided by readers through intonation and side remarks during reading.

(3) Some of the latter were later simply included where they seemed to fit, without much editorial effort or skill being exerted when less accomplished scribes mechanically copied the work onto a new scroll.

---

25. A possible objection to this statement is the observation that ancient scrolls, for example ones from among the Dead Sea Scrolls, contain significant amounts of empty space in the form of large margins at the edges of the scrolls. In my opinion, these margins do not indicate a lack of concern over space. Rather, the willingness of scribes and those who commissioned these texts to commit such considerable amounts of space to the production of margins suggests aesthetic and practical concerns. Aesthetically, the margins served an ornamental role in order to indicate the importance that was accorded the written contents of the scrolls. Practically, the margins served a protective role, preserving the written contents of the scrolls from destruction, whether accidental or that caused by natural processes that occurred over time, as ancient scrolls typically were damaged or decayed at the edges (most commonly at the beginnings, ends, and bottoms of the scrolls, as the extant examples of the Dead Sea Scrolls amply demonstrate). Rather than suggesting a lack of concern over space, this costly investment in space-consuming margins further increased the pressure to save space. See Tov's comments on "*de luxe* editions" with larger margins and low levels of scribal intervention, many of which were scriptural scrolls (idem, *Scribal Practices and Approaches*, 125–29).

26. Dorsey, *Literary Structure*, 16.

27. Ibid., 15.

(4) Lengthier additions and more elegant editorial adjustments were incorporated where there was space to do so when entire works were copied onto new writing materials. This gave expert editors the opportunity to make larger and more systematic revisions and improvements. Some editing of significant sections may have occurred through exchanging individual sheets within a scroll, using a smaller sheet (like Sheet 8 of 1QIsa[a]) to leave out sections of material, and using larger sheets (like Sheet 12 of 1QIsa[a]) to add extra material.

Evidence supporting this explanation can be found through tracing editorial activities in the writings from Qumran. Emanuel Tov reached similar conclusions in his recent study of scribal practices in the writing of Qumran scrolls. Summarizing his findings, he states:

> [A]ssuming that the external shape of the earliest scrolls of Hebrew Scripture was no different from that of the Qumran scrolls, we set out to analyze the procedures for writing and rewriting ancient scrolls. We noted that the inscribed area in scrolls was not a flexible entity. In fact, after the scroll was inscribed, there simply was no technical possibility for a scribe to insert any substantial addition into the text or to delete or rewrite segments larger than a few words or a line. We therefore suggested that editors or scribes did not use earlier copies as the basis for their content changes, but instead, constantly created fresh scrolls for expressing their new thoughts. . . . Each layer of rewriting probably involved the penning of a new copy. This hypothesis involves the further assumption of linear development of Scripture books and probably also the depositing, writing, and rewriting of Scripture scrolls in a central place, viz., the temple.[28]

These suggestions by Tov help to account for the uneven distribution of highly integrated editorial sections interspersed with less sophisticated ones. Going beyond Tov, however, it seems that at least some rewriting of more substantial portions of the text could have been done without producing entirely new copies, as Tov suggests. If the Great Isaiah Scroll (1QIsa[a]) is in any way representative, a medium-length section of text could have been rewritten, and either shortened or expanded by substituting the relevant sheet of parchment, rather than an entirely new copy of the entire composition needing to be produced.

Tov's conclusions and my own observations may explain why those who shaped the book of Isaiah into its final, canonical form left not only subtle traces of their editorial work in the shape of editorial seams (as Childs suggests) but also much more obvious signs of diachronic development. Texts such as the ones discussed above show *overt* signs of development, bright-colored editorial patches sewn on, as it were, in order to signal development, ambiguity, and thus openness of signification—an invitation for creative interpretation. In Tov's view, since the realia of rewriting were formerly beyond the scholarly horizon, we are now obligated to take our new understanding of ancient editorial processes into consideration in our historical-critical analysis of Hebrew Scripture.[29]

---

28. Tov, "Writing of Early Scrolls," 347.

29. Ibid. Cf. also Jesper Høgenhaven, "The Isaiah Scroll and the Composition of the Book of Isaiah," in *Qumran between the Old and New Testaments*, ed. Frederick H. Cryer and Thomas L. Thompson, JSOTSup 290 (Sheffield: Sheffield Academic, 1998), 151–58.

Earlier Prophecies in the Book Called Isaiah

In the following section, I will consider how the topos of "former things" is used in the book of Isaiah to demonstrate divine sovereignty over international affairs. This will provide examples of later editorial work of a more systematic nature that consciously employs diachronic references to authenticate the prophetic message in Isaiah 40–66. Two kinds of texts are relevant here: those that relate former things to the present or the future, and those that authenticate the antiquity of earlier prophecies.

The "Former Things" in Isaiah

The following texts appear to relate former things to the present and/or the future: Isa 37:26–27; 40:27–41:4; 41:21–29; 42:9; 43:8–13; 43:15–21; 44:6–8; 44:26–45:1; 46:8–11; 48:3–8; 48:14–16; 65:16–17. All but the first and the last of these appear in the part of the book commonly referred to as "Second Isaiah." Since an examination of all these texts lies outside the scope of the present study,[30] I will use 41:21–29 as a case study to illustrate the synchronic purpose to which diachronic features in a text could be put, with special focus on the relationship between Israel and the nations. With the God of Israel addressing rival gods, Isa 41:21–29 reads:

> Set forth your case, says the LORD; bring your proofs, says the King of Jacob. Let them bring them, and tell us what is to happen. Tell us the former things, what they are, so that we may consider them, and that we may know their outcome; or declare to us the things to come. Tell us what is to come hereafter, that we may know that you are gods; do good, or do harm, that we may be afraid and terrified. You, indeed, are nothing and your work is nothing at all; whoever chooses you is an abomination. I stirred up one from the north, and he has come, from the rising of the sun, *one who calls on my name*.[31] He shall trample on rulers as on mortar, as the potter treads clay. Who declared it from the beginning, so that we might know, and beforehand, so that we might say, "He is right"? There was no one who declared it, none who proclaimed, none who heard your words. I first have declared it to Zion, and I give to Jerusalem a herald of good tidings. But when I look there is no one; among these there is no counselor who, when I ask, gives an answer. No, they are all a delusion; their works are nothing; their images are empty wind.

Verse 25 presents a specific example of "former things," prophecies originally given by the God of Israel to Isaiah of Jerusalem that are now seen to have been fulfilled. As Childs notes, "the description of God's 'stirring up' Cyrus from the north (41:25) picks up the same verb used in 13:17, 'I am stirring up the Medes.'"[32] In other words,

---

30. Cf. Carr, "Reaching for Unity," 69–70, and the references to relevant work of other scholars in note 15 there. See also Christopher R. Seitz, *Zion's Final Destiny: The Development of the Book of Isaiah; A Reassessment of Isaiah 36–39* (Minneapolis: Fortress, 1991), 37–46.

31. The italics here indicate that I have followed the Masoretic text, against the NRSV's conjecture "he was summoned by name" (following an ingenious but unnecessary emendation by Elliger); see Childs, *Isaiah*, 321, and John Goldingay, *The Message of Isaiah 40–55: A Literary-Theological Commentary* (London: T&T Clark, 2005), 144.

32. Childs, *Introduction to the Old Testament as Scripture*, 330, cited in Seitz, *Zion's Final Destiny*, 43n27. See also Childs, *Isaiah*, 322–23, and John Goldingay and David F. Payne, *A*

the overthrow of the Babylonian empire at the hands of Cyrus the Mede is seen as the fulfillment of a prophetic word from the past, preserved in a part of the book that is commonly referred to as "First Isaiah" and supposedly first uttered more than a century earlier by Isaiah of Jerusalem.[33]

In this and the other passages that mention "former things," the issue at stake is whether it is the God of Israel or other gods who control(s) past, present, and future events. Consequently, these texts are regularly set in the forensic language of lawsuits in which Israel's God presents his case for superiority to the other gods and/or their worshippers. The argument repeatedly turns on evidence surrounding one central issue: Who has in the past foretold what has now come, is now coming, or will soon come to pass? According to the reasoning of these passages, the answer to this question determines which deity is in control of events and thus more worthy of worship than the others. Beyond such "trials" of other gods and the question of religious adherence, however, a more profound question is answered for the suffering, doubting, and hesitant exiles. They are comforted, their election is confirmed, and their hope for an imminent return from exile is kindled.[34] The present time of crisis and decision is part of God's long-term planning, and present circumstances can be understood in the light of Israel's history (the past) and final destiny (the future). God's sovereignty includes all nations, including the most powerful empires of the time (Babylon and Persia).

Another example of a potential former prophecy—Isaiah of Jerusalem's prophecy to Hezekiah concerning the exile to Babylon in Isaiah 39—further illustrates the point. Roy Melugin suggests that this passage comes the closest to providing a setting for Isaiah 40–55, envisaging a redactor placing the material of Second Isaiah next to the last concrete historical reference in the book of Isaiah as it then existed.[35] Agreeing with Melugin on this point, Seitz concludes:

> Why is there so substantial a book associated with the prophet Isaiah? The answer would turn on the fulfillment of the divine word. Why?—because Isaiah spoke of the future assault on Zion by Babylon (39:5–7), and because he also spoke of God's abiding protection over that same Zion (37:35). The first was fulfilled, allowing God to speak again from the divine counsel about a judgment that had been rendered (40:2). Concerning the second there were serious questions, but here too the "former things" were the witness to which the prophet turned to defend the cause of Zion (44:26).[36]

Critical and Exegetical Commentary on Isaiah 40–55, vol. 1, *Introduction and Commentary on Isaiah 40–44:23*, ICC (London: T&T Clark, 2006), 200.

33. See Seitz, *Zion's Final Destiny*, 41–45, and Christopher R. North, "The 'Former Things' and the 'New Things' in Deutero-Isaiah," in *Studies in Old Testament Prophecy, Presented to Professor Theodore H. Robinson by the Society for Old Testament Study on his Sixty-fifth Birthday, August 9th, 1946*, ed. H. H. Rowley (Edinburgh: T&T Clark, 1950), 111–26, esp. 119–20, 124.

34. See Childs, *Isaiah*, 317.

35. Roy F. Melugin, *The Formation of Isaiah 40–55*, BZAW 141 (Berlin: de Gruyter, 1976), 177.

36. Seitz, *Zion's Final Destiny*, 45.

Isaiah 42:9—which declares, "See, the former things have come to pass, and new things I now declare; before they spring forth, I tell you of them"—could thus be a theme verse for the line of argumentation used in the passages mentioning "former things." Because the fulfillment of the previously declared "former things" is set forth as evidence of God's control over Israel's destiny, the exiles addressed in Isaiah 40–55 are encouraged to heed the prophetic summons to get ready for their imminent return to the homeland, for Israel's God "confirms the word of his servant, and fulfills the prediction of his messengers; [he] says of Jerusalem, 'It shall be inhabited,' and of the cities of Judah, 'They shall be rebuilt, and I will raise up their ruins'" (44:26). The argument presented in these passages hinges on a diachronic dimension in the text, and the importance of this diachronic dimension cannot be underestimated. "[T]he corpus of Second Isaiah presupposes that of First Isaiah," not just editorially, in the sense that the latter comes first in the book (synchronic level), but historically (diachronic level). The prophecies of First Isaiah that are now being fulfilled were given long ago by Isaiah of Jerusalem, and this diachronic level plays the crucial role in Second Isaiah's argument.[37]

The "Sealed Book" in Isaiah

But if so much editing was going on, how could the recipients of the message and the readers of the book know that such "ancient" prophecies were really as old as they were said to be? The book of Isaiah itself provides an eloquent answer. The first reference to the production and "sealing" of prophetic utterances in written form is found in Isa 8:16–17: "Bind up the testimony, seal the teaching among my disciples. I will wait for the LORD, who is hiding his face from the house of Jacob, and I will hope in him." Note here the reference to waiting and to the prophet's hope that is grounded in the existence of the sealed teaching that is to be kept by his disciples. In a similar situation in which the prophet's message is rejected again, Isaiah is also directed to write it down—on a tablet, the most durable writing surface—so that it will be preserved for the time of the message's fulfillment: "Go now, write it before them on a tablet, and inscribe it in a book, so that it may be for the time to come as a witness forever" (30:8). Blenkinsopp comments on the relationship between these two passages as follows:

> Isaiah confided his testimonies and teachings to his disciples in order to guarantee the authenticity of the predictions they contained after the failure of his first incursion into Judean foreign affairs (Isa 8:16). This written copy is called a "testimony" *(tĕ῾ûdâ)*, an indication that predictive prophecies could take on a quasilegal status when written and notarized for purposes of authentication, comparable to the prophetic "witness" written in a "book" alluded to at Isa 30:8–11.[38]

---

37. Cf. Childs, *Isaiah*, 322, and Williamson, *Book Called Isaiah*, 2–3.

38. Blenkinsopp, *Opening the Sealed Book*, 6–7. A similar argument can be found in Williamson, *Book Called Isaiah*, 94–115.

After his first intervention in international affairs failed to alter political and religious behavior, Isaiah was told to preserve his message in writing and charge his disciples to keep his prophetic teachings in sealed form in the expectation of the eventual vindication of their truth and relevance. But why a *sealed* book? Important documents, such as legal contracts, were sealed with wax or clay to avoid tampering and some would require validation by witnesses, like the tablet on which Isaiah was told to write "Belonging to Maher-shalal-hash-baz" (8:1–2). Isaiah 29:11–12 reads:

> The vision of all this has become for you like the words of a sealed document. If it is given to those who can read, with the command, "Read this," they say, "We cannot, for it is sealed." And if it is given to those who cannot read, saying, "Read this," they say, "We cannot read."

Blenkinsopp explains:

> [S]ealing a predictive prophecy had the purpose of providing irrefutable proof of its authenticity, and therefore its divine origin, at the time of fulfillment. When that happened, and the prophet was sure that it would, the situation envisaged in 29:11–12 would be reversed. The book would be unsealed and its meaning would become clear to those now capable of hearing and understanding.[39]

Blenkinsopp's point is supported by Isa 29:18: "On that day the deaf shall hear the words of a scroll, and out of their gloom and darkness the eyes of the blind shall see." Since there are only two references to a sealed document in Isaiah, "it seems likely that the sealed 'vision of all these things' is a reference to Isaiah's sealed testimony confided to his disciples. . . . The passage about the sealed book, therefore, deals with the reception or nonreception of *written* prophecy."[40]

As Blenkinsopp notes, Isa 29:11–12 initially concerned Israel's "failure to grasp the prophetic message, but its more precise import can be determined only in the context of the book as a whole."[41] Recognizing the secondary nature of 29:11–12 (a prose addition to the preceding poetic material), Blenkinsopp suggests that this and other such "addenda are attached to and are generated by reflection on existing prophetic sayings, updating earlier pronouncements in light of later situations, creating in effect new prophecy out of old."[42] Blenkinsopp understands the passage as simply another way of expressing, through the metaphor of a sealed book, the public's lack of comprehension when confronted with the prophet's oral message. Since the book of Isaiah as a whole is also presented as a vision, the expression "the vision of all this" in 29:11 may refer to the book of Isaiah in whatever shape it existed at the time of writing.[43]

---

39. Blenkinsopp, *Opening the Sealed Book*, 14.

40. Ibid., 13; emphasis original.

41. Ibid., 9.

42. Ibid., 9. Cf. Childs' comment, "[D]ivine revelation has now been carefully related to the vehicle of a written scroll. The effect of hardening is that Israel can no longer understand its scriptures. Certainly this development would indicate a later stage in the history of the text's growth" (Childs, *Isaiah*, 218).

43. Blenkinsopp, *Opening the Sealed Book*, 11–12.

The statement in 48:16—"Draw near to me, hear this! From the beginning I have not spoken in secret, from the time it came to be I have been there. And now the Lord God has sent me and his spirit"—may seem to contradict the preceding argument. However, the point of "sealing" the prophetic teachings was not to keep them secret, but rather to preserve them in unaltered form and thus prove, at a later time, that the predictive prophecy contained in them had been fulfilled.

Conclusion

In this study of diachronic and synchronic features in the book of Isaiah, I have developed a model of the textual genesis of the book called Isaiah that attempts to explain the puzzling juxtaposition of highly edited materials with less integrated materials and the overlapping phenomenon of the presence of apparently contradictory statements in close proximity (e.g., Isa 2:21–22 and 17:1–14). How can we account for the coexistence of heavily edited sections that exhibit textual tensions that not only have been preserved but also at times have even been highlighted?

In my discussion of writing and copying, I have suggested a process of annotation, copying, and more extensive editing that has explanatory power for some of these texts. I have also argued that more consistency *could* have been achieved with relative ease. The question thus presents itself: Why are such inconsistencies as we find not only so pronounced but also so pervasive? Two possible answers suggest themselves: (1) There were so many different layers of reinterpretation and so many different copyists and redactors involved in the production of the text in its present form that consistency was simply impossible to achieve. (2) Most of the tensions and their accentuations are deliberately and skillfully built into the final form of the book.

To what extent can these two answers respond satisfactorily to two additional questions regarding the book of Isaiah? Namely: Why, then, does the book retain such a high literary quality, and why are there also so many highly sophisticated and well-executed cross-links in the book, features that have been demonstrated in two important recent volumes of collected essays?[44] In my view, the first answer cannot account for these features. The second answer, by contrast, can account for salient features of the book as a whole as well as for the specific passages studied here.

First, the book of Isaiah in its final, highly edited form contains diachronic and other contrasting features as a consequence of ancient writing processes. Second, the book has a concept of time that differs markedly from modern, Western conceptions, specifically with regard to a "layered" understanding of several possible futures. Third, the various contributors to the book not only had different perceptions of the many complex theological themes in the book, but they also

---

44. See the essays in Everson and Kim, *The Desert Will Bloom*, and in J. Todd Hibbard and Hyun Chul Paul Kim, eds., *Formation and Intertextuality in Isaiah 24–27*, SBLAIL 17 (Atlanta: SBL, 2013).

shared a nuanced understanding of their complexity, and consequently recognized the validity and complementarity of each other's contributions to the ongoing conversation.

What the evidence points to is that the book called Isaiah is a multi-author work, and later contributors to the book did not seek to hide that fact, even accentuating features of the book that provide clues to this effect for later readers. The book is—and wants to be—self-consciously polyphonic.

This consciously dialogical approach to communicating the complex theological issues at stake arose from awareness among many of the contributors to the book of the changing relational dynamics between Israel and its God, as evidenced in the cataclysmic historical developments leading up to, through, and beyond exile. The result is the beautifully complex and poetically ambiguous yet theologically rich and compelling compendium called "the book of Isaiah." It gathers the voices and insights of its many contributors into a larger, more voluminous choir of witnesses testifying to a theological vision that emerged over time, producing the timeless message of a larger "oratorio" in which the combined voices of all communicate much more than the sum of the individual parts.

The book of Isaiah wants to be read as a unified composition inspired by the historical figure of the prophet Isaiah of Jerusalem. It also wants to be read as a "prophetic chronicle." The book as a whole intersperses the original compositions from Isaiah's own lifetime with divinely inspired theological and equally prophetic reflections in the form of shorter comments *and* carefully crafted, longer literary units, in both prose and poetic form. This prophetic chronicle constitutes an account of faithful prophetic reflection through time, informed by and responding to the fulfillment of Isaiah of Jerusalem's prophecy and new historical circumstances long after his lifetime. It includes new prophecy based on fresh divine revelation and informed by faithful theological and historical reflection that providentially guides later generations of Israelite (and Christian) believers through the challenges they face in their own generations and beyond.

7

Isaiah as Prophet and Isaiah as Book in Their Ancient Near Eastern Context

John W. Hilber

Introduction

In 2000, Philip Davies wrote: "the indisputable evidence that the so-called 'prophetic' books were created as literary artifacts, and indeed were mostly brought into their present shape by scribal editing, surely places the burden of proof on those who want to associate them primarily with the spoken words of many individuals."[1] In the light of relatively recent expansion in our knowledge of ancient Near Eastern prophetism, I have discussed in a general way this "burden of proof" in an earlier essay.[2] In the present article, the emphasis lies on the contribution that the study of ancient Near Eastern prophecy can make to questions about the prophet Isaiah and the book that bears his name.

Isaiah as Prophet

Relevance and Possibility of Prophetic Portraits

The historicity of the prophet Isaiah might appear relatively unimportant to the message of the book of Isaiah. Yet, even a canonical approach that often sidesteps historical questions is deeply concerned with the reality of the experience of the prophets, exemplified, for example, in call narratives, the prophets' role in intercession, or their inner struggles that gave birth to their messages.[3] Authenticity and theological truth are inseparable. The existence and character of Isaiah the prophet is of interest for understanding the composition history of the book of Isaiah.

---

1. Philip R. Davies, "'Pen of Iron, Point of Diamond' (Jer. 17:1): Prophecy as Writing," in *Writings and Speech in Israelite and Ancient Near Eastern Prophecy*, ed. Ehud Ben Zvi, Michael H. Floyd, and Christopher R. Matthews, SBLSymS 10 (Atlanta: Society of Biblical Literature, 2000), 66.

2. John W. Hilber, "The Culture of Prophecy and Writing in the Ancient Near East," in *Do Historical Matters Matter to Faith? A Critical Appraisal of Modern and Postmodern Approaches to Scripture*, ed. James K. Hoffmeier and Dennis R. Magary (Wheaton, IL: Crossway, 2012), 219–41.

3. Brevard S. Childs, *Old Testament Theology in a Canonical Context* (Philadelphia: Fortress, 1985), 123–28.

When attempting to examine the features of a prophet as an individual, one must address the methodological question of whether the writings attributed to prophets in the Old Testament are reliable sources for reconstructing anything historical about the prophets themselves.[4] With characteristic clarity, Martti Nissinen writes, "Prophecy as it appears in the biblical texts ('biblical prophecy') is a literary construct related to the historical phenomenon of prophetic intermediation ('ancient Hebrew prophecy') but not identical with it."[5] How then does one bridge the gap without assuming the historical authenticity of the texts? While demonstrating historical plausibility is helpful, it is not sufficient to establish that the portrait of a prophet in literature corresponds to an actual prophet's life. Many would agree that ancient texts indicate *some* reality about the world they describe, but this in itself does not entail that specific events or persons so described are more than fiction.[6] But there is another consideration that should not be overlooked. All available information leads to the conclusion that the ancients regarded the source of prophecy and accuracy of reporting to be important (see below). Would mere correspondence to a *realistic* story (i.e., it "rang true") satisfy an audience weighing the credibility and authority of the divine word? The implied "contractual agreement" between author and audience was different for prophecy than for narrative text (e.g., epic). Therefore, for a prophetic text to have been acceptable to an ancient audience, we should expect an authentic link between prophet and text. One's ability to evaluate the *degree* of correlation between the text and historical reality depends in part on how one understands the commitment of the ancient culture in question to preserving original prophetic speech and what freedom was acceptable to alter or elaborate on that speech. So, in addition to historical plausibility, it is important to evaluate the relationship between prophetic speech and its transmission in writing.

Prophetic Portraits

Although scholars tend to understate differences between prophets in Israel and those in neighboring cultures—particularly regarding the degree of ethical criticism, judgment, and stance against religious pluralism found among the bibli-

---

4. For an overview of the methodological debate, see Martti Nissinen, "The Historical Dilemma of Biblical Prophetic Studies," in *Prophecy in the Book of Jeremiah*, ed. Hans M. Barstad and Reinhard G. Kratz, BZAW 388 (Berlin: de Gruyter, 2009), 103–20, and, with a different emphasis, Hilber, "Culture of Prophecy and Writing," 219–21.

5. Nissinen, "Historical Dilemma of Biblical Prophetic Studies," 108, 114; cf. idem, "What is Prophecy? An Ancient Near Eastern Perspective," in *Inspired Speech: Prophecy in the Ancient Near East; Essays in Honour of Herbert B. Huffmon*, ed. John Kaltner and Louis Stulman, JSOTSup 378 (London: T&T Clark, 2004), 31.

6. Hans M. Barstad, "What Prophets Do: Reflections on Past Reality in the Book of Jeremiah," in *Prophecy in the Book of Jeremiah*, ed. Hans M. Barstad and Reinhard G. Kratz, BZAW 388 (Berlin: de Gruyter, 2009), 22–24, 31–32; Nissinen, "Historical Dilemma of Biblical Prophetic Studies," 109.

cal prophets—Robert Gordon's conclusion remains a fair assessment: "In the end the difference between Israelite prophecy and the rest may simply have to be expressed in terms of its conception of its God."[7] The important point is that the Old Testament portrait coheres well with what is known of prophetic phenomena in the broader ancient Near East. This extends to the prophet Isaiah in several particulars.

Like other ancient Near Eastern prophets, Isaiah served as a "sign" (Isa 8:18; cf. ARM 26 207:4–7)[8] and performed symbolic actions (Isa 20:2–3; cf. ARM 26 206:1–18). His ministry to kings illustrates the function of a prophet as intercessor and one who responds to inquiry and lament (Isa 37:1–7; 38:1–8; cf. SAA 9 1.8 v 14–21).[9] Isaiah's call brought him into the divine council, which was a prerogative of extrabiblical prophets as well (Isa 6:1–9; cf. SAA 12 69 [rations for prophetesses in the divine council]).[10] His messages included oracles of encouragement and announcements of the destruction of enemies, and were intended to influence political decision-making in the interest of the state. In these contexts, conflict between Isaiah and other Judean leaders is not without parallel among prophets and other functionaries in Mesopotamian society.[11] The text of the book of Isaiah contains considerable criticism directed at society and the monarchy, whereas there is comparatively less emphasis on this in ancient Near Eastern prophecy; nevertheless, some similarity exists (Isa 7:9; cf. Mari A.1121+A.2731; A.1968).[12] These

---

7. Robert P. Gordon, "Where Have All the Prophets Gone? The 'Disappearing' Israelite Prophet Against the Background of Ancient Near Eastern Prophecy," *BBR* 5 (1995): 86. For a concise survey of the data, see Hilber, "Culture of Prophecy and Writing," 222–23. For a more complete comparison and commentary, see Martti Nissinen, "Biblical Prophecy from a Near Eastern Perspective: The Cases of Kingship and Divine Possession," in *Congress Volume, Ljubljana 2007*, ed. André Lemaire, VTSup 133 (Leiden: Brill, 2010), 441–68.

8. See Matthijs J. de Jong, *Isaiah among the Ancient Near Eastern Prophets: A Comparative Study of the Earliest Stages of the Isaiah Tradition and the Neo-Assyrian Prophecies*, VTSup 117 (Leiden: Brill, 2007), 264. However, *ittātim* ("signs") could refer to the substance of a drink given to the prophets to induce their oracles rather than a reference to the prophets themselves. See Martti Nissinen, C. L. Seow, and Robert K. Ritner, *Prophets and Prophecy in the Ancient Near East*, SBLWAW 12 (Atlanta: Society of Biblical Literature, 2003), 41. This volume offers convenient access to almost all sources cited in this essay.

9. Compare ARM 26 207, 212, 216; Hittite plague prayers; Zakkur stela; Assurbanipal Prism B v 46–49; SAA 3 13, 31; SAA 10 294. See also John W. Hilber, *Cultic Prophecy in the Psalms*, BZAW 352 (Berlin: de Gruyter, 2005), 62–74.

10. See ARM 26 196, 208, and the Deir ʿAlla Plaster (the prophets are party to dialogue among the gods); cf. Robert P. Gordon, "From Mari to Moses: Prophecy at Mari and in Ancient Israel," in *Of Prophets' Visions and the Wisdom of Sages: Essays in Honour of R. Norman Whybray on His Seventieth Birthday*, ed. Heather A. McKay and David J. A. Clines, JSOTSup 162 (Sheffield: JSOT Press, 1993), 71–74; cf. 1 Kgs 22:19; Jer 23:22; Zech 3:1–10.

11. Martti Nissinen, *References to Prophecy in Neo-Assyrian Sources*, SAAS 7 (Helsinki: University of Helsinki Press, 1998), 93–95, 150–53; de Jong, *Isaiah among the Ancient Near Eastern Prophets*, 265–66.

12. Mari text A.1121+A.2731 constitutes the only extant example from extra-biblical prophecy where a king's enthronement is threatened. Milder admonitions for social justice and cultic duty are also evident (e.g., A.1968; ARM 26 194, 199, 206, 215, 220, 221, 232; SAA 9 2.3 ii 24–27; 9 3.5 iii 26–27; SAA 13 144). Further, see Martti Nissinen, "Das kritische Potential

comparisons support the supposition that a prophetic tradition begun by a prophet named Isaiah is historically plausible.[13]

Prophets and Writing

In the ancient Near East, prophetic texts were associated closely with the prophets themselves.[14] These societies held divine revelation in high regard and carefully transmitted prophetic speech in a variety of written genres: correspondence, citations embedded in literary works, oracle reports and collections, divine letters, and cultic liturgy.

Correspondence

Perhaps the best known excerpts of prophecy are those found in the Mari correspondence. In these citations, the correspondents carefully indicated the circumstances in which the prophecies originated, identifying as well some important details about the prophets who uttered them. One finds within this correspondence a range of citation techniques, from paraphrase (e.g., ARM 26 207:40–43)[15] to verbatim quotations (e.g., ARM 26 217:27–28).[16] Suggestions that correspondents felt at liberty to alter prophetic oracles to suit their own interests have overstated the evidence—especially when this leads to assertions that we have no confidence that we possess the actual words of the prophets.[17] The royal archive from Nineveh

---

in der altorientalischen Prophetie," in *Propheten in Mari, Assyrien und Israel*, ed. Matthias Köckert and Martti Nissinen, FRLANT 201 (Göttingen: Vandenhoeck and Ruprecht, 2003), 1–32; Nissinen, "Biblical Prophecy from a Near Eastern Perspective," 453.

13. One might add the observation that the book of Isaiah attests the name Isaiah in passages generally assigned to the eighth century, as well as in the historical tradition also preserved in Kings (see de Jong, *Isaiah among the Ancient Near Eastern Prophets*, 263, 269).

14. What follows is a summary of the arguments set forth in Hilber, "Culture of Prophecy and Writing," 223–39. The organization by genre follows Martti Nissinen, "Spoken, Written, Quoted, and Invented: Orality and Writtenness in Ancient Near Eastern Prophecy," in *Writings and Speech in Israelite and Ancient Near Eastern Prophecy*, ed. Ehud Ben Zvi, Michael H. Floyd, and Christopher R. Matthews, SBLSymS 10 (Atlanta: Society of Biblical Literature, 2000), 235–71.

15. Simon B. Parker, "Official Attitudes toward Prophecy at Mari and in Israel," *VT* 43 (1993): 60–62.

16. Dominique Charpin, "Prophètes et rois dans le Proche-Orient Amorrite," in *Prophètes et rois: Bible et Proche-Orient*, ed. André Lemaire, Lectio Divina hors série (Paris: Cerf, 2001), 31–32.

17. The oft-cited example involves three different letters that presumably report the same prophecy and that are linked together by their use of the aphorism "under the straw water runs" (ARM 26 197, 199, 202). Parker represents the first of many who follow this line of argument (Parker, "Official Attitudes toward Prophecy," 57, 62n26). However, careful examination of the context of these three letters shows that they were uttered by two different individuals, and the two oracles delivered by the same prophet originated in two different performance contexts. Therefore, these are not three differing citations of the same oracle; rather, they are three different oracles all directed at the same historical situation.

also preserves letters citing prophetic speech. As at Mari, some citations are close, if not verbatim (e.g., SAA 10 352:25–4′), while others are looser, preserving only the tenor of the original oracle (e.g., SAA 10 284).[18] An important example from late seventh-century Judah is Lachish Ostracon 3, which suggests that prophetic messages were in public circulation outside the elite circles of society.[19] One might expect paraphrase in a genre such as a letter, but in such correspondence the illocution, if not the actual wording, of the prophetic message is faithfully transmitted.

Citations Embedded in Literary Works

A variety of literary works from Mesopotamia, Egypt, and the Levant cite prophetic speech.[20] They exhibit the same range of citation techniques as correspondence, but there is no evidence of free invention.

Oracle Reports and Collections

Unlike the genres just discussed, which cite prophecy as one part of a text with broader purposes, the design of oracle reports was to record and preserve prophetic speech directly, thus offering close access to the oral performance of prophets.[21] The oracles preserved in the Nineveh archive give evidence of direct transcription of oral prophecy with little if any editing. They exhibit formal elements common to biblical prophecy, which will be examined below relative to oracles in Isaiah. Here it is important to note the care with which scribes recorded in colophons the name and place of origin of the oracle, and, in one instance, its exact date. As with reports of prophetic speech in correspondence, the link between divine speech and the identity of the prophet was regarded as crucial to the authority and accountability of the prophecy.

Some of the tablets from Nineveh record only a single oracle, but three tablets contain collections of individual oracles, sometimes from more than one prophet (SAA 9 1–3). In spite of the diversity of prophetic origin, the collections appear to be organized according to chronological and thematic considerations. Although the length of any one of these collections does not exceed that of even the smallest of the biblical prophetic books, the process of oracle collection has led many to draw a parallel with shorter collections within biblical prophetic books.[22] The Nineveh archive

---

18. Nissinen, "Spoken, Written, Quoted, and Invented," 261–63.

19. Nissinen, Seow, and Ritner, *Prophets and Prophecy in the Ancient Near East*, 213.

20. *Epic of Zimri Lim*, *Story of Wenamon*, Zakkur stela, Amman Citadel inscription, the *Marduk Ordeal*, a lament liturgy of Assurbanipal, and the Akitu rituals.

21. Nissinen, "Spoken, Written, Quoted, and Invented," 244.

22. E.g., John Van Seters, "Prophetic Orality in the Context of the Ancient Near East: A Response to Culley, Crenshaw and Davies," in *Writings and Speech in Israelite and Ancient Near Eastern Prophecy*, ed. Ehud Ben Zvi, Michael H. Floyd, and Christopher R. Matthews, SBLSymS 10 (Atlanta: Society of Biblical Literature, 2000), 86; Nissinen, "Spoken, Written, Quoted, and Invented," 254; idem, "How Prophecy Became Literature," *SJOT* 19 (2005): 165–66; Karel van der Toorn, *Scribal Culture and the Making of the Hebrew Bible* (Cambridge: Harvard University Press, 2007), 123.

is significant because it shows that prophetic oracles were inscribed soon after oral delivery, were given shape as collections within a decade of recording, and remained associated with the person of the prophet who actually spoke the oracles. The Deir ʿAlla plaster texts show that literary transmission of prophecy was possible in the region of Jerusalem at a time earlier than that purported for the biblical prophetic books. They contain an interlacing of narrative passages with oracular visions, suggesting to Nissinen a scribal editing process parallel to the one that produced the biblical prophetic books, where final editors accessed written prophetic sources.[23]

Divine Letters

Correspondence between deities and kings is known from Mesopotamia, and some of these texts are form-critically indistinguishable from oral prophecy. Mari text ARM 26 194 originates from a prophet who sends a letter of divine speech directly to the king with the assistance of a scribe (cf. ARM 26 414:31–32). Since other examples (ARM 26 192; FLP 1674; SAA 3 47) offer no definitive evidence regarding the role of scribes, it is not known whether they originated as oral prophecy or were composed in writing. In each case, the original recipient would have conceived of these letters as legitimate, inspired speech. Charpin concludes that divine letters were "an integral part of the dossier of prophecy."[24] Whether or not there was a scribal intermediary, divine letters show that bifurcation between prophet and scribe is unwarranted.[25]

Egyptian Royal Cult

While most Egyptian texts considered in past discussion are properly classified as a subspecies of wisdom literature (e.g., the *Prophecies of Neferti*), when examining prophecy scholars have overlooked numerous royal inscriptions that record first-person divine speech that was framed with introductory speech formulas and was delivered to the king in a cultic setting.[26] These texts, emerging from corona-

---

23. Nissinen, "How Prophecy Became Literature," 164. However, he also regards the literary shape and expansion of biblical books to be a scribal process disassociated from the prophet.

24. Charpin, "Prophètes et rois dans le Proche-Orient Amorrite," 101.

25. An interesting analogy is offered by Kelle, who suggests that Israel's prophets were similar to Greek orators in social function: "In sum, the Hebrew Bible characteristically presents prophets as engaged in discourse that is argumentative public address, which relates to specific, contextual needs and employs a wide variety of styles for persuasive effect" (Brad E. Kelle, "Ancient Israelite Prophets and Greek Orators: Analogies for the Prophets and Their Implications for Historical Reconstruction," in *Israel's Prophets and Israel's Past: Essays on the Relationship of Prophetic Texts and Israelite History in Honor of John H. Hayes*, ed. Brad E. Kelle and Megan Bishop Moore, LHBOTS 446 [London: T&T Clark, 2006], 63). The extensive discourses of Greek orators came into writing and "show evidence of having been reworked after their original oral delivery," probably in some cases by the orators themselves (ibid., 79). So, Kelle suggests, prophets may have done some of their own editing.

26. John W. Hilber, "Prophetic Speech in the Egyptian Royal Cult," in *On Stone and Scroll: Essays in Honour of Graham Ivor Davies*, ed. James K. Aitken, Katharine J. Dell, and Brian A. Mastin, BZAW 420 (Berlin: de Gruyter, 2011), 39–53.

tions, victory celebrations, and building dedications, were adapted for the next five hundred years in live performance during royal cultic rituals. It seems that Egyptian priests functioned prophetically in the royal cult. No care was given to preserve the name(s) of the functionaries, but this is not surprising in view of the exclusive place of the Egyptian king in all relief texts and art. The length, literary artistry, and repeated use of these divine speeches might suggest written composition; however, as with divine letters, one must be careful not to set prophet and scribe in mutually exclusive roles. My personal hypothesis is that these were prophetic speeches composed in advance for liturgical performance.

Summary with Relevance to Isaiah as Prophet

An extensive collection of texts offers insight into prophets and prophetism in the ancient Near East. The biblical presentation of Isaiah conforms well to the image of historical prophets we know of apart from the Bible. Furthermore, as noted above, ancient societies held divine revelation in high regard and carefully transmitted prophetic speech in a variety of literary genres. Both correspondents and scribes transmitted oracles in letters and literary texts with relative accuracy. Oracle reports and collections demonstrate that direct recording of oral prophecy was common at least in seventh-century Assyria, close to the time of Isaiah of Jerusalem. Divine letters and Egyptian cultic texts suggest that prophecy could also originate in writing. With the exception of Egyptian prophecy and brief excerpts cited secondarily in contexts other than prophetic ones, care was taken to maintain an identifying link between written oracle and prophet. Therefore, heuristically, one should expect the book of Isaiah to be linked with oracles authentic to the prophet, the debate being not whether, but to what extent, this is the case.[27]

Isaiah as Book

Cultural Capacity for Prophetic Books

Whether one dates the whole of the book of Isaiah to the preexilic period or extends the composition into the postexilic period, the key phenomenon to explain is the length and literary sophistication of the book. Comparative studies of prophetic texts only highlight the uniqueness of biblical prophetic literature in this regard. Specifically relevant to the date for the composition of Isaiah is the question whether a social context existed in preexilic Israel with both the capacity

---

27. Ben Zvi challenges the assumption that superscriptions should be trusted (Ehud Ben Zvi, "Studying Prophetic Texts against Their Original Backgrounds: Pre-ordained Scripts and Alternative Horizons of Research," in *Prophets and Paradigms: Essays in Honor of Gene M. Tucker*, ed. Stephen Breck Reid, JSOTSup 229 [Sheffield: Sheffield Academic Press, 1996], esp. 128–29), but the comparative evidence appears to justify accepting *a priori* that superscriptions were important and therefore likely to be authentic.

and disposition to produce prophetic texts, and, in addition, to generate complex prophetic *literature*. Regarding capacity, an established scribal culture with the capacity to generate books existed by the later monarchy.[28] Regarding disposition, the Assyrian crisis could have generated interest in promoting the prophetic message connected with the demise of the north.[29] Indeed, at this time the south also experienced covenant sanctions, including partial exile under Sennacherib. Even apart from the institutional support of palace or temple, the writing of prophetic speech could still come from the support of individual scribes.[30] So, if the production of "books" is granted to preexilic Israel, then the production of *prophetic* books might be expected. While nothing comparable to the biblical prophetic literature exists in extrabiblical texts,[31] the importance of preserving prophecy for the benefit of future generations does find a parallel in the Neo-Assyrian oracle collections.[32]

Redaction of Prophetic Literature

The existence in ancient Israel of the capacity and disposition to produce prophetic literature does not imply that the books this culture produced necessarily originated as single-author compositions, whether such an author wrote a composition himself or employed the help of a scribe. Erhard Blum, for example,

---

28. Alan R. Millard, "Books in Ancient Israel," in *D'Ougarit à Jérusalem: Recueil d'études épigraphiques et archéologiques offerts à Pierre Bordreuil*, ed. Carole Roche, Orient & Méditerranée 2 (Paris: De Boccard, 2008), 255–64.

29. William M. Schniedewind, *How the Bible Became a Book* (Cambridge: Cambridge University Press, 2004), 40–45, 64, 84–90; David M. Carr, *Writing on the Tablet of the Heart: Origins of Scripture and Literature* (Oxford: Oxford University Press, 2005), 113–15, 131, 164–65; Richard S. Hess, "Questions of Reading and Writing in Ancient Israel," *BBR* 19 (2009): 1–9. For temple sponsorship, see van der Toorn, *Scribal Culture*, 87–88, 183–84. Babylonian and Persian backdrops have been proposed: see, respectively, Nissinen, "How Prophecy Became Literature," 156–57, and Ehud Ben Zvi, "The Concept of Prophetic Books and Its Historical Setting," in *The Production of Prophecy: Constructing Prophecy and Prophets in Yehud*, ed. Diana V. Edelman and Ehud Ben Zvi (London: Equinox, 2009), 93–95; but the Assyrian crisis offered sufficient impetus.

30. Carr, *Writing on the Tablet of the Heart*, 287–88; Alan R. Millard, " 'Take a Large Writing Tablet and Write on it': Isaiah—a Writing Prophet?," in *Genesis, Isaiah and Psalms: A Festschrift to Honour Professor John Emerton for His Eightieth Birthday*, ed. Katharine J. Dell, Graham Davies, and Yee Von Koh, VTSup 135 (Leiden: Brill, 2010), 114–15; idem, "Writing and Prophecy," in *Dictionary of the Old Testament: Prophets*, ed. Mark J. Boda and J. G. McConville (Downers Grove, IL: InterVarsity Press, 2012), 887. Individual scribal professionals are attested in Mesopotamia (Laurie E. Pearce, "The Scribes and Scholars of Ancient Mesopotamia," *CANE*, 4:2273) but not clearly in Egypt (Edward F. Wente, "The Scribes of Ancient Egypt," *CANE*, 4:2217).

31. But then, most genres of biblical literature have no *complete* ancient Near Eastern parallels, except perhaps Proverbs and Song of Songs.

32. Beate Pongratz-Leisten, *Herrschaftswissen in Mesopotamien: Formen der Kommunikation zwischen Gott und König im 2. und 1. Jahrtausend v. Chr.*, SAAS 10 (Helsinki: University of Helsinki Press, 1999), 285, 315; Millard, " 'Take a Large Writing Tablet,' " 116.

describes the fundamental reorientation in current mainstream scholarship from form-critical investigation of actual prophetic speech to analysis of redactional layers of scribal theologians who expanded prophetic writings over extended periods of time.[33] Since there are no extrabiblical examples of prophetic literature, comparative studies offer no analogies. However, the various sociological models that are proposed to provide settings for the plethora of competing redactional models are not supported by what is known of the cultural ethos of prophecy, which is one that suggests closer connection between prophet and text than these models acknowledge. This presents a problem not only for complex redactional models, but also for proposals of anonymous authorship of Deutero-Isaiah. Ulrich Berges, for example, announces "farewell" altogether to Deutero-Isaiah, arguing that the absence of an author's name in this part of the book is the very reason for positing a more complex redactional process for composition (quoting Becker that "real prophets do not remain anonymous").[34] But, if real prophets do not remain anonymous, one can equally question the proposal that an anonymous *series* of scribes fabricated substantial additions to a core prophetic text and presented them as direct divine speech. Since prophetic speech was equivalent to diplomatic communication from the divine realm, this sort of activity would amount to religious-political treason.[35] Unlike other genres, prophetic speech was necessarily anchored to the authority of the prophetic spokesperson who functioned individually as a divine ambassador.

The Redactional Model of M. J. de Jong for the Book of Isaiah

One significant effort to establish a comparative link between the composition of the book of Isaiah and ancient Near Eastern prophetic phenomena is that of Matthijs de Jong.[36] De Jong utilizes prophetic texts, particularly from the Neo-Assyrian corpus, to illustrate the plausibility of his redactional analysis of First Isaiah. Adapting previous redactional models, de Jong proposes four stages in the development of the Isaiah tradition:

---

33. Erhard Blum, "Israels Prophetie im altorientalischen Kontext: Anmerkungen zu neueren religionsgeschichtlichen Thesen," in *"From Ebla to Stellenbosch": Syro-Palestinian Religions and the Hebrew Bible*, ed. Izak Cornelius and Louis Jonker, ADPV 37 (Wiesbaden: Harrassowitz, 2008), 84. Cf. Michael H. Floyd, "'Write the Revelation!' (Hab 2:2): Reimagining the Cultural History of Prophecy," in *Writings and Speech in Israelite and Ancient Near Eastern Prophecy*, ed. Ehud Ben Zvi, Michael H. Floyd, and Christopher R. Matthews, SBLSymS 10 (Atlanta: Society of Biblical Literature, 2000), 143; idem, "The Production of Prophetic Books in the Early Second Temple Period," in *Prophets, Prophecy, and Prophetic Texts in Second Temple Judaism*, ed. Michael H. Floyd and Robert D. Haak, LHBOTS 427 (London: T&T Clark, 2006), 292; Nissinen, "Historical Dilemma of Biblical Prophetic Studies," 117.

34. Ulrich F. Berges, "Farewell to Deutero-Isaiah or Prophecy without a Prophet," in *Congress Volume, Ljubljana 2007*, ed. André Lemaire, VTSup 133 (Leiden: Brill, 2010), 579.

35. For prophetic delivery, whether oral or written, as diplomatic communication, see Hilber, "Culture of Prophecy and Writing," 223–24, 234–35.

36. De Jong, *Isaiah among the Ancient Near Eastern Prophets.*

(Stage 1) During the Assyrian crisis, Isaiah of Jerusalem delivered short salva-tion oracles to encourage Hezekiah not to resist Assyria but to await YHWH's intervention.

(Stage 2) During the period of Assyria's demise, a late seventh-century revi-sion recontextualized Isaiah's original message of salvation by prophesying, *ex eventu*, Assyria's destruction at the international level and Josiah's rise as the ideal king.

(Stage 3) After the destruction of Jerusalem, a literary composition trans-formed the tradition of Isaiah from that of a prophet of salvation to a prophet of doom; this redaction highlighted the people's disobedience to Isaiah's warn-ings as the explanation of the failure of Isaiah's vision of peace.[37]

(Stage 4) Postexilic visions of eschatological salvation were added to existing material.

According to de Jong, the exilic reworking of Isaiah material was the "formative stage" for transforming "small textual compilations" from the late seventh century into "substantial literary complexes."[38]

It lies outside the scope of this essay to comment on de Jong's redactional model, which, as he argues, must stand or fall independent of his application of the extrabiblical prophetic material.[39] The ancient Near Eastern prophetic texts only provide, in his words, "an analogy to the literary character of the development of the Isaiah tradition."[40] The issue relevant to this essay, then, is how well de Jong's proposed analogies cohere with his stages of redaction. For Stage 1 (eighth-century oracles), de Jong maintains that the prophetic portrait of Isaiah conforms to the characteristics of ancient Near Eastern prophets, except that Isaiah's "dominant

---

37. De Jong discusses the fact that differences between biblical and extrabiblical prophecy on the subject of judgment have been overstated (ibid., 307–13). Nevertheless, he maintains that the emphasis on judgment in Israelite prophetic books is a later redactional component (Matthijs J. de Jong, "Biblical Prophecy—A Scribal Enterprise: The Old Testa-ment Prophecy of Unconditional Judgment Considered as a Literary Phenomenon," *VT* 61 [2011]: 39–70). However, as Blum maintains, there is ample precedent for judgment proph-ecy in the eighth century based upon Mesopotamian parallels and the Deir 'Alla plaster texts; and, indeed, it was the resistance to this word of judgment that prompted the inscrip-turation of some of these early prophetic messages of Isaiah (Blum, "Israels Prophetie im altorientalischen Kontext," esp. 107). See further H. G. M. Williamson, "Isaiah: Prophet of Weal Or Woe?," in *"Thus Speaks Ishtar of Arbela": Prophecy in Israel, Assyria, and Egypt in the Neo-Assyrian Period*, ed. Hans Barstad and Robert P. Gordon (Winona Lake, IN: Eisen-brauns, 2013), 273–300.

38. De Jong, *Isaiah among the Ancient Near Eastern Prophets*, 83–84; cf. 41–47, 169–70, 394.

39. He writes, "One must determine on exegetical and historical, and not on compara-tive grounds, which parts of the book represent the earliest prophetic tradition and its first development in the Assyrian period" (ibid., 39).

40. Ibid., 188.

critical tone" sets him apart.[41] This echoes conclusions drawn earlier in this essay. For Stages 3 and 4 (exilic literary redaction and postexilic visions), because there are no extrabiblical prophetic texts comparable in length or literary sophistication to biblical prophetic books, there is no material for comparison to these stages of growth in the book of Isaiah. However, for Stage 2 (Josianic revision), de Jong draws upon three main types of texts as analogies to this stage of growth in the Isaiah tradition.

Reformulation of Oracles

De Jong's first comparison is with the Neo-Assyrian oracle collections, which he draws upon to serve as examples of literary development.[42] He observes that the Neo-Assyrian oracle collections represent "a secondary stage . . . dissociated from their original context . . . [that] became part of a new constellation of meaning . . . looking back on a longer episode of connected events."[43] This observation about how texts find new relevance with changing historical contexts is valid, and it is true of biblical material as well. However, it is one thing to assert that a scribe creates new significance when archiving oracle reports into a collection, that is, "characterized by editorial selection and stylisation of the oracles," but it is quite another to suggest, as de Jong does for the Josianic redaction of Isaiah, that this editorial process materially altered the original intent of the oracle in order to transform it into saying something different from the original.[44]

The difficulty with de Jong's proposal is that the Neo-Assyrian oracle collections show little evidence of editing other than their being made to conform to the conventional layout that characterizes these reports, the addition of colophons, and the organization of oracles around liturgical rubrics (SAA 9 3.2:8–9; 3.3:26–32). In one case, there is likely an insertion of a descriptive comment by the scribe: "He [the prophet] said (this) five, six times, and then (he said [quote sign, *mā*]) '. . .'" (SAA 9 8:4–5).[45] If anything, this insertion suggests that the scribe was taking great

---

41. Ibid., 347–48, 352–56.

42. Ibid., 357.

43. Ibid., 397. De Jong cites Pongratz-Leisten (*Herrschaftswissen in Mesopotamien*, 283) and van der Toorn (*Scribal Culture*, 15) as well. Nissinen suggests that once prophecy was put into writing by scribes, it was subject to literary refinement, in terms of both style and interpretation (Nissinen, "Spoken, Written, Quoted, and Invented," 241, 244; cf. Pongratz-Leisten, *Herrschaftswissen in Mesopotamien*, 267).

44. For example, de Jong proposes that an Isaianic oracle to Ahaz (Isa 7:4–9a) received an addition in the late seventh century (Isa 7:9b) that transformed the original salvation oracle into a threat. Likewise, a rereading of the original oracle of salvation to Ahaz (Isa 7:14b, 16) expanded the context with verses 10–13 and 17 (the addition of Isa 7:14a ["therefore"] links the verse with the accusation of unbelief) in order to transform it into a judgment. The end result is criticism of the policies of the Davidic dynasty that led to disaster, "prophesying" hope in an ideal king, Josiah, who would restore peace (Isa 9:1–6[ET 2–7]) (De Jong, *Isaiah among the Ancient Near Eastern Prophets*, 58–63, 163–66).

45. Pierre Villard, "Les prophéties à l'époque néo-assyrienne," in *Prophètes et rois: Bible et Proche-Orient*, ed. André Lemaire, Lectio Divina hors série (Paris: Cerf, 2001), 76–77.

care to affirm exactly what the prophet spoke, differentiating his own comment from the words of the prophet.[46] In addition, quite different from the Standard Babylonian customarily used in scribal composition and copying, the prophecies are in an oral dialect of Neo-Assyrian. Consequently, Parpola states that "they were written down from oral performance and apparently not subjected to any substantial editing."[47] Nissinen offers the reasonable suggestion that due to space limitation the oracles may have been abbreviated,[48] but otherwise there is no evidence of *change* or *expansion* in the prophetic message. Therefore, the Neo-Assyrian collections do not offer a valid parallel to the sort of literary development that de Jong proposes for the Josianic redaction of Isaiah's oracles.

In addition to oracle collections, de Jong also lists quotations in letters and in royal inscriptions as secondary uses of prophecy. Regarding letters, he maintains that "the formulation of the prophecies was probably adapted to serve a new purpose."[49] This is clear in one letter from a scholar to Assurbanipal cited by de Jong.[50] The correspondent reminds the king of a prophetic oracle delivered to Assurbanipal's father, Esarhaddon, and then he uses that oracle as a basis to affirm the future success of Assurbanipal. However, this actually provides a counterexample to the type of resignification de Jong envisions for Isaiah's oracles, since in this letter the scholar maintains the identity of the referent (Esarhaddon) and the meaning of the original oracle as he applies it to the new situation of Assurbanipal. The new application is merely an inference from the original oracle. The same applies to examples of prophecy in royal inscriptions; while they are indeed "scribal adaptations" of prophecy embedded *within* literature, they should not be characterized as "evidence [of] the transition from prophecy *into* literature" (italics mine), as de Jong proposes.[51]

De Jong presents a number of examples of "oracles that received literary elaboration" resulting in their becoming larger texts.[52] However, none of these offers evidence of alteration or expansion of oracles. The first, SAA 9 2.4, is best understood as one oracle incorporating two strophes.[53] The second, SAA 3 47, is a divine letter. Whether it originated orally or as written composition is unknown; but even if it was an oral text that received a literary elaboration, there is no reason to think that the substance of the oral message was altered in any way. The third, SAA 9 5, offers

---

46. Throughout these texts, the use of the quotation particle *mā* suggests to Parpola that the scribes were reporting prophetic speech and that the texts were not written by the prophets themselves (Simo Parpola, *Assyrian Prophecies*, SAA 9 [Helsinki: University of Helsinki Press, 1997], lv).

47. Ibid., lxviii.

48. Nissinen, "How Prophecy Became Literature," 165.

49. De Jong, *Isaiah among the Ancient Near Eastern Prophets*, 400.

50. SAA 10 174; de Jong, *Isaiah among the Ancient Near Eastern Prophets*, 401.

51. De Jong, *Isaiah among the Ancient Near Eastern Prophets*, 404. De Jong uses better nuanced wording elsewhere: "Both reworked oracles and the literary derivatives of prophecy testify to the phenomenon of prophecy finding its way into literature" (ibid., 419–20).

52. Ibid., 404–12.

53. See Hilber, *Cultic Prophecy in the Psalms*, 78.

no evidence that it is a "literary derivative of prophecy," de Jong's alternate translations notwithstanding.[54] Rather, its style and content are comparable to those of
other oracles. The fourth example, SAA 9 9, need not be "a literary text."[55] Careful
execution of script and archival preservation mean only that this oracle was particularly important to Assurbanipal. The presence of doxological elements or allusions to the *Epic of Gilgamesh* should not be ruled *a priori* beyond the competence
of a prophet.[56] The oracle collection SAA 9 3 does incorporate liturgical rubrics;
and it was probably performed in conjunction with the enthronement rituals of
Esarhaddon. Thus, it illustrates a secondary use of prophetic oracles for a new context, and, as a whole, constitutes a literary composition.[57] However, as in the case
of letters and royal inscriptions, there is no evidence that the oracular messages in
this composition were altered or augmented by the scribe.

Literary Derivatives of Prophecy

A step beyond texts having undergone "elaboration" are ones that de Jong
classifies as "literary derivatives of prophecy." Rather than adapting oral prophecies, these examples *originated* as literary compositions.[58] The first, SAA 3 13, is a
dialogue between Assurbanipal and the god Nabû. This text shares many affinities
with the prophetic oracle SAA 9 9 and likely emerged from the same historical setting.[59] Pongratz-Leisten suggests that SAA 3 13 is a fictive dialogue that employs a
literary technique similar to the one used in the exchange of letters between deity
and king.[60] In similar fashion, de Jong describes this text as a scribal imitation of
oracular style.[61] However, given its affinity to the prophetic oracle preserved in
SAA 9 9, the text more likely reflects an actual exchange of lament and oracular

---

54. Cf. de Jong, *Isaiah among the Ancient Near Eastern Prophets*, 174–75.

55. Ibid., 406.

56. See Martti Nissinen, "The Socioreligious Role of the Neo-Assyrian Prophets," in
*Prophecy in Its Ancient Near Eastern Context: Mesopotamian, Biblical, and Arabian Perspec-
tives*, ed. Martti Nissinen, SBLSymS 13 (Atlanta: Society of Biblical Literature, 2000), 97–98;
idem, "Spoken, Written, Quoted, and Invented," 244. De Jong argues that the literary parallel between SAA 9 9 and the *Epic of Gilgamesh* must allude to the death of Assurbanipal's
brother Šamaš-šum-ukin, which necessitates that this allusion is a literary elaboration in
SAA 9 9 that was composed *after* the date of the oracle (oracle dated 650 BCE in the colo-
phon; Šamaš-šum-ukin's death and literary elaboration dated around 648 BCE). However,
the literary allusion in SAA 9 9 draws a parallel between Ištar's efforts to defend Assurbanipal's life and Gilgamesh's hardships when seeking life for *himself*, not necessarily alluding
to Enkidu, who had died (cf. *Epic of Gilgamesh* ix.i.1–5). Hence, de Jong has over-read the
extent of the analogy intended by the prophet in this allusion. Even if the allusion includes a
parallel between Šamaš-šum-ukin's and Enkidu's deaths, this does not necessitate dating the
allusion *after* Šamaš-šum-ukin's death; it could just as easily be a literary way of promising
Assurbanipal victory over his brother.

57. De Jong, *Isaiah among the Ancient Near Eastern Prophets*, 411.

58. Ibid., 412–20.

59. Hilber, *Cultic Prophecy in the Psalms*, 70–74.

60. Pongratz-Leisten, *Herrschaftswissen in Mesopotamien*, 273n37.

61. De Jong, *Isaiah among the Ancient Near Eastern Prophets*, 412–13.

response that characterized the general crisis facing Assurbanipal. Although it may be a condensation of different, related performances, real cultic speech lies behind the composition.[62] The three other texts categorized by de Jong as "literary derivatives" are divine letters (SAA 3 44, 45, and 46). As discussed above, some texts of this genre consist of a repetition of the contents of a campaign report from the king, with the deity's affirmation in response (e.g., SAA 3 41).[63] Other divine letters are indistinguishable from oral prophecy (e.g., ARM 26 194; SAA 3 47). It appears that recipients of divine letters accepted these communications as divine speech. Therefore, even though these messages might have originated to varying degrees as written compositions from the outset, they represent prophetic communication. This contributes no support for the idea that oracles underwent alteration or expansion, nor for the idea that they were merely imitations of divine speech. As noted above, in view of the fact that divine speech, whether delivered orally or in writing, was regarded as diplomatic exchange between the deity and the king, any scribal fabrication would have been religious and political treason. The texts came from socially recognized mediators of the divine word.

Literary Predictions (Pseudo-Prophecy)

De Jong presents another genre of texts, "literary predictive texts" (e.g., the Marduk Prophecy; the Uruk Prophecy; [similarly] the *Song of Erra*), "in order to provide a counterpart to the seventh-century revision of the Isaiah tradition."[64] In particular, it is the employment of "pseudo-prophecy" (i.e., *ex eventu* predictions) and the utilization of the "ideal king" motif that draws his interest.[65] There are several problems in associating these texts with Isaiah, however. A more in-depth discussion is found below; at this point, suffice it to say that literary predictive texts constitute a different genre from that of prophecy, one that utilizes a distinctly different compositional technique.

In sum, this criticism of de Jong's analogies does not negate the possibility of a Josianic (or any other) redaction; however, it denies that there is evidence from ancient Near Eastern parallels that scribes, in an effort to recontextualize, rewrote or expanded prophetic oracles in any substantial way. De Jong insists that beyond Stage 1 (Isaiah's original oracles) there is no oral backdrop; rather, "the three compilations are to be regarded as literary composition, originating from a

---

62. Jason Atkinson, "Prophecy in K1285: Re-evaluating the Divine Speech Episodes of Nabû," in *"Thus Speaks Ishtar of Arbela": Prophecy in Israel, Assyria, and Egypt in the Neo-Assyrian Period*, ed. Hans Barstad and Robert P. Gordon (Winona Lake, IN: Eisenbrauns, 2013), 59–89; cf. Meindert Dijkstra, *Gods voorstelling: Predikatieve expressie van zelfopenbaring in oudoosterse teksten en Deutero-Jesaja*, Dissertationes Neerlandicae, Series Theologica 2 (Kampen: Kok, 1980), 147–48.

63. Even de Jong's primary example, SAA 3 44, ends with reference to a letter that had been sent from the king (line 28′), which may allude to the initiation by the king of an exchange of letters.

64. De Jong, *Isaiah among the Ancient Near Eastern Prophets*, 420.

65. Ibid., 433.

scribal milieu."[66] Yet, what he construes as a "literary derivative of prophecy" may be conceived of simply as another mode of prophetic expression that became manifest in written composition. The Mesopotamian texts discussed above illustrate the manifold ways in which divine speech was mediated (orally delivered prophecy preserved in written form; prophecy quoted or paraphrased in another genre; divine speech composed originally in various written forms). While one might wish to use manifestations of prophecy in Mesopotamian texts to demonstrate that biblical prophetic books are a form of scribal prophecy to be distanced from "real" prophets, these texts illustrate the opposite, namely, that individuals who were recognized as prophets produced written prophecy, even if they enlisted the *assistance* of a scribe.

Literary Predictive Texts

De Jong is not the only scholar to propose that "literary predictive texts" illustrate the mechanism of "scribal prophecy," by which more complex prophetic texts are generated by scribes, not prophets. Because of the implications of this for the production of prophetic *literature* in Israel, and specifically the book of Isaiah, this proposal merits careful consideration. The phenomenon of pseudepigraphy associated with these texts is also relevant to the question of authorship.

Five texts that early on were designated "Akkadian Prophecies" by A. Kirk Grayson and Wilfred Lambert, and "Akkadian Apocalypses" by William Hallo, have in recent decades been described with more careful nuance as "Literary Predictive Texts" by Maria de Jong Ellis.[67] Tremper Longman's classification of "autobiography" suits two of the texts, the Marduk and Shulgi Prophecies,[68] but the genre association of the other three texts is not as clear.[69]

It is not difficult to understand the earlier nomenclature "prophecy" or "apocalypse." The texts purport to predict the distant future. For example, the Uruk

---

66. Ibid., 379.

67. A. K. Grayson and W. G. Lambert, "Akkadian Prophecies," *JCS* 18 (1964): 7–30; William W. Hallo, "Akkadian Apocalypses," *IEJ* 16 (1966): 231–42; Maria de Jong Ellis, "Observations on Mesopotamian Oracles and Prophetic Texts: Literary and Historiographical Considerations," *JCS* 41 (1989): 148. One of Grayson and Lambert's four original texts may not fall within this "genre," but the Uruk Prophecy (published by Hunger and Kaufman, see note 70 below) and the Dynastic Prophecy (A. K. Grayson, *Babylonian Historical-Literary Texts*, Toronto Semitic Texts and Studies 3 [Toronto: University of Toronto Press, 1975]) have since been included—hence the known number of texts in the genre is five.

68. Tremper Longman III, *Fictional Akkadian Autobiography: A Generic and Comparative Study* (Winona Lake, IN: Eisenbrauns, 1991), 131–90.

69. Indeed, whether they even constitute a unified genre remains to be seen; see Ellis, "Observations on Mesopotamian Oracles," 154, and, most recently, Matthew Neujahr, *Predicting the Past in the Ancient Near East: Mantic Historiography in Ancient Mesopotamia, Judah, and the Mediterranean World*, BJS 354 (Providence: Brown University Press, 2012), 8, 110, 114–15.

Prophecy states: "He will exercise rule and kingship in Uruk and his dynasty will be established forever. The kings of Uruk will exercise rulership like the gods."[70] But, differentiating this from biblical prophecy, Stephen Kaufman has observed that "the Mesopotamian idea of the ideal future would seem to be (for those in power, at least) nothing more than an indefinite continuation of the status quo."[71] Joyce Baldwin offers the similar comment that this view of the future is for an unending succession of kings, not a climactic endpoint of history.[72] The parallels, then, to the sort of kingdom envisioned by Isaiah (e.g., Isa 11 and 65–66) are conceptually different.

The classification "apocalypse" is also understandable. Because of the common formula "a king shall arise . . ." (or similar expression), used repeatedly for a series of future, changing kingdoms, many scholars of both mainstream and conservative stripes have compared these predictive texts to Dan 8:23–25 and 11:2–45 (esp. 11:2). The comparison is reinforced for those who view the pseudonymity of these Akkadian texts in the light of Jewish apocalyptic literature[73] and especially of the presence of *ex eventu* prophecy that is also presumed for Daniel. Helmer Ringgren claimed that these texts "provide some of the stones out of which the structure of apocalypticism is built up."[74] However, as Matthew Neujahr stresses, dissimilarities must be recognized, especially in ideology, which means that direct dependence is doubtful.[75]

Nissinen correctly argues that the texts in question are neither prophecies nor apocalypses, properly speaking.[76] Nevertheless, he stresses that they all share an interest in predicting the future. This feature has given rise in recent years to pro-

---

70. Hermann Hunger and Stephen A. Kaufman, "A New Akkadian Prophecy Text," *JAOS* 95 (1975): 372–73.

71. Stephen A. Kaufman, "Prediction, Prophecy, and Apocalypse in the Light of New Akkadian Texts," *Proceedings of the Sixth Congress of Jewish Studies*, ed. A. Shinan (Jerusalem: World Union of Jewish Studies, 1977), 1:226.

72. Joyce G. Baldwin, "Some Literary Affinities of the Book of Daniel," *TynBul* 30 (1979): 90.

73. The presence of "heavenly drama" is another common feature. See, for example, the access to the divine council portrayed in 1 Kgs 22 and the vision from the Shulgi Prophecy. Jack M. Sasson notes this for Mari prophecy in his "Mari Apocalypticism Revisited," in *Immigration and Emigration within the Ancient Near East: Festschrift E. Lipiński*, ed. K. Van Lerberghe and A. Schoors (Leuven: Peeters, 1995), 285–88.

74. Helmer Ringgren, "Akkadian Apocalypses," in *Apocalypticism in the Mediterranean World and the Near East: Proceedings of the International Colloquium on Apocalypticism, Uppsala, August 12–17, 1979*, ed. David Hellholm (Tübingen: Mohr, 1983), 386. The thousand-year span (Kassite to Seleucid periods) from which these Akkadian texts derive renders influence all the more plausible for William Hallo ("The Expansion of Cuneiform Literature," *PAAJR* 46–47 [1979]: 307–22).

75. Neujahr, *Predicting the Past in the Ancient Near East*, 146–51.

76. Martti Nissinen, "Neither Prophecies nor Apocalypses: The Akkadian Literary Predictive Texts," in *Knowing the End from the Beginning: The Prophetic, the Apocalyptic, and Their Relationship*, ed. Lester L. Grabbe and Robert D. Haak, JSPSup 46 (London: T&T Clark, 2003), 143.

posals that the Akkadian literary predictive texts provide the best model for understanding the creation of prophetic *literature* in Israel, which supposedly originated by the same process of scribal composition that produced Akkadian predictive texts. And since the Akkadian texts are predictions after the fact, so too, it is argued, are many biblical counterparts.

This reasoning is utilized by de Jong regarding analogies for a scribal, pseudo-prophetic redaction of Isaiah's oracles. He writes that "the examples of literary prediction . . . are characterised by pseudo-prophetic, predictive style, similar to that of the revision of the Isaiah tradition."[77] For de Jong, both portray a future reign of an ideal king who at the purported time of the prophecy is anonymous. Applying this thinking more broadly than just to the prophet Isaiah, he argues that "biblical prophecy of unconditional and total judgment [is] essentially a scribal phenomenon created *ex eventu*."[78]

Stuart Weeks proposes that for biblical prophecy one needs to draw a distinction between prophetic speech and prophetic literature.[79] In his view, as one searches for the closest analogies to prophetic literature, one thinks of Akkadian predictive texts and Egyptian texts such as the *Prophecies of Neferti*.[80] Thus, Egyptian literature has also been invoked in the discussion.

In response, as noted above with respect to divine letters, prophetic functionaries are known in some cases to have conveyed their revelations in written form from the outset, even working in conjunction with scribes if necessary. In addition, since oral performance was often transcribed, one need not propose literary predictive texts as a forerunner of biblical prophetic literature. Also, there are a number of reasons to *differentiate* biblical prophetic literature from literary predictive texts.

First, there is a significant difference in origin. Mesopotamian literary predictive texts derive from omen literature, a feature texts of this kind share that was recognized early in the study of them.[81] With others, Nissinen observes that prophecy and omen divination belong to the same conceptual world, that is, both work under the assumption that divine knowledge ("secrets of the gods"; participation in the

---

77. De Jong, *Isaiah among the Ancient Near Eastern Prophets*, 438.

78. Idem, "Biblical Prophecy—A Scribal Enterprise," 40.

79. Stuart Weeks, "Predictive and Prophetic Literature: Can *Neferti* Help Us Read the Bible?," in *Prophecy and the Prophets in Ancient Israel*, ed. John Day, LHBOTS 531 (London, New York: T&T Clark, 2010), 25–26.

80. This accords with the earlier suggestion by Lester L. Grabbe in *Priests, Prophets, Diviners, Sages: A Socio-Historical Study of Religious Specialists in Ancient Israel* (Valley Forge, PA: Trinity, 1995), 86–87. See further JoAnn Scurlock, "Prophecy as a Form of Divination: Divination as a Form of Prophecy," in *Divination and Interpretation of Signs in the Ancient World*, ed. Amar Annus, OIS 6 (Chicago: Oriental Institute of the University of Chicago, 2010), 282.

81. Ellis, "Observations on Mesopotamian Oracles," 131–32, 159, 162; Nissinen, "Neither Prophecies nor Apocalypses," 140. Grayson argues that the relationship between these Akkadian "prophecies" and omen literature is purely stylistic (Grayson, *Babylonian Historical-Literary Texts*, 16, 22).

divine council) is transmitted to the human realm.[82] However, he notes that prophets and diviners employed different techniques in their gaining access to revelation,
bore different "identity-markers" whereby society recognized their mediation, and
often operated in different social contexts.[83] In spite of superficial similarities in
their making of predictive claims, literary predictive texts and biblical prophetic
literature arose from distinctly different forms of mediation: scholarly meditation
upon omen series, on the one hand, and prophetic speech, on the other.[84] In addition, apart from Dan 8:23–25 and Dan 11, Old Testament prophetic literature
bears little stylistic similarity to Akkadian literary predictive texts. Regarding Egyptian counterparts (e.g., the *Prophecies of Neferti*; the *Admonitions of Ipuwer*), Nili
Shupak has demonstrated that, although these texts have a component of future-
telling, they belong to a class of wisdom literature.[85] Most important in her analysis
are the observations that in these Egyptian texts divine messenger speech is absent
and the element of prediction stems from the employment of magic by priests
and sages.[86] These differences from biblical prophetic literature are reminiscent of
the limitations in the analogy between Mesopotamian literary-predictive texts and
biblical prophetic texts.

Second, literary predictive texts may be closer to a form of historiography than
to prophecy, having been constructed from historical sources but using the style
of omen apodoses.[87] While it is generally assumed that these texts are intentionally
deceptive, this merits further consideration. Baldwin notes that Akkadian Text
A has interest in chronological detail, which makes it more akin to royal annals.[88]
Without the beginning and end of the text, it is difficult to understand exactly its
overall purpose or genre (predictive prophecy or a chronology predicated upon a
series of omens?). In other words, combined with their origin in omen analysis,
the presence of historical *reflection* in these texts may place them closer to historiography than pseudo-prediction. This would be analogous to someone recon-

---

82. Martti Nissinen, "Prophecy and Omen Divination: Two Sides of the Same Coin," in
Divination and Interpretation of Signs in the Ancient World, ed. Amar Annus, OIS 6 (Chicago: Oriental Institute of the University of Chicago, 2010), 342, 345.

83. Ibid., 343.

84. Cf. Ellis, "Observations on Mesopotamian Oracles," 146–47.

85. Nili Shupak, "Egyptian 'Prophecy' and Biblical Prophecy: Did the Phenomenon
of Prophecy, in the Biblical Sense, Exist in Ancient Egypt?," *JEOL* 31 (1989–1990): 5–40.
More recently, Shupak has classed these texts as "admonitory (or critical) wisdom litera-
ture" (idem, "The Egyptian 'Prophecy'—A Reconsideration," in *"Von reichlich ägyptischem
Verstande": Festschrift für Waltraud Guglielmi zum 65. Geburtstag*, ed. Hans-Werner Fischer-
Elfert and Karola Zibelius-Chen, Philippika: Marburger Altertumskundliche Abhandlungen
[Wiesbaden: Harrassowitz, 2006], 133–44).

86. Shupak, "Egyptian 'Prophecy' and Biblical Prophecy," 24, 27. Cf. Bernd Ulrich Schipper, "'Apokalyptik,' 'Messianismus,' 'Prophetie'—Eine Begriffsbestimmung," in *Apokalyptik
und Ägypten: Eine kritische Analyse der relevanten Texte aus dem griechisch-römischen Ägypten*, ed. Andreas Blasius and Bernd Ulrich Schipper, OLA 107 (Leuven: Peeters, 2002), 38.

87. Neujahr, *Predicting the Past*, 98–101, 245.

88. Baldwin, "Some Literary Affinities of the Book of Daniel," 82–83. Cf. Ellis, "Observations on Mesopotamian Oracles," 162–63.

structing the events leading up to the attacks on September 11, 2001, on the basis of intelligence sources that show in retrospect what was unfolding.

Third, the issue of pseudepigraphic intent needs to be reconsidered. As a matter of observation, the Akkadian literary predictive texts in question are *anonymous* but they are not *pseudepigraphic*. The difference is immensely important. The pseudepigraphic ascription is derived from the fact that the "Marduk Prophecy" and "Shulgi Prophecy" cannot actually have come from these divine individuals. This evaluation presupposes that deities do not speak. *We* may judge that Marduk does not exist or that Shulgi is not a deified king, but we cannot deny that the *author* of these texts believed that divine knowledge is transmittable. In other words, from an *emic* rather than an *etic* point of view, it is far from clear that in the worldview of the original authors and audience these predictive texts were fictive. However, Weeks argues,

> This is not a matter of authors pretending to be someone else, but of authors speaking through and about their main character . . . Unless prophetic literature constitutes a significant exception to this very common convention, it is a reasonable assumption that the original readership would have understood the attributes of the prophetic books in this way. . . . [So] attribution and characterization . . . must surely undercut traditional assumptions about the centrality of the historical prophets to the concerns of prophetic literature.[89]

But in this essay I argue that prophetic literature is indeed different from these literary predictive texts. And in order for prophetic literature to *function* in society, it must be linked with an authoritative prophetic source. Whether oral or literary, the function is to impose the divine will on the community. So on closer inspection, there is little to commend the proposal that literary predictive texts provide an analogy to the composition of prophetic literature. These Mesopotamian and Egyptian texts were never regarded as "prophetic" in the same sense as the biblical books; rather, they were divine revelation mediated and composed through a mechanism that differs from prophecy.

Form Criticism and Second Isaiah[90]

For a hundred years, scholars have drawn comparisons between the salvation oracles of Isa 40–55 and those of Neo-Assyrian prophecies, touching on the form,

---

89. Weeks, "Predictive and Prophetic Literature," 34–35, 40.

90. Barstad has described the many parallels between the oracles of First Isaiah and those found in Mari texts (Hans M. Barstad, "*Sic dicit dominus*: Mari Prophetic Texts and the Hebrew Bible," in *Essays on Ancient Israel in Its Near Eastern Context: A Tribute to Nadav Naʾaman*, ed. Yairah Amit, Ehud Ben Zvi, Israel Finkelstein, and Oded Lipschits [Winona Lake, IN: Eisenbrauns, 2006], 21–52). While he himself would not endorse any model of preexilic authorship for the whole of Isaiah, he does conclude that these parallels point to an origin of prophetic traditions (generally) "long before the final editing of the Hebrew Bible" (p. 47). More pertinent to the purposes of this essay are comparisons to Second Isaiah.

setting, and rhetoric of these texts.[91] This discussion has bearing on the composition of this portion of the book of Isaiah in at least two ways.[92] First, if passages such as Isa 41:8–16, 43:1–7, and 44:1–5 have their setting in the cult, this might lend support to the notion that these passages in Second Isaiah depended on Isaianic oracles delivered in the first-temple setting. Second, the close form-critical parallel between the salvation oracles of Isa 40–55 and seventh-century Neo-Assyrian oracles merits special comment, since the Assyrian prophets are roughly contemporary with Isaiah of Jerusalem. As will be argued, however, these two considerations contribute little to discussion of the composition history of the book of Isaiah.

Cultic Origins?

As early as 1914, Hugo Gressmann argued that Second Isaiah depended on the pattern of Assyrian prophetic oracles.[93] But as Nissinen has noted, his view became overshadowed by Joachim Begrich's theory of a *priestly* salvation oracle, and the prophetic nature of the Assyrian sources was mostly overlooked in subsequent scholarship.[94] It is now recognized that elements of Isaiah's salvation oracles, par-

---

91. The most striking common elements are the "fear not" formula and the divine self-predication formula ("I am X"). One difficulty in the comparison is the fact that the Assyrian oracles do not follow any standard *structure*, even though they share many of the same formal *elements*. Parpola observes that the Neo-Assyrian oracles "consist of a limited inventory of structural and thematic elements," although the arrangement is quite variable (Parpola, *Assyrian Prophecies*, lxiv–lxv; cf. Dijkstra, *Gods voorstelling*, 164, 368). This is true for both the Assyrian and Old Testament forms (Manfred Weippert, "Assyrische Prophetien der Zeit Asarhaddons und Assurbanipals," in *Assyrian Royal Inscriptions: New Horizons in Literary, Ideological, and Historical Analysis*, ed. F. M. Fales, OAC 17 [Rome: Istituto per l'Oriente, 1981], 89–90).

92. "At least," since form-critical considerations have been used to differentiate redactional layers within Deutero-Isaiah. Weippert, for example, argues that the homogeneity of prophetic style in Isa 40–48 and Assyrian oracles, over against the lack of similar forms in Isa 49–55, suggests that an outline of individual authorship can be ascertained for Isa 40–48, which isolates this core from later accretions in Isa 49–55 (Manfred Weippert, " 'Ich bin Jahwe'—'Ich bin Ishtar von Arbela': Deuterojesaja im Lichte der neuassyrischen Prophetie," in *Prophetie und Psalmen: Festschrift für Klaus Seybold zum 65. Geburtstag*, ed. Beat Huwyler, Hans-Peter Mathys, and Beat Weber, AOAT 280 [Münster: Ugarit-Verlag, 2001], 55–56).

93. Hugo Gressmann, "Die literarische Analyse Deuterojesajas," *ZAW* 34 (1914): 289–90.

94. Martti Nissinen, "Fear Not: A Study on an Ancient Near Eastern Phrase," in *The Changing Face of Form Criticism for the Twenty-First Century*, ed. Marvin A. Sweeney and Ehud Ben Zvi (Grand Rapids: Eerdmans, 2003), 123–26. Cf. Joachim Begrich, "Das priesterliche Heilsorakel," *ZAW* 54 (1934): 81–92. For example, even though Zimmerli referred to Esarhaddon's oracle collections, he categorically denied that the "fear not" expression and the self-predication formula ("I am X") could have emerged from prophetic speech (Walther Zimmerli, "I Am Yahweh," in *I Am Yahweh*, ed. Walter Brueggemann, trans. Douglas W. Scott [Atlanta: John Knox, 1982], 15, 17, 22–23.). Similarly, Harner used Assyrian sources to support Begrich's position and suggested that Second Isaiah's oracles were similar to priestly oracles, in this case delivered in the lamentable context of exile (Philip B. Harner, "The Salvation Oracle in Second Isaiah," *JBL* 88 [1969]: 419–22).

ticularly the "fear not" formula, are typical of prophetic speech.[95] But the question of the priestly versus prophetic origin is not crucial, since there is no *functional* distinction between prophet and priest if either is speaking in a prophetic capacity. What is important is the question whether the divine speech of the oracles in question is related specifically *to the cult.* Jean Vincent, who did not miss the implications of the Assyrian sources, recognized that much of the material in Second Isaiah stemmed from actual prophetic tradition, which he located in the cult; and he inferred from this that some oracles in Isa 40–55 might be associated with the circles of Isaiah of Jerusalem.[96] Of course, Vincent did not argue that the composition of Isa 40–55 was preexilic, but only that some materials are authentic to the traditions of the preexilic cult rather than mere imitations of cult-prophetic speech by an exilic author. But doubt remains whether the appearance of the *form* necessitates preexilic cultic practice. Meindert Dijkstra, for example, who considered at length the Neo-Assyrian data, regarded passages in Second Isaiah (e.g., Isa 42:18–43:7; 43:22–45:5; 48:16b–19) as finding "inspiration through the imitation of a cultic ceremony."[97] Similarly, Manfred Weippert concluded that Second Isaiah's announcements were patterned on royal *prophetic* oracles (including Neo-Assyrian examples), albeit with a previously unattested application to a foreign king or democratized in view of a rejected hope for the Davidic dynasty. Thus, they may be traced back to preexilic oracular style, albeit adapted by Second Isaiah to the exilic context.[98]

Thus, while one might be tempted to argue on the basis of *Sitz im Leben* that portions of Second Isaiah are preexilic, methodological problems abound. First, Vincent maintained that there was significant continuity between the preexilic and postexilic cults to allow for the origin of some cultic material with postexilic cult prophets.[99] Second, the setting for the oracles in Second Isaiah could well have been

---

95. Martti Nissinen, "Die Relevanz der neuassyrischen Prophetie für die alttestamentliche Forschung," in *Mesopotamica—Ugaritica—Biblica: Festschrift für Kurt Bergerhof zur Vollendung seines 70. Lebensjahres am 7. Mai 1992,* ed. Manfried Dietrich and Oswald Loretz, AOAT 232 (Kevelaer: Butzon & Bercker, 1993), 248. This formula is common even in secular contexts (idem, "Fear Not: A Study on an Ancient Near Eastern Phrase," 132–45), but when associated with divine speech, it is a distinctly prophetic formula (ibid., 128–29, 160–61).

96. Jean M. Vincent, *Studien zur literarischen Eigenart und zur geistigen Heimat von Jesaja, Kap. 40–55,* BBET 5 (Frankfurt: Peter Lang, 1977), 129–31, 187, 256. With the support of the Neo-Assyrian texts, Vincent expanded on the conclusions of von Waldow, who argued that Deutero-Isaiah was not merely imitating a priestly oracle but rather was an actual prophet living among the exiles, whose oracles followed the tradition of the Jerusalem cult-prophets (Hans Eberhard von Waldow, "Anlass und Hintergrund der Verkündigung des Deuterojesaja" [PhD diss., Bonn, 1953]).

97. Dijkstra, *Gods voorstelling,* 365–68, 375–76, with citation from p. 375.

98. Weippert, "Assyrische Prophetien der Zeit Asarhaddons und Assurbanipals," 91–92, 109–10; idem, "Aspekte israelitischer Prophetie im Lichte verwandter Erscheinungen des Alten Orients," in *Ad bene et fideliter seminandum: Festgabe für Karlheinz Deller zum 21. Februar 1987,* ed. Gerlinde Mauer and Ursula Magen, AOAT 220 (Kevelaer: Butzon & Bercker, 1988), 312–14; idem, " 'Ich bin Jahwe'—'Ich bin Ishtar von Arbela,' " 36–37, 56.

99. Vincent, *Studien zur literarischen Eigenart,* 258.

Jerusalem, though during the exilic period.[100] So one might consider these oracles related to remnants of cultic life around Jerusalem but still exilic. Third, in a model such as von Waldow's, an exilic prophet in Babylon might have addressed oracles to the worshipping community there.[101] This would be "cultic" but in a non-sacrificial context. Finally, and most significant, there is Nissinen's description of the various settings in which the "fear not" formula appears. His survey shows that, while connected to genuinely *prophetic* oracles when combined with divine speech, the setting is not always cultic.[102] What remains of form-critical consideration is that evidence presses against models of scribal imitation, since the form is linked to actual prophetic performance scenarios.

Genetic Relationship to Assyrian Oracles?

Underlying the above discussion is the recognition that the salvation oracles in Isa 40–48 are similar to those of Neo-Assyrian prophecies to a degree unparalleled in other Old Testament prophetic books.[103] Nevertheless, beyond the *similarity in form* and the possibility of a shared *Sitz im Leben* is the question whether there is any *direct* link between the two corpora of texts. The similarities are so striking that Weippert poses the hypothetical possibility that Deutero-Isaiah learned the form through contact with Neo-Babylonian prophets, who in turn had been trained in a prophetic tradition stemming back to Neo-Assyrian times.[104] One might ask why such a circuitous course should be proposed when a more direct explanation is that the ground source of Isa 40–48 is none other than Isaiah of Jerusalem, who was a near contemporary with the Neo-Assyrian prophets at a time of close contact between Assyria and Judah. However, the form is so widespread chronologically and geographically that Weippert is correct to conclude that both Neo-Assyrian prophets and the biblical prophet whose oracles are preserved in Isa 40–48 are simply part of the same broad stream of Syrian-Mesopotamian prophetic tradition.[105]

---

100. Hans M. Barstad, *The Babylonian Captivity of the Book of Isaiah: "Exilic" Judah and the Provenance of Isaiah 40–55* (Oslo: Novus, 1997).

101. Von Waldow maintained that Deutero-Isaiah responded to communal laments uttered during commemorations of the destruction of the temple (von Waldow, "Anlass und Hintergrund," 89, 123; idem, ". . . *Denn ich erlöse dich": Eine Auslegung von Jesaja 43*, BibS(N) 29 [Neukirchen: Neukirchener, 1960], 56–57).

102. Nissinen, "Fear Not: A Study on an Ancient Near Eastern Phrase," 159–60.

103. Nissinen correctly notes that, aside from Isa 40–55, the closest parallels occur in historical books and psalms, not other writing prophets (idem, "Die Relevanz der neu-assyrischen Prophetie," 249; cf. idem, "Fear Not: A Study on an Ancient Near Eastern Phrase," 148). For detailed comparison, see Weippert, " 'Ich bin Jahwe'—'Ich bin Ishtar von Arbela,' " 37–55.

104. Weippert, " 'Ich bin Jahwe'—'Ich bin Ishtar von Arbela,' " 57–58. The formal characteristics are constitutive enough to suggest to Weippert that Isa 40–48 stems from an individual prophet and can be differentiated from extrapolations in "Dtr Isa. B" (Isa 49:1–52:12), "DtrIsa. C" (Isa 54 and following), and Isa 52:13–53:12 (ibid., 55–56).

105. Ibid., 58.

Rhetoric of Prediction

Another feature of comparison between Neo-Assyrian oracles and Second Isaiah is a type of intertextuality in which the deity refers to previous prophetic announcements that have been fulfilled as a basis for strengthening faith in current promises. Weippert points to Assyrian examples such as: "Could you not rely on the previous utterance which I spoke to you? Now you can rely on this later one too" (SAA 9 1.10:7–12).[106] This is comparable to Isa 42:9, "Behold, the former things have come to pass; now I declare new things" (cf. Isa 41:21–29; 48:3–6, 12–16).[107] One might note that there is a significant difference in the temporal gap between prophecy and fulfillment in these respective prophetic corpora. In the case of Ishtar's oracles, it is a matter of years between the initial promises of kingship for Esarhaddon and his victory in the midst of civil war. In the case of Isaiah, more than a century separates the announcements of the preexilic prophets from the deliverance from exile through YHWH's anointed, Cyrus.[108] This difference, of course, comes into the debate in competing models of the composition history of the book of Isaiah. But merely observing similarities in rhetorical use of the fulfillment motif cannot help, and the *capacity* of biblical prophets to predict the distant future is not necessarily denied by advocates of an exilic date for Second Isaiah.

Conclusion

None of this discussion denies the nature of biblical prophetic books as "literary artifacts," the book of Isaiah being a supreme example. But the evidence supports a close link between prophetic books and the individual prophets whose oracles make up these literary masterpieces.[109] Ancient Near Eastern prophetic

---

106. Ibid., 51–52. Also SAA 9 1.1:15–17; 1.4:34–36; 2.2:17–18; 9 7:3–7.

107. Weippert, "Aspekte israelitischer Prophetie," 316–17; idem, "'Das Frühere, siehe, ist eingetroffen . . .': Über Selbstzitate im altorientalischen Prophetenspruch," in *Oracles et prophéties dans l'antiquité: Actes du Colloque de Strasbourg, 15–17 Juin 1995*, ed. Jean-Georges Heintz, Travaux du Centre de Recherche sur le Proche-Orient et la Grèce Antiques 15 (Paris: Boccard, 1997), 147–69; idem, "'Ich bin Jahwe'—'Ich bin Ishtar von Arbela,'" 53–55.

108. This is not to say that Mesopotamians did not have a *concept* of divine determination of the future and revelation revolving around such plans. For example, Assurbanipal (Prism A vi 107–117) states that he had been preordained by the gods "from distant days" to restore Nanaya's temple. Even though the will of the gods was not revealed until a future generation, this text exhibits the thought-category of a long-term divine plan, similar to what we find in literary predictive texts, which exhibit the same sense of predetermination and subsequent revelation by the gods (Nissinen, *References to Prophecy*, 40–41; cf. de Jong, *Isaiah among the Ancient Near Eastern Prophets*, 403).

109. Unfortunately, the following article by Martti Nissinen came to my attention too late to be integrated into the discussion of this paper: "Since When Do Prophets Write?," in *In the Footsteps of Sherlock Holmes: Studies in the Biblical Text in Honour of Anneli Aejmelaeus*, ed. Kristin de Troyer, Michael T. Law, and Marketta Liljeström [Leuven: Peeters, 2014], 585–606. Nissinen would not likely agree with my conclusion here. Nevertheless, while he

phenomena provide a model for partial collection and editing of prophetic speech that preserves the integrity of the original prophetic words while at the same time contextualizing their significance for new settings. Because prophetic *literature* in the Bible has no analogy in the ancient Near East, the comparative method does not lend direct support to arguments in favor of the composition of this book *as a whole* in preexilic, exilic, or postexilic times. But the evidence does lead one to expect that the final form of the book consists substantially of authentic Isaianic material.

---

argues that there is no firm evidence in the Hebrew Bible that biblical prophets *wrote* prophecy before the time of Ezekiel (perhaps Jeremiah), he observes that there is broad evidence from the ancient Near East that prophets worked in close conjunction with scribes (p. 592), which is the minimal dynamic necessary for my conclusion.

8

Cyrus or Sennacherib? Historical Issues Involved in the Interpretation of Isaiah 40–55

GARY V. SMITH

Introduction

Historical hints about the setting of the audience in Isa 40–55 are largely hidden from the view of most readers because (1) the theological messages contained in these chapters are about God's power, his deeds of comfort, and what he will do for Israel and the nations; (2) relatively few historical people, events, and places are mentioned in these chapters; and (3) when possible indicators of a historical situation are present, it is not always clear how the audience was temporally or geographically related to them. In addition, conclusions about the historical setting of Isa 40–55 vary significantly because interpreters use different assumptions, insights, and methods in dealing with the evidence.

Many critical scholars have concluded that Isa 40–55 was composed not by the prophet Isaiah, but by one or more authors/editors who were living in Babylon toward the end of the exilic period (550–540 BCE).[1] Because chapters 40–55 were included as part of the canonical scroll of Isaiah, many evangelical scholars believe that the prophet Isaiah was the author, but they agree with the critical interpretation that Isa 40–55 was addressed to the Jewish community living in the Babylonian exile around 150 years later.[2]

New proposals have raised questions about these conclusions, and the variations in these approaches expose some weaknesses in the "accepted perspectives" on the temporal and geographical location of the audience in Isa 40–55. For example, Hendrik Spykerboer's investigation of chapters 40–55 leads him to conclude that the author was in Babylon, but "the coherence of 40:12–55:5 as demonstrated in our study must also lead to the conclusion that the whole work is meant for

---

1. Samuel R. Driver sets forth the key reasons for attributing chs. 40–55 to a later author in Babylonian exile: the twin claims that prophets normally address their contemporaries and that the prophet here is addressing an exilic audience, as well as the different historical setting, literary style, and theological ideas in these chapters in comparison with those in Isa 1–39 (*An Introduction to the Literature of the Old Testament* [1897; repr., Cleveland: World, 1956], 230–46).

2. John N. Oswalt believes that the critical opinions about the authorship of Isa 40–66 stumble over the issue of whether it is possible to prophesy about the future (*Isaiah 40–66*, NICOT [Grand Rapids: Eerdmans, 1998], 3–6).

the same group of people, i.e., primarily for the Israelites in Jerusalem."[3] Klaus Baltzer concludes that "Jerusalem is most likely the place where DtIsa's work was composed . . . but [it] was performed for the *golah*" in Babylon as well as for the people in Jerusalem.[4] Christopher Seitz's study of Isaiah leads him to the conclusion that the provenance of chapters 40–55 was likely in Judah.[5] Lena-Sofia Tiemeyer's evaluation of evidence for a geographic location in Babylon suggests that it is more likely that chapters 40–55 were written in Judah after the people returned from exile.[6] John Goldingay and David Payne are forthright in stating that the arguments for a Babylonian location for chapters 40–55 are "circumstantial. . . . Many features of the material are intelligible on any hypothesis regarding its audience's location."[7] Brevard Childs believes that most of the original historical markers in chapters 40–66 were removed by canonical editors, so the message "no longer can be understood as a specific commentary on the needs of exiled Israel."[8] Joseph Blenkinsopp admits that "the arguments for a Babylonian location are not as firm as some proponents think . . . [but] an origin in the Babylonian diaspora is marginally preferable."[9] Menahem Haran's investigation supports the view that chapters 40–48 reflect a Babylonian setting, while chapters 49–55 had their origin in Judah because they directly address the people of Jerusalem in the second person, the reproof of sins in this section relates to people in Judah, and the background of 52:1–12 is Jerusalem.[10]

---

3. According to Spykerboer, "it is most probable that DI lived in Babylon. . . . the situation in exile is never a prerequisite as far as the addresses are concerned. . . . We thus conclude that DI wrote his work and sent it to people in Jerusalem to comfort and encourage them" (*The Structure and Composition of Deutero-Isaiah: With Special Reference to the Polemics against Idolatry* [Meppel: Krips, 1976], 187–88).

4. Klaus Baltzer believes this drama was performed "on the southeast slopes of Jerusalem" (*Deutero-Isaiah*, Hermeneia [Minneapolis: Fortress, 2001], 24).

5. "The relationship between Isaiah 40–66, Lamentations, Zechariah 1–8, and numerous of the Psalms suggests for this writer that Judah is the most likely provenance" (Christopher R. Seitz, "Divine Council: Temporal Transition and the New Prophecy in the Book of Isaiah," *JBL* 109 [1990]: 230n5).

6. Lena-Sofia Tiemeyer, *For the Comfort of Zion: The Geographical and Theological Location of Isaiah 40–55*, VTSup 139 (Leiden: Brill, 2011).

7. John Goldingay and David F. Payne, *A Critical and Exegetical Commentary on Isaiah 40–55*, ICC (London: T&T Clark, 2006), 1:31.

8. Brevard S. Childs, *Introduction to the Old Testament as Scripture* (Philadelphia: Fortress, 1979), 325.

9. Joseph Blenkinsopp, *Isaiah 40–55: A New Translation with Introduction and Commentary*, AB 19A (New York: Doubleday, 2002), 103–4. Martien A. Halvorson-Taylor agrees with Blenkinsopp's position (*Enduring Exile: The Metaphorization of the Exile in the Hebrew Bible*, VTSup 141 [Leiden: Brill, 2011], 107).

10. Haran attributes the Palestinian background to the period after the return of the exiles ("The Literary Structure and Chronological Framework of the Prophecies in Is. XL–XLVIII," in *Congress Volume, Bonn 1962*, VTSup 9 [Leiden: Brill, 1963], 127–55). He notes his disagreement with M. H. Segal (ibid., 153n1), who held that all of Isa 40–66 was composed in Palestine (*Mebô' Hammiqra'*, vol. 2, 1946).

Following a redactional analysis of Isa 40–55, Klaus Kiesow finds three layers in this text: (1) 40:13–48:20 was written in Babylon for the exiles because it is about God's ability to bring the exiles home; (2) 49:1–52:10 was penned in Judah for the returnees because it discusses the fate of Jerusalem and God's glory in Jerusalem; and (3) 52:13–55:13, which is eschatological in nature, was composed in Judah.[11] Ulrich Berges' redactional analysis of these same chapters, however, yields five layers: (1) a group of core messages in 40:12–46:1 that were written in Babylon from 550 to 539 BCE; (2) a *golah* redaction by returning exiles that completed chapters 40–48 around 521–520 BCE; (3) a Jerusalem redaction that added chapters 49–52 in 521 BCE; (4) a second Jerusalem redaction in chapters 54–55 that invites the worshippers of YHWH among the nations to return to Zion, plus a few other scattered texts; and (5) a fourth servant song from Jerusalem in Isa 52:13–53:12.[12] While some scholars have raised serious questions about the fine distinctions that such approaches make between various redactional layers,[13] what is interesting for our purposes is that several modern critical scholars (as well as some early critics) identify the location of the audience in some sections of Isa 40–55 as Judah or someplace other than Babylon.[14] Thus it is essential to evaluate the degree to which possible Babylonian influence has left any temporal or geographical imprint on Isa 40–55.

The Weakness of Arguments for a Mesopotamian Exilic Setting for Isaiah 40–55

It seems fair to conclude that the Neo-Assyrian and, later, the Neo-Babylonian empire exercised considerable influence on the lives of the common people in Judah, as well as of the governmental and educated class, given the fact that they interacted over many years in a number of ways—through travel, trade, wars, and treaties.

11. Klaus Kiesow, *Exodustexte im Jesajabuch: Literarkritische und motivgeschichtliche Analysen*, OBO 24 (Freiburg: Editions Universitaires, 1979), 158–202.

12. Ulrich F. Berges, *Jesaja 40–48*, HThKAT (Freiburg: Herder, 2008), 338–413.

13. For example, see the insightful and critical review by Marvin A. Sweeney, "Review of R. G. Kratz, *Kyros im Deuterojesaja-Buch*," *JBL* 113 (1994): 129–32.

14. Karl Marti rejected a Babylonian setting because the author of Isa 40–55 shows no knowledge of Ezekiel and has no knowledge of living conditions in Babylon (*Das Buch Jesaja*, KHC 10 [Tübingen: Mohr Siebeck, 1900], xv). John H. Maynard argued for a Palestinian location because of the references to Palestinian trees and the lack of reference to the popular Babylonian palm tree, the author's lack of knowledge concerning Babylon, his statement to "go out from there" in 52:11, and his calling Mesopotamia "the ends of the earth" in 41:9 ("The Home of Deutero-Isaiah," *JBL* 36 [1917]: 213–24). Bernhard Duhm thought that the prophet lived in Phoenicia (*Das Buch Jesaia*, Göttinger HKAT 3.1, 4th ed., [Göttingen: Vandenhoeck & Ruprecht, 1922], 18, 373). Mitchell J. Dahood also supported a Phoenician origin for these chapters ("Phoenician Elements in Isaiah 52:13–53:12," in *Near Eastern Studies in Honor of William Foxwell Albright*, ed. Hans Goedicke [Baltimore: Johns Hopkins University Press, 1971], 63–73).

Through these means of contact, the leaders in Judah had relationships with Meso-potamian governments, institutional officials, military leaders, and troops for ap-proximately 150 years before the fall of Jerusalem. The discovery of ninety-two objects in Judah inscribed with cuneiform writing testifies to this long period of contact.[15] Judah and the Neo-Assyrian and Neo-Babylonian empires shared com-mon Semitic vocabulary and idioms, and interrelated cultural ways of doing things. It should not automatically be assumed that one's knowledge of another nation's ex-pressions implies that he or she lives in that foreign land. For example, it is unlikely that the detailed information concerning all the nations addressed in the oracles against the foreign nations in Isa 13–23, Jer 46–51, and Ezek 25–32 indicates that the authors of these materials and their audiences lived in these foreign countries. For this reason, several common arguments for locating the audience of Isa 40–55 in Babylonian exile are not very persuasive. These include arguments concerning (1) knowledge of Babylonian gods and religion, (2) the influence of the Akkadian language on the language and literature of these chapters, (3) references to activity in Babylon, (4) comments about the destruction of Judah, (5) reconstructions of a time of great fear in exile but peace in Judah, (6) references to God as Redeemer, and (7) the idea that 39:1–8 creates a bridge to the exilic era in chapters 40–55. I will consider each of these arguments separately.

(1) The inclusion of occasional references to the history, culture, and religion of Mesopotamia would not be unusual for an Israelite prophet writing during the Neo-Assyrian or the Neo-Babylonian periods.[16] During these times Jehu submit-ted to the Assyrian king Shalmaneser III,[17] Ahaz submitted to Tiglath-pileser III (2 Kgs 16; 2 Chr 28), Hezekiah formed a coalition with Merodach-baladan of Babylon (Isa 39), Manasseh was a vassal of Assyria and spent some time in Assyria (2 Chr 33:10–13), and Judah was controlled by Babylon from 605 until the fall of Jerusalem in 586 BCE (2 Kgs 24–25; Jer 39–40; 52).

When Isa 46:1–2 and 47:12–13 refer, derogatorily, to Babylonian gods and re-ligious officials (see also 44:25), this is not surprising, since one would expect the Israelite prophets to know the names of the gods of other nations. Determining the

---

15. Horowitz, Oshima, and Sanders discuss ninety-two cuneiform-inscribed objects from twenty-eight places in Israel, including literary texts, letters, school exercises, and magical texts (Wayne Horowitz, Takayoshi Oshima, and Seth Sanders, eds., *Cuneiform in Canaan: Cuneiform Sources for the Land of Israel in Ancient Times* [Jerusalem: Israel Ex-ploration Society, 2006]). David S. Vanderhooft discusses the influence of the Babylonian imperial administration on its vassals and how that influence affected the prophets (*The Neo-Babylonian Empire and Babylon in the Latter Prophets*, HSM 59 [Atlanta: Scholars Press, 1999], 61–202).

16. A number of other prophetic texts that I would date to the time of the Neo-Assyrian or Neo-Babylonian empires refer to God's plans for these nations: Isa 7:17–20; 10:5–34; 13–14; 20:1–6; 21:1–10; 36–37; 39; Jer 21; 24–25; 27–29; 39–40; Hos 5:13; 7:11; 8:9; 9:3; 10:6; 11:5, 11; 12:2; Mic 4:10; 5:5–6; Hab 1:6–11; 2:6–20; and the book of Nahum.

17. Amihai Mazar, *Archaeology of the Land of the Bible: 10,000–586 B.C.E.*, ABRL (New York: Doubleday, 1992), 404. Jehu's submission to Shalmaneser III is recorded on the Black Obelisk but not in the book of Kings.

precise historical background(s) of such texts is not so easy, however. When foreign religious officials are mentioned, for example, it is not always easy to determine if they are Assyrian or Babylonian (44:25). It is difficult to distinguish religious and cultural features from the time of Tiglath-pileser III (the overlord of Ahaz) and the time of Sennacherib (during Hezekiah's reign), and to distinguish either from Babylonian religious and cultural features from the time of Nebuchadnezzar (the time of Jehoiakim and Zedekiah). Based on the long period of contact between Judah and the Mesopotamian empires, the prophets in Judah probably had more than a rudimentary knowledge of the religions of Mesopotamia and the methods its peoples used to divine the will of their gods (44:25; 47:12–13). This kind of religious knowledge would not require a prophet or his audience to live in Assyria or Babylon.

In contrast, James Muilenburg believes that the movement of the two main Babylonian gods, Bel and Nebo, as described in Isa 46:1–2, represents the experience of "one who has seen the sacred procession"[18] in Babylon, and Klaus Baltzer views this text as a parody of the New Year's Festival.[19] Although Babylon's *akītu* festival was likely well known in all the surrounding nations and could have been the object of a parody, it seems unlikely that Isa 46:1–2 describes this festival, for this text does not depict the idols being joyfully paraded in a procession.[20] Instead, they are burdens carried into captivity, a common image in the ancient Near East for communicating the defeat of a nation's gods.[21]

(2) Some conclude that Akkadian influence on words, metaphors, and phrases in Isa 40–55 betrays a Babylonian setting, since only people living in Babylon would have known Akkadian. However, given the long period of social, governmental, and military contact between Israel and Mesopotamia during the Neo-Assyrian and Neo-Babylonian eras, it is hard to prove a Babylonian exilic setting for Isa 40–55; Akkadian influence on Hebrew could have occurred during either the Neo-Assyrian period or the Neo-Babylonian period before the Judeans went into exile (605–586 BCE). To prove an exilic setting for these chapters, one would need to show that the Akkadian influence on them involved unique linguistic features that developed in Babylon only after 586 BCE. Shalom Paul finds only ten examples in Isa 40–66 of influence from the Akkadian language and literature written in this language.[22] Furthermore, Peter Machinist identifies significant

---

18. James Muilenburg, "The Book of Isaiah: Chapters 40–66," *IB* 5:397.

19. Baltzer, *Deutero-Isaiah*, 255. Hanspeter Schaudig thinks the prophet is addressing Israelites in exile who are seeing this event ("'Bēl Bows, Nabû Stoops!': The Prophecy in Isaiah xlvi 1–2 as a Reflection of Babylonian 'Processional Omens,'" *VT* 58 [2008]: 557–72).

20. Another weakness of this theory is that Nabonidus did not celebrate the *akītu* festival.

21. Norman Whybray believes this refers to the defeat of Babylon in 539 BCE. He writes, "this is a further example of a prophecy that was not fulfilled; in the event Cyrus proclaimed himself a follower of Marduk" (R. N. Whybray, *Isaiah 40–66*, NCB [London: Marshall, Morgan & Scott, 1975], 113–14).

22. Shalom M. Paul, *Isaiah 40–66: Translation and Commentary*, ECC (Grand Rapids: Eerdmans, 2012), 61–63; idem, "Deutero-Isaiah and Cuneiform Royal Inscriptions," in *Essays*

linguistic influences from Assyrian specifically in Isa 1–39, which should probably be ascribed to the propaganda of the Assyrian empire and the direct impact of the Assyrians on the royal Israelite court.[23] This does not lead him to conclude, however, that the prophet Isaiah or the audience in Isa 1–39 lived in Assyria. However, it is almost impossible to determine whether these influences came through direct contact with Assyria, or indirectly, through Israel's contact with neighboring nations like Aram/Syria.

After a thorough study of the Akkadian influences on Isa 40–55, Hans Barstad concludes that "we have not a single word in Isa 40–55 that may indicate any Akkadian influence on the writer of this text."[24] This seems to overstate the case, for Jacob Behr claims a close connection between chapters 40–55 and the language, phraseology, and ideology of Babylonian literature.[25] Nevertheless, Tiemeyer has shown that many of the phrases that Behr mentions were common Semitic expressions and that many of these phrases have earlier biblical parallels that would be a more likely source for the prophet's phraseology. Thus she does not find that the linguistic and cultural similarities between Isa 40–55 and Babylonian literature

---

in Memory of E. A. Speiser, ed. William W. Hallo, *JAOS* 88 (New Haven: American Oriental Society, 1968), 180–86. These include "calling a monarch by name," designating a king as a "favorite/beloved," the expression "I grasped his arm," and the movement of people "on horses, chariots, and wagons." According to Nahum M. Waldman, the idea of "clearing a way in the wilderness" derives from Assyrian royal inscriptions ("A Biblical Echo of Mesopotamian Royal Rhetoric," in *Essays on the Occasion of the Seventieth Birthday of Dropsie University, 1909–1979*, ed. Abraham I. Katsh and Leon Nemoy [Philadelphia: Dropsie University Press, 1979], 449–55). However, Tiemeyer rejects this influence because the phraseology in Isaiah is not identical to that found in Assyrian documents and because the idea of journeying through the wilderness is a part of the exodus story and is present in the preexilic era, as evidenced in Jer 2:2; 31:8 (*For the Comfort of Zion*, 86–92).

23. Machinist provides six connections with Neo-Assyrian royal inscriptions, in addition to several other comparisons ("Assyria and Its Image in the First Isaiah?," *JAOS* 103 [1983]: 719–34). For example, both the Assyrians themselves and the book of Isaiah picture the Assyrian armies as lions (Isa 5:29) and Assyrian control as a "yoke" (Isa 10:27; 14:25). Since most of these connections can be found in earlier writings in the Hebrew Bible (e.g., people and their armies are compared to lions in Num 23:24; 24:9; and Ps 17:8–12; and control over a people is described as a "yoke" in Gen 27:40; Lev 26:13; and Deut 28:48), it seems hard to identify them all as borrowings.

24. Barstad questions the validity of a Babylonian setting in the following publications: "Akkadian 'Loanwords' in Isaiah 40–55 and the Question of the Babylonian Origin of Deutero-Isaiah," in *Text and Theology: Studies in Honour of Dr. Theol. Magne Sæbø, Presented on the Occasion of His 65th Birthday*, ed. Arvid Tångberg (Oslo: Verbum, 1994), 36–48; "On the So-called Babylonian Literary Influence in Second-Isaiah," *SJOT* 2 (1987): 90–110; and *The Babylonian Captivity of the Book of Isaiah* (Oslo: Novus, 1997), 59–76.

25. Behr investigates (1) the contrast between light and darkness, which points to contact with Persian Zoroastrianism, (2) God's knowledge of the past, which is similar to Nabu's knowledge, and (3) similar expressions like "called by name" in Isa 43:1 and the Cyrus Cylinder, and "clearing a way through the wilderness" in Isa 40:3–4 and several royal inscriptions (Jacob W. Behr, *The Writings of Deutero-Isaiah and the Neo-Babylonian Royal Inscriptions: A Comparison of the Language and Style* [Pretoria: University of Pretoria, 1937], 15–32).

require the author or the audience of the former to be located in Babylon.[26] In addition, she observes that the common people in Babylon actually spoke Aramaic at the time of the exile, with Akkadian being limited primarily to royal decrees and cultic rituals.[27] Thus Aramaic would be expected to have exercised a greater influence than Akkadian on a Judean author/editor and his audience living in Babylon during this period.

(3) References to activity in Babylon in Isa 40–55 may point to the location of the author or his audience. In 43:8–15 YHWH defends the claim that he alone is God and that he acts on behalf of his people. One justification for this claim is that YHWH will "send to Babylon and bring down all the Babylonians as fugitives" (43:14). Claus Westermann interprets this as a reference to God sending Cyrus to defeat Babylon in 539 BCE,[28] but according to Blenkinsopp this interpretation of the verse does not match the peaceful takeover of Babylon described in the Cyrus Cylinder.[29] Although the Hebrew text of the end of 43:14 seems damaged and almost beyond reconstruction, it appears to describe a flight of Babylonian fugitives in boats. There is no indication of the date or location of the audience listening to this proclamation. However, since Babylon was not destroyed, and Cyrus took no captives, this may refer instead to the fall of Babylon pictured in 21:1–10.

Some connect the reference in Isa 48:14 to what God will accomplish against Babylon to the events described in 46:1–2 and 47:1–15. But since Cyrus neither destroyed Babylon nor sent Bel (Marduk) and Nebo into captivity in 539 BCE (46:1–2), it is unlikely that any of these texts describes the fall of Babylon in that year. Thus Isa 48:14 was not a message of comfort to people living in the Babylonian exile.

Finally, in 48:20 the prophet calls his audience to "go forth from Babylon, flee from Chaldea,"[30] an appeal whose geographical indicators can be interpreted literally if one assumes the author was speaking to exiles shortly after Cyrus' decree in 538 BCE. Nevertheless, 48:2 indicates that the author was speaking to people who called themselves the citizens of the holy city. Isaiah 46:1–47:15 likely refers to Sennacherib's total annihilation of Babylon in 689 BCE or the later conquest by

---

26. Tiemeyer, *For the Comfort of Zion*, 86–92. For example, she argues that since the expression "to call by name" is used in Exod 31:2 and 35:30, the prophet probably did not borrow this from Assyrian inscriptions. According to Paul V. Mankowski, seventeen Akkadian loanwords are found in Isaiah, in comparison with fifteen in Jeremiah, eleven in Ezekiel, twelve in the Psalms, and thirteen in 2 Chronicles (*Akkadian Loanwords in Biblical Hebrew*, HSS 47 [Cambridge: Harvard University Press, 2000]). Strangely, the book that bears the name of the prophet Jeremiah, who was not in Babylon, contains more loanwords than the book that bears the name of Ezekiel, who was in Babylon.

27. Tiemeyer, *For the Comfort of Zion*, 84.

28. Claus Westermann, *Isaiah 40–66: A Commentary*, trans. David M. G. Stalker, OTL (Philadelphia: Westminster, 1969), 125.

29. Blenkinsopp (*Isaiah 40–55*, 227) rejects the connection with the Cyrus Cylinder, but maintains that Isa 43 refers generally to the defeat of Babylon at some point in time.

30. All subsequent biblical citations in this article are from the NASB.

Xerxes in 482 BCE.[31] If this is correct, 48:20 focuses on the disobedience and stubbornness of God's people (48:4, 8) and argues that Judah should reject any talk of an alliance with Babylon (cf. 39:1–8). Judah should trust YHWH their Redeemer for deliverance from Sennacherib (48:9, 20b), reject the uncleanness of a Babylonian alliance (52:11), and flee from the temptation to trust the Chaldeans (48:20).

(4) References in Isa 40–55 to destruction in Judah are often automatically connected to the fall of Jerusalem in 586 BCE, even though there were several other occasions when Judah or Jerusalem suffered serious ruin and the deportation of its citizens.[32] Since Isa 40–55 does not identify who put Judah in ruins, it is difficult to know whether the perpetrator was, for example, Shishak/Egypt, Hazael/Aram, Israel, Assyria, or Babylon. Without firm evidence regarding which defeat is in view, many commentators simply assume that the text addresses the Babylonian exiles about Jerusalem's being destroyed in 586 BCE. The references to ruin or destruction in chapters 40–55 fall into three general groups: (a) references to past or present plunder, desolation, and war (41:11–12; 42:22–25; 51:13–14, 17–19; 52:3–5); (b) references to Cyrus rebuilding the ruins of Jerusalem (44:26; 45:13); and (c) the eschatological restoration and rebuilding of the ruins of Jerusalem (49:8, 17–19, 24–26; 52:9; 54:3). If this understanding is correct, only two references (44:26; 45:13) refer to the fall of Jerusalem, and these two appear in the context of a future rebuilding of the city. The examples listed above do not offer much support for assuming that the fall of Jerusalem has already taken place.

Isaiah 40–55 presents the big picture of Israel's past, present, and future. According to this panoramic perspective, Israel was sinful and blind (41:19–20; 43:8), performed useless worship (43:22–24), made idols (44:9–20), argued with God (45:9), was stubborn (48:4, 8), and falsely accused God (49:14). The prophet recognized that the people in Judah were attacked in war (41:11–12; 42:22–25) and

---

31. Goldingay admits that, "As in the case of ch. 46, it cannot be said that there was a close correspondence between the events envisaged here and the actual events surrounding the fall of Babylon in 539" (*The Message of Isaiah 40–55: A Literary-Theological Commentary* [London: T&T Clark, 2005], 317). The events described in ch. 46 could refer to the conquests by Xerxes in 482 BCE (according to Philip R. Davies, "God of Cyrus, God of Israel: Some Religio-historical Reflections on Isaiah 40–55," in *Words Remembered, Texts Renewed: Essays in Honor of J. F. A. Sawyer*, ed. J. Davies et al. [JSOTSup 195; Sheffield: Sheffield Academic, 1995], 207–25) or to Sennacherib's conquest of Babylon in 701 BCE (according to Gary V. Smith, *Isaiah 40–66* [NAC 15B; Nashville: Broadman & Holman, 2009], 283–89, 295).

32. The Egyptian pharaoh Shishak attacked Jerusalem, taking gold from the house of God and the king, around 925 BCE (1 Kgs 14:25–28; 2 Chr 12:1–12); the Philistines, Arabs, and Ethiopians took possessions from the king's house and took some of his sons and wives as captives (2 Chr 21:16–17); Hazael of Syria came to Jerusalem and took "all the sacred things" and gold from the house of God and the king's palace sometime between 835 and 797 BCE (2 Kgs 12:17–18; 2 Chr 24:23); Jehoash of Israel defeated Jerusalem, tore down part of the wall, and took gold, silver, and some captives around 783 BCE (2 Kgs 14:8–14; 2 Chr 25:22–24); Rezin and Pekah defeated all Judah except Jerusalem in 734–732 BCE and took 200,000 captives (2 Kgs 16:5–9; 17–18; 2 Chr 28:5–18); Sennacherib defeated all of Judah except Jerusalem in 701 BCE and claims to have taken 200,150 captives (2 Kgs 18–19; *ANET*, 288); and 2 Kgs 24:10–17 refers to gold and hostages being taken in 605 BCE, during the Babylonian control of Judah.

predicted a future judgment of Judah (43:28; 48:9–11). This yields an overarching metanarrative of (a) cycles of past/present sins and past/present judgments, (b) future judgment (43:28), (c) restoration by Cyrus (44:26–28), and (d) a final, marvelous eschatological restoration. Although some believe that the wars mentioned in Isa 40–55 refer to Babylon's defeat and ruin of Jerusalem in 586 BCE, this does not fit some texts. In Isa 41:8–14 YHWH promises that Israel's enemies will "become nothing and perish, you will look for them but you will not find them" (41:11–12). This promise matches only one Israelite experience—YHWH's miraculous deliverance of Jerusalem from Sennacherib when an angel defeated the Assyrian army.[33]

(5) The messages of hope and comfort in Isa 40–55 are often seen as the prophet's encouragement of those who were fearful and hopeless in Babylonian captivity. John Oswalt, for example, believes that

> chapters 40–55 are not addressed to a people looking to avoid destruction. These chapters address a people in despair, a people who believe their condition was hopeless. The affirmations that Isaiah made answer questions that would arise from the destruction of Jerusalem and the onset of the exile, not conditions existing between 739 and 701 BCE.[34]

Oswalt rejects the notion that Isa 40–55 was addressed to a preexilic "people living with a measure of security in their own land,"[35] which apparently reflects his understanding of life during the time of the prophet Isaiah (739–701 BCE).

However, this picture of despair and fear in exile is not reflected in the actual biblical evidence.[36] Jeremiah's letter to the exiles never mentions exilic slavery, imprisonment, abuses by the Babylonians, or that the exiles experienced hopeless despair (Jer 29). His letter encourages people to settle in for seventy years, to "seek the welfare of the city" where they live, and to pray for it (Jer 29:7). In addition, Jehoiachin, the exiled king of Judah, seems to have lived quite well in the Babylonian court, and was eventually released and granted a regular allowance by the Babylonians (Jer 52:31–34). The book of Daniel explains how some exiles rose to high positions in government and how, in one case, the Babylonian king sent out a decree against anyone who might offend the God of Shadrach, Meshach, and Abednego (Dan 3:29). The prophet Ezekiel's portrayal of living conditions in Babylon lacks

---

33. Smith, *Isaiah 40–66*, 104, 135–36.

34. John N. Oswalt, "Who Were the Addressees of Isaiah 40–66?," *BSac* 169 (2012): 33–47.

35. Ibid., 37.

36. Poor translations sometimes create a negative picture of exile. The NASB rendering of Isa 51:14 creates a false impression: "The exile will soon be set free, and will not die in the dungeon, nor will his bread be lacking." The HCSB translates the first clause here instead as "The prisoner is soon to be set free." While this verse could picture the people of Jerusalem as imprisoned by Sennacherib in the capital, YHWH promises their release without a long period of starvation (51:14b). The interpretation of 51:14b as a reference to imprisonment in Jerusalem (not in exile) is consistent with 51:17–19, which describes Judah drinking the curse from God's cup, resulting in the desolation of Judah (probably by the Assyrian army), as well as the reference in 51:21–23 to the enemy drinking from the cup of God's wrath (regarding the destruction of the Assyrian army at Jerusalem).

any reference to despair, fear of being put to death, or persecution of the Judean exiles. Since the elders of Israel were able to meet together (Ezek 8:1; 14:1; 20:1), they must have enjoyed considerable religious freedom. In addition, when the opportunity to leave Babylon came after Cyrus' decree in 538 BCE, many Judeans chose to stay rather than return to Jerusalem (Ezra 1–2). To summarize, the evidence available does not picture great despair among those living in Babylonian exile.

In contrast, the Assyrian attack on Jerusalem in 701 BCE involved the decimation of forty-six major walled cities, the taking of more than 200,000 captives, and a hopeless situation in which an Assyrian army of more than 185,000 troops besieged the city of Jerusalem.[37] In this context it would not be surprising to hear the prophet speak of people feeling helpless because of this war (Isa 41:10–13), people hiding in holes with no one to rescue them (Isa 42:22), and God pouring out his wrath on his people (Isa 42:25), while delaying his full anger so that his people would be refined but not destroyed (Isa 48:9–10). Having observed many other strong cities (e.g., Lachish, Libnah in Isa 37:8) attacked by a vastly superior Assyrian army, the Judeans saw no hope for Jerusalem. One would expect intense fear and hopelessness at such a time (Isa 36:22; 37:1–3; 40:27; 41:10; 43:1). This created an occasion for a prophet to declare God's power over the nations (Isa 40:15, 17; 41:12; 49:25b–26) as well as the news that their enemies would perish and become nothing (41:11–12; 51:22b–23). Many of the prophecies in Isa 40–55 seem less applicable to the relatively peaceful situation in Babylonian exile, in which some exiled individuals rose to high government positions (Dan 1–3), than to the hopelessness resulting from Judah's defeat before a vastly superior army.

Since Sennacherib's general Rab-shakeh repeatedly questioned whether Hezekiah's God was able to "deliver" (Isa 36:15, 18, 20; 37:11, 13) and Jerusalem and Hezekiah prayed for YHWH's deliverance (Isa 37:20), the messages about God's ability to deliver his people in Isa 40–55 were very fitting messages of hope for this occasion. Because Rab-shakeh also claimed that his gods and his army had defeated all the gods and armies of other nations (Isa 36:19–20; 37:12–13), the prophet's declaration that the idol gods were nothing and his trial speeches against these powerless gods (40:18–20; 41:21–24; 44:9–20) were very appropriate to that context. They provided encouragement to the Judeans who had not seen God intervene in earlier battles against the Assyrians.

(6) The frequency of references in Isa 40–55 to God as Redeemer is the fundamental reason that Martien Halvorson-Taylor locates the audience of these chapters in an exilic setting.[38] She believes the author is picturing the exiles when using the metaphors of prisoners, desolate children, a mother without children, and debt slaves, with the exile being their prison sentence. Thus Halvorson-Taylor's thematic reasoning based on associated terminology that is only tangentially related to the exile or redemption is unconvincing.[39] According to Halvorson-Taylor, Judah

---

37. *ANET*, 288.

38. Halvorson-Taylor, *Enduring Exile*, 107.

39. Halvorson-Taylor discusses the exodus and associated terminology in 40:1–2, but the term "redeemer" is not found there (ibid., 119–26). Terms she associates with exile and

needed a Redeemer (from the root ג-א-ל, *g-ʾ-l*, which occurs seventeen times in Isa 40–55; cf. the root פ-ד-ה, *p-d-h*, which occurs once) who would deliver them and return them to their land in a new exodus experience.[40] Although Deuteronomy uses פ-ד-ה (*p-d-h*) six times, always to refer to the exodus, it never uses ג-א-ל (*g-ʾ-l*) (which it uses twice) this way.[41] The book of Exodus uses ג-א-ל (*g-ʾ-l*) only twice, both times to refer to the exodus.[42] In Isa 41:14 and 49:26 the term Redeemer (גֹּאֵל, *gōʾēl*) serves as a title for a God, who would help his people in war (42:11–14; 49:25–26); it has nothing to do with an exodus or deliverance from exile. Isaiah 54:5, 8 include "Redeemer" as one of the titles of God, Isa 52:9 tells the "ruins of Jerusalem" that God has redeemed (ג-א-ל, *g-ʾ-l*) them, and God's plan to redeem his people mentioned in 43:1 and 51:10 relates to the eschatological gathering of Israel. Isaiah 44:22 connects the word "redeem" (ג-א-ל, *g-ʾ-l*) to redemption from sin, and other texts that use the word "Redeemer" (גֹּאֵל, *gōʾēl*) lack any direct connection to an exodus experience (43:14; 44:6, 24; 47:4; 48:17; 49:7). Isaiah 48:20 is the only verse that associates fleeing Babylon with God's redemption.

In contrast to Halvorson-Taylor, Tiemeyer questions the claim that the use of exodus imagery proves a Babylonian setting, since the general concepts associated with exodus events could be used in various settings to illustrate God's care for his people.[43] Hans Barstad maintains that the exodus imagery in Isa 40–55 is metaphorical and thus not a major emphasis in these chapters.[44] Furthermore, some parts of this text describe God's return to Jerusalem (40:5; 52:7–12), not an exodus of Judeans. Although exodus imagery is widely used in Isaiah, it is often a reminder of YHWH's powerful past actions in the original exodus (e.g., Isa 42:13; 43:16–17; 48:21; 51:10; 52:3–4) or metaphorical imagery for what God will do eschatologically (e.g., Isa 41:17–18; 43:2–3, 20; 49:10; 51:3; 52:12) when he gathers many people from all nations to Zion.

(7) Some interpreters view the reference to Judeans going into exile in Babylon in Isa 39:6–7 as a natural "bridge from the Babylon of Merodach-baladan to the Babylon of Nebuchadnezzar."[45] They believe that the chronological displacement

---

redemption are service/debt; guilt/punishment; and forgiven/paid—but these expressions are not always used in the context of an exile.

40. The occurrences of the root ג-א-ל (*g-ʾ-l*) in Isa 40–55 are found at 41:14; 43:1, 14; 44:6, 22–24; 47:4; 48:17, 20; 49:7, 26; 51:10; 52:3, 9; 54:5, 8; the one instance of פ-ד-ה (*p-d-h*) is found in 51:11.

41. ג-א-ל (*g-ʾ-l*) is found in Deut 19:6, 12, but neither time with reference to the exodus. פ-ד-ה (*p-d-h*) occurs in Deut 11:8; 12:31, 41; 13:3–4, 8; 19:1.

42. פ-ד-ה (*p-d-h*) occurs eight times in Exodus but none of these occurences is related to the event of the exodus. ג-א-ל (*g-ʾ-l*) is found in Exod 6:6; 15:13.

43. Tiemeyer, *For the Comfort of Zion*, 155–67.

44. Barstad, *A Way in the Wilderness: The "Second Exodus" in the Message of Second Isaiah*, JSS Monograph 12 (Manchester: University of Manchester Press, 1989), 1–101.

45. Brevard S. Childs, *Isaiah: A Commentary*, OTL (Louisville: Westminster John Knox, 2001), 286. See also Goldingay, *Message of Isaiah 40–55*, 4; Blenkinsopp, *Isaiah 40–55*, 47.

of chapter 39 vis-à-vis 36–37[46] creates a bridge that prepares the reader to under-stand the messages in chapters 40–55 as one of comfort for the exiles in Babylon. But this proposed bridge from one period in Babylonian history to another lacks beams to support it, for there are no references either to Babylon or to exiles liv-ing in Babylon in chapters 40, 41, or 42. Babylon is not mentioned until 43:14, and even there it is not the home of exiled Judeans but a city under attack (a theme not mentioned in 39:6–7). If the prophecy in 39:6–7 intended to create a conscious line of thought connecting it to chapters 40–55, there should be some explicit echoes of the themes of 39:6–7 in one of the succeeding chapters. However, Isa 40–43 never mentions the destruction of Jerusalem or the exile of the people in Babylon, both of which are key themes in 39:6–7.

Evidence for a Preexilic Location in Judah

Since the evidence commonly cited to support a Babylonian exilic audience for Isa 40–55 is inconclusive at best, what evidence from these chapters can we cite in support of a non-Babylonian and non-exilic setting for these chapters?[47]

(1) Isaiah 41:8–14 offers two hints about the locations of the prophet and his audience: First, God claims he took Israel ("the offspring of Abraham," v. 8) "from the far ends of the earth" (v. 9), a phrase that a prophet living in Babylon would probably not use if he was addressing an exilic audience.[48] Second, in 41:10, 13, 14, God encourages his people to "fear not," even though they are at war with some enemy (vv. 11–12).[49] A war setting does not coincide with any known Babylonian event while the people were in exile. The promise in 41:12 that God will cause the enemy to "become nothing" (יִהְיוּ כְאַיִן, *yihyû kĕʾayin*) and perish is reminiscent of only one war that Judah fought: YHWH's defeat of the Assyrian army at Jerusalem

---

46. Many have wondered why Isa 38–39, which concerns events that happened prior to the events depicted in chs. 36–37, were placed after chs. 36–37. Although it is impossible to get into the mind of the author/editor who placed these chapters in this order, this placement may have been meant to bring the reputation of Hezekiah down to earth. He demonstrated great faith in 37:14–20, but he was not the Messiah. Instead, he was a fallible man who struggled with trusting God (Isa 30–31; 39).

47. Since I have published my initial thoughts on this subject in an earlier article, here I will merely summarize the evidence cited there. See Gary V. Smith, "Isaiah 40–55: Which Audience Was Addressed?," *JETS* 54 (2011): 701–14.

48. Blenkinsopp recognizes that "the language does not point necessarily or exclusively to a Babylonian location" (*Isaiah 40–55*, 201). William H. Cobb has a similar understanding of the implication of this phrase. People do not usually describe a nearby location as "the far ends of the earth" ("Where Was Isaiah 40–66 Written?," *JBL* 27 [1908]: 48–64).

49. Martti Nissinen traces the form-critical understanding of this phrase in the Bible and its use in Neo-Assyrian texts ("Fear Not: A Study of an Ancient Near Eastern Phrase," in *The Changing Face of Form Criticism for the Twenty-First Century*, ed. Marvin A. Sweeney and Ehud Ben Zvi [Grand Rapids: Eerdmans, 2003], 122–61). Not every usage in the Bible or the ancient Near East is in a war context, but Isa 41:10–12 does mention war.

in 701 BCE (Isa 37:36).[50] Thus the setting here is preexilic, and this war coincides with events happening in Jerusalem in the time of Hezekiah.

(2) Isaiah 42:22 describes a people "plundered and looted, all of them trapped in holes." Since these images of war (cf. 1 Sam 14:11) do not match any known setting from the Babylonian exile, they must refer to some preexilic event.[51] These circumstances match the references to war against and the destruction/ruin of Jerusalem in 51:13–14, 17–19. This prophecy predicts that the cup of God's judgment that Jerusalem is now consuming will soon be drunk by her tormentors (51:22–23). This war could refer to Judah's defeat when Sennacherib conquered forty-six walled cities. The great reversal of destinies when the enemy will drink the cup of God's wrath (51:22–23) could refer to the angel from God defeating the Assyrian army (185,000 troops) around Jerusalem in 701 BCE (37:36).[52]

(3) The future destruction of the temple referred to in Isa 43:28 indicates that this prophecy was issued at some time before the fall of Jerusalem and the destruction of the temple in 586 BCE. The two verbs וַאֲחַלֵּל (wa'ăḥallēl), "and I will pollute," and וְאֶתְּנָה (wĕ'ettĕnâ), "and I will give," point to the future plan of God, which requires a preexilic dating and is most naturally understood as a warning to the people in Jerusalem.

(4) Although the defeat of Babylon and the removal of its gods mentioned in 46:1–2 and 47:1–15 are often connected to Cyrus' defeat of Babylon in 539 BCE, the Cyrus Cylinder claims that Cyrus did not destroy Babylon in that conquest; instead, he entered the city peaceably. Therefore, this prophecy probably refers to Sennacherib's complete leveling of Babylon in 689 BCE, a preexilic event. This prophecy argues that Hezekiah should not trust in an alliance with Babylon (cf. 39:1–8), because God will soon destroy that city.

(5) The lack of a specific mention of Babylon in the eschatological messages of the prophet that predict that God will bring people back to their land from the north and the south, the east and the west, and even from the ends of the earth (Isa 43:5–6), also argues against a Babylonian, exilic setting.[53] This orientation to Judah does not seem to refer to events at the time of Cyrus, when the Judeans returned from captivity in Babylon, but to the final restoration of God's people when God establishes his kingdom.

---

50. Jan L. Koole thinks Isa 41:8–14 refers to the Babylonian defeat of Jerusalem (*Isaiah III*, vol. 1, *Isaiah 40–48*, HCOT [Kampen: Pharos, 1997], 160–61), but God did not make the Babylonians "nothing" in that war.

51. According to Westermann, it is difficult to connect this verse to conditions in exile because people did not live in prisons or holes in Babylon (*Isaiah 40–66*, 112).

52. A less clear example of a reference to YHWH's victory in 701 is Isa 43:3, according to which God gave Cush, Seba, and Egypt as a ransom for Israel. This is often thought of as a reward to Cyrus for letting the Israelites go home, but the Persians did not take control of Egypt until seventeen years later. In addition, 45:13 notes that God gave Cyrus no reward. Isaiah 43:3 does not seem to relate to the exile. John Calvin suggested that it could refer to the preexilic occasion when God gave Sennacherib victory over Egypt ("Commentary on the Book of the Prophet Isaiah," *Calvin's Commentaries* [Grand Rapids: Baker, 2003], 8:321).

53. A similar Jerusalem point of view is present in a similar prophecy in 49:12.

A preexilic Jerusalem/Zion is reflected in the comment, "the destroyers and devastators will depart from you" (49:17). This does not describe Judeans departing from some peaceful Babylonian location. The departing of the destroyers mentioned here could refer to the flight of the remaining Assyrian troops after 185,000 were killed at Jerusalem (Isa 37:36).[54]

(6) In most of Isa 40–55, the audience is identified as Jacob/Israel (mainly in chs. 40–48) or Zion/Jerusalem (mainly in chs. 49–55). From the very beginning, the prophet offers "comfort" to "Jerusalem" and "my people" (40:1–2), who are to go up on a high mountain to spread the good news to "the cities of Judah" (40:9). Norman Whybray turns things upside down with his statement that "Jerusalem (and also 'Zion') is often used by Deutero-Isaiah to designate the exiles rather than the actual city."[55] The names Israel and Jacob in the titles "the God of Israel/Jacob" and "the Holy One of Israel" (41:14, 16; 44:6; 45:15; 47:4; 48:17; 49:7, 26; 52:12; 55:5) offer little help in resolving this issue. Of relevance here is Tiemeyer's examination of the use of "Jacob/Israel" in Isa 40–55, which "little favours identifying Jacob-Israel with the exilic community in Babylon."[56] Some of these texts in Isa 40–55 that mention Jacob and Israel lack evidence for defining the location of the speaker or audience (40:27; 44:23), while the contexts of others apparently point to a literal location of Jacob/Israel in Palestine (41:8; 42:24; 43:22, 28; 44:21; 45:19; 46:3). A third group of texts offers encouragement on the basis of God's eschatological deeds to fearful individuals whose geographical location is unknown (43:1, 5; 44:1–2; 46:13; 49:6). One text does refer to people in exile (45:4).

Scholars who have carried out a similar examination of the combination of the names Jerusalem and Zion (or of either term used alone) found in 49–55 suggest that these names can point to people in the literal city of Jerusalem, people in exile, or people in both locations.[57] Even though these terms point to a place, in some

---

54. One might add to this the indication in 52:4 that the Israelites were oppressed "at first" in Egypt and then "at the end" by Assyria and the fact that in this context there is no clear reference to oppression in Babylon (apparently it had not yet happened). Whybray believes the phrase "and now, what have I here" in 52:5 means "what have I here in Babylon" (*Isaiah 40–66*, 165–66). However, "Babylon" is not mentioned in the text. One could just as easily add "Jerusalem" instead of Babylon here, though both insertions are inappropriate. "And now, what have I here" could refer to the taking away of people by any nation (e.g., the Assyrians or the Babylonians). Since the clause "and now, what have I here?" in 52:5a apparently refers to people taken away by the enemy rulers mentioned in 52:5b, it could refer to the 200,000 captives taken by Sennacherib. His mocking of YHWH is well known from Isa 36–37. There is little evidence that the Israelites in exile were mocked by the Babylonian rulers. On the contrary, Nebuchadnezzar repeatedly praised their God (Dan 2:47; 3:28–29, 32–33[ET 4:2–3]; 4:31–34[ET 34–37]).

55. Whybray, *Isaiah 40–66*, 49. Michael Goulder has rightly questioned this interpretation ("Deutero-Isaiah of Jerusalem," *JSOT* 28 [2004]: 351–62).

56. Tiemeyer, *For the Comfort of Zion*, 249.

57. According to George A. F. Knight, when Jerusalem is addressed in the singular, this refers to the city in exile, but when it is plural, this refers to the exiles themselves (*Isaiah 40–55: Servant Theology* [Grand Rapids: Eerdmans, 1984], 15). See also Willem A. M. Beuken, "Isaiah liv: The Multiple Identity of the Person Addressed," in *Language and Meaning:*

texts this place may be a theological symbol (i.e., the place of God's presence), suggesting that they may not refer primarily to a geographic place or to the Israelite inhabitants who live there (48:2). These terms can refer to a literal geographic place (40:1, 9;[58] 49:14; 51:16, 17; 52:9), though some examples are unclear (41:27; 46:13; 51:16), while others seem to point to a place (and people) in Judah in an eschatological setting (51:3, 11; 52:1, 2, 7, 8, 9). Only two examples refer to a place (i.e., the city of Jerusalem) after the exile in Babylon (44:26, 28).

What Do the References to Cyrus Imply?

The references to Cyrus (Koresh) in Isa 44:28 and 45:1 indicate that God was determined to rebuild and restore the ruins of Jerusalem and that he would use a strong military ruler who did not know him to make a decree to rebuild Jerusalem (44:26, 28; 45:1). This section has to do primarily with what God will do and only secondarily with what Cyrus/Koresh will accomplish because of God's help.

This prophecy presents a conundrum for many interpreters because (1) it gives such a specific prophecy, including the name of the king who will fulfill it, and (2) if it came from the prophet Isaiah, it was given more than 150 years before it was fulfilled. There is only one similar biblical example: in 1 Kgs 13:2, a prophet announced more than a century in advance that a man named Josiah would destroy the altar built by Jeroboam I at Bethel. According to 2 Kgs 23:15–17, this prophecy was fulfilled about 150 years later by King Josiah. Of course, when these predictions were made, the prophets and their audiences had no idea how long it would be before these words would be fulfilled. Therefore, the only unusual feature about both was the advance naming of an individual who was not then known. If prophets can predict eschatological events that will be fulfilled in the distant future,[59] prophets should also be able to predict events that will happen only 150 years later—though this was not their usual practice. Charles Torrey, Klaus Baltzer, and R. K. Harrison sought to eliminate this problem by suggesting that the name Cyrus (Koresh) was a later scribal addition to Isa 44:28 and 45:1 after the prophecy was fulfilled.[60] In

---

Studies in Hebrew Language and Biblical Exegesis, ed. James Barr, OtSt 19 (Leiden: Brill, 1974), 55, 63–66.

58. Paul takes "my people . . . Jerusalem" in 40:1 to refer to Israelite exiles in Babylon, but views the "cities of Judah" in 40:9 to be literal cities in Judah (*Isaiah 40–66*, 127, 136). Concerning 40:1, Oswalt comments, "It is significant that there is no trace of a Babylonian milieu here. . . . Nor is there any reason in the context to think that 'Jerusalem' is merely a metaphor for the exiled people" (*Isaiah 40–66*, 49n18). Blenkinsopp claims that 40:1–2 "is an assurance of a proximate return to the homeland addressed to Judeo-Babylonians" (*Isaiah 40–55*, 180).

59. Even in the non-eschatological setting of Gen 15, God told Abram that his enslaved people would return to the land 400 years later, a period much longer than 150 years.

60. C. C. Torrey, *Second Isaiah: A New Interpretation* (New York: Scribner's, 1928), 41; Baltzer, *Deutero-Isaiah*, 223; Roland K. Harrison, *Introduction to the Old Testament* (Grand Rapids: Eerdmans, 1969), 794–95. Since there is no evidence to support this hypothesis, it is only a convenient theory that attempts to eliminate a problem.

my opinion, this solution is unnecessary. Isaiah 40–55 cannot be dated on the basis of the prophecy about Cyrus (whether or not his mention by name is original or a later scribal addition) simply because it predicts an event that took place during the late exilic period.

The prophecy about Cyrus in Isa 44:24–45:7 should not be interpreted as the key to placing chapters 40–55 in an exilic setting. As both Brevard Childs and Hugh Williamson conclude, the central issue in determining a date for Isa 40–55 is the claim that the prophet's audience could verify that the first stage of Cyrus' work had been completed (implying a date after 550 BCE) and that the second stage lay in the near future (implying the fall of Babylon in 539 BCE).[61] Childs says,

> On the basis of his former prophecies concerning Cyrus, which have been realized and can readily be confirmed by all, the prophet then makes a future prediction in 44:24ff. and 45:1ff. The logic of the prophetic argument demands that the audience of the prophet's words stands at a point in the sixth century when the former prediction is viewed as part of history.[62]

The former predictions that were already accomplished are usually connected to the prophecy in which God "stirs up" and "calls" a strong "one from the east" and "delivers up nations to him, and subdues kings before him" (41:2–3; cf. v. 25). Many commentators believe that these verses describe Cyrus' early victories as he rose to power.[63] The Hiphil perfect verb הֵעִיר (hēʿîr), "he aroused, stirred up, awakened," in 41:2 (cf. הַעִירוֹתִי, haʿîrôtî, "I stirred up," in v. 25) points to a past event. The same verbal form is used to describe God's "awakening, arousing" of Cyrus in 2 Chr 36:22 and Ezra 1:1; and a similar form of the same verb is used in Isa 45:13, which many relate to Cyrus' work. Although the presence of the same verb in all of these passages might argue for connecting them, an initial caution is raised when one notes that the same verb (ע-ו-ר, ʿ-w-r) is used for God's "stirring up" of the Assyrian king Tiglath-pileser III (1 Chr 5:26); his "stirring up" the Philistines and Arabs against Jehoram (2 Chr 21:16); and his promise to "stir up" (Polel of ע-ו-ר, ʿ-w-r) a scourge against the Assyrians (Isa 10:26). Nevertheless, many simply assume that the one who was "aroused, stirred up" in 41:2–3, 25 must be the military conqueror Cyrus. But what evidence is there to support this view, and how can the events described in these verses be firmly related to Cyrus' victories in 550 BCE? It is clear that the strong ruler will do God's work, but it is not clear from 41:2–3, 25 how this conquering king will deal with Israel. While it is possible that the one God calls and uses to subdue nations in 41:2 and Cyrus, who is described similarly in 45:1, 4, are the same person, the similar descriptions in these two texts may point to parallels between two different kings rather than to the same person.

Problems with identifying the king in 41:2–3, 25 with Cyrus arise when one tries to develop a holistic picture of the military issues mentioned in 41:2–3, 10–13,

---

61. Childs, *Isaiah*, 322. H. G. M. Williamson, *The Book Called Isaiah: Deutero-Isaiah's Role in Composition and Redaction* (Oxford: Clarendon, 1994), 2–3.

62. Childs, *Isaiah*, 290.

63. Paul, *Isaiah 40–66*, 158; Childs, *Isaiah*, 318; Oswalt, *Isaiah 40–66*, 81.

25. All of these verses describe a military conflict. Verses 2–3 and 25 emphasize God's use of a strong military commander from the east, while verses 10–13 focus on God strengthening those who were being attacked. Since the army that attacks God's people in 41:10–13 will "become nothing," this army cannot be a Babylonian army (since it was successful) or a Persian army (since they never attacked Jerusalem or the Judeans in exile). Therefore, it can only refer to the Assyrian army that was very successful in conquering forty-six walled cities in Judah but was later reduced to nothing when an angel from God killed 185,000 soldiers (Isa 37:36). Thus, if Isa 41 describes a single military event, Sennacherib must be the one from the east whom YHWH arouses to defeat various nations in order to accomplish his will (cf. 10:5; 36–37). Another reason for not viewing the king in 41:2–3, 25 as Cyrus is the statement that this king "will call on my name" (41:25), which conflicts with God's claim that Cyrus "did not know me" (45:4, 5).

Consequently, if Cyrus is not the king referred to in 41:2–3, 10–13, 25, then it seems unwarranted to date the composition of Isa 40–55 to the period between Cyrus' victories in 550 BCE and his victory over Babylon in 539 BCE. Instead, the prophet appears to argue that the Judeans should trust YHWH because of his overwhelming power over the Assyrians, as described in chapters 36–37. The oracles in chapters 40–55 argue that, since YHWH has raised up a strong king like Sennacherib (41:2–3, 25) and will redeem his people from the power of this great king (41:10–13; cf. chs. 36–37), certainly his people should be able to trust in God's ability to use the unknown king Cyrus to restore the people of Jerusalem in the future (44:24–45:7).

Does the Message of Isaiah 40–48 Fit a Judean, Preexilic Perspective?

The real test of the plausibility of a proposed setting for Isa 40–48 is whether it makes sense of the messages the prophet gives to his audience. Is it possible to relate Isa 40–48 to an audience in preexilic Judah?[64] Based on the war imagery in several passages in these chapters, I have argued that the prophecies were given to promote hope in the context of Sennacherib's attack on Jerusalem (chs. 36–37) when Hezekiah was considering an alliance with Babylon (ch. 39). If this situation is correct, these messages would give three positive motivations for Hezekiah and the nation to trust God: (1) YHWH alone is God, Creator, Savior, Redeemer, King, and in control of history. Therefore, the Assyrian gods are powerless, and an alliance with Babylon would show a lack of trust in God. (2) YHWH will allow Judah to be afflicted (by the Assyrians), but he will defeat the Assyrian army that is presently at war with them, defeat Judah's allies from Babylon, and ultimately rebuild Jerusalem to prove that he alone is God. (3) In the future YHWH will come to earth to restore, reign over, and reward people from all nations who trust in him and his Servant.

---

64. Space limitations prevent the inclusion of Isa 49–55 in this analysis.

In the remainder of this section, I will summarize the message of Isa 40–48, indicating how well it fits an eighth-century situation. One can understand why, as Sennacherib destroyed one fortified city after another, some people in Jerusalem might have complained that YHWH was hidden and was not acting justly (40:27). Although this massive attack caused some to question YHWH, the prophet proclaimed that the nations were nothing before him (40:15, 17, 23–24) and that the man-made gods of the Assyrians (cf. 36:18–20; 37:11–12) could not be compared to Israel's God, who will give knowledge, power, and care to those who trust in him (40:12–14, 18–20, 25–26, 28–31). Although YHWH raised up Sennacherib from the east to subdue many nations (41:1–4), YHWH's larger purpose was to show the powerlessness of the gods of the nations (41:5–7) and to demonstrate his ability to strengthen his people by later making the Assyrian army into nothing (41:8–14). In the distant future YHWH will completely restore both creation and the nation to demonstrate that he has not forsaken them (41:17–20). At some point YHWH's chosen royal Servant will establish justice for the whole earth (42:1–4) by enlightening the blind eyes of people in all nations (42:5–9).

Initially YHWH was silent as the Assyrians brought great destruction upon Judah (42:14; 42:18–25; cf. 37:3), but soon he would come to guide his blind servants (42:16) and destroy those who trust in idols (42:17). The Judeans need not fear as if everything seems hopeless, for YHWH created and redeemed his people in the past and promised to gather them together from all over the world because he loves them and wants to declare his glory to everyone (43:1–7). Consequently, YHWH's blind people should declare to the nations that he alone is Savior and that the idol gods are nothing (43:8–13). Israel should not trust in an alliance with Babylon (cf. 39:1–8), for YHWH their Creator and King will destroy the capital of that empire (43:14–15; 46–47). Because Judah did not call on YHWH and did not worship him truly with their sacrifices at the temple, even though their God was able to forgive their sins, his place of worship and its officials will be defiled (43:22–28; 44:26).

The Judeans should not live in fear, for in the distant future YHWH will bless them through his Spirit and transform their world (44:1–5). Therefore, they should trust in YHWH, their Redeemer and King (44:6–8), and not fear deceptive idols made out of trees (44:9–20). Since YHWH's plan is for Jerusalem to be inhabited in the future, he will cause Cyrus to decree that the city will be rebuilt (44:24–28). Cyrus himself will not know YHWH, but the latter will use him to subdue many nations (45:1–7). Although some people may question YHWH's actions, he is in control of the future rebuilding of Jerusalem (45:9–13). In the distant future many nations will come and acknowledge YHWH as Savior (45:14–17). So the call is put forth for all nations to turn to YHWH and be saved (45:18–25). Israel should not trust in Babylonian alliances (cf. 39:1–8), for Babylon and its gods will be defeated (46:1–2; 47:1–15). Through these developments YHWH will bring salvation to Zion (46:3–13). His plan involves delaying the venting of his wrath in full military destruction (the Babylonian exile), so that he can refine the Judeans in the furnace of Assyrian affliction and prevent his name from being profaned (48:1–11). If Judah would only listen and follow God's leading, they could avoid the threatened destruction (48:12–19). They must reject Babylon and flee from all that it represents (48:20), for its claim to power will fail (48:14). YHWH will lead his people and redeem them, just as he did when their ancestors lived in the wilderness (48:17–19, 21).

Conclusion

In this essay I have argued that both the common critical and the traditional evangelical treatments of the historical background of Isa 40–55 do not adequately address the probability or even the possibility that Sennacherib's attack on Jerusalem, which is described in Isa 36–39, provides the historical background to Isa 40–55. An exilic setting for these chapters can no longer simply be assumed, but must be tested in light of the historical references to an enemy army becoming nothing (41:11–12) in a war with Judah. Sennacherib's attack on Judah and Jerusalem provides the logical context for the prophet to explain that Judah's sins had brought them to a crisis event (42:22) and to encourage the nation to trust YHWH for deliverance from the Assyrians. The prophet's claims about the sovereignty of God and the uselessness of man-made idols counter the claims of the Assyrians, who are convinced that YHWH cannot deliver Jerusalem from the power of their army or the will of their gods (36:10–20). Isaiah 40–55 declares a resoundingly different message: Judah should trust their all-powerful Redeemer, Savior, and King, who will turn the Assyrians into nothing (41:12; 37:36), establish justice for all nations through the Servant (42:4), and one day dwell in Zion (40:9), where people from the ends of the earth will bend the knee, recognizing that there is no other God (45:22–23).

Characteristics of the Hebrew of the
Recognized Literary Divisions of Isaiah

MARK F. ROOKER

Introduction

One plausible way to address the issue of the authorship and unity of the book of Isaiah is to examine the language of the book.[1] Particularly in mind here is the employment of what has been called the diachronic method, an analysis of a portion of the biblical text to determine whether the text—for example, a book such as Isaiah—contains primarily preexilic or postexilic features.

Early Diachronic Observations[2]

In a sense, the diachronic, or historical, approach to the study of Biblical Hebrew began in 1815, with the publication of *Geschichte der hebräischen Sprache und Schrift*[3] by Wilhelm Gesenius. In this work, Gesenius analyzed the language of the biblical books, frequently drawing attention to late linguistic features. After Gesenius made these early observations, little was done to continue this investigation until the beginning of the twentieth century, when Samuel R. Driver widened the scope of inquiry in observing that Biblical Hebrew contained chronologically distinct linguistic layers. Along with a few other, less-known, scholars, Driver observed that books such as Chronicles, Ecclesiastes, Esther, Daniel, Ezra, and Nehemiah differ linguistically from earlier books of the Hebrew Bible.[4] In his Old Testament *Introduction*, in

---

1. Portions of the present article reproduce or otherwise draw on material from my book *Biblical Hebrew in Transition: The Language of the Book of Ezekiel*, JSOTSup 90 (Sheffield: Sheffield Academic, 1990).

2. A more comprehensive treatment of this history may be found in Mark F. Rooker, "The Diachronic Study of Biblical Hebrew," *JNSL* 14 (1988): 199–214, and *Biblical Hebrew in Transition*, 23–33.

3. Leipzig: Vogel.

4. S. R. Driver, *An Introduction to the Literature of the Old Testament*, 9th ed. (Edinburgh: T&T Clark, 1913), 455, 505, 518, 525, 530–31, 535–40; idem, *A Treatise on the Use of the Tenses in Hebrew*, 3rd ed. (Oxford: Clarendon, 1892), 108, 196; idem, "On Some Alleged Linguistic Affinities of the Elohist," *Journal of Philology* 11 (1882): 201–36. See also D. S. Margoliouth, "Language of the Old Testament," in *A Dictionary of the Bible*, ed. James Hastings

particular, he presented a thorough analysis of the language of each biblical book, frequently describing the language of exilic and postexilic writers as "New Hebrew."[5]

Perhaps of equal importance for the diachronic study of Hebrew was Arno Kropat's *Syntax des Autors Chronik verglichen mit der seiner Quellen*, published in 1909.[6] Kropat's landmark study was devoted to analyzing the linguistic features of Chronicles. His *modus operandi* was contrasting the books of Chronicles with the parallel passages in Samuel-Kings. Presupposing that the Chronicler had as his source a masoretic prototype of Samuel-Kings,[7] Kropat was able to identify the language of the Chronicler by means of his linguistic adjustments where the Chronicler's text differed from Samuel-Kings in parallel passages.

In subsequent years, though still early in the twentieth century, many Hebrew grammarians, like Hans Bauer and Pontus Leander, and Paul Joüon, were generally aware of the differences between preexilic and postexilic Hebrew but did not focus on the specific features of these two phases of the language.[8] This all changed with the discovery of the greatest archaeological find of the twentieth century, the Dead Sea Scrolls.

The Dead Sea Scrolls

The Dead Sea Scrolls, found at Qumran, catapulted Gesenius' and Kropat's earlier findings into greater prominence. In particular, after the early publications of the literature from Qumran, Abba Bendavid and Edward Kutscher brought the diachronic study of the Bible back into the scholarly consciousness. *Biblical Hebrew and Mishnaic Hebrew*, a two-volume study written in Hebrew by Abba Bendavid, appeared in 1951 and made full use of the linguistic data of the Dead Sea Scrolls in a discussion of the typologies of Biblical and Mishnaic Hebrew.[9] Kutscher also

---

(Edinburgh: T&T Clark, 1900), 3:31; Leo Metmann, *Die Hebräische Sprache: Ihre Geschichte und lexikalische Entwicklung seit Abschluss des Kanons* (Jerusalem: A. M. Luncz, 1904), 5.

5. The same phrase was also used by Ewald to describe the language of late biblical books. See H. Ewald, *Ausführliches Lehrbuch der hebräischen Sprache des Alten Bundes*, 8th ed. (Göttingen: Dieterich, 1870), 25 (§3d). Equally significant was Driver's description of the earlier Biblical Hebrew stratum as "classical." See, e.g., Driver, *Introduction to the Literature of the Old Testament*, 454n.

6. BZAW 16, Giessen: Weimer.

7. See John Van Seters, "The 'Shared Text' of Samuel-Kings and Chronicles Re-Examined," in *Reflection and Refraction: Studies in Historiography in Honour of A. Graeme Auld*, ed. Robert Rezetko, Timothy H. Lim, and W. Brian Aucker, VTSup 113 (Leiden: Brill, 2007), 503–15, esp. 515. In addition, Sara Japhet affirms that "the book of Kings is the most important of the Chronicler's biblical sources," but that Ezra-Nehemiah was also used as a source (Sara Japhet, *I & II Chronicles: A Commentary*, OTL [Louisville: Westminster John Knox, 1993], 16, 18 [quotation from p. 16]).

8. See H. Bauer and P. Leander, *Historische Grammatik der hebräischen Sprache des Alten Testaments* (Halle: Georg Olms, 1922), 26 (§2q); and P. Joüon, *Grammaire de l'hébreu biblique* (Rome: Pontifical Biblical Institute, 1923), 4–6 (§§3a–b).

9. *Biblical Hebrew and Mishnaic Hebrew*, 2 vols. (1951; 2nd ed., Tel Aviv: Dvir, 1967).

made full use of the finds from Qumran and observed that the differences between 1QIsaᵃ and the MT of Isaiah are much like the differences between the MT texts of Samuel-Kings and Chronicles.[10] His vast contribution to this field can be seen in his posthumous works *The Language and Linguistic Background of the Isaiah Scroll (1QIsaᵃ)*[11] and *A History of the Hebrew Language.*[12]

Avi Hurvitz

Since the 1970s, Avi Hurvitz has dominated the field of the diachronic study of the Hebrew Bible.[13] Hurvitz's approach to the history of Biblical Hebrew is harmonious with the work of Kropat. Like Kropat, he insists that parallel chapters in the Bible are the most important aids for diachronic research.[14] Again like Kropat, Hurvitz affirms that the differences between parallel texts in Chronicles and Samuel-Kings are due to different phases of the Hebrew language rather than to the stylistic tendencies of different authors. With well over sixty publications devoted to this subject, perhaps Hurvitz's greatest contribution has been his consistent effort to fashion an objective methodology for the diachronic study of Biblical Hebrew.[15]

Hurvitz identified four basic criteria in the diachronic study of the Hebrew Bible: distribution, opposition, extrabiblical attestation, and accumulation.[16] According to the principle of linguistic distribution, a postexilic Hebrew feature would occur predominantly in biblical books that are considered late, such as Esther–Chronicles.[17] Also, for a linguistic feature to be considered late it must replace an equivalent feature in the preexilic biblical literature, particularly Genesis–Kings. This is the principle or criterion of linguistic opposition. If the linguistic feature predominates in books that are considered late, and if this feature begins to be used in place of the corresponding Early Biblical Hebrew (EBH) feature, we would expect the feature to continue to appear in Postbiblical Hebrew writings, such as rabbinic literature, Sirach, and the Dead Sea Scrolls. This is the principle of extrabiblical attestation. The last criterion of the diachronic approach is the principle

---

10. See Avi Hurvitz, "The Recent Debate on Late Biblical Hebrew: Solid Data, Experts' Opinions, and Inconclusive Arguments," *HS* 47 (2006): 196.

11. Leiden: Brill, 1974.

12. Jerusalem: Magnes, 1982.

13. His first major work was *The Transition Period in Biblical Hebrew: A Study in Post-Exilic Hebrew and its Implications for the Dating of Psalms* (Jerusalem: Mosad Bialik, 1972) [Heb.].

14. Ibid., 16n10.

15. Cf., see Avi Hurvitz, "Linguistic Criteria for Dating Problematic Biblical Texts," *Hebrew Abstracts* 14 (1973): 74–79.

16. Avi Hurvitz, "The 'Linguistic Dating of Biblical Texts': Comments on Methodological Guidelines and Philological Procedures," in *Diachrony in Biblical Hebrew*, ed. Ziony Zevit and Cynthia Miller-Naudé, LSAWS 8 (Winona Lake, IN: Eisenbrauns, 2012), 276.

17. Following the order of the last books of the Hebrew canon: Esther, Daniel, Ezra, Nehemiah, 1–2 Chronicles.

of accumulation. This is the most comprehensive criterion, since it involves the previous three criteria of distribution, opposition, and extrabiblical attestation. For a text to be judged as late on linguistic grounds, it must contain an accumulation of linguistic features that meet the first three criteria.[18]

As an objective operating principle, Hurvitz maintains that one must deal exclusively with the Masoretic Text in its present form—in spite of the fact that various textual alterations, literary developments, and editorial activities may have occurred during the long history of transmission. We know from rabbinic testimony and the practice of scribes from Qumran that great care was taken in the transmission process and that this would have nullified any concept of a linguistic revision.[19]

Challenges to Hurvitz

In the last dozen years, some have challenged Hurvitz's methodology and procedure and called into question his results. These challenges have appeared in two major publications: *Biblical Hebrew: Studies in Chronology and Typology*,[20] edited by Ian Young, and *Linguistic Dating of Biblical Texts*, a two-volume work by Ian Young, Robert Rezetko, and Martin Ehrensvärd.[21] Many of the contributors to these volumes insist that the differences between EBH and LBH (Late Biblical Hebrew) do not reflect different chronological periods; rather, the differences are merely stylistic. These scholars consider EBH conservative and LBH non-conservative in style. These studies have made a great contribution to the overall discussion, calling for clarification with regard to diachronic analysis in general and specific studies in particular. The final part of the two-volume work by Young, Rezetko, and Ehrensvärd contains an extremely helpful list of eighty-eight grammatical features and 372 lexical features that have been designated LBH by any one of twelve works of scholarship that have appeared since the beginning of the twentieth century.[22]

---

18. See Ian Young, Robert Rezetko, and Martin Ehrensvärd, *Linguistic Dating of Biblical Texts*, 2 vols. (London: Equinox, 2008), 1:21–23. Hurvitz adds: "This accumulation is relative. It is very doubtful whether we can mechanically apply statistical criteria to linguistic issues like these" ("Linguistic Criteria for Dating Problematic Biblical Texts," 76).

19. See Avi Hurvitz, *A Linguistic Study of the Relationship Between the Priestly Source and the Book of Ezekiel: A New Approach to an Old Problem*, CahRB 20 (Paris: J. Gabalda, 1982), 19, 21; idem, "The Relevance of Biblical Hebrew Linguistics for the Historical Study of Ancient Israel," in *Proceedings of the Twelfth World Congress of Jewish Studies: Jerusalem, July 29–August 5, 1997*, ed. Ron Margolin (Jerusalem: World Union of Jewish Studies), 31 (cited in Young, Rezetko, and Ehrensvärd, *Linguistic Dating of Biblical Texts*, 1:17–18). See also Richard M. Wright, *Linguistic Evidence for the Pre-exilic Date of the Yahwistic Source*, LHBOTS 419 (London: T&T Clark, 2005), 13–15.

20. London: T&T Clark, 2003.

21. See note 18 above.

22. A. Kropat, *Die Syntax des Autors der Chronik verglichen mit der seiner Quellen: Ein Beitrag zur historischen Syntax der Hebräischen*, BZAW 16 (Giessen: Töpelmann, 1909);

The essays in a book called *Diachrony in Biblical Hebrew*, which appeared in 2012, have raised questions regarding the methods employed by those who have challenged Hurvitz's conclusions.[23] The authors in this volume question whether the challengers have followed sound linguistic principles. It is of interest that this recent work includes a chapter, by Shalom Paul, on "Signs of Late Biblical Hebrew in Isaiah 40–66." This is the most extensive linguistic analysis of the language of Isaiah 40–66 to date, and thus the most important study related to our topic.[24]

Shalom Paul and Isaiah 40–66

In the beginning of his study, Paul refers to his work in his recent commentary,[25] where he provides his view about the authorship and date of Isa 40–66. He asserts that, since the prophecies in these chapters are clearly dated to the transitional period between the late exilic and early postexilic eras, it is to be expected that "the seeds of linguistic change toward LBH gradually and sporadically had already begun to make their debut."[26] In addition, because it is not feasible to distinguish precisely between exilic and postexilic Hebrew, Paul treats Isa 40–66 as one corpus. More specifically, Paul maintains that "chaps. 40–66 are one coherent opus composed by a single prophet."[27] Our study of Paul's work confirms this.

It goes without saying that Paul compares features of Isa 40–66 to LBH because, in his understanding, Isa 40–66 was written either in the exilic or postexilic period. However, if it can be demonstrated that the language of Isa 1–39 and 40–66

Hurvitz, *Transition Period in Biblical Hebrew* (1972); R. Polzin, *Late Biblical Hebrew: Toward an Historical Typology of Biblical Hebrew Prose*, HSM 12 (Missoula, MT: Scholars Press, 1976); Hurvitz, *Linguistic Study of the Relationship Between the Priestly Source and the Book of Ezekiel* (1982); E. Y. Kutscher, *A History of the Hebrew Language* (Jerusalem: Magnes, 1982); R. Bergey, "The Book of Esther: Its Place in the Linguistic Milieu of Post-Exilic Biblical Hebrew Prose; A Study in Late Biblical Hebrew" (PhD diss., Dropsie College for Hebrew and Cognate Learning, 1983); E. Qimron, *The Hebrew of the Dead Sea Scrolls*, HSM 29 (Atlanta: Scholars Press, 1986); Rooker, *Biblical Hebrew in Transition* (1990); A. Sáenz-Badillos, *A History of the Hebrew Language*, trans. J. Elwolde (Cambridge: Cambridge University Press, 1993); W. Van Peursen, *The Verbal System in the Hebrew Text of Ben Sira*, Studies in Semitic Languages and Linguistics 41 (Leiden: Brill, 2004); Wright, *Linguistic Evidence for the Pre-exilic Date of the Yahwistic Source* (2005); P. Joüon and T. Muraoka, *A Grammar of Biblical Hebrew* (Rome: Pontifical Biblical Institute, 2006).

23. Ziony Zevit and Cynthia Miller-Naudé, eds., *Diachrony in Biblical Hebrew*, LSAWS 8 (Winona Lake, IN: Eisenbrauns, 2012).

24. In ibid., 293–300. My earlier study "Dating Isaiah 40–66: What Does the Linguistic Evidence Say?" (*WTJ* 58 [1996]: 303–12) focused primarily on LBH features in Ezekiel and compared these with the language of Isa 40–66. Thus, Paul's work is much more comprehensive (Paul, "Signs of Late Biblical Hebrew," 295n3).

25. Shalom M. Paul, *Isaiah 40–66: Translation and Commentary*, ECC (Grand Rapids: Eerdmans, 2012).

26. Paul, "Signs of Late Biblical Hebrew," 293.

27. Paul, *Isaiah 40–66*, 12.

come from the same basic historical period, that is, the preexilic period, and as a consequence are typologically related, this understanding would constitute an argument for the overall unity of the book.

Shalom Paul discusses six broad linguistic categories: syntactic features, grammar, Aramaic lexical features, verbal lexical features, nominal lexical features, and phrases and expressions. In this essay, I will examine at least two language features from each category: one that will tend to support Paul's position and another that will expose some weaknesses in it. I will also examine whether these same "signs" of LBH occur in Isa 1–39, in order to gain greater perspective and to assess whether the signs actually demonstrate the later provenance of Isa 40–66. The remainder of the features Paul examines are categorized with comment in three appendices.

Syntactic Features

ה-י-ה (*h-y-h*) + Participle

The use of the copula ה-י-ה (*h-y-h*) with the participle, a common feature of Mishnaic Hebrew,[28] is found more frequently in the literature of LBH than in earlier periods.[29] Examples of this LBH feature, which connotes the durative or iterative aspect, include the following:

Neh 2:13

וָאֱהִי שֹׂבֵר בְּחוֹמֹת יְרוּשָׁלַם

wā’ĕhî śōbēr bĕḥômōt yĕrûšālaim

I inspected the walls of Jerusalem.[30]

2 Chr 24:12

וַיִּהְיוּ שֹׂכְרִים חֹצְבִים וְחָרָשִׁים

wayyihyû śōkĕrîm ḥōṣĕbîm wĕḥārāšîm

They hired masons and carpenters.

---

28. See M. H. Segal, *A Grammar of Mishnaic Hebrew* (Oxford: Clarendon Press, 1927), 156–57.

29. A point made by F. E. König: "so ist es doch zweifellos, dass in den späteren Schriften des ATs. mehr, als früher, היה mit dem Particip gesetzt worden ist" (*Historisch-kritisches Lehrgebäude der hebräischen Sprache*, 3 vols. [Leipzig: Hinrichs, 1881–97], 2:132 [§239c]). So also G. Bergsträsser, *Hebräische Grammatik* (Leipzig: Vogel, 1918), 2:73 (§13i); P. Joüon, *Grammaire de l'hébreu biblique*, 340–41 (§121g); and S. Morag, "Qumran Hebrew: Some Typological Observations," *VT* 38 (1988): 160. Driver stated that this construction was commonly used by later biblical writers (*A Treatise on the Use of the Tenses in Hebrew*, 198 [§135]).

30. All translations of Hebrew and other languages in this article are my own.

The increased likelihood that this expression would be employed in LBH, relative to earlier periods, may be illustrated by the following passages:

1 Kgs 8:7

כִּי הַכְּרוּבִים פֹּרְשִׂים כְּנָפַיִם

kî hakkĕrûbîm pōrĕśîm kĕnāpayim

For the cherubs spread (their) wings.

2 Chr 5:8

וַיִּהְיוּ הַכְּרוּבִים פֹּרְשִׂים כְּנָפַיִם

wayyihyû hakkĕrûbîm pōrĕśîm kĕnāpayim

And the cherubs spread (their) wings.

Isa 59:2

כִּי אִם־עֲוֺנֹתֵיכֶם הָיוּ מַבְדִּלִים בֵּינֵכֶם לְבֵין אֱלֹהֵיכֶם

kî ʾim-ʿăwōnōtêkem hāyû mabdīlîm bênēkem lĕbên ʾĕlōhêkem

But your iniquities have separated you from your God.

This late feature is similar to the construction found in Biblical Aramaic in the phrase וַהֲוָת בָּטְלָא עַד שְׁנַת תַּרְתֵּין (*wahăwāt bāṭĕlāʾ ʿad šĕnat tartên*), "it (the work) stopped until the second year" (Ezra 4:24).

In postbiblical literature, ה-י-ה (*h-y-h*) + participle constructions were even more widespread. This construction, for example, is one of the prominent features of the Temple Scroll.[31] The following are examples of this feature in the Dead Sea Scrolls:[32]

1QM IV, 11

הכוהן האחד יהיה מהלך

hkwhn hʾḥd yhyh mhlk

The first priest shall advance.

11QTemple XXXIV, 7

יהיו טובחים אותמה ויהיו כונסים

yhyw ṭwbḥym ʾwtmh wyhyw kwnsym

They shall slaughter them and collect (them).

---

31. See Elisha Qimron, "The Vocabulary of the Temple Scroll," in *Shnaton* 4 (1980): 244 [Heb.].

32. For other illustrations, see 1QM IX, 1; XVI, 8; XVIII, 15; 11QTemple XXXIV, 7. For additional postbiblical examples, see Paul, "Signs of Late Biblical Hebrew," 294–95.

The following semantically parallel phrase from the Babylonian Talmud illustrates both the prevalence of this feature in the Talmud and the manner in which the later practice differed from the EBH convention:[33]

b. Zebaḥ. 56b

יכול יהו נאכלין

ykwl yhw nʾklyn

They may be eaten.

Compare this with:

Lev 7:15

בְּיוֹם קָרְבָּנוֹ יֵאָכֵל

bĕyôm qorbānô yēʾākēl

It shall be eaten on the day of its offering.

We may suspect that the construction in *b. Zebaḥ.* 56b reflects Aramaic influence. This feature was widespread in Aramaic, being attested in the Biblical Aramaic illustration quoted above, as well as in various Aramaic dialects, including Syriac, Palmyrene, and the language of the Babylonian Talmud.[34] Shalom Paul's assertion that the usage of this formula in Isa 59:2 is uniquely a sign of LBH for the book of Isaiah is undermined by the fact that the phrase is more prominent in Isa 1–39 than in 40–66, as indicated, for example, by the following texts:

Isa 10:14

וְלֹא הָיָה נֹדֵד כָּנָף

wĕlōʾ hāyâ nōdēd kānāp

And there was none that moved a wing.

Isa 14:2

וְהָיוּ שֹׁבִים לְשֹׁבֵיהֶם

wĕhāyû šōbîm lĕšōbêhem

And they shall take their captors captive.

---

33. Cited by Bendavid in *Biblical Hebrew and Mishnaic Hebrew*, 1:381. For additional postbiblical examples of this phenomenon, see ibid., 1:380–81, 2:540–42.

34. See Joseph A. Fitzmyer, *The Syntax of Imperial Aramaic* (PhD diss., Johns Hopkins University, 1956), 221–22; Theodor Nöldeke, *Kurzgefasste syrische Grammatik* (Leipzig: T. O. Weigel, 1880), 277, 190–92; Jean Cantineau, *Grammaire du palymyrénien épigraphique* (Cairo: Imprimerie de l'Institut Français d'Archaéologie Orientale, 1935), 144; Michael Schlesinger, *Satzlehre der aramäischen Sprache des babylonischen Talmuds* (Leipzig: Georg Olms, 1928), 28, 42; David Marcus, *A Manual of Babylonian Jewish Aramaic* (Washington, DC: University Press of America, 1981), 8; and David M. Golomb, *A Grammar of Targum Neofiti* (Chico, CA: Scholars Press, 1985), 188–201. According to Japhet, Aramaic exercised the strongest influence on LBH (*I & II Chronicles*, 41).

Isa 30:20

וְהָיוּ עֵינֶיךָ רֹאוֹת אֶת־מוֹרֶיךָ

wĕhāyû ʿênêkā rōʾôt ʾet-môrêkā

But your eyes will see your teacher.

Isa 37:38

וַיְהִי הוּא מִשְׁתַּחֲוֶה בֵּית נִסְרֹךְ אֱלֹהָיו

wayĕhî hûʾ mištaḥăwê bêt nisrōk ʾĕlōhāyw

And while he was worshipping in the temple of Nisroch his god . . .

וַיִּקְבְּרוּ אֹתוֹ (*wayyiqbĕrû ʾōtô*) > וַיִּקְבְּרֻהוּ (*wayyiqbĕrūhû*)

Another syntactic feature Paul regards as a sign of linguistic change in Isa 40–66 has to do with the increased tendency in LBH to connect a pronominal object suffix directly to a finite verb, instead of the verb being followed by a direct object marker with a suffix.[35] Notice the following diachronic contrasts:

2 Kgs 9:28

וַיִּקְבְּרוּ אֹתוֹ

wayyiqbĕrû ʾōtô

And they buried him.

2 Chr 22:9

וַיִּקְבְּרֻהוּ

wayyiqbĕrūhû

And they buried him.

2 Kgs 14:20

וַיִּשְׂאוּ אֹתוֹ

wayyiśʾû ʾōtô

And they brought him.

2 Chr 25:28

וַיִּשָּׂאֻהוּ

wayyiśśāʾūhû

And they brought him.

---

35. See Paul, "Signs of Late Biblical Hebrew," 294.

Paul observes that this phenomenon is common in Isa 40–66, occurring approximately three hundred times, and claims that it is a sign of LBH. However, there may be a better explanation for this much higher occurrence of the direct object suffixed to the finite verb that Paul does not entertain. The use and occurrences of the direct object marker may be directly related to the differences in style between Isa 1–39 and Isa 40–66. Isaiah 40–66 exhibits more affinities with Hebrew poetry than does Isa 1–39. This is demonstrated by the higher concentration of prose particle accumulation (use of direct object marker, the article, and the relative pronoun) in Isa 1–39. According to Andersen and Forbes, narrative prose particles occur 851 times in Isa 1–39 (thus accounting for 8.6 percent of the text) and 347 times in Isa 40–66 (4.9 percent); that is, the percentage of prose particles in Isa 1–39 is nearly twice what it is in Isa 40–66. In addition, Andersen and Forbes argue that less than 5 percent prose particle accumulation indicates a poetic text.[36] This would explain the avoidance of the direct object marker in Isa 40–66.

Grammar

הָלַךְ (hālak) > הִלֵּךְ (hillēk)

The Qal of the root ה-ל-ךְ (h-l-k) occurs more than 1,400 times in the Hebrew Bible, in virtually every conceivable genre and context. However, this root occurs in the Piel only twenty-five times and these occurrences are virtually restricted to late and poetic texts.[37] The increased use of the Piel should be considered a linguistic development.[38] The following parallel passages illuminate the הָלַךְ (hālak) > הִלֵּךְ (hillēk) shift in Postbiblical Hebrew.[39]

Lev 26:3

אִם־בְּחֻקֹּתַי תֵּלֵכוּ

’im-bĕḥuqqōtay tēlēkû

If you walk in my statutes . . .

---

36. See Francis I. Andersen and A. Dean Forbes, " 'Prose Particle' Counts of the Hebrew Bible," in *The Word of the Lord Shall Go Forth: Essays in Honor of David Noel Freedman in Celebration of His Sixtieth Birthday*, ed. Carol L. Meyers and M. O'Connor (Winona Lake, IN: Eisenbrauns, 1983), 166, 174.

37. The Piel occurs in Isa 59:9; Ezek 18:9; Hab 3:11; Pss 38:7[ET 6]; 55:15[ET 14]; 81:14[ET 13]; 85:14[ET 13]; 86:11; 89:16[ET 15]; 104:3, 10, 26; 115:7; 131:1; 142:4[ET 3]; Job 24:10; 30:28; Prov 6:11, 28; 8:20; Eccl 4:15; 8:10; 11:9; Lam 5:18. The Piel of ה-ל-ךְ occurs in only one nonpoetic text, 1 Kgs 21:27, which is clearly preexilic.

38. BDB, 235.

39. See Bendavid, *Biblical Hebrew and Mishnaic Hebrew*, 1:376; and Hurvitz, *Linguistic Study*, 50.

Ezek 18:9

בְּחֻקּוֹתַי יְהַלֵּךְ

běḥuqqôtay yěhallēk

If he walks in my statutes . . .

Isa 8:6

מֵי הַשִּׁלֹחַ הַהֹלְכִים לְאַט

mê haššilōaḥ hahōlěkîm lě'aṭ

the gently flowing waters of Shiloah

Siloam 4–5

וילכו המים מן המוצא

wylkw hmym mn hmwṣ'

The water flowed from the spring.

m. Kelim 22:9[40]

אלא שיהוא המים מהלכין תחתיהן

'l' šyhw' hmym mhlkyn tḥtyhn

But it is the waters flowing under them.

The Piel of ה-ל-ך (*h-l-k*) is frequent not only in Postbiblical Hebrew, but also in the targumim:

Gen 7:18

וַתֵּלֶךְ הַתֵּבָה עַל־פְּנֵי הַמָּיִם

wattēlek hattēbâ 'al-pěnê hammāyim

And the ark floated on the surface of the waters.

Tg. Onq.

ומהלכא תיבותא על אפי מיא

wmhlk' tybwt' 'l 'py my'

And the ark floated on the surface of the waters.

---

40. See W. H. Lowe, *The Mishnah on Which the Palestinian Talmud Rests* (Cambridge: Cambridge University Press, 1883). The Piel of ה-ל-ך (*h-l-k*) is frequent in the Mishnah: *m. 'Erub.* 4:1, 7; *Yoma* 5:1; *Ned.* 2:1; *'Erub.* 5:8; *Naz.* 5:5; *B. Qam.* 3:4; *Roš Haš.* 1:9. See Paul, "Signs of Late Biblical Hebrew," 295.

Exod 2:5

וְנַעֲרֹתֶיהָ הֹלְכֹת עַל־יַד הַיְאֹר

wĕnaʿărōtêhā hōlĕkōt ʿal-yad hayĕʾōr

. . . while her young women walked alongside the Nile.

Tg. Onq.

ועולימתהא מהלכן על כיף נהרא

wᶜwlymthʾ mhlkn ʿl kyp nhrʾ

. . . while her young women walked on the shore of the Nile.

Numerous examples of the Piel of ה-ל-ך (*h-l-k*) are found in rabbinic literature.[41] The extensive use of ה-ל-ך (*h-l-k*) in the Piel in Aramaic texts might indicate that its occurrence in Biblical Hebrew reflects Aramaic influence. Thus, the occurrence of this form in Isa 59:9 could be classified as a potential sign of LBH.

פ-ח-ד (*p-ḥ-d* Piel)

Paul lists the Piel of פ-ח-ד (*p-ḥ-d*) as illustrating this same phenomenon. The term occurs in this stem only in Isa 51:13 and Prov 28:14. No further examples from LBH are attested and this form does not appear to have replaced a corresponding EBH term. Furthermore, no occurrences are attested in the Dead Sea Scrolls or in the Mishnah. Thus the Piel of פ-ח-ד (*p-ḥ-d*) is not a certain sign of LBH.[42]

Aramaic Lexical Features

יַחְדָּו (*yaḥdāw*) > כְּאֶחָד (*kĕʾeḥād*)

כְּאֶחָד (*kĕʾeḥād*) "together" (which occurs in Isaiah only in 65:25) is a calque of כחדא (*kḥdʾ*), the Aramaic translation of יַחְדָּו (*yaḥdāw*). The claim that this is a sign of LBH may be supported from the contrast of a comparative phrase within Isaiah itself:

Isa 11:7

וּפָרָה וָדֹב תִּרְעֶינָה יַחְדָּו

ûpārâ wādōb tirʿênâ yaḥdāw

The cow and the bear will graze together.

---

41. For further examples, see E. Ben-Yehuda, *Thesaurus totius hebraitatis*, 8 vols. (New York: Thomas Yoseloff, 1947–59), 2:1097–98 [Heb.]; M. Jastrow, *A Dictionary of the Targumim, the Talmud Babli and Yerushalmi, and the Midrashic Literature*, 2 vols. (New York: P. Shalom, 1967), 1:352–53.

42. None of the twelve sources Young, Rezetko, and Ehrensvärd cite in their *Linguistic Dating of Biblical Texts* lists this form as an example of LBH.

Isa 65:25

זְאֵב וְטָלֶה יִרְעוּ כְאֶחָד

zĕʾēb wĕṭālê yirʿû kĕʾeḥād

The wolf and the lamb will graze together.

The term כְאֶחָד (*kĕʾeḥād*) occurs in other texts not considered to represent EBH, including Eccl 11:6; Ezra 2:64; 3:9; 6:20; Neh 7:66; and 2 Chr 5:13. In the Aramaic targum to Isa 40–66, כחדא (*kḥdʾ*) appears sixteen times. It is frequent in rabbinic literature and the Dead Sea Scrolls. Of the twelve sources cited in Young, Rezetko, and Ehrensvärd's *Linguistic Dating of Biblical Texts*, only Robert Polzin's *Late Biblical Hebrew* mentions this term and claims that it was standard in Mishnaic Hebrew.[43] While it occurs very frequently in Mishnaic Hebrew, it does not always seem to mean "together." It could also be rendered "one of them" (*m. Peʾah* 8:9), "as one" (*m. ʿErub.* 5:3; *m. Yebam.* 4:7), "at the same time" (*m. Neg.* 3:1), or "at once" (*m. Mak.* 3:5).[44] It seems significant that even though the LBH term does occur in Isa 40–66 (Isa 65:25), the EBH equivalent, יַחְדָו (*yaḥdāw*) / יַחַד (*yaḥad*), occurs more frequently in Isa 40–66 than in Isa 1–39: יַחְדָו (*yaḥdāw*) occurs ten times in 1–39 and seventeen times in 40–66, and יַחַד (*yaḥad*) occurs two times in chapters 1–39 and five times in 40–66.[45] The concentration of כחדא (*kḥdʾ*) in the targum may indicate the Aramaic provenance of כְאֶחָד (*kĕʾeḥād*) in the biblical texts in which it occurs.

מַס (*mas*) > מִדָּה (*middâ*)

Another Aramaic lexical feature, according to Paul, is reflected in the occurrence of the word מִדָּה (*middâ*), "tax, tribute," in Isa 45:14. This term occurs in late biblical books (Ezra 4:20; 6:8; Neh 5:4) and is cognate to the Aramaic term מנדה (*mndh*), found in Ezra 4:13 and 7:24. The Aramaic word also occurs in rabbinic literature, as in *b. Ned.* 62b and *Gen. Rab.* 64:29. The term was used in lieu of מַס (*mas*), which occurs twenty-three times in the Hebrew Bible, virtually always in EBH. However, scholars have generally understood מִדָּה (*middâ*) in Isa 45:14 as a different term. The Hebrew noun מִדָּה (*middâ*), "large, tall," is from the root מ-ד-ד (*m-d-d*).[46] Thus, the traditional reading of the phrase אַנְשֵׁי מִדָּה in this verse has been something like "men of stature":

---

43. See Polzin, *Late Biblical Hebrew*, 139.

44. Jastrow translates the Aramaic phrase "at the same time" (*Dictionary of the Targumim*, 1:38). Martin Ehrensvärd declares more emphatically that כְאֶחָד (*kĕʾeḥād*) does not mean "together" in Postbiblical Hebrew ("Linguistic Dating of Biblical Texts," in *Biblical Hebrew: Studies in Chronology and Typology*, ed. Ian Young [London: T&T Clark, 2003], 181).

45. This occurrence of the EBH terms in Isa 40–66 is even more impressive because Isa 1–39 is substantially longer than Isa 40–66.

46. *HALOT*, 547–48; BDB, 551.

MT Isa 5:14

אַנְשֵׁי מִדָּה

>’anšê middâ

men of stature

LXX

ἄνδρες ὑψηλοὶ

andres hypsēloi

men of stature

Vulgate

viri sublimes

exalted men

Paul's understanding of מִדָּה (*middâ*) as "tax, tribute" forces him to emend the Hebrew text from אנשי מדה (*’nšy mdh*) "men of stature" to נשאי מדה (*nś'y mdh*), "bearing tribute." However, this is sheer conjecture, lacking any textual support. The Masoretic Text and the versions all read "men of stature."

Verbal Lexical Features

י-ר-ה (*y-r-h* Hiphil), ל-מ-ד (*l-m-d* Piel) > ב-י-ן (*b-y-n* Hiphil)

Following Hurvitz, Polzin, and Qimron, Paul cites the Hiphil of ב-י-ן (*b-y-n*), meaning "to teach," in Isa 40:14 as a sign of LBH.[47] In support of this understanding, he lists Ps 119:27, 34, 73, 125, 130, 144, 169; Job 6:24; 32:8; Dan 1:17; 8:16, 27; 9:22; 10:14; 11:33; Ezra 8:6; Neh 8:8; and 2 Chr 35:3 as additional LBH examples of this meaning; he also cites the use of the Hiphil participle מֵבִין (*mēbîn*) with the meaning "teacher" in 1 Chr 15:22; 25:7, 8; 27:32.[48] First Chronicles 25:8 is particularly significant because it distinguishes "teacher" (מֵבִין, *mēbîn*) from "student" (תַּלְמִיד, *talmîd*). While the meaning "teacher" in 1 Chr 25:8 seems clear from context, none of the occurrences of the verb ב-י-ן (*b-y-n*) in the Hiphil in the books of Chronicles has a synoptic counterpart in Samuel-Kings.

In addition, we might question many of the examples that Paul gives, since the Hiphil of ב-י-ן (*b-y-n*) does not necessarily refer to "conveying knowledge" (i.e., "to

---

47. Hurvitz, *Transition Period in Biblical Hebrew*, 136, 138–39; Polzin, *Late Biblical Hebrew*, 142–43; Qimron, *Hebrew of the Dead Sea Scrolls*, 88.

48. Hurvitz, *Transition Period in Biblical Hebrew*, 138n184; Paul, "Signs of Late Biblical Hebrew," 297. The NJPS translation renders all the participle forms as "master," a possible equivalent of "teacher."

teach"); rather, it may mean "to possess knowledge."[49] On the other hand, 2 Chr 35:3 offers a clear example of the use of ב-י-ן (*b-y-n*) with the meaning "teach":

2 Chr 35:3

וַיֹּאמֶר לַלְוִיִּם המבונים (הַמְּבִינִים) לְכָל־יִשְׂרָאֵל

wayyōʾmer lalĕwiyyīm hmbwnym (hammĕbînîm) lĕkol-yiśrāʾēl

He said to the Levites who taught all Israel . . .

The meaning of the Hiphil form הַמְּבִינִים here is equivalent to that of the corresponding EBH verbs י-ר-ה (*y-r-h*) in the Hiphil and ל-מ-ד (*l-m-d*) in the Piel:

Exod 24:12

לֻחֹת הָאֶבֶן וְהַתּוֹרָה וְהַמִּצְוָה אֲשֶׁר כָּתַבְתִּי לְהוֹרֹתָם

lūḥōt hāʾeben wĕhattôrâ wĕhammiṣwâ ʾăšer kātabtî lĕhôrōtām

. . . stone tablets with the law and the commandment that I have written to teach them.

Deut 17:11

עַל־פִּי הַתּוֹרָה אֲשֶׁר יוֹרוּךָ

ʿal-pî hattôrâ ʾăšer yôrûkā

. . . according to the instructions that they teach you.

Deut 33:10

יוֹרוּ מִשְׁפָּטֶיךָ לְיַעֲקֹב וְתוֹרָתְךָ לְיִשְׂרָאֵל

yôrû mišpāṭêkā lĕyaʿăqōb wĕtôrātĕkā lĕyiśrāʾēl

They will teach Jacob your ordinances and Israel your law.

Dan 1:4

וּלְלַמְּדָם סֵפֶר וּלְשׁוֹן כַּשְׂדִּים

ûlĕlammĕdām sēper ûlĕšôn kaśdîm

. . . and to teach them the literature and language of the Chaldeans.

The roots י-ר-ה (*y-r-h*) and ל-מ-ד (*l-m-d*) occur together in parallelism in Prov 5:13. In the Hebrew Bible, it is only in Isa 40:14 that the Piel of ל-מ-ד (*l-m-d*) and the Hiphil of ב-י-ן (*b-y-n*) occur in parallelism.[50] In Dan 1:4 the two terms occur together in the same verse. However, as in Isa 40:14, in Dan 1:4 the root ל-מ-ד (*l-m-d*) more

---

49. See the ESV, NRSV, and NJPS translations of ב-י-ן (*b-y-n*) in Ps 119; Job 32:8; Dan 1:17; Neh 8:8. A distinction *may* exist between "teaching," in order "to make someone understand," and "explaining."

50. ל-מ-ד (*l-m-d*) actually occurs two times in Isa 40:14.

clearly means "to teach" than the parallel ב-י-ן (*b-y-n*). Furthermore, Hurvitz has pointed out that while in the wisdom books (as well as other books of the Hebrew Bible) the verbs ב-י-ן (*b-y-n*), ל-מ-ד (*l-m-d*), and י-ר-ה (*y-r-h*) are used in relation to "teaching" the Law or commandments, except for in Nehemiah the Hiphil of ב-י-ן (*b-y-n*) is not used in relation to a teacher; rather, the words מְלַמֵּד (*mĕlammēd*) and מוֹרֶה (*môrê*) are preferred.[51] Nevertheless, the use of ב-י-ן (*b-y-n*) to mean "to teach" may still qualify as a sign of LBH. But, once again, this usage is not distinctive to Isa 40–66, since the Hiphil of י-ר-ה (*y-r-h*) and of ב-י-ן (*b-y-n*) occur in parallelism in Isa 28:9 (not mentioned by Paul) as well.[52]

ק-ו-ם (*q-w-m*) > ע-מ-ד (*ʿ-m-d*)

In the later history of Biblical Hebrew, the verb ע-מ-ד (*ʿ-m-d*) was employed more commonly in contexts where EBH had used the verb ק-ו-ם (*q-w-m*). This can be observed already in EBH, where it is possible to recognize the "intrusion" of ע-מ-ד (*ʿ-m-d*) into the semantic domain of the lexeme ק-ו-ם (*q-w-m*).[53] The use of ע-מ-ד (*ʿ-m-d*) in a context where in an EBH text we would expect ק-ו-ם (*q-w-m*) is illustrated in Isa 66:22:

Isa 66:22

כִּי כַאֲשֶׁר הַשָּׁמַיִם הַחֲדָשִׁים וְהָאָרֶץ הַחֲדָשָׁה אֲשֶׁר אֲנִי עֹשֶׂה עֹמְדִים לְפָנַי

kî kaʾăšer haššāmayim haḥŏdāšîm wĕhāʾāreṣ hahădāšâ ʾăšer ʾănî ʿōśê
ʿōmĕdîm lĕpānay

For just as the new heavens and the new earth that I make shall endure before me . . .

The semantic similarity of ק-ו-ם (*q-w-m*) and ע-מ-ד (*ʿ-m-d*), as well as the diachronic shift from ק-ו-ם (*q-w-m*) to ע-מ-ד (*ʿ-m-d*), can be observed in the following parallel usages of the two terms:[54]

Exod 1:8

וַיָּקָם מֶלֶךְ־חָדָשׁ עַל־מִצְרָיִם

wayyāqom melek-ḥādāš ʿal-miṣrāyim

And a new king arose over Egypt.

---

51. Hurvitz, *Transition Period in Biblical Hebrew*, 138–39.

52. Technically, both Polzin and Qimron argue that the LBH (and the Dead Sea Scrolls) formula involves ב-י-ן (*b-y-n*) followed by the preposition בְּ (*bĕ*) (Polzin, *Late Biblical Hebrew*, 142–3; Qimron, *Hebrew of the Dead Sea Scrolls*, 88).

53. E. Y. Kutscher, "Aramaic Calque in Hebrew," *Tarbiz* 33 (1964): 124 [Heb.].

54. See Hurvitz, *Linguistic Study*, 95; and Bergey, "Book of Esther," 126–27.

Dan 8:23

יַעֲמֹד מֶלֶךְ עַז־פָּנִים וּמֵבִין חִידוֹת

yaʿămōd melek ʿaz-pānîm ûmēbîn ḥîdôt

A king bold in countenance and understanding riddles shall arise.

Deut 19:15

עַל־פִּי שְׁלֹשָׁה־עֵדִים יָקוּם דָּבָר

ʿal-pî šĕlōšâ-ʿēdîm yāqûm dābār

On the testimony of three witnesses a matter will be established.

Esth 3:4

לִרְאוֹת הֲיַעַמְדוּ דִּבְרֵי מָרְדֳּכַי

lirʾôt hăyaʿamdû dibrê mordŏkay

. . . in order to see whether the words of Mordecai would stand.

The meanings "rise up," "appear," "rise up against," and "be established" expressed in EBH by the verb ק-ו-ם (*q-w-m*) were represented in LBH by ע-מ-ד (*ʿ-m-d*).

The trend to use ע-מ-ד (*ʿ-m-d*) in contexts where EBH employed ק-ו-ם (*q-w-m*) continued in Postbiblical Hebrew as well. The following representative examples from the Dead Sea Scrolls and Sirach illustrate this proclivity:

1QM X, 2

ועמד הכוהן ודבר אל העם

wʿmd hkwhn wdbr ʾl hʿm

The priest will arise and speak to the people.

CD I, 14[55]

בעמוד איש הלצון

bʿmwd ʾyš hlṣwn

When the man of mockery appeared . . .

11QTemple LVI, 9

שמוע אל הכוהן העומד שמה לשרת

šmwʿ ʾl hkwhn hʿwmd šmh lšrt

Listen to the priest who stands there to serve.

---

55. Chaim Rabin observed that the usage of ע-מ-ד (*ʿ-m-d*) in the Zadokite Document reflects LBH usage (*Zadokite Documents*, 2nd ed. [Oxford: Clarendon, 1958], 14n2).

Sir 47:1

וגם אחרין עמד נתן

wgm ʾḥryn ʿmd ntn

After him Nathan rose up.

However, the shift from ק-ו-ם (*q-w-m*) to ע-מ-ד (*ʿ-m-d*) in Postbiblical Hebrew is best illustrated by contrasting the following two EBH passages with the following two postbiblical passages:[56]

Judg 10:1

וַיָּקָם אַחֲרֵי אֲבִימֶלֶךְ לְהוֹשִׁיעַ אֶת־יִשְׂרָאֵל תּוֹלָע

wayyāqom ʾaḥărê ʾăbîmelek lĕhôšîaʿ ʾet-yiśrāʾēl tôlāʿ

After Abimelech Tola arose to save Israel.

4QFlor 1:13

דויד יעמוד להושיע את ישראל

dwyd yʿmwd lhwšyʿ ʾt yśrʾl

David arose to save Israel.

Ps 1:5

לֹא־יָקֻמוּ רְשָׁעִים בַּמִּשְׁפָּט

lōʾ-yāqūmû rĕšāʿîm bammišpāṭ

The wicked will not arise in judgment.

m. Sanh. 10:3

ואין עומדין בדין . . . שנאמר על כן לא יקומו רשעים במשפט

wʾyn ʿwmdyn bdyn . . . šnʾmr ʿl kn lʾ yqwmw ršʿym bmšpṭ

And they shall not stand in judgment . . . as it is said, *therefore the wicked will not arise in judgment.*

The last two pairs of citations are particularly significant because the postbiblical texts are closely parallel to the EBH passages. In both instances, the EBH verb ק-ו-ם (*q-w-m*) is replaced by ע-מ-ד (*ʿ-m-d*).[57] And while Isa 66:22 seems to have this af-

---

56. Cf. Bendavid, *Biblical Hebrew and Mishnaic Hebrew*, 1:332, 360; Hurvitz, *Linguistic Study*, 95–96; and Bergey, "Book of Esther," 127.

57. In Tannaitic times, ע-מ-ד (*ʿ-m-d*) was used almost exclusively (Kutscher, *History of the Hebrew Language*, 84 [§123]; Bendavid, *Biblical Hebrew and Mishnaic Hebrew*, 1:2, 62, 65–66, 84, 114, 132, 327). The root ק-ו-ם (*q-w-m*) occurs in the Mishnah only about five times in all stems, whereas the root ע-מ-ד (*ʿ-m-d*) occurs over two hundred times. The same state of affairs is reflected in the Tosefta. See C. Kasovsky, *Thesaurus Mishnae*, 4 vols. (Jerusalem: Massadah Publications, 1956–1960), 3:1380–83, 4:1566.

finity with LBH, once again this feature is not foreign to Isa 1–39. Isaiah 3:13 may even be a clearer example of this characteristically LBH phenomenon:

Isa 3:13

נִצָּב לָרִיב יְהוָה וְעֹמֵד לָדִין עַמִּים

niṣṣāb lārîb yhwh wĕʿōmēd lādîn ʿammîm

The LORD stands to contend; he rises to judge peoples.

מ-צ-ץ (*m-ṣ-ṣ*)

In contrast to the widespread use of ע-מ-ד (*ʿ-m-d*) in LBH and beyond, Paul argues that the occurrence of the root מ-צ-ץ (*m-ṣ-ṣ*), "to suck," in Isa 66:11 reflects a LBH tendency. עמד occurs profusely in LBH and in later Hebrew and מצץ occurs but rarely in these same linguistic strata. Thus מ-צ-ץ (*m-ṣ-ṣ*) as LBH is problematic. Although the root occurs in *Targum Pseudo-Jonathan* at Ps 75:9[ET 8], as well as in rabbinic literature, in *m. Parah* 9:3 (מוצצת, *mwṣṣt*) and *m. Šabb.* 19:2 (ומוצצין, *wmwṣṣyn*), the term occurs in the Hebrew Bible only in Isa 66:11. As a *hapax legomenon*, this one usage does not meet the criterion of linguistic distribution in other biblical books of the Hebrew Bible deemed to be late.[58]

Nominal Lexical Features

יָם (*yām*) > מַעֲרָב (*maʿărāb*)

The noun מַעֲרָב (*maʿărāb*), "west," occurs seventeen times in the Hebrew Bible. It appears three times in Isa 40–66 (in 43:5; 45:6; 59:19), and also in other poetic texts (Pss 75:7[ET 6]; 103:12; 107:3) and other texts considered to be late (Dan 8:5; 1 Chr 7:28; 12:16; 26:16, 18, 30; 2 Chr 32:30; 33:14).[59] The term began to be used in lieu of יָם (*yām*).

Josh 12:7

הִכָּה יְהוֹשֻׁעַ וּבְנֵי יִשְׂרָאֵל בְּעֵבֶר הַיַּרְדֵּן יָמָּה

hikkâ yĕhôšuaʿ ûbĕnê yiśrāʾēl bĕʿēber hayyardēn yāmmâ

. . . (whom) Joshua and the sons of Israel defeated on the west side of the Jordan.

---

58. For other *hapax* terms in Paul's article, see Appendix A below.

59. However, none of the seven occurrences in Chronicles has parallels in Samuel-Kings. The term may also occur in Judg 20:33, though this possible occurrence involves an interpretive issue. Ehrensvärd considers Pss 75 and 107 to be preexilic, which makes him hesitant to consider the term postexilic (see Yigal Bloch, "The Third-Person Masculine Plural Suffixed Pronoun *-mw* and Its Implications for the Dating of Biblical Hebrew Prose," in *Diachrony in Biblical Hebrew*, 164n32).

1 Chr 26:30

מֵעֵבֶר לַיַּרְדֵּן מַעְרָבָה

mē‘ēber layyardēn ma‘rābâ

west of the Jordan

The use of מַעְרָב (*ma‘ărāb*) in the targumim in place of the EBH יָם (*yām*) also clearly indicates a diachronic shift.

Gen 28:14 MT

וּפָרַצְתָּ יָמָּה וָקֵדְמָה וְצָפֹנָה וָנֶגְבָּה

ûpāraṣtā yammâ wāqēdmâ wĕṣāpōnâ wānegbâ

And you will spread out to the west and to the east and to the north and to the south.

Gen 28:14 *Tg. Onq.*

ותתקף מערבא וצפונא ודרומא ומדנחא

wttqp m‘rb’ wṣpwn’ wdrwm’ wmdnḥ’

And you will conquer to the west and to the north and to the south and to the east.

The LBH term is also common in rabbinic literature:

m. Ma‘aś. Š. 5:2

לוד מן המערב

lwd mn hm‘rb

Lod to the west

m. ‘Erub. 3:5

מזרח . . . מערב

mzrḥ . . . m‘rb

from the east side . . . on the west side

Sipre Numbers 73

תוקע לצפון ולמעבר

twq‘ lṣpwn wlm‘br

Conquer north and west.

מַעְרָב (*ma‘ărāb*) occurs frequently in the Dead Sea Scrolls, twelve times as a noun (e.g., in 3Q15 VIII, 11; 4Q274 I, 2; 11Q19 XXX, 7) and five times as an adjective (3Q15 III, 10; VI, 12; X, 8, 13; XI, 16).[60] The use of מַעְרָב (*ma‘ărāb*) for "west" clearly marks

---

60. See Paul, "Signs of Late Biblical Hebrew," 298.

a LBH innovation.[61] While the term occurs three times in Isa 40–66, it does not occur in Isa 1–39. However, the EBH equivalent יָם (*yām*) occurs twenty times in Isa 1–39 and eleven times in Isa 40–66.[62]

עוֹלָם (*ʿōlām*), נֶצַח (*neṣaḥ*), עַד (*ʿad*) > עוֹלָמִים (*ʿōlāmîm*)

Paul also suggests that the plural term עוֹלָמִים (*ʿōlāmîm*), "eternity," is a late Hebrew noun. The expression occurs three times in Isa 40–66, twice in 45:17 and once in 51:9. In LBH, the plural form replaces earlier forms such as עוֹלָם (*ʿōlām*), נֶצַח (*neṣaḥ*), and עַד (*ʿad*).[63] While the plural occurs in Pss 51:9[ET 7]; 145:13; and Eccl 1:10, the following parallel passages illustrate the diachronic shift:[64]

1 Kgs 1:31

יְחִי אֲדֹנִי הַמֶּלֶךְ דָּוִד לְעֹלָם

yĕḥî ʾădōnî hammelek dāwid lĕʿōlām

May my lord King David live forever.

Dan 2:4

מַלְכָּא לְעָלְמִין חֱיִי

malkāʾ lĕʿolmîn ḥĕyî

O king, live forever.

The targumim also illustrate this shift:

Exod 15:18 MT

יְהוָה יִמְלֹךְ לְעֹלָם וָעֶד

yhwh yimlōk lĕʿōlām wāʿed

The Lord will reign forever and ever.

---

61. However, Rezetko and Ehrensvärd express doubt that מַעֲרָב (*maʿărāb*) is late, since the word is attested in Ugaritic. See Robert Rezetko, "'Late' Common Nouns in the Book of Chronicles," in *Reflection and Refraction: Studies in Historiography in Honour of A. Graeme Auld*, ed. Robert Rezetko, Timothy H. Lim, and W. Brian Aucker, VTSup 113 (Leiden: Brill, 2007), 407, and M. Ehrensvärd, "Linguistic Dating of Biblical Texts," in *Biblical Hebrew: Studies in Chronology and Typology*, 164–88.

62. In Isa 1–39 the occurrences are found at 5:30; 8:23; 10:22, 26; 11:9, 11, 14–15; 16:8; 17:12; 18:2; 19:5; 21:1; 23:2, 4, 11; 24:14–15; 27:1. In Isa 40–66 the occurrences are found at 42:10; 43:16; 48:18; 49:12; 50:2; 51:10 (2x), 15; 57:20; 60:5; 63:11. However, of these only the occurrences in Isa 11:14; 24:14; and 49:12 clearly mean "west."

63. Hurvitz, *Transition Period in Biblical Hebrew*, 100–104; Qimron, *Hebrew of the Dead Sea Scrolls*, 68, 93; Wright, *Linguistic Evidence for the Pre-exilic Date*, 68–71, 129.

64. See also Dan 2:24; 6:27, 29; 9:24; 2 Chr 6:2 (// 1 Kgs 8:13).

Exod 15:18 *Tg. Onq.*

יוי מלכותיה קאים לעלמא ולעלמי עלמיא

ywy mlkwtyh qʾym lʿlmʾ wlʿlmy ʿlmyʾ

The kingdom of the Lord will arise forever and ever.

Deut 32:40 MT

וְאָמַרְתִּי חַי אָנֹכִי לְעֹלָם:

wěʾāmartî ḥay ʾānōkî lěʿōlām

And say, I live forever.

Deut 32:40 *Tg. Onq.*

ואמרית קיים אנא לעלמין

wʾmryt qyym ʾnʾ lʿlmyn

And say, I am alive forever.

עוֹלָמִים (*ʿōlāmîm*) occurs dozens of times in Qumran texts. Note the following diachronic contrast:

Gen 9:16

בְּרִית עוֹלָם

běrît ʿôlām

eternal covenant

1QS IV, 22

ברית עולמים

bryt ʿwlmym

eternal covenant

As would be expected, the late term עוֹלָמִים (*ʿôlāmîm*) is not absent from earlier texts, being attested in 1 Kgs 8:13 as well as Isa 26:4. While the plural עוֹלָמִים (*ʿôlāmîm*) occurs three times in Isa 40–66, it occurs once in Isa 1–39 (Isa 26:4). However, the earlier, singular form, עוֹלָם (*ʿôlām*), occurs twenty-nine times in Isa 40–66, but only ten times in Isa 1–39.[65] Thus, Isa 40–66 prefers the earlier singular עוֹלָם (*ʿôlām*) to a greater degree than the earlier form's attestation in Isa 1–39. The later plural form עוֹלָמִים (*ʿôlāmîm*) occurs only four times in Isaiah, once in Isa 1–39 and three times in Isa 40–66. Thus the evidence is somewhat mixed, and it is not

---

65. In Isa 1–39 the occurrences are found at 9:6[ET 7]; 14:20; 25:2; 30:8; 32:14, 17; 33:14; 34:10, 17; 35:10. In Isa 40–66 the occurrences are found at 40:8, 28; 42:14; 44:7; 46:9; 47:7; 51:6, 8, 11; 54:8; 55:13; 56:5; 57:11, 16; 58:12; 59:21; 60:15, 19, 20, 21; 61:4, 7; 63:9, 11–12, 16, 19; 64:3–4.

clear from this evidence that Isa 40–66 decidedly reflects LBH when compared to Isa 1–39. However, it cannot be denied that עוֹלָמִים (ʿōlāmîm) is a sign of LBH.

מַסְמְרִים (masměrîm)

A more problematic example of a LBH noun cited by Paul is the Hebrew term מַסְמְרִים (masměrîm), "nails," in Isa 41:7. This word also appears in works considered to be late, namely, Jer 10:4; Eccl 12:11 (מַשְׂמְרוֹת, maśměrôt); 1 Chr 22:3; and 2 Chr 3:9. While it is true that the term is used in postbiblical texts—such as b. B. Bat. 7b; Gen. Rab. 68:13; y. Ḥag. 3:1, 78d; y. Pesaḥ. 5.32b;[66] and in the Damascus Document at Qumran (CD XII, 17)—an EBH counterpart cannot be established. Given the absence of synoptic passages in Samuel-Kings for 1 Chr 22:3 and 2 Chr 3:9, an uncontested word for "nail" in EBH is lacking.[67]

Phrases and Expressions

פְּרִי בֶטֶן (pěrî beṭen) > בֶּן בֶּטֶן (ben beṭen)

Paul argues that the phrase בֶּן בֶּטֶן (ben beṭen), "child of the womb," in Isa 49:15, which occurs elsewhere only in Job 19:17 and in the Aramaic equivalent בַּר בִּטְנִי (bar biṭnî) in Prov 31:2, is characteristic of LBH, replacing the earlier phrase פְּרִי בֶטֶן (pěrî beṭen), found, for example, in Gen 30:2; Deut 28:4; Isa 13:18; and Mic 6:7.[68] Neither פְּרִי בֶטֶן (pěrî beṭen) nor בֶּן בֶּטֶן (ben beṭen) is attested in Postbiblical Hebrew. Thus, even though בֶּן בֶּטֶן (ben beṭen) does not occur in later Hebrew, the diachronic contrast within the Bible would appear tentatively to suggest that this phrase is a sign of LBH.

רוּחַ הַקֹּדֶשׁ (rûaḥ haqqōdeš), "The Holy Spirit"

The phrase רוּחַ הַקֹּדֶשׁ (rûaḥ haqqōdeš), "the holy spirit," occurs in the Hebrew Bible only in Isa 63:10–11 (רוּחַ קָדְשׁוֹ, rûaḥ qodšô) and Ps 51:3[ET 1] (רוּחַ קָדְשֶׁךָ, rûaḥ qodšěkā). However, it is used widely in rabbinic literature (m. Soṭah 9:6, 15; t. Soṭah 12:5; 13:3) and in the Dead Sea Scrolls (1QHᵃ IV, 26; VI, 13; VIII, 11, 16, 21; 1QSᵇ II, 24; CD II, 12; V, 11; VII, 4; 1QS IV, 21; VIII, 16; IX, 3).[69] While it could be argued that this is a late phrase widely used in postbiblical literature, to classify it as LBH is ruled out because there is no corresponding phrase in EBH literature that could

---

66. Numerous examples occur in Mishnaic Hebrew. See Kasovsky, *Thesaurus Mishnae*, 3:1280.

67. The word for "tent-peg," יָתֵד (yātēd), which frequently occurs in the context of the tabernacle, is a different term. See BDB, 450.

68. Paul, "Signs of Late Biblical Hebrew," 299. See also Deut 28:11, 18, 53; 30:9; Pss 127:3; 132:11.

69. Paul, "Signs of Late Biblical Hebrew," 299.

suggest a diachronic contrast. It appears there was no occasion in EBH for this phrase to occur. Moreover, the possibility that a phrase conveying the notion of "*a* holy spirit" could exist in the earlier biblical period is theologically doubtful.

One Final Word

דָּוִד (*dāwīd*) > דָּוִיד (*dāwîd*)

We close this study by examining orthography, that of the name David. Many argue that, in general, the writings of LBH have more plene, or fuller, spellings than EBH compositions.[70] For example, the personal name David occurs 1,023 times in the Old Testament, with both the defective and plene spellings. It has long been recognized that, in contrast to the orthography of Samuel-Kings, a characteristic feature of the orthography of the Chronicler is his insistence in writing this name with the plene spelling, דָּוִיד (*dāwîd*).[71] The plene form is absent from Samuel and occurs in Kings only three times (1 Kgs 3:14; 11:4, 36).[72] Thus, of the 671 occurrences of the name "David" in Samuel-Kings, only three are written plene, while the remainder are written defectively. By contrast, in Ezra, Nehemiah, and Chronicles, the name David occurs 271 times, always written with the plene spelling. A few illustrations are sufficient to indicate the diachronic nature of this orthographic shift:[73]

2 Sam 7:26

וּבֵית עַבְדְּךָ דָוִד יִהְיֶה נָכוֹן לְפָנֶיךָ

ûbêt ʿabdĕkā dāwīd yihyê nākôn lĕpānêkā

And the house of your servant David will be established before you.

1 Chr 17:24

וּבֵית־דָּוִיד עַבְדְּךָ נָכוֹן לְפָנֶיךָ

ûbêt-dāwîd ʿabdĕkā nākôn lĕpānêkā

And the house of David your servant will be established before you.

---

70. See Kutscher, *History of the Hebrew Language*, 81; and Francis I. Andersen and A. Dean Forbes, *Spelling in the Hebrew Bible* (Rome: Biblical Institute Press, 1986), 110. The tendency to increase the use of plene spellings is particularly prominent among the Dead Sea Scrolls. See Takamitsu Muraoka, "Hebrew," *EDSS*, 1:340. For a different interpretation of the variable spelling of the name "David" than what is defended here, see James Barr, *The Variable Spellings of the Hebrew Bible* (Oxford: Oxford University Press, 1989), 197, 201. Barr suggests that the different spellings of the name David may reflect a change in pronunciation.

71. For full discussion, see David Noel Freedman, "The Spelling of the Name 'David' in the Hebrew Bible," *HAR* 7 (1983): 89–102; Andersen and Forbes, *Spelling in the Hebrew Bible*, 4–9. Passages that Andersen and Forbes suggest were subject to editorial activity (*Spelling in the Hebrew Bible*, 5).

72. Passages that Andersen and Forbes suggest were subject to editorial activity (*Spelling in the Hebrew Bible*, 5).

73. See also 2 Sam 6:16 // 1 Chr 15:29; 1 Kgs 12:19 // 2 Chr 10:19.

1 Kgs 7:51

וַיָּבֵא שְׁלֹמֹה אֶת־קָדְשֵׁי דָּוִד אָבִיו

wayyābēʾ šĕlōmô ʾet-qodšê dāwīd ʾābîw

Solomon brought in the sacred things of his father David.

2 Chr 5:1

וַיָּבֵא שְׁלֹמֹה אֶת־קָדְשֵׁי דָּוִיד אָבִיו

wayyābēʾ šĕlōmô ʾet-qodšê dāwîd ʾābîw

Solomon brought in the sacred things of his father David.

The trend of LBH toward the plene spelling of the personal name David is evident in the Dead Sea Scrolls. This tendency can be demonstrated best by looking at occurrences of this name in the biblical manuscripts of Samuel and Isaiah from Qumran. These are always written plene, against the corresponding passages in Isaiah and Samuel, where the name is always written defectively in MT:[74]

Isa 29:1 MT

קִרְיַת חָנָה דָוִד

qiryat ḥānâ dāwīd

city where David camped

Isa 29:1 1QIsaᵃ

קרית חנה דויד

qryt ḥnh dwyd

city where David camped

Isa 55:3 MT

חַסְדֵי דָוִד הַנֶּאֱמָנִים

ḥasdê dāwīd hanneʾĕmānîm

the faithful mercies of David

---

74. For these and other examples, see Kutscher, *Language and Linguistic Background of the Isaiah Scroll,* 99. Compare also 2 Sam 5:13; 8:17; 12:15 in the MT and in 4QSamᵃ. For these texts, see Emanuel Tov, "Determining the Relationship between the Qumran Scrolls and the LXX: Some Methodological Problems," in *The Hebrew and Greek Texts of Samuel,* ed. Emanuel Tov (Jerusalem: Magnes, 1980), 55; and Eugene C. Ulrich, *The Qumran Text of Samuel and Josephus* (Missoula, MT: Scholars Press, 1978), 45, 83, 138, 143. For additional plene spellings of the name David in 4QSamᵃ, see ibid., 45, 56, 82, 86, 88, 196–97.

Isa 55:3 1QIsaᵃ

חסדי דויד הנאמנים

    ḥsdy dwyd hnᵓmnym

    the faithful mercies of David

2 Sam 3:1 MT

וְדָוִד

    wĕdāwīd

    and David

2 Sam 3:1 4QSamᵃ

ודויד

    wdwyd

    and David

Ezekiel 34:23 provides early evidence of the trend to write the name David plene, a tendency that increased in the exilic period. Ezekiel appears to occupy an intermediate or transitional status in the דָוִד (*dāwīd*) > דָוִיד (*dāwîd*) shift.[75] This is what David Noel Freedman concluded:

> The viewpoint propounded here is that the books of the Hebrew Bible which contain the name of David reflect, in the predominant spelling of each book, the period during which they were compiled and formally published. Thus the books containing the three letter spelling should be assigned to the First Temple period, the books with the four letter spelling to the Second Temple period, and those with mixed spelling to the transitional period between the two others.[76]

In Isa 40–66, the name David occurs only once, in Isa 55:3, where we find the defective spelling that characterizes preexilic usage and that is also the spelling of the name throughout Isa 1–39. Although not too much should be made from an isolated example, if Freedman is correct, so-called Second Isaiah fits better with the preexilic literature, as reflected in Isa 1–39, than with the period of the exile or the postexilic period.

Conclusion

Shalom Paul's treatment of the language of Isa 40–66 in his article in the book *Diachrony in Biblical Hebrew* is unique within this important volume. The article

---

75. Freedman, "Spelling of the Name 'David,'" 92n7, 95, 96, 99, 102; and Rooker, *Biblical Hebrew in Transition*, 68–71. See also Saénz-Badillos, *History of the Hebrew Language*, 116.

76. "Spelling of the Name 'David,'" 99.

has no footnotes and only four references in the bibliography, two of which, it could be argued, undermine his attempt to isolate LBH features.

Paul cites thirty-four features or signs of LBH in Isa 40–66. He finds twenty possible signs of LBH in Isa 40–55 and sixteen possible examples in Isaiah 56–66. This roughly evenly divided set of attestations indicates that linguistically Isa 40–55 and 56–66 are very similar and reinforces Paul's assertion that Isa 40–66 should be dealt with as a unit. It may also suggest that these chapters were composed in the same time period.

Twenty-one of the features Paul analyzes are not included in any of the other twelve sources that analyze LBH that are cited in *Linguistic Dating of Biblical Texts*.[77] Ten of these are *hapax legomena* occurring only in Isaiah and thus have no distribution in LBH, though they are attested in postbiblical writings. Indeed, on eleven occasions Paul fails to identify an EBH equivalent for an alleged LBH sign. While he acknowledges Hurvitz's contribution to the diachronic study of Biblical Hebrew and appears to follow his methodology, Paul consistently fails to take distribution into account.

In spite of the potential late signs in Isa 40–66, there is a virtual consensus that Isa 40–66 represents Classical or preexilic Biblical Hebrew. Chaim Rabin characterized the Hebrew of Isa 40–66 as almost perfect Classical Hebrew.[78] As a consequence, indisputable marks of LBH in Isaiah are scanty. On the contrary, Isa 40–66 is clearly aligned with EBH. Stated differently, Bloch observes that "the overall concentration of typologically archaic linguistic features in these books (Ezekiel, Jeremiah, Haggai, and First Zechariah [1–8]) is much less pronounced than in Deutero-Isaiah."[79] Since the language of Isa 40–66 does not diverge from preexilic Hebrew,[80] it provides no evidence that Isa 40–66 was composed in the exilic and/ or postexilic periods. From a linguistic standpoint, the evidence suggests that Isa 40–66 was composed at roughly the same time as Isa 1–39.

The diachronic method cannot provide an absolute date for the composition of the book of Isaiah. However, it provides a good comparison between the nature of the Hebrew language in the broad chronological categories of the preexilic and postexilic periods. The language of Isa 40–66 does not fit the language of the exilic and postexilic periods. Features of LBH that we observe in Esther, Ezra-Nehemiah, and Chronicles are missing. The language of Isa 1–39 and 40–66 strongly suggests that both sections come from the same time period. As such, the book of

---

77. *Linguistic Dating of Biblical Texts* is one of only four references that Paul mentions in his bibliography.

78. See C. Rabin, *Die Entwicklung der hebräischen Sprache*, Veröffentlichungen der Hochschule für jüdische Studien Heidelberg 2 (Wiesbaden: Reichert, 1988), 16 (cited by Ehrensvärd, "Linguistic Dating of Biblical Texts," 175); see also ibid., 176, 185, and Young, Rezetko, and Ehrensvärd, *Linguistic Dating of Biblical Texts*, 87).

79. Bloch, "Third-Person Masculine Plural Suffixed Pronoun *-mw*," 163.

80. See David Talshir, "The Habitat and History of Hebrew during the Second Temple Period," in *Biblical Hebrew: Studies in Chronology and Typology,* ed. Ian Young (London: T&T Clark, 2003), 254.

Isaiah should be read as a unity.[81] While this alone will not convince scholars that Isa 40–66 was written by the prophet Isaiah in the eighth century BCE, its significance should not be disregarded when proposing other explanations based on preinterpretive grids.

Appendix A: Biblical *Hapax Legomena* and/ or Words Unique to Isaiah[82]

4.1.3. The Hebrew word שׁ-שׁ-ג (*g-š-š*), "to grope," occurs only in Isa 59:10 (2x). The word appears in the targumim, but does not appear in the Dead Sea Scrolls.

4.1.4. The verb שׁ-שׁ-א (*ʾ-š-š*), "be strong/firm" (Isa 46:8), is a *hapax legomenon* in the Bible. The root occurs in Aramaic and in rabbinic literature but apparently not at Qumran.

4.1.5.1. נ-ט-ל (*n-ṭ-l*), "to lift, raise," occurs in the Piel only in Isa 63:9. The root occurs twice at Qumran but apparently as a Qal form.

4.1.5.3. ס-ג-ר (*s-g-r*), "to bow down," occurs in the Hebrew portions of the Bible only in Isa (46:4, 7; 53:4, 11). The verb does occur in Biblical Aramaic (Dan 2:46; 3:5–7, 10–12, 14–15 [2x], 18, 28) and in the targumim and in rabbinic literature.

4.1.5.4. ב-ח-ר (*b-ḥ-r*), a common Hebrew word, means "to test" only in Isa 48:10. The term does occur with this meaning in the targumim.

4.1.5.5. כ-ו-ל (*k-w-l*), "to measure," is a *hapax legomenon* in the Bible (Isa 40:12). It occurs in the targumim and rabbinic literature.

4.3.1. שׁ-ר-ב (*š-r-b*), "parched ground," is unique in the Bible to Isa in 49:10 and 35:7. The term has the meaning "the parched ground" in the targumim and rabbinic literature. It does not occur in Mishnaic Hebrew.

4.3.4. זִיקוֹת (*zîqôt*), "firebrands, sparks," is a biblical *hapax legomenon*, occurring only in Isa 50:11. It does occur in rabbinic literature and in the Dead Sea Scrolls.

5.5. זְבֻל קָדְשֶׁךָ (*zĕbūl qodšĕkā*), "your holy heights," occurs in the Bible only in Isa 63:15. The phrase occurs occasionally in the Dead Sea Scrolls.

---

81. This conclusion can also be drawn from an impartial *prima facie* reading of the New Testament (John 12:38–40).

82. In the appendices, the entries are numbered according to the numbering system in Paul, "Signs of Late Biblical Hebrew," 294–99.

5.8. בֵּית תְּפִלָּה (*bêt tĕpillâ*), "house of prayer," occurs in the Bible only in Isa 56:7 (2x). It occurs in rabbinic literature.

Appendix B: Problematic Entries

2.1. Many agree with Paul that the use of the Hebrew infinitive absolute as a substitute for a finite verb occurs more often in LBH than in EBH. Paul cites almost forty examples outside of Isaiah where this appears in books often considered late. The infinitive absolute is used for a finite verb six times in Isa 40–66 (Isa 42:20 [2x, if one includes the Qere reading רָאוֹת (*rāʾôt*)]; 59:4 [4x]).[83] While Paul seems to be correct in his analysis, a study of Isa 1–39 reveals that this feature is more frequent in this first major section of Isaiah. The use of the infinitive absolute for a finite verb occurs possibly thirteen times in Isa 1–39 (Isa 5:5 [2x]; 21:5 [4x]; 22:13 [2x]; 31:5 [2x]; 37:19, 30; 38:5).

4.1.5.2. Paul argues that the Hebrew verb ס-ב-ל (*s-b-l*), which occurs in Isa 46:4, 7; 53:4, 11, is an example of LBH because this verb also occurs in Lam 5:7; Ps 144:14; Eccl 12:5, and because in the targumim this same root consistently translates Hebrew נ-שׂ-א (*n-ś-ʾ*) (Deut 24:15; 32:11; Job 21:3). The verb ס-ב-ל (*s-b-l*) occurs twice in the Dead Sea Scrolls (4Q200 II, 2; 4Q525 V, 12). While the root is not common, it does occur in Mishnaic Hebrew (*m. Zebaḥ.* 12:6; *m. Kelim* 28:9). There is some positive evidence that this verb could be considered a sign of LBH in Isa 40–66. Paul failed to note that the verb occurs as an infinitive in Gen 49:15.

4.2.1. Paul argues that the verb ע-ו-ר (*ʿ-w-r*) in the Hiphil stem means "to raise up a conquering nation, individual, or instrument of destruction."[84] He finds four examples of this usage in Isa 40–66, namely, in Isa 41:2, 25; 42:13; 45:13. As examples of the possible lateness of the meaning of this term, he cites examples in Jer 50:9; 51:1, 11; Ezek 23:22; Hag 1:14; Dan 11:2, 25; Ezra 1:1; 1 Chr 5:26; and 2 Chr 21:16. Paul suggests that the verb is the LBH equivalent of the EBH Hiphil of ק-ו-ם (*q-w-m*). The verb also occurs at Qumran and in rabbinic literature. However, Paul does not show any direct diachronic contrast of this root with EBH usage. None of the twelve sources cited in *Linguistic Dating of Biblical Texts* cites this as an example of LBH. Indeed, other studies have concluded that the Piel of ק-ו-ם (*q-w-m*) is the EBH equivalent of the Hiphil of ק-ו-ם (*q-w-m*) and not the root ע-ו-ר (*ʿ-w-r*). Furthermore, while Paul notes that the Hiphil of ע-ו-ר (*ʿ-w-r*) appears in Isa 13:17, it may be equally significant that the Hiphil of ק-ו-ם (*q-w-m*) occurs in Isa 14:9 and 23:13, as well as in Isa 44:26; 49:6, 8.

---

83. Another possibility is Isa 57:17.
84. Paul, "Signs of LBH," 296.

4.3.2. The term צֶאֱצָאִים (ṣeʾĕṣāʾîm), "offspring," occurs in Isa 1–39 (22:24; 34:1) and Isa 40–66 (42:5; 44:3; 48:19; 61:9; 65:23), and elsewhere in the Hebrew Bible only in the book of Job (5:25; 21:8; 27:14; 31:8). The term is common at Qumran, occurring seventeen times. The term also occurs in rabbinic literature, although it is absent in the Mishnah. According to Paul, צֶאֱצָאִים (ṣeʾĕṣāʾîm) replaces EBH זֶרַע (zeraʿ), בָּנִים (bānîm), and בְּנֵי בָנִים (bĕnê bānîm). However, Paul does not establish the diachronic contrast with what he asserts are the earlier forms in EBH. Moreover, outside of Isaiah, the other examples of צֶאֱצָאִים (ṣeʾĕṣāʾîm) all come from the poetic book of Job; examples are lacking from Esther–Chronicles, where we normally find examples of LBH. In addition, while the term צֶאֱצָאִים (ṣeʾĕṣāʾîm) occurs four times in Isa 40–66, the EBH term זֶרַע (zeraʿ) occurs only seven times in Isa 1–39 but eighteen times in Isa 40–66.

4.3.5. Another proposed sign of LBH in Isa 40–66 is the use of לְאָחוֹר (lĕʾāḥôr) in the sense of "future" in Isa 41:23; 42:23 (see also Jer 7:24 and Ps 114:3, 5). Paul admits that most of the occurrences of לְאָחוֹר (lĕʾāḥôr) and אַחַר (ʾaḥar) in the Hebrew Bible mean something like "backward, back part, behind," and in some of the texts just mentioned Paul admits that the words arguably retain this meaning. The term לְאָחוֹר (lĕʾāḥôr) also occurs in Sir 6:28 and 12:12, and in Mishnaic Hebrew in *m. Ḥag.* 2:1. There is no diachronic contrast between the words, nor do they have sufficient distribution in any books written in LBH to be classified as a LBH feature.

5.3. The phrase אָמַר יְהוָה צְבָאוֹת (ʾāmar yhwh ṣĕbāʾôt), "says YHWH of Hosts," occurs in Isa 45:13, and numerous times in Jeremiah (51x), Haggai (7x), Zechariah (21x), and Malachi (21x), as well as in 1 Chr 17:7. This common phrase could not have been expressed differently in EBH. In fact, it occurs in 1 Sam 15:2 and 2 Sam 7:8, preceded by the particle כֹּה (kô), "thus." The phrase is not listed as a feature of LBH in *Linguistic Dating of Biblical Texts*. The evidence for considering this a LBH innovation or sign is weak.

5.6. Paul proposes that the phrase עִיר הַקֹּדֶשׁ (ʿîr haqqōdeš), "the holy city, city of the temple," in Isa 48:2; 52:1; and 64:9 should be considered late. Admittedly, the phrase occurs in some late texts, such as Dan 9:24 and Neh 11:1, 18, and in postbiblical texts, such as Sir 36:18 and the Dead Sea Scrolls (CD XX, 220; 4Q176 8–11), and in rabbinic literature (*b. B. Qam.* 97b; *b. Soṭah* 47a). However, once again there is no diachronic contrast with a similar phrase in earlier books, nor is there evidence for a corresponding phrase or concept such as "a holy city." This phrase also is not attested in Mishnaic Hebrew.

5.7. The phrase בֵּית קֹדֶשׁ (bêt qōdeš), "holy temple," occurs only once in Isaiah, in the form בֵּית קָדְשֵׁנוּ (bêt qodšēnû), "our holy temple" (Isa 64:10), but its position as a LBH phrase is reinforced in that the other three biblical references all occur in the late books of Chronicles (1 Chr 29:3; 2 Chr 3:8, 10: בֵּית קֹדֶשׁ הַקֳּדָשִׁים [bêt qōdeš haqqŏdāšîm]). Furthermore, the phrase appears in postbiblical literature, such as the Dead Sea Scrolls (1QS VIII, 5; IX, 6; 4Q176 XVI, 3), and in rabbinic literature, where we find בית קדש הקדשים (*byt qdš hqdšym*), "house of the Holy of Holies" (*m. Mid.* 4:7; *y. Ber.* 4.5.8c; *y. Kil.* 8.4.31c). Nevertheless, the likelihood that this is a LBH phrase is diminished by the absence of an EBH equivalent and the logical fact that there is no indefinite phrase such as "a holy temple" in the Hebrew Bible. None of the twelve sources cited in *Linguistic Dating of Biblical Texts* suggests that this is an example of LBH.

Appendix C: Possible Late Biblical Hebrew Features

4.2.3. A Hebrew verb that perhaps should be classified as LBH is ג-א-ל (*g-ʾ-l*) with the meaning "to (be) defile(d)" (Isa 59:3; 63:3). While this root never bears this meaning in EBH, Paul claims it has this meaning in Zeph 3:1; Mal 1:7 (2x); Lam 4:14; Ezra 2:62 (= Neh 7:64); and Dan 1:8 (2x). Moreover, it is possible that this root bears this meaning in the Dead Sea Scrolls (CD XII, 16; 1QM IX, 8). However, this meaning does not carry over into Mishnaic Hebrew, and the sense of "defiling" for ג-א-ל (*g-ʾ-l*) is not recorded in Jastrow's *Dictionary*.[85]

5.2. The phrase עַם הַקֹּדֶשׁ (*ʿam haqqōdeš*), "the holy people," occurs in Isa 62:12 and 63:18 and, in a slightly variant form, in Dan 12:7 (עַם קֹדֶשׁ [*ʿam qōdeš*], "a holy people"). Most occurrences of the phrase in the Dead Sea Scrolls are definite rather than indefinite, but the opposite is the case in EBH. In EBH we find עַם קָדוֹשׁ (*ʿam qādôš*), "a holy people", in Deut 7:6; 14:2, 21; 26:19; 28:9, and גּוֹי קָדוֹשׁ (*gôy qādôš*), "a holy nation," in Exod 19:6. Although the phrase עַם הַקֹּדֶשׁ (*ʿam haqqōdeš*) exhibits a diachronic contrast with EBH, it is limited in its distribution and its classification as LBH is questionable. None of the twelve sources cited in *Linguistic Dating of Biblical Texts* refers to this phrase as a characteristic of LBH.

---

85. Jastrow, *Dictionary of the Targumim*, 1:202, 261. With respect to Biblical Hebrew, both BDB (p. 146) and *HALOT* (pp. 169–70) state that this meaning of ג-א-ל (*g-ʾ-l*) is late. Qimron also gives this meaning for the root in the Dead Sea Scrolls (*Hebrew of the Dead Sea Scrolls*, 89).

10 | The Literary Macrostructures of the Book of Isaiah and Authorial Intent

Peter J. Gentry

Introduction

Generally speaking, during the last two hundred years scholarship on the book of Isaiah has not focused on the literary structure of the work as a unitary whole. However, the last thirty years have witnessed a movement away from viewing this book as a patchwork of sources to considering the meaning of the entire work as a unity.[1] This unity, however, is often perceived as only a *redactional* unity and not an *authorial-compositional* unity.

Ulrich Berges' 1998 monograph, entitled *Das Buch Jesaja: Komposition und Endgestalt*, belongs to this recent trend.[2] The analysis of Berges retains all the usual divisions of the text according to different authors/sources and their redactional stages (i.e., the literary structure of the individual sections). However, Berges does not think it is possible to go beyond that to find an overall coherence to the work. Nonetheless, an approach that assumes several authors and redactions radically affects interpretation, as I will illustrate shortly.

Adele Berlin speaks clearly of the relationship between the literary structure of a text and its meaning: "Poetics makes us aware of how texts achieve their meaning. Poetics aids interpretation. If we know *how* texts mean, we are in a better position to discover *what* a particular text means."[3] To be more specific, perhaps as much as 50 percent of the "meaning" of a text is communicated by the literary forms and micro- and macrostructures (i.e., arrangement) of the constituent parts, and only 50 percent by the actual words or statements in the text or the assembly of texts that make up the larger work. The literary structure of the whole—i.e., the macro-arrangement of the constituent parts of the text— creates a metanarrative, a larger plot structure that is key to interpretation of the individual parts. If such can be demonstrated, then an alternative arrangement

---

1. See the first essay in this volume by Richard Schultz.

2. Herders Biblische Studien 16, Freiburg: Herder. This book recently appeared in English as Ulrich Berges, *The Book of Isaiah: Its Composition and Final Form*, trans. Millard C. Lind, Hebrew Bible Monographs 46 (Sheffield: Sheffield Phoenix, 2012).

3. Adele Berlin, *Poetics and Interpretation of Biblical Narrative* (Winona Lake, IL: Eisenbrauns, 1983), 17 (emphasis hers).

of the materials would alter the meaning of any segment of text. Thus, if an eighth-century prophet named Isaiah spoke/wrote some or all of the words but the editorial arrangement of the individual parts comes from a much later time, this may provide an alternative metanarrative for understanding the details in the individual texts that comprise the present prophecy. Therefore, by saying that the book of Isaiah possesses a literary unity I mean that the book's larger literary structure and the statements in the text reflect the same authorial intent, whether they come from the author himself or were communicated by him to disciples contemporary with him.

The Enlightenment exaltation of reason yielded an exegetical method and commentaries that excel in detailed lexical, syntactical, and textual analyses of the book of Isaiah, but that lack a bird's-eye perspective on the overall literary structure and coherence of the work. This atomistic exegesis essentially fails since the interpretive task requires interpreters to move back and forth from a view of the whole to the analysis of the parts and conversely from analysis of the parts to a view of the whole. An inadequate view of the whole leaves only endless analyses of the parts without adequate context for understanding them.

Interpreting the Bible may not be straightforward for *modern* and *Western* readers, since the biblical texts are *ancient* and *Eastern* in origin. My main thesis in this essay is that critical scholarship has not asked with sufficient rigor: "What are the Hebrews' own rules for literature and prophecy?" Instead, it has imposed modern, Western approaches to literature upon ancient, Eastern texts.

Although an essay such as this must be limited in scope, I intend to explore four areas where the ancient Hebrews have not been allowed to speak for themselves. These concern four features of the book of Isaiah that affect our grasp of its literary macrostructures and in turn determine how we understand its parts: (1) the role of text linguistics, (2) the nature of Hebrew discourse/literature, (3) the character of the author, and (4) the nature of Hebrew prophecy.

Four Features of the Book of Isaiah

The Role of Text Linguistics

Text linguistics is a branch of linguistics, the modern science of language, that has been developing since its embryonic stage in the early 1900s.[4] Prior to this, grammar was normally divided into phonology, morphology, and syntax. Text linguistics, or discourse grammar, considers features of the language that operate beyond the boundary of the sentence and that involve the text as a whole. Just as higher levels inform lower levels in grammar, so text linguistics informs syntax, as illustrated by the following Latin paradigm:

---

4. A pioneering work is G. Pilhofer, *Grammatik der Kate-Sprache in Neuguinea* (Berlin: Dietrich Reimer, 1933).

puella	*puellae*
puellae	*puellarum*
puellae	*puellis*
puellam	*puellas*
puella	*puellis*

From a purely morphological viewpoint, there are only seven different forms here, but from a syntactical viewpoint there are ten. Therefore, it is unwise to discuss morphology apart from syntax. Similarly, the distinction in Classical Hebrew between an adverb and a direct object is frequently not morphological but syntactical, involving a different order or positioning of a word in the sentence. Just as syntax informs and necessitates a revision of morphology, so awareness of macro-syntax may improve knowledge of clause-level syntax as well as issues of coherence and literary structure at the compositional level.

Recent attention to discourse grammar in biblical Hebrew has helped us recognize specific sentence types that mark the beginnings and endings of sections. As a general rule, verbless clauses at the margins of discourse mark the setting. A verbal sentence may also function this way, but in such situations it is asyndetic and the adverbial modifier precedes a perfect verb rather than a clause initiated by a *wāw*-consecutive verb form.[5] The most obvious example is the first sentence in Gen 1, but we may illustrate this point by comparing and contrasting several parallel texts from 2 Kgs 18:13–20:19 and Isa 36–39.

2 Kgs 18:13	Isa 36:13
וּבְאַרְבַּע עֶשְׂרֵה שָׁנָה לַמֶּלֶךְ חִזְקִיָּה עָלָה סַנְחֵרִיב מֶלֶךְ־אַשּׁוּר עַל כָּל־עָרֵי יְהוּדָה הַבְּצֻרוֹת וַיִּתְפְּשֵׂם׃	וַיְהִי בְּאַרְבַּע עֶשְׂרֵה שָׁנָה לַמֶּלֶךְ חִזְקִיָּהוּ עָלָה סַנְחֵרִיב מֶלֶךְ־אַשּׁוּר עַל כָּל־עָרֵי יְהוּדָה הַבְּצֻרוֹת וַיִּתְפְּשֵׂם׃

ûbĕ'arba' 'eśrê šānâ lammelek ḥizqîyâ	*wayĕhî bĕ'arba' 'eśrê šānâ lammelek ḥizqîyāhû*
'ālâ sanḥērîb melek-'aššûr 'al kol-'ārê yĕhûdâ	*'ālâ sanḥērîb melek-'aššûr 'al kol-'ārê yĕhûdâ*
habbĕṣūrôt wayyitpĕśēm	*habbĕṣūrôt wayyitpĕśēm*

2 Kgs 19:1 // Isa 37:1

וַיְהִי כִּשְׁמֹעַ הַמֶּלֶךְ חִזְקִיָּהוּ וַיִּקְרַע אֶת־בְּגָדָיו

wayĕhî kišmōa' hammelek ḥizqîyāhû wayyiqra' 'et-bĕgādāyw

2 Kgs 20:1 // Isa 38:1

בַּיָּמִים הָהֵם חָלָה חִזְקִיָּהוּ לָמוּת וַיָּבֹא אֵלָיו יְשַׁעְיָהוּ בֶן־אָמוֹץ הַנָּבִיא

bayyāmîm hāhēm ḥālâ ḥizqîyāhû lāmût wayyābō' 'ēlāyw yĕša'yāhû ben-'āmôṣ hannābî'

---

5. As demonstrated in recent works, but also earlier, by Stephen G. Dempster, in his dissertation, "Linguistic Features of Hebrew Narrative: A Discourse Analysis of Narrative from the Classical Period" (PhD diss., University of Toronto, 1985).

The prayer of Isa 38:7–20 is inserted between verses 6 and 7 of 2 Kgs 20. Then 2 Kgs 20:8–11 is summarized in Isa 38:7–8, while 38:21–22 picks up 2 Kgs 20:7. Finally, 2 Kgs 20:12–19 is identical to Isa 39:1–8.

2 Kgs 20:12	Isa 39:1
בָּעֵת הַהִיא שָׁלַח בְּראדַךְ בַּלְאֲדָן בֶּן־בַּלְאֲדָן מֶלֶךְ־בָּבֶל סְפָרִים וּמִנְחָה אֶל־חִזְקִיָּהוּ	בָּעֵת הַהוּא שָׁלַח מְרֹדַךְ בַּלְאֲדָן בֶּן־בַּלְאֲדָן מֶלֶךְ־בָּבֶל סְפָרִים וּמִנְחָה אֶל־חִזְקִיָּהוּ
bāʿēt hahîʾ šalaḥ bĕrōʾdak balʾădān ben-balʾădān melek-bābel sĕpārîm ûminḥâ ʾel-ḥizqîyāhû	*bāʿēt hahîʾ šalaḥ mĕrōdak balʾădān ben-balʾădān melek-bābel sĕpārîm ûminḥâ ʾel-ḥizqîyāhû*

We cannot accept an approach to these parallels based solely on theories of who borrowed from whom. The question is rather: What function do the discourse markers have in the text in which they are now embedded? The difference between 2 Kgs 18:13 and Isa 36:13 shows that regardless of sources used by either the author of the book of Isaiah or the author of Kings, their works in their final form treat the same events differently. The fact that both chapters 38 and 39 of Isaiah begin with asyndeton and a verbal clause in which the adverbial phrase is pre-posed to a perfect verb indicates that these begin new sections. Conversely, while many see Isa 40:1 as the beginning of a new section, in Hebrew literature it would be odd to commence a major unit so abruptly without an introduction. Therefore, from the perspective of discourse grammar in ancient Hebrew, the standard approach of dividing the book between chapters 39 and 40 is highly suspect.

In my analysis below, I will suggest that a new section begins at 38:1, not at 40:1.[6] In a similar analysis in the notes to the *ESV Study Bible*, Raymond C. Ortlund Jr. states:

> Chapters 36–37 look back to chs. 28–35, proving through Hezekiah that faith in God is met by his blessing. Chapters 38–39 provide context for chs. 40–55, as Hezekiah's folly dooms his nation to Babylonian exile. Concerning the backdrop of divine faithfulness (chs. 36–37) and human inconstancy (chs. 38–39), God stands forth as the only hope of his people.[7]

The Nature of Hebrew Discourse/Literature

Repetition is at the heart of Hebrew discourse. A common pattern in Hebrew literature is to consider topics in a recursive manner. While this approach seems monotonous and repetitive to those who do not understand how these texts communicate, normally a Hebrew author begins a discourse on a topic, develops it from a particular angle, and then ends that conversation. Next, he begins another conversation, taking up the same topic again and considering it from a different perspective. When we hear these two discourses on the same topic in succession,

---

6. So also J. A. Motyer, *The Prophecy of Isaiah: An Introduction and Commentary* (Downers Grove, IL: InterVarsity Press, 1993), 289.

7. In Lane T. Dennis, ed., *The ESV Study Bible* (Wheaton, IL: Crossway, 2008), 1302.

they function like the left and right speakers of a stereo system. The speakers of a stereo system simultaneously provide both the same and different music. In one sense the music from the left speaker is identical to that of the right, but in another sense they are slightly different, so that when we hear the two together the effect is a sound that is in stereo instead of being one-dimensional. Similarly, in Hebrew literature ideas being discussed can be experienced like stereo sound or even DTS 5.1 Surround Sound.

This approach is followed in any given genre of literature and across genres, whether prose or poetry, and at both the macroscopic and microscopic levels. As an illustration, in Exod 19:5–6 YHWH announces his purpose in the covenant at Sinai:

> You will be my treasured possession more than/out of all the nations, . . .
> and you will be for me a kingdom of priests and a holy nation.

Two clauses joined by the conjunction *wāw* constitute the declaration by YHWH. If we begin with the second clause, the phrases "kingdom of priests" and "holy nation" are like the sound coming out of the left and right speakers of a stereo system. Taken individually and together, they constitute another way of saying "God's personal treasure." The two parts of the second clause in turn become sound from a right speaker for which the first clause is sound from the left speaker.[8]

We also see this phenomenon across genres. Exodus 14 and 15 present a prose and then a poetic account of the crossing of the Red Sea. The same is true of Judg 4 and 5, which recount the destruction of Sisera and his iron chariots. Genesis 1:1–2:3 and 2:4–3:24 present an example of two different styles within the same narrative genre. These do not represent different sources, but reflect a common characteristic of a single author's communication.

This also explains why most Hebrew poetry is based on the couplet; this is the minimalist version of the left and right speakers to create a stereo effect. When an author works in threes we have tricola or triplets of discussions in discourse (e.g., three panels portraying the future king in Isa 7–12 and three songs about the servant in Isa 49–53).

This approach to literature is also the basis for chiasm in literary structures. Faced with two or three topics to discuss and the need to treat every topic twice, they may be presented in an A B C :: A′ B′ C′ order. But they may also be arranged differently, for example, A B C :: C′ B′ A′.[9] Admittedly, many chiastic structures

---

8. For a full exposition of this text, see Peter J. Gentry and Stephen J. Wellum, *Kingdom through Covenant: A Biblical-Theological Understanding of the Covenants* (Wheaton, IL: Crossway, 2012), 315–27.

9. The most important studies of chiasm and recursive discourse in Hebrew literature are H. C. Brichto, *Toward a Grammar of Biblical Poetics* (New York: Oxford University Press, 1992), 13–14, 75–76, 86, 118, 165; Victor M. Wilson, *Divine Symmetries: The Art of Biblical Rhetoric* (Lanham, MD: University Press of America, 1997); M. H. Woudstra, *The Book of Joshua*, NICOT (Grand Rapids: Eerdmans, 1981), 78; and esp. Charles Lock, "Some Words after Chiasmus," in *The Shape of Biblical Language: Chiasmus in the Scriptures and Beyond*, ed. John Breck (Crestwood, NY: St. Vladimir's Seminary Press, 1994), 361–67. The most recent book-length study of chiasm is Mary Douglas, *Thinking in Circles: An Essay on Ring*

proposed by scholars are mere mirages, as Mark Boda has rightly noted.[10] Within the overall exegetical enterprise, discovering the literary structure of a text is often difficult. However, contrary to the claims of James Kugel, chiastic or episodic literary structures are not the subjective creations of interpreters, but belong to the objective phenomena of the text.[11] The differences between and among scholars' structural analyses frequently result from differing methods or some scholars' shallow study of the text.[12] Because limitations of space preclude treatment of the structure of the entire book of Isaiah, this essay can only illustrate, rather than prove, my thesis that the book of Isaiah is a literary unity.

The Character of the Author

One feature that characterizes the entire book of Isaiah is the author's tendency to introduce a new topic in a mysterious manner and then to delay exposition of it until later key information that enables readers to understand what is being described has been provided. Several illustrations will clarify this point.

Isaiah 13 commences the section commonly known as the Oracles concerning Foreign Nations (chs. 13–27). Based on its title, the first oracle concerns Babylon. This prophecy consists of three sections arranged in an A B A′ pattern:

A   YHWH Summons His Warriors (vv. 1–5)
  B   The Day of YHWH: Judgment upon the Arrogant (vv. 6–16)
A′ YHWH Summons His Warriors—the Coming of the Medes (vv. 17–22)

Given the prose heading ("Oracle concerning Babylon"), the reader knows the topic. In verses 1–5, YHWH summons his warriors, but the reader is not told why. In 13:6–16 we learn that these warriors will be used to punish Babylon, but at this point we do not know who they are. Verses 17–22 finally identify them as the Medes. In this passage we must read to the end before we find out the key information. The first and last paragraphs are the left and right speakers that bring the information to the reader in stereo sound.

The Oracles concerning Foreign Nations are constructed in three groups of five. In chapter 21, which begins the second set of five, Isaiah uses a mysterious title: "Oracle concerning the Desert by the Sea." But where on earth is that? The reader recognizes all the places mentioned in the first five oracles, but this designation is

---

Composition (New Haven: Yale University Press, 2007). None of these studies connects the approach to literature just described with the propensity for chiasm in literary structures.

10. Mark J. Boda, "Chiasmus in Ubiquity: Symmetrical Mirages in Nehemiah 9," *JSOT* 71 (1996): 55–70.

11. James L. Kugel, "On the Bible and Literary Criticism," *Prooftexts* 1 (1981): 99–104. For episodic versus chiastic progression, see Byron Wheaton, "Focus and Structure in the Abraham Narratives," *TJ* 2/27 (2006): 143–62.

12. I have often acknowledged that others perceived the structure of a text better than I had. For example, Mark Boda's proposed chiastic structure for Isa 56–66 fits the data better than my own analysis. See Mark J. Boda, *A Severe Mercy: Sin and Its Remedy in the Old Testament*, Siphrut 1 (Winona Lake, IN: Eisenbrauns, 2009), 213.

unknown. This forces the reader to continue reading. Not until verse 9 do we learn that the author is describing Babylon. In the wake of divine judgment, Babylon will be a desolate spot on the Persian Gulf, a desert by the sea, inhabited by various types of owls (13:21–22). Isaiah 21:11–12 contains an oracle concerning דּוּמָה (*dûmâ*). This geographic epithet is also enigmatic. Does the author mean Dumah (along with Dedan and Tema in 21:13–14), an oasis on the North Arabian trade route? Since the word can mean "silence," this may be a play on words concerning Edom; the devastation in Edom will result in eternal silence. Isaiah 21:13–15 involves an oracle concerning עֲרָב (*ʿărāb*). Is this Arabia, or is it a noun meaning "desert," a play on the word for "evening"? This oracle is followed by an oracle concerning the Valley of Vision, but again, this place is unknown. However, as we continue reading, we find out that this refers to Jerusalem and the plans that YHWH has for it.

The four Servant Songs also contain an element of mystery. While the first Song, in chapter 42, forms part of the introduction to this entire section, the last three Servant Songs are grouped together in rapid succession in chapters 49, 50, and 52–53. The first of these songs introduces the mystery: Who is this servant? Is it Israel? Given the calling of Israel in Exod 19–24, such an interpretation appears plausible. Moreover, Israel is affirmed as the servant in Isa 49:3, though earlier the reader has learned that Israel as a nation is a blind, deaf, and disobedient servant (42:18–25), which creates tension in the plot structure.

The parable of the Song of the Vineyard in 5:1–7 offers a final example. This parable consists of four stanzas. The first stanza (vv. 1–2) relates a story of a farmer preparing a vineyard and expecting good vintage, but instead the vineyard yields rotten, stunted grapes. In the second stanza (vv. 3–4) the listeners are asked for a verdict. The third stanza (vv. 5–6) confirms the rhetorical question posed in the second stanza by relating the decision of the vineyard's owner. He will do exactly what the listeners expect; he will destroy this useless vineyard. The last stanza (v. 7) represents the shocking punch line, applying the parable to Judah and Jerusalem; they are the bad grapes! Once again, the initial mystery is clarified at the end. As in Nathan's parable to David concerning the poor man and his one ewe lamb (2 Sam 12:1–6), the author engages the listeners and gets them to declare the verdict before revealing that they are condemning themselves.

The parable genre also fits what readers discover in the call of Isaiah in chapter 6. In chapters 5–12, which constitute the third section of the book, Isaiah uses recursive technique to deal with the topic of corruption in the old Zion and the path of transformation that will lead to the new Zion. Rejecting the prophet's message, his audience has by now tired of being scolded. Isaiah 6:8–10 specifies that Isaiah was sent to a people who will not hear, see, or understand. Accordingly, his communicative techniques will suit the audience and their situation.

The Nature of Hebrew Prophecy

The Israelite prophet characterized his experience as a חָזוֹן (*ḥāzōn*), i.e., a vision. Nonetheless, the expression may apply to any or all of the prophet's five senses (cf. Isa 21:3). His prophetic experience gave him access to the heavenly court where YHWH is enthroned.[13] The prophet heard and saw the divine decisions that concern the governing of particular individuals, nations, or situations. Isaiah in particular does not necessarily understand what he is reporting. With broad strokes he paints a panoramic picture in which the near and distant futures are set side by side.

When Jesus cited Isa 61:1–2 in the Nazareth synagogue (Luke 4:16–21), he ended his reading with "Proclaim the year of the Lord's favor" (v. 2a), omitting "and the day of judgment of our God" (v. 2b). From the viewpoint of the New Testament, the former is already and the latter is not yet. Following the lead of Jesus, it seems that certain elements of Isa 60 are being fulfilled today, while others await a future fulfilment.

Although this phenomenon can be found throughout the book of Isaiah, it has not been sufficiently noted. Isaiah 20 presents another clear example. In this short oracle Isaiah predicts Assyria's defeat of the Philistines and Egypt[14] by means of a symbolic drama in which he goes around barefoot and naked. The prophecy was fulfilled when Sargon II attacked Ashdod in 711 BCE and when Esarhaddon took his campaign to Egypt in 671 BCE. Although these two events are separated by forty years, they are presented in a single, panoramic vision.

The Literary Coherence of the Book of Isaiah

Having briefly described four features of the book of Isaiah as a construct of ancient Hebrew literature, I will argue for the literary coherence of the entire work. An analogy may be useful here. The Honda Acura RL was a full-size luxury sedan equipped with a sound system producing DTS 5.1 surround sound, distributed from ten Bose speakers (two speakers per channel). Analogously, the book of Isaiah develops its plot structure by presenting the central theme of the transformation of Zion seven times.[15] The "music" of Isaiah is like that of a DTS 5.1 surround sound system with Bose speakers; or, even better, Isaiah resembles a DTS 7.1 surround sound system, describing the transformation of Zion in all seven of its major sections like a seven-channel audio system. Isaiah details the path from a corrupt Zion in the old creation to a renewed and transformed Zion in the new creation.

---

13. First Kings 22:13–23 and Zech 3 show the connection between the heavenly court and speaking for God. Indeed, the first person plural in "Who will go for *us*?" in Isa 6:8 confirms that as a prophet Isaiah has access to the heavenly council.

14. The literary unit represented by Isa 20 is signaled by the shift to prose, in contrast to the poetry of the adjacent chapters (i.e., Isa 19 and 21).

15. See Barry G. Webb, "Zion in Transformation: A Literary Approach to Isaiah," in *The Bible in Three Dimensions: Essays in Celebration of Forty Years of Biblical Studies in the University of Sheffield*, ed. D. J. A. Clines, Stephen E. Fowl, and Stanley E. Porter, JSOTSup 87 (Sheffield: Sheffield Academic, 1990), 65–84.

The Book of Isaiah: From Zion in the Old Creation to Zion in the New[16]

1. The Judgment and Transformation of Zion—Part 1 (1:2–2:4)
2. The Judgment and Transformation of Zion—Part 2 (2:5–4:6)
3. The Judgment of the Vineyard, and the Coming King (5:1–12:6)
4. The City of Man versus the City of God (13:1–27:13)
5. Trusting the Nations versus Trusting the Word of YHWH (28:1–37:38)
6. Comfort and Redemption for Zion and the World (38:1–55:13)
7. The Servants of YHWH and the New Creation (56:1–66:24)

Sections One and Two: Isaiah 1–4

I will consider the first two divisions of the book together. Isaiah 1:2–2:4 and 2:5–4:6 can be outlined as follows:

Outline of Isaiah 1:2–2:4

I. Disloyalty and Discipline (1:2–9)
    A. Accusation of Covenant Disloyalty (1:2–4)
    B. Discipline Has Reached Desperate Measures (1:5–9)
II. The Adjudication of Israel's Offenses (1:10–20)
    A. Rejection of Hypocritical Worship (1:10–15d)
    B. Invitation to Repent and Practice Righteousness (1:15e–17)
    C. Promise of Forgiveness and Restoration/Judgment (1:18–20)
III. The Purification of Zion (1:21–31)
    A. Lament over the Corruption of Zion (1:21–23)
    B. Promise of Punishment and Restoration (1:24–26)
    C. Purification of Zion and Judgment of Sinners (1:27–31)
IV. Vision of Future Zion (2:1–4)

Outline of Isaiah 2:5–4:6

I. The Purification of Zion (2:5–4:1)
    A. The Need for Purging (2:5–9)
    B. The Process of Purging (2:10–21)
    C. The Application to Judah (2:22–4:1)

---

16. Some of the outlines and charts in this chapter have been inspired or influenced by the exemplary structural analyses of Motyer, *Prophecy of Isaiah*, and are used by permission. My subdivisions have been determined by the discourse grammar of the texts and by Michael O'Connor's analysis of poetics. See Michael P. O'Connor, *Hebrew Verse Structure* (Winona Lake, IL: Eisenbrauns, 1982).

    1. Judgment of Zion's Leaders (3:1–15)
        (a) The Act of the Lord, YHWH of Armies (3:1a)
        (b) Collapse of Leadership (3:1b–5)
        (c) Cameo of Social Disorder (3:6–7)
        (d) Collapse of Zion (3:8)
        (d´) Judgment of Zion (3:9–11)
        (b´) Corruption of Leadership (3:12)
        (c´) Cameo of Judgment (3:13–15a)
        (a´) The Word of the Lord, YHWH of Armies (3:15b)
    2. Judgment of Zion's Women (3:16–4:1)
  II. Vision of Future Zion (4:2–6)
    A. Growth by the Lord (4:2)
    B. A Holy City (4:3–4)
    C. Canopy, Glory, and Shelter (4:5–6)

In simplified terms, chapter 1 introduces the charge of covenant disloyalty, and, after describing how this will be dealt with, culminates, in 2:1–4, in a glorious vision of the future Zion. Isaiah 2:5–4:6 returns to the lack of social justice and the process of judgment and restoration planned by YHWH. This section also ends, in chapter 4, with a glorious vision of the future Zion.

Some may object to my analysis of the first two sections of the book, since chapter 5 is commonly taken with the preceding section, resulting in a major break between chapters 5 and 6. For example, in Isa 2–5 Oswalt observes four sections that follow a pattern of hope/judgment/hope/judgment (2:1–5; 2:6–4:1; 4:2–6; 5:1–30).[17] Although special discourse markers that could adjudicate whether 5:1–30 belongs to the preceding or following section are lacking, from a theological perspective the pattern of hope/judgment/hope/judgment seems backwards. Regardless of the origin of chapter 1, if we include this chapter the pattern is judgment/hope/judgment/hope/judgment/hope, a pattern we find throughout the book. Oswalt's analysis also fails to account for the close connection between the vision in Isa 6 and the judgment in 5:1–30.[18]

Isaiah 1 as the Introduction to the Book

Many view Isa 1 as a prologue to the book, in part because similar headings are found in Isa 1:1 and 2:1. However, the heading in 2:1 is shorter, and instead of announcing "the vision that he saw" (1:1), it announces "the word that he saw." Isaiah 2:1 also omits the chronological reference to the period identified with the four kings of Judah. Suggestions on what the heading in 2:1 introduces have varied among commentators: verses 1–4, chapters 2–4, 2–5, 2–10, or 2–12. A prose rubric at 13:1

---

17. See John N. Oswalt, *The Book of Isaiah: Chapters 1–39*, NICOT (Grand Rapids: Eerdmans, 1986), 113, 120, 150–51.

18. See Peter J. Gentry, "Isaiah and Social Justice," *Midwestern Journal of Theology* 12.1 (2013): 1–15; and idem, "No One Holy Like the Lord," *Midwestern Journal of Theology* 12.1 (2013): 17–38.

indicates that 2:1 might introduce chapters 2–12. It is also possible that it originally served as a heading for the whole work, for which Isaiah later wrote chapter 1 as a prologue. This last suggestion is bolstered by the many parallels between the beginning and ending of the book and the way major themes are adumbrated in 1:2–2:4.

A primary example of this is the introduction of "social justice" in Isa 1:27, which I will now expound in some detail. Isaiah 1 concludes by twice addressing the topic of judgment and purification-restoration (vv. 24–26 and 27–31); the latter occurrence does this in reverse order (i.e., A B :: B′ A′). In the concluding unit, verses 27–31, Isaiah speaks first of renewal and redemption before describing divine judgment. Verse 27 in particular is difficult: "Zion will be ransomed by justice and those who repent by righteousness."[19] The key to interpreting this statement is understanding its poetic form along with its thematic function within the book as a whole.

According to the basic form of Hebrew poetry—lines cast as parallel pairs—the word "justice" in the first line of Isa 1:27 is matched by "righteousness" in the second. Normally in prose, when these two words are coordinated by means of a figure of speech known as a hendiadys, they represent a single concept, in this case best expressed in English by the phrase "social justice." The word-pair expresses idiomatically a single idea that is both different from and greater than that created by simply conjoining the two words. However, Hebrew poetry allows such a word-pair to be split so that half is in one line of the couplet and half in the other. The word-pair "justice" and "righteousness" is central to the discourse of the book of Isaiah, occurring at least sixteen times.[20]

When the ancient Israelites tried to boil down the more than six hundred instructions given in the old covenant to a single statement, the word-pair מִשְׁפָּט וּצְדָקָה (mišpāṭ ûṣĕdāqâ) provided a key to expressing the character required by the stipulations in the covenant as a whole.[21]

The word-pair of "justice" and "righteousness" split over parallel lines also occurs in Isa 5:7, which is the key statement and charge against Israel in the Vineyard Parable, as well as in 5:16. The word-pair is only found at critical junctures in the literary structure. So, what does it mean to be ransomed by social justice in 1:27? Significantly, in the introduction to the work as a whole, certain ideas are only hinted at or given in germ form. A careful reading of the book as a whole is required to see how this program of salvation unfolds. Not until the commencement of the last section of the book, in 56:1–8, does this finally become clear.

---

19. For example, H. G. M. Williamson notes four options for understanding "the precise force of the preposition בְּ [bě], 'in, with, by', which links the verb with *justice* and *righteousness*" (*A Critical and Exegetical Commentary on Isaiah 1–27*, vol. 1, *Isaiah 1–5*, ICC [London: T&T Clark, 2006], 156; italics original).

20. Isaiah 1:21, 27; 5:7, 16; 9:6[ET 7]; 16:5; 26:9; 28:17; 32:1, 16; 33:5; 56:1; 58:2 (2x); 59:9, 14. Three additional verses (11:4, 51:5, and 59:4) employ verbal forms of the root שׁ-פ-ט (š-p-ṭ) instead of the noun מִשְׁפָּט (mišpāṭ). See Thomas L. Leclerc, *YHWH Is Exalted in Justice: Solidarity and Conflict in Isaiah* (Minneapolis: Augsburg Fortress, 2001), esp. pp. 10–13, 88, 157.

21. Gentry and Wellum, *Kingdom through Covenant*, 565–87. Another summary word-pair is חֶסֶד וֶאֱמֶת (ḥesed we'ĕmet).

The first half of 56:1 involves a call and a command to observe justice and do righteousness. Here again, the words "justice" and "righteousness" are distributed over the two parallel lines. The second half of verse 1 provides the motive for the command: "because my salvation is about to happen and my righteousness is about to be revealed." The first half of verse 1 is a call to practice social justice, while the second half bases the command on the sovereign work of God, who demonstrates righteousness through his act of salvation.

Accordingly, the first verse of the final section of Isaiah is linked thematically with the previous sections by its use of the "social justice" word-pair. Remarkably, this pair occurs six times in the book's final eleven chapters (56:1; 58:2 [2x]; 59:4, 9, 14),[22] but not once in the section that comprises chapters 38–55. The word-pair "righteousness–salvation" or "salvation–righteousness" in the second half of Isa 56:1 speaks of righteousness as an attribute of God; it is the way he works in all his relationships. Since humans do not possess this characteristic in their relationships, it must come from God, as a gift of deliverance. This word-pair occurs within section six (Isa 38–55) in 45:8, 21; 46:13; 51:5, 6, 8. The first verse of the seventh section of Isaiah (Isa 56–66) combines phrases that are found only in the first five (Isa 1–37) and seventh (Isa 56–66) sections, respectively, with a phrase found only in the sixth section (Isa 38–55). This testifies to the unity of the book and signals that the book's final section will build on these two ideas. It is unlikely that the occurrences of these word-pairs split over parallel lines are either accidental or due to the redactional work of the disciples of Isaiah, rather than reflecting a coherence deriving from a single mind.

To summarize, in the first five (Isa 1–37) and seventh (Isa 56–66) sections of the book, we see that social justice is necessary to live in God's presence, because it is fundamental to acting as a faithful covenant partner. In the sixth section of the book (Isa 38–55), social justice comes as a divine gift, through the work of a mysterious Servant of YHWH. This structure enables us to understand correctly the statement in 1:27 that Zion will be ransomed by social justice, since it is a germ idea that requires the entire book to unfold. Any exegetical effort that focuses on Isa 1 in isolation will fail.[23]

Themes, like social justice, that are found at both the beginning and the end of the book function like bookends. To cite another example from Isa 1, verses 27b–31 portrays the future judgment to be experienced by those who pursue their own desires, power, and human-designed worship. We do not know precisely what verse 29 means by "sacred-oaks" and "gardens," but these clearly represent idolatrous practices in Isaiah's time. Remarkably, the only other clear references to these oaks and gardens are found in the book's final two chapters (65:3–5; 66:3–4, 17).

---

22. Leclerc, *YHWH Is Exalted in Justice*, esp. pages 10–13, 88, 157.

23. John Oswalt has defended a similar conclusion in "Righteousness in Isaiah: A Study of the Function of Chapters 56–66 in the Present Structure of the Book," in *Writing and Reading the Scroll of Isaiah: Studies of an Interpretive Tradition*, vol. 1, *Formation and Interpretation of Old Testament Literature*, ed. C. Broyles and C. Evans, VTSup 70 (Leiden: Brill, 1997), 177–91.

The powerlessness of these gardens is compared to trees dying for lack of water and sparks landing in tow, resulting in an unquenchable fire (1:30–31). The book concludes with similar words (66:24). Interestingly, throughout the book trees serve as a metaphor for kings and kingdoms, another idea introduced in germ form in chapter 1.[24] Just as the book begins with a broken covenant expressed in idolatrous worship and social injustice, these themes are taken up in 66:22–23. And just as the beginning chapter suggests that there will be a renewed covenant marked by true worship and social justice, so does the concluding chapter. Isaiah 66:19 contains the notion of a remnant, along with a portrayal of transformed Zion (66:7–8). To be castigated for the oaks in 1:29 is matched by being put to shame in 66:5, and the judgment is also described as fire in 66:15–16, 24. Just as Isa 1:18, 27 offers forgiveness and redemption by righteousness, so 66:2 contains a commendation of the humble and contrite in spirit. And the book appropriately begins and ends with the words of YHWH (1:2, 20; 66:2, 4).

To conclude, the numerous parallels between the beginning and ending of the book, as well as the extra heading in 2:1, suggest that chapter 1 was written at the end of the writing process as a prologue to the book. Having added chapter 1, the A B A′ structure of chapters 2–4 (Future Zion / Corrupt Zion / Future Zion) becomes an A B A′ B′ structure.

Section Three: Isaiah 5–12

We may now resume our whirlwind exploration of the literary coherence of the book by considering the third section, which continues the theme of the transformation of Zion in the context of the Syro-Ephraimite crisis.[25]

Outline of Isaiah 5:1–12:8

    I. Covenant Violation: Lack of Social Justice (5:1–30)
        A. Song of the Vineyard (5:1–7)
            1. Story of a Vineyard and Its Fruit (5:1–2)
            2. Listeners Asked for a Verdict (5:3–4)
            3. The Owner's Decision (5:5–6)
            4. Application to Judah (5:7)

---

24. Some examples are as follows (though this list is not exhaustive): trees in general (עֵץ יַעַר, ʿēṣ yaʿar): 10:19; cf. vv. 33–34; cedars (אַרְזֵי הַלְּבָנוֹן, ʾarzê hallĕbānôn): 2:13; 14:8; firs (בְּרוֹשִׁים, bĕrôšîm): 14:8; oaks (אַלּוֹנֵי הַבָּשָׁן, ʾallônê habbāšān): 2:13; root (שֹׁרֶשׁ, šōreš): 11:1, 10; 53:2; stump (גֶּזַע, gezaʿ): 11:1; branch (חֹטֶר, ḥōṭer): 11:1; shoot (יוֹנֵק, yônēq): 53:2; shoot (נֵצֶר, nēṣer): 11:1; 14:19; "from these two tails of smoking sticks" (מִשְּׁנֵי זַנְבוֹת הָאוּדִים הָעֲשֵׁנִים הָאֵלֶּה, miššĕnê zanbôt hāʾûdîm hāʿăšēnim hāʾēllê): 7:4; shade (צֵל, ṣēl): 30:3.

25. Foundational to my structural analysis of this section is the work of Christophe Rico, *La mère de l'Enfant-Roi, Isaïe 7,14: "Almâ" et "Parthenos" dans l'univers biblique; un point de vue linguistique*, La Bible en ses Traditions—Études (Paris: Cerf, 2013). Rico rightly argues that עַלְמָה (ʿalmâ) in Isa 7:14 can only refer to a "young virgin." Accordingly, Isaiah hereby gives a direct prediction of the coming king, a prediction that is unrelated to any circumstances in Isaiah's time.

    B. Bad Grapes: Indictment of God's People (5:8–24)
       1. Round One: The Primary Issues (5:8–17)
         a. Woe #1: Land-Grabbing (5:8–10)
         b. Woe #2: Partying and Revelry (5:11–12)
            i. Therefore #1: Punishment (5:13)
            ii. Therefore #2: Punishment (5:14–17)
       2. Round Two: Expansion and Explanation (5:18–24)
         a. Woe #3: Mocking Divine Justice (5:18–19)
         b. Woe #4: Inverting God's Standards (5:20)
         c. Woe #5: Relying on Human Technology (5:21)
         d. Woe #6: Partying and Inverting Social Justice (5:22–23)
            Therefore #3: Punishment (5:24)
    C. The Vineyard Ravaged (5:25–30)
        Therefore #4: Punishment
II. Commission of Isaiah (6:1–13)
    A. Vision of YHWH (6:1–4)
    B. Response of Isaiah (6:5–6)
    C. Commission of the Prophet (6:7–13)
III. The Immanuel Cycle (7:1–8:18)
    A. The Threat to the Davidic House [N][26] (7:1–9)
       1. Conspiracy against the Davidic House (7:1–2)
       2. Response of the Prophet (7:3–6)
       3. The Conspiracy Will Fail (7:7–9)
    B. Oracle Concerning Immanuel (7:10–25)
       1. Birth of Immanuel / Difficult Future [F] (7:10–17)
       2. Invasion of Egyptians and Assyrians [N] (7:18–20)
       3. Famine in Judah [N] (7:21–22)
       4. Desolation in Judah [N] (7:23–25)
    C. Oracle Concerning Maher-Shalal-Hash-Baz [N] (8:1–4)
    B.´ Second Mention of Immanuel [N] (8:5–10)
       1. Rising River: Invasion of Assyrians (8:5–8)
       2. The Anti-Assyrian Coalition Plot Foiled (8:9–10)
    C.´ Second Mention of Maher-Shalal-Hash-Baz [N] (8:11–18)
       1. Oracle: Put Your Trust in YHWH (8:11–15)
       2. Response: Isaiah and Sons Signs for Israel (8:16–18)
IV. The Cycle of El-Gibbor (8:19–10:19)
    A. Introduction (8:19–22)
       1. Oracle: Only YHWH Knows the Future (8:19)
       2. Response: No Hope Apart from Trusting God's Word (8:20)
       3. Comment: Despair of Those Who Rely on Themselves (8:21–22)
    B. The Promise of El-Gibbor [F] (8:23–9:6[ET 9:1–7])
    C. Judgment upon Israel [N] (9:7–10:4[ET 9:8–10:4])
       1. Foreign Invasion (9:7–11[ET 8–12])
       2. Corrupt Society (9:12–16[ET 13–17])
       3. Anarchy (9:17–20[ET 18–21])
       4. Exile (10:1–4)

---

26. On the meaning of the symbols [N] and [F] in this outline, see p. 242 below.

D. Divine Use of and Judgment upon Assyria [N] (10:5–19)
    1. Assyria's Plans and YHWH's Plans (10:5–11)
    2. Assyria's Pride: Evaluated by Her and the Lord (10:12–15)
    3. Divine Judgment upon Assyria (10:16–19)
V. The Cycle of the Remnant: Deliverance from Assyria /
Future Salvation for Judah (10:20–11:16)
  A. Deliverance for a Remnant [N/F] (10:20–26)
    1. A Remnant Will Rely on YHWH (10:20–23)
    2. Deliverance for the Remnant (10:24–26)
  B. Fall of Assyrian Tree and Rebirth of the Davidic Tree (10:27–11:16)
    1. Assyria Will Be Judged [N] (10:27–34)
      a. Deliverance for Judah in Assyrian Attack (10:27–32)
      b. The Lord Lops Off / Cuts Down the Forest (10:33–34)
    2. Rebirth of the Davidic Tree [F] (11:1–16)
      a. Reign of a Future King (11:1–9)
        i. Gifts Given to a Future King (11:1–3a)
        ii. The Rule of the Future King (11:3b–5)
        iii. The Harmony of the Future Kingdom (11:6–7)
        iv. The Victory of the Knowledge of YHWH (11:8–9)
      b. Nations Recognize the Davidic Monarch (11:10)
      c. Future Restoration of Israel: Return of Exiles (11:11–16)
VI. Hymn of Praise and Thanksgiving (12:1–8)

The following markers in the text were key in establishing the structure.

7:1–6	וַיְהִי בִּימֵי אָחָז	wayhî bîmê ʾāḥāz
7:7–9	כֹּה אָמַר אֲדֹנָי יְהוִה	kô ʾāmar ʾădōnāy yhwh
7:10–27	וַיּוֹסֶף יְהוָה דַּבֵּר אֶל־אָחָז לֵאמֹר	wayyôsep yhwh dabbēr ʾel-ʾāḥāz lēʾmōr
7:18	וְהָיָה בַּיּוֹם הַהוּא	wĕhāyâ bayyôm hahûʾ
7:20	בַּיּוֹם הַהוּא	bayyôm hahûʾ
7:21	וְהָיָה בַּיּוֹם הַהוּא	wĕhāyâ bayyôm hahûʾ
7:23	וְהָיָה בַּיּוֹם הַהוּא	wĕhāyâ bayyôm hahûʾ
8:1–4	וַיֹּאמֶר	wayyōʾmer
8:5–8	וַיֹּסֶף יְהוָה דַּבֵּר אֵלַי עוֹד לֵאמֹר	wayyôsep yhwh dabbēr ʾēlay ʿôd lēʾmōr
8:9–10	רֹעוּ . . . עֻצוּ	rōʿû . . . ʿūṣû
8:11–15	כִּי כֹה אָמַר יְהוָה אֵלַי כְּחֶזְקַת הַיָּד	kî kô ʾāmar yhwh ʾēlay kĕhezqat hayyād
8:16–18	צוֹר תְּעוּדָה חֲתוֹם תּוֹרָה בְּלִמֻּדָי	ṣôr tĕʿûdâ ḥătôm tôrâ bĕlimmūdāy
8:19–23a[ET 9:1a]	וְכִי־יֹאמְרוּ אֲלֵיכֶם	wĕkî-yōʾmĕrû ʾălêkem

8:23b–9:6[ET 1b–7]	כָּעֵת הָרִאשׁוֹן הֵקַל	kā'ēt hārī'šôn hēqal
9:7–11[ET 8–12]	דָּבָר שָׁלַח אֲדֹנָי בְּיַעֲקֹב	dābār šālaḥ 'ădōnāy bĕya'ăqōb
9:12–20[ET 13–21]	וְהָעָם לֹא־שָׁב עַד־הַמַּכֵּהוּ	wĕhā'ām lō'-šāb 'ad-hammakkēhû
10:1–4	הוֹי הַחֹקְקִים חִקְקֵי־אָוֶן	hôy haḥōqĕqîm ḥiqqê-'āwen
10:5–11	הוֹי אַשּׁוּר שֵׁבֶט אַפִּי	hôy 'aššûr šēbeṭ 'appî
10:12–19	וְהָיָה כִּי־יְבַצַּע אֲדֹנָי אֶת־כָּל־מַעֲשֵׂהוּ בְּהַר צִיּוֹן	wĕhāyâ kî-yĕbaṣṣa' 'ădōnāy 'et-kol-ma'ăśēhû bĕhar ṣiyyôn
10:20–23	וְהָיָה בַּיּוֹם הַהוּא	wĕhāyâ bayyôm hahû'
10:24–26	לָכֵן כֹּה־אָמַר אֲדֹנָי יְהוִה צְבָאוֹת	lākēn kô-'āmar 'ădōnāy yhwh ṣĕbā'ôt
10:27–32	וְהָיָה בַּיּוֹם הַהוּא	wĕhāyâ bayyôm hahû'
10:33–34	הִנֵּה הָאָדוֹן יְהוָה צְבָאוֹת	hinnê hā'ādôn yhwh ṣĕbā'ôt
11:1–9	וְיָצָא חֹטֶר מִגֵּזַע יִשָׁי	wĕyāṣā' ḥōṭer miggēza' yišāy
11:10–16	וְהָיָה בַּיּוֹם הַהוּא	wĕhāyâ bayyôm hahû'

The third section of the book of Isaiah runs from the beginning of chapter 5 through the end of chapter 12 and expands on previously identified themes a third time, in the context of the Syro-Ephraimite crisis. This section concludes by describing a renewed Zion, and in focusing on a future king and a second exodus, it offers a glorious vision of the future. Isaiah 5–12 introduces a central component in the plot structure: the first of two kings, Ahaz and Hezekiah. This royal theme continues to the end of the book: chapters 38–39 introduce the sixth section, which concerns Hezekiah, followed by chapters 40–55, which focus on the servant king. The conquering/saving king is also prominent in 61:1–63:6, at the center of the seventh and final section, Isa 56–66.

I have marked the outline of chapters 7–12 with two symbols, [F] and [N]. [F] identifies predictions concerning the distant future, while [N] identifies those concerning the near future. In these chapters, oracles concerning the distant and near futures are placed side by side, creating a single, panoramic scene. As the outline above suggests, just as the promise of El-Gibbor occurs next to an announcement of Israel's imminent judgment and the promise of the shoot from David's stump occurs next to an announcement of Assyria's imminent judgment, so the oracle concerning the birth of Immanuel appears side by side with the predicted defeat of the Syro-Ephraimite coalition at the hands of the Assyrians. The result is three panels, each depicting a coming king from a different perspective. The oracles concerning Maher-Shalal-Hash-Baz and Immanuel relate to different children but are placed side by side.

The oracles concerning the distant and near futures are intentionally set side by side for good reason. First, according to Deut 18:22, "When a prophet speaks in the LORD's name, and the message fails to be fulfilled, that is a message the LORD has not spoken. The prophet has spoken it presumptuously. Do not be afraid of him" (author's translation). This text is fundamental, paving the way for the structures we find in this and other books, such as Daniel and Zechariah. Each book contains predictions concerning the near future that come true, attesting to the genuineness of the prophet and encouraging confidence in his predictions concerning the distant future, which his immediate audience could not possibly have evaluated. This explains the bipartite structure of books like Daniel (1–6 / 7–12), Isaiah (1–39 / 40–66), and Zechariah (1–8 / 9–14).

Second, as will be evident from the outline of the book of Isaiah's sixth section, chapters 38–55, presented below, the deliverance predicted for God's people involves two stages: (1) release from Babylonian exile, and (2) redemption from sin. The second stage will require much more time than the first stage. Based on Jer 25, Daniel thought the exile would end in his day, but as he learns in chapter 9 of the book of Daniel, another Egyptian bondage of sorts was coming before the people would experience a new exodus.

Section Four: Isaiah 13–27

Alec Motyer has provided an overall outline for the Oracles concerning the Foreign Nations that is firmly rooted in the literary features of the text.[27] He divides the text into three groups of five oracles, with the fourth oracle in each section focusing to a greater or lesser degree on Israel, the people of God:

A	B	C
Babylon (13:1–14:27)	The Desert by the Sea (Babylon) (21:1–10)	The City of **Wasteland** (24:1–20)
Political overthrow	*Religious overthrow*	*Broken **covenant** (5) Broken city gates (12)*
Philistia (14:28–32)	Silence (**Dumah**) (21:11–12)	Zion's King (24:21–23)
A Davidic king will yet reign in Zion	*Indefinite continuance of **circumstances** as they are*	*"After many days"*
Moab (15:1–16:14)	Evening (Arabia) (21:13–17)	The Great Banquet (25:1–12)
Moab in need, but through pride refuses shelter in Zion	*Desert tribes in need: no ultimate refuge in mutual security*	*All nations feasted in Zion save Moab, excluded by pride*

27. I reproduce a stylistically modified version of Motyer's chart from *Prophecy of Isaiah*, 133, below. I have modified several of his headings, indicated here in bold font. According to Motyer, *Prophecy of Isaiah*, 131–34, the words in normal font indicate the addressee or basic subject of the oracle or subsection, while the words in italic font indicate the theme(s).

Damascus/Ephraim (17:1–18:7)	The Valley of Vision (Jerusalem) (22:1–25)	The City of God (26:1–20)
Strong cities forsaken (9); the forgotten rock (10)	*The city torn down (10)*	*The strong city (1); the everlasting rock (4)*
Egypt (19:1–20:6)	Tyre (23:1–18)	The Final Gathering (27:1–13)
Co-equal membership: Egypt, Assyria, and Israel (19:24–25)	*Holiness to the Lord (23:18)*	*The harvest from Egypt and Assyria (27:12–13)*

Space constraints allow me to examine only the first group of five oracles. In the following remarks I will seek to demonstrate how Isa 13–20 is connected to chapters 7–12, namely, in developing the promise of a future deliverance and king and relating these to the nations. Foundational to the flow of thought here are the covenants YHWH made with Abraham and David, since the covenant made at Sinai has been violated and is now at an end. I will briefly consider the literary structures of the first five oracles concerning the foreign nations to see how the nations' relationship to Zion becomes central to their blessing and judgment, in accordance with Gen 12:1–3.

Oracle concerning Babylon (13:1–14:27)

    A The Day of YHWH (13:2–16)
        B Overthrow of Babylon (13:17–22)
            C Restoration of YHWH's People (14:1–2)
        B′ Overthrow of Babylon (14:3–23)
    A′ The End of Assyrian Power (14:24–27)

As is common in Hebrew literature, this oracle concerning Babylon and Assyria (two world powers associated at that time) is divided into two larger subunits, 13:2–22 and 14:3–27. The passage 14:1–2 occurs at the center of a chiastic structure that portrays Israel as restored and the nations among it as male and female servants. This second point may be construed as many of Jesus' disciples understood it.[28] They foresaw Israel on top and all nations subject to it. However, since Isa 14:1–2 should be interpreted in light of Isa 38–55 and 56–66, this is a misinterpretation. First, chapters 38–55 introduce a future servant who will do for Israel what she has failed to do herself in service to YHWH. Second, Isa 54:17 clearly demonstrates that the servant will spawn *servants* as a result of his finished work. Finally, chapters 56–66 declare that these future servants will include eunuchs and foreigners who function as Levites and priests in the restored worshipping community on Mount Zion. Thus, in 14:1–2 Isaiah baits his readers by speaking of the inclusion of the Gentiles.

---

28. Cf. Acts 1:6 and the expectations of Ps 2:9; cf. Rev 2:27.

Oracle against Philistia (14:28–32)

The oracle concerning Philistia also divides into two sections, each half of which is repeated, creating an overall A B A′ B′ structure. Following his pronouncement of judgment upon the Philistines, the prophet announces future safety for the wretched in Zion.

A Future Destruction for the Philistines (14:29)
  B Future Safety for the Wretched in Zion (14:30)
A′ Future Destruction for the Philistines (14:31)
  B′ Future Safety for the Wretched in Zion (14:32)

At the beginning of this oracle, the Philistines are told not to celebrate because the rod that struck them is broken. Using mixed metaphors involving plants and different kinds of snakes, the oracle warns them of a future ruler who will force them to submit. While some scholars associate this with a coming Assyrian king, others see a future descendant of Ahaz. Although the interpretation of several details is uncertain, the main points are clear. With the death of the king, whether Judean or Assyrian, the Philistines are not to think they have escaped judgment. God promises safety for those in Zion but warns of total destruction for the nations who have not sought refuge with the anointed king who rules in Zion.

Oracle against Moab (15:1–16:14)

A The Sudden Destruction of Moab (15:1)
  B The Lament of the Moabites (15:2–4)
    C Grief over Moab (15:5–9)
      D A Plea for Safety in Zion and Moab's Pride (16:1–6)
  B′ The Lament of the Moabites (16:7–8)
    C′ The Grief of the Lord over Moab (16:9–12)
A′ The Imminent Destruction of Moab (16:13–14)

All three of the topics found in Isa 15–16 are dealt with twice, and although the structure in which they are presented and represented is not a perfect chiasm, 16:1–6 is clearly central. There we find this remarkable statement:

> And a throne will be established in *ḥesed*,
>   and one will sit on it in *'ĕmet*,
>   in the tent of David judging
>   and seeking justice
> and swift in righteousness. (v. 5)

This short declaration promises a descendant of David whose rule will exhibit perfectly all the instructions in the Covenant. The word-pairs חֶסֶד (*ḥesed*) and אֱמֶת (*'ĕmet*) and "justice" and "righteousness" are split, in both cases, over parallel lines that form bookends for the central statement, offering another example of

the latter word-pair being found at significant points within the literary sections
in which it is found.

The oracle concerning Moab is emotionally charged. Not only the nation itself, but YHWH also, is grieved over the judgment of Moab. Moab is commanded
to pay tribute to the commander of Israel, because only there will it find safety.
YHWH calls the people of Moab "my fugitives" and commands Zion to allow the
fugitives to stay with her, although pride unfortunately prevents them from doing
so. The focus of the chiastic center of the oracles, however, is on the social justice
established by the Davidic king.

Oracle against the Superpowers of This World and the Northern Kingdom (17:1–18:7)

> A The Superpowers of This World (17:1–3)
>   B Judgment on the Northern Kingdom (17:4–6)
>   C People Will Turn from Idols to Creator (17:7–8)
>   B′ Judgment on the Northern Kingdom (17:9–11)
> A′ The Superpowers of This World (17:12–18:7)

Like the first oracle (13:1–14:27), the fourth (17:1–18:7) consists of two corresponding sections (AB and B′A′) that are placed on either side of a central section (C). The first section (A) focuses on destruction brought to Syria and the
Northern Kingdom by the eastern and western superpowers of the world, Assyria
and Nubia. The last section (A′) takes up the topic again and shows that this ter-
ror will be limited (by God). The second section (B) deals specifically with the
judgment on the Northern Kingdom. The fourth section (B′) matches the second
and gives the reason for this judgment. In the central section (C), metaphors from
the agricultural harvest in 17:5–6 anticipate the salvation of a remnant, which is
portrayed in 17:7 not in particularistic terms, but rather in terms of humanity in
general (אָדָם, 'ādām).

Oracle concerning Egypt (19:1–20:6)

> A The Smiting of Egypt in General Terms (19:1–15)
>   B The Healing of Egypt (19:16–25)
> A′ The Smiting of Egypt in Detailed Terms (20:1–6)

Motyer correctly observes that the oracle concerning Egypt is divided into
three parts, with the healing of Egypt at the center of the chiasm. The future portrayed for Egypt involves five cities, including Heliopolis, which will speak the
language of Canaan. The prophet also envisions an altar to YHWH in the midst
of Egypt and a memorial pillar of stone at the border, the latter similar to the one
set up by the newly established nation of Israel in the book of Joshua (22:10–11).
Accordingly, in the future Egypt will become a country like Israel. The climax appears in 19:24–25:

In that day Israel will be the third with Egypt and Assyria, a blessing in the midst of the earth, whom the Lord of hosts has blessed, saying, "Blessed be Egypt my people, and Assyria the work of my hands, and Israel my inheritance." (ESV)

Here Isaiah predicts that the renewal and restoration of Zion will involve taking Israel's worst enemies and incorporating them into the one people of God, giving names to Assyria and Egypt that once were used only of Israel.

Noting Motyer's division of Isa 13–27 into three sections, each containing five oracles, we observe a clear plan in the overall structure of the Oracles concerning the Foreign Nations. The oracles in the first group of five all have headings that refer to geographical entities well known to the average Israelite. As discussed earlier, the headings of the second set of five use enigmatic titles. Finally, the last group of five lacks prose headings. These features correlate with a progression in the groups of oracles. The first set of five basically addresses the near future, the second set concerns the distant future, and the third portrays a future that is even further removed.

This progression correlates with the use of apocalyptic language, metaphors, and symbols in the various oracles. Were I to describe events in the United States one year from now, the cultural setting, people, and places would probably remain consistent with the present. Were I to describe events five hundred years in the future, new metaphors and symbols would be required. Were I to describe the even more distant future, everything would have to be communicated via metaphors and symbols. It would be like explaining to a man I met in the jungle of Papua New Guinea how my Macintosh computer worked.

Some scholars have dated the apocalyptic section (chs. 24–27) to a later time than the lifetime of Isaiah of Jerusalem. This dating fails to consider the fact that apocalyptic language is based on metaphors and symbolism drawn from the creation account in Gen 1–2, used and developed more fully by Isaiah than any other prophet. Just as Jer 4 describes the attack of the armies of Babylon and the coming destruction of Jerusalem as a kind of reversal of the creation events portrayed in Gen 1, so Isaiah uses similarly colorful metaphors in Isa 13 and 24–27. This progression of thought is completely natural for a people whose theology is based on the notion of one *creator god*.[29] Moreover, Isa 24–27, the final group of oracles in the fourth section of the book, contemplates the future in general terms, which makes the dating of these chapters fully compatible with that of the oracles concerning the foreign nations in Isa 13–23, given the intertwining of the futures of Israel and the nations in the first two groups of five (for example, in Isa 19:25).

In the fifth and sixth sections of the "seven Bose speakers" of Isaiah, ideas that have only been previously introduced as seed thoughts receive extended discussion. First, the issue of trusting in YHWH rather than in humans—the City of God versus the City of Man—is treated in six woes in Isa 28–35.

---

29. See ch. 8 of N. T. Wright, *The New Testament and the People of God*, Christian Origins and the Question of God 1 (Minneapolis: Fortress, 1992).

Section Five: Isaiah 28–37

The structure of Isa 28–35 can be described as follows:[30]

Principles	Applications
28:1–29 When God's people reject his word (9–13)[31] and covenant (14–15), destruction follows (18–22), held within divine purposes (23–29)	30:1–33 Refuge is sought in Egypt (1–7), rejecting the Lord's word (8–12), but his ultimate (13–26) and immediate (27–33) purposes are settled
29:1–14 There is disaster and deliverance (1–8) but historical deliverance does not change people spiritually. This needs a further divine action (9–14), which is already planned	31:1–32:20 Divine deliverance scorns both Egypt's help and Assyria's enmity (31:1–9). Beyond lies the perfect kingdom with true king (32:1) and transformed people (2–8). The pattern of history will be repeated: overthrow (9–14) and transformation (15–20)
29:15–24 People may think to run the world without God (15), but he is the sovereign and his transforming purposes (16–17) will work out spiritually (18–19), morally and socially (20–21), fulfilling what began in Abraham (22) and establishing a truly renewed people (23–24)	33:1–35:10 Treacherous people (33:1, 8) may seem to rule but divine sovereignty remains (33:3, 10). The perfect kingdom (33:13–24), morally and socially (33:15) and spiritually (33:24), will come. The enemy will finally be destroyed (chapter 34) and the redeemed will gather to Zion (chapter 35)

The prose of chapters 36–37 concludes the fifth section of the book of Isaiah, and the prose of chapters 38–39 introduces the sixth section. Prose is used similarly elsewhere, in shorter sections.[32]

---

30. The following outline is copied from Motyer, *Prophecy of Isaiah*, 228.

31. *Sic* (Motyer, *Prophecy of Isaiah*, 228). 1–13 or 7–13 may be intended here instead.

32. Isaiah 13 is headed by a prose rubric. The chiastic center of the oracle against Babylon (13:1–14:27), namely, 14:1–2, is prose, and the parable in 14:4b–21 is introduced by a prose statement (14:3–4a). The end of this oracle (14:24–27) is also prose. Isaiah 15, which begins the oracle against Moab (15:1–16:14), is headed by a prose rubric. The center of the chiasm in this oracle is not a bicolon or couplet. The end (16:13–14) is prose. Isaiah 17, which begins the oracle against Syria and the northern kingdom (17:1–18:7), is also headed by a prose rubric. Like 14:1–2, the chiastic center of this oracle, 17:7–8, is prose. This oracle also concludes

Section Six: Isaiah 38–55

Isaiah 38–55 can be outlined as follows:

Outline of Isaiah 38–55[33]

    A. Historical prologue: Hezekiah's fatal choice (38:1–39:8)
        B. Universal consolation (40:1–42:17)
            1. The consolation of Israel (40:1–41:20)
            2. The consolation of the Gentiles (41:21–42:17)
        C. Promises of redemption (42:18–44:23)
            1. Release **from Babylon** (42:18–43:21)
            2. Forgiveness **of Sins** (43:22–44:23)
        C'. Agents of redemption (44:24–53:12)
            1. Cyrus: liberation (44:24–48:22)
            2. The Servant: atonement (49:1–53:12)
        B'. Universal proclamation (54:1–55:13)
            1. The call to Zion (54:1–17)
            2. The call to the world (55:1–13)

Isaiah 38–55 looks farther into the future, beyond the judgment of exile to the comfort and consolation of Israel, that is, the return of the people from exile. Then YHWH will establish Zion as the people/place where all nations may seek his instruction for social justice. This scene is described in the language of the exodus, though the return from the Babylonian exile is portrayed as an even greater exodus![34] This new exodus also involves the term "redeem" (ג-א-ל, *g-ʾ-l*), which refers to the duties of one's nearest relative. Since, by virtue of the Israelite covenant, YHWH is Israel's nearest relative, he will "buy back" his people from exile as he once delivered them from bondage and slavery in Egypt. However, the return from exile is not a chronologically singular event. The promises of redemption envision two distinct events: release (42:18–43:21) and forgiveness (43:22–44:23). Release involves bringing the people physically out of exile in Babylon and back to their own land; forgiveness entails dealing fully and finally with their sin and the broken covenant. To adapt a common expression, you can take the people out of

---

in prose (18:7). For Isa 19–20, a prose rubric heading appears again, but the entire central section of the chiasm in this oracle (19:16–25), as well as the final section (20:1–6), is prose. Hebrew literature typically encases poetry in prose settings. We observe these structures in macro-sections as well as in micro-sections. The norms of Hebrew literature do not support interpreting Isa 40 as the beginning of a new section.

33. Reproduced from Motyer, *Prophecy of Isaiah*, 289. I have modified a number of the headings in minor ways, indicated here by bold font.

34. For a discussion of exodus language and themes in Isaiah, see Bernhard W. Anderson, "Exodus Typology in Second Isaiah," in *Israel's Prophetic Heritage: Essays in Honor of James Muilenburg*, ed. Bernhard W. Anderson and Walter Harrelson (New York: Harper, 1962), 177–95.

Babylon, but how do you get Babylon out of the people?[35] The books of Ezra and Nehemiah depict a people that had returned from exile but had not changed in their relationship to God; the failure to practice social justice remained a central problem. For this reason, for the postexilic prophet Zechariah the return from exile was both a present reality and a future hope.[36] The exile would be over only when YHWH dealt with the people's sin and renewed the covenant, the temple was rebuilt, and YHWH returned to dwell in their midst as King. In the book of Isaiah, the two agents of redemption, Cyrus and the Servant, are linked to these two stages of redemption. Furthermore, the oracles concerning the foreign nations in chapters 13–27 have prepared the reader for the new relationship between Israel and the nations that we see in the B-sections of the outline found immediately above.

This interpretation of these chapters differs radically from that of Berges, who sees 42:1–4 as an original Cyrus oracle reinterpreted to suit the Servant of YHWH. Moreover, Berges does not view 42:5–9 as an expansion of the first Servant Song but as Cyrus' commissioning. He states:

> After the self-predication of Yhwh in 42.5 and 8, which frames the Cyrus oracle, v. 9 brings the unit to a close, on the one hand once more emphasizing the end of the past salvation history (הנה באו הראשנות), and on the other hand, proclaiming a "new" thing (חדשות). What the exilic prophet means by this new thing is clarified by the recasting in 42:14–16 and by the close parallels of 43:18–19. "Remember not the former things! Have no regard for the things of old! Behold I am doing a new thing; now it springs forth, do you not perceive it? Indeed I will make a path through the wilderness, and rivers in a dry land." The exilic prophet does not conceive of the new things as specific events, such as the return from exile, but rather as the continual implementation of the divine will for Israel's salvation; he makes no vague announcement that has to be deciphered, but rather uses these metaphors in order to relieve the exilic community of their anxiety about the future.[37]

Berges discusses the literary structure of Isa 40–55 in terms of a basic "Isaianic" stratum with a Golah redaction and a first and second Jerusalem redaction. Because he does not view 42:5–9 as a recursive and repetitive treatment of the Servant of YHWH, these verses can be severed from it. Consequently, in his analysis of verse 9 Berges fails to understand the former things as referring to the events of the exodus and the new things as referring to the new exodus, that is, as two stages of restoration whose chronology in Isaiah is unclear. In addition, he does not correlate Isa 43:18–19, in which God makes a way in the desert for the blind (see 42:18–19), with Isa 6:9–10 and new exodus language, a correlation that leads to the conclusion that the blind are the remnant from Isaiah's Jerusalem who are brought not only out of Babylon, but eventually also out of slavery to sin. Berges' interpretation of 42:9 also puts it at odds with 46:9–11 (understanding the "bird of prey" "from the east" in 46:11 as Cyrus), which connects the new things directly with Cyrus.

---

35. The vision in Zech 5:5–11 of the woman in a basket carried by flying women back to Babylon apparently symbolizes the task of removing Babylon from the people.

36. In a book addressed to returned exiles, Zech 2:7[ET 3] calls for the exiles to escape from Babylon.

37. Berges, *Book of Isaiah*, 322.

Section Seven: Isaiah 56–66

The seventh and final section of Isaiah consists of chapters 56–66. As noted previously, typical of Hebrew prophecy, some parts focus on the people of God in Isaiah's time and some focus on the distant future.

Outline of Isaiah 56:1–66:24[38]

A   Universal vision (56:1–8)
  B   Problems (56:9–59:15a)
    C   Divine warrior (59:15b–21)
      D   Nucleus (servant, Israel, Zion) (60–62)
    C′ Divine warrior (63:1–6)
  B′ Problems (63:7–66:17)
A′ Universal vision (66:18–24)

Detailed Outline of 65:1–66:24[39]

A   YHWH's Call to Those Who Had Not Sought Him (65:1)
  B   YHWH's Repayment of a Rebellious People (65:2–7)
    C   Promise of a Preserved Remnant (65:8–10)
      D   Those Who Forsake YHWH Destined for Slaughter (65:11–12)
        E   Joys of YHWH's Servants in the New Creation (65:13–25)
      D′ Where Is the True Temple of YHWH and Its Worship? (66:1–4)
    C′ Assurance for Those Who Tremble at YHWH's Word (66:5–14)
  B′ Divine Judgment upon the False Worshippers (66:15–17)
A′ Worldwide Pilgrimage to the Temple of YHWH (66:18–24)

Earlier in the essay, I noted that Isa 56:1 connects the word-pair "justice" and "righteousness," which is found in the book's first five sections and seventh sections, with the word-pair "righteousness" and "salvation," which occurs in the sixth section. Since the practice of social justice characterizes those who are faithfully in covenant with YHWH, the emphasis on true worship in Isa 56–66 is not surprising. In these concluding chapters, the prophet contrasts the righteous and the wicked, as well as the blessings awaiting the former and the everlasting judgments awaiting the latter. Central to the seventh section (Isa 56–66) is the warrior king portrayed in C and C′ (Isa 59:15b–21 and 63:1–6).

---

38. This outline is reproduced from Boda, *Severe Mercy*, 213, by permission of Eisenbrauns.

39. The textual subdivisions in the following outline are those of Motyer (*Prophecy of Isaiah*, 522–23) but I have offered different summaries for the nine subsections. Motyer also distinguishes a tenth and final subsection: "Conclusion: Jerusalem, pilgrimage center for the whole world" (66:22–24).

Conclusion

Fundamental to the approach advocated here is a recognition of the recursive, resumptive character of Hebrew discourse and literature. Once one realizes that these texts are written using this ancient eastern convention, it becomes clear that this convention is a hermeneutical key to understanding difficult passages, not one that should prompt one to attribute different passages to different redactors or sources. Several brief examples will suffice:

> All the stars of the heavens will be dissolved
>> and the sky rolled up like a scroll;
>> all the starry host will fall
>>> like withered leaves from the vine,
>>> like shriveled figs from the fig tree.
> My sword has drunk its fill in the heavens;
>> see, it descends in judgment on Edom,
>> the people I have totally destroyed.
>>> (Isa 34:4–5, NIV 1984)

> In that day the LORD will punish
> the powers in the heavens above
> and the kings on the earth below.
>> (Isa 24:21, NIV 1984)

Isaiah 34:4–9 pictures Edom as a sacrifice. This section contains the strange statement: "My sword has drunk its fill in the heavens; see, it descends in judgment upon Edom." In the ancient world, people—including the biblical writers—assumed a close connection between events on earth and events in heaven. Daniel 9 portrays heavenly princes behind the activities of the nations. Isaiah also mentions the heavenly powers who must be punished, in 24:21 and 27:1. Just as in 24:21 God first punishes the evil spiritual powers ruling over the nations and then the nations themselves, so in 34:4–5 he punishes the dark powers in the heavens before his sword comes to the earth to deal with nations in rebellion against him. The language in 34:5 draws on that of Deut 32:40–42, where the nations whom God has used to discipline his own people have wrongly concluded that they achieved this by their own power and the power of false gods. Here a difficult text (Isa 34:5) is clarified by appealing to the resumptive technique employed in parallelism.

> The fortress will be abandoned,
>> the noisy city deserted;
> citadel and watchtower will become a wasteland forever,
>> the delight of donkeys, a pasture for flocks,
> till the Spirit is poured on us from on high,
>> and the desert becomes a fertile field,
>> and the fertile field seems like a forest.
> Justice will dwell in the desert,
>> his righteousness live in the fertile field.
>>> (Isa 32:14–16, NIV 1984)

This is another difficult passage. The Spirit is poured out from heaven and the desert becomes fertile; justice will dwell in the desert. This is reminiscent of 11:1–9, where the Spirit of God is given without measure to a future king, and the king's gifts are used to establish justice in the land, resulting in a new creation. As in 32:14–16, the giving of the Spirit is linked with the new world inhabited by justice. Accordingly, we may interpret 32:15–16 as an abbreviated reference to 11:1–9, which also associates the giving of the Spirit with a new creation where righteousness dwells.

> Then the eyes of those who see will no longer be closed,
>   and the ears of those who hear will listen.
> The fearful heart will know and understand,
>   and the stammering tongue will be fluent and clear.
>   (Isa 32:3–4, NIV 1984)

Isaiah 32:3–4 describes what will happen when a righteous king rules. If one compares 29:11 and 6:9–13 with this passage, its meaning becomes clearer. Since Isaiah's audience had already rejected his message, their ears will not hear, their eyes will not see, and their heart will not understand. 32:3–4 declares simply that when the broken covenant is renewed in the new creation, the people of God will grasp his messages to them through Isaiah.

Finally, grasping Isaiah's vision of the future Zion requires putting all the visions of 2:1–4, 4:2–6, 11:1–9, chapter 25, and chapter 65—texts that are found in the first, second, third, fourth, and seventh sections of the book and that portray a mountain paradise—together into one holographic image. That only the fifth and sixth sections of the book do not reach their climax in a mountain paradise suggests they serve a different purpose in the larger literary structure.

The evidence marshalled here indicates that the larger literary structures within a book contribute as significantly to its message as the individual texts of which they are comprised. The elaborate structures in Isaiah and the literary coherence of the book reflect the work of a single literary genius. To attribute them to a later editor rather than to Isaiah of Jerusalem is to posit an unknown and unidentified genius in Israel as the creator of this remarkably unified work. This is unconvincing. The literary structures of Isaiah are so intricate and intertwined with the message of the book that to attribute parts of the book to the disciples of Isaiah or later redactors is implausible.

11

Authors and Readers (Real or Implicit) and the Unity/Disunity of Isaiah

Mark J. Boda

Watching the Game from the Balcony

During the NBA finals of 1991 Michael Jordan and his Chicago Bulls lost only two games. The more famous of the two was the opening game of their final series against the Lakers. But there was another, long forgotten by most: one played on May 10, 1991, the 99–97 victory of Charles Barkley and his 76ers in the Philadelphia Spectrum. Why do I remember? Because I was there.

It was truly a highlight of that summer between seminary and doctoral studies, a bright spot in the midst of my short-lived painting career in the inner city of Philadelphia. A seminary buddy called me up with the offer of tickets to an NBA playoff game. My response was one of disbelief and he was honest enough to tell me that we would be in the fourth balcony, immediately assuring me that we would be in the second row, so at least we would only have one row in front of us. We arrived that night with great anticipation and began our ascent to our loft; up and up we climbed until we entered into the fourth balcony. As we stood at the entrance it dawned on us that we were indeed in the second row of the fourth balcony, but unfortunately the second row turned out to be the final row of that great stadium with a concrete wall directly behind us. As we sat in our perch far above the basketball court, we could see the balconies below us and wondered what it would be like to sit in a seat in one of those closer balconies, let alone in the microscopic courtside seats. That night we watched the game from a distance and took in what turned out to be an epic battle between two superstars, a piece of history that would contrast with most of the games played that May by Jordan and his Bulls.

It appears to me that my experience that night was in some ways akin to our experience of reading certain books within the Scriptures. As readers we sit at varying levels of remove from the action taking place on the court below us. Whether it is Luke depicting for us the ministry of Jesus or the Chronicler presenting the exploits of David, we as an audience sit with ancient authors and audiences in a balcony at varying levels of remove from the events being described. In my teaching and writing I have come to distinguish between what I call referential historical context and compositional historical context, the former referring to the historical context of the events found in a text, the latter to the historical context of the one(s) responsible for relating these events.[1] In Scripture we are nearly always watching the game from the balcony, and while this is true for historiographical works, it is also true for prophetic material.

Voices and Writers

Evidence for our position in the balcony is readily seen in the various voices in the book of Isaiah that present the material to the reader. The superscriptions found in Isa 1:1, 2:1, and 13:1, for instance, highlight a voice presenting the words of Isaiah to the audience. These superscriptions are distinct from the autobiographical depiction found, for instance, in Isa 6, in which Isaiah speaks in the first person about one of his revelatory experiences. The use of the first-person style makes clear the distinction between the third-person voice and the prophet. Throughout Isaiah one also finds narratives that depict Isaiah in action and within these narratives the prophet's words are set in a context of dialogue with other characters and events. Some of these narratives are expressed in the third person, as a voice speaks about Isaiah (e.g., Isa 7, 36–39), while others are expressed in the first person, as the prophet speaks autobiographically (Isa 6, 8).[2] This modulation between first and third person highlights the presence of a voice in the text distinct from the prophet that is presenting to the reader the words and actions of the prophet. While it is possible that the prophet himself is both biographer and autobiographer, shifting between third and first person, this does not appear to me to be the simplest reading of the text.[3]

Other biblical books provide insight into such modulation between third- and first-person accounts.[4] At the outset of Ecclesiastes a third-person voice identifies

---

1. For an example, see Mark J. Boda, "Judges," in *The Expositor's Bible Commentary*, vol. 2, *Numbers–Ruth*, rev. ed., ed. Tremper Longman III and David E. Garland (Grand Rapids: Zondervan, 2012), 1047–52.

2. Scholars have often posited a memoir of the prophet (*Denkschrift*) as foundational for the book form or at least an early book form; cf. Karl Budde, *Jesaja's Erleben: Eine gemeinverständliche Auslegung der Denkschrift des Propheten (Kap. 6,1–9,6)* (Gotha: L. Klotz, 1928); R. E. Clements, *Isaiah 1–39*, NCB (Grand Rapids: Eerdmans, 1980), 4.

3. For the diversity in evangelical approaches to these various voices in the book, compare the following: Edward J. Young, who argues that "the prophet Isaiah himself was the author of the entire book; he himself committed it to writing, and he was responsible for collecting his messages and placing them in the present book which bears his name" (*The Book of Isaiah*, NICOT [Grand Rapids: Eerdmans, 1965], 1:8); John N. Oswalt, who speaks of "brief editorial or transitional materials . . . added, either by Isaiah himself or those working with him," and who is open to the possibility that Isaiah used "amanuenses" (*The Book of Isaiah, Chapters 1–39*, NICOT [Grand Rapids: Eerdmans, 1986], 26); and John Goldingay, who distinguishes between the "Ambassador" (Isaiah, who is the "I" as well as the one who introduces YHWH's words) and the "Disciple" ("someone speaking about Isaiah in the third person in order to introduce him"), but also adds the "Poet" (40:6; 50:4) and the "Preacher" (61:1) (*Isaiah*, NIBC [Peabody, MA: Hendrickson, 2001], 3–4).

4. See David M. Carr, "Isaiah 40:1–11 in the Context of the Macrostucture of Second Isaiah," in *Discourse Analysis of Biblical Literature: What It Is and What It Offers*, ed. Walter

what follows as "the words of Qoheleth, the son of David, king in Jerusalem" (1:1) and even summarizes a key component of that message in 1:2 ("says Qoheleth").[5] This third-person voice reemerges at a key point in the presentation of Qoheleth's words in 7:27 ("says Qoheleth"), and again at the conclusion of the presentation with a summary in 12:8 matching that found in 1:2. What follows in 12:9–14 reveals that this third-person voice is not Qoheleth himself, but rather a sage presenting Qoheleth's teaching to a disciple. Similar to this is the book of Ezra-Nehemiah.[6] Autobiographical speech occurs at various places within the book in the sections focused on the activities of Ezra and Nehemiah. While Ezra 7–10 begins and ends with third-person description about Ezra, at a certain point there is a shift into first-person speech, beginning in 7:27 and extending to the end of chapter 9. A similar trend can be seen in Neh 1–13, which begins in the third person in 1:1a and then, in 1:1b, shifts into the first person, which is most likely the voice through Neh 7:5. Following the citation of the list of early returnees in chapter 7, Neh 8 depicts Nehemiah in the third person (see v. 9), as also do Neh 10 (v. 1) and Neh 12 (v. 26). The first-person account recommences in 12:31 and continues to the end of the book (13:31). In Ezra-Nehemiah autobiographical material is included within a larger literary complex presented by someone distinguished from the first-person autobiographical voice.

Although they are similar to Isaiah in their common use of autobiographical speech, these two examples are culled from material distinct from Isaiah in terms of genre (wisdom, historiography). But examples closer to Isaiah in terms of both genre and autobiographical voice are the prophetic books of Jeremiah, Ezekiel, and the Twelve.

Jeremiah 1:1–3 contains a third-person voice introducing us to Jeremiah and his historical context.[7] The first-person voice of Jeremiah is clearly evident throughout the book, beginning straightaway with Jer 1:4 ("Now the word of the LORD came to me saying . . ."). But this first-person voice alternates with a third-person voice that at times introduces the prophetic speech, for example, in Jer 11:1: "The word which came to Jeremiah from the LORD, saying . . ." This voice presents itself as drawing on the autobiographical account of Jeremiah, for example, as Jer 11:5 notes, "Then I said . . ." Not only do we hear the third-person voice in the introductions to prophetic declarations, but this voice also breaks into the book at

---

R. Bodine, SemeiaSt (Atlanta: Scholars Press, 1995), 55–56, on the role of first-person meta-communicative statements as a structural marker.

5. See further, Mark J. Boda, "Speaking into the Silence: The Epilogue of Ecclesiastes," in *The Words of the Wise Are Like Goads: Engaging Qoheleth in the 21st Century*, ed. Mark J. Boda, Tremper Longman III, and Cristian Rata (Winona Lake, IN: Eisenbrauns, 2013), 257–79.

6. See further Mark J. Boda, "Redaction in the Book of Nehemiah: A Fresh Proposal," in *Unity and Disunity in Ezra–Nehemiah: Redaction, Rhetoric, and Reader*, ed. Mark J. Boda and Paul L. Redditt, Hebrew Bible Monographs (Sheffield: Sheffield Phoenix, 2008), 25–54.

7. There has been much discussion of the role of the third- and first-person voices in Jeremiah and the authenticity of the first-person voice: e.g., A. R. Pete Diamond, "Jeremiah," in *Eerdmans Commentary on the Bible*, ed. James D. G. Dunn and J. W. Rogerson (Grand Rapids: Eerdmans, 2003), 543–49.

certain points for shorter or longer stretches to depict Jeremiah through narrative accounts (shorter examples: Jer 19:14; 20:1–3; a longer example: Jer 39–42). Among the prophets, the book of Ezekiel is the one most dominated by the autobiographical voice.[8] Even here, however, one finds a third-person voice breaking into the account at the outset, in 1:2–3.

In several of the books within the Twelve one finds both biographical and autobiographical speech. The books of Hosea (1:1–4), Amos (1:1–2), and Micah (1:1) all begin with a superscription as a third-person voice introduces the reader to the prophetic figure. In each case, the autobiographical voice emerges in the later sections of the book (Hos 3:1–3; Amos 5:1; 7:1, 2, 4, 5, 7, 8, 12, 14; 8:1, 2; 9:1; Mic 3:1, 8; 6:6, 7; 7:1, 7, 8, 9–10). Similarly, Habakkuk contains two superscriptions (1:1; 3:1), yet in the prayer of chapter 3 first-person speech emerges (3:2, 7, 16, 18–19). In Zechariah one finds someone presenting the experiences and words of Zechariah the prophet, signaled by the historiographical introductions found at 1:1, 7, and 7:1.[9] The autobiographical voice is clearly presented throughout 1:8–6:15 as the prophet relates his experience of a series of visions. In Zech 7–8, however, one can discern a clear distinction between the voice of one presenting Zechariah's prophetic words and actions (7:4; 8:18) and the autobiographical voice of Zechariah himself (7:1, 8).[10] The book of Zechariah is thus presented to the reader by a voice distinct from the first-person voice of the prophet. A first-person voice emerges at the center of the second half of Zechariah as well (11:4–16).

These examples reveal that wherever autobiography is found in Old Testament books, there is always a third-person voice playing some role in the presentation of the material to the reader.

How do we deal with these various voices that we encounter in the text? In the twentieth century, traditional interpretation tended to eradicate the distance between these voices, identifying the third-person voice with the first-person voice. The diachronic approaches that dominated the first half of the twentieth century explained these various voices through the historical methodologies of source, form, and redaction criticism.[11] The synchronic approaches that eventually

---

8. See esp. D. Nathan Phinney, "Life Writing in Ezekiel and First Zechariah," in *Tradition in Transition*, ed. Mark J. Boda and Michael H. Floyd, LHBOTS 475 (London: T&T Clark, 2008), 83–103; idem, "Portraying Prophetic Experience and Tradition in Ezekiel," in *Thus Says the Lord: Essays on the Former and Latter Prophets in Honor of Robert R. Wilson*, ed. John J. Ahn and Stephen L. Cook, LHBOTS 502 (London: T&T Clark, 2009), 234–43; cf. idem, "The Prophetic Persona in the Book of Ezekiel: Autobiography and Portrayal" (PhD diss., Yale University, 2004).

9. These are not superscriptions in the classic sense since they include finite verbs, and, in the case of 1:1, this historical account continues in 1:6b with the depiction of the response of the people.

10. Zechariah 8:1 has no indirect object. See further Mark J. Boda, *The Book of Zechariah*, NICOT (Grand Rapids: Eerdmans, forthcoming).

11. For redaction criticism in the prophets, see Paul L. Redditt, "Editorial/Redaction Criticism," in *Dictionary of the Old Testament: Prophets*, ed. Mark J. Boda and J. Gordon McConville (Downers Grove, IL: InterVarsity Press, 2012), 171–78.

dominated the second half of the twentieth century explained these various voices through the literary methodologies of narrative and rhetorical criticism.

Evangelicals have struggled with both of these strategies.[12] Diachronic approaches appeared to distance the text from the experiences related in the text, in particular, those of the prophetic figures and their oral pronouncements.[13] These diachronic approaches often used contradiction within the literature to identify the various levels of development. Synchronic approaches, while treating biblical books as literary wholes in their final form, also in some cases distanced the text from the experiences related in the text, treating the books as fictive.[14]

It appears to me that one needs to take seriously the distinction within the biblical witness between the first-person and third-person voices we have been discussing. Whether one adopts a diachronic or synchronic hermeneutic or some combination of the two, the simplest explanation for the distinct voicing that we discover in the text is that the prophetic voice is being presented to us by someone other than the prophet. Whether we call this other voice the redactor, the author, the implicit author, or the narrator, in the end there is a distinction: we are watching the game from the balcony.[15]

Audiences and Readers

This discussion of these various voices begs the question of the ears of those with whom we sit in the balcony. For those adopting a diachronic hermeneutic, such ears are real and multiple, ranging from original oral audiences to audiences of later redactors. Adopting a synchronic hermeneutic requires that one articulate a single

---

12. Cf. Michael A. Grisanti, "The Present State of Old Testament Scholarship," in *The World and the Word: An Introduction to the Old Testament*, ed. Eugene H. Merrill, Mark F. Rooker, and Michael A. Grisanti (Nashville: Broadman & Holman, 2011), 149–62.

13. Cf. Randall K. J. Tan, "Recent Developments in Redaction Criticism: From Investigation of Textual Prehistory Back to Historical-Grammatical Exegesis?," *JETS* 44 (2001): 599–614; Paul E. Hughes, "Compositional History: Source, Form, and Redaction Criticism," in *Interpreting the Old Testament: A Guide to Exegesis*, ed. Craig Broyles (Grand Rapids: Baker Academic, 2001), 221–44; D. A. Carson, "Redaction Criticism: On the Legitimacy and Illegitimacy of a Literary Tool," in *Scripture and Truth*, ed. D. A. Carson and John Woodbridge (Grand Rapids: Zondervan, 1983), 119–46; Grant R. Osborne, "Historical Criticism and the Evangelical," *JETS* 42 (1999): 193–210; Stephen Smith, "The Evangelical and Redaction Criticism," *Chm* 107 (1993): 130–45; Lawson G. Stone, "Redaction Criticism: Whence, Whither, and Why? Or, Going Beyond Source and Form Criticism without Leaving Them Behind," *LTQ* 27 (1992): 105–18.

14. Cf. Carl F. H. Henry, "Narrative Theology: An Evangelical Approach," *TJ* 8 (1987): 3–19; although see J. Daniel Hays, "An Evangelical Approach to Old Testament Narrative Criticism," *BSac* 166 (2009): 3–18.

15. On implied authors and readers, see Jerome T. Walsh, *Old Testament Narrative: A Guide to Interpretation* (Louisville: Westminster John Knox, 2010), 1–11. For recent discussion and defense of the concept of the implied author in literary studies, see vol. 45 of the journal *Style* (Spring 2011), 1–190.

implicit audience or reader, although in literary studies the role of the modern reader admits a variety of implicit audiences.[16] However one views this audience, the reality is that the text evidences or implies certain audiences and these audiences are distinct from any oral audience that may be discerned behind the text.

It is not odd to me that the book of Isaiah has been conventionally divided into three major sections, with transition points noted at Isa 40 and 56.[17] Chapters 1–39 contain historical notations that identify for us an audience in the Assyrian period. The final historical notation and its attendant narrative in Isa 39 build expectation for the transition to an audience in the Babylonian period that appears beginning in Isa 40 and continues throughout the ensuing chapters. The dominant picture of the audience in these chapters is of a community in exile from a city in ruins, with the exiles and their city needing both comfort and renewal, whether spiritual or physical. This audience is called to leave (48:20–21) a judged Babylon (ch. 47) and enter into a Jerusalem restored by the Persian Cyrus (44:26–45:13). With Isa 56, however, there appears to be a shift to a new literary collection, one whose rhetorical shape has often been described as chiastic in design, at the core of which is material closely aligned with that seen throughout Isa 40–55. It is in Isa 56 that we find reference to a new audience. In Isa 56:8 the Lord God is described as one who gathers the dispersed of Israel and who will gather yet more scattered ones to Israel. This suggests a context in the Persian period after the initial waves of returnees had settled in the land, when there was need for and expectation of further returns.

If this articulation of the various audiences in Isaiah can be accepted, it is then important to note that while earlier audiences can still be discerned in the text and play a role in meaning making, the meaning determined by a later audience should dominate the meaning of texts originally addressed to a different audience.[18] This does not mean that the meaning of the text to the later audience contradicts the meaning of the text directed to the earlier audience. It only means that the text is now being used in a different historical or literary context, among a different community or set of readers with different needs, by composers seeking to address a new configuration of issues, even if similar to those of an earlier audience.

Thus, for example, while there are many reasons to see the oracles against the nations in Isa 13–23 as a collection embedded within the geopolitics of the Assyrian

---

16. See David J. A. Clines, "The Many Voices of Isaiah 40," in *Let Us Go Up to Zion: Essays in Honour of H. G. M. Williamson on the Occasion of His Sixty-Fifth Birthday*, ed. Iain Provan and Mark J. Boda, VTSup 153 (Leiden: Brill, 2012), 113–26, for recent discussion of implicit readers of Isaiah.

17. See further Mark J. Boda, "Walking in the Light of Yahweh: Zion and the Empires in the Book of Isaiah," in *Empire in the New Testament*, ed. Stanley E. Porter and Cynthia Long Westfall, McMaster New Testament Studies (Grand Rapids: Eerdmans, 2010), 54–89.

18. See H. G. M. Williamson, *The Book Called Isaiah: Deutero-Isaiah's Role in Composition and Redaction* (Oxford: Clarendon, 1994) for the role played by the one(s) responsible for Isa 40–55 in the present form of Isa 1–39; see also Jacob Stromberg, *Isaiah after Exile: The Author of Third Isaiah as Reader and Redactor of the Book*, Oxford Theological Monographs (Oxford: Oxford University Press, 2011) for the role played by the one(s) responsible for Isa 56–66 in the present form of the book.

period,[19] the opening oracle related to Babylon appears to be targeted at the implicit audience found in Isa 40 and following, one comforted by a message of judgment concerning Babylon's destruction at the hands of the Medo-Persians (Isa 13:17–22) and a message of salvation looking to the restoration of Israel to the land (14:1–3).[20] Similarly the message of the "remnant" of Israel returning in 10:20–23 would have significance for the audience signaled in Isaiah 40 and following.

It is this later audience that appears to be in mind in the shaping of the entire complex found in Isa 1–39. For instance, Isa 1 appears to contain two distinct pericopes. The first, in 1:1–20, reflects the conditions of the Assyrian invasion of Hezekiah's kingdom (esp. 1:8) and lays out an agenda of repentance (1:16–17), which if embraced will lead to blessing (1:19) but if rejected will lead to destruction (1:20). It is this latter scenario that comes into view in the second pericope, 1:21–31, as a severe judgment is envisioned for Jerusalem that will refine it into a faithful city once again. The *telos* of both pericopes is a community faithfully pursuing the priorities of YHWH, with the first accomplishing this through the response of the community to the prophetic call to repentance, and the second through the divine act of judgment announced by the prophet. While the message of repentance can be discerned throughout Isa 1–39, it is the message of refinement that emerges in the end as the outcome of Isaiah's ministry, as he predicts the Babylonian judgment in the closing depiction of chapter 39.

Isaiah 6 is another superb example of how the audiences signaled by Isa 40 and following emerge within the section of Isaiah where an Assyrian audience is most obvious. As Isaiah takes up his commission received within the heavenly court, it is made clear from the outset that the penitential process so foundational to the prophetic tradition (the first scenario of Isa 1) would be frustrated, leaving the refinement agenda (the second scenario of Isa 1) as the way forward. That refinement agenda in Isa 6 has two phases, the first of which is laid out in verses 11–12, which will leave a tenth portion in the land (v. 13a), and the second of which is found in in verse 13b–c and which will see the burning of even that tenth until all that remains is but a memory (memorial) preserved through "holy seed" from a once mighty tree. This double phase reflects the progression of the closing chapters of Isa 1–39, which describe the destructive force of Assyria sweeping into Hezekiah's kingdom (ch. 36) and a remnant emerging as Jerusalem is spared (ch. 37), but whose message in the end is of a greater destruction at the hands of Babylon (ch. 39).

This evidence from chapters 1–39 provides a few indications that these chapters should be read ultimately in light of the perspective of the audience of Isa 40 and following. The one(s) responsible for the final form of Isaiah have (had) in mind the entire message of Isaiah and that entire message needs to be taken into account as we interpret earlier messages declared by Isaiah to his Assyrian-period audience.

---

19. See, e.g., Seth Erlandsson, *The Burden of Babylon: A Study of Isaiah 13:2–14:23*, ConBOT 4 (Lund: GWK Gleerup, 1970); Oswalt, *Book of Isaiah, Chapters 1–39*, 300–1.

20. See, e.g., Williamson, *Book Called Isaiah*, 156–83; Brevard S. Childs, *Isaiah: A Commentary*, OTL (Louisville: Westminster John Knox, 2001), 116, 123.

The Autobiographical Voice in Isaiah

While the discussion to this point has distinguished between autobiographical and biographical voices within the book of Isaiah and between the book's different audiences, no clear statement has been made on the presence of an autobiographical voice in the second half of the book (Isa 40–66). Is there any evidence for a distinction between the autobiographical voice linked to the Assyrian period and the autobiographical voice(s) found after texts conventionally linked to the Assyrian period?

To consider this issue we will begin with a closer look at one of the key transitions in the book of Isaiah: 40:1–11. Some have suggested that this text is part of the larger prophetic call narrative tradition exemplified by Exod 3–4, Isa 6, Jer 1, Ezek 1–3, and possibly also Amos 7 and Judg 6.[21] John Watts and Ronald Clements both discern two streams within this narrative tradition, one tagged as the "Word of God" type that emphasizes the prophetic figure's reluctance (e.g., Moses and Jeremiah) and the other the "Theophany of the Divine Court" type that emphasizes the appearance of YHWH in his court (e.g., Isaiah and Ezekiel).[22] This latter type is reflective of the Jeremianic assertion that the true prophet was one who had stood and listened in God's council (Jer 23:16–22). It is also reflected in texts often referred to as "Divine Court Protocol," such as Zech 3, 1 Kgs 22, and Job 1–2, where messenger figures (human and/or heavenly) caucus around YHWH. While the elements of the Word of God type of prophetic call narrative tradition are not prominent in Isa 40:1–11, one can discern elements that suggest the influence of the Theophany of the Divine Court type or, at the least, the Divine Court Protocol tradition.[23] There is continuity between Isa 40:1–11 and the call scene in Isa 6 in the reference to the "glory of the LORD" (40:5), the sense of human frailty before YHWH (40:6–8), and the destruction of vegetation before YHWH's judgment (40:6–8). At the same time there is discontinuity, and this discontinuity highlights the fundamental shift in tone towards the audience (now, in ch. 40, there is comfort and tender speech spoken "to the heart," in contrast to Isa 6, where speech results in hardened hearts).[24]

---

21. See e.g., Carr, "Isaiah 40:1–11," 59–61.

22. Cf. Walther Zimmerli, *Ezekiel: A Commentary on the Book of the Prophet Ezekiel*, Hermeneia (Philadelphia: Fortress, 1979), 99–100; Clements, *Isaiah 1–39*, 72–73; and John D. W. Watts, *Isaiah 1–33*, rev. ed., WBC 24 (Nashville: Nelson, 2005), 103–5.

23. The following scholars see a heavenly court scene in this text: J. A. Motyer, *The Prophecy of Isaiah: An Introduction & Commentary* (Downers Grove: InterVarsity Press, 1993), 299; R. N. Whybray, *Isaiah 40–66*, NCB (London: Marshall, Morgan, & Scott, 1975), 48; John D. W. Watts, *Isaiah 34–66*, rev. ed., WBC 25 (Nashville: Nelson, 2005), 607. Christopher R. Seitz notes the "mixed" character of this passage (call narrative/divine council scene) ("The Divine Council: Temporal Transition and New Prophecy in the Book of Isaiah," *JBL* 109 [1990]: 236).

24. On continuity and discontinuity, see further Seitz, "Divine Council," 238–40; John N. Oswalt, *The Book of Isaiah: Chapters 40–66*, NICOT (Grand Rapids: Eerdmans, 1998); Francis Landy, "The Ghostly Prelude to Deutero-Isaiah," *BibInt* 14 (2006): 332–35, 357–58; Roy F. Melugin, "Poetic Imagination, Intertextuality, and Life in a Symbolic World," in *The*

Evidence that Isa 40:1–11 is a reflection of the Divine Court Protocol motif may be discerned in the modulation of voices and audiences throughout the text.[25] The first speaker is "your God"—or, better, a proxy speaking on behalf of "your God"[26]—who calls a masculine plural audience to comfort, speak, and proclaim to a group called "my people" and Jerusalem (40:1–2). The act of proclaiming (ק-ר-א, *q-r-ʾ*) is one associated with the messenger tradition of the Old Testament, which is commonly associated with human figures called prophets but which could also be associated with the heavenly figures that we often refer to as angels. Thus in verses 1–2 YHWH or his proxy calls out to a masculine plural group that could be a group of prophets but that is most likely the divine council, in which one finds both heavenly and human messenger figures.[27] The כִּי (*kî*) that follows the verb וְקִרְאוּ (*wĕqirʾû*) does not introduce the content of the speech to be proclaimed, but rather the reason for the proclamation, namely, the completion of the exilic discipline.[28]

Verse 3 introduces another speaker, described as a "voice" (קוֹל, *qôl*). Since this voice is described as "proclaiming" (קוֹרֵא, *qôrēʾ*), a participle that echoes the imperative וְקִרְאוּ (*wĕqirʾû*) addressed to the masculine plural audience of verses 1–2, one may assume that the text is now providing the content that a voice should proclaim to the people/Jerusalem, calling them to "prepare" (פ-נ-ה, *p-n-h*, Piel masc. pl.) and "make straight" (י-שׁ-ר, *y-š-r*, Piel masc. pl.) the way/highway for YHWH their God. However, a "voice" (קוֹל, *qôl*), also linked to a participle of a speaking verb (א-מ-ר, *ʾ-m-r*), will emerge in verse 6 and address the prophetic figure directly, and so function as part of the series of verbal exchanges that began in verse 1. In

Desert Will Bloom: Poetic Visions in Isaiah, ed. A. Joseph Everson and Hyun Chul Paul Kim, SBLAIL (Atlanta: SBL, 2009), 7–15; Shalom M. Paul, *Isaiah 40–66: Translation and Commentary*, ECC (Grand Rapids: Eerdmans, 2012), 127–28.

25. For two recent analyses of voicing in Isa 40:1–11, see Landy, "Ghostly Prelude to Deutero-Isaiah," 332–63, and Clines, "Many Voices," 113–26. For a review of past research on the structure of Isa 40:1–11, see Carr, "Isaiah 40:1–11," 52–54. See Lena-Sofia Tiemeyer, *For the Comfort of Zion: The Geographical and Theological Location of Isaiah 40–55*, VTSup 139 (Leiden: Brill, 2011), 337–39, on the integrity and structure of 40:1–11, contrasting R. G. Kratz, "Der Anfang des Zweiten Jesaja in Jes 40,1f und seine literarischen Horizonte," *ZAW* 105 (1993): 404–5, who sees diverse perspectives in the various sections.

26. Clines calls this "the reporting voice of the narrator" ("Many Voices," 113).

27. See, e.g., Seitz, "Divine Council," 230; Paul, *Isaiah 40–66*, 127; Tiemeyer, *For the Comfort of Zion*, 16–17, for the divine council (a view based firmly on the earlier work of F. M. Cross, "The Council of Yahweh in Second Isaiah," *JNES* 12 [1953]: 274–77); and, e.g., Joseph Blenkinsopp, *Isaiah 40–55: A New Translation with Introduction and Commentary*, AB 19A (New York: Doubleday, 2002), 180, for prophets, the latter a view held by the targumim and key commentators in the Jewish tradition (Rashi, Ibn Ezra, Kimchi); cf. Paul, *Isaiah 40–66*, 127. For approaches claiming that a broader audience is in view, see David Noel Freedman, "The Structure of Isaiah 40:1–11," in *Perspectives on Language and Text: Essays and Poems in Honor of Francis I. Andersen's Sixtieth Birthday, July 28, 1985*, ed. Edgar W. Conrad and Edward G. Newing (Winona Lake, IN: Eisenbrauns, 1987), 167–93; John D. W. Watts, *Isaiah*, Word Biblical Themes (Dallas: Word, 1989), 85–87. OG inserts "O priests."

28. See *HALOT*, 1129, which reminds us that the content of the speech follows directly without an introductory particle (contra, e.g., Clines, "Many Voices," 113).

light of this, the voice in verse 3 may be better understood as a participant in the divine council who most likely is not YHWH, but rather one who speaks with YHWH's authority—since this voice speaks of YHWH in the third person, refers to "our God," and ends its speech with "the mouth of YHWH has spoken" (v. 5).[29] The masculine plural audience, indicated by the imperatives "prepare" (פ-נ-ה, *p-n-h*, Piel masc. pl.) and "make straight" (י-שׁ-ר, *y-š-r*, Piel masc. pl.), may be "my people" from verses 1–2, in light of the appearance of a "voice" in verse 6 who addresses (speaking verb participle) a prophetic figure with a command (imperative). However, it is more likely that this audience is the divine council addressed in verses 1–2. A call to transform the cosmos in preparation for the arrival of YHWH is something appropriate for discussion within the divine council, where heavenly beings would have the necessary resources.[30]

With 40:6a there is another shift.[31] Although again the speaker is a "voice" (קוֹל, *qôl*), the audience is now masculine singular, reflected in the masculine singular imperative "proclaim" (קְרָא, *qěrāʾ*). This audience appears to be the first person voice ("I") who responds in verse 6b.[32] The meaning of what then follows in verses 6c–8 is disputed.[33] On the one hand, it may be the content of the proclamation commanded in verse 6a, since, as noted above, the content of a speech introduced by the verb ק-ר-א (*q-r-ʾ*) follows directly without an introductory particle. However, in verse 6b, the interjection of the prophetic "I" figure ("And I said, 'What shall I proclaim?'") stands between the imperatival ק-ר-א (*q-r-ʾ*) and what follows in verses 6c–8. The repetitious character of verses 6c–8, together with the use of the strong asseverative אָכֵן (*ʾākēn*) at its center point (v. 7c), suggests that verses 6c–8 represents a dialogue between the "voice" and the "I" of verse 6a–b.[34] Inter-

---

29. Landy notes how the use of "our" "displays a certain solidarity, in contrast to the distance implied by אלהיכם (*ʾlhykm*), 'your God,' in v. 1" ("Ghostly Prelude to Deutero-Isaiah," 340–1).

30. On vv. 3–5 as addressed to the divine council, see, e.g., Klaus Baltzer, *Deutero-Isaiah: A Commentary on Isaiah 40–55*, Hermeneia (Minneapolis: Fortress, 2001), 53, and Clines, "Many Voices," 119.

31. I see no need to identify vv. 6–8 as a later addition, as does, e.g., Kratz, "Der Anfang des Zweiten Jesaja," 406–7.

32. MT reads *wāw*-copulative with Qal suffix conjugation 3 masc. sg. of א-מ-ר (*ʾ-m-r*), while OG understands the form as *wāw*-copulative with Qal prefix conjugation 1 com. sg. of the same root (there is no difference between these two forms in a text without vowels). In either case, both of these texts have a first-person voice (Seitz argues that the Qumran [1QIsaª] reading, ואומרה, "may support" a first-person reading, but ואומרה could be understood as a fem. sg. participle; cf. Seitz, "The Divine Council," 234n19, who cites David L. Petersen, *Late Israelite Prophecy: Studies in Deutero-Prophetic Literature and in Chronicles*, SBLMS 23 [Missoula, MT: Scholars Press, 1977], 20; see Tiemeyer, *For the Comfort of Zion*, 15, who rejects the fem. sg. and masc. sg. readings in favor of a 1 com. sg. reading).

33. See Landy, "Ghostly Prelude to Deutero-Isaiah," 345.

34. See further Mark J. Boda, "'Uttering Precious Rather Than Worthless Words': Divine Patience and Impatience with Lament in Isaiah and Jeremiah," in *Why? . . . How Long? Studies on Voice(s) of Lamentation Rooted in Biblical Hebrew Poetry*, ed. LeAnn Snow Flesher, Carol J. Dempsey, and Mark J. Boda, LHBOTS 552 (London: Bloomsbury, 2014), 83–99; cf.

estingly, in the section following the asseverative אָכֵן (ʾāken), reference is made to "our God," as was the case in the speech of the "voice" in verses 3–5. After asking "What shall I proclaim?", the prophetic figure laments the ephemeral condition of the potential human audience before the disciplinary wind/spirit of YHWH ("All flesh is grass and all its durability/faithfulness like the flower of the field. Grass withers and flower falls, because the wind/spirit of YHWH blows on it") and the "voice" responds with a contrastive speech (introduced by אָכֵן [ʾāken]) that agrees that the people are grass that withers and flower that falls, but also states that the "word of our God stands forever."

If verses 6c–8 represent a lament and response dialogue between the "voice" and the "I," what then is the answer to the question of the identity of the first-person "I" in verse 6b? We are left with the final section of 40:1–11, which is introduced by a final shift in audience in verse 9.[35] While verse 1 identified YHWH or his proxy as the speaker, verses 3a and 6a identified a "voice" as the speaker, and verse 6b identi-fied "I" as the speaker (with verses 6c–8 representing a dialogue that ends with the "voice" responding to the "I"), one does not find an explicit reference to a speaker at the beginning of verse 9.[36] The audience of this verse, however, is feminine singular, as is indicated by the five feminine singular imperatives ("go up," "lift up" [twice], "do not be afraid," and "say"). This audience consists of one(s) called "messenger" (Piel fem. sg. participle of ב-שׂ-ר, b-ś-r). The precise relationship between this "mes-senger" and Zion/Jerusalem, whether objective ("messenger to Zion/Jerusalem") or explicative ("Messenger Zion/Jerusalem"), is not clear.[37] However, the use of the feminine singular participle in a context where the only feminine figure is the city, as well as the fact that this messenger is called to address other cities ("the cities

---

Claus Westermann, *Isaiah 40–66: A Commentary*, trans. David M. G. Stalker, OTL (Phila-delphia: Westminster, 1969), 40–43; Seitz, "Divine Council," 235; Carr, "Isaiah 40:1–11," 59; Baltzer, *Deutero-Isaiah*, 57; Clines, "Many Voices," 115, 125.

35. So also Richard J. Clifford, *Fair Spoken and Persuading: An Interpretation of Second Isaiah*, Theological Inquiries (Toronto: Paulist Press, 1984), 76, and Clines, "Many Voices," 119. On debate over the character of vv. 9–11 within Isa 40:1–11, see Carr, "Isaiah 40:1–11," 54, 62–63. Carr sees vv. 9–11 as representing a shift from the divine council dialogue to enact-ment on the earthly plane. The same follows from understanding vv. 9–11 as the message to be delivered by the prophet. In my view of the structure of Isa 40–55, vv. 9–11 do not set up the message of chs. 40–48, but rather the message of 49:14–55:13. The emergence of the prophetic servant comes first (40:27–49:13, thus akin to 40:6–8) and then has an impact on Zion/Jerusalem (49:14–55:13, thus akin to 40:9–11). My view also contrasts with that of Tiemeyer (*For the Comfort of Zion*, 17–18), who identifies the 1 com. sg. voice in 40:6b with the messenger to Zion in 40:9, a conclusion that is untenable, in my opinion, because of the masc. sg. imperative in 40:6a.

36. On this ambiguity, see Terry W. Eddinger, "An Analysis of Isaiah 40:1–11 (17)," *BBR* 9 (1999): 131.

37. See e.g., Paul, *Isaiah 40–66*, 135, and Tiemeyer, *For the Comfort of Zion*, 17, for the objective (Paul suggesting Jeremiah's Rachel), and, e.g., Childs, *Isaiah*, 301, and Blenkinsopp, *Isaiah 40–55*, 184–85, for the explicative. Landy treats this messenger as "an aspect of Zion that is returning to itself," but also as the prophet's "female counterpart to itself" ("Ghostly Prelude to Deutero-Isaiah," 350).

of Judah"), suggests that the messenger is indeed the city Zion/Jerusalem. Zion/Jerusalem is instructed to assume the role of mountain messenger who declares the victory of God and the presence of the King, in both his powerful presence and tender care (notice the play on the word "arm" in vv. 10–11). Most important to the present discussion is the fact that this call to Messenger Jerusalem/Zion appears to be the content of the proclamation of the "I" of verse 6b.[38] Thus, the prophetic "I" is commissioned to relay a message to another figure (Messenger Zion/Jerusalem) to be proclaimed. The message that will be proclaimed is then provided in verses 9c–11, beginning with הִנֵּה אֱלֹהֵיכֶם (hinnê ʾĕlōhêkem), "behold, your God."

These many voices clearly fit the ethos of the divine court, reminiscent of the discussion format in the heavenly scene in 1 Kgs 22:19–22. Caucusing with the divine council the prophet hears of an impending era as the divine council is told to comfort the people and Jerusalem and to prepare the cosmos for YHWH's arrival. The "I" figure of the prophet is singled out in the midst of the divine council and called to proclaim. This figure's proclamation, however, is to be directed to "Zion/Jerusalem," who is to be commissioned to proclaim to "the cities of Judah" the arrival of YHWH as sovereign and shepherd Lord.

What are the implications of this reading of Isa 40:1–11 for our understanding of the autobiographical voice in the book as a whole?[39] First-person voices are found throughout the book of Isaiah. Of course, YHWH speaks regularly in the first person, as do various characters within the narratives (e.g., Ahaz in 7:12), and first person voice is found in apostrophic material in prophetic speeches (as in the statement made by the king of Babylon in 14:13–14). At certain points, however, a prophetic voice speaks in the first person: 6:1, 5–8, 11; 8:1, 3, 5, 11, 17, 18; 18:4; 21:2–4, 6, 10, 11, 16; 22:3; 24:16; 25:1; 26:9, 20; 28:22, 23; 31:4; 32:9, 13, 18; 33:2, 20, 22; 40:6; 48:16b;[40] 49:1–5; 50:4–9; 51:1; 61:1, 10; 62:1;[41] 63:15.[42] The autobiographical "I" found

---

38. Contra Landy, who considers that in vv. 9–11 "the prophet speaks for himself, and through the posited herald of Zion and Jerusalem" ("Ghostly Prelude to Deutero-Isaiah," 350).

39. See the earlier work of Peter R. Ackroyd, "Isaiah 1–12: Presentation of a Prophet," in *Congress Volume, Göttingen 1977*, ed. Walther Zimmerli, VTSup 29 (Leiden: Brill, 1978), 16–48; idem, "Isaiah 36–39: Structure and Function," in *"The Place Is Too Small for Us": The Israelite Prophets in Recent Scholarship*, ed. R. P. Gordon, Sources for Biblical and Theological Study 5 (Winona Lake, IN: Eisenbrauns, 1995), 478–94; and Francis Landy, "I and Eye in Isaiah, or Gazing at the Invisible," *JBL* 131 (2012): 85–97. Landy speaks of the fictive identification of the second prophet with the first through first-person speech. Note also Childs, *Isaiah*, 296.

40. Possibly 48:15–16a also, but it is also possible that the speaker here is God; see Oswalt, *Book of Isaiah, Chapters 40–66*, 277–78.

41. Possibly 62:6–7 also, though it is also possible that the speaker here is God; see Oswalt, *Book of Isaiah, Chapters 40–66*, 583–85.

42. For first-person plural, see 42:24; 47:4; 53:1, 5, 6, 8; 59:9–13; 63:16–17; 64:5–8, 10. The speaker in the references in ch. 53 appears to be the prophet embedded within the community, since 53:1 refers to "our message." But the references in chs. 59 and 63–64 appear to be citing the voice of the community to which YHWH responds; that is, these texts constitute a prophetic liturgy.

in chapters 1–39 is in a few places explicitly linked to the Assyrian period and to the prophet Isaiah of Jerusalem (see Isa 6 and 8). The reader encountering Isa 40:6 would assume initially that the "I" here is the same "I" first encountered in Isa 6–8, that is, Isaiah of Jerusalem.[43] However, Isa 40–66, and especially 40–55, is well known for its progressive revelation of a figure or figures.[44] It is interesting that the autobiographical voices in chapters 49, 50 and 61 are all linked to the figure of the servant who emerges in the course of chapters 40–66. The structure of Isa 40–55 highlights two main characters: the servant Jacob/Israel and the city Zion/Jerusalem.[45] It is the emergence of the servant figure, which comes first in Isa 40:27–49:13, that results in the explosion of the cosmos' praise in 49:13. This praise in 49:13 prompts the lament, in 49:14, of Zion/Jerusalem, whose pain is addressed through the proclamation of a prophetic figure who declares a message to Zion (52:7–10), but then through the redemptive suffering of the servant figure whose actions result in the call to joy to Zion in chapter 54. So also within chapters 56–66, the witness of the servant figure in 61:1 lies at the center of a literary complex focused on hope for Zion/Jerusalem (chs. 60–62), made explicit by 62:1, in which the autobiographical "I" says: "For Zion's sake I will not keep silent, and for Jerusalem's sake I will not keep quiet . . ." The connection between the autobiographical servant figure and Zion/Jerusalem in Isa 40–66 echoes the link established between the autobiographical prophetic figure and Zion/Jerusalem at the outset of the literary complex in Isa 40:1–11.[46] Thus, just as the first-person accounts in Isa 6–8 shape the reader's expectations for other references to the autobiographical voice in chapters 1–39, so the servant's first-person declarations in Isa 40–66 shape the reader's understanding of the autobiographical voice in Isa 40:6. What some may suggest is confusion between Isaiah and the servant figure is better understood as a creative fusion of two key figures within the Isaiah tradition.[47] Most interpreters of Isaiah understand the servant figure(s) as distinct from Isaiah of Jerusalem, and the rhetorical flow and development of Isa 40–66 suggests that the servant figure follows in the tradition of Isaiah, taking up the prophet's mantle and declaring hope

---

43. As noted by Oswalt, *Book of Isaiah, Chapters 40–66*, 48. See also Seitz, "Divine Council," 238, 241–43, who calls this "the last gasp from 'the former day'" (p. 243) and who writes that "the objecting voice of vv. 6b–7 speaks as though he were Isaiah himself" (ibid.).

44. See also Tiemeyer, *For the Comfort of Zion*, 14–25, for a review of non-divine first-person speech in Isa 40–55. She notes close ties between the first-person voice in Isa 40, the servant figure, and a female messenger. She presents evidence for a female author of Isa 40–55, but in the end makes no definitive statement on this matter (pp. 26–30).

45. For my view of the structure of Isa 40–66, see Boda, "Walking in the Light of Yahweh," 54–89; idem, *A Severe Mercy: Sin and Its Remedy in the Old Testament*, Siphrut: Literature and Theology of the Hebrew Scriptures 1 (Winona Lake, IN: Eisenbrauns, 2009), 212–13; idem, "'Uttering Precious Rather Than Worthless Words.'"

46. Tiemeyer, *For the Comfort of Zion*, 333–43, also provides evidence for the way "40:1–11 foreshadows many of the themes in Isa. 40–55" (p. 343), esp. noting 52:7–10 and 55:6–11, as the collection comes to an end.

47. See Landy, "Ghostly Prelude to Deutero-Isaiah," 333, who in describing Isa 40:1–11 writes: "As a prologue, it introduces a new poetic voice and vision; at the same time, it cannot but be infused by the voices of the past."

for Zion/Jerusalem and ultimately the people of God. For readers of the book of Isaiah, there is an experience of delayed revelation, as the identity of the "I" of Isa 40:6 is provided. The presence of this new and emerging identity is suggestive of a later figure or figures functioning in continuity with the earlier tradition of Isaiah. Although even this figure, or these figures, may be portrayed as a revelation of Isaiah of Jerusalem, it seems most natural to see him/them as one(s) articulating the Isaianic message anew for those who survived the exilic nightmare.

Theology of Revelation

The evidence presented above has highlighted the presence of not only the voice of a prophet in the book of Isaiah, but also the voice of a narrator or editor(s) distinct from the prophet, as well as that of another first-person figure (or other first-person figures) progressively unveiled in the second half of the book. I also have noted evidence for different audiences that dominate the various parts of the book. For some these are not radical statements. Others may be uncomfortable with where this leads the evangelical scholar and especially how such an approach relates to an orthodox view of Scripture.

The doctrine of divine involvement in the revelatory processes related to inscripturation has always been key to evangelical hermeneutics. Traditionally this doctrine has been discussed under two sub-topics: inspiration and illumination. Typically, the first sub-topic focuses on the processes that resulted in the production of Scripture in antiquity, while the second focuses on the processes that result in the interpretation of Scripture in the present day. While in general the first part of the twentieth century was dominated by articulations of the first of these sub-topics, the second part of that century saw a shift to the second sub-topic. Thus the "battle for the Bible" shifted from issues related to divine and human involvement in the production of Scripture, in which inerrancy was an important concern,[48] to issues related to the divine and human involvement in the interpretation of the final product, in which hermeneutics came to the fore.[49] Another way to view this shift is through the speaker-word-audience or author-text-reader hermeneutical continuum. In any communicative act one must distinguish between intention (speaker/author), expression (word/text), and impression (audience/reader). While one can speak about an actual oral or literary expression of word or text, the limitations of human cognition, language, and communication mean that there is inevitable dissonance between intention and impression.

The doctrine of divine involvement in the revelatory processes related to inscripturation is relevant to each of these stages in the communicative act. Second Peter 1:21 ("no prophecy was ever made by an act of human will, but people moved by the Holy Spirit spoke from God," NASB revised) focuses on the divine involve-

---

48. E.g., Harold Lindsell, *The Battle for the Bible* (Grand Rapids: Zondervan, 1976).

49. E.g., Kevin J. Vanhoozer, *Is There a Meaning in This Text? The Bible, the Reader, and the Morality of Literary Knowledge* (Grand Rapids: Zondervan, 1998).

ment in oral prophetic utterance. While it was truly people who made prophetic utterances, such prophecies were motivated not by human will but by the Holy Spirit, so that the oral word could be confidently identified as "from God," that is, as truly divine (cf. Heb 1:1). Thus the prophetic experience that underlies the prophecies we now possess in Scripture is inspired by God while truly mediated through human experience and expression.

While 2 Pet 1:21 focuses on the oral prophetic utterance (what this verse denotes by the word "prophecy"),[50] 2 Tim 3:16 provides insight into the inscripturated text, for there the focus is on "Scripture" (γραφή, graphē), also called "sacred writings" (ἱερὰ γράμματα, hiera grammata) in 3:15. Both of these terms focus on the textual dimension of the revelatory process, the very letters and words that constitute the Scriptures. While these letters and words are truly human language, they are identified as "God-breathed/inspired" (θεόπνευστος, theopneustos). Thus, not only is the prophetic experience that underlies inscripturated prophecy inspired by God, but, according to 2 Tim 3:16, the subsequent written prophetic witness is also inspired.

The doctrine of divine involvement in the revelatory processes related to inscripturation addresses not only the underlying prophetic revelatory experiences and the resulting written record of those experiences, but also the interpretation of this Scripture, the aspect of the communicative process that concerns the reader. Helpful in this regard is the Gospel of John and its articulation of the role of the Spirit to guide the new covenant community into all truth.[51] While John 16:13–14 speaks of this Spirit of truth who guides into "all truth," John 14:26 makes clear that part of this teaching role of the Spirit is to bring to remembrance the words Jesus shared with his disciples. In light of John 2:22 and especially 12:16 it is clear that this "act of remembrance that the Spirit enables . . . is not so much an exercise in recollection as an understanding of things said and done in the past from the perspective of the death and resurrection of Jesus."[52] It is thus "a Spirit-directed understanding of the past,"[53] which involves not only interpretation of Jesus' words and actions (e.g., John 2:22; 7:39) but also the Scriptures that preceded his ministry (e.g., John 2:17; 12:16). These texts in John are foundational for the doctrine often called illumination.

These exemplary New Testament witnesses highlight divine involvement in the revelatory processes related to inscripturation. It is important to note that, for all of these revelatory processes, human involvement is celebrated within the

---

50. Understanding the reference to "prophecy of Scripture" in 2 Pet 1:20 as meaning "prophecies that eventually were included in Scripture." Notice how 2 Pet 1:21 refers to "speaking" (λαλέω, laleō).

51. See further Mark J. Boda, "Word and Spirit, Scribe and Prophet in Old Testament Hermeneutics," in Spirit & Scripture: Examining a Pneumatic Hermeneutic, ed. Kevin L. Spawn and Archie T. Wright (London: T&T Clark, 2011), 41; and esp. Stephen E. Fowl, Engaging Scripture: A Model for Theological Interpretation, Challenges in Contemporary Theology (Malden, MA: Blackwell, 1998), 99–100.

52. Fowl, Engaging Scripture, 100.

53. Ibid., 101.

Christian articulation of this doctrine. Scripture as a whole is never treated as having dropped out of heaven, like the Ten Commandments, as words directly written by God (Exod 31:18; 32:15, 16; 34:1, 28; Deut 9:10). Nevertheless, God is the dominant partner in the revelatory experiences of those responsible for Scripture (author), sovereignly superintending the processes that resulted in the inscripturation of these revelatory experiences (text), as well as the ongoing processes of interpretation of these inscripturated texts (reader). As noted above, the term usually used for the processes related to reception and inscripturation is *inspiration*, while that used for the processes related to inscripturation and interpretation is *illumination*. Attempts to blur the line between these two sub-topics of the doctrine of inscripturation have been met with great resistance in evangelical circles, for obvious reasons, but the shift to deeper reflection on hermeneutics demands greater attention to the topic of illumination, although this will not be our focus here.[54]

The traditional doctrine of inscripturated revelation outlined above has implications for the evangelical study of the Old Testament prophetic corpus. It appears to me that some Evangelicals have focused on the inspired experiences of the Old Testament prophetic figures named in the various Old Testament books at the expense of the inspired processes that resulted in the inscripturation of these experiences. The book of Jeremiah provides some insight into the role played by a supportive figure (Baruch the scribe) in the preservation and production of the book that bears Jeremiah's name. For some reason, within certain streams of evangelical hermeneutics there has been little difficulty granting a role to the gospel writers (none of which are named in their respective books) as purveyors of the revelatory words and redemptive acts of Jesus, but great difficulty envisioning a role for the (mostly) unnamed figures responsible for preserving and interpreting the words and deeds of the Old Testament prophets. The fact is that we do not know the identities of those responsible for much of Old Testament historiography and many psalms, and yet this does not call into question the inspired character of these works. God can work through the nameless individuals responsible for biblical revelation.

In light of the evidence culled from books in the Old Testament that contain autobiography, it appears to me that the most natural reading of these books entails at least distinguishing between autobiographical and biographical voices. This honors the processes involved in inscripturation, and in the end it is the inscripturated text that is deemed authoritative for the Christian community, not the experiences of those who received the revelation. This distinction between autobiographical and biographical voices also reminds us that the audiences of the oral speeches of the prophets are distinct from those who received the written forms of the prophetic books. A prophetic book was formed by a person or group living after the completion of the prophet's ministry and was addressed to a group that would read the prophecies and narratives in a period distinct from that of the prophet. In the case of a prophetic book like Isaiah, whose contents clearly look

---

54. See further Boda, "Word and Spirit."

beyond the period of Isaiah of Jerusalem, the issue of audience and reception is paramount for our understanding of the meaning of the text.

These shifting audiences and thus contexts of interpretation appear to be matched by shifting autobiographical prophetic voices that, while sharing in common the tradition first articulated in Judah by Isaiah of Jerusalem, reflect new personalities with new perspectives for these shifting audiences. This development of the autobiographical personality in the book of Isaiah is key to the revelation of Jesus the Messiah, since it establishes a typological pattern that begins with Isaiah of Jerusalem in Isa 1–39 (note ch. 6) and continues through the servant of Isa 40–55, as well as the figure at the heart of Isa 56–66 (ch. 61). In addition, the development of the autobiographical personality in Isaiah would also prove key to the identity of those who follow Jesus the Messiah (Isa 6 // Acts 28:25–28; Isa 40 // 1 Pet 1:22–25; Isa 49:6 // Acts 13:47).

12

The Implications of an Evangelical View of Scripture for the Authorship of the Book of Isaiah

John N. Oswalt

Introduction

Many biblical scholars take it for granted that the present book of Isaiah is the result of the work of multiple authors and editors. On the surface, this is not an unreasonable possibility, even for those who take the Bible to be divine revelation. For instance, the books of 1–2 Kings are without question the work of several different hands over several centuries. The issue that this paper will explore is whether a distinctly evangelical view of Scripture calls the current view concerning Isaiah into question.

First, since "evangelical" views of Scripture vary greatly today, it will be necessary to survey the range of possibilities and to suggest a view that has at least some claim to the sobriquet "evangelical" and might also claim some broad acceptance. Second, there is complete disagreement in the field of Old Testament studies about what degree of coherence or incoherence may exist in the book of Isaiah, and there is even less agreement on the relationship between whatever degree of coherence one is willing to grant and the matter of authorship. So, again, it will be necessary to give some account of the possibilities on these issues and to evaluate how the view of Scripture one espouses might bear upon them. In the end, because one's conclusions about authorship have so much to do with one's conclusions about coherence or incoherence, I will focus on the implications of multiple authorship for one's understanding of the book of Isaiah.

An Evangelical View of Scripture

For the first three-quarters of the last century, there was little doubt as to what an evangelical view of Scripture affirmed; it was that the Bible was without error in the original manuscripts. This was the view that Charles Hodge and Benjamin Warfield had hammered out at the beginning of the twentieth century.[1] They and their followers maintained with some degree of success that, while the language "without

---

1. Benjamin B. Warfield, *The Inspiration and Authority of the Bible* (Philadelphia: Presbyterian & Reformed, 1948).

error in the original manuscripts" might not be the wording that the church fathers used, it expressed the viewpoint of orthodoxy. Although various caveats were put forward modifying their position (for example, concerning whether "infallible" is a better term than "inerrant"), there was still general agreement among the fundamentalists and their various descendant groups that the Bible is utterly reliable not merely in its theological and ethical teachings but also in its assertions about history, geography, and claims concerning authorship.[2]

The first "hole in the dike," as it were, may be seen in the work of Rogers and McKim in 1979.[3] They certainly did not originate the questions they raised, but their work brought those questions to the fore in a direct and comprehensive way. In particular, they called attention to the supposedly Aristotelian way in which Hodge and Warfield had placed reason before faith. Thus, they argued, the Princetonians had framed the discussion in ways the fathers would never have done. Furthermore, Rogers and McKim claimed that the argument that the Bible was "inerrant in the autographs" was essentially meaningless since we do not have— and probably never will have—access to those documents.

Since 1979, the leak in the dike has become a flood, with the result that the concept of "inerrancy" has become so amorphous today as to be meaningless. Persons with as diverse views as John Woodbridge[4] and Peter Enns[5] could both claim to be "inerrantists."[6] Along the way, the word "evangelical" has suffered a similar fate. Whereas once "evangelical" connoted common views on certain scriptural teachings—the deity and resurrection of Christ, the substitutionary atonement of Christ, the necessity of personal faith in Christ for salvation from sin, and the reality of heaven and hell—today there is very little common ground on these issues among those calling themselves "evangelical."[7] It appears that if one feels warmly about Jesus as a present reality in one's life, this qualifies one to be called an Evangelical, whatever else such a person may believe about Jesus and the Scriptures that testify to him.

---

2. A point of view strongly put forward by Harold Lindsell, *The Battle for the Bible* (Grand Rapids: Zondervan, 1976).

3. Jack B. Rogers and Donald K. McKim, *The Authority and Interpretation of the Bible: An Historical Approach* (San Francisco: Harper & Row, 1979).

4. John D. Woodbridge, *Biblical Authority: A Critique of the Rogers/McKim Proposal* (Grand Rapids: Zondervan, 1982).

5. Peter Enns, *Inspiration and Incarnation: Evangelicals and the Problem of the Old Testament* (Grand Rapids: Baker Academic, 2005).

6. See G. K. Beale, *The Erosion of Inerrancy in Evangelicalism: Responding to New Challenges to Biblical Authority* (Wheaton, IL: Crossway, 2008).

7. A similar thing has happened to the word "myth." It is a counsel of despair to claim, as Kenton Sparks does, that, since the current definitions of "myth" are so many and so diverse, we can only say that a myth is a tale of the gods (*Ancient Texts for the Study of the Hebrew Bible: A Guide to the Background Literature* [Peabody, MA: Hendrickson, 2005], 306). Thus, any narrative about a deity is labeled a myth, even if one of those narratives is diametrically opposite in content, nature, and intent from all the rest. See my *The Bible among the Myths: Unique Revelation or Just Ancient Literature?* (Grand Rapids: Zondervan, 2009) for further discussion.

So, is it even worthwhile to attempt to define an evangelical view of Scripture? I believe it is, perhaps especially so in the present chaotic situation. There are legitimate and illegitimate uses of ideas as determined by their origins and historic usage, and it is always appropriate to call people back to the legitimate ones. Furthermore, it is essential that those of us who share common views stand together, not allowing differences on lesser issues to divide us.

Obviously, a full treatment of this complex topic would demand a volume or more, not merely a section of a short paper. Thus, I am fully aware of the summary nature of what I propose here. Because of its necessary terseness, my presentation will pass over important nuances, the discussion of which would need to be part of a fuller treatment. But my hope is that what I offer here may find broad acceptance among those of us who affirm Scripture as the inspired word of God and thus form a general basis for our ongoing discussion of Isaiah.

First of all, let us remember that the idea that the Bible is completely truthful and reliable, and thus "without error," is a very ancient one, extending from Ignatius to individuals as diverse as Augustine and Wesley. Even if we cannot locate precise earlier roots for the particular Hodge/Warfield way of formulating this thought, the concept itself is by no means one that first originated in the nineteenth century CE.[8] Why was this position on the Bible's truthfulness and reliability taken? Undoubtedly it was because of the prior conviction on the part of those who espoused it that the Bible is divine revelation. Whence came that conviction? The reasons leading to it are both objective and subjective. Objectively, there is simply no other literature like it anywhere else. While one can find numerous connections with other literatures in terms of details, the whole is simply *sui generis*. What other explanation can be given for this phenomenon than the one it gives itself? It is from YHWH, I Am.

The subjective evidence is directly coupled with the objective evidence. In stories that can be multiplied thousands of times over, we hear of individuals who read the Bible and find their lives transformed. This book has a unique capacity to address people. Other books capture the imagination; other books seize the mind; other books inspire to action. This book addresses people and calls them out of whatever it is that holds them in captivity. YHWH, most especially in the person of Christ, speaks to people out of this book.

So, on the basis of both the objective and the subjective evidence, which are consistent with each other, the conviction arose that this collection is the revelation of God.[9] When we then recognize the fact that it is YHWH's absolute reliability, along with his *ḥesed* and his goodness, that defines his nature, it certainly follows

---

8. See the data presented by Woodbridge, *Biblical Authority*.

9. Any lesser understanding of the nature of the Bible has disastrous results for the concept of revelation, as Brevard Childs and James Barr, among others, argued so devastatingly in the 1970s (James Barr, "Revelation through History in the Old Testament and in Modern Theology," in *New Theology No. 1*, ed. Martin Marty and Dean G. Peerman [New York: Macmillan, 1964], 60–74; Brevard S. Childs, *Biblical Theology in Crisis* [Philadelphia: Westminster, 1970]). If the Bible only *contains* revelation, we have no sure way to distinguish what is revealed from what is not. On the other hand, if the Bible only *witnesses to* revelation, and it is granted that the witnesses are fallible, then we have no access to the revelation itself.

that what he says, or directs to be said, is true. But here comes the sticking point: true in what sense? Can the Bible not convey theological truth to us in narratives that are not themselves historically factual? Surely we do not reduce truth to mere facts, it will be said.

The problem with this argument is that it dismisses the Bible's own warrant for its theology. William F. Albright, who was no Evangelical, despite what his modern detractors say, had it right. He said that the only way we can explain Israel's distinctive ideas is if they had some distinctive experiences.[10] And this is exactly what the Israelites (and, later, the Jews and the early Christians) claim. From Genesis to Revelation, the biblical writers make their theological claims on the basis of YHWH's having intruded into their experience and having subsequently explained to them the significance of those intrusions. If YHWH did not act and speak in those very ways, we are left with no explanation for their unique theology. If that theology was only an accident of history, as those who refuse to accept the possibility of revelation claim, then we should expect that accident, or a similar one, to have been produced elsewhere. But the stunning fact is that it was not. Thus, we can only conclude that, if the Bible's theology is true, then the historical basis for that theology must be true as well.[11]

So what does the Bible's reliability entail? In the end the word one uses (whether "reliability" or another) is less important than one's hermeneutical approach. An "inerrancy hermeneutic" would assume the following: (1) no biblical writer knowingly falsified any statement of fact; (2) claims of authorship are to be taken at face value; (3) statements are completely reliable when understood in the light of genre and current usage; and (4) apparent discrepancies would disappear if all the data were known. This, it seems to me, is the right direction in which to proceed. The question is not whether a person uses a certain word (e.g., "inerrancy") to define him- or herself. The question is what one holds the text to be and what implications concerning the entire truthfulness of the text that conviction leads one to affirm.[12]

Many Evangelicals look favorably upon canonical criticism as a way past the impasse that exists between reading the Bible as the word of God and the increasing skepticism concerning its worth as a historical document. So it is thought that one can say in faith that the Bible has been given to us in its present form as the word of God and that it can be interpreted as such in spite of the incorrectness of its statements about its origins. I find it somewhat ironic that this approach owes the most to Brevard Childs, since it was Childs who, along with James Barr, so thoroughly demolished G. Ernest Wright's proposal that a fallible witness can

---

10. William F. Albright, *History, Archaeology and Christian Humanism* (New York: McGraw-Hill, 1964), 83–100.

11. See *Do Historical Matters Matter to Faith? A Critical Appraisal of Modern and Postmodern Approaches to Scripture*, ed. James K. Hoffmeier and Dennis R. Magary (Wheaton, IL: Crossway, 2012).

12. See James I. Packer, "Infallible Scripture and the Role of Hermeneutics," in *Scripture and Truth*, ed. D. A. Carson and John D. Woodbridge (Grand Rapids: Zondervan, 1983), 353–54.

nonetheless convey true theology. It also seems ironic to me that canonical criticism rests on the very same premise upon which the Biblical Theology Movement was built, namely, that the validity of theology can be separated from the reliability of the claims about the origins of the theology.[13] I cannot see how the theology of the Abraham narrative can have any claim over me if the narrative itself is legendary.[14] Furthermore, I do not understand what led the proponents of this theology to cast it in narrative form at all if these events never took place, especially when no other people ever cast their theology in such a form. I do not believe that one can have a valid theology if that theology is cut loose from what the theology claims as its origin and warrant.

The Importance of the Biblical Claims Concerning a Book's Origins

If one grants what has been stated in the preceding section, it is vitally important to see what a biblical book both says and implies about its origins. If the book makes no explicit or implicit claims about authorship or date (as for instance, the book of Joel), an evangelical approach does not impose any demands upon the interpreter. On the other hand, if such claims are made, then we must shape our interpretations according to those claims. Of course, if we approach the book as non-Evangelicals, these claims will have no *a priori* impact upon us, and we can treat them on strictly rational grounds, accepting them or dismissing them at will.

In my view, what is happening with regard to the book of Isaiah is like the clam's response to the starfish tugging on its shell. Many Evangelicals have become tired of resisting the unrelenting pressure of the so-called critical consensus regarding Isaiah's date and composition and are accepting multiple authorship without adequate consideration of the implications of that decision.[15] Too often, on this

---

13. In this regard, it is very interesting to compare Childs' commentary on Isaiah (*Isaiah: A Commentary*, OTL [Louisville: Westminster John Knox, 2001]), one of his last works, with his earlier commentary on Exodus (*The Book of Exodus: A Critical, Theological Commentary*, OTL [Philadelphia: Westminster, 1974]). On the one hand, in the Exodus commentary he devotes a considerable amount of space to reconstructing the supposed history of the text, on the apparent assumption that knowing its "actual" history will aid the reader in interpreting the final form of the text (to which relatively little attention is given). In the Isaiah commentary, on the other hand, he gives almost no attention to hypothetical earlier forms of the text and interprets the final form with relatively little attention to historical settings. In two different ways, he seems to be testifying to the difficulty that results from removing the final meaning of a text from its claimed historical origins.

14. A legendary account certainly could convey moving and inspirational content worthy of reflection. But that is very different from saying that the content is a divine revelation demanding my allegiance to the God whom it reveals.

15. As in Pentateuchal studies, "consensus" in the case of Isaiah is a rather misleading term. The only real consensus is that the present book is not the work of a single author. Once one affirms one's critical "orthodoxy" on that point, then there is almost total freedom.

and other critical questions, they only ask whether it is still possible to retain their faith in Jesus Christ after having adopted the position. Concluding in most cases that it is, they gratefully accept the majority position and are deeply grieved when someone questions not their piety but their orthodoxy. The fact is, the wrong question has been asked. The question is not whether faith can be retained in spite of accepting prevailing critical reconstructions of the Bible (faith can be remarkably tenacious), but whether faith can be promulgated *from* such a Bible. Will such a Bible ever provide an adequate basis for faith?

Today, as early twenty-first-century "Evangelicals," we are all too unconsciously replaying events from a century ago. At that time, persons of undoubted piety and faith (such as George Adam Smith,[16] W. Robertson Smith,[17] and Charles A. Briggs[18]) were asserting that a vital experience with God was not dependent upon one's judgments concerning the way in which the Scriptures came to be. Over against them, persons like Benjamin Warfield,[19] Robert Dick Wilson,[20] and J. Gresham Machen[21] asserted with equal vigor that the then-emerging critical positions so undermined any concept of divine involvement in the creation of the Bible that the Bible's claims for the revealed nature of its theology were rendered meaningless. They argued that the effect of the new biblical criticism would be to destroy the Bible's ability to create faith. What they were saying was that Smith, Briggs, and others like them had not adequately considered the implications of the positions they were enthusiastically adopting. That these individuals were able to retain their personal faith (usually entered into during the pre-critical stage of their lives) did not prove that a critically decimated Bible retained the capacity to call others to that same faith.[22]

The result is that there are almost as many proposals for the composition of the book as there are scholars in the field. If there is any unanimity at present, it is that Isaiah of Jerusalem probably wrote what is now chapters 6–12 and perhaps some other parts of chapters 15–33; that the anonymous prophet of the exile probably wrote chapters 40–55 (although there is still lingering doubt among some over the so-called Servant Songs); and that chapters 56–66 are a collection of postexilic writings. On the questions of how long the process actually took and who was responsible for the final form, there is no agreement at all.

16. George A. Smith, *The Book of Isaiah*, ed. W. R. Nicholl, 2 vols., Expositor's Bible (London: Hodder & Stoughton, 1910).

17. W. Robertson Smith, *The Old Testament in the Jewish Church*, 2nd ed. (New York: D. Appleton, 1892).

18. Charles A. Briggs, *The Higher Criticism of the Hexateuch*, 2nd ed. (New York: Scribner's, 1897).

19. Warfield, *Inspiration and Authority*.

20. Robert D. Wilson, *A Scientific Investigation of the Old Testament* (Philadelphia: Sunday School Times, 1926).

21. J. Gresham Machen, *Christianity and Liberalism* (New York: Macmillan, 1923), 69–79.

22. On the illogicality of faith based on what is taught in a critically reconstructed Bible, see the comments of Bart Ehrman and William Dever in "Losing Faith: Who Did and Who Didn't," *BAR* 33.2 (2007): 50–57.

I wish here to raise that challenge again, because, in my opinion, history has proven the fundamentalists, for all their defects, to be correct on this point. Where is saving faith today among the descendants of the critics of a century ago?[23] Wherever vigorous faith exists in the world today, it is a direct consequence of a high view of Scripture, whether of a pre-critical sort (as in the Orthodox churches, for example) or of a fundamentalist sort (as in Britain and America and all those lands touched by the British and American missionary enterprises). This is true in both Wesleyan and Calvinist circles.[24] If we are convinced that the origins of the biblical message are quite different from what a plain reading of the text would lead us to believe and that these origins are not only different but are also artfully concealed, inevitably the veracity of that message as religious truth cannot be maintained. To this extent the fundamentalists were correct: faith and a kind of criticism that denies the Bible's own claims about its origins cannot coexist to the second generation.

I realize that by taking this approach I open myself to the charge of trying to foreclose all critical investigation with an appeal to philosophical and theological arguments. This is not my purpose. The Bible by its very nature calls us to historical and literary inquiry. For instance, it is obvious that the canon arose over a long period of time. This fact invites us to make serious attempts to understand that historical and literary process. We must carry out such inquiries as best we can. In some cases, perhaps many, they will demand that we revise some dearly held positions. However, the Bible's character as the "mother" of the Christian faith *also* must be taken into account in these inquiries; to fail to do so is to leave out a vital part of the equation. It may sound courageous to claim that we will not allow matters of faith to enter into our investigations as we only go where the data lead us, but, in fact, the Bible's character as a faith document is a part of the data. To leave this out, therefore, is not courageous but simply wrong.

---

23. Neo-orthodoxy was a short-lived attempt to bridge the gap between criticism and authority by saying that God revealed himself to Israel and the church and that, while we no longer have direct access to that revelation, the Bible's theology is still directly inspired by YHWH. The logical contradiction between a fallible source and an infallible result doomed the attempt in Europe by 1965 and America by 1975. It is significant that the people who have the most vital interest in this theology today are American Evangelicals who bring to it an *a priori* faith commitment. (Cornelius Van Til's critique of Brunner in his introduction to the 1948 edition of Warfield, *Inspiration and Authority*, is very apropos.)

24. It is popular among Wesleyans today to attempt to disassociate themselves from "fundamentalist" understandings of the Bible. It is pointed out that Wesleyans in the 1880s and 1890s did not insist on biblical authority in the ways in which scholars in the Reformed tradition did, and it is suggested that the adoption of the verbal-plenary theory of inspiration by such theologians as H. Orton Wiley (*Christian Theology*, 3 vols. [Kansas City: Beacon Hill, 1940–43]) was an unfortunate mistake. In fact, when conservative Wesleyans awakened to the modernist threat in the first two decades of the twentieth century, they had to decide who their real friends were and who shared their convictions. It is understandable that they chose Warfield, since he expressed what they believed. It is significant that when the Methodist Episcopal Church, South, wanted to print a defense against modernism, it chose Robert Dick Wilson's popular tract *Is the Higher Criticism Scholarly?* (Nashville: Methodist Publishing House, 1924; original, Philadelphia: Sunday School Times, 1922).

It must also be noted that many of the data related to the major critical problems are notably slippery. We do not have objective evidence to support any of the major critical reconstructions of the Bible. This means that leaving out faith questions immediately tends to direct the results toward conclusions that exclude any direct divine intervention in the final product. If I begin to investigate some phenomenon or event by excluding matters of faith, it will not be surprising if I come up with an explanation for that event that is destructive of faith. To admit the question of faith may not finally issue in an explanation that demands faith, but it at least leaves open that possibility, if it should be called for. Accordingly, this is what I am calling for Evangelicals to do: before we accept the logic of a theory that claims to explain biblical phenomena in a certain way, let us also consider where that theory will take us. If it takes us to a place where the Bible can no longer fulfill the function that it undeniably has done for at least three thousand years, namely, creating faith in YHWH, the God and Father of our Lord Jesus Christ, let us approach that theory with the highest degree of skepticism.

Current Views on the Unity of Isaiah and the Question of Authorship

It is particularly appropriate to consider these questions with regard to the book of Isaiah because of the very profound change that has come over Isaiah studies during the last thirty years. From the appearance, in 1892, of Bernard Duhm's epochal commentary *Das Buch Jesaia*—epochal because from that time onward the majority opinion was solidly fixed on multiple authorship—the basic thrust was toward greater and greater fragmentation of the book.[25] Although the rise of form criticism altered the way in which this breaking up of the book into smaller and smaller fragments was carried out, it still furthered the same cause.[26]

---

25. Bernhard Duhm, *Das Buch Jesaia* (Göttingen: Vandenhoeck & Ruprecht, 1892).

26. Such early form-critical work as that of the following scholars gave reason to believe that some of the blocks of material that had been divided by previous methods should, in fact, be read together: Hugo Gressmann, "Die literarische Analyse Deuterojesajas," *ZAW* 34 (1914): 254–97; Sigmund Mowinckel, "Die Komposition des deuterojesajanischen Buches," *ZAW* 49 (1931): 87–112, 242–60; and Joachim Begrich, *Studien zu Deuterojesaja*, BWANT 4/25 (Stuttgart: Kohlhammer, 1938). But form criticism also has added its own measure of subjectivism, in that its proponents have not been able to produce enough evidence for the structure and development of many of the supposed forms to enable different people to reach the same conclusions when analyzing the same pieces of literature. Thus, between 1945 and 1975 a great deal of attention was given to attempts to determine authenticity on the basis of whether certain sentences or words were part of the original form or not. The best expressions of this work in commentary form are those of the Das Alte Testament Deutsch and the Biblischer Kommentar, Altes Testament, series: Otto Kaiser, *Der Prophet Jesaja: Kapitel 1–12*, ATD 17 (Göttingen: Vandenhoeck & Ruprecht, 1960); idem, *Der Prophet Jesaja: Kapitel 13–39*, ATD 18 (Göttingen: Vandenhoeck & Ruprecht, 1973); Claus Westermann, *Das Buch Jesaja: Kapitel 40–66*, ATD 19 (Göttingen: Vandenhoeck & Ruprecht, 1966); Hans

But by the early 1970s, a change in direction began to appear. Further effort in subdividing pericopes (e.g., the work of Antoon Schoors[27] and Rosario Merendino[28]) seemed to have reached the point of dwindling results. There was an attitude abroad of "so what?" How did all of the immense effort expended help us to achieve a better understanding of what the book of Isaiah is actually saying? Undoubtedly, Childs' emphasis on the importance of the canonical form of the text was an important catalyst, especially with the appearance of his foundational works in this regard.[29] In the early 1980s, a number of works exploring ways in which the book might be interpreted as a whole appeared. Among the authors were Carroll Stuhlmueller,[30] Ronald Clements,[31] Walter Brueggemann,[32] Rolf Rendtorff,[33] and others.[34] Christopher Seitz gave special focus to these concerns in the 1988 volume that he edited, *Reading and Preaching the Book of Isaiah*.[35] The various chapters in this book all speak to the issues of the wholeness of the canonical text. What all the authors in this volume were seeking to do was to understand better what the final shape of the book is intending to say. Furthermore, these authors all agreed that the later parts of the book were written with full knowledge of the earlier parts. They traced the development of these parts throughout and showed how materials in some early chapters presuppose the existence of the conclusions that later chapters reach. So thorough was the change that Rolf Rendtorff stated in a paper on the composition of Isaiah read at the 1991 annual meeting of the Society of Biblical Literature that it was no longer possible to approach the study of the book as was done fifteen years earlier (i.e., as a collection of essentially unrelated pericopes).[36]

Wildberger, *Jesaja: Kapitel 1–39*, 3 vols., BKAT 10 (Neukirchen-Vluyn: Neukirchener, 1965–82); Karl Elliger and Hans-Jürgen Hermisson, *Deuterojesaja*, 3 vols., BKAT 11 (Neukirchen-Vluyn: Neukirchener, 1970–2014).

27. Antoon Schoors, *I Am God Your Saviour: A Form-Critical Study of the Main Genres in Is. XL–LV*, VTSup 24 (Leiden: Brill, 1973).

28. Rosario P. Merendino, *Der Erste und Letzte: Eine Untersuchung von Jes 40–48*, VTSup 31 (Leiden: Brill, 1981).

29. Brevard S. Childs, *Old Testament Theology in a Canonical Context* (Philadelphia: Fortress, 1986).

30. Carroll Stuhlmueller, "Deutero-Isaiah: Major Transitions in the Prophet's Theology and in Contemporary Scholarship," *CBQ* 42 (1980): 1–29.

31. Ronald E. Clements, "The Unity of the Book of Isaiah," *Int* 36 (1982): 117–29.

32. Walter Brueggemann, "Unity and Dynamic in the Isaiah Tradition," *JSOT* 29 (1984): 89–107.

33. Rolf Rendtorff, "Zur Komposition des Buches Jesaja," *VT* 34 (1984): 295–320.

34. Although Roy F. Melugin's *The Formation of Isaiah 40–55*, BZAW 141 (Berlin: de Gruyter, 1976) is an intensely form-critical study, his continual concern for the function of the pericopes in their present relation to each other is an expression of these emerging concerns.

35. Christopher R. Seitz, ed., *Reading and Preaching the Book of Isaiah* (Philadelphia: Fortress, 1988; repr., Eugene, OR: Wipf & Stock, 2002).

36. Rolf Rendtorff, "The Book of Isaiah: A Complex Unity; Synchronic and Diachronic Reading," in *Society of Biblical Literature 1991 Seminar Papers*, ed. Eugene H. Lovering Jr., SBLSP 30 (Atlanta: Scholars Press, 1991), 8–20 (subsequently revised and reprinted in Roy

This was quite an admission from the foremost student of a leading form critic, Gerhard von Rad.

While some of the earlier enthusiasm for this way of understanding the book has waned, its continuing influence can be seen in such works as Hugh Williamson's *The Book Called Isaiah*[37] and, most strikingly, in Brevard Childs' commentary in the Old Testament Library series.[38] This is the first critical commentary in more than a century to treat the entire book as a canonical whole. It is especially significant that this volume replaces the three volumes by Otto Kaiser and Claus Westermann in the Old Testament Library series, which treated Isa 1–39 and 40–66 as distinct from one another.[39]

As encouraging as this trend is for those of us concerned for the theological integrity of the book of Isaiah in its present, canonical form, we must not lose sight of the fact that there has been no real shift from the conviction of multiple authorship. Christopher Seitz is as convinced as Duhm was that the book is the product of many authors/editors who wrote from many different perspectives. Seitz also believes that the unity of the present book is not the result of the original vision but rather of progressive editorial development.[40] Critical scholars continue to reject emphatically earlier arguments for unity of authorship.[41] Rather, we have a Wellhausen-like synthesis for Isaiah. Sometime during the fifth, or perhaps the fourth, century BCE, the book appeared in its final form. This utilized several preexisting collections, which, in turn, had also incorporated older pieces. There is wide disagreement about the number and extent of those various pieces. The whole was combined with appropriate transitional segments to produce a coherent theological statement, a theology that, some would say, was incipient in the very first pieces. The two-volume commentary by John Watts in the Word Biblical

---

F. Melugin and Marvin A. Sweeney, eds., *New Visions of Isaiah*, JSOTSup 214 [Sheffield: Sheffield Academic, 1996], 32–49).

37. H. G. M. Williamson, *The Book Called Isaiah: Deutero-Isaiah's Role in Composition and Redaction* (Oxford: Clarendon, 1994).

38. Childs, *Isaiah*.

39. Otto Kaiser, *Isaiah 1–12: A Commentary*, trans. John Bowden, 2nd ed., OTL (Philadelphia: Westminster, 1983); idem, *Isaiah 13–39: A Commentary*, trans. R. A. Wilson, OTL (Philadelphia: Westminster, 1974); Claus Westermann, *Isaiah 40–66*, trans. David M. G. Stalker, OTL (Philadelphia: Westminster, 1969).

40. Christopher R. Seitz, "Introduction: The One Isaiah // The Three Isaiahs," in *Reading and Preaching the Book of Isaiah*, ed. Christopher R. Seitz (Philadelphia: Fortress, 1988; repr., Eugene, OR: Wipf & Stock, 2002), 17–18. This is not to denigrate his efforts. The final chapter of the book just mentioned reveals that Seitz is as concerned about the theological unity and integrity of the book as I am. But he is trying to maintain these after having become convinced of multiple authorship. While I remain skeptical of the viability of that effort, if multiple authorship is the only option, his is a laudable effort.

41. As contained, for instance, in Oswald T. Allis, *The Unity of Isaiah: A Study in Prophecy* (Philadelphia: Presbyterian & Reformed, 1950); Edward J. Young, *Who Wrote Isaiah?* (Grand Rapids: Eerdmans, 1958); and Rachel Margalioth, *The Indivisible Isaiah: Evidence for the Single Authorship of the Prophetic Book* (New York: Yeshiva University, 1964).

Commentary series incorporates some of this understanding, as does Williamson's volume mentioned above.[42]

The significance of this development for the concern of this paper is that it brings to the forefront the question, "How does the present form of the book ask us to understand what the book as a whole is saying?" Can an after-the-fact unity explain and undergird the revelational theology of the book?[43] This question is of critical importance in assessing the theological implications of multiple authorship. Can the book be understood as a theological whole if it is the result of a long redactional process? Presumably, the answer could be affirmative; the question is whether the book will allow us to do so in view of its own internal claims. It is to that problem that we now turn.

The Evidence of the Book of Isaiah in Regard to Its Authorship

At the outset, we must be careful not to assume more for Isaiah than it claims for itself. This was one major fault of the fundamentalist apologetic for inspiration— the tendency to construct philosophical models of what divine inspiration would entail and then to impose those findings upon the text. When it became clear, in case after case, that the text itself did not make such sweeping claims, the whole attempt was called into question. There is nothing about the Bible's message that, in and of itself, rules out a theology developing over hundreds of years. In fact, that is an apt description of the whole biblical-theological enterprise. From Genesis to Revelation, biblical theology manifests a continuous development that still remains within the broad parameters that make that theology unique. Thus, the idea that a given book, or group of books, might show this same process in microcosm is not impossible. For example, there can be no question that the texts that make up the book of Kings (1 and 2 Kings in English versions) went through a long collection period extending from Solomon (970 BCE) to the destruction of Jerusalem (586 BCE) and that the final collection exhibits a clearly unified theological perspective. Nor is there is anything *a priori* that says that the kind of development of Hebrew religion that the Documentary (i.e., JEDP) theory of Pentateuchal origins hypothesizes could not have been the actual way in which God revealed himself to the Hebrew people. But the problem comes with the repeated insistence of the text of the Pentateuch that this is *not* the way that revelation took place. Here is the problem. If, for whatever reason, conscious or unconscious, the Hebrew people felt it necessary to create a fictional explanation of the origins of their nation and faith,

---

42. John D. W. Watts, *Isaiah 1–33*, WBC 24 (Waco, TX: Word, 1985); *Isaiah 34–66*, WBC 25 (Waco, TX: Word, 1987); Williamson, *Book Called Isaiah*. For a good summary of various approaches to the book's unity, see Williamson, "Isaiah: Book of," in *Dictionary of the Old Testament: Prophets*, ed. Mark J. Boda and J. Gordon McConville (Downers Grove, IL: InterVarsity Press, 2012), 366–71.

43. That it cannot do so is seen in a gradual lessening of interest in the unity of the book during the past decade.

what grounds does that faith have for the sweeping claims it makes for its God and his demands upon the human heart?

That, then, is the issue in Isaiah: not what could have been the case, but what does the present form of the text claim to have been the case. Does the text invite us to read it as the end-product of two or three hundred years of theological reflection and editing, having been sparked by the initial writings of Isaiah son of Amoz, with its final form having been incipient from the beginning but only given to the whole at the end of the process? My own studies have convinced me, somewhat against my will, that a plain reading of the text will not permit this. In fact, I am now convinced that the book is at pains to deny such an account of its origins.[44] That being the case, I am driven to conclude that acceptance of multiple authorship of Isaiah in any of its popular forms is finally incompatible with faith in the Bible as the inerrant Word of God.[45]

What are the claims of Isaiah regarding its origins? As has been frequently noted, there is no mention of the prophet Isaiah after chapter 39. Furthermore, there is no historical reportage that would undeniably link chapters 40–66 with the Judah of 700 BCE.[46] The hints of historical context in chapters 40–55 all point to the exile, while similar hints in chapters 56–66 point (although with less clarity) to the postexilic period.[47] This is unlike the Pentateuch, in which the insistence upon Mosaic authorship is found repeatedly from Exod 24:3 to Deut 31:22. Where, then, do I find the claims that I think have faith implications?[48]

First of all, if Isaiah is not specifically referred to after chapter 39, neither is any other writer. Given the superscription, the lack of any other name in the book

---

44. For a capable, contemporary defense of single authorship, see Richard L. Schultz, "How Many Isaiahs Were There and What Does It Matter? Prophetic Inspiration in Recent Evangelical Scholarship," in *Evangelicals and Scripture: Tradition, Authority and Hermeneutics*, ed. Vincent Bacote, Laura C. Miguélez, and Dennis L. Okholm (Downers Grove, IL: InterVarsity Press, 2004), 150–70; idem, "Isaiah, Isaiahs, and Current Scholarship," in *Do Historical Matters Matter to Faith? A Critical Appraisal of Modern and Postmodern Approaches to Scripture*, ed. James K. Hoffmeier and Dennis R. Magary (Wheaton, IL: Crossway, 2012), 243–61.

45. This is not to "de-Christianize" those who are convinced of multiple authorship. One's position on this subject is certainly not one of the essentials for salvation!

46. However, it should be noted that the references to idolatry in chapters 56–66 are not in the same vein as those in the undeniably postexilic books. In books like Haggai, Zechariah, and Malachi, the issue seems to center more on syncretism and sorcery rather than on actual idol worship, as Isa 57:1–10 does, for instance. Nevertheless, this constitutes only suggestive, not hard, evidence.

47. John N. Oswalt, "Who Were the Addressees of Isaiah 40–66?," *BSac* 169 (2012): 33–47.

48. This absence of repeated statements of authorship in Isaiah demands that I give more latitude on this question than I do on the authorship of the Pentateuch. There, it seems to me, the text forecloses the options very severely. Although the evidence for Isaiah seems conclusive to me, the absence of repeated statements in this book means that room for sincere difference of opinion concerning authorship must be left. I am concerned with the basis for those opinions, however. See below.

is significant. Thus there is no reason to doubt that the superscription is intended to qualify the entire following document, no matter what the latter's length may be. "Isaianic" responsibility for all that follows is thus the "default" position, unless there is a specific deviation from that, which there is not.

With regard to the provenance of chapters 40–66, Brevard Childs makes a vital observation. Assuming multiple authorship, he looks for the identification of these other authors as well as for the specific historical events that, on the pattern of the other Hebrew prophets, should form a framework for their messages. Strangely to him, he finds none of the former, and, with the single exception of references to the historic personage Cyrus, only the most general forms of the latter. This leads Childs to conclude that the final editors have consciously deleted any material that would point away from Isaianic authorship. They have removed any references to authors and events that would give the reader any context for the interpretation of the book other than that of Jerusalem in 700 BCE.[49]

While we may disagree with Childs' conclusions here, his observations are of the greatest importance, since, in my opinion, he is absolutely correct. For whatever reason, the supposed authors/editors of the second part of the book (chs. 40–66) did not wish either their name or their location to be identified. An instructive contrast is found in the book of Ezekiel, where the author, the setting, and, frequently, the audience are defined for every address and often reiterated within the address. But this is not only the case for Ezekiel; this kind of identification is characteristic of all the prophets.[50] This makes its absence all the more striking in Isaiah. We can only conclude that the failure to identify the hypothetical additional contributors is highly significant.[51]

The lack of explicit historical and geographical settings for chapters 40–66 is equally significant. To be sure, as mentioned above, we may believe that these chapters have exilic and postexilic readers in view, but that is very different from saying that the material was written during those times.[52] Other biblical prophecies go far beyond what "Second" and "Third Isaiah" demonstrate in rooting their

---

49. See Childs' 1972 James Sprunt Lectures at Union Theological Seminary, "Canon and Criticism: The Old Testament as Scripture of the Church." See also Brevard S. Childs, *Introduction to the Old Testament as Scripture* (Philadelphia: Fortress, 1979), 325–27.

50. Joel presents a possible exception in that it does not specify its place or time in a way that we can now define. However, in its own day, the locust plague almost certainly provided very specific identification of those factors. In its present form, Isaiah does not give any information that would have been any more useful then than it is now.

51. For a compelling argument for the importance of the New Testament's identification of Isaiah as the author of the entire book, see G. K. Beale's article in the present volume.

52. This is the only place where an Old Testament prophet would be speaking *to* people in the future and not merely about them. I suggest that the reason for this is twofold. In the first place, the exile of the northern tribes in 721 BCE and following demanded theological address, particularly in view of Isaiah's sweeping statements about YHWH's absolute trustworthiness and his realization that Judah's exile was only deferred. In the second place, the theology of chapters 6–39 demanded a rounding out and completion that could only be seen in the light of what the coming generations would endure. See Oswalt, "Who Were the Addressees," for further discussion of these points. See also note 62 below.

pronouncements in specific settings.[53] No persons are named (with the exception of Cyrus, which is made more striking by this uniqueness); no locations are given; and no particular historical events are made the basis of the statements. Thus, Childs' observations are correct.

How can we account for this? Four possible explanations present themselves. The first is the most easily dismissed: all of this is an accident. This is hardly possible, given the clear intentionality of the rest of the prophetic corpus. In light of the evident care with which the texts were studied and transmitted, it cannot be supposed that such an "accident" could have crept past the editor(s) without correction.

A second possibility is that these omissions were intentional, but that we no longer know what that intention was. This is the counsel of despair. Again, given the univocal approach of the prophetic writers to historical rootage, such an omission can hardly have been of such casual concern as to have the reasons for it be left unclear to the readers of the material.

The third and fourth possibilities share the same rationale but not the same explanation. The rationale is that the present form of the book testifies to a single author. But from this point the two hypotheses part company. The first is that of Childs. He assumes that the original forms of "Second" and "Third Isaiah" did identify their authors and settings, just as we would expect, but that these were consciously removed during the redaction process in order to express the conviction that the far-reaching theological perspective of the final form of the book is indeed a whole and not a composite one.

But what this means is that a fiction (regarding authorship) has been resorted to in support of what the authors/editors considered to be a truth (regarding message). Does that in and of itself make the "truth" untrue? Perhaps not, but then one must also ask why the authors/editors did this. Did they believe that their "truth" was not convincing unless they created a fictional context for it? Did they believe that an open admission of the actual origins of their conclusions about the nature of reality would call into question the validity of those conclusions? This question is of the utmost importance and will be considered further below.

Like the third hypothesis, the fourth argues that the present form of the book testifies to single authorship. But, unlike the third, it accepts that the data may be taken at face value rather than being the result of alteration in support of a fictional conclusion. Materials identifying the date(s) of other authors are not present for the simple reason that there were no other authors. By the same token, specific details of the exilic and postexilic periods are missing from chapters 40–66 because these materials were not spoken/written during those time periods. The lack of specificity found in those chapters would be exactly what might be expected of a person who only knew the most general features of those future periods. This

---

53. This absence is why Paul D. Hanson was able to deconstruct chapters 56–66 so thoroughly and then reconstruct them to fit a completely hypothetical setting (*The Dawn of Apocalyptic* [Philadelphia: Fortress, 1979]). This would have been much more difficult if the material were as rooted in an explicit historical setting as most other biblical prophecies are.

is not to overlook the startling exception of Cyrus, but this is a case of the exception proving the rule. If the author was sufficiently at home in his exilic situation to want to include Cyrus in his prophecy, it is inconceivable that he would not include additional details from his exilic experience as well. What that suggests is that the mention of Cyrus in the absence of other specific details is either evidence of predictive prophecy or an attempt to make the reader believe that it is predictive prophecy when it is not.

This latter point directs our attention toward another important claim of Isaiah. From the very beginning of the book, the reality of predictive prophecy is affirmed. This is the import of chapters 1–5, which virtually all commentators agree are, as a unit, designed as an introduction to the book in its present form. In these chapters, two themes are interchanged. First, both in sequence and proportion, is the announcement of the imminent destruction of the godless people of YHWH, the Holy One of Israel (1:1–31; 2:6–4:1; 5:1–30). But coupled directly with that announcement of judgment is the assurance of cleansing and a mission of Israel to the whole world (4:2–6 and 2:1–5). It is clear that this interchange is intended to tell the reader that the present book is to be read as a whole and that the prediction of near judgment in chapters 1–39 is one piece with the prediction of more distant hope in chapters 40–66.

Could one instead argue that chapters 1–5 were written sometime in the fourth or even the third century, after the redaction of the other Isaianic material had been completed? Could these chapters have been written as a retrospect rather than a prospect? Of course, that is possible, but, if so, the redactors have done their best to hide that that was the case. For, just as chapter 1 begins with a superscription identifying Isaiah as the author of what follows, so the segment 2:1–5:30 is identified as "the word that Isaiah son of Amoz saw concerning Judah and Jerusalem" (2:1). Thus, the introduction tells us that Isaiah son of Amoz saw the outlines of Judah's entire future in advance and that what follows in the remainder of the book is to be read in that light. The book intends that we understand that God is able to communicate to his prophets both general and specific information about the future. This is further supported by the prediction of the fall of Babylon in so-called "First Isaiah," in chapters 13–14, 21, and 39.[54] What the book is telling the reader is that we should believe that God is indeed the Lord of the Nations, the One who can be trusted because he knows both the immediate future and the distant future, and that nothing that happens will be either a surprise to him or beyond his direct control.

---

54. Critical scholars, for most of whom the impossibility of specific inspired prediction is a dictum, must excise such predictions from the work of Isaiah son of Amoz and ascribe them to some later figure. What, then, were the redactors trying to accomplish by putting these words in Isaiah's mouth? Williamson seeks to avoid this question by saying that much of so-called "First Isaiah" is the work of "Second Isaiah" from the late exilic period and that, therefore, nothing is being put in anyone's mouth (*Book Called Isaiah*; see esp. pp. 156–57 and 209–11). In my opinion, while this might be said of chapters 13–14 and 21, it definitely cannot be said of chapter 39, where some of the words are clearly described as coming from Isaiah's mouth.

Is this merely a faith statement that appropriate after-the-fact observations have been interpolated to support, or is it to be taken at face value? Much depends on the answer to this question. If we do not have actual evidence supporting our conviction that God knows the future, what claim upon human hearts does such a conviction have? What is the value of an argument for which the evidence has to be manufactured?

The insistence that God had predicted Judah's future far in advance is made even stronger in chapters 40–48. Again and again in those chapters we are told that YHWH's superiority over the idol-gods of Babylon is grounded in his ability to announce the future in advance and then bring the prediction to pass in history. This point is made repeatedly (41:21–24; 43:8–12; 44:6–8, 24–28; 45:21; 46:8–11; 48:4–8). The first of these texts will serve as an example:

> Set forth your case, says the LORD;
>   bring your proofs, says the King of Jacob.
> Let them bring them, and tell us
>   what is to happen.
> Tell us the former things, what they are,
>   that we may consider them,
> that we may know their outcome;
>   or declare to us the things to come.
> Tell us what is to come hereafter,
>   that we may know that you are gods;
> do good, or do harm,
>   that we may be dismayed and terrified.
> Behold, you are nothing,
>   and your work is less than nothing;
>   an abomination is he who chooses you.
>   (Isa 41:21–24 ESV)[55]

This passage explains the significance of the Cyrus prophecies.[56] They are the *pièce de résistance* in proof of these claims. Cyrus had been predicted long in advance, so that during the exile the Judeans would see the evidence coming forward in all its force. Some commentators try to gloss over the importance of this point by ignoring it.[57] Others suggest that the anonymous prophet of the exile had made the original predictions about Cyrus (which for some reason are not included in

---

55. Most treatments of this feature of the book do not do justice to the force of the argument. See, for instance, Carroll Stuhlmueller, "'First and Last' and 'YHWH-Creator' in Deutero-Isaiah," *CBQ* 29 (1967): 495–511. They relate it to statements about creation and the exodus instead of to the issue of the prediction of the return from exile.

56. Note in particular the linkages between predictive prophecy and the calling of Cyrus in the so-called Cyrus Oracle (44:24–27). Here all the themes of YHWH's unique divinity that appear in the "first" and "last" theme noted above occur in the specific context of the prediction of Cyrus.

57. See, for instance, Watts, *Isaiah 34–66*, 114–15, who *de facto* disallows the point by devoting most of the comment to a discussion of supposedly similar predictions ascribed

the present corpus) in 546 BCE, after Cyrus had become prominent and four or five years before the material now found in chapters 40–55 was written.[58]

But even this latter suggestion, which preserves some appearance of prediction, will not do, for it continues to deny the substance of prediction. According to advocates of this view, "Second Isaiah" made his so-called prediction after everyone knew about Cyrus and after even the Babylonians had begun to see him as a heaven-sent savior.[59] Such a "prediction" would be of little worth in the lawsuit against the idol-gods that is repeatedly presented in chapters 41–46.[60] Unless the captives could be led to believe that this Persian emperor had been predicted by their God long before he was even born, the oft-repeated arguments on behalf of YHWH's absolute superiority would have been worthless.[61]

The Theological Issues Relating to the Authorship of the Book of Isaiah

These then are the theological issues relating to the authorship (and by extension, the unity) of the book of Isaiah. If the book is the product of a redactional process

---

to Marduk in the Babylonian Nabonidus Chronicle. A comparison of the two literatures reveals significant differences.

58. So Christopher R. North, "The 'Former' Things and the 'New' Things in Deutero-Isaiah," in *Studies in Old Testament Prophecy Presented to Professor Theodore H. Robinson by the Society for Old Testament Study on His Sixty-fifth Birthday, August 9th 1946*, ed. H. H. Rowley (Edinburgh: T&T Clark, 1950), 111–26.

59. Cf. the translation of the Cyrus Cylinder in *ANET*, 315–16.

60. It is interesting to note how many commentators, in their discussions of the lawsuit, admit that "Second Isaiah" really did not have grounds for his absolutistic claims, since the idol-gods also foretold the future. So, for example, Duhm, *Das Buch Jesaia*, 307; John L. McKenzie, *Second Isaiah*, AB 20 (Garden City: Doubleday, 1968), 28; R. N. Whybray, *Isaiah 40–66*, NCB (London: Marshall, Morgan & Scott, 1975), 69. Westermann also claims that the gods foretold the future, but he insists that it is the centuries-old prophecies of the exile that make possible "Second Isaiah's" arguments (*Isaiah 40–66*, 90–91). According to Westermann, Isaiah's point here is that no idol ever gave a *specific* prediction (such as that regarding Cyrus). Williamson denies the force of the argument made above with regard to predictive prophecy, saying that "there is still predictive prophecy in all parts of the book even on the most radical of critical positions" ("Isaiah: Book of," 370). In my view, this statement is both overly general and overstated. It is unclear what kind of prediction Williamson is talking about, and, in most cases, it has been a hallmark of critical scholarship to declare that all "prediction" is after the event.

61. A frequent charge is that, if Isaiah son of Amoz addressed part of his message primarily to people living 150 years in the future, then he was speaking about things that were meaningless to his own day (so Williamson, "Isaiah: Book of," 370). That is hardly the case, since, just as we receive as meaningful for our own day revelation from scriptures addressed to people thousands of years ago, so people in Isaiah's own day could receive revelation from scriptures addressed to people in the future. At the same time, the reference to the sealing up of the testimony (Isa 8:16–17) suggests that words can be given at one time that are intended for a future time.

extending over hundreds of years, the redactors involved have done everything in their power to hide this fact. They have not only systematically removed all traces of any author except Isaiah son of Amoz, but they have also specifically framed the introduction to the book to make it appear that the entire work comes from this one author. This has been done, it is claimed, for theological purposes. First, the redactors have sought to make it appear that Israel's God is different from all other beings that the world may call gods because of his ability to foretell the future, even 150 years in advance. Their second purpose is to make it appear that Judah's exile and return were not just accidents of history. Instead, in contrast to this view, these events were part of the outworking of a preexisting divine plan expressed in a single process of election, judgment, cleansing, restoration, and sanctification, all of which finds its fulfillment in the coming Messiah. In sum, the book, as redacted, insists that the concept of God it presents is not the result of after-the-fact reflection and integration, but rather something that was revealed *before* the facts and then confirmed *by* the facts. This is the whole thrust of the anti-idolatry polemics: only the true God, the Creator, has a consistent purpose in creation so as to have the long-term goals necessary for implementing such a program.

But, if the modern theories of the redaction of the book are correct, then all of this is merely fabrication. The redactors knew that God had not foretold anything to Isaiah son of Amoz about captivity in Babylon, let alone about deliverance from Babylon. They knew that he had said nothing about Cyrus, let alone about the conditions that the returnees would encounter back in their land. They knew that the prophetic predictions regarding the future were only slightly less general than anything that the prophets of other nations could produce. They knew that the stunning sweep of meaning that the book gives to life was nothing more than theological speculation. They also knew that the only way to convince people to accept this theology was to deny or conceal everything that has just been conceded.

Now, someone may object that such a judgment is overly harsh and also artificial.[62] Perhaps the redaction process was a long, slow process, the result of many almost-unconscious decisions made along the way by many different individuals. Thus, no one sat down at any point and decided to falsify the record. The falsification simply happened as a matter of course, layer by layer. Indeed, later redactors may have believed that Isaiah son of Amoz had said some of the things that earlier redactors had added to his writings. This, in turn, would have encouraged them to add more things that Isaiah should have said or that were valid implications of what they thought Isaiah had said.

But the process, as commonly conceived by current scholarship, was neither smooth nor unconscious. For example, most Anglo-American commentators agree that chapters 40–55, with the possible exception of the "Suffering Servant" passages, were the work of one person. If that person was not Isaiah son of Amoz, then someone made the decision to make it appear that it was, and for what other

---

62. So Childs (see note 49 above). While I respect his purpose and his concerns, it still seems to me that to attempt to make something appear to be so when it is manifestly not so is to create fiction, not compelling theology.

reason could this be than to make it appear that Isaiah had, under the inspiration of YHWH, foretold both the Babylonian captivity and the Persian release? Furthermore, if Isaiah did not predict the Babylonian captivity and the subsequent destruction of Babylon, then someone had to insert the statements about these matters where they now appear, and that was surely a conscious decision.

But even if we were to grant the assumption that the process of redaction did not involve a conscious decision to falsify the evidence for the theology of Isaiah, the outcome is the same: we know today that it has been falsified. How is it possible to affirm a theology when the only support its originators could adduce for it is false? How much better it would have been if they had only admitted that the way they arrived at this stunning theological construction was the same way their neighbors arrived at theirs—by philosophical speculation on the basis of the available data of the cosmos. But they do not do that. Instead, they have, at least somewhat consciously, constructed an elaborate argument resting on fallacious evidence. We may ask why they did this, but, much more to the point, why should we accept a theology resting on contrived evidence? I think this is a question that every Evangelical prepared to adopt the historical-critical reconstruction of the compositional history of the book of Isaiah must answer.

13

Binding Up the Testimony: Concluding Reflections on the Origins of the Book of Isaiah

Daniel I. Block

Introduction: The Problem

The essays in this volume reflect the ongoing debate within Evangelicalism concerning critical scholarly reconstructions of the growth of the book of Isaiah.[1] The responses represent three basic approaches:

(1) The oracles in the book all come from the late eighth- to early seventh-century BCE prophet identified in the superscription of the book (Isaiah son of Amoz), and they all address the historical period specified in the superscription of the book. They are characterized as "the vision concerning Judah and Jerusalem" that he saw "in the days of Uzziah, Jotham, Ahaz, and Hezekiah, kings of Judah" (Isa 1:1). This interpretation assumes that the temporal modifier applies both to the time the prophet received and delivered the oracles contained in the book and to the substance of the oracles. Although some oracles set their sights on the distant future, they were all addressed to the remnant of the people of Israel in Judah under threat by the Neo-Assyrians.

(2) The oracles in the book all come from the late eighth- to early seventh-century BCE prophet identified in the superscription of the book (Isaiah son of Amoz), but they address two different contexts. For the most part, chapters 1–39 concern the people of Judah during the reigns of the kings specified and while under threat by the Neo-Assyrians, while chapters 40–66 look far beyond the prophet's own day and are intended to provide hope for the exiles of Judah during and after the Babylonian exile (anticipated in Isa 39:5–8). This interpretation assumes that the temporal modifier in the superscription applies only to the time the prophet received and delivered the oracles contained in the book and not necessarily to the substance of all the oracles.

1. I am grateful to Richard Schultz and Franklin Wang for reading an earlier version of this essay and their suggestions for its improvement. Of course, any infelicities in content or presentation are my own.

(3) Most of the oracles in chapters 1–39 come from the late eighth- to early seventh-century BCE prophet identified in the superscription of the book (Isaiah son of Amoz) and address Judah during the Neo-Assyrian crisis, though they may have been edited significantly later. More significantly, the oracles in chapters 40–66 derive from a later prophet (or prophets) who was (or were) thoroughly imbued with the spirit of Isaiah ben Amoz but who lived and prophesied during the days of Judah's exile in Babylon and during the early Persian period. This interpretation assumes that the entire superscription applies only to the first thirty-nine chapters and that chapters 40–66 were later attached to the "Book of Isaiah" because they reflect the prophet's theological vision for Judah and the world.

The purpose of the colloquium at which these papers were presented was to consider whether or not these various perspectives are compatible with an evangelical view of Scripture. This issue is complex, and the range of opinions expressed in the papers suggests that Evangelicals are not agreed on the matter. On the surface, the first option summarized above is the simplest and the last option is the most complex, but internal data create difficulties for each solution proposed.

The current standard position within critical circles is that the book of Isaiah exhibits a remarkable literary and theological unity and that the eighth-century prophet Isaiah of Jerusalem stands behind much of chapters 1–39. However, most scholars view the present book as a whole as the product of a literary process that transpired over several centuries, the final stages coming from the Persian era (though some identify elements that come from even later times). Although the entire book is recognized as a literary-compositional whole, few are willing to concede chapters 40–66 to the eighth-century prophet of Jerusalem. This approach attempts to address several serious issues with which the traditional unitarian view has difficulty dealing. At the risk of being overly simplistic, this involves three major points:

(1) Isaiah 40–55 appears to reflect a Persian-era situation (cf. 40:2) and the explicit references to Cyrus (44:28; 45:1–2; cf. 45:13; 48:14–15) seem to describe a figure who has already appeared. Chapters 56–66 seem to derive from an even later context, perhaps the time of Malachi.

(2) The style of and emotions expressed in chapters 40–66 differ radically from those of 1–39. Messages of the imminent judgment of Israel and Judah are replaced by promises of imminent restoration.

(3) In "Deutero-Isaiah" and "Trito-Isaiah," Israelite theology proper reaches its zenith; the person behind chapters 40–55 is the theologian of the Hebrew Bible par excellence. He speaks more than any other on the nature of God. In his infinitude, YHWH is Creator, Sustainer, Life-Giver, the First and Last, the Incomparable One, and Israel has the glorious privilege of being his elect.

Furthermore, no longer is the Messiah presented as Davidic king (chs. 1–39) or Anointed Conqueror (chs. 56–66); rather, he appears as a humble Servant.

Based on these and other considerations, many conclude that the source of chapters 40–55 moves in a world quite different from that of Isaiah ben Amoz of Jerusalem. We have here (and in chs. 56–66) one or more disciples of Isaiah who have drunk deeply at their mentor's theological well, but who, in addressing new situations, have superseded their teacher.

However, this solution is not without its own obstacles, and adherents of the current scholarly consensus on these points must address three major issues of their own:

(1) Dating the oracles of Isa 40–66 to the exilic period or later negates one of the most important motifs in this part of the book, namely, that YHWH's divinity is proved by his ability to declare in advance distant future events and then to have them transpire exactly as predicted: 41:21–23; 42:8–9; 43:8–9, 18–19; 44:6–8, 24–28. If texts like these are dated to the periods to which they refer, this fundamental conviction is emptied of its rhetorical force.

(2) While the standard critical position highlights the theological contribution of chapters 40–66, it leaves the greatest theologian in Israel's history without identity or name. The only appropriate comparison would be the Sinaitic revelation without a real Moses.

(3) The opening superscription of the book invites us to read all the prophecies in it as the words of the eighth-century prophet Isaiah ben Amoz. Some have compared the book of Isaiah to the Book of the Twelve, which combines the twelve Minor Prophets within a single book, suggesting that, just as these prophecies derive from different hands and were written over the span of four centuries, the book of Isaiah is the result of a centuries-long redactional process that involved a number of writers. However, the fact that similar superscriptions head the individual Minor Prophets[2] distinguishes the Book of the Twelve from Isaiah. Although the present canonical arrangement of the Twelve *invites* us to read each of these books in light of its literary neighbors, the retention of the superscriptions in the collection *mandates* that we interpret each prophetic book first and foremost within the historical and cultural context the oracles address and from which they emerged. The singular heading to the book of Isaiah certainly *invites*, if not *mandates*, us to read the oracles in this book as essentially the work of Isaiah ben Amoz of Jerusalem.

---

2. Hos 1:1; Joel 1:1; Amos 1:1; Obad 1; Mic 1:21; Nah 1:1; Hab 1:1; Zeph 1:1; Hag 1:1; Zech 1:1; Mal 1:1. Jonah 1:1 functions as an introduction to a narrative (as opposed to an oracular) prophetic work. Technically, Hag 1:1 and Zech 1:1 function as date notices for specific oracles, but, like superscriptions to prophetic books, they identify the prophet and establish the context for the prophecy.

A Way Forward

Resolving all these issues in accord with an evangelical high view of Scripture is difficult. At the outset, we should acknowledge the two temptations that may short-circuit the enterprise: making the Scriptures say more than they claim, and rejecting the claims that the Scriptures actually make.

The first temptation is especially strong in fundamentalist circles. In truth, the book of Isaiah does not identify its author. But this is not that remarkable, especially if we consider that this problem applies to virtually all of the Hebrew Bible.[3] Although few would doubt that the book of Amos contains the authentic words of this eighth-century BCE prophet, the fact is that we do not know who was responsible for transcribing, gathering, and arranging his oracles in their present form. Like Amos 1:1, the third-person narrative preamble in Isa 1:1, at least, appears to come from a different hand.

But we should not be puzzled by the anonymity of Isaiah any more than we are puzzled by the anonymity of other books in the Hebrew Scriptures for a second reason.[4] This anonymity accords perfectly with what we know (or do not know!) of the composition of literary texts in the ancient Semitic world. Although ancient Mesopotamian documents often identify scribes who copied traditional and economic texts, those that explicitly identify their authors are extremely rare. In 1957, Wilfred G. Lambert could cite only two literary texts that mention the name of their authors:[5] the myth of "Erra and Ishum," which claims to be the divinely inspired composition of Kabti-ilani-Marduk,[6] and "The Babylonian Theodicy," a complex, autobiographical acrostic poem consisting of twenty-seven stanzas each made up of eleven lines beginning with the same syllable.[7] Our understanding of the authorship of ancient Mesopotamian literature

---

3. A point also made by Bruce K. Waltke, "Oral Tradition," in *A Tribute to Gleason Archer*, ed. Walter C. Kaiser Jr. and Ronald F. Youngblood (Chicago: Moody, 1986), 30.

4. I related the observations that follow to the book of Deuteronomy in an earlier essay, "Recovering the Voice of Moses: The Genesis of Deuteronomy," *JETS* 44 (2001): 385–408, at 386–87; reprinted in *The Gospel according to Moses: Theological and Ethical Reflections on the Book of Deuteronomy* (Eugene, OR: Cascade, 2012), 21–51, at 22–23.

5. W. G. Lambert, "Ancestors, Authors, and Canonicity," *JCS* 11 (1957): 1. For a discussion of an ancient text that lists the names of several authors, see idem, "A Catalogue of Texts and Authors," *JCS* 16 (1962): 59–77.

6. For English translations, see Stephanie Dalley, in *COS* 1.113:404–16; Benjamin R. Foster, *Before the Muses: An Anthology of Akkadian Literature* (Bethesda, MD: CDL, 1993), 2:771–805. Kabti-ilani-Marduk's name has also surfaced in the "Catalogue of Texts and Authors" from the library of Assurbanipal, published in Lambert, "A Catalogue of Texts and Authors," *JCS* 16 (1962): 65. Cf. his comments on pp. 73–74.

7. The author does not identify himself outright, but when the opening syllables of each stanza are pieced together they yield the sentence "I, Sagilkinamubbib, am adorant of god and king." See the translation by Benjamin R. Foster in *COS* 1.154:492–95 (also found in idem, *Before the Muses*, 2:790–98). For the Akkadian text, translation, and commentary, see W. G. Lambert, *Babylonian Wisdom Literature* (Oxford: Clarendon, 1960), 63–89.

has not changed much since 1957,[8] and no additional compositions naming their authors have been discovered.[9]

The reticence of ancient authors of literary texts to identify themselves presumably derives from their (or their communities') placement of a higher value on the message of their compositions than on the identity of the composer. Whatever the reason, the same phenomenon is evident in the Hebrew Bible. While one text may attribute literary activity that led to the creation of another text to a specific person,[10] and while characters in biblical books may attribute prophetic declarations to earlier individuals,[11] not a single book in the Hebrew Bible names its author. As a result, until the recent awakening of interest in literary approaches to biblical texts, both critical and conservative scholars were preoccupied with trying to answer questions of authorship and provenance. But the fact remains: nowhere do the Scriptures expressly identify Isaiah as the author of the book that goes by his name.

Despite the reticence of ancient authors, both inside and outside the Bible, to identify themselves, some scholars declare in unequivocal terms that Isaiah was the author of the book of Isaiah in its entirety. Although other biblical sources ascribe scribal activity to Isaiah, neither the book itself nor any other book or character within a book claims that Isaiah wrote the entire book. Concerning this point, we should not overstate the claims of the New Testament. In Mark 1:2, the Evangelist quotes a statement that he says "is written in Isaiah the prophet" (γέγραπται ἐν τῷ Ἠσαΐᾳ τῷ προφήτῃ; *gegraptai en tō Ēsaia tō prophētē*)." The preposition "in" does not identify the author of the book, but signals the location of the citation. In Mark 7:6, Jesus cites a specific statement (Isa 29:13) that he says Isaiah wrote, but this is not quite the same as declaring him to be the author of the book.[12] Luke 3:4 cites another part of the book of Isaiah (40:3): "As it is written in the book of the words of Isaiah, 'A voice of one calling in the desert, "Prepare the way for the Lord"'" (ὡς γέγραπται ἐν βίβλῳ λόγων Ἠσαΐου τοῦ προφήτου; *hōs gegraptai en biblō logōn Ēsaiou tou prophētou*). Here the narrator perceives the book as a written record of Isaiah's prophetic pronouncements, but does not identify the author of the book. According to Luke 4:17–18, Jesus received "the scroll of the prophet Isaiah" (βιβλίον τοῦ προφήτου Ἠσαΐου; *biblion tou prophētou Ēsaiou*) and read,

---

8. We have learned that the legendary Adapa was recognized as the author of written texts, presumably produced via dictation by the gods, and that the Etana Epic is attributed to a certain Lunanna. See Lambert, "Catalogue of Texts and Authors," 67, and cf. his discussion on pp. 72–76.

9. For a discussion of the present awareness of ancient authors, see Foster, *Before the Muses*, 1:19–21.

10. Second Chronicles 26:22 reports that the prophet Isaiah the son of Amoz produced a complete written record (כָּתַב, *kātab*) of the accomplishments of King Uzziah.

11. Note the references to the following prophets: Jeremiah (Ezra 1:1; Dan 9:2); Micah (Jer 26:18); Jonah (2 Kgs 14:25); Haggai and Zechariah (Ezra 5:1; 6:14).

12. Mark 7:6 reads: "He [Jesus] said to them, 'Isaiah prophesied rightly about you hypocrites, as it is written, "This people honors me with their lips, but their hearts are far from me."'"

"The Spirit of the Lord is upon me, because he has anointed me to proclaim good news to the poor. . . ." Significantly, while the quoted text is from Isa 61:1–2 (which critical scholars deny to Isaiah ben Amoz) and the scroll itself is identified by the name of the prophet, Luke 4:17 does not attribute the authorship of the scroll to Isaiah. Although it is possible that in this verse "the scroll of the prophet Isaiah" means "the scroll that Isaiah produced," it could also mean "the scroll that contains the prophecies of Isaiah" or "the scroll about the prophet Isaiah."[13] Consequently, although the New Testament consistently associates the prophecies in the book of Isaiah with Isaiah ben Amoz, the New Testament texts that refer to the book of Isaiah provide little warrant for insisting that Isaiah was the author of the book.

If conservatives are tempted to make biblical texts say more than they actually do, the temptation in critical scholarship is the opposite, not letting the text mean what it actually says, which neutralizes the witness of the only secure source of data.[14] Accordingly, critical scholars stifle both the character and the voice of Moses in the book of Deuteronomy by attributing the book's speeches to an eighth- to seventh-century BCE Deuteronomistic preacher and by dismissing the statements in the book concerning Moses' scribal activity as pseudepigraphic rhetoric.[15] Although knowledge of ancient scribal practices requires that we leave room for later updating of earlier texts,[16] for Isaiah this approach is particularly problematic. Whether or not the statements in this book come from Isaiah ben Amoz, to assign texts that declare YHWH's distinctive ability to predict the distant future—and even to name characters who will not appear for a century or more[17]—to a date

---

13. Analogous to the book of Jeremiah, which contains many stories about the prophet and refers to him by name in the third person more than 120 times.

14. Michael Fox describes precisely the nature of the suspicion that pervades much of critical scholarship: "Indeed the willingness *not* to take a text at face value is the essence of critical scholarship" (*Character and Ideology in the Book of Esther* [Columbia: University of South Carolina Press, 1991], 148–49; emphasis original).

15. See most recently the commentary by Jack R. Lundbom, *Deuteronomy: A Commentary* (Grand Rapids: Eerdmans, 2013). For a response to this approach, see Block, "Recovering the Voice of Moses."

16. For the book of Deuteronomy, note (a) expressions like "across the Jordan, in the wilderness in the Arabah, opposite Suph" (1:1), and "unto this day" (2:22; 3:14; 10:8; 11:4; 29:3[ET 4]); (b) parenthetical historical notes (2:10–12, 20–23; 3:9, 11, 13b–14); (c) the use of the past tense in 2:12, "just as Israel did to the land of their possession which YHWH gave them"; (d) the obituary of Moses (32:48–52; 34:1–12); (e) the reference to Dan as a northern extremity (34:1); (f) the use of Israelite tribal names for geographic regions of Canaan (34:1–3); (g) the observation that since the death of Moses no prophet like him has arisen in Israel, that is, no one whom YHWH knew face to face (34:10), which makes sense only if the narrator was aware of the historical significance of Moses' own prediction concerning the prophetic institution in 18:14–22 and knew at least a few prophetic figures with whom Moses could be compared. For a brief discussion of this issue and its implications for an evangelical view of Scripture, see John H. Walton and D. Brent Sandy, *The Lost World of Scripture: Ancient Literary Culture and Biblical Authority* (Downers Grove, IL: InterVarsity Press, 2013), 62–63.

17. E.g., Cyrus in Isa 44:28 and 45:1; cf. Josiah in 1 Kgs 13:2.

after the events described in the texts have transpired is to neuter the rhetorical force of these passages and transform their message.

Given our evangelical commitments, how, then, may we proceed in our discussions of the genesis of the book of Isaiah? It strikes me that, even though we affirm the superintending presence of the Holy Spirit in the process of writing, we need to recognize that the Scriptures are the product of a magnificent divine-human symbiosis. Under the inspiration of the Spirit of God, the biblical authors performed the creative compositional exercises that are involved generally in the composition of literary works. Indeed, in the process of the production of a prophetic book we may recognize at least seven stages of growth.

(1) *The prophetic event:* the prophet receives his/her message from God. The superscription to the book of Isaiah classifies Isaiah's prophetic experience as a "vision" (חָזוֹן, *ḥāzôn*). Although the book provides only a single autobiographical report of an actual vision (Isaiah's call to prophetic ministry, 6:1–13), the expression "vision" in Isa 1:1 should be interpreted more generally as referring to "divine revelation" of realities that are beyond the ken of ordinary sight. Specific prophetic events are signaled by prophetic formulae like "YHWH said [to Isaiah/me],"[18] "thus YHWH / Adonai YHWH has declared,"[19] "the declaration of YHWH / Adonai YHWH,"[20] and "the word of YHWH came to Isaiah, saying,"[21] as well as references to the voice of YHWH speaking (Isa 6:8; 40:3, 6).[22]

(2) *The rhetorical event:* the prophet transmits a divine message to his audience. The narrative segment of the book (chs. 36–39) describes Isaiah speaking as a prophet (in 37:6; 38:1, 21; 39:3, 5), but elsewhere he is portrayed performing sign acts (20:1–6). Rhetorical moments are also signaled by Isaiah's calls to attention with "Hear" followed by a vocative reference to the audience or a notice of an impending oracle.[23]

(3) *The transcriptional event:* the oracle is committed to writing. While references to scribal activity in Isaiah are rare, on several occasions Isaiah is portrayed as engaged in writing. In 8:1, YHWH commands the prophet to take a large scroll and write on it, in common script, the name "Maher-shalal-hash-baz." And in 30:8–9, YHWH tells him to write on a tablet and on a scroll a prophecy concerning the animals of the Negev, which is actually an oracle against Egypt.

---

18. The divine declaration formula: Isa 3:16; 7:3; 8:1, 3; 18:4; 20:3; 21:6, 16; 29:13; 31:4; 36:10.

19. The citation formula: Isa 7:7; 8:11; plus more than forty other times.

20. The signatory formula: Isa 1:24; 3:15; plus more than twenty other times.

21. The word event formula: Isa 38:4.

22. For discussion of these and other prophetic formulae, see Daniel I. Block, *The Book of Ezekiel*, vol. 1, *Chapters 1–24*, NICOT (Grand Rapids: Eerdmans, 1997), 32–36.

23. Isa 1:2, 10; 7:13; 28:14, 23; 32:9; 33:13; 34:1; 39:5; 42:18; 44:1; 46:3, 12; 47:8; 48:1, 16; 49:1; 51:1, 7, 21; 55:2–3; 66:5.

In the future, this written document will serve as a witness against Israel for their hard-heartedness and refusal to listen to YHWH. Texts like these at least raise the possibility that Isaiah might have committed individual prophetic messages to writing.

(4) *The narratorial event:* the account of the circumstances of the prophetic event are added to the transcribed oracle, creating a complete literary unit. Compared to Ezekiel and Jeremiah, in Isaiah these narratival notes occur inconsistently. Such notes generally appear at the head of an oracle, but were not a part of the message itself. In Isaiah, they appear simply as an announcement of an "oracle [מַשָּׂא, *maśśāʾ*] concerning X,"[24] or as notes specifying the occasion of the prophecy (6:1; 7:1–2; 20:1–2; 38:1; 39:1–2). The problem of recovering the origins of the oracles in chapters 40–66 is exacerbated by the total absence of narratival notes in this section.

(5) *The compilation event:* the individual literary units are gathered. Any comments we make concerning this phase in the production of the book of Isaiah are speculative. However, some find an allusion to this stage in the enigmatic statement of Isa 8:16, "Bind up the testimony; seal the teaching among my disciples" (NRSV). While it is unclear whether the suffix "my" on לִמֻּדָי (*limmūḏāy*) refers to those who learn from YHWH's own teaching (NJPS) or to Isaiah's disciples, many find here evidence that the prophet had followers who were charged with the task of preserving written copies of his oracles.

(6) *The editorial event:* the collection is organized and the individual oracles are stitched together by means of connective and correlative notes, resulting in a more or less coherent book. For some books, we have evidence of this stage transpiring in more than one track,[25] but the text-critical data give no signs that this was the case with Isaiah. The book of Isaiah gives clear evidence of intentional arrangement in its grouping of oracles: oracles of judgment against Israel/Judah (chs. 1–11), oracles against the nations (chs. 13–23), "apocalyptic" oracles (chs. 24–27), oracles of woe (chs. 28–33), the Hezekiah narratives (chs. 36–39), and oracles of hope after judgment (chs. 40–66).

(7) *The nominal event:* a composition is specifically associated with the name of a person. Evidence for this final stage in the process is typically found in the superscription to a book, where someone has declared the genre of the material that follows and attributed it to a specific individual, who is identified by

---

24. Isa 13:1; 15:1; 17:1; 19:1; 21:1, 11, 13; 22:1; 23:1; 30:6.

25. The MT and LXX versions of Jeremiah attest to two significantly different versions. We may speculate that the former represents a Seraiah collection (cf. Jer 51:59–64) and the latter a Baruch collection. Cf. Jack R. Lundbom, *Jeremiah 1–20: A New Translation with Introduction and Commentary,* AB 21A (New York: Doubleday, 1999), 92–101. For an alternative approach, see Andrew Shead, *A Mouth Full of Fire: The Word of God in the Words of Jeremiah,* NSBT (Downers Grove, IL: InterVarsity Press, 2012), 65–86.

name. Except for the enigmatic Ezek 1:2–3, where a nominal note was inserted to clarify the "thirtieth year" referred to in verse 1, this information is typically provided in the opening statement of the book. As is the case with the Ezekiel anomaly, the prophet whom the person who inserted the nominal note wants hearers/readers to associate with the oracles is generally introduced by name and, as occasion demands, is referred to with a third-person pronoun; this suggests that hearers are to distinguish between the person responsible for this final stage in the production of a prophetic book and the prophet whose oracles and activities are reported in the book. The same is true of Isa 1:1 and its relationship to the rest of the book that bears this prophet's name. After this, changes in the composition involve largely advertent and inadvertent alterations in the process of transmission.

Whether or not the stages described above represent an accurate picture of the process whereby the book of Isaiah was produced, they provide a heuristic model for comparing scholars' proposals for its composition. Isaiah scholars obviously part company in the level of involvement they would ascribe to Isaiah ben Amoz of Jerusalem (Fig. 1).

A Comparison of Interpreters' Assessment of Isaiah's Level of Involvement in the Production of the Book that Bears His Name (based on internal evidence)			
	Fundamentalist	Medial	Critical
Least	7. The nominal event	7. The nominal event	7. The nominal event
	6. The editorial event	6. The editorial event	6. The editorial event
	5. The narratorial event	5. The narratorial event	5. The narratorial event
	4. The compilation event	4. The compilation event	4. The compilation event
	3. The transcriptional event	3. The transcriptional event	3. The transcriptional event
	2. The rhetorical event	2. The rhetorical event	2. The rhetorical event
Greatest	1. The prophetic event	1. The prophetic event	1. The prophetic event
Note: Shading reflects the level of certainty, from greatest (light) to least (dark).			

Figure 1

While the fundamentalist position requires that Isaiah of Jerusalem be credited with the authorship of the book that bears the prophet's name, the darker shading in ##1 and 2 of the "critical" column reflects critical scholars' denial of any role for him in chapters 40–66. The best course seems to be a medial position by which we separate the prophet's public role from his role as scribe. This allows us to credit Isaiah ben Amoz with virtually all the prophecies in the book[26] without considering him the author of the book. It is illuminating to compare his role in this book, as conceived by those holding to the medial position just referred to, with the

---

26. With some—though minimal—allowance for post-Isaianic updating.

roles of Jeremiah and Ezekiel in the books that go by their names, also considering these from a medial position on this matter (Fig. 2).

A (Medial Position) Comparison of the Levels of the Major Prophets' Involvement in the Production of the Books that Bear Their Names (based on internal evidence)			
	Isaiah	Jeremiah	Ezekiel
Least	7. The nominal event (1:1)	7. The nominal event (1:1)	7. The nominal event (1:2–3)
	6. The editorial event	6. The editorial event	6. The editorial event
	5. The narratorial event	5. The narratorial event	5. The narratorial event
	4. The compilation event	4. The compilation event	4. The compilation event
	3. The transcriptional event	3. The transcriptional event	3. The transcriptional event
	2. The rhetorical event	2. The rhetorical event	2. The rhetorical event
Greatest	1. The prophetic event	1. The prophetic event	1. The prophetic event
	Note: Shading reflects the level of certainty, from greatest (light) to least (dark).		

Figure 2

Given the prominent roles that associates, especially Baruch and Seraiah, played in Jeremiah's prophetic service, it seems his involvement in the production of his book may have been minimal (perhaps even analogous to that of Jesus in the Gospels). The two references to Isaiah actually transcribing oracular pronouncements (8:1; 30:8–9), on the one hand, and the absence of references to a secretary, on the other, lead me to be slightly more generous with respect to the role that Isaiah might have played in the transcriptional and compilation events. The internal evidence of the book of Ezekiel differs drastically from that of both Isaiah and Jeremiah. It appears that Ezekiel had no associates or disciples; by 586 BCE he had lost even his wife (Ezek 24:18), leaving him alone to compile the texts containing his oracles and to do his own editorial work. Isaiah's references to "disciples" (לִמֻּדִים, limmûdîm; cf. Isa 8:16; 50:4) opens the possibility to some assistance for this prophet. Whether they functioned as compilers and editors during his own lifetime or whether these were later adherents to a "theological school" of Isaiah is unclear. Indeed, it is unclear when the book was put together in more or less its present form.

Although the references to Cyrus in 44:28 and 45:1 remain a problem, it is quite conceivable that Merodach-Baladan's visit to Jerusalem in Hezekiah's time (cf. 2 Kgs 20:12–19; Isa 39:1–7) precipitated the restoration oracles of chapters 40–66. The detail and thoroughness of Isaiah's vision of restoration is extraordinary. However, inasmuch as earlier threats of the curse for Israel's persistent rebellion against her covenant Suzerain were repeatedly followed up with declarations that the nation's judgment would not be the final word and that YHWH had guaranteed Israel's ultimate restoration within the covenant structure (Lev 26:40–46; Deut 4:26–31; 29:1[ET 2]–30:10), that Isaiah would or could have predicted the nation's return from Babylon is not in itself surprising. Furthermore, given ancient declarations of the universal, if not cosmic, nature of Israel's mission, the foundations for the final chapters had been laid long before Isaiah's time. If these chapters actually derive from Isaiah ben Amoz, they could have been assembled and the book produced within decades of the prophet's lifetime.

On the other hand, it is equally conceivable that the prophet's oracles were preserved as separate literary documents until after the restoration, and that the editor(s) did his (their) work *ex eventu* and intentionally arranged the oracles to reflect the sequence of Israel's experience—namely, judgment and exile followed by restoration—and then concluded with the oracles that envision the nation's fulfillment of its universal and cosmic mission. Deuteronomy provides a precedent not only for this sequence, but also for external factors determining the shape of a book: we do not know how many speeches Moses delivered on the Plains of Moab, but the arrangement of those that have been preserved accords with second-millennium imperial Hittite suzerain-vassal treaties: historical preamble (chs. 1–4); stipulations (chs. 5–26); covenant blessings and curses (ch. 28); plus allusions to a document clause (31:9–13) and to witnesses to the treaty (4:26; 30:19).[27]

Conclusion

Although the data provided by the book of Isaiah regarding its own origins are limited but fixed, in the absence of clear internal signals and external descriptions of how prophetic books were produced in the ancient world, any reconstructions of the genesis of this book are speculative. The challenge facing Evangelicals in trying to answer the question of how this book came to be is not to force the text to say more than it says while simultaneously allowing the text to have its own full voice. As a basic premise, we seek to read biblical texts with the grain established by the authors, rather than against that grain. This requires a hermeneutic of trust of the text that we have received, rather than a hermeneutic of suspicion. When we interpret the book of Isaiah as the prophet whose authority stands behind the book and those responsible for its composition intended, we are confident that we will have both grasped its meaning and come to understand the mind of God, who through his Spirit inspired the text. In the meantime, we proceed humbly and with eyes wide open to all the data provided by the text itself, along with the inner- and extrabiblical sources that bear on its interpretation. Fortunately, to a remarkably large extent, we need not be too distracted by these scholarly debates in order to explore the profound theology of the book and to preach its message with exegetical integrity and authority.[28]

---

27. Cf. Kenneth A. Kitchen, *On the Reliability of the Old Testament* (Grand Rapids: Eerdmans, 2003), 283–94; Markus Zehnder, "Building on Stone? Deuteronomy and Esarhaddon's Loyalty Oaths (Part 1): Some Preliminary Observations," *BBR* 19 (2009): 341–74; "(Part 2): Some Additional Observations," *BBR* 19 (2009): 511–35.

28. This is also the opinion of H. G. M. Williamson, who holds to the critical viewpoint but has published a fine essay on "Preaching from Isaiah," in *Reclaiming the Old Testament for Christian Preaching*, ed. G. J. R. Kent, P. J. Kissling, and L. A. Turner (Downers Grove, IL: InterVarsity Press, 2010), 141–56.

Bibliography

Abramson, Shraga. *Talmud Babli: Masekhet Baba Batra*. Talmud Babli, edited by J. N. Epstein. Jerusalem: Debir and Massadah, 1958.

Ackroyd, Peter R. "Isaiah 1–12: Presentation of a Prophet." In *Congress Volume, Göttingen 1977*, edited by Walther Zimmerli, 16–48. VTSup 29. Leiden: Brill, 1978.

———. "Isaiah 36–39: Structure and Function." In *"The Place Is Too Small for Us": The Israelite Prophets in Recent Scholarship*, edited by Robert P. Gordon, 478–94. Sources for Biblical and Theological Study 5. Winona Lake, IN: Eisenbrauns, 1995.

Albright, William F. *History, Archaeology and Christian Humanism*. New York: McGraw-Hill, 1964.

Alexander, Joseph A. *The Prophecies of Isaiah*. 1865. Reprint, Grand Rapids: Zondervan, 1977.

Alexander, Philip S. "The Formation of the Biblical Canon in Rabbinic Judaism." In *The Canon of Scripture in Jewish and Christian Tradition*, edited by Philip S. Alexander and J.-D. Kaestli, 57–80. Lausanne: Éditions du Zèbre, 2007.

Allis, Oswald T. *The Unity of Isaiah: A Study in Prophecy*. Philadelphia: Presbyterian and Reformed, 1950.

Andersen, Frances I., and A. Dean Forbes. "'Prose Particle' Counts of the Hebrew Bible." In *The Word of the Lord Shall Go Forth*, edited by Carol L. Meyers and M. O'Connor, 165–183. Winona Lake, IN: Eisenbrauns, 1983.

———. *Spelling in the Hebrew Bible*. Rome: Biblical Institute Press, 1986.

Anderson, Bernhard W. "Exodus Typology in Second Isaiah." In *Israel's Prophetic Heritage: Essays in Honor of James Muilenburg*, edited by Bernhard W. Anderson and Walter Harrelson, 177–95. New York: Harper, 1962.

Arnold, Bill T., and Bryan E. Beyer. *Encountering the Old Testament*. Grand Rapids: Baker Books, 1999.

Assis, Elie. *The Book of Joel: A Prophet between Calamity and Hope*. LHBOTS 581. New York: Bloomsbury, 2013.

Atkinson, Jason. "Prophecy in K1285: Re-Evaluating the Divine Speech Episodes of Nabû." In *"Thus Speaks Ishtar of Arbela": Prophecy in Israel, Assyria, and Egypt in the Neo-Assyrian Period*, edited by Hans M. Barstad and Robert P. Gordon, 59–89. Winona Lake, IN: Eisenbrauns, 2013.

Avigad, Nahman. *The Dead Sea Scrolls of the Hebrew University*. Jerusalem: Magnes, 1955.

Bacher, Wilhelm. "Synagogue, The Great." In *JE*, new ed., edited by I. Singer, 11:640–43. New York: Funk & Wagnall's, 1925.

Baldwin, Joyce G. "Some Literary Affinities of the Book of Daniel." *TynBul* 30 (1979): 77–99.

Baltzer, Klaus. *Deutero-Isaiah: A Commentary on Isaiah 40–55*. Hermeneia. Minneapolis: Fortress, 2001.

Barr, James. "Revelation through History in the Old Testament and in Modern Theology." In *New Theology No 1*, edited by Martin Marty and Dean G. Peerman, 60–74. New York: Doubleday, 1964.

———. *The Variable Spellings of the Hebrew Bible*. Oxford: Oxford University Press, 1989.

Barstad, Hans M. "Akkadian 'Loanwords' in Isaiah 40–55 and the Question of the Babylonian Origin of Deutero-Isaiah." In *Text and Theology: Studies in Honour of Dr. Theol. Magne Sæbø, presented on the occasion of his 65th birthday*, edited by Arvid Tångberg, 36–48. Oslo: Verbum, 1994.

———. *The Babylonian Captivity of the Book of Isaiah: 'Exilic' Judah and the Provenance of Isaiah 40–55*. Oslo: Novus, 1997.

———. "On the So-called Babylonian Literary Influence in Second-Isaiah," *SJOT* 2 (1987): 90–110.

———. "Sic dicit dominus: Mari Prophetic Texts and the Hebrew Bible." In *Essays on Ancient Israel in Its Near Eastern Context: A Tribute to Nadav Na'aman*, edited by Yairah Amit, Ehud Ben Zvi, Israel Finkelstein, and Oded Lipschits, 21–52. Winona Lake, IN: Eisenbrauns, 2006.

———. *A Way in the Wilderness: the "Second Exodus" in the Message of Second Isaiah*, JSS Monograph 12. Manchester: University of Manchester Press, 1989.

———. "What Prophets Do. Reflections on Past Reality in the Book of Jeremiah." In *Prophecy in the Book of Jeremiah*, edited by Hans M. Barstad and Reinhard G. Kratz, 10–32. BZAW 388. Berlin: Walter de Gruyter, 2009.

Barthélemy, Dominique. *Critique textuelle de l'Ancien Testament*. OBO 50.3. Göttingen: Vandenhoeck & Ruprecht, 1992.

Bauer, Hans, and Pontus Leander. *Historische Grammatik der hebräischen Sprache des Alten Testamentes*. Halle: Georg Olms, 1922.

Beale, G. K. *The Erosion of Inerrancy in Evangelicalism: Responding to New Challenges to Biblical Authority*. Wheaton, IL: Crossway, 2008.

———. "Isaiah 6:9–13: A Retributive Taunt against Idolatry." *VT* 41 (1991): 257–278.

———. "Other Religions in New Testament Theology." In *Biblical Faith and Other Religions: An Evangelical Assessment*, edited by D. W. Baker, 79–105. Grand Rapids: Kregel, 2004.

———. "A Specific Problem Confronting the Authority of the Bible: Should the New Testament's Claim That the Prophet 'Isaiah' Wrote the Whole Book of Isaiah Be Taken at Face Value?" In *Resurrection and Eschatology: Theology in Service of the Church; Essays in Honor of Richard B. Gaffin Jr.*, edited by Lane G. Tipton and Jeffrey C. Waddington, 135–76. Phillipsburg: P&R, 2008.

———. *We Become What We Worship: A Biblical Theology of Idolatry*. Downers Grove, IL: InterVarsity Press, 2008.

Beckwith, Roger. *The Old Testament Canon of the New Testament Church*. Grand Rapids: Eerdmans, 1985.

Begg, Christopher T. "The 'Classical Prophets' in Josephus' Antiquities." *LS* 13 (1988): 341–57.

————. *Josephus' Story of the Later Monarchy (AJ 9,1–10,185)*. Leuven: Peeters, 2000.

Begrich, Joachim. "Das priesterliche Heilsorakel." *ZAW* 54 (1934): 81–92.

————. *Studien zu Deuterojesaja*. BWANT 4/25. Stuttgart: Kohlhammer, 1938.

Behr, J. W. *The Writings of Deutero-Isaiah and the Neo-Babylonian Royal Inscriptions: A Comparison of the Language and Style*. Pretoria: University of Pretoria, 1937.

Ben Zvi, Ehud. "The Concept of Prophetic Books and Its Historical Setting." In *The Production of Prophecy: Constructing Prophecy and Prophets in Yehud*, edited by Diana V. Edelman and Ehud Ben Zvi, 73–95. London: Equinox, 2009.

————. "Studying Prophetic Texts against Their Original Backgrounds: Pre-Ordained Scripts and Alternative Horizons of Research." In *Prophets and Paradigms: Essays in Honor of Gene M. Tucker*, edited by Stephen Breck Reid, 125–35. JSOTSup 229. Sheffield: Sheffield Academic, 1996.

Bendavid, Abba. *The Biblical Language and the Rabbinic Language*. 2 vols. Tel Aviv: Dvir, 1967 [in Hebrew].

Ben-Yehuda, E. *Thesaurus Totius Hebraitatis*. 8 vols. New York: Thomas Yoseloff, 1947–59 [in Hebrew].

Berges, Ulrich F. *The Book of Isaiah: Its Composition and Final Form*. Translated by Millard C. Lind. Hebrew Bible Monographs 46. Sheffield: Sheffield Phoenix, 2012.

————. "Farewell to Deutero-Isaiah Or Prophecy Without a Prophet." In *Congress Volume, Ljubljana 2007*, edited by André Lemaire, 575–95. VTSup 133. Leiden: Brill, 2010.

————. *Jesaja 40–48*. HThKAT. Freiburg: Herder, 2008.

Bergey, Ronald. "The Book of Esther: Its Place in the Linguistic Milieu of Post-Exilic Biblical Hebrew Prose: A Study in Late Biblical Hebrew." PhD diss., Dropsie College for Hebrew and Cognate Learning, 1983.

————. "The Song of Moses (Deuteronomy 32.1–43) and Isaianic Prophecies: A Case of Early Intertextuality?" *JSOT* 28 (2003): 33–54.

Bergsträsser, Gotthelf. *Hebräische Grammatik*. Vol. 2, *Verbum*. Leipzig: Vogel, 1929.

Berlin, Adele. *Poetics and Interpretation of Biblical Narrative*. Winona Lake, IN: Eisenbrauns, 1983.

Beuken, Willem A. M. "Isaiah liv: The Multiple Identity of the Person Addressed," in *Language and Meaning: Studies in Hebrew Language and Biblical Exegesis*, edited by James Barr, 29–70. OtSt 19. Leiden: Brill, 1974.

————. *Jesaja 1–12*. HthKAT. Freiburg: Herder, 2003.

Blau, Ludwig. "Bible Canon." In *JE*, new ed., edited by I. Singer, 3:140–50. New York: Funk & Wagnall's, 1925.

Blenkinsopp, Joseph. "The Formation of the Hebrew Bible Canon: Isaiah as a Test Case." In *The Canon Debate*, edited by Lee M. McDonald and James A. Sanders, 53–67. Peabody, MA: Hendrickson, 2002.

————. *Isaiah 40–55: A New Translation with Introduction and Commentary*. AB 19A. New York: Doubleday, 2002.

————. *Opening the Sealed Book: Interpretations of the Book of Isaiah in Late Antiquity*. Grand Rapids: Eerdmans, 2006.

Bloch, Yigal. "The Third-Person Masculine Plural Suffixed Pronoun -*mw* and Its Implications for the Dating of Biblical Hebrew Prose. In *Diachrony in Biblical Hebrew*, edited by Ziony Zevit and Cynthia Miller-Naudé, 147–70. LSAW 8. Winona Lake, IN: Eisenbrauns, 2012.

Block, Daniel I. "Recovering the Voice of Moses: The Genesis of Deuteronomy." *JETS* 44 (2001): 385–408. Reprinted in *The Gospel according to Moses: Theological and Ethical Reflections on the Book of Deuteronomy*, 21–51. Eugene, OR: Cascade, 2012.

———. *The Book of Ezekiel*. Vol. 1, *Chapters 1–24*. NICOT. Grand Rapids: Eerdmans, 1997.

———. *The Book of Ezekiel*. Vol. 2, *Chapters 25–48*. NICOT. Grand Rapids: Eerdmans, 1998.

Blum, Erhard. "Israels Prophetie im altorientalischen Kontext: Anmerkungen zu neueren religionsgeschichtlichen Thesen." In *"From Ebla to Stellenbosch": Syro-Palestinian Religions and the Hebrew Bible*, edited by Izak Cornelius and Louis Jonker, 81–115. ADPV 37. Wiesbaden: Harrassowitz, 2008.

Boda, Mark J. "Chiasmus in Ubiquity: Symmetrical Mirages in Nehemiah 9." *JSOT* 71 (1996): 55–70.

———. "Judges," in *The Expositor's Bible Commentary*. Vol. 2, *Numbers–Ruth*, rev. ed., edited by Tremper Longman III and David E. Garland, 1047–52. Grand Rapids: Zondervan, 2012.

———. "Redaction in the Book of Nehemiah: A Fresh Proposal." In *Unity and Disunity of Ezra-Nehemiah: Redaction, Rhetoric, Reader*, edited by Mark J. Boda and Paul Redditt, 25–54. Hebrew Bible Monographs 17. Sheffield: Sheffield Phoenix, 2008.

———. *A Severe Mercy: Sin and Its Remedy in the Old Testament*. Siphrut: Literature and Theology of the Hebrew Scriptures 1. Winona Lake, IN: Eisenbrauns, 2009.

———. "Speaking into the Silence: The Epilogue of Ecclesiastes." In *The Words of the Wise Are Like Goads: Engaging Qoheleth in the 21st Century*, edited by Mark J. Boda, Tremper Longman III, and Cristian Rata, 257–79. Winona Lake, IN: Eisenbrauns, 2013.

———. "'Uttering Precious Rather than Worthless Words': Divine Patience and Impatience with Lament in Isaiah and Jeremiah." In *Why? How Long? Studies on Voice(s) of Lamentation Rooted in Biblical Hebrew Poetry*, edited by Mark J. Boda, Carol Dempsey, and LeAnn Snow Flesher, 83–99. LHBOTS. London: Bloomsbury, 2014.

———. "Walking in the Light of Yahweh: Zion and the Empires in the Book of Isaiah." In *Empire in the New Testament*, edited by Stanley E. Porter and Cynthia Long Westfall, 54–89. McMaster New Testament Studies. Grand Rapids: Eerdmans, 2010.

———. "Word and Spirit, Scribe and Prophet in Old Testament Hermeneutics." In *Spirit & Scripture: Examining a Pneumatic Hermeneutic*, edited by Kevin L. Spawn and Archie T. Wright, 25–45. London: T&T Clark, 2011.

———. *Zechariah*. NICOT. Grand Rapids: Eerdmans, forthcoming.

Boda, Mark J., and Michael H. Floyd, eds. *Bringing out the Treasure: Inner Biblical Allusion in Zechariah 9–14.* JSOTSup 370. New York: Sheffield Academic, 2003.

Bredenkamp, Conrad J. *Der Prophet Jesaia.* Erlangen: Andreas Deichert, 1887.

Brendsel, Daniel J. *'Isaiah Saw His Glory': The Use of Isaiah 52–53 in John 12.* BZNW 208. Berlin: de Gruyter, 2014.

Brichto, Herbert C. *Toward a Grammar of Biblical Poetics: Tales of the Prophets.* New York: Oxford University Press, 1992.

Briggs, Charles A. *The Higher Criticism of the Hexateuch.* 2nd ed. New York: Scribner's, 1897.

Brooke, G. J. "Isaiah in the Pesharim and Other Qumran Texts." In *Writing and Reading the Scroll of Isaiah: Studies of an Interpretive Tradition,* edited by Craig C. Broyles and Craig A. Evans, 609–32. VTSup 70,2. Leiden: Brill, 1997.

———. "On Isaiah at Qumran." In *"As Those Who Are Taught": The Interpretation of Isaiah from the LXX to the SBL,* edited by Claire Mathews McGinnis and Patricia K. Tull, 69–85. SBLSymS 27. Atlanta: Society of Biblical Literature, 2006.

Brownlee, William H. "The Literary Significance of the Bisection of Isaiah in the Ancient Scroll of Isaiah from Qumran." In *Trudy Dvardtsat Pyatogo Mezhdunarodnogo Kongressa Vostokokovedov,* 431–47. Tome 1. Moscow: Tzolatel'stvo Vostochnoi Literatary, 1962.

Brueggemann, Walter. "Unity and Dynamic in the Isaiah Tradition." *JSOT* 29 (1984): 89–107.

Budde, Karl. *Jesaja's Erleben: Eine gemeinverständliche Auslegung der Denkschrift des Propheten (Kap. 6, 1–9, 6).* Gotha: L. Klotz, 1928.

Burrows, M. "Orthography, Morphology, and Syntax in the St. Mark's Isaiah Manuscript." *JBL* 68 (1949): 195–211.

Calvin, John. "Commentary on the Book of the Prophet Isaiah." *Calvin's Commentaries.* Grand Rapids: Baker, 2003.

Cantineau, J. *Grammaire du Palymyrenien Epigraphique.* Le Caire: Imprimerie de l'Institute Français d'Archaéologie Orientale, 1935.

Carr, David M. "Isaiah 40:1–11 in the Context of the Macrostucture of Second Isaiah." In *Discourse Analysis of Biblical Literature: What It Is and What It Offers,* edited by Walter R. Bodine, 51–74. SemeiaSt. Atlanta: Scholars Press, 1995.

———. "Reaching for Unity in Isaiah." *JSOT* 57 (1993): 61–80.

———. *Writing on the Tablet of the Heart: Origins of Scripture and Literature.* Oxford: Oxford University Press, 2005.

Carson, D. A. *Matthew, Chapters 13 through 28.* Expositor's Bible Commentary. Grand Rapids: Zondervan, 1995.

———. "1 Peter." In *Commentary on the New Testament Use of the Old Testament,* edited by G. K. Beale and D. A. Carson, 1015–45. Grand Rapids; Baker, 2007.

———. "Redaction Criticism: On the Legitimacy and Illegitimacy of a Literary Tool." In *Scripture and Truth,* edited by D. A. Carson and John Woodbridge, 119–46. Grand Rapids: Zondervan, 1983.

Carson, D. A., and H. G. M. Williamson, eds. *It is Written—Scripture Citing Scripture, Essays in Honour of Barnabas Lindars, SSF.* Cambridge: University Press, 1988.

Charpin, Dominique. "Prophètes et rois dans le Proche-Orient Amorrite," In *Prophètes et rois: Bible et Proche-Orient*, edited by André Lemaire, 21–53. Lectio divina Hors série. Paris: Les éditions du Cerf, 2001.

Cheyne, T. K. *The Prophecies of Isaiah: A New Translation with Commentary and Appendices*. Vol. 2. New York: Thomas Whittaker, 1890.

Childs, Brevard S. *Biblical Theology in Crisis*. Philadelphia: Westminster, 1970.

———. *Biblical Theology of the Old and New Testaments: Theological Reflection on the Christian Bible*. London: SCM, 1992.

———. *The Book of Exodus: A Critical, Theological Commentary*. OTL. Philadelphia: Westminster, 1974.

———. "Canon and Criticism: The Old Testament as Scripture of the Church." James Sprunt Lectures. Union Theological Seminary, 1972.

———. *Introduction to the Old Testament as Scripture*. Philadelphia: Fortress / London: SCM, 1979.

———. *Isaiah: A Commentary*. OTL. Louisville: Westminster John Knox, 2001.

———. *Old Testament Theology in a Canonical Context*. Philadelphia: Fortress, 1985.

Clements, Ronald E. "Beyond Tradition-History: Deutero-Isaianic Development of First Isaiah's Themes." In *The Prophets*, edited by Philip R. Davies, 128–46. BibSem 42. Sheffield: Sheffield Academic, 1996.

———. *Isaiah 1–39*. NCB. Grand Rapids: Eerdmans, 1980.

———. "Patterns in the Prophetic Canon: Healing the Blind and the Lame." In *Canon, Theology, and Old Testament Interpretation: Essays in Honor of Brevard S. Childs*, edited by Gene M. Tucker, David L. Petersen, and Robert R. Wilson, 189–200. Philadelphia: Fortress, 1988.

———. "The Unity of the Book of Isaiah." *Int* 36 (1982): 117–129.

Clifford, Richard J. *Fair Spoken and Persuading: An Interpretation of Second Isaiah*. Theological Inquiries. Toronto: Paulist, 1984.

Clines, David J. A. "The Many Voices of Isaiah 40." In *Let Us Go Up To Zion: Essays in Honour of H. G. M. Williamson on the Occasion of his Sixty-Fifth Birthday*, edited by Iain Provan and Mark J. Boda, 113–126. VTSup 153. Leiden: Brill, 2012.

Cobb, William H. "Where was Isaiah 40–66 Written?," *JBL* 27 (1908): 48–64.

Coggins, Richard J. "Do We Still Need Deutero-Isaiah?" *JSOT* 81 (1998): 77–92.

Cohen, Menachem, ed. *Mikra'ot Gedolot 'Haketer': Exodus, part 1*. Ramat-Gan, Israel: Bar Ilan University, 2012.

———, ed. *Mikra'ot Gedolot 'Haketer': Isaiah*. Ramat-Gan, Israel: Bar Ilan University, 1996.

Conrad, Edgar W. *Reading Isaiah*. OBT. Minneapolis: Fortress, 1991.

Cross, Frank M. "The Contribution of the Qumran Discoveries to the Study of the Biblical Text." *IEJ* 16 (1966): 81–95.

———. "The Council of Yahweh in Second Isaiah." *JNES* 12 (1953): 274–277.

Dahood, Mitchell J. "Phoenician Elements in Isaiah 52:13–53:12." In *Near Eastern Studies in Honor of William Foxwell Albright*, edited by Hans Goedicke, 63–73. Baltimore: Johns Hopkins University Press, 1971.

Dalley, Stephanie, trans. "Erra and Ishum." In *The Context of Scripture*. 3 vols, edited by William W. Hallo, and K. Lawson Younger, 1:404–16. Leiden: Brill, 1997–2002.

Davies, Philip R. "'Pen of Iron, Point of Diamond' (Jer 17:1): Prophecy as Writing." In *Writings and Speech in Israelite and Ancient Near Eastern Prophecy*, edited by Ehud Ben Zvi, Michael H. Floyd, and Christopher R. Matthews, 65–81. SBLSymS 10. Atlanta: Society of Biblical Literature, 2000.

———. "God of Cyrus, God of Israel: Some Religio-historical Reflections on Isaiah 40–55." In *Words Remembered, Texts Renewed: Essays in Honor of J. F. A. Sawyer*, edited by J. Davies *et al*, 207–25. JSOTSup 195. Sheffield: Sheffield Academic, 1995.

Dempster, Stephen G. "Linguistic Features of Hebrew Narrative: A Discourse Analysis of Narrative from the Classical Period." PhD diss., University of Toronto, 1985.

Dennis, Lane T., ed. *The ESV Study Bible*. Wheaton, IL: Crossway Bibles, 2008.

Diamond, A. R. Pete. "Jeremiah." In *Eerdmans Commentary on the Bible*, edited by James D. G. Dunn and J. W. Rogerson, 543–616. Grand Rapids: Eerdmans, 2003.

The Digital Sea Scrolls project (http://dss.collections.imj.org.il/isaiah.

Dijkstra, Meindert. *Gods voorstelling: Predikatieve expressie van zelfopenbaring in Oudoosterse teksten en Deutero-Jesaja*. Dissertationes Neerlandicae, Series Theologica 2. Kampen: Kok, 1980.

Dillard, Raymond B., and Tremper Longman III. *An Introduction to the Old Testament*. Grand Rapids: Zondervan, 1994.

Diodore of Tarsus. *Commentary on Psalm 118*. In *Biblical Interpretation in the Early Church*, edited and translated by Karlfried Froehlich. Philadelphia: Fortress, 1984.

Döderlein, Johann Christoph. *Esaias ex recensione textus hebraie ad fidem codicum manuscriptorum et versionum antiquarum latine vertit notasque varii argument*. 2nd ed. Altorf: Officina Schupfeliana, 1780. 3rd Altorf: Georg. Petr. Monath, 1789.

Dorsey, David A. *The Literary Structure of the Old Testament: A Commentary on Genesis–Malachi*. Grand Rapids: Baker, 1999.

Douglas, Mary. *Thinking in Circles: An Essay on Ring Composition*. New Haven: Yale University Press, 2007.

Driver, S. R. *An Introduction to the Literature of the Old Testament*. 9th ed. Edinburgh: T&T Clark, 1913.

———. "On Some Alleged Linguistic Affinities of the Elohist." *Journal of Philology* 11 (1882): 201–236.

———. *A Treatise on the Use of the Tenses in Hebrew*. 3rd ed. Oxford: Clarendon, 1892.

Driver, S. R., and A. Neubauer. *The Fifty-Third Chapter of Isaiah according to the Jewish Interpreters*. Oxford: James Parker, 1877.

Duhm, Bernhard. *Das Buch Jesaia*. Göttinger HKAT 3.1, 4th ed. Göttingen: Vandenhoeck & Ruprecht, 1922; 1st ed. 1892.

Eddinger, Terry W. "An Analysis of Isaiah 40:1–11 (17)." *BBR* 9 (1999): 119–135.

Ehrensvärd, Martin. "Linguistic Dating of Biblical Texts," in *Biblical Hebrew: Studies in Chronology and Typology*, edited by Ian Young, 164–88. London: T&T Clark, 2003.

Ehrman, Bart, and William Dever. "Losing Faith: Who Did and Who Didn't." *BAR* 33 (2007): 50–57.

Eichhorn, Johann Gottfried. *Einleitung ins Alte Testament: Dritter Theil.* 2nd ed. Leipzig: Weidmanns Erben und Reich, 1787.

Elliger, Karl, and Hans-Jürgen Hermisson. *Deuterojesaja.* 2 vols. BKAT. Neukirchen-Vluyn: Neukirchener, 1970.

Ellis, Maria de Jong. "Observations on Mesopotamian Oracles and Prophetic Texts: Literary and Historiographical Considerations." *JCS* 41 (1989): 127–86.

Enns, Peter. *Inspiration and Incarnation: Evangelicals and the Problem of the Old Testament.* Grand Rapids: Baker Academic, 2005.

Erlandsson, Seth. *The Burden of Babylon: A Study of Isaiah 13:2–14:23.* ConBOT 4. Lund: GWK Gleerup, 1970.

Eslinger, Lyle M. "Inner-Biblical Exegesis and Inner-Biblical Allusion: The Question of Category." *VT* 42 (1992): 47–58.

Evans, Craig A. "The Function of Isaiah 6:9–10 in Mark and John." *NT* 24 (1982): 124–38.

———. "On the Unity and Parallel Structure of Isaiah." *VT* 38 (1988): 129–47.

Everson, A. Joseph, and Hyun Chul Paul Kim, eds. *The Desert Will Bloom: Poetic Visions in Isaiah.* SBLAIL 4. Atlanta: Society of Biblical Literature, 2009.

Ewald, Heinrich. *Ausführliches Lehrbuch der hebräischen Sprache des Alten Bundes.* 8th ed. Göttingen: Dieterich, 1870.

———. *Die Propheten des Alten Bundes.* 3 vols. Göttingen: Vandenhoeck & Ruprecht, 1867–68.

———. *Die Propheten des Alten Bundes.* 2nd ed. Vol. 3, *Die jüngsten Propheten des alten Bundes mit den Büchern Barukh und Daniel.* Göttingen: Vandenhoeck & Ruprecht, 1867–68.

Firth, David G. and H. G. M. Williamson, *Interpreting Isaiah: Issues and Approaches.* Downers Grove, IL: InterVarsity Press, 2009.

Feldman, Louis H. *Studies in Josephus' Rewritten Bible.* JSJSup 58. Leiden: Brill, 1998.

Fischer, Irmtraud. "World Peace and 'Holy War'—Two Sides of the Same Theological Concept: 'YHWH as Sole Divine Power' (A Canonical-Intertextual Reading of Isaiah 2:1–5, Joel 4:9–21, and Micah 4:1–5)." In *Isaiah's Vision of Peace in Biblical and Modern International Relations: Swords into Plowshares*, edited by Raymond Cohen and Raymond Westbrook, 151–65. Culture and Religion in International Relations. New York: Palgrave Macmillan, 2008.

Fishbane, Michael A. *Biblical Interpretation in Ancient Israel.* Oxford: Clarendon, 1985.

Fitzmyer, Joseph A. "The Syntax of Imperial Aramaic." PhD diss., John Hopkins University, 1956.

Flint, Peter W. "The Isaiah Scrolls from the Judean Desert." In *Writing and Reading the Scroll of Isaiah: Studies of an Interpretive Tradition*, edited by Craig C. Broyles and Craig A. Evans, 481–489. VTSup 70,2. Leiden: Brill, 1997.

———. "Non-Masoretic Variant Readings in the Hebrew University Scroll (IQ-Isab) and the Text to be Translated." In *The Dead Sea Scrolls and Contemporary Culture: Proceedings of the International Conference Held at the Israel Museum, Jerusalem (July 6–8, 2008)*, edited by Adolfo D. Roitman, Lawrence H. Schiffman, and Shani Tzoref, 105–17. STDJ. Leiden: Brill, 2011.

Floyd, Michael H. "'Write the Revelation!' (Hab 2:2): Re-Imagining the Cultural History of Prophecy." In *Writings and Speech in Israelite and Ancient Near Eastern Prophecy*, edited by Ehud Ben Zvi and Michael H. Floyd, 103–43. SBLSymS 10. Atlanta: Society of Biblical Literature, 2000.

———. "The Production of Prophetic Books in the Early Second Temple Period." In *Prophets, Prophecy, and Prophetic Texts in Second Temple Judaism*, edited by Michael H. Floyd and Robert D. Haak, 276–97. LHBOTS 427. New York, London: T&T Clark International, 2006.

Foster, Benjamin R. *Before the Muses: An Anthology of Akkadian Literature.* 2 vols. Bethesda: CDL, 1993.

Fowl, Stephen E. *Engaging Scripture: A Model for Theological Interpretation.* Challenges in Contemporary Theology. Malden: Blackwell, 1998.

Fox, Michael. *Character and Ideology in the Book of Esther.* Columbia: University of South Carolina Press, 1991.

Freedman, David N. "The Spelling of the Name 'David' in the Hebrew Bible." *HAR* 7 (1983): 89–102.

———. "The Structure of Isaiah 40:1–11." In *Perspectives on Language & Text: Essays and Poems in Honor of Francis I. Andersen's Sixtieth Birthday July 28, 1985*, edited by Edgar W. Conrad and Edward G. Newing, 167–193. Winona Lake, IN: Eisenbrauns, 1987.

Friedländer, M. *Commentary of Ibn Ezra on Isaiah, Edited from MSS. and Translated, with Notes, Introductions, and Indexes.* New York: Philipp Feldheim, 1873.

Friedman, Theodore. "Isaiah: Introduction." In *EncJud*, edited by F. Skolnik, 10:57–60. 2nd ed. Detroit: Thomson Gale, 2007.

Gärtner, Judith. *Jesaja 66 und Sacharja 14 als Summe der Prophetie: Eine traditions- und redaktionsgeschichtliche Untersuchung zum Abschluss des Jesaja- und des Zwölfprophetenbuches.* WMANT 114. Neukirchen-Vluyn: Neukirchener Verlag, 2006.

Gentry, Peter J. "Isaiah and Social Justice." *Midwestern Journal of Theology* 12 (2013): 1–15.

———. "No One Holy Like the Lord." *Midwestern Journal of Theology* 12 (2013): 17–38.

Gentry, Peter J., and Stephen J. Wellum. *Kingdom through Covenant: A Biblical-Theological Understanding of the Covenants.* Wheaton, IL: Crossway, 2012.

Gesenius, D. Wilhelm. *Geschichte der hebräischen Sprache und Schrift.* Leipzig: Vogel, 1815.

———. *Der Prophet Jesaia.* Vol. 2, bk. 1, *Einleitung und Commentar über Kapitel 1–12.* Leipzig: Vogel, 1821.

———. *Der Prophet Jesaia.* Vol. 3. *Commentar über Kapitel 40–66, nebst einigen Beylagen und den Registern.* Leipzig: Vogel, 1821.

Gevaryahu, H. M. I. "Biblical Colophons: A Source for the 'Biography' of Authors, Texts and Books." In *Congress Volume, Edinburgh 1974*, 42–59. VTSup 28. Leiden: Brill, 1975.

Ginsberg, H. L. "The Oldest Interpretation of the Suffering Servant." *VT* 3 (1953): 400–404.

Ginsburg, Christian D. *Introduction to the Massoretico-Critical Edition of the Hebrew Bible*. London: Trinitarian Bible Society, 1897.

Ginzberg, Louis. *The Legends of the Jews*. 7 vols. Philadelphia: JPS, 1938. Reprint, Baltimore: Johns Hopkins University Press, 1998.

Goldingay, John, and David F. Payne. *A Critical and Exegetical Commentary on Isaiah 40–55*. Vol. 1, *Introduction and Commentary on Isaiah 40–43:23*. ICC. London: T&T Clark, 2006.

———. *Isaiah*. NIBC. Peabody, MA: Hendrickson, 2001.

———. *The Message of Isaiah 40–55: A Literary-Theological Commentary*. London: T&T Clark, 2005.

———. "What Are the Characteristics of Evangelical Study of the Old Testament?" *EvT* 73 (2001): 99–117.

Golomb, David M. *A Grammar of Targum Neofiti*. Chico, CA: Scholars Press, 1985.

Gordon, Robert P. "From Mari to Moses: Prophecy at Mari and in Ancient Israel." In *Of Prophets' Visions and the Wisdom of Sages: Essays in Honour of R. Norman Whybray on His Seventieth Birthday*, edited by Heather A. McKay and David J. A. Clines, 63–79. JSOTSup 162. Sheffield: JSOT, 1993.

———. "Where Have All the Prophets Gone? The 'Disappearing' Israelite Prophet against the Background of Ancient Near Eastern Prophecy." *BBR* 5 (1995): 67–86.

Goshen-Gottstein, Moshe H., ed. *The Book of Isaiah*. Jerusalem: Magnes, 1995.

Goulder, Michael. "Deutero-Isaiah of Jerusalem," *JSOT* 28 (2004): 351–62.

Grabbe, Lester L. *Priests, Prophets, Diviners, Sages: A Socio-Historical Study of Religious Specialists in Ancient Israel*. Valley Forge, PA: Trinity, 1995.

Graetz, H. "Isaiah XXXIV and XXXV." *JQR* 4 (1891): 1–8.

Grayson, A. K. *Babylonian Historical-Literary Texts*. Toronto Semitic Texts and Studies. Toronto: University of Toronto Press, 1975.

Grayson, A. K., and W. G. Lambert. "Akkadian Prophecies." *JCS* 18 (1964): 7–30.

Gressmann, Hugo. "Die literarische Analyse Deuterojesajas." *ZAW* 34 (1914): 254–297.

Grisanti, Michael A. "The Present State of Old Testament Scholarship." In *The World and the Word: An Introduction to the Old Testament*, edited by Eugene H. Merrill, Mark F. Rooker, and Michael A. Grisanti, 149–61. Nashville: Broadman & Holman, 2011.

Haag, Herbert. *Der Gottesknecht bei Deuterojesaja*. EdF 233. Darmstadt: Wissenschaftliche Buchgesellschaft, 1985.

Halivni, David Weiss. *The Formation of the Babylonian Talmud*. Translated by J. L. Rubenstein. Oxford: Oxford University Press, 2013.

Hallo, William W. "Akkadian Apocalypses." *IEJ* 16 (1966): 231–42.

———. "The Expansion of Cuneiform Literature." *PAAJR* 46–47 (1979): 307–22.

Hallo, William W., and K. Lawson Younger, eds. *The Context of Scripture*. 3 vols. Leiden: Brill, 1997–2002.

Halvorson-Taylor, Martien A. *Enduring Exile: The Metaphorization of the Exile in the Hebrew Bible*. VTSup 141. Leiden: Brill, 2011.

Hannah, Darrell D. "Isaiah within Judaism of the Second Temple Period." In *Isaiah in the New Testament*, edited by Steven Moyise and Maarten J. J. Menken, 7–33. NTSI. New York: T&T Clark, 2005.

Hanson, Paul D. *The Dawn of Apocalyptic*. Philadelphia: Fortress, 1979.

Haran, Menahem. "Archives, Libraries, and the Order of the Biblical Books." *JANESCU* 22 (1993): 51–61.

———. "The Literary Structure and Chronological Framework of the Prophecies in Isa. XL–XLVIII." In *Congress Volume, Bonn 1962*, 127–55. VTSup 9. Leiden: Brill, 1963.

Harner, Philip B. "The Salvation Oracle in Second Isaiah." *JBL* 88 (1969): 418–34.

Harrison, Roland K. *Introduction to the Old Testament*. Grand Rapids: Eerdmans, 1969.

Hayes, John H., and Frederick C. Prussner. *Old Testament Theology: Its History and Development*. London: SCM, 1985.

Hays, J. Daniel. "An Evangelical Approach to Old Testament Narrative Criticism." *BSac* 166 (2009): 3–18.

Hays, Richard B. "'Who Has Believed Our Message?' Paul's Reading of Isaiah." In *The Conversion of the Imagination: Paul as Interpreter of Israel's Scripture*, 34–45. Grand Rapids: Eerdmans, 2005.

Heim, Knut M. "The (God-)Forsaken King of Psalm 89: A Historical and Intertextual Enquiry." In *King and Messiah in Israel and the Ancient Near East*, edited by John Day, 296–322. JSOTSup 270. Sheffield: Sheffield Academic, 1998.

Heinemann, Isaac. *Darkhei ha-Aggadah*. Jerusalem: Magnes, 1954.

Hengstenberg, Ernst W. *Christology of the Old Testament and a Commentary on the Messianic Predictions*. Translated by Reuel Keith. Abridged reprint ed., Grand Rapids: Kregel, 1970.

Henkind, Sol, and Evelyn Henkind. Talmud Text Databank, at the Saul Lieberman Institute of Talmud Research of the Jewish Theological Seminary of America (http://www.lieberman-institute.com).

Henry, Carl F. H. "Narrative Theology: An Evangelical Approach." *TJ* 8 (1987): 3–19.

Hess, Richard S. "Questions of Reading and Writing in Ancient Israel." *BBR* 19 (2009): 1–9.

Hibbard, J. Todd. *Intertextuality in Isaiah 24–27*. FAT 2, 16. Tübingen: Mohr Siebeck, 2006.

Hibbard, J. Todd, and Hyun Chul Paul Kim, eds. *Formation and Intertextuality in Isaiah 24–27*. SBLAIL 17. Atlanta: Society of Biblical Literature, 2013.

Hilber, John W. *Cultic Prophecy in the Psalms*. BZAW 352. Berlin: de Gruyter, 2005.

———. "The Culture of Prophecy and Writing in the Ancient Near East." In *Do Historical Matters Matter to Faith? A Critical Appraisal of Modern and Postmodern Approaches to Scripture*, edited by James K. Hoffmeier and Dennis Magary, 219–41. Wheaton: Crossway, 2012.

————. "Prophetic Speech in the Egyptian Royal Cult." In *On Stone and Scroll: Essays in Honour of Graham Ivor Davies*, edited by James K. Aitken, Katharine J. Dell, and Brian A. Mastin, 39–53. BZAW 420. Berlin: de Gruyter, 2011.

Hill, Andrew E. *Malachi*. AB 25D. New York: Doubleday, 1998.

Höffken, Peter. *Jesaja: Der Stand der theologischen Diskussion*. Darmstadt: Wissenschaftliche Buchgesellschaft, 2004.

Hoffmeier, James K., and Dennis R. Magary, eds. *Do Historical Matters Matter to Faith? A Critical Appraisal of Modern and Postmodern Approaches to Scripture*. Wheaton: Crossway, 2012.

Høgenhaven, Jesper. "The First Isaiah Scroll from Qumran (1QIsa) and the Massoretic Text. Some Reflections with Special Regard to Isaiah 1–12." *JSOT* 28 (1984): 17–35.

————. "The Isaiah Scroll and the Composition of the Book of Isaiah." In *Qumran between the Old and New Testament*, edited by Frederick H. Cryer and T. L. Thompson, 151–58. LHBOTS. Sheffield: Sheffield Academic, 1998.

Holm-Nielsen, S. *Hodayot: Psalms from Qumran*. ATDan 2. Aarhus: Universitetsforlaget, 1960.

Holmes, Michael W., ed. and trans., *The Apostolic Fathers: Greek Texts and English Translations*, 3rd ed. Grand Rapids: Baker, 2007.

Horowitz, Wayne, Takayoshi Oshima, and Seth Sanders, eds., *Cuneiform in Canaan: Cuneiform Sources for the Land of Israel in Ancient Times*. Jerusalem: Israel Exploration Society, 2006.

Hughes, Paul E. "Compositional History: Source, Form, and Redaction Criticism." In *Interpreting the Old Testament: A Guide to Exegesis*, edited by Craig Broyles, 221–244. Grand Rapids: Baker Academic, 2001.

Hunger, Hermann, and Stephen A. Kaufman. "A New Akkadian Prophecy Text." *JAOS* 95 (1975): 371–75.

Hurvitz, Avi. *A History of the Hebrew Language*. Jerusalem: Magnes, 1982.

————. *The Language and Linguistic Background of the Isaiah Scroll (1QIsaᵃ)*. Leiden: Brill, 1974.

————. "Linguistic Criteria for Dating Problematic Biblical Texts." *Hebrew Abstracts* 14 (1973): 74–79.

————. "The 'Linguistic Dating of Biblical Texts': Comments on Methodological Guidelines and Philological Procedures," in *Diachrony in Biblical Hebrew*, edited by Ziony Zevit and Cynthia Miller-Naudé, 265–80. LSAW 8. Winona Lake, IN: Eisenbrauns, 2012.

————. *A Linguistic Study of the Relationship between the Priestly Source and the Book of Ezekiel: A New Approach to an Old Problem*. CahRB 20. Paris: J. Gabalda, 1982.

————. "The Recent Debate on Late Biblical Hebrew: Solid Data, Experts' Opinions, and Inconclusive Arguments." *HS* 47 (2006): 191–210.

————. "The Relevance of Biblical Hebrew Linguistics for the Historical Study of Ancient Israel." In *Proceedings of the Twelfth World Congress of Jewish Studies, Jerusalem, July 29–August 5, 1997: Division A: The Bible and Its World*, 21–33. Jerusalem: World Union of Jewish Studies, 1999.

————. *The Transition Period in Biblical Hebrew: A Study in Post-Exilic Hebrew and its Implications for the Dating of Psalms.* Jerusalem: Mosad Bialik, 1972 [in Hebrew].

Ibn Ezra, Abraham. *The Commentary of Ibn Ezra on Isaiah.* Edited and translated by M. Friedländer. New York: Philipp Feldheim, 1964.

Jacobs, Louis. "Are There Fictitious Baraitot in the Babylonian Talmud?" *HUCA* 42 (1971): 185–96.

————. *Structure and Form in the Babylonian Talmud.* Cambridge: Cambridge University Press, 1991.

Jain, Eva. "Die materielle Rekonstruktion von 1QJes^b (1Q8) und einige bisher nicht edierte Fragmente dieser Handschrift." *RevQ* 20/79 (2002): 389–409.

Japhet, Sara. *I & II Chronicles: A Commentary.* OTL. Louisville: Westminster/John Knox, 1993.

Jastrow, M. *A Dictionary of the Targumim, the Talmud Babli and Yerushalmi, and the Midrashic Literature.* 2 vols. New York: P. Shalom, 1967.

Jong, Matthijs J. de. "Biblical Prophecy—a Scribal Enterprise: The Old Testament Prophecy of Unconditional Judgment Considered as a Literary Phenomenon." *VT* 61 (2011): 39–70.

————. *Isaiah among the Ancient Near Eastern Prophets: A Comparative Study of the Earliest Stages of the Isaiah Tradition and the Neo-Assyrian Prophecies.* VTSup 117. Leiden: Brill, 2007.

Josephus. *The Works of Flavius Josephus.* Translated by William Whiston. New updated ed. Peabody, MA: Hendrickson, 1987.

Joüon, Paul. *Grammaire de l'Hébreu Biblique.* Rome: Institut Biblique Pontifical, 1923.

Joüon, Paul, and T. Muraoka, *A Grammar of Biblical Hebrew.* Roma: Editrice Pontificio Institut Biblio, 2006.

Kahle, Paul. *Die hebräischen Handschriften aus der Höhle.* Stuttgart: Kohlhammer, 1951.

Kaiser, Otto. *Isaiah 1–12: A Commentary.* 2nd ed. Translated by John Bowden. OTL. Philadelphia: Westminster, 1983.

————. *Isaiah 13–39: A Commentary.* Translated by R. A. Wilson. OTL. Philadelphia: Westminster, 1974.

————. *Der Prophet Jesaja: Kapitel 1–12.* ATD 17. Göttingen: Vandenhoeck & Ruprecht, 1960.

————. *Der Prophet Jesaja: Kapitel 13–39.* ATD 18. Göttingen: Vandenhoeck & Ruprecht, 1973.

Kasovsky, C. *Thesaurus Mishnae.* 4 vols. Jerusalem: Massadah, 1956–60.

Kaufman, Stephen A. "Prediction, Prophecy, and Apocalypse in the Light of New Akkadian Texts" In *Proceedings of the Sixth Congress of Jewish Studies*, edited by A. Shinen, 1:221–28. 3 vols. Jerusalem: Jerusalem Academic, 1977: 221–28.

Keil, Carl F. *Introduction to the Old Testament.* Vol. 2. Edinburgh: T&T Clark, 1869.

Keiser, Thomas A. "The Song of Moses as a Basis for Isaiah's Prophecy." *VT* 55 (2005): 486–500.

Kelle, Brad E. "Ancient Israelite Prophets and Greek Orators: Analogies for the Prophets and their Implications for Historical Reconstruction." In *Israel's*

Prophets and Israel's Past: Essays on the Relationship of Prophetic Texts and Israelite History in Honor of John H. Hayes, edited by Brad E. Kelle and Megan Bishop Moore, 57–82. LHBOTS 446. London: T & T Clark, 2006.

Kiesow, Klaus. *Exodustexte im Jesajabuch: Literarkritische und motivgeschichtliche Analysen*. OBO 24. Fribourg: Editions Universitaires. 1979.

Kim, Brittany D. "'Enlarge the Place of Your Tent': The Metaphorical World of Israel's Household in the Book of Isaiah." PhD diss., Wheaton College, 2014.

Kim, Hyun Chul Paul. "The Song of Moses (Deuteronomy 32:1–43) in Isaiah 40–55." In *God's Word for Our World*, edited by J. Harold Ellens, Deborah L. Ellens, Isaac Kalimi, and Rolf Knierem, 1:141–71. JSOTSup 388. London: T&T Clark, 2004.

Kitchen, Kenneth A. *On the Reliability of the Old Testament*. Grand Rapids: Eerdmans, 2003.

Knibb, M. A. "Martyrdom and Ascension of Isaiah." In *The Old Testament Pseudepigrapha*, edited by J. H. Charlesworth, 2:143–76. Garden City: Doubleday, 1985.

Knight, George A. F. *Isaiah 40–55: Servant Theology*. Grand Rapids: Eerdmans, 1984.

König, F. E. *Historisch-kritisches Lehrgebäude der hebräischen Sprache*. 3 vols. Leipzig: Hinrichs, 1881–97.

Koole, Jan L. *Isaiah III*. Vol. 1, *Isaiah 40–48*. HCOT. Kampen: Pharos, 1997.

Korpel, Marjo C. A., "Introduction to the Series Pericope." In *Delimitation Criticism: A New Tool in Biblical Scholarship*, edited by Marjo Korpel and Joseph Oesch, 1–50. Pericope: Scripture as Written and Read in Antiquity 1. Assen: Van Gorcum, 2000.

Korpel, Marjo C. A., and Joseph Oesch, eds. *Studies in Scriptural Unit Division*. Pericope: Scripture as Written and Read in Antiquity 3. Assen: Van Gorcum, 2002.

Kratz, R. G. "Der Anfang des Zweiten Jesaja in Jes 40,1f und seine literarischen Horizonte." *ZAW* 105 (1993): 400–19.

Kraus, Hans-Joachim, *Geschichte der historisch-kritischen Erforschung des Alten Testaments*. 3rd ed. Neukirchen-Vluyn: Neukirchener, 1982.

Krochmal, Nachmann. *More Nebuche ha-seman*. Leopoli: Joseph Schnayder, 1851.

Kropat, Arno. *Die Syntax des Autors der Chronik verglichen mit der seiner Quellen: Ein Beitrag zur historischen Syntax des Hebräischen*. BZAW 16. Giessen: Töpelmann, 1909.

Kugel, James L. "On the Bible and Literary Criticism." *Prooftexts* 1 (1981): 99–104.

Kutscher, E. Y. "Aramaic Calque in Hebrew." *Tarbiz* 33 (1964): 118–30 [Hebrew].

———. *Biblical Hebrew and Mishnaic Hebrew*, 2 vols. 2nd ed., Tel Aviv: Dvir, 1967.

———. *A History of the Hebrew Language*. Jerusalem: Magnes, 1982.

———. *The Language and Linguistic Background of the Isaiah Scroll (1QIsaᵃ)*. Leiden: Brill, 1974.

Kynes, Will. "Job and Isaiah 40–55: Intertextualities in Dialogue." In *Reading Job Intertextually*, edited by Katharine Dell and Will Kynes, 94–106. LHBOTS 574. London: Bloomsbury: 2013.

Lambert, W. G. "Ancestors, Authors, and Canonicity," *JCS* 11 (1957): 1–14.

———. *Babylonian Wisdom Literature*. Oxford: Clarendon, 1960.

———. "A Catalogue of Texts and Authors." *JCS* 16 (1962): 59–77.

Landy, Francis. "I and Eye in Isaiah, or Gazing at the Invisible." *JBL* 131 (2012): 85–97.

———. "The Ghostly Prelude to Deutero-Isaiah." *BibInt* 14 (2006): 332–363.

Lau, Wolfgang. *Schriftgelehrte Prophetie in Jes 56–66*. BZAW 225. Berlin: de Gruyter, 1994.

Lawee, Eric. "Don Isaac Abarbanel: Who Wrote the Books of the Bible?" *Tradition* 30 (1996): 65–73.

Leclerc, Thomas L. *Yahweh is Exalted in Justice: Solidarity and Conflict in Isaiah*. Minneapolis: Augsburg Fortress, 2001.

Leiman, Sid Z. *The Canonization of Hebrew Scripture: The Talmudic and Midrashic Evidence*. 2nd ed. Transactions of the Connecticut Academy of Arts and Sciences 47. New Haven: Connecticut Academy of Arts and Sciences, 1991.

Levine, Etan. "The Land of Milk and Honey." *JSOT* 87 (2000): 43–57.

Lightstone, J. N. "The Rabbi's Bible: The Canon of the Hebrew Bible and the Early Rabbinic Guild." In *The Canon Debate*, edited by Lee M. McDonald and James A. Sanders, 163–84. Peabody, MA: Hendrickson, 2002.

Lim, Timothy H. *The Formation of the Jewish Canon*. AYBRL. New Haven: Yale University Press, 2013.

Lindsell, Harold. *The Battle for the Bible*. Grand Rapids: Zondervan, 1976.

Lock, Charles. "Some Words after Chiasmus." In *The Shape of Biblical Language: Chiasmus in the Scriptures and Beyond*, edited by John Breck, 361–67. Crestwood: St. Vladimir's Seminary Press, 1994.

Longman III, Tremper. *Fictional Akkadian Autobiography: A Generic and Comparative Study*. Winona Lake, IN: Eisenbrauns, 1991.

Lowe, W. H. *The Mishnah on Which the Palestinian Talmud Rests*. Cambridge: Cambridge University Press, 1883.

Lowth, Robert. *Isaiah: A New Translation; With a Preliminary Dissertation, and Notes, Critical, Philological, and Explanatory*. London: J. Dodsley & T. Cadelle, 1778. 14th ed. London: William Tegg, 1848.

———. *De sacra poesi Hebraeorum: praelectiones academicae*. Oxford: Clarendon, 1753. Published in English in 1787.

Lundbom, Jack R. *Deuteronomy: A Commentary*. Grand Rapids: Eerdmans, 2013.

———. *Jeremiah 1–20: A New Translation with Introduction and Commentary*. AB 21A. New York: Doubleday, 1999.

Machen, J. Gresham. *Christianity and Liberalism*. New York, Macmillan, 1923.

Machinist, P. "Assyria and Its Image in the First Isaiah?" *JAOS* 103 (1983): 719–34.

Mankowski, Paul V. *Akkadian Loanwords in Biblical Hebrew*. HSS 47. Cambridge: Harvard University Press, 2000.

Marcus, David. *A Manual of Babylonian Jewish Aramaic*. Washington, DC: University Press of America, 1981.

Margalioth, Rachel. *The Indivisible Isaiah: Evidence for the Single Authorship of the Prophetic Book*. New York: Yeshiva University, 1964.

Margoliouth, D. S. "Language of the Old Testament." In *A Dictionary of the Bible*, edited by James Hastings, 3:25–35. Edinburgh: T&T Clark, 1900.

Margolis, Max L. *The Hebrew Scriptures in the Making*. Philadelphia: JPS, 1922.

Marti, Karl. *Das Buch Jesaja*. KHC 10. Tübingen: Mohr Siebeck, 1900.

Martin, Malachi. *The Scribal Character of the Dead Sea Scrolls*. 2 vols. Louvain: Publication Universitaires, 1958.

Martínez, F. García. "Le livre d'Isaïe à Qumrân: Les textes. L'influence." *MdB* 49 (1987): 43–45.

Maynard, John H. "The Home of Deutero-Isaiah." *JBL* 36 (1917): 213–24.

Mazar, Amihai. *Archaeology of the Land of the Bible: 10,000–586 B.C.E.* ABRL. New York: Doubleday, 1992.

McKenzie, John L. *Second Isaiah*. AB 20. Garden City: Doubleday, 1968.

McLaughlin, John L. "Their Hearts *Were* Hardened: The Use of Isaiah 6,9–10 in the Book of Isaiah." *Bib* 75 (1994): 1–25.

Melugin, Roy F. *The Formation of Isaiah 40–55*. BZAW 141. Berlin: de Gruyter, 1976.

———. "Poetic Imagination, Intertextuality, and Life in a Symbolic World." In *The Desert Will Bloom: Poetic Visions in Isaiah*, edited by A. Joseph Everson and Hyun Chul Paul Kim, 7–15. SBLAIL. Leiden: Brill; Atlanta: Society of Biblical Literature, 2009.

Melugin, Roy F., and Marvin A. Sweeney, eds. *New Visions of Isaiah*. LHBOTS 214. Sheffield, England: Sheffield Academic, 1996.

Merendino, Rosario P. *Der Erste und Letzte: Eine Untersuchung von Jes 40–48*. VTSup 31. Leiden: Brill, 1981.

Metmann, Leo. *Die Hebräische Sprache: Ihre Geschichte und lexikalische Entwicklung seit Abschluss des Kanons*. Jerusalem: A. M. Luncz, 1904.

Millard, Alan R. "'Take a Large Writing Tablet and Write on it': Isaiah—a Writing Prophet?," In *Genesis, Isaiah and Psalms: A Festschrift to Honour Professor John Emerton for His Eightieth Birthday*, edited by Katharine J. Dell, Graham Davies, and Yee Von Koh, 105–17. VTSup 135. Leiden: Brill, 2010.

———. "Books in Ancient Israel." In *D'Ougarit à Jérusalem: Recueil d'études épigraphiques et archéologiques offerts à Pierre Bordreuil*, edited by Carole Roche, 255–64. Orient and Méditerranée 2. Paris: De Boccard, 2008.

———. "Writing and Prophecy." In *Dictionary of the Old Testament: Prophets*, edited by Mark J. Boda and J. Gordon McConville, 883–88. Downers Grove, IL: InterVarsity Press, 2012.

Miller-Naudé, Cynthia, and Ziony Zevit, eds. *Diachrony in Biblical Hebrew*. LSAW 8. Winona Lake, IN: Eisenbrauns, 2012.

Miscall, Peter D. *Isaiah*. Readings. 2nd ed. Sheffield: Sheffield Phoenix, 2006.

de Moor, Johannes C., ed. *Synchronic or Diachronic: A Debate on Method in Old Testament Exegesis*. OtSt 34. Leiden: Brill, 1995.

Morag, S. "Qumran Hebrew: Some Typological Observations." *VT* 38 (1988): 148–64.

Morgenstern, Julian. *The Message of Deutero-Isaiah in its Sequential Unfolding*. Cincinnati: Hebrew Union College Press, 1961.

Motyer, J. A. *The Prophecy of Isaiah: An Introduction and Commentary*. Downers Grove, IL: InterVarsity Press, 1993.

———. "Three in One or One in Three: A Dipstick into the Isaianic Literature," *Chm* 108 (1994): 22–36.

Mowinckel, Sigmund. "Die Komposition des deuterojesajanischen Buches." *ZAW* 49 (1931): 87–112.

Muilenburg, James. "The Book of Isaiah: Chapters 40–66." In *Interpreter's Bible*, edited by G. A. Buttrick et al, 5.381–773. Nashville: Abingdon, 1956.

Muraoka, Takamitsu. "Hebrew." In *EDSS*, edited by Lawrence H. Schiffman and James C. VanderKam, 1:340–45. Oxford: Oxford University Press, 2000.

Neujahr, Matthew. *Predicting the Past in the Ancient Near East: Mantic Historiography in Ancient Mesopotamia, Judah, and the Mediterranean World.* BJS 354. Providence: Brown University Press, 2012.

Neusner, Jacob. "Rabbinic Literature: Mishnah and Tosefta." In *Dictionary of New Testament Background*, edited by Craig A. Evans and Stanley E. Porter, 893–97. Downers Grove, IL: InterVarsity Press, 2000.

———. *The Rabbis and the Prophets*. Studies in Judaism. Lanham: University Press of America, 2011.

Niese, Benedict, ed. *Flavii Iosephi Opera*. 2nd ed. 6 vols. Berlin: Weidmann, 1955.

Nissinen, Martti. "Biblical Prophecy from a Near Eastern Perspective: The Cases of Kingship and Divine Possession." In *Congress Volume, Ljubljana 2007*, edited by André Lemaire, 441–68. VTSup 133. Leiden: Brill, 2010.

———."Das kritische Potential in der altorientalischen Prophetie." In *Propheten in Mari, Assyrien und Israel*, edited by Matthias Köckert und Martti Nissinen, 1–32. FRLANT 201. Göttingen: Vandenhoeck and Ruprecht, 2003.

———. "Fear Not: A Study on an Ancient Near Eastern Phrase." In *The Changing Face of Form Criticism for the Twenty-First Century*, edited by Marvin A. Sweeney and Ehud Ben Zvi, 122–61. Grand Rapids, Cambridge: Eerdmans, 2003.

———. "The Historical Dilemma of Biblical Prophetic Studies." In *Prophecy in the Book of Jeremiah*, edited by Hans M. Barstad and Reinhard G. Kratz, 103–20. BZAW 388. Berlin: Walter de Gruyter, 2009.

———. "How Prophecy Became Literature." *SJOT* 19 (2005): 153–72.

———. "Neither Prophecies nor Apocalypses: The Akkadian Literary Predictive Texts." In *Knowing the End from the Beginning: The Prophetic, the Apocalyptic, and Their Relationship*, edited by Lester L. Grabbe and Robert D. Haak, 134–48. 46. London: T&T Clark, 2003.

———. "Prophecy and Omen Divination: Two Sides of the Same Coin." In *Divination and Interpretation of Signs in the Ancient World*, edited by Amar Annus, 341–51. OIS 6. Chicago: Oriental Institute of the University of Chicago, 2010.

———. *References to Prophecy in Neo-Assyrian Sources*. SAAS 7. Helsinki: University of Helsinki Press, 1998.

———. "Die Relevanz der neuassyrischen Prophetie für die alttestamentliche Forschung." In *Mesopotamica, Ugaritica, Biblica: Festschrift für Kurt Bergerhof zur Vollendung seines 70. Lebensjahres am 7. Mai, 1992*, edited by Manfred Dietrich and Oswald Loretz, 217–58. AOAT 232. Kevelaer: Butzon and Bercker, 1993.

———. "Since When Do Prophets Write?" In *In the Footsteps of Sherlock Holmes: Studies in the Biblical Text in Honour of Anneti Aejmelaus*, edited by Kristen de Troyer, Michael T. Law, and Marketta Liljeström, 585–606. Leuven, Peeters, 2014.

———. "The Socioreligious Role of the Neo-Assyrian Prophets." In *Prophecy in Its Ancient Near Eastern Context: Mesopotamian, Biblical, and Arabian Perspectives*, edited by Martti Nissinen, 89–114. SBLSymS 13. Atlanta: Society of Biblical Literature, 2000.

———. "Spoken, Written, Quoted, and Invented: Orality and Writtenness in Ancient Near Eastern Prophecy." In *Writings and Speech in Israelite and Ancient Near Eastern Prophecy*, edited by Ehud Ben Zvi and Michael H. Floyd, 235–71. SBLSym S 10. Atlanta: Society of Biblical Literature, 2000.

———. "What is Prophecy? An Ancient Near Eastern Perspective." In *Inspired Speech: Prophecy in the Ancient Near East (Essays in Honour of Herbert B. Huffmon)*, edited by John Kaltner and Louis Stulman, 17–37. JSOTSup 378. London, New York: T&T Clark, 2004.

Nissinen, Martti, C. L. Seow, and Robert K. Ritner. *Prophets and Prophecy in the Ancient Near East*. SBLWAW 12. Atlanta: Society of Biblical Literature, 2003.

Noble, Paul R. *The Canonical Approach: A Critical Reconstruction of the Hermeneutics of Brevard S. Childs*. BibInt 16. Leiden: Brill, 1995.

Nöldeke, Theodor. *Kurzgefasste syrische Grammatik*. Leipzig: T. O. Weigel, 1880.

North, Christopher R. "The 'Former Things' and the 'New Things' in Deutero-Isaiah." In *Studies in Old Testament Prophecy, Presented to Professor Theodore H. Robinson by the Society for Old Testament Study on his Sixty-fifth Birthday, August 9th 1946*, edited by H. H. Rowley, 111–26. Edinburgh: T&T Clark, 1950.

Nurmela, Risto. "The Growth of the Book of Isaiah Illustrated by Allusions in Zechariah." In *Bringing out the Treasure: Inner-Biblical Allusion in Zechariah 9–14*, edited by Mark J. Boda and Michael H. Floyd, 245–59. London: Sheffield Academic, 2003.

———. *The Mouth of the Lord Has Spoken: Inner-Biblical Allusions in Second and Third Isaiah*. Studies in Judaism. Lanham: University Press of America, 2006.

———. *Prophets in Dialogue: Inner-Biblical Allusions in Zechariah 1–8 and 9–14*. Åbo, Finland: Åbo Akademi University Press, 1996.

O'Connor, Michael P. *Hebrew Verse Structure*. Winona Lake, IN: Eisenbrauns, 1982.

Oesch, Josef. M. *Petucha und Setuma: Untersuchungen zu einer überlieferten Gliederung im hebräischen Text des Alten Testaments*. OBO 27. Göttingen: Vandenhoeck & Ruprecht, 1979.

Olley, John W. " 'Hear the Word of YHWH.' " *VT* 43 (1993): 19–49.

Osborne, Grant R. "Historical Criticism and the Evangelical." *JETS* 42 (1999): 193–210.

Oswalt, John N. *The Bible Among the Myths: Unique Revelation or just Ancient Literature?* Grand Rapids: Zondervan, 2009.

———. *The Book of Isaiah: Chapters 1–39*. NICOT. Grand Rapids: Eerdmans, 1986.

———. *The Book of Isaiah: Chapters 40–66*. NICOT. Grand Rapids: Eerdmans, 1998.

———. "Righteousness in Isaiah: A Study of the Function of Chapters 56–66 in the Present Structure of the Book." In *Writing and Reading the Scroll of Isaiah:*

Studies of an Interpretive Tradition, edited by Craig C. Broyles and Craig A. Evans, vol. 1, *Formation and Interpretation of Old Testament Literature*, 177–191. VTSup 70. Leiden: Brill, 1997.

———. "Who were the Addressees of Isaiah 40–66?" *BSac* 169 (2012): 33–47.

Packer, James I. *"Fundamentalism" and the Word of God*. Grand Rapids: Eerdmans, 1957.

———. "Infallible Scripture and the Role of Hermeneutics." In *Scripture and Truth*, edited by D. A. Carson and John D. Woodbridge, 325–56. Grand Rapids: Zondervan, 1983.

Pao, David. *Acts and the Isaianic New Exodus*. WUNT 2/130. Tübingen: Mohr Siebeck, 2002.

Parker, Simon B. "Official Attitudes toward Prophecy at Mari and in Israel." *VT* 43 (1993): 50–68.

Parpola, Simo. *Assyrian Prophecies*. SAA 9. Helsinki: University of Helsinki Press, 1997.

Parry, Donald W., and Elisha Qimron. *The Great Isaiah Scroll (1QIsaᵃ): A New Edition*. STDJ 32. Leiden: Brill, 1999.

Paul, Shalom M. "Deutero-Isaiah and Cuneiform Royal Inscriptions." In *Journal of the Oriental Society 88: Essays in Memory of E. A. Speiser*, edited by William W. Hallo, 180–86. New Haven: Cambridge, 1968.

———. *Isaiah 40–66: Translation and Commentary*. ECC. Grand Rapids: Eerdmans, 2012.

———. "Signs of Late Biblical Hebrew." In *Diachrony in Biblical Hebrew*, edited by Ziony Zevit and Cynthia Miller-Naudé, 293–300. LSAWS 8. Winona Lake, IN: Eisenbrauns, 2012.

Payne, David F. *A Critical and Exegetical Commentary on Isaiah 40–55*. Vol. 1, *Introduction and Commentary on Isaiah 40–44:23*. ICC. London: T&T Clark, 2006.

Pearce, Laurie E. "The Scribes and Scholars of Ancient Mesopotamia," *Civilizations of the Ancient Near East*, edited by Jack M. Sasson, 4:2265–78. Peabody, MA: Hendrickson, 1995.

Petersen, David L. *Late Israelite Prophecy: Studies in Deutero-Prophetic Literature and in Chronicles*. SBLMS 23. Missoula, MT: Scholars Press, 1977.

Pfeiffer, Robert H. *Introduction to the Old Testament*. New York: Harper & Brothers, 1941.

Philo. *The Works of Philo*. Translated by C. D. Yonge. Peabody, MA: Hendrickson, 1993.

Phinney, D. Nathan. "Life Writing in Ezekiel and First Zechariah." In *Tradition in Transition*, edited by Mark J. Boda and Michael H. Floyd, 83–103. LHBOTS 475. London: T&T Clark, 2008.

———. "Portraying Prophetic Experience and Tradition in Ezekiel." In *Thus Says the Lord: Essays on the Former and Latter Prophets in Honor of Robert R. Wilson*, edited by John J. Ahn and Stephen L. Cook, 234–243. LHBOTS 502. New York; London: T&T Clark, 2009.

———. "The Prophetic Persona in the Book of Ezekiel: Autobiography and Portrayal." PhD diss., Yale University, 2004.

Pilhofer, Georg. *Grammatik der Kâte-Sprache in Neuguinea*. Berlin: Dietrich Reimer, 1933.

Polaski, Donald C. *Authorizing the End: The Isaiah Apocalypse and Intertextuality*. BibInt 50. Leiden: Brill, 2001.

Polzin, Robert. *Late Biblical Hebrew: Toward an Historical Typology of Biblical Hebrew Prose*. HSM 12. Missoula: Scholars Press, 1976.

Pongratz-Leisten, Beate. *Herrschaftswissen in Mesopotamien: Formen der Kommunikation zwischen Gott und König im 2. und 1. Jahrtausend v. Chr.* SAAS 10. Helsinki: University of Helsinki Press, 1999.

Pope, Marvin H. "Isaiah 34 in Relation to Isaiah 35, 40–66," *JBL* 71 (1952): 235–43,

Pritchard, James B., ed. *Ancient Near Eastern Texts: An Anthology of Texts and Pictures*. 3rd ed. Princeton: Princeton University Press, 1955.

Pulikottil, Paulson. *Transmission of Biblical Texts in Qumran: The Case of the Large Isaiah Scroll 1QIsa[(a)]*. JSPSup 34. Sheffield: Sheffield Academic, 2001.

Qimron, Elisha. *The Hebrew of the Dead Sea Scrolls*. HSM 29. Atlanta: Scholars Press, 1986.

———. "The Vocabulary of the Temple Scroll." *Annual for the Study of the Bible and Ancient Near East* 4 (1980): 239–262 [in Hebrew].

Rabin, Chaim. *Die Entwicklung der hebräischen Sprache*. Veröffentlichungen der Hochschule für jüdische Studien Heidelberg 2. Wiesbaden: Reichert, 1988.

———. *The Zadokite Documents: I. The Admonitions; II. The Laws*. 2nd rev. ed. Oxford: Clarendon, 1958.

Redditt, Paul. "Editorial/Redaction Criticism. " In *Dictionary of the Old Testament: Prophetic Books*, edited by Mark J. Boda and J. Gordon McConville, 171–78. Downers Grove, IL: InterVarsity Press, 2012.

Rendtorff, Rolf. "The Book of Isaiah: A Complex Unity. Synchronic and Diachronic Reading." In *Society of Biblical Literature Seminar Papers*, edited by Eugene H. Lovering, 8–20. Atlanta: Society of Biblical Literature, 1991. Reprinted in Rolf Rendtorff, *New Visions of Isaiah*, edited by Roy F. Melugin and Marvin A. Sweeney, 32–49. JSOTSup 214. Sheffield: Sheffield Academic Press, 1996.

———. "Zur Komposition des Buches Jesaja." *VT* 34 (1984): 295–320.

Renger, Johannes. "Authors: I. Ancient Orient and Egypt," *BNP (Antiquity)*, edited by H. Cancik and H. Schneider, 2:399. Leiden: Brill, 2003.

Rezetko, Robert. " 'Late' Common Nouns in the Book of Chronicles," in *Reflection and Refraction: Studies in Historiography in Honour of A. Graeme Auld*, edited by Robert Rezetko, Timothy H. Lim, and W. Brian Aucker, 379–418. VTSup 113. Leiden: Brill, 2007.

Rico, Christophe. *La mère de l'Enfant-Roi, Isaïe 7,14: "'Almâ" et "Parthenos" dans l'univers biblique; un point de vue linguistique*. La Bible en ses Traditions—Études . Paris: Cerf, 2013.

Ridderbos, N. H. "Isaiah: Book of." In *New Bible Dictionary*, edited by I. Howard Marshall et al, 512–518. 3rd ed. Leicester: InterVarsity Press, 1996.

Ringgren, Helmer. "Akkadian Apocalypses." In *Apocalypticism in the Mediterranean World and the Near East: Proceedings of the International Colloquium on Apocalypticism, Uppsala, August 12–17*, edited by David Hellholm, 379–86. Tübingen: Mohr Siebeck, 1983.

Roberts, Bleddyn J. "The Second Isaiah Scroll from Qumrân (1QIsb)." *BJRL* 42 (1959): 132–44.

Robinson, George L. "Isaiah." In *The International Standard Bible Encyclopaedia*, edited by James Orr, 3:1495–1508. Chicago: Howard Severance, 1915.

Rogers, Jack B., and Donald McKim. *The Authority and Interpretation of the Bible: An Historical Approach*. San Francisco: Harper and Row, 1979.

Rogerson, John W. *Old Testament Criticism in the Nineteenth Century: England and Germany*. London: SPCK, 1984.

Rooker, Mark F. *Biblical Hebrew in Transition: The Language of the Book of Ezekiel*. JSOTSup 90. Sheffield: Sheffield Academic, 1990.

———. "Dating Isaiah 40–66: What Does the Linguistic Evidence Say?" *WTJ* 58 (1996): 303–12.

———. "The Diachronic Study of Biblical Hebrew." *JNSL* 14 (1988): 199–214.

Rosenberg, A. J. *Mikraoth Gedoloth: The Book of Isaiah*. Vol. 1, *Translation of Text, Rashi and Other Commentaries*. Judaica Books of the Prophets. Brooklyn: Judaica, 1982. Reprint, 2007.

Rosenmüller, Ernst Friedrich Karl. *Scholia in VT Partis Tertiae Jesajae Vaticinia Complectensus Volumen Tertium*. 2nd ed. Leipzig: Joh. Ambros. Barthii, 1820.

Sáenz-Badillos, Angel. *A History of the Hebrew Language*. Translated by John Elwolde. Cambridge: Cambridge University Press, 1993.

———. "Abraham Ibn Ezra: Between Tradition and Philology." *Zutot* 2 (2002): 85–94.

Sanders, Paul. *The Provenance of Deuteronomy 34*. OtST 37. Leiden: Brill, 1996.

Sandys-Wunsch, John. "Early Old Testament Critics on the Continent." In *Hebrew Bible/Old Testament: The History of Its Interpretation*, vol. 2, *From the Renaissance to the Enlightenment*, edited by Magne Sæbø, 971–84. Göttingen: Vandenhoeck & Ruprecht, 2008.

Sarna, Nahum M. "The Order of the Books." In *Studies in Jewish Bibliography, History, and Literature in Honor of I. Edward Kiev*, edited by C. Berlin, 407–413. New York: Ktav, 1971.

Sasson, Jack M. "Mari Apocalypticism Revisited." In *Immigration and Emigration within the Ancient Near East: Festschrift E. Lipiński*, edited by K. Van Lerberghe and A. Schoors, 285–88. Leuven: Peeters, 1995.

Sawyer, John F. A. *The Fifth Gospel: Isaiah in the History of the Church*. Cambridge: Cambridge University Press, 1996.

Schaudig, Hanspeter. "'Bēl Bows, Nabû Stoops!': The Prophecy in Isaiah xlvi 1–2 as a Reflection of Babylonian 'Processional Omens,'" *VT* 58 (2008): 557–72.

Scheidweiler, F. "The Gospel of Nicodemus/Acts of Pilate and Christ's Descent into Hell." In *New Testament Apocrypha*, edited by Wilhelm Schneemelcher, translated by A. J. B. Higgins, George Ogg, Richard E. Taylor, and R. McL. Wilson. Vol. 1, *Gospels and Related Writings*, 444–484. Philadelphia: Westminster, 1963.

Schipper, Bernd Ulrich. "'Apokalyptik,' 'Messianismus,' 'Prophetie': Eine Begriffs-bestimmung." In *Apokalyptik und Ägypten: Eine kritische Analyse der rele-vanten Texte aus dem griechisch-römischen Ägypten*, edited by Andreas Blasius and Bernd Ulrich Schipper, 21–40. OLA 107. Leuven: Peeters, 2002.

Schlesinger, Michael. *Satzlehre der aramäischen Sprache des babylonischen Tal-muds*. Leipzig: Georg Olms, 1928.

Schmitzer, Ulrich E. "Authors." In *BNP (Antiquity)*, edited by H. Cancik, H. Schnei-der, C. F. Salazar, et al, 2:399–403. Leiden, Brill, 2003.

Schniedewind, William M. *How the Bible Became a Book*. Cambridge: Cambridge University Press, 2004.

Schoors, Antoon. *I Am God Your Saviour: A FormCritical Study of the Main Genres in Is XL–LV*. VTSup 24. Leiden: Brill, 1973.

Schultz, Richard L. "How Many Isaiahs Were There and What Does it Matter? Prophetic Inspiration in Recent Evangelical Scholarship." In *Evangelicals and Scripture: Tradition, Authority, and Hermeneutics*, edited by Vincent Bacote, Laura C. Miguélez, and Dennis L. Okholm, 150–70. Downers Grove, IL: Inter-Varsity Press, 2004.

———. "How Many Isaiahs Were There?" *Areopagus Journal: The Journal of the Apologetics Resource Center*, Spring 2012: 16–23.

———. "Intertextuality, Canon, and 'Undecidability': Understanding Isaiah's 'New Heavens and New Earth (Isa 65:17–25)." *BBR* 20 (2010): 19–38.

———. "Isaiah, Isaiahs, and Current Scholarship." In *Do Historical Matters Matter to Faith?: A Critical Appraisal of Modern and Postmodern Approaches to Scrip-ture*, edited by James K. Hoffmeier and Dennis R. Magary, 243–61. Wheaton: Crossway, 2012.

———. "Qoheleth and Isaiah in Dialogue." In *Reading Ecclesiastes Intertextu-ally*, edited by Katherine Dell and Will Kynes, 57–70. LHBOTS 574. London: Bloomsbury: 2014.

———. *The Search for Quotation*. JSOTSup 180. Sheffield: Sheffield Academic, 1999.

———. "The Ties that Bind: Intertextuality, The Identification of Verbal Parallels, and Reading Strategies." In *Thematic Threads in the Book of the Twelve*, edited by Paul Redditt and Aaron Schart, 39–57. BZAW 325. Berlin, New York: de Gruyter, 2003.

Schürer, Emil, Gese Vermes, Fergus Millar, and Martin Goodman, eds. *The History of the Jewish People in the Age of Jesus Christ*. Rev. ed. 3 vols. London: T&T Clark, 1993.

Scurlock, JoAnn. "Prophecy as a Form of Divination: Divination as a Form of Prophecy." In *Divination and Interpretation of Signs in the Ancient World*, edited by Amar Annus, 277–316. OIS 6. Chicago: Oriental Institute of the University of Chicago, 2010.

Segal, M. H. *A Grammar of Mishnaic Hebrew*. Oxford: Clarendon, 1927.

Seitz, Christopher R. "The Divine Council: Temporal Transition and New Proph-ecy in the Book of Isaiah." *JBL* 109 (1990): 229–47.

———. "Introduction: The One Isaiah // The Three Isaiahs," *Reading and Preach-ing the Book of Isaiah*, edited by Christopher R. Seitz, 13–22. Philadelphia: Fortress, 1988. Repr., Eugene, OR: Wipf & Stock, 2002.

———. "Isaiah, Book of (First Isaiah), (Third Isaiah)." In *Anchor Bible Dictionary*, edited by David N. Freedman, 3:472–88, 501–7; Garden City, NY: Doubleday, 1992.

———. *Isaiah 1–39*. IBC. Philadelphia: Westminster John Knox, 1993.

———. "Prophecy in the Nineteenth Century Reception." In *Hebrew Bible/Old Testament: The History of Its Interpretation*, Vol. III/1, *The Nineteenth Century*, edited by Magne Sæbø, 556–581. Göttingen: Vandenhoeck & Ruprecht, 2013.

———. ed. *Reading and Preaching the Book of Isaiah*. Philadelphia: Fortress, 1988.

———. *Zion's Final Destiny: The Development of the Book of Isaiah; A Reassessment of Isaiah 36–39*. Minneapolis: Fortress, 1991.

Seligsohn, Max. "Samuel David (ShaDaL) Luzzatto." In *JE*, new ed., edited by I. Singer, 8:224–26. New York: Funk & Wagnall's, 1925.

Seow, Choon-Leong. "Qoheleth's Eschatological Poem." *JBL* 118 (1999): 209–34.

Shead, Andrew. *A Mouth Full of Fire: The Word of God in the Words of Jeremiah*. NSBT. Downers Grove, IL: InterVarsity Press, 2012.

Shupak, Nili. "Egyptian 'Prophecy' and Biblical Prophecy: Did the Phenomenon of Prophecy, in the Biblical Sense, Exist in Ancient Egypt?" *Jaarbericht van het Vooraziatisch-egyptisch Genootschap Ex Orient Lux* 31 (1989): 5–40.

Shupak, Nili. "The Egyptian 'Prophecy'—a Reconsideration." In *Von reichlich ägyptischem Verstande: Festschrift für Waltraud Guglielmi zum 65. Geburtstag*, edited by Hans-Werner Fischer-Elfert and Karola Zibelius-Chen, 133–44. Philippika: Marburger Altertumskundliche Abhandlungen. Wiesbaden: Harrassowitz, 2006.

Simon, Maurice, trans. *The Babylonian Talmud: Baba Bathra*. The Babylonian Talmud, edited by I. Epstein. London: Soncino, 1938.

Simon, Uriel. "Ibn Ezra between Medievalism and Modernism: The Case of Isaiah XL–LXVI." *VTSup* 36 (1985): 257–71.

Skehan, Patrick W. "The Qumran Manuscripts and Textual Criticism." In *Volume du Congrès Strasbourg*, 148–60. VTSup 4. Leiden: Brill, 1957.

———. "Qumran, Littérature de Qumran, A. Texts bibliques." *Dictionnaire de la Bible: Supplément* 9 (1979): 805–22.

Smith, Gary V. *Isaiah 1–39*. NAC 15A. Nashville: Broadman & Holman, 2007.

———. "Isaiah 40–55: Which Audience was Addressed?" *JETS* 54 (2011): 701–14.

———. *Isaiah 40–66*. NAC 15B. Nashville: Broadman & Holman, 2009.

Smith, George A. *The Book of Isaiah*. Edited by W. R. Nicholl. 2 vols. The Expositor's Bible. London: Hodder & Stoughton, 1910.

Smith, Stephen. "The Evangelical and Redaction Criticism." *Chm* 107 (1993): 130–145.

Smith, W. Robertson. *The Old Testament in the Jewish Church: A Course of Lectures in Biblical Criticism*. 2nd ed. New York: D. Appleton, 1892.

Sommer, Benjamin D. "Allusions and Illusions: The Unity of the Book of Isaiah in Light of Deutero-Isaiah's Use of Prophetic Tradition." In *New Visions of Isaiah*, edited by Roy F. Melugin and Marvin A. Sweeney, 156–86. JSOTSup 214. Sheffield: Sheffield Academic, 1996.

———. *A Prophet Reads Scripture: Allusion in Isaiah 40–66*. Contraversions. Palo Alto: Stanford University Press, 1998.

Sparks, Kenton L. *Ancient Texts for the Study of the Hebrew Bible: A Guide to the Background Literature*. Peabody, MA: Hendrickson, 2005.

———. *God's Word in Human Words: An Evangelical Appropriation of Critical Biblical Scholarship*. Grand Rapids: Baker Academic, 2008.

Spinoza, Benedict. *A Theological-Political Treatise and a Political Treatise*. Translated by R. H. M. Elwes. London: G. Bell, 1883.

Spykerboer, Hendrik C. *The Structure and Composition of Deutero-Isaiah: With Special Reference to the Polemics against Idolatry*. Meppel: Krips, 1976.

Stanley, Christopher D. *Paul and the Language of Scripture*. SNTSMS 69. Cambridge: Cambridge University Press, 1992.

Stansell, Gary. *Micah and Isaiah: A Form and Tradition Historical Comparison*. SBLDS 85. Atlanta: Scholars Press, 1988.

———. "The Poet's Prophet: Bishop Robert Lowth's Eighteenth-Century Commentary on Isaiah." In *"As Those Who Are Taught": The Interpretation of Isaiah from the LXX to the SBL*, edited by Christine M. McGinnis and Patricia K. Tull, 223–42. SBLSymS 27. Atlanta: Society of Biblical Literature, 2006.

Steck, Odil H. "Beobachtungen zu Jesaja 56–59." *BZ* 2/31 (1987): 236–37.

———. *Bereitete Heimkehr: Jesaja 35 als redaktionelle Brücke zwischen dem Ersten und dem Zweiten Jesaja*. SBS 121. Stuttgart: Katholisches Bibelwerk, 1985.

———. *Die erste Jesajarolle von Qumran (1QIsa)*. 2 vols. SBS 173. Stuttgart: Katholisches Bibelwerk, 1998.

———. *Gottesknecht und Zion: Gesammelte Aufsätze zu Deuterojesaja*. FAT 4. Tübingen: Mohr Siebeck, 1992.

———. *The Prophetic Books and their Theological Witness*. St. Louis: Chalice, 2000.

———. *Studien zu Tritojesaja*. BZAW 203. Berlin: de Gruyter, 1991.

Stone, Lawson G. "Redaction Criticism: Whence, Whither, and Why? Or Going Beyond Source and Form Criticism without Leaving Them Behind." *LTQ* 27 (1992): 105–18.

Stonehouse, N. B. *The Witness of Matthew and Mark to Christ*. Philadelphia: Presbyterian Guardian, 1944. Reprint, Grand Rapids: Eerdmans, 1958.

Strauss, Mark L. *The Davidic Messiah in Luke-Acts: The Promise and Its Fulfillment in Lukan Christology*. JSNTSup 110. Sheffield: JSOT, 1995.

Stromberg, Jacob, *An Introduction to the Study of Isaiah*. T&T Clark Approaches to Biblical Studies. London: T&T Clark, 2011.

———. *Isaiah After Exile: The Author of Third Isaiah as Reader and Redactor of the Book*. Oxford Theological Monographs. Oxford: Oxford University Press, 2011.

Stuhlmueller, Carroll. "Deutero-Isaiah: Major Transitions in the Prophet's Theology and in Contemporary Scholarship." *CBQ* 42 (1980): 1–29.

———. "'First and Last' and 'Yahweh-Creator' in Deutero-Isaiah." *CBQ* 29 (1967): 495–511.

Sukenik, Eliezer L. *The Dead Sea Scrolls of the Hebrew University*. Jerusalem: Magnes, 1955.

Swanson, Dwight. "The Text of Isaiah at Qumran." In *Interpreting Isaiah*, edited by David G. Firth and H. G. M. Williamson, 191–212. Downers Grove, IL: InterVarsity Press 2009.

Sweeney, Marvin A. "On the Road to Duhm: Isaiah in Nineteenth-Century Critical Scholarship." In *"As Those Who Are Taught": The Interpretation of Isaiah from the LXX to the SBL*, edited by Christine M. McGinnis and Patricia K. Tull, 243–62. SBLSymS 27. Atlanta: Society of Biblical Literature, 2006.

———. "Review of R. G. Kratz, *Kyros im Deuterojesaja-Buch*," *JBL* 113 (1994): 129–32.

———. *TANAK: A Theological and Critical Introduction to the Jewish Bible*. Minneapolis: Fortress, 2012.

———. "Textual Citations in Isaiah 24–27: Toward an Understanding of the Redactional Function of Chapters 24–27 in the Book of Isaiah." *JBL* 107 (1988): 39–52.

Talshir, David. "The Habitat and History of Hebrew during the Second Temple Period," in *Biblical Hebrew: Studies in Chronology and Typology*, edited by Ian Young, 251–75. London: T&T Clark, 2003.

Tan, Randall K. J. "Recent Developments in Redaction Criticism: From Investigation of Textual Prehistory Back to Historical-Grammatical Exegesis?" *JETS* 44 (2001): 599–614.

Tasker, R. V. G. *The Old Testament in the New Testament*. Grand Rapids: Eerdmans, 1954.

Tate, Marvin E. "The Book of Isaiah in Recent Study." In *Forming Prophetic Literature: Essays on Isaiah and the Twelve in Honor of John D. W. Watts*, edited by James W. Watts and Paul R. House, 22–56. JSOTSup 235. Sheffield: Sheffield Academic, 1996.

Thackeray, H. St. J. *The Septuagint and Jewish Worship: A Study in Origins*. The Schweich Lectures. London: Oxford University Press, 1921.

Theodore of Mopsuestia. *Commentary on the Twelve Prophets*. Translated by Robert C. Hill, Fathers of the Church (Washington: Catholic University of America Press, 2004).

Theodoret of Cyrus. *Commentaries on the Prophets*. Vol. 1, *Commentary on Jeremiah*. Translated by Robert C. Hill. Brookline: Holy Cross Orthodox, 2006).

Thompson, John A. "The Book of Joel." In *Interpreter's Bible*, edited by G. A. Buttrick et al, 6:727–60. Nashville: Abingdon, 1956.

Tiemeyer, Lena-Sofia. *For the Comfort of Zion: The Geographical and Theological Location of Isaiah 40–55*. VTSup 139. Leiden: Brill, 2011.

Tooman, William A. *Gog of Magog*, FAT 52. Wiesbaden, Harrassowitz Verlag, 2011.

———. "Transformation of Israel's Hope: The Reuse of Scripture in the Gog Oracles." In *Transforming Visions: Transformations of Text, Tradition, and Theology in Ezekiel*, edited by William Tooman and Michael Lyons, 50–110. Princeton Theological Monograph Series 127. Eugene, OR: Pickwick/Wipf & Stock, 2010.

Toorn, Karel van der. *Scribal Culture and the Making of the Hebrew Bible*. Cambridge: Harvard University Press, 2007.

Torrey, C. C. *The Second Isaiah*. New York: Scribner's Sons; Edinburgh: T&T Clark, 1928.

Tov, Emanuel. "The Background of the Sense Divisions in the Biblical Texts." In *Delimitation Criticism: A New Tool in Biblical Studies*, edited by Marjo Korpel and Joseph Oesch, 312–50. Pericope: Scripture as Written and Read in Antiquity 1. Assen: Van Gorcum, 2000.

———, ed. *The Dead Sea Scrolls on Microfiche: A Comprehensive Fascimile Edition of the Texts from the Judean Desert, Companion Volume.* Leiden: Brill, 1993.

———. "Determining the Relationship between the Qumran Scrolls and the LXX: Some Methodological Problems." In *The Hebrew and Greek Texts of Samuel*, edited by Emanuel Tov, 45–67. Jerusalem: Magnes, 1980.

———. *Scribal Practices and Approaches Reflected in the Texts Found in the Judean Desert.* STDJ 54. Brill: Leiden, 2004.

———. "Sense Divisions in the Qumran Texts, the Masoretic Text, and Ancient Translations of the Bible." In *The Interpretation of the Bible: The International Symposium in Slovenia*, edited by Joze Krasovec, 121–46. Sheffield: Sheffield Academic, 1998.

———. "The Text of Isaiah at Qumran." In *Writing and Reading the Scroll of Isaiah: Studies of an Interpretive Tradition*, edited by Craig C. Broyles and Craig A. Evans, 491–511. VTSup 70, 2. Leiden: Brill, 1997.

———. *Textual Criticism of the Hebrew Bible.* 2nd ed. Minneapolis: Fortress, 1992.

———. "The Writing of Early Scrolls and the Literary Analysis of Hebrew Scripture." *DSD*13 (2006): 339–347.

Tull, Patricia. "One Book, Many Voices: Conceiving of Isaiah's Polyphonic Message." In *"As Those Who Are Taught": The Interpretation of Isaiah from the LXX to the SBL*, edited by Christine M. McGinnis and Patricia K. Tull, 279–314. SBLSymS 27. Atlanta: Society of Biblical Literature, 2006.

Tull Willey, Patricia. *Remember the Former Things: The Recollection of Previous Texts in Second Isaiah.* SBLDS 161. Atlanta: Scholars Press, 1997.

Ulrich, Eugene. "Isaiah." In *EDSS*, edited by Lawrence H. Schiffman,and James C. VanderKam, 348–88. New York: Oxford University Press, 2000.

———. *The Qumran Text of Samuel and Josephus.* Missoula, MT: Scholars Press, 1978.

Ulrich, Eugene and Peter W. Flint. *Qumran Cave 1: II. The Isaiah Scrolls.* 2 vols. DJD 32. Oxford: Clarendon, 2010.

Van Peursen, W. *The Verbal System in the Hebrew Text of Ben Sira.* SSLL 41. Leiden: Brill, 2004.

Van Seters, John. *The Edited Bible: The Curious History of the "Editor" in Biblical Criticism.* Winona Lake, IN: Eisenbrauns, 2006.

———. "Prophetic Orality in the Context of the Ancient Near East: A Response to Culley, Crenshaw and Davies." In *Writings and Speech in Israelite and Ancient Near Eastern Prophecy*, edited by Ehud Ben Zvi and Michael H. Floyd, 83–88. SBLSymS 10. Atlanta: Society of Biblical Literature, 2000.

———. "The 'Shared Text' of Samuel–Kings and Chronicles Re-Examined." In *Reflection and Refraction: Studies in Historiography in Honour of A. Graeme Auld*, edited by Robert Rezetko, Timothy H. Lim, and W. Brian Aucker, 503–517. VTSup 113. Leiden, Boston: Brill, 2007.

Van Til, Cornelius, "Introduction" to Benjamin B. Warfield, *The Inspiration and Authority of the Bible,* edited by Samuel G. Craig. 1948. 2nd ed. Nutley: Presbyterian & Reformed, 1970.

Vanderhooft, David S. *The Neo-Babylonian Empire and Babylon in the Latter Prophets*. HSM 59. Atlanta: Scholars Press, 1999.

Vanhoozer, Kevin J. *Is There a Meaning in This Text? The Bible, the Reader, and the Morality of Literary Knowledge*. Grand Rapids: Zondervan, 1998.

Vargon, Shmuel. "Isaiah 56:9–57:13: Time of the Prophecy and Identity of the Author According to Samuel David Luzzatto." *JSQ* 6 (1999): 218–33.

———. "S. D. Luzzatto's Approach Regarding the Unity of the Book of Isaiah." *Review of Rabbinic Judaism* 4 (2001): 272–96.

Villard, Pierre. "Les prophéties à l'époque néo-assyrienne." In *Prophètes et rois: Bible et Proche-Orient*, edited by André Lemaire, 55–84. Lectio divina Hors serie. Paris: Les éditions du Cerf, 2001.

Vincent, Jean M. *Studien zur literarischen Eigenart und zur geistigen Heimat von Jesaja, Kap. 40–55*. BBET 5. Frankfurt: Peter Lang, 1977.

Waldman, Nahum M. "A Biblical Echo of Mesopotamian Royal Rhetoric," in *Essays on the Occasion of the Seventieth Birthday of Dropsie University, 1909–1979*, edited by Abraham I. Katsh and Leon Nemoy, 449–55. Philadelphia: Dropsie University Press, 1979.

Waldow, Hans Eberhard von. "Anlass und Hintergrund der Verkündigung Deuterojesajas." Diss., Bonn, 1953.

———. ". . . denn ich erlöse dich.": Eine Auslegung von Jesaja 43. BibS(N) 29. Neukirchen: Neukirchener, 1960.

Wall, Ernestine van der. "The 'Theologica Prophetica' of Campegius Vitringa." In *Hugo Grotius, Theologian: Essays in Honour of G. H. M. Posthumus Meyjes*, edited by Henk J. M. Nellen and Edwin Rabbie, 195–216. Studies in the History of Christian Traditions 55. Leiden: Brill, 1994.

Walsh, Jerome T. *Old Testament Narrative: A Guide to Interpretation*. Louisville: Westminster John Knox, 2010.

Waltke, Bruce K. *An Old Testament Theology: An Exegetical, Canonical, and Thematic Approach*. Grand Rapids: Zondervan, 2007.

———. "Oral Tradition." In *A Tribute to Gleason Archer*, edited by Walter C. Kaiser and Ronald F. Youngblood, 17–34. Chicago: Moody, 1986.

Walton, John H., and D. Brent Sandy. *The Lost World of Scripture: Ancient Literary Culture and Biblical Authority*. Downers Grove, IL: InterVarsity, 2013.

Warfield, Benjamin B. *The Inspiration and Authority of the Bible*. Edited by Samuel G. Craig. 1948. 2nd ed. Nutley: Presbyterian & Reformed, 1970.

Warhurst, Amber, Seth B. Tarrer, and Christopher M. Hays. "Problems with Prophecy." In *Evangelical Faith and the Challenge of Historical Criticism*, edited by Christopher M. Hays and Christopher B. Ansberry, 95–124. London: Society for Promoting Christian Knowledge, 2013.

Watts, John D. W. *Isaiah 1–33*. Rev. ed. WBC 24. Nashville: Thomas Nelson, 2005.

———. *Isaiah 34–66*. Rev. ed. WBC 25. Nashville: Thomas Nelson, 2000.

———. *Isaiah*. Word Biblical Themes. Dallas: Word, 1989.

Watts, Rikki E. *Isaiah's New Exodus in Mark*. WUNT 88. Tübingen: Mohr Siebeck, 1997.

Webb, Barry G. "Zion in Transformation: A Literary Approach to Isaiah." In *The Bible in Three Dimensions: Essays in Celebration of Forty Years of Biblical Stud-*

ies in the University of Sheffield, edited by David J. A. Clines, Stephen E. Fowl, and Stanley E. Porter, 65–84. JSOTSup 87. Sheffield: Sheffield Academic, 1990.

Weeks, Stuart. "Predictive and Prophetic Literature: Can *Neferti* Help Us Read the Bible?" In *Prophecy and the Prophets in Ancient Israel*, edited by John Day, 25–46. LHBOTS 531. London, New York: T&T Clark International, 2010.

Weippert, Manfred. "Aspekte israelitischer Prophetie im Lichte verwandter Erscheinungen des Alten Orients." In *Ad bene et fideliter seminandum: Festgabe für Karlheinz Deller zum 21. Februar 1987*. Edited by Gerlinde Mauer and Ursula Magen, 287–319. AOAT 220. Kevelaer: Butzon and Bercker, 1988.

———. "Assyrische Prophetien der Zeit Asarhaddons und Assurbanipals." In *Assyrian Royal Inscriptions: New Horizons in Literary, Ideological and Historical Analysis*, edited by F. M. Fales, 71–115. OAC 17. Rome: Istituto per L'Orient, 1981.

———. " 'Das Frühere, siehe, ist eingetroffen. . . .': Über Selbstzitate im altorientalischen Prophetenspruch." In *Oracles et prophéties dans l'antiquité: Actes du colloque de Strasbourg 15–17 Juin 1995*, edited by Jean-Georges Heintz, 147–69. Travaux du Centre de Recherche sur le Proche-Orient et la Grèce Antiques 15. Paris: Université des Sciences Humaines de Strasbourg, 1997.

———. " 'Ich bin Jahwe'—'Ich bin Ishtar von Arbela': Deuterojesaja im Lichte der neuassyrischen Prophetie." In *Prophetie und Psalmen: Festschrift für Klaus Seybold zum 65. Geburtstag*, edited by Beat Huwyler, Hans-Peter Mathys, and Beat Weber, 31–59. AOAT 280. Münster: Ugarit-Verlag, 2001.

Wente, Edward F. "The Scribes of Ancient Egypt." In *Civilizations of the Ancient Near East*, edited by Jack M. Sasson, 4:2211–21. New York: Scribner's, 1995.

Westermann, Claus. *Das Buch Jesaja: Kapitel 40–66*. ATD 19. Göttingen: Vandehoeck & Ruprecht, 1966.

———. *Isaiah 40–66: A Commentary*. Translated by David M. G. Stalker. OTL. Philadelphia: Westminster, 1969.

Weyde, Karl W. "Inner-Biblical Interpretation: Methodological Reflections on the Relationship between Texts in the Hebrew Bible." *SEÅ* 70 (2005): 287–300.

Wheaton, Byron. "Focus and Structure in the Abraham Narratives." *TJ* 2/27 (2006): 143–162.

Whybray, R. N. *Isaiah 40–66*. NCB. London: Marshall, Morgan, & Scott, 1975.

Wildberger, Hans. *Jesaja. Kapitel 1–39*. 3 vols. BKAT. Neukirchen-Vluyn: Neukirchener, 1965–82.

Wiley, H. Orton. *Christian Theology*. 3 vols. Kansas City: Beacon Hill, 1940–43.

Williamson, H. G. M. *The Book Called Isaiah: Deutero-Isaiah's Role in Composition and Redaction* . Oxford: Clarendon, 1994.

———. *A Critical and Exegetical Commentary on Isaiah 1–27*. Vol. 1, *Isaiah 1–5*. ICC. London: T&T Clark, 2006.

———. "Deuteronomy and Isaiah," in *For Our Good Always: Studies on the Message and Influence of Deuteronomy in Honor of Daniel I. Block*, edited by Jason S. DeRouchie, Jason Gile, and Kenneth J. Turner, 251–69. Winona Lake, IN: Eisenbrauns, 2014.

———. "In Search of the Pre-exilic Isaiah." In *In Search of Pre-Exilic Israel*, edited by John Day, 181–206. London: T&T Clark, 2004.

———. "Isaiah: Book of." In *Dictionary of the Old Testament Prophets*, edited by Mark J. Boda and J. Gordon McConville, 366–71. Downers Grove, IL: InterVarsity Press, 2012.

———. "Isaiah: Prophet of Weal or Woe?" In *"Thus Speaks Ishtar of Arbela": Prophecy in Israel, Assyria, and Egypt in the Neo-Assyrian Period*, edited by Hans M. Barstad and Robert P. Gordon, 273–300. Winona Lake, IN: Eisenbrauns, 2013.

———. "Poetic Vision in Isaiah 7:18–25." In *The Desert Will Bloom: Poetic Visions in Isaiah*, edited by A. Joseph Everson and Hyun Chul Paul Kim, 77–89. SBLAIL 4. Atlanta: Society of Biblical Literature, 2009.

———. "Preaching from Isaiah." In *Reclaiming the Old Testament for Christian Preaching*, edited by Grenville J. R. Kent, Paul J. Kissling, and Laurence A. Turner, 141–56. Downers Grove, IL: InterVarsity Press, 2010.

———. "Recent Issues in the Study of Isaiah." In *Interpreting Isaiah: Issues and Approaches*, edited by David G. Firth and H. G. M. Williamson, 21–39. Downers Grove, IL: InterVarsity Press, 2009.

———. "Synchronic and Diachronic in Isaian Perspective." In *Synchronic or Diachronic? A Debate on Method in Old Testament Exegesis*, edited by Johannes C. de Moor, 211–26. OtSt 34. Leiden: Brill, 1995.

———. *Variations on a Theme: King, Messiah and Servant in the Book of Isaiah*. The Didsbury Lecture Series. Carlisle: Paternoster, 1998.

Willi-Plein, Ina. *Vorformen der Schriftexegese innerhalb des Alten Testamentes*. BZAW 123. Berlin:Walter de Gruyter, 1971.

Wilson, Robert Dick. *Is the Higher Criticism Scholarly?* Philadelphia: Sunday School Times, 1922.

———. *A Scientific Investigation of the Old Testament*. Philadelphia: Sunday School Times, 1926.

Wilson, Victor M. *Divine Symmetries: The Art of Biblical Rhetoric*. Lanham: University Press of America, 1997.

Wise, Michael O., Martin G. Abegg, and Edward M. Cook, eds. *The Dead Sea Scrolls: A New English Translation*. New York: Harper Collins, 1996; rev. ed. San Franciso: HarperOne, 2005.

Wood, John H. "Oswald T. Allis and the Question of Isaianic Authorship." *JETS* 48 (2005): 249–261.

Woodbridge, John D. *Biblical Authority: A Critique of the Rogers/McKim Proposal*. Grand Rapids: Zondervan, 1982.

Woudstra, Marten H. *The Book of Joshua*. NICOT. Grand Rapids: Eerdmans, 1981.

Wright, N. T. *The New Testament and the People of God*. Christian Origins and the Question of God 1. Minneapolis: Fortress, 1992.

Wright, Richard M. *Linguistic Evidence for the Pre-exilic Date of the Yahwistic Source*. LHBOTS 419. London: T&T Clark, 2005.

Wyrick, Jed. *The Ascension of Authorship*. Cambridge: Harvard University Press, 2004.

Young, Edward J. *The Book of Isaiah*. 3 vols. Grand Rapids: Eerdmans, 1965–1972.

———. *Who Wrote Isaiah?* Grand Rapids: Eerdmans, 1958.

Young, Ian. *Biblical Hebrew: Studies in Chronology and Typology*. LHBOTS 369. London: T&T Clark, 2003.

Young, Ian, Robert Rezetko, and Martin Ehrensvärd. *Linguistic Dating of Biblical Texts*. 2 vols. London: Equinox, 2008.

Zehnder, Markus. "Building on Stone? Deuteronomy and Esarhaddon's Loyalty Oaths (Part 1): Some Preliminary Observations." *BBR* 19 (2009): 341–74.

———. "Building on Stone? Deuteronomy and Esarhaddon's Loyalty Oaths (Part 2): Some Additional Observations." *BBR* 19 (2009): 511–35.

Zevit, Ziony, and Cynthia Miller-Naudé, eds. *Diachrony in Biblical Hebrew*. LSAWS 8. Winona Lake, IN: Eisenbrauns, 2012.

Ziegler, Joseph. *Sapientia Iesu Filii Sirach*. Septuaginta: VT Graecum Auctoritate Societatis Litterarum Gottingensis editum XII.2. Göttingen: Vandenhoeck & Ruprecht, 1965.

Zimmerli, Walther. *Ezekiel: A Commentary on the Book of the Prophet Ezekiel*. Hermeneia. 2 vols. Philadelphia: Fortress, 1979/1983.

———. "I Am Yahweh." In *I Am Yahweh*, translated by Douglas W. Scott, edited by Walter Brueggemann, 1–28. Atlanta: John Knox, 1982. Originally published as "Ich bin Jahwe." In *Geschichte und Altes Testament*, edited by Gerhard Ebeling, 179–209. BHT 16. Tübingen: J. C. B. Mohr, 1953

———. "Prophetic Proclamation and Reinterpretation." In *Tradition and Theology in the Old Testament*, edited by Douglas Knight, 69–100. Philadelphia: Fortress, 1977.

Index of Modern Authors

Index of Ancient Sources